# AMERICANA GERMANICA

Paul Ben Baginsky's Bibliography
of German Works Relating to
America, 1493–1800

*Don Heinrich Tolzmann*

HERITAGE BOOKS
2019

# HERITAGE BOOKS
*AN IMPRINT OF HERITAGE BOOKS, INC.*

**Books, CDs, and more—Worldwide**

For our listing of thousands of titles see our website
at
www.HeritageBooks.com

A Facsimile Reprint
Published 2019 by
HERITAGE BOOKS, INC.
Publishing Division
5810 Ruatan Street
Berwyn Heights, Md. 20740

Copyright © 1994 Don Heinrich Tolzmann

— Publisher's Notice —
In reprints such as this, it is often not possible to remove blemishes from the original. We feel the contents of this book warrant its reissue despite these blemishes and hope you will agree and read it with pleasure.

International Standard Book Numbers
Paperbound: 978-0-7884-0151-0
Clothbound: 978-0-7884-6852-0

## Table of Contents

| | |
|---|---|
| Editor's Introduction | v |
| Preface | xi |
| The Fifteenth Century | 1 |
| The Sixteenth Century | 1 |
| The Seventeenth Century | 15 |
| The Eighteenth Century | 31 |
| Supplementary List | 169 |
| Index | 173 |
| Selective Bibliography | 219 |

Editor's Introduction

From December 1938 through January 1939, the New York Public Library held an exhibit on "Early German Works Relating to America," which was based on the bibliography compiled by Paul Ben Baginsky. (1) The exhibit was held simultaneously with the annual meetings of the American Association of Teachers of German and the Modern Language Association, which was in part responsible for the substantial number of visitors. (2) The exhibit itself reflected the lively interest that Germans took in America, and how this interest grew, changed, and evolved as the decades past.

The earliest German publication dealing with America (1493) followed swiftly after the voyage of Columbus to the New World, and works dealing with America, and various aspects thereof, would steadily increase so that by 1800, more than 1,500 works had appeared.

Almost midway in this three century period, the general interest in America became increasingly focused on North America as a result of the settlements there. (3) In 1608, the first permanent German settlers arrived at Jamestown, Virginia, and in the years thereafter, Germans settled in New York and elsewhere throughout the colonies, and then in 1683, the first permanent German settlement was established at Germantown, Pennsylvania. (4) These events were decisive in directing German interest and attention to North America as a place not only of discovery, exploration, and adventure, but as a place for immigration and settlement.

In his preface, Baginsky notes that in his attempt to write a study of the German view of America from the time of the Columbian discovery to 1800, he encountered a major problem by the lack of a bibliographical reference source on the topic. To rectify this situation, he set out to examine pre-1800 German-language publications to index them with regard to any references they might contain to America.

This work contains not only books, but also articles, essays, and reviews. The basis for his research were the extensive holdings of the New York Public Library. His work, hence, amounts not only to a bibliography of the holdings there, but also a periodical index to pre-1800 German periodical literature. Moreover, he expanded this substantial base by including relevant titles from Joseph Sabin, Dictionary of Books Relating to America, as well as from Christian Kayser, Vollständiges Bücher-Lexikon. (5)

All of these works are organized in chronological arrangement by the date of publication. The work also contains a detailed subject, author, and title index. It, hence, can be utilized for the location of works by specific authors, for works on specific subjects, and for specific titles. The subject index, of course, is of great value for providing access to German works on particular persons, or on particular places.

My reason for editing this volume for re-publication were the following. First, anyone interested in pre-1800 German-American history will find this work not only valuable, but essential. (6) By means of this work, one can locate, for example, works dealing with various locales where Germans had settled. Second, after making use of this work extensively for pre-1800 German-American historical researches, it became apparent that this work needed again to be made available for those interested in the history, literature, and culture of German-Americans before 1800. (7)

Finally, this work is of value not only for German-American history, but for a number of other areas as well. It will useful for those interested in the general topic of relations between Germany and America before 1800. (8) It will be of interest for anyone seeking information on pre-1800 America may find that the only publication available on a given topic may have been a German-language publication. (9) And, last but not least, it will be of use for those interested in the image of

America in German Literature before 1800. (10) In short, this work has a wide variety of uses with regard to the relations between Germany and America before 1800.

viii

Notes

1. This bibiliography originally appeared as: Paul H. Baginsky, **German Works Relating to America, 1493-1800: A List Compiled from the Collections of the New York Public Library**. (New York: New York Public Library, 1942).

2. For further information on the exhibit, see Paul H. Baginsky, "Early German Interest in the New World, 1494-1618," **American-German Review**. (1939): 8-9, 36.

3. Regarding the early period of German-American history, see Don Heinrich Tolzmann, ed., **Germany and America (1450-1700): Julius Friedrich Sachse's History of the German Role in the Discovery, Exploration, and Settlement of the New World**. (Bowie, MD: Heritage Books, Inc. 1991).

4. Regarding the earliest Germans in America, see Don Heinrich Tolzmann, ed., **The First Germans in America, With a Biographical Directory of New York Germans**. (Bowie, MD: Heritage Books, Inc., 1992).

5. See pp. 169-72.

6. For references to works dealing with German-American history, see Don Heinrich Tolzmann, **German-Americana: A Bibliography**. (Metuchen, NJ: Scarecrow Pr., 1975) and Don Heinrich Tolzmann, **Catalog of the German-Americana Collection, University of Cincinnati**. (München: K.G. Saur, 1990).

7. See a recent catalog of the publications of Heritage Books, Inc., Bowie, Maryland, for a list of works by the Editor dealing with various aspects of German-American history, including the early period.

8. Regarding the early period of German-American relations, see Tolzmann, **Germany and America**.

9. It should be noted that valuable supplements to

this work can be found in the following works: Philip M. Palmer, "German Works on America," in: In Honorem Lawrence Marsden Price: Contributions by his Colleagues and by His Former Students. (Berkeley: University of California Pr., 1952), pp. 271-412, and Horst Dippel, **Americana Germanica: 1770-1800: Bibliograpie deutscher Amerikaliteratur.** (Stuttgart: J. B. Metzler, 1976).

10. With regard to the image of America in German Literature, see Don Heinrich Tolzmann, ed., In der **Neuen Welt: Deutsch-Amerikanische Festschrift zur 500-Jahrfeier der Entdeckung von Amerika, 1492- 1992.** New German-American Studies, Vol. 5. (New York: Peter Lang Pub. Co., 1992).

# GERMAN WORKS RELATING TO AMERICA

## 1493-1800

A List Compiled From the Collections of
The New York Public Library

*By* PAUL BEN BAGINSKY
German Department, Brooklyn College

NEW YORK
THE NEW YORK PUBLIC LIBRARY
1942

# PREFACE

"I cling to the illusion that it is vitally important that the United States understand itself as a factor in world civilization. Historians have not given sufficient attention to the part we have had in European life and opinion." — R. H. Heindel, in his *The American Impact on Great Britain, 1898–1914*, preface.

LIKE many a similar undertaking this check list was not compiled for bibliographical reasons only. More than four years ago the compiler started to gather material for a book on what he then called "the development of the notion of America in Germany." This gathering had not progressed very far, however, before it was practically stopped by insufficient bibliographical data, and it became clear that he could not progress much further with his enterprise until more adequate bibliographical foundations had been laid. Thus began the work which finally led to the publication of this check list.

This remark should not be taken as an indication of gross immodesty. No one has more admiration than the compiler for the achievements of Harrisse, Sabin, and other bibliographers who have already contributed so largely to this field. His indebtedness to them is evident in many of the descriptive notes in this list, especially in those for the earlier books, which are frequently quotations or adaptations from the standard works of American bibliography. Those works, however, are more general in their scope than the present compilation, and have been limited to the listing of books and pamphlets. Only here and there do they record a periodical containing articles on America, and they have neglected almost completely the multitude of book reviews which are so important in any evaluation of contemporary public opinion and knowledge. This is true even of Meynen's excellent bibliography which appeared while work for this list was far advanced.

In order to bridge this gap, at least in part, all files of German periodicals of the time available in The New York Public Library were examined for the attitude of the German people towards America. As a guide, the *Allgemeines Repertorium der Literatur,* and similar works proved most useful. The search was not confined to periodicals devoted to literature and Geisteswissenschaft at large, but included those concerned with science. The magazines containing articles on medicine and forestry yielded much unsuspected material, and many forgotten titles have been gathered in and listed.

Although obviously proud of the productivity of this method, the compiler knows full well that this list, limited to the collections of The New York Public Library, is only a contribution to a more complete bibliography which must take into account those of all American as well as European libraries. The supplementary section (pages 169–172) gives some indications toward this end.

But the list, even in its present form, shows clearly the various phases and historical development to 1800 in the relation between Germany and America. The purpose of this introduction, however, forbids more than a general indication of the nature and extent of both. Although this relation is naturally reciprocal, the role Germans have had in America is more widely known and has been more thoroughly discussed; so emphasis will be focussed on the other side of the sea, where the Western hemisphere from the day of its discovery has had a fascination and challenge for the German reader.

As one would expect, much of the early information about the New World reached the Germans indirectly, since they were basically neither explorers nor colonizers. Yet a scant five years after Columbus had written his letter to Luis de Santangel, a German translation appeared (no. 6), to be followed in a decade by Jobst Ruchamer's translation of the *Paesi Novamente Retrovati* (no. 31). This interest in geography and travel is evident by an increasing number of translations of the better known contemporary accounts, some of which were concerned with Mexico, and especially with the missionary activities among the native tribes. One practical aspect of the interest was directed toward the making and reading of maps. It has been said with more acumen than accuracy that the Germans worked out the maps by which other nations could undertake voyages for colonization.

By the middle of the century there were some firsthand accounts of life in the Americas, notably that of Hans Staden which recorded both his adventurous travels and something of the manners and customs of his captors, the Tupi Indians of Brazil (no. 69). But in the main, Germans received their expanding knowledge about the distant land from the multiplying encyclopedias of geographical and historical information and through the "voyages," such as those edited by Theodor de Bry and Levinus Hulsius.

The rapid increase of information on America becomes clearly manifest through a superficial comparison of the two editions of Sebastian Franck's *Weltbuch*, a general geography of the known world in four books, devoted to Asia, Africa, Europe, and America. In the first edition (1534; no. 56), the section on America comprises only twenty-six out of two hundred and thirty-seven pages. The edition of 1567 (nos. 72, 73) consists of two volumes, the first dealing with the "countries recently found," the second, with navigation; and America occupies a large proportion of each.

The Thirty Years War (1618-1648) brought at least a partial break in the continuity of cultural development for Germans; moreover, the concern of Europe with America had turned from discovery and exploration to settlement and exploitation. The beginning of real participation by Germans in this second phase may be conveniently dated by the journey of William Penn through their provinces in 1673 to discuss the settlement of indigent families in his proposed colony; and with the prospect of escape from religious and political persecution came new vistas of new homes. Although these colonists were a fresh source of direct information on the New World, they were relatively few in number before well into the first quarter of the eighteenth century. Some of the earliest accounts of these German emigrants stress the hardships of the ocean voyage and privations suffered after their arrival. The description of the misery of some three thousand of them who had gone to New York with Governor Hunter, by Anton Wilhelm Boehme, Chaplain to the Consort of Queen Anne (no. 240), and the publication by a returning German (no. 249) of a register of the survivors in 1717 of a group which had left the Palatinate seven years earlier, and who thus sent back greetings to "their dear relatives" whom they never expected to see again on this earth, testify to the difficulties and discouragement these settlers endured. Even in 1756, Gottlieb Mittelberger (no. 359) included with his firsthand description of Pennsylvania a "detailed account of the sad and unfortunate circumstances of most of the Germans who have emigrated or are emigrating to that country."

While such publications were undoubtedly creating apathy toward America, if not an unfavorable impression, other factors were at work among certain circles to counteract this. More extensive reports were beginning to come back from various religious groups. The University and people of Halle, for instance, were deeply interested in the Salzburgers who had gone to Georgia in 1732 and founded Eben Ezra. The orphanage at Halle became the model for the first institution of its kind in the Colonies. In 1744, the initial issue of the so-called Hallische Nachrichten (no. 317) appeared. To Johann Caspar Velthusen, superintendent of churches and connected with the University of Helmstädt (later dissolved by Napoleon) came word from North Carolina of the lack of school books for the children, which must be printed in Germany and sent on the long voyage. And the settlers needed many other kinds of help from their homeland. Affiliations like these, as they became more numerous, brought through letters and particularly through church reports an ever richer flow of details about life in the Colonies, quite aside from the activities of the congregations. But, illuminating as these records are to us today, we cannot assume that they aroused a widespread interest in the New World, although we know that they contributed and diffused among their small circle of readers a more accurate idea of the problems of everyday living that these settlers resolutely faced.

A wider public, however, became interested in America in the 1750's, at the time of the French and Indian War. Several publications were issued of an entirely different character from the church reports of the previous decades, which were limited to individual congregations as well as in locale. America was now treated as a conglomerate of colonies of different nations and the German settlements were recognized only as part of a larger unit. Yet it should be noted that most of the material on the non-Germanic colonies still came from indirect sources.

The American struggle for independence intensified an interest already thoroughly kindled; publications and articles dealing with America not only began to multiply rapidly, but they embraced more varied topics, indicating a livelier curiosity about many other aspects of American life. Literature, political theory, geography, agriculture, medicine — even the common affairs of daily living — were influenced by events and ideas from across the ocean.

The "Amerika-Bild," or the concept of America in German literature and especially the influence of the American Revolution on it, has been competently discussed several times. The poets of the Storm and Stress school, weighted with the burdens of a timeworn Europe, built up a rather romanticized picture of the vast reaches of the New World. Stimulated by eighteenth-century rationalism and the philosophy of a return to nature, they were longing for emigration to the frontier where they could live and perfect the simple life. Writers of fiction were finding in escape to the distant shores the *deus ex machina* with which to solve all the problems of their characters. The earlier zeal to bring the American "heathen," the Indians, the benefits of Christianity was replaced by a sentimental concern with slaves and Indians. Herder, finding in primitive peoples and their folklore the fullest expression of the poetic and race "soul," saw in the Indians an example of his faith in unity through variety. For the idealist, Columbus became the symbol of what might be realized by fidelity to the aspirations of the inner man, while Benjamin Franklin and George Washington achieved the heroic stature of legendary figures. Washington became the symbol not only of American liberty, but also of the liberty of all nations. On the whole, however, as others have said, the enthusiasm for the American Revolution manifest in German literature was not so extensive as one might assume offhand; yet one phase should perhaps receive more attention than it has been accorded.

Although belonging to literature in only a limited sense, the songs of the mercenaries, deliberately composed to foster courage, should be contrasted with the many expressions of bitter irony and lamentation for the youths who had been sent at the will of a tyrannical ruler to fight in a foreign war. Whatever their artistic value, the latter reflect the democratic tendency and indicate the very great influence of the American Revolution on political thought in Germany.

In scarcely any other instance did the brutality of absolute government become so obvious even to the unpolitically minded. But the sale of the auxiliary troops to the English was only one of many topics connected with the American Revolution that aroused the German public and helped develop its political ideas. The scarcity of enthusiastic statements — especially during the period when the American cause was yet undecided — should not mislead as to the extent of that interest. In many German countries where the rulers feared the discussion or even the publication of news regarding these events, rigid censorship was applied, and only the desired opinion could be expressed with impunity. Then, too, many of the German princes, as in Hanover, were closely related to or even identical with the English royal family. In German states where there was antagonism to England, more enthusiasm over the American struggle was voiced. Prussia under Frederick the Great seems to have permitted the most freedom (note on no. 511C). In most cases it is possible from the place of publication, always given in this list in references to periodical articles, to guess correctly the point of view of the journal towards the conflict.

As a generalization it can be said that the Germans — especially the bourgeois class to which most of the leading scholars belonged — sympathized with democratic ideals, but disliked revolution as the means to attain them. Only a very small group favored this method. The concept of benevolent despotism, then so prominent, branded revolution as something alien. The nobility, as the ruling class, of course sided with the English. But even though published enthusiasm is scarce, we know the actual interest in the American struggle was tremendous. It was by no means mere interest in a significant contemporary historical event, but one in the very idea of democracy itself, whose spreading power and power to spread were already being felt. All groups — those who wished it to spread through the German states and those who feared that it might — were stimulated by the thrill that stemmed from dealing with such dangerous matters. A considerable number of publications in the following list reveal that the authors wanted to escape the sharp eye and penalties of the censor, while others show with equal clarity that the hiding itself was enjoyed as an exciting experience. The flood of translations and adaptations of foreign works issued by German publishers with an eye to business, the reprinting of the most obsolete works, frequently without benefit of revision, can be fully understood only when we take into account the thrill that the reading of every text concerning seditious America brought.

The desire to read about American events is closely connected with the rapid development of German periodicals. The list proves how prominently news about

America figured in them and also shows their range of viewpoint. The "Stats-Anzeigen," edited by Professor August Ludwig Schloezer of the University of Göttingen in Hanover, which at times had the unusually large circulation of 4,400, read and approved by such rulers as Maria Theresa and the Emperor Joseph, was pro-British. The "Berliner Monatsschrift" (not in the Library; see no. 744) took the opposite side, while the "Teutscher Merkur," issued in Weimar (no. 479), held to the middle course. It was, moreover, through periodicals that the German public became acquainted with letters, reports, and diaries of officers and surgeons in the auxiliary troops and with such items as would never have been published otherwise. So another channel of direct information was opened.

But it was a scholarly movement, seemingly very remote from the stimulating events of the American Revolution (though historians can easily show that both have similar roots), which more than anything else spread information among the Germans. Its center was the University of Göttingen, established in 1734, and thus one of the youngest German institutions of higher learning. Here in opposition to the humanistic approach still being followed by other German universities, a group of professors sought to promote a more practical knowledge. Following Conring's lead, Professor Gottfried Achenwall had created the branch of science, known as "Statistik als Staatskunde," which aimed to collect and to grasp all those facts and figures about a country that might be of practical value to the politician. It was Anton Friedrich Büsching — first a professor of theology in Göttingen, then the principal of the famous Gymnasium zum grauen Kloster in Berlin — who applied Achenwall's method to geography and thus became the "father of modern geography."

It is suggestive to see how the scholarship at the University of Göttingen, in contrast to the output of the commercial publishers, was responsible for the valuable books on America and for the encouragement of German translation of the most noteworthy foreign treatises on the New World. Schloezer, whose merits have been competently described, was a full professor there; Matthias Christian Sprengel, his disciple, occupied the post of an "ausserordentlicher Professor," before he was offered a full professorship at Halle by Freiherr von Zedlitz, Frederick the Great's minister of education. It was he who later wrote: "The revolution just finished will be of great importance for Europe. Our fortunate descendants will benefit from the results of which we cannot even have a presentiment. It is by no means disadvantageous to our continent. Even if individual states should suffer and the fame of America should increase emigration from Germany and Great Britain, Europe as a whole will profit, and centuries will not suffice to limit her growing greatness."

Whereas the endeavors of Schloezer and Sprengel have been noted by the historians, those of others have been entirely neglected. This list, for example, offers material to evaluate the contribution of August Friedrich Crome, who took his doctor's degree in Göttingen in 1785, one year after the publication of his work on America. He was the first to show the relative size of land and population by squares.

An earlier, but equally forgotten man, whose achievements in the field of American-German relations will be treated shortly by the compiler of this list, is Friedrich Wilhelm von Taube. Born in London, where his father was physician to Queen Karoline Wilhelmine, wife of King George II, he studied law at Göttingen. Taube did not live long enough to see the outcome of the American Revolution, but as a scion of a Hanover family serving the Royal Court in London, he sided with the British, as the following title indicates: "Thoughts on the Present State of Our Colonies in North America, on Their Behaviour to Their Mother Country, and on the True Interest of the Nation in regard of the Colonies" (London, 1766). In contrast to his later works this tract is written in English. Taube was also a frequent contributor to Büsching's *Magazin für die Historie und Geographie* (not in the Library). The work is especially significant because he had traveled in America before settling down to practice law in Hanover. In this respect the writing contrasts with that of most of his contemporaries, who sought to produce practical information on America, but who had never set foot on its soil. In fact, many of them felt this no handicap, but considered their treatises, the result of elaborate and critical reading of the accounts of travelers, more exact than their source material. The sciolism of the previous century had yielded to a more critical approach, and although much remained to be accomplished, a comparison of the works on America by Johann Jakob Moser (no. 795) and by Christian Daniel Ebeling (no. 1163) shows the progress which resulted from Büsching's new method in geography.

Ebeling's five volumes which remained for decades the standard German work on America, is an immediate continuation of Büsching's geographical studies. Ebeling, who had also been a student at Göttingen and in later years a teacher in History and Greek at the Gymnasium in Hamburg, was commissioned to write the geography and history of America which Büsching had planned before his death. Though Ebeling never saw this country, he was the first German in his field to have the aid of Americans. Joel Barlow, then United States consul in Hamburg, arranged an introduction to Ezra Stiles, president of Yale College, to whom he wrote: "Every attempt to instruct the European world in whatever concerns America deserves our warmest encouragement, as it serves the oppressed of all nations to come to us: a migration which at once augments our prosperity and their felicity. And I know no man who possesses more ability and inclination to serve the cause of humanity in this way than he whom I have the honour to recommend to your correspondence." Thus a correspondence and exchange of books was arranged. At his death Ebeling's library consisted of 4,000 volumes on America and 10,000 maps. His own enthusiasm for America misled him to overrate the general interest among the German public. At a time when it shifted to the events in France, he started his *Amerikanisches Magazin* (no. 1267), one of the few German periodicals devoted entirely to American matters. The magazine lasted two years, 1795–1797, before it ceased publication because of lack of support. His thorough knowledge of and personal connections with the youthful United States, linked with a great pedagogical zeal to popularize the subject of his learning, made Ebeling the head of the group of admirers of this country; and in all cases where his own favorable opinion was contradicted or attacked, America had no more aggressive advocate.

The veneration which hailed America as the land of freedom awakened a national German patriotic opposition in the last decade of the eighteenth century. A reaction against the "Americophiles" arose, and opprobrium was heaped upon the States. The most derogatory account was written by Dietrich Freiherr von Bülow (no. 1363) who twice visited the new republic. In the intensity of his monomania he was akin to his contemporary Heinrich von Kleist, but his nagging and faultfinding was not compensated by a great poetic genius. Today we know that much of his bitterness was the result of an ill-advised business venture, in which he lost his inheritance. As a true romanticist he made his personal disappointment the measurement for this country, and declared that the New World was not the utopia many had conceived it to be. The heterogeneous character of the population, the commercialism, the lack of systematic education, the prevalence of crime — even the unhealthy climate — were all subjects of his censure. Nor did he foresee a glowing future for the young country. Despite the unequivocal challenge to these views by Ebeling and others, this well-known controversy did much to establish a hostile trend in opinion on America. There were, of course, other contributory factors, such as the disillusionment over the efficacy of popular government and the immediate results of the French Revolution. Then, too, the Romanticists were already turning to the past and to sanctuary in the esthetic from the distraction of political turmoil.

While this American impact on German political life and thought has been hinted at before, the American impact on everyday activity of Germans has received practically no attention. Even a superficial glance through the subjects of the index of this check list, however, will show into how many ramifications

# GERMAN WORKS RELATING TO AMERICA   xix

of ordinary life this influence reached. Germans inquire and learn how the English transport beer overseas so that it does not become sour. They import seeds of American plants, labor to grow American trees not only for ornamental purposes, but for the reforestation of depleted German woods, then threatening a serious shortage of fuel. The breeding of horses in America, the grinding of flour, the manufacturing of maple sugar are all carefully studied; and a minor German poet sings the praise of the man who made hats from the sheared fur of Canadian beavers. The question of how the spruce beer of Canada and New England could be made in Germany is spiritedly discussed, and the results of experiments exchanged. Other topics only slightly more removed from everyday living also undergo sober investigation. American drugs, which have been a recurring subject of research since the early sixteenth century, when a cure was sought for the King's Evil, continue to receive attention. An especially interesting item in this record is the effort to make tobacco useful in medicine. Tracts on the yellow fever and tropical diseases in the West Indies are abundant. Toward the close of the eighteenth century, the treatment of inmates in the Philadelphia prison is held up as an example by which German penitentiaries might profit. Meteorological observations in the New World and the accounts of American anatomists on the dissection of both animals and plants are carefully studied. The German learned societies did much to extend the knowledge resulting from research work in this country, for they were in friendly contact with the societies in Philadelphia and New England and read and reviewed their proceedings, thus making familiar to the general public the names of American scholars.

German children, too, shared in this more ample knowledge of the New World. In fact, this bibliography points the way to sufficient material for a study on the fascinating subject of how America was represented in German schoolbooks and taught to the young. With the expanding and diversified information about this continent during the eighteenth century, the almost exclusive emphasis on the German settlements such as Philadelphia, gave way on the one hand to the tendency for encyclopedic generalization and on the other to a stress on geography in its practical aspects. Even geographical card games were used to make such material popular with boys and girls. But perhaps the most significant contribution to the information on America among children was the work of the eminent pedagogue Joachim Heinrich Campe, and his history of the discovery of the western hemisphere (see nos. 762, 1304). The popularity of Campe's work is easily judged by the number of editions and translations issued which continued far beyond the period treated in this check list.

The brief analysis in the preceding paragraphs has been only a hint of the kind and scope of the published information from which Germans formulated their concept of America during the three centuries following the voyage of Columbus, and a suggestion of how the emphasis shifted during this period. Fairly meager at first, the stream broadened and branched out until it reached into many fields of thought and activity. The reader of today will not see in the multitude of "unfair" and erroneous statements about America to be found in the items in this check list mere "curiosa," quaint and amusing, but will understand and evaluate them in their relation to the cultural history of Germany. Each step is a significant one, for the increasing knowledge, both true and false, was not only the acquisition of facts by the German people, but gradual and steady growth of their own world of thought — and an important page in the fascinating story of the reciprocal intellectual relations of the Old World and the New.

A few technical aspects of the list should be noted:

Only foreign material published before 1800 (chiefly in German) is included. "America," before 1600, is taken to mean the Western Hemisphere. After that date, the term applies here only to North America, including the West Indies, but excluding the Arctic regions. Material pertaining to Arctic voyages is recorded only when it concerns attempts to find the so-called Northwest, or Northeast, passage.

The list is arranged chronologically and is followed by a supplementary alphabetical list of works which the compiler did not find in the Library, and by a general index.

Line titles are given for publications before 1700. Short titles, adapted to bring out the relationship of each work to the subject of the compilation, are used for later publications, in many cases.

Throughout the list, content, rather than bibliographical detail, is stressed, though the amount of bibliographical detail in each entry depends to a considerable extent on the amount given on the Library's catalogue cards, from which such information was generally transcribed. Inconsistencies in technical features, as the record of size of volumes (sometimes indicated in the conventional "4°," "f°," sometimes in centimetres) are due to the fact that the Library has changed its form of catalogue entry a number of times during the past fifty or sixty years; no attempt has been made to systematize such variations. Typography has been "levelled"; old-style S's, R's, etc., and the shortened oblique "shilling mark" used in early books for the comma, have been reduced to the current typographical mode. Imprints are conventionalized, and descriptions of the physical book is brief.

A special word about the works represented only by German reviews in this list. Two categories are present. The first consists of German works which the compiler did not locate in the Library's collections. The second includes works in other languages (especially English and French) noticed in German reviews. As the Library has an outstanding representation of early works relating to America, it would be misleading to give no indication of their presence. Therefore, class marks of such works have usually been appended in notes.

As a naturalized citizen, the compiler could speak at length of how his devotion for his adopted country has inspired this work, but he can be less reticent concerning the persons whose inspiration he wishes to acknowledge. He owes a debt of gratitude to the staff of The New York Public Library for their courtesy and unfailing help, especially to F. Ivor D. Avellino, Karl Brown, Deoch Fulton, Daniel C. Haskell, Robert W. Hill, Gerald D. McDonald and Henry Meier, who have assisted him in so many ways. As for the index, Karl Brown's aid makes him in fact a coauthor.

In compiling the index an unfortunate typographical error in the text of the list was discovered. For the second line of no. 1259, read "Philosophical Society, held at Philadelphia, for."

The work as it appears here is dedicated as a token of gratitude to the staff of the German Department of Brooklyn College, Brooklyn, N. Y., of which the compiler has been a member for the past eight years. The friendly atmosphere of the College has done much to keep up his good spirits and strength during the years of strenuous labor.

# GERMAN WORKS RELATING TO AMERICA
## 1493–1800

### 1493

1. SCHEDEL, HARTMANN. [Das Buch der Chroniken. Nürnberg: A. Kolberger, 1493.] 10 p.l., cc lxxxvi f., 1 l. illus. (incl. maps, plans, ports.) 43½ cm. (f°.) †* KB 1493
l. 1ᵃ: Register Des | buchs der Cro- | nikeṅ vnd geschichten | mit figureṅ vnd pildnus | sen von anbegiñ der welt | bis auf dise vṅsere Zeit.
The New World is not yet mentioned. However, the mention of Martin Behaim (Blatt cclxxxv, verso) becomes important later.
See notes on nos. 274A, 382.

### 1494

2. BRANT, SEBASTIAN. Das Narren schyff | Ad Narragonia... [Basel, 1494.] Faksimile der Erstausgabe von 1494 mit einem Anhang enthaltend die Holzschnitte der folgenden Originalausgaben und solche der Locherschen Übersetzung und einem Nachwort von Franz Schultz. Strassburg: Verlag von Karl J. Trübner, 1913. 2 p.l., 327, lv (i) p. illus. 8°. (Gesellschaft für elsässische Literatur. Jahresgaben. [Nr.]1.)
Harrisse Add. 2.                        Reserve 1494
Ouch hatt man sydt jnn Portigal
Vnd jnn hyspanyen vberall
Golt jnslen funden, vnd nacket lüt
Von den man vor wust sagen nüt.
This verse on 1. iiij, verso, evidently refers to the newly discovered world. Harrisse quotes the same lines in the first editions in Latin, French, and English, all of which differ in interpretation of the original passage.

3. —— Das Narrenschiff von Dʳ. Sebastian Brant, nebst dessen Freiheitstafel. Neue Ausgabe, nach der Original-Ausgabe besorgt und mit Anmerkungen versehen von Adam Walther Strobel... Quedlinburg und Leipzig: Gottfr. Basse, 1839. xiii(i), 312 p. 8°. (Bibliothek der gesammten deutschen National Literatur von der ältesten bis auf die neuere Zeit. Bd. 17.)
NGT

4. —— Das Narrenschiff von Sebastian Brant. Herausgegeben von Karl Goedeke. Leipzig: F. A. Brockhaus, 1872. xxxvi, 265 p. 18½ cm. (Deutsche Dichter des sechzehnten Jahrhunderts. Bd. 7.)                  NFN (Deutsche)

5. —— Sebastian Brants Narrenschiff. Herausgegeben von Dr. F. Bobertag. Berlin und Stuttgart: W. Spemann [188–?]. 2 p.l., xxvi, 329 p. 8°. (Deutsche National Litteratur... herausgegeben von Joseph Kürschner. Bd. 16.)  NGT

### 1497

6. COLUMBUS, CHRISTOPHER. Eyn schön hübsch lesen von etlichen insslen | die do in kurtzen zyten funden synd durch dē | künig von hispania, vnd sagt võ grossen wun | derlichen dingen die in dē selbē insslen synd. [Strasbourg: Bartholomäus Kistler, 1497.] 8 l. illus. 20 x 15½ cm. (4°.)                          * KB 1497
Sabin 14638. JCB, 1919, 1, 29.
l. 2ᵃ: (D)Er houptman der schiffung des mörs Cristoferus co- | lon von hispania schribt dem künig von hispania võ | den insslen des lands ]ndie vff dem fluss gangen ge | nant...
Colophon: l. 7ᵃ: Getruckt zũ strassburg vff gruneck võ meister Bartlomess | küstler ym iar .M.CCCC.XCVIJ. vff sant Jeronymus tag.
"Getüetschet vss der katilonischen zungen vndvss dem latin | zũ Ulm." — l. 7ᵃ.
See no. 7.

7. —— Der deutsche Kolumbus-Brief. In Facsimile-Druck. Herausgegeben mit einer Einleitung von Konrad Häbler. Strassburg: J. H. E. Heitz (Heitz & Mündel), 1900. 24 p.; facsim.: 1 l. [12] p. 19 cm.              * KB 1497
"Der deutsche Text besitzt also nicht nur insofern einen Werth, als er bekundet, wie weit das Interesse an den Entdeckungen des grossen Genuesen selbst in denjenigen Kreisen Deutschlands verbreitet war, die der Gelehrten-Sprache nicht theilhaftig waren, sondern er ist ausserdem bis auf weiteres auch noch der einzige Repräsentant eines unabhängigen und anscheinend an Gewissenhaftigkeit den anderen eher überlegenen Zweiges der Ueberlieferung dieses überaus wichtigen Dokumentes... Leider lässt sich nun aber fast gar nichts darüber ermitteln, wo, wie und durch wen diese deutsche Uebersetzung zustande gekommen ist." — Haebler.
See no. 6.

### 1505

8. DEN RECHTEN weg auss zu faren võ Liss- | bona gen Kallakuth von meyl zu meyl | Auch wie der Kunig von Portigal yetz newlich vill Galeen vnd | naben wider zu ersuchen vnd bezwingen newe landt vnd Insellen, | durch kallakuth in Indien zu faren, Durch sein haubtman also be | stelt als hernach getruckt stet gar von seltzsamen dingen. [Nürenberg: Georg Stuchs, 1505?] 4 l. illus. 4°.     Reserve 1505
Sabin 68353.
Woodcut on title repeated on recto of last leaf.
The tract describes the water route to India around Africa and gives Portuguese plans of new explorations. The cut of the globe on the second page shows Africa surrounded by water.
"Man findt auch darin verzeychnet Nurnberg, Liszbona vñ kallakuth." "...ce petit livre n'a pas paraitre avant 1505, car il contient des instructions pour la recherche de deux grands- vaisseaux perdus dans le courant de l'année 1505."— From an unidentified book catalogue. There is an allusion to the new lands and islands lately discovered in the inscription of the woodcut, but no notice of America in the text itself.

9. —— The same. Photographic reproduction of the original edition, in the Library of Congress, made in 1886.            Reserve 1505

10. VESPUCCI, AMERIGO. Von der neü gefunden | Region so wol ein welt genempt mag werden, | durch den Cristēlichen künig, von Portigal, | wunderbarlich erfunden. [Basel: Michael Furter, 1505.] Photostat reproduction. 16 p. illus. 8°.                              Reserve 1505
Sabin 99340. Harrisse 37.
First edition in German of the Basel translation made from the first edition in Latin (Lambert's edi-

[1]

*1505, continued*

**10. VESPUCCI, AMERIGO,** *continued*

tion). This is expressed as follows: "Uss ytalischer sprach in latin der hüpsch Tollmetsch dyss | epistel gezogē hat vmb das alle latiner verstandē wie vil | grosser wunderlichen dingen von tag zů tag fundē | ...Uss latin ist diss missiue in Tütsch gezogen vss dem exem | plar das von Pariss kam im Meyen monet mitle Nach | Cristus geburt .xv. hundert vnd fünff iar." — *p. 16.*

**11.** —— Von der neüw gefunden Region | die wol ain welt genent mag werden, durch den Cristenlichen | künig von portugal, wunderbarlich erfunden. [n.p., 1505? Boston, 1921.] 7 l. illus. 12°. (Americana series; photostat reproductions by the Massachusetts Historical Society. no. 43.) Reserve 1505
Sabin 99341. Harrisse 34.
One of the ten photostat copies reproduced from the original in the British Museum.
In fine: Auss ytalischer sprach in latein der hübsch Tolmetsch dise Epi | stel gezogen hat... Auss latein ist diss missiue in Teutsch | gezogen auss dem Exemplar das von Pariss kam im mayen mo | net nach Christi geburt .xv. hundert vnd fünff jar.
Second edition in German of the Basel translation.

**12.** —— —— The same. Photostat reproduction. Reserve 1505

**13.** —— ⁌ Von der neüwen gefundē | Region, die wol ein wellt genennt mag werden. | durch den Cristenlichen künig von Portugal, gar | wunderlich vnd seltzam erfunden. [n.p., 1505.] Photostat reproduction. 10 l. 4°. Reserve 1505
Sabin 99342. Harrisse Add. 21.
In fini: Auss ytalischer sprach in latein der hübsch Tull- | metsch dise Epistel gezogen hat... Auss la | tein ist diss missiue in teütsch gezogen auss dem ex- | emplar das von Pariss kam jm Mayen monat na | ch Cristi gepurdt xv. hundert vnd fünff jar.
Third edition in German of the Basel translation.

**14.** —— Von der neu gefunden Region die wol | ein welt genent mag werden, durch den Cristenlichen künig | von portigal, wunderbarlich erfunden. [Augsburg? 1505.] 8 L, incl. 1 blank. 4°. Reserve 1505
Sabin 99343. Harrisse 38.
Translation of the Novus Mundus by Johann Schönsperger (see *Allgemeine deutsche Biographie*, v. 32, p. 320). Voyage began 14th May 1501.
At the end of the text is the following information: "Auss lateyn ist dyss missiue in Teusch | gezogen auss dem Exemplar das von Paryss kam im meyen mo- | net Nach Christi geburt .xv. hundert vnd funff jar."

**15.** —— —— The same. Photostat reproduction. Reserve 1505

**16.** —— Von den nüwē In- | sulē vnd lāden so yetz kürtzlichē er | funden synt durch den Künig von Portugall. [Strassburg: Mathis Hupfuff, 1505.] Facsimile. Boston, 1926. 15 l. illus. 23½ cm. (Americana series; photostat reproductions by the Massachusetts Historical Society. no. 176.) *KB 1505
Sabin 99345.
Colophon: Getrůckt zů Strassbůrg von Mathis hůpf | vff. in dem Füntzehenhundertsté vn̄ fünfftē Jar.
One of ten photostat copies. The original is in the Henry E. Huntington Library.
Two woodcuts below title.

**17.** —— Von den nawen Jnsulen vnnd | Landen so itzt kurtzlichē erfun | den sint durch den Konigk von | Portugal. [Leipzig: Wolfgang Müller, 1505.] Photostat reproduction. 8 l. 4°. Reserve 1505
Sabin 99346. Harrisse Add. 20.
Colophon: Getruckt tzů Leybsigck durch Wolfgangk Müller (sunst Stöcklin) nach Cristgeburth | ym funfftzehenhundertisten vnd funfften iare
Wolfgang Stöckel's edition in German of the Strassburg translation, reprinted from Hupfuff's first edition. See no. 16.

**18.** —— Das sind die new gefundē menschē od' volcker In form vn̄ gestalt Als sie hie stend durch dē Cristenlichen | Künig von Portugall | gar wuunderbarlich erfunden. [Nürenberg: Georg Stuchs, 1505?] broadside. illus. f°. Photostat reproduction. Broadside 1505
Sabin 99360.
The narrative is an abridgment of, or rather an extract from, the Basel German translation, made apparently from Schönsperger's Augsburg edition. It relates almost entirely to the natives and their manner of living. Large woodcut of the Indian natives and three ships entering a bay.

**19. WOODCUT** of South American Indians. Dise figur anzaigt vns das volck vnd insel die gefunden ist durch den christenlichen künig zů Portugal oder von seinen vnderthonen. Die leüt sind also nacket hübsch. braun wolgestalt von leib. ir heübter. | halss. arm. scham. füss. frawen vnd mann ain wenig mit federn bedeckt. Auch haben die mann in iren angesichten vnd brust vid [*sic!*] edel gestain. Es hat auch nyemantz nichts sunder sind alle ding gemain. | Vnnd die mann habendt weyber welche in gefallen. es sey mütter, schwester oder freüudt [*sic!*], darjnn haben sy kain vnderschayd. Sy streyten auch mit einander. Sy essen auch ainander selbs die erschlagen | werden. vnd hencken das selbig fleisch in den rauch. Sy werden alt hundert vnd fünftzig iar. Vnd haben kain regiment. [Augsburg: Johann Froschauer, 1505?] broadside. 35½ x 25 cm. (In: Wilberforce Eames, Description of a wood engraving illustrating the South American Indians «1505». New York, 1920.) Spencer Coll. Ger. 1505
Harrisse BAV 20. Sabin 99362, where detailed information can be found.
Woodcut, 33½ x 22 cm., colored by hand, above four lines of text printed in Gothic type. The cut is printed from the same block as that in the Munich library. See no. 20.
Most of the statements in the text appear to be taken from the Basel translation of Vespucci's account of his third voyage. See no. 10.
One of two impressions known of the earliest xylographic picture relating to America; without doubt it is a very few years after the letter of Columbus announcing his discovery. It represents savages of Brazil (a country just then discovered) in a hut with their wives and children, dressed in their native dress and headgear. Hanging between two trees are the head and shoulder of a man roasting over a fire. In the distance on the sea are two ships. In the foreground are three warriors, two children playing, and a mother nursing another. In the background are a man and a woman making love, and beside them is another figure engaged in making a meal of a human arm, while a younger Indian looks on. The woodcut is probably founded on or a copy of an actual sketch made on the spot. It is thus the first authentic pictorial representation of the American aborigines.

**20.** —— Same title. ††* KVB 1505
Sabin 99361.
Photostat reproduction from a photograph of the original in the Staatsbibliothek, Munich.

GERMAN WORKS RELATING TO AMERICA 3

1506

21. VESPUCCI, AMERIGO. Von der new gefunndē Region die wol | ein welt genennt mag werden, Durch den Cristenlichen Kü | nig von Portugall, wunnderbarlich erfunden. [Nürnberg: Wolffganng Hueber, 1506.] Facsimile. 11 p. 4°.
Sabin 99344. Harrisse 33. Reserve 1506
Colophon: Gedruckt yn Nüremberg | durch Wolffganng | Hueber.
Original in the Commerz-Bibliothek in Hamburg.
This also is an account of the third voyage, in 1501, and was translated from the Latin in 1505. It gives in full the date of Vespucci's sailing, the fourteenth of May 1501, while the Latin and Italian editions say the tenth or the thirteenth.

22. —— —— The same. Photostat reproduction. Stuart *KB 1506

23. —— —— The same. Photostat reproduction. Reserve 1506

24. —— —— Another copy. Facsimile. Paris: Pilinski, 1861. 6 l. illus. 4°. Reserve 1506

25. —— Von den nüwē In | sulē vnd landen so yetz kürtzlichen | erfunden synt durch den Künig von Portugall. [Strassburg, 1506.] 8 l. illus. 4°. Reserve 1506
Sabin 99347. Harrisse 40.
Colophon: Getruckt zū Strassburg in dem fünfftzē hundersten vnd sechst Jar.

26. —— —— The same. Facsimile. Boston, 1921. 8 l. illus. 8°. (Americana series; photostat reproductions by the Massachusetts Historical Society. no. 49.) Reserve 1506

27. —— —— The same. Photostat reproduction. Reserve 1506

28. —— Von den newen Jnsulen vnd lan- | den so yttz kurtzlichen erfundenn | seynd durch den kunigk von Portigal. [Leipzig: B. Martin Landsberg, 1506.] Photostat reproduction. 12 p. 4°. Reserve 1506
Sabin 99348. Harrisse 41.
Colophon: Gedruckt tzu Leypsick durch Baccalariū Martinū | Landessbergk Jm iar Tausentfunffhundert vnd sechs.
Martin Landsberg's first edition in German of the Strassburg translation, reprinted from Hupfuff's first edition. See No. 19.

29. —— Von den newen Jusulen[sic!] vnd lan- | den so yetz kurtzlichen erfundenn | seynd durch den Kunig von Portygal. [Leipzig: B. Martin Landsberg, 1506.] Photostat reproduction. 12 p. 4°. Reserve 1506
Sabin 99349.
Colophon: Gedruckt tzu Leypsick durch Baccalariū Martinum Landessberg Jm iar Ttausentfunfhundert vnd sechs.
Martin Landsberg's second edition in German of the Strassburg translation; reprinted from the first edition. See no. 28.

30. —— Van den nygē Jnsulen vnd | landen so ytzundt kortliken | befunden sindt dorch den koningk van Portugal. [Magdeburg: Jacob Winter, 1506.] Photostat reproduction. 15 p. 4°. Reserve 1506
Sabin 99350.
Colophon: Gedruckt to Magdeborch van Jacob | Winter. Na Cristi vnses leuen heren ge | borth Tusent veffhundert vnd sess Jar.
In fine: ..."Uth welscher tungen in de latinische

vñ ytzund | in düdes ein guder dichter dysse Epistel gekert | heft..."
Jacob Winter's edition in German of the Strassburg translation, reprinted from Stöckel's Leipzig edition of 1505. See no. 17.

1508

31. FRACANZANO DA MONTALBODDO, COMPILER. Newe vnbekanthe landte Und ein newe weldte in kurtz verganger zeythe erfunden. [Nürnberg: Stuchs, 1508.] 68 l. f°. Reserve 1508
Sabin 50056.
Title on a scroll encircling a globe.
Colophon: Also hat ein endte dieses Büchlein, wel- | ches auss wellischer sprach in die dewtschen | gebrachte vnd gemachte ist worden, durch | den wirdigē vnd hochgelartben herrē Job- | sten Ruchamer...Vnd durch mich Geor- | gen Stüchssen zu Nüreinbergk, Gedrückte | vnd volendte nach Christi vnsers lieben her- | ren geburdte. M.CCCC.VIIJ. Jare, am Mit- | woch sancti Mathei, des heiligen apostols | abenthe, der do was der zweyntzigste tage | des Monadts Septembris.
This is the first collection of voyages printed in German. Translation of his Paesi nouamente retrouati.
"The table of contents is not reliable. The third book is therein called the second; the fourth is taken for the third. The chapters 80-90, 91-101, and 105-108, contain the first three voyages of Columbus. The fourth voyage is not inserted at all. The work presents a remarkable peculiarity in the spelling of names. Columbus is called Dawber (male pigeon), Alonzo Niño, der Schwartze (the black), Lorenzo de Medicis, Laurentz artzt (L. the physician). As to Vespuccius, the reader will find only the third voyage." — Harrisse, no. 57. The Low Saxon version (Sabin 50057) by Henning Ghetel of Lübeck is not in The New York Public Library.

32. —— —— Another copy. Reserve 1508

1509

33. VESPUCCI, AMERIGO. Diss büchlin saget wie die zwē | durchlüchtigstē herrē her Fernandus. K. zū Castilien | vnd herr Emanuel. K. zū Portugal haben das weyte | mōr ersūchet vnnd funden vil Insulen, vnnd ein Nüwe | welt von wilden nackenden Leüten, vormals vnbekant. [Strassburg: Joh. Grüniger, 1509.] 32 l. illus. 4°. Reserve 1509 Vespucci
Sabin 99356.
Colophon: Gedruckt zū Strassburg durch Johānē Grüniger Jm iar. M.CCCC.IX. vff mitfast.
Title page has a pen facsimile by Harris after the copy in the British Museum.
First edition in German of the Four Voyages, translated from the Latin of Jean Basin.

34. —— —— Another issue. Reserve 1509 Vespucci
Sabin 99357.
Colophon: Getruckt zu Strassburg durch Johānē Grüniger Im jar. M.CCCC.IX. vff Letare.

35. DER WELT kugel | Beschrybūg der welt vnd desz gā | tzē Ertreichs hie angezōgt vñ vergleicht einer rotundē | kuglen, die dan sunderlich gemacht hie zū gehōrēde, dar | in der kauffmā vnd ein ietlicher sehen vñ mercken mag | wie die menschen vndē gegē vns wonē vñ wie die Son | vmbgang, herin beschriben mit vil seltzamē dingē. [Strassburg: Johann Grüniger, 1509.] 16 l., incl. diagrs. maps. illus. 19 cm. *KB 1509
Photostat reproduction of the original in the Austrian National Library.
Sabin 102623. Harrisse Add. 32. Schmidt, 1, 103.
Woodcut of globe on title page; l. 10[b] and 14[b] include a portion of the "nüw welt."

## 1515

**36.** COPIA der Newen eytung [sic!] auss Presilg Landt. [Augsburg: Erhart Oeglin, 1515?] Photostat reproduction. 4 l. 20 cm. (4°.)
\*KB 1515
Harrisse, BAV, 100. JCB, 1919, 1, 63.
Colophon: Gedruckt zū Augspurg durch Erhart öglin.
Original in the Bavarian Staatsbibliothek.
"This extremely curious and interesting plaquette purports to be a translation into German of a letter describing the arrival of a vessel from Brazil to a port not mentioned." — *Harrisse.*

**37.** COPIA der newen zeytung auss Presillg landt; [1515] ; Facsimileabdruck herausg. von Dr. Hans H. Bockwitz. Leipzig: Deutsches Museum für Buch und Schrift, 1920. 15 p. incl. facsims., 2 woodcut illus. (incl. coat of arms). 21 cm. (Dokumente des Zeitungswesens. No. 1.)
\*KSC Dokumente
Reproductions from the originals in the Bavarian Staatsbibliothek.
Nachweis der Ausgaben, Fundorte und Fundstellen, der Facsimile-Ausgaben, Textabdrucke und Übersetzungen, p. 13-15.

**38.** COPIA der Newen Zeytung | auss Presillg Landt. [n.p., 1515?] 4 l. 20 cm. (4°.) \*KB 1515
Harrisse, BAV 99.
No colophon.

**39.** COPIA der Newen Zeytung | auss Presilg Landt. [Augsburg: E. Oeglin, 1515?] 4 l. 20 cm. (4°.)
\*KB 1515
Harrisse, BAV 100.
Colophon: Getruckt zū Augspurg durch Erhart öglin.

**40.** COPIA der Newen Zeytung | auss Presillg Landt. [n.p., 1515?] Photostat reproduction. 4 l. 20 cm. (4°.)
\*KB 1515
Original in the Leipzig University Library.

**41.** NEW zeutung auss presillanndt. Facsimile einer handschriftlichen "Neuen Zeitung" aus dem Anfange des 16. Jahrhunderts. Mit einem Geleitwort von Geh. Reg.-Rat Prof. Dr. Konrad Haebler. Herausgegeben von Dr. Hans H. Bockwitz. Leipzig: Deutsches Museum für Buch und Schrift, 1920. 5 p., 2 facsims. (4 l.) 31 x 22 cm. (Dokumente des Zeitungswesens. No. 5.)
\*KSC Dokumente
At head of title: 1515.
"Die vielfach erörterte Frage nach der *Neuen Zeitung aus Presilg Land* hatte mit Konrad Haeblers Entdeckung einer Handschrift im Fuggerarchiv zu Augsburg im Jahre 1895 eine neue Wendung erfahren. Rund 20 Jahre später (1914) bezweifelte ein brasilianischer Gelehrter, Rodolpho B. Schuller, die Ergebnisse der Haeblerschen Arbeit in einem Schriftchen, gegen das Haebler im Folgenden Stellung nimmt. Aus der umfaugreichen Literatur, die sich an die *Neue Zeitung* knüpft ist neuerdings das Wichtigste in der *Zeitschrift des Deutschen Vereins für Buchwesen und Schrifttum.* Jahrgang 3, Heft 1-2, 1920 zusammengestellt worden." — *H. H. Bockwitz.*
See also Paul Roth, *Die neuen Zeitungen in Deutschland im 15. und 16. Jahrhundert,* Leipzig, 1914.

## 1518

**42.** AIN RECEPT von ainem holtz zu brauchen für die kranckhait | der frantzosen vnnd an- | der flüssig offen schäden | aus hispanischer sprach | zu teütsch gemacht, dar- | zū das Regimennt wie | man sich darinn halten | vnd auch darzū schickñ soll. [Augsburg, 1518.] 4 l. 8°.
Reserve 1518 Recept
Colophon: Gedruckt vnd volendt in der Kaiserlichen Statt | Augspurg an dem ersten tag des Monadts Decembris, des jars nach der geburt Cri | sti vnsers herrn Tausent fünffhun | dert vnd achtzehen jare.
Has been attributed to Leonardus Schmaus, whose Latin pamphlet, *Lucubrati uncula,* 1518 (Reserve: 1518), is listed in Sabin (no. 77661). Both booklets deal with the "Lignum Indicum" (Guaicum wood) as a remedy for syphilis.
See no. 43.

## 1519

**43.** AIN RECEPT von | ainem holtz zū brauchen für die | kranckhait der Frantzosen vnd | ander flüssig offen schäden auss | hispanischer sprach zū Teütsch | gemacht, darzū das Regiment | wie man sich darinn halten vnd | auch darzū schicken soll. [Augsburg, 1519.] 4 l. 4°.
Reserve 1519 Recept
Colophon: Gedruckt vnnd volendt in der Kayserlich- | en Statt Augspurg durch Hanns von | Erffort der jar zal nach der geburt | Cristi vnsers herren: im Tau | sent fünffhundert vñ neün | zehenden jahre.
See no. 42.

## 1520

**44.** ANGLIARA, JUAN DE. Die schiffung mitt | dem Lanndt der | Gulden Insel gefundē durch | Hern Johan võ Angliara | Hawptman des Cristen | lichen Künigs võ His | pania. gar hübsch | ding zū hõrē mit | allen yren leben | vnd sit- | ten. [Augsburg? 1520?] 4 l., incl. 1 blank (wanting). 4°.
Reserve 1520
The book describes a voyage to Calicut in 1519 and the discovery of a rich island under the sovereignty of Prester John, probably Ceylon. — *Harrisse* 102.
Harrisse supposes identity of the author and Pietro Martire d'Angbiera.
See no. 82.

**45.** EIN AUSZUG ettlicher | sendbrieff dem aller durchleüchtigisten | grossmechtigistē Fūrsten vnd Herren Herren Carl Rōmischen vnd | Hyspanischē König &c vnserm gnedigen hern durch ire verordent | Hauptleut, von wegen einer newgefundē Inseln, der selbē gelegen | heit vnd jnwoner sitten vñ gewonheitē inhaltend vor kurtzuerschi- | nen tagen zugesandt. [Nürnberg, 1520.] 71., 1 blank. 4°. Reserve 1520 Auszug
Sabin 2442.
Colophon: Getruckt in der keiserlichen Stat Nūrmberg durch | Fryderichen Peypus, vnd seliglich volend | am 17. tag Marcij des jars do man | zalt nach Christi vnsers lieben | herren geburt. M.D.XX.
This contains a relation of the expedition of de Córdoba, Grijalva and Cortés to Yucatan.

## 1522

**46.** CORTÉS, HERNANDO. Translation vss hi- | spanischer sprach zū Frantzôsisch gema | cht, so durch dē Vice Rey in Neapols, | Fraw Margareten Hertzogiñ in Bur | gundi zū geschriben. [n. p., 1522.] 4 l. 4°.
Reserve 1522 Translation
Sabin 16954. Harrisse 113.
In fine: Geben Validolyff vff dē .vij. tag Octo | bris..Anno xxiy.
The conquest of Mexico is alluded to on verso of Aiij, as follows: "Nit weit võ der selben insel haben | sy erobert ein stat genant Tenustitan, iñ deren gezalt sind sächtzig tausent hārdstetten mit ei- | ner gūten rinckthmauren ingefasst."

## GERMAN WORKS RELATING TO AMERICA

*1522, continued*

47. NEWE zeittung: von dem lande. das die | Sponier funden haben ym 1521. iare genant Jucatan. | Newe zeittung vō Prussla, vō Kay: Ma: hofe 18 Martze. 1522. | Newe zceyt von des Turcken halben von Offen geschrieben. [n. p., 1522.] Facsimile. Boston, 1928. 11 p. illus. 22½ cm. (Americana series; photostat reproductions by the Massachusetts Historical Society. no. 201.) *KB 1522
See JCB, 1919, I, 82. Harrisse BAV Add. 70.
One of eleven photostat copies reproduced from the original in the Augsburg library.
See no. 49.
See also Paul Roth, *Die neuen Zeitungen in Deutschland im 15. und 16. Jahrhundert*, Leipzig, 1914.

48. EIN SCHÖNE | Newe zeytung so Kayserlich | Mayestet auss India yetz | nemlich zůkommen seind. | Gar hüpsch võ den Newen | ynseln, vnd von yrem sytten | gar kurtzweylig zůleesen. [Augsburg: Sigmund Grimm, 1522?] 8 l. 20 x 16½ cm. (4°.) *KB 1522
Sabin 16956.
Brunet II, 165. Harrisse BAV 115. JCB, 1919, I, 81. Ternaux no. 22.
"Contains abridged account of voyages of Columbus and of the 'Conquest of Mexico,' down to 1522." — *Sabin 16956.*

49. ZUR "NEUEN ZEITUNG" aus dem Lande Yucatan vom Jahre 1522; Facsimileabdruck herausg. von Dr. H. H. Bockwitz. Leipzig: Deutscher Verein für Buchwesen und Schrifttum, 1928. 8, xi p. incl. facsims., 6 l. illus. 24 cm. (Dokumente des Zeitungswesens. No. 6.)
Harrisse BAV Add. 70. *KSC Dokumente
Includes facsimile reproduction of the original in the Augsburg Library of: Newe zeittung von dem lande, das die Sponier funden haben ym 1521. iare genant Jucatan. Newe zceyt von des Turcken halben võ Offen geschrieben. [n.p., 1522?] 6 l. illus. 16½ cm. (4°.) Without reproduction of the blank verso of the last leaf.
"Zum Inhalt und dokumentarischen Wert der *Neuen Zeitung aus Jucutan* ist zu sagen, dass sie unverkennbar auf den Briefen beruht, die Cortès nach seinem Einmarsch in Mexiko (August 1519), aber vor der Ankunft des Narvaez und vor der noche triste (1. auf 2. Juli 1520) an Kaiser Karl v. geschrieben hat." — p. 6.
See also Paul Roth, *Die neuen Zeitungen in Deutschland im 15. und 16. Jahrhundert*, Leipzig, 1914; Sophus Ruge, *Die Entdeckungsgeschichte der Neuen Welt*, Hamburg, 1892, v. 1, p. 84.
See no. 47.

### 1524

50. EIN BEWERT RECEPT wie man | das holtz Guagacam für | die krannckheit der | Frantzosen brau | chen sol. [Germany?] 1524. 6 p. 4°. Reserve 1524
Syphilis.

### 1525

51. FRIES, LORENZ. Yslegung der Mer | carthen oder Cartha Marina | Darin man sehen mag, wa einer in der welt sey, vnd wa ein ietlich | Land, Wasser vnd Stat gelegē ist. Das als in dē büchlin zefindē. [Strassburg: Joh. Grieninger, 1525.] 1 p.l., 29 l. map. illus. f°.
†* KB 1525
Sabin 25964. Harrisse 133. Ruge 117.
Colophon: Getruckt zů Strassburg von | Johannes Grieninger, vnd | vollendet vff vnser Lie | hen Frawen abent der | geburt. Im. Jar | 1525.
The first chapter relates wholly to America, beginning "Das neuw land hie beschriben, America genant, ist gar nackendt als gros als ein vierdes teil der gantzen welt..."
See no. 52.

### 1527

52. FRIES, LORENZ. Yslegung der Mercar | then oder Carta Marina Darin | man sehen mag, wo einer in der wellt sey, vnd wo | ein yetlich Landt, Wasser vnd Stadt | gelegen ist. Das alles in dem | büchlin zū finden... [Strassburg: Johannes Grieninger, 1527.] Photostat reproduction. 26 l. map. illus. f°. *KB 1527
Colophon: Getruckt zū Strassburg von Johannes Grieninger, vnd | vollendet vff sant Erasi | mus tag. Jm Jar. 1527.
See no. 51.

### 1530

53. FRIES, LORENZ. Ynderweisung | vnd vsslegunge | Der Cartha Marina oder die mer | cartē | Darin man sehen mag, wa einer in d'welt sy, vnd wa ein ytlich | land, wasser vnd stet ligē, als in dē büchlin angezōgt vñ in d'chartē zůsehen. [Strassburg: Johannes Grieninger, 1530.] 22 l. illus. f°. Reserve 1530
Sabin 25964. Harrisse 158.
Colophon: Getruckt zū Strassburg von | Johannes Grieninger vnd | vollendet vff Sant Jörgē | abent. Jm. jar. MDXXX.
This is an abridged edition of the *Yslegung der Mercharten* of 1525 (see no. 51). Only three woodcuts are retained, one of which is on the title page.

### 1533

54. ZUMARRAGA, JUAN DE, BISHOP OF MEXICO. Ein Sendbrieff des Bischoffs der grossem [*sic!*] | stadt Temixtitan in der Newen erfundenn | welt, gen Tolosa in Franck | reich geschriben. 4°. (In: Bottschafft des Grossmechtigsten Konigs Dauid...[n.p., 1533?] l. 18b-19b.) *KB 1533 Bottschafft
No colophon. Possibly printed at Dresden or Leipzig.
See Harrisse BAV 177. JCB, 1919, I, 107.
Missionary activities in Mexico.

55. —— Ein Sendbrieff des Bischoffs der gros | sen stadt Temixtitan in der Newen erfunden welt | gen Tolosa in Franckreich geschriben. 4°. (In: Bottschafft des Grossmechtigsten | Konigs Dauid... [Dresden: W. Stoeckel, 1533.] 1. 23b-24b.) *KB 1533 Bottschafft
Colophon: Gedrugkt zu Dressden durch Wolffgang Stöckel. 1533.

### 1534

56. FRANCK, SEBASTIAN. Weltbůch: spiegel | vñ bildtniss des gantzen erd- | bodens von Sebastiano Franco Wōr- | densi in vier bůcher, nemlich in Asiam | Aphricam, Europam vnd Americam, gestelt vnd abteilt,... Auch etwas võ new | gefundenen welten vnd Jnseln, ... auss vilen weitleüffigen büchern in | ein handtbůch eingeleibt vnd ver- | fasst, vormals dergleichen | in Teütsch nie auss- | gangen. | Mit einem zů end angehenckten Register alles innhalts. | ... [Tübingen: Ulrich Morhart, Anno 1534.] 6 p.l., iii-ccxxxvij f., 7 l. f°. Reserve 1534
Sabin 25468. Harrisse 197.
A general geography of the then known world. "America das vierdt Bůch...," p. ccxi-ccxxxvij.

*1534, continued*

57. NOVUS ORBIS REGIONUM. Die New | welt, der landschaf- | ten vnnd Insulen, so | bis hie her allen Altweltbeschrybern vnbekant | Jungst aber von den Portugalesern vnnd Hispaniern jm | Nider- | genglichen Meer herfunden. Sambt den sitten vnnd gebreuchen der Inwonenden | völcker. Auch was Gütter oder Waren man bey jnen funden, vnd jnn | vnsere Landt bracht hab... Strassburg: durch Georgen Vlricher | von Andla, am viertzehenden tag des Mertzens. An. M.D.XXXIII. 6 p.l., 242 [i.e. 252] f. f°.     Reserve 1534 Novus
Sabin 34106. Harrisse 188.
Translation by Michael Herr of Huttich's Novus Orbis and supplementary material. Edited by Simon Grynaeus.

58. NEWE Zeytung | aus Hispanien und | Italien. Mense Februario. | 1534. [n.p., 1534.] 4 l. 21 cm. (4°.)     *KB 1534
Sabin 54945. Harrisse BAV 195.
Contains news from Turkey and Peru. The latter seems to be taken from the letters of Pizarro. Its accounts of the wealth of Peru are greatly exaggerated.
See also Paul Roth, *Die neuen Zeitungen in Deutschland im 15. und 16. Jahrhundert*, Leipzig, 1914.

*1535*

59. COPEY etlicher brieff | so auss Hispania kummē | seindt, anzaygent die eygenschafft des, | Newen Lands, so newlich von Kay. | May. Armadi auff dem newen | Môr gefunden ist worden, | durch die Hispanier. [n.p.,] D.M.XXXV. 4 l. 4°.     Reserve 1535
Harrisse Add. 108.
Relating to Peru. "Solche zeyttung ist auss | Hyspanischer sprach, in die Frantzösische getransfertirt worden, darnach in Nyderlendisch vnd Hoch- | teusch sprach. Dise zway schryff bat ein glaubwür- | diger Mann mit nammen Mayster Adolff Kay. May. Secretari in Hispania abladen sehen." — *l. 4°.*

60. EGENOLF, CHRISTIAN. Chronica, Beschrei- | bung vnd gemeyne anzeyge, Vonn | aller Wellt herkommen, Fürnämen | Lannden, Stande, Eygenschafften | Historien, wesen, manier, sitten, an vnd abgang. Auss den glaubwir | digsten Historiē, On all Glos | se vnd Zůsatz, Nach Hi- | storischer Warheit | beschriben. Franckenfort am Meyn: Bei Christian Egenolffen [1535]. 6 l., cxxxvii [i.e. 139] f., 1 blank. woodcut. f°.     Reserve 1535
Sabin 12957. Harrisse 211.
On verso of ciii, the writer treats "Von America dem vierdten Theyl der Welt, Anno MCCCCXCVII erfunden."
Harrisse is of the impression that this is an edition of Steinhoewel's Chronicle, compiled by Christian Egenolf.
The book contains many illustrations and portraits, the latter in form of medallions.

*1541*

61. RYFF, WALTHER HERMANN. Ejn wolgegründt nutzlich vnd | heylsam handtbüchlin gemeyner Practick | der gantzen leibartzney,... Allen denen zunutz, trost | vnd hilff, die mit kranckheytten vnd gepresten des | leibs beladen seind, auss sunderlichem ge- | neygtem willen, in Teütsche sprach | verfassst [*sic!*] vnd in Truck | geben... [Strassburg: bey Balthassar Beck,] 1541. 482 l. 12°.     Reserve 1541
Colophon: Getruckt zu Strassburg bey Balthassar Beck. 1541.
Refers to Guaicum wood as a remedy for syphilis.

62. —— New erfundne | Heylsame, vnd bewårte artzney, gewisse hilff vnnd radt, nit al- | lein die Frantzosen oder bösen blatern, sunder | auch anders sorgliche schwere kräckheyt man- | gel vnd gebrechē, menschlichs leibs, so sich eüs | serlichen oder innerlichen erheben, aber bissher | für vnheylbar geacht worden, gründtlichen | vnd gentzlichen zů vertreiben,... mit vormals vnbekanter, vnd biss auff | dise zeit vnbewisster bereytung, gebrauch vnd | würckung des Indianischen holtz Gua- | iacum oder Frantzosen holtz genen | net, yetz und newlich erfundē, | vnd an tag geben. | Durch M. Gualtherum H. Ryff in Teütsche | sprach verfassst [*sic!*], vnd in truck verordnet. [Strassburg: Balthassar Beck,] MDXLI. 110 l., 4 blank. illus. 8°.     Reserve 1541
Colophon: Getruckt zů Strassburg bey Balthassar Beck.
See no. 61.

*1542*

63. FRANCK, SEBASTIAN. Weltbůch, spie- | gel vnd bildtnis des gan- | tzen Erdtbodens, von Sebastiano | Franco Wördensi inn vier bůcher | nåmlich in Asiam, Aphricam, Eu- | ropam vnd Americam, gestelt und abteylt... nit ausz... fablen, sunder auss | angenomnen, glaubwürdigen, erfarnen Weltbe- | schreibern, můselig zuhauff getragen, vnnd | auss vilen weitleüffigen bůchern, in ein | handtbůch eyngeleibt vnd verfas- | set, vormals dergleichen inn | Teütsch nie auss- | gangen. | Mit einem zuend angehenckten Register alles innhalts. [Frankfurt am Main?] 1542. 5 p.l., iii–cxxxvii f., 7 l. f°.     Reserve 1542
Sabin 25469. Harrisse 238.
"This edition is not merely a reissue of the original, with a fresh title, as Harrisse asserts, but is entirely a new setting-up of the text." — *B. Quaritch.* The alterations are slight, however.
See no. 56.

*1543*

64. LUCIDARIUS. M. Elucidarius, Von al | lerhandt geschöpffen Gottes, den Engeln | den Hymmeln, Gestirns, Planeten, vnd wie alle Creaturen | geschaffen seind auff erden. Auch wie die Erd inn drey thail | gethailt, vnd dero Länder, sampt der Völcker darīn, aigen | schafften, vnnd wunderbarlichen Thieren, auss Plinio | Secundo, Solino, vnnd andern Weldtbeschrey | bern, ain kurtze vnnd lustige anzaygung. Augspurg: Gedruckt durch Hainrich Stayner. Anno MDXLIII. 40 l. incl. diagr. illus. 20 cm. (4°.)
*KB 1543
There is a reference to America in Chapter 8.
See no. 51 (p. 102) in K. Schorbach, *Studien über das deutsche Volksbuch Lucidarius*... Strassburg, 1894. 8°. (Quellen und Forschungen zur Sprach- und Culturgeschichte der germanischen Völker, v. 74, NFF.)

## 1544

**65. MUENSTER, SEBASTIAN.** Cosmographia. | Beschreibūg | aller Lender Dūrch | Sebastianum Munsterum | in welcher begriffen | Aller vőlcker, Herrschafften | Stetten, vnd namhafftiger flecken, herkommen: | Sitten, gebreüch, ordnung, glauben, secten, vnd hantierung, durch die gantze welt, vnd fürnem- | lich Teütscher nation. | Was auch besunders in iedem landt gefunden | vnnd darin beschehen sey. | ... Basel: durch Henrichum Petri. Anno M.D.XLIIII. 6 l., dclix(i) p., 24 maps. illus. f°.

Sabin 51385. Harrisse 258.   Reserve 1544

The mappemund has the words, "America seu insula Brasilij;" and map xxiiii, the following inscription on the verso, "Die newe | weldt der grossen | und vilen Inse- | len von den Spa | niern gefunden." America is described under the heading, "Von den neüwen inseln," pages dcxxxvi to dcxlii.

## 1546

**66. LERCHER, LAUX.** Ein neüwe zeitung, wie des Künigs auss Portugals Schiffleüt einen | grossen mann haben zū wegen bracht, heisst Christian gross | Jndia, wie er sich vermåhelt hat, mit einer Junckfrawen die | Christenheit Europa genannt... Dises grossen mans vnd seines gemahels bedeüttung | würt Christenlich aussgelegt, durch Laux Lerchern | von Riedlingen. [n.p., 1546.] 7 l. 4°.   Reserve 1546

Sabin 40134.

Colophon: Getruckt vnd volendt auff das tausent fünff hun- | dert vnd sechs vnd viertzigst jar, auff den | andern tag des Jenners.

"It strictly belongs...to a 'Bibliotheca Africana.' " — *Sabin.*

## 1550

**67. CORTÉS, HERNANDO.** Ferdinandi | Cortesii. |. Von dem Newen Hispanien, so im | Meer gegem Nidergang, Zwo gantz lustige vnnd | fruchtreiche Historien, an den grossmåchtigisten vnüberwindt- | lichisten Herren, Carolvm. v. Rőmischen | Kaiser &c. Künig in Hispanien &c. | Die erst im M.D.XX. jar zůgeschriben, in wellicher grundt- | lich vnd glaubwirdig erzelt wirdt, der Abendtlåndern, vnnd | sonderlich der Hochberümpten statt Temixtitan eroberung. | Die andere im 1524. jar, Wie Temixtitan so abgefallen, wider erobert, Nachmals andere herrliche Syg, sampt der erfindung des Meers SVR, | So man für das Jndianisch Meer achtet. | Darzů auch von vilen andern Landtschafften Jndiæ, | So erfunden von dem 1536. biss auf das 42. Jar. | ...Erstlich in Hispanischer Sprach von Cortesio selbst beschriben, Nachmals | von Doctor Peter Sauorgnan auss Friaul in Lateinische sprach Transferiert, | Entlich aber in Hochteütsche sprach, ...von Xysto Betuleio vň Andrea | Diethero von Augspurg,... Augspurg: durch Philipp Vlhart, Jn der Kirchgassen, bey S. Vlrich Anno Domini M.D.L. 6 p.l., xxxix f., 3 l., lx f. 32 cm.   †* KB 1550

Sabin 16957.

The first part, translated by Sixt Birck (xxxix f.) contains the second narration. The "Ander histori" (2 p.l., lx f.) is translated by Andreas Diether; the first twelve chapters (f. i–xi*) being taken from Peter Martyr's fourth "Decade," followed by Cortés's third narration (Chapter 13–44, f. xi*–l). The remainder of the work (f. li–lx) contains a letter by Oviedo, dated San Domingo, Jan. 20, 1543.

## 1557

**68. FEDERMANN, NICOLAUS.** Indianische Historia. | EIn schőne kurtz- | weilige Historia Niclaus Fe | dermanns des Jüngern von | Vlm erster raise so er von Hispania vň | Andolosia auss in Indias des Occea- | nischen Mőrs gethan hat, vnd | was ihm allda ist begegnet biss auff sein | widerkunfft inn Hispaniam, auffs | kurtzest beschriben, gantz | lustig zů lesen. [Hagenau: S. Bund,] MDLVII. 63 l. 4°.

Sabin 23997.   Reserve 1557

Colophon: Getruckt zů Hagenaw bei Sigmund Bund, etc.

This is the narrative of Federmann's first trip only, 1529–1532. He commanded part of the German troops sent by the Welsers, of Augsburg, to Venezuela. See Victor Hautzsch, *Die überseeischen Unternehmungen der Augsburger Welser* [Altenburg], 1895, *TLC p.v.139, no. 5;* Otfrid von Hanstein, *Auf der Jagd nach dem goldenen Kaziken; die erste deutsche Kolonie der Welser in Venezuela, 1527 bis 1555,* Leipzig [cop. 1929] (Sammlung interessanter Entdeckungsreisen, Bd. 7, *HDN*); K. H. Panhorst, *Deutschland und Amerika, ein Rückblick auf das Zeitalter der Entdeckungen und die ersten deutsch-amerikanischen Verbindungen, unter besonderer Beachtung der Unternehmungen der Fuger und Welser,* München, 1928, *HCP.*

The original account of Federmann's expedition, written in Spanish by a "notario scribano publico" (an edition of 1916 is in *HDN*) was translated into German by Federmann and published for the first time (with his additions) by his brother-in-law, Hans Kiffhaber (or Jean Kiefhaber). See the reprint in Literarischer Verein in Stuttgart, *Bibliothek,* Bd. 47, *NFF;* also M. Weinhold, *Ueber Nicolaus Federmann's Reise in Venezuela 1529–1531,* in Verein fuer Erdkunde zu Dresden, *Jahresbericht,* Dresden, 1866, No. 3, p. 91–112, *KL;* and Arnold Federmann, *Deutsche Konquistadoren in Südamerika,* Berlin [cop. 1938], *HDN.*

**69. STADEN, HANS.** Varhaftige. be- | schreibung eyner Landschafft der wilden | nacketen, grimmigen menschenfresser leuthen, in der newen | welt America gelegen. Vor vnd nach Christi geburt im Land | zů Hessen vnbekant, biss vff dise zwey negst vergangene jar | Da sie Hans Staden von Homberg auss Hessen durch sein | eygne erfarung erkant, vnd ytzt durch den truck an tag gibt. | Vnd zum andern mal fleissig corrigiret vnd gebessert. | ...Mit eyner vorrede D. Joh. Dryandri, genant Eychman | [Marburg: Andres Colben, 1557.] 89 l. illus. 19½ x 15½ cm. (4°.)   *KB 1557

Sabin 90039.

Colophon: Getruckt zū Marpurg in Hessen land, bei Andres Colben, Vff Mariae Geburts tag, Anno MDLVII.

For later German editions, see nos. 73, 92, 93, 125A.

The work is in two sections, the first describing Staden's voyages and adventures, and nine months' captivity in Brazil; the second giving an account of the manners and customs of the Tupi Indians whose prisoner he was.

See R. F. Burton's annotations and the bibliography (p. xcv–xcvi), in *The captivity of Hans Stade of Hesse, in A. D. 1547–1555, among the wild tribes of eastern Brazil; translated by Albert Tootal,* London: Hakluyt Society, 1874, *KBD (Hakluyt);* and Hans Staden, *Ein deutscher Landsknecht in der Neuen Welt; bearbeitet von Professor Dr. R. Lehmann-Nitsche,* Leipzig, 1929 (Alte Reisen und Abenteuer), *HBC.*

*1557, continued*

70. STADEN, HANS. Warhaftige | Historia vnd beschreibung eyner Landt- | schafft der Wilden, Nacketen, Grimmigen Menschfresser | Leuthen, in der Newenweldt America gelegen, vor vnd nach | Christi geburt im Land zū Hessen vnbekannt, biss vff dise ij. nechst vergangene jar, Da sie Hans Staden von Homberg auss Hessen durch sein eygne erfarung erkant | vnd yetzo durch den truck an tag gibt. | ...Mit eyner vorrede D. Joh. Dryandri, genant Eychman | ... Marpurg, im jar M.D.LVII. 89 l. map. illus. 20 x 16 cm. (4°.) *KB 1557
Sabin 90036, JCB, 1919, I, 199.
Colophon: Zū Marpurg im Kleeblatt, bei Andres Kolben, vff Fastnacht. 1557. Dedication and preface dated 1556. This is probably the first edition. (See Sabin 90037.)

71–72. —— Warhafftige Historia | vnnd beschreibung einer Landschafft | der Wilden, Nacketen, Grimmigen Menschfres- | ser Leuthen, in der Newen Welt America gelegen, vor vnd | nach Christi geburt im Land zu Hessen vnbekant, biss auff diese ij. nechst vergangene jar, Da sie Hans Staden von Homberg auss Hessen | durch sein eygene erfarung erkant, vnd jetzund | durch den truck an tag | gibt. | ...Mit einer vorrede D. Joh. Dryandri, genant Eychman | ... [Franckfurt: Weygandt Han, 1557?] 84 l. illus. 19½ x 15 cm. *KB 1557
Sabin 90038.
Colophon: Gedruckt zu Franckfurdt am Mayn durch Weygandt Han, in der Schnurgassen zum Krug.

**1567**

73. FRANCK, SEBASTIAN. Ander theil dieses Welt- | buchs von Schiff- | fahrten. | Warhafftige Be- | schreibunge aller | vnd mancherley sorgfeltigen Schif- | farten, auch viler vnbekanten erfundnen Landtschafften,... Item von erschrecklicher, seltzamer Natur vnd Eygenschafft der Leuthfresser,...zusamen getragen. | Durch Vlrich Schmidt von Straubingen, vnd andern mehr, so daselbst | in eigener Person gegenwertig gewesen, vnd solches erfaren | ... Franckfurt am Mayn: [Sigmund Feirabends und Simon Hûters,] Anno 1567. 6 l. (one blank), 110, 59 f., 1 l. f°. Reserve 1567
Sabin 25471.
Staden's narrative (see Nos. 69, 70, 71) is reprinted on folios 27–59 of the second Buch.
Bound with his *Erst Theil* (no. 74).

74. —— Erst theil dieses Welt- | buchs, von Newen | erfundnen Landt- | schafften. | Warhafftige Be- | schreibunge aller | theil der Welt, darinn nicht allein etli- | che alte Landschafften, ...beschrieben werden, sondern auch sehr viel neuwe, so zu vnsern zeiten, ...erfunden seyn, ...Dessgleichen auch etwas von New gefundenen Welten, vnd aller darinn gelegnen Võlcker, ...auss etlichen glaubwirdigen...Bûchern, ... Durch Sebastian Franck von Wõrd, zum ersten an tag | geben, jetzt aber...auff ein neuwes vbersehen, | vnd in ein wolgeformtes Handt- | buch verfasset. [Frankfurt: M. Lechler,] Anno M.D.LXVII. 6 l., ccxlii f., 8 l. (one blank.) f°. Reserve 1567
Sabin 25471.

A large portion of this volume relates to America.
Note also *Wahrhaftige Beschreibung aller und mancherley sorgfältigen Schiffahrten auch viler unbehandten Landschaften, etc.; durch Ulrich Schmidt von Straubingen und andern mehr*, Francfurt, 1567. — *cf.* Ternaux 106.

**1570**

75. GIOVIO, PAOLO, BISHOP OF NOCERA. Pauli Jouij, von | Com, Bischoffs | zu Nucera: | Warhafftige Be- | schreibunge aller | Chronickwirdiger namhafftiger Hi- | storien vnd Geschichten, so sich bey Menschen gedåchtnuss, von | dem tausend vier hundert vnd vier vnd neuntzigsten, biss auff das tausend fünff | hundert vnd siben vnd viertzigste jar, hin vñ wider in der gantzen Welt,...zugetragen... Von dem ... Herrn Paulo Jouio...in Lateinischer Sprach...beschrieben, Vnd jetzund zum theil durch...Georgium Forberger... Vnd in | den vbrigen Theilen, durch...Hieronymū Halueriũ...in die hohe Teutsche Sprach verdolmetscht,... Franckfurt am Mayn, im jar | M.D.LXX. 3 parts in 1 v. illus. f°. †*KB 1570
Colophon: Gedruckt zu Franckfurt am | Mayn, bey Georg Raben, in verlegung | Petri Perne, Bürgers vnd Buchdru- | ckers zu Basel. M.D.LXX.
Contains brief accounts of early discoveries in America. See part 2, p. 315–316.

**1571**

76. JESUITS. Sendtschreyben vnd | warhaffte zeytungen. | Von Auffgang | vnd erweiterung des Chri- | stenthumbs, bey den Hayden inn | der newen welt: Auch von veruolgung | vnnd hailigkait, der Gaistlichen Apo- | stolischen Vorsteher daselbs, so erst di- | ses jar, auss den Orientischen Jn- | dien kommen, vnd jetzt inn | teutsche spraach transs- | feriert worden. | Durch D. Philipp Dobereiner | von Tûrschenreut. | ... [München: A. Berg,] Anno M.D.LXXI. 111 l. 16°. Reserve 1571 Drey
Colophon: Gedruckt zu München, bey Adam Berg. Anno 1571.
Bound with: Drey Christliche Predigten. 1571.
Missionary activities of the Jesuits.

**1576**

77. FEYERABEND, SIGMUND. Cosmographia | Das ist: | Warhaffte eigent- | liche vnd kurtze Beschreibung | dess gantzen Erdbodems, nemlich, Europe, ...vnd die | nach Petolomeo neuw erfundnen Jnseln, Americe vnd Magellane (so jetzt die neuwe | Welt genennt) ... Franckfurt am Mayn [P. Reffeler,] M.D.LXXVI. 73 l. f°. Reserve 1576
Colophon: Gedruckt zu Franckfurt am | Mayn, durch Paulum Reffelern, in Ver- | legung Sigmund Feyerabends. M.D.LXXVI.
"Die Spanier nennen jre Neuwe welt America | auch Jndien | aber vnrecht | dann dieses Jndien hat seinen Namen nach dem fuernemesten vnd namhafften Fluss Jndus | so darinnen laufft. Vand wölte man America auch nach jrem fuernemesten Flüssen einen Namen geben | so würde sie ehe Oreliana | oder Amonsonia | dann Jndia heissen." — *p. 65*. No further mention of America.
As to Sigmund Feyerabend, see Heinrich Pallmann, in *Archiv für Frankfurts Geschichte und Kunst*, Neue Folge, Bd. 7, 1881, EKZ.

## GERMAN WORKS RELATING TO AMERICA

*1576, continued*

77A. FISCHART, JOHANN. Das Glückhafft Schiff | von Zürich. | ... [Augsburg, 1576.] 8°. (In his: Werke. Stuttgart: Union deutsche Verlagsgesellschaft [1895]. Teil 1, p. 131-197.)
NGT
Added title page: Deutsche National-Litteratur. Bd. 18, Abt. 1.
Note verses 327-330:
Weren dise am Meer geseasen,
So lang wer vnersûch nicht gwesen
America, die newe Welt
Dan jr Lobgir het dahin gstellt.

78. NEWE Zeyttung | auss den New erfundnen | Jnseln, wie daselbst gros- | ser Schaden durch Erdbi- | dem geschehen, im Jar nach der Geburt | vnsers Erlösers vnd Seligmachers Je- | su Christj M.D.LXXVJ. den XX. Brachmo- | nats. [n.p., 1577.] 4 l. 20½ cm. (4°.)  *KB 1577
See Paul Roth, *Die neuen Zeitungen in Deutschland im 15. und 16. Jahrhundert*, Leipzig, 1914.
Note: Cosmographia: das ist: wahrhaffte Beschreibung des gantzen Erdbodems, nemlich Europe, 1576, is not in the Library.

### 1579

79. BENZONI, GIROLAMO. Der | Newenn | Weldt vnd In- | dianischen Königreichs, newe vnnd | wahrhaffte History, von allen Geschichten, Handlungen | Thaten, Strengem vnnd Ernstlichem Regiment der Spanier gegen den | Indianern,...Desgleichen, | Von der Indianer wunderbarlichen Sitten, Statuten, Glauben, | ... Erstlich, | durch Hieronymum Bentzon von Meyland in Welscher Spraach | wahrhafftig beschrieben, vnnd selbs persônlich in XIII, Jaren durchwanderet. | Vorhin nie in Teutscher Spraach dessgleichen gesehen: Erst jetzt mit sonderm Fleiss | allen Regenten vnd Oberherrn, sambt liebhabern der Historien, | zu nutz auss dem Latein in das Teutsch | gebracht. | Durch | Nicolaum Höniger von Königshofen an der Tauber. Basel: durch Sebastian Henricpetri [1579]. 4 p.l., 220 p. f°. Reserve 1579
Sabin 4797.
The colophon contains the date of 1579.
For details, see note on no. 82A.

### 1580

80. SETTLE, DIONYSE. Beschreibung | Der schiffart des Haubt- | mans Martini Forbissher auss Engel- | land, in die Lender gegen West vnd Nordt- | west, im Jar 1577. Darinnen diser Lender Inwohner ˚sit- | ten vnd weiss zu leben, sampt jren Trachten vnd | Waffen Abcontrefeiung, auch andern, zuuor | vnbekandten vnd sonderlichen sachen, | angezeigt wirdt. Auss dem Frantzôsischen auffs trewlichste in | das Teutsche gebracht. Nûrnberg. | M.D.LXXX. 13 l. 1 illus. 20 x 15 cm.  *KB 1580
Sabin 25996, 79344 (improved entry). JCB, 1919, I, pt. 2, 279.
Colophon: Gedruckt zu Nürnberg durch Katharinam Gerlachin vnd Johanns vom Berg Erben.
Full-page woodcut of natives brought back to England. Rare first edition of the German translation of Dionyse Settle's account of the second voyage of Frobisher. Settle accompanied Frobisher on this voyage in 1577. His account appeared in English in the same year. In 1578 it was published in French, translated by N. Pithou, and in 1580 the Latin and German editions (from the French) were printed.
See also "Dionyse Settle's account of the second voyage," in V. Stefansson's *The three voyages of Martin Frobisher*, 1938, v. 2, p. 1-25, * KP *(Argonaut)*, and G. B. Parks's "The two versions of Settle's Frobisher narrative," in *Huntington Library quarterly*, v. 2, p. 59-65, *HND.

### 1581

81. FEYERABEND, SIGMUND, EDITOR. General Chronica | Das ist: | Warhaffte eigent- | liche vnd kurtze Beschreibung | vieler namhaffter, vnd zum theil biss daher vnbekannter Landtschaff- | ten...vnd...ein | kurtzer Summarischer doch verstendlicher Ausszug vnd Beschreibung der neuw erfun- | denen Inseln, Americe vnd Magellane, so man die neuwe Welt pflegt zu nennen. | Darinnen alle Völker vnd Nationen...fûr die Augen gestelt werden. | Jetzt auffs neuw mit sonderm grossen fleiss, besser als zuvor, beschrieben vnd verteutscht ... Franckfurt am Mayn, M.D.LXXXI. 3 p.l., 142 [i.e. 143] f. f°. Reserve 1581
Ternaux 2897.
The third part treating the "neuwen Inseln" is wanting in this copy.
See no. 77.

### 1582

82. ANGHIERA, PIETRO MARTIRE D'. Ander Theil, | Der Newen Welt vnd Indiani- | schen Nidergängischen Königsreichs... Erstlich | Durch Petrum Martyrem...beschrieben...Verteuschet, | Durch | Nicolaum Höniger von Kônigshofen | an der Tauber. | ... Basel: Durch Sebastian Henricpetri [1582]. 12 p.l., ccxlvdcij p., 1 l. f°. (In: G. Benzoni. Erste Theil... Basel, 1582.) Reserve 1582 Benzoni
For another German edition of the same place and year, see Sabin 45012.
As to Pietro Martire d'Anghiera, see H. A. Schumacher, *Petrus Martyr der Geschichtsschreiber des Weltmeeres*, New York, 1879, H; Theodore Maynard, "Peter Martyr d'Anghiera: humanist and historian," in the *Catholic historical review*, 1931, v. 16, p. 435-448, IAA; J. H. Sinclair, "Bibliografía de Pedro Martir de Anghiera," in *Academia nacional de historia, Quito, Boletín*, 1930, v. 10, January / May, p. 18-43, †HCA.
See nos. 44, 82A.

82A. BENZONI, GIROLAMO. Erste Theil | Der | Newenn | Weldt vnd In- | dianischen Nidergängischen König- | reichs, Newe vnd Wahrhaffte History, von allen Geschichten, Handlungen, Thaten, Strengem vnd sträfflichem Regiment der Spanier gegen den Indianern, ...Durch Hieronymum Bentzon von Meylandt in Lateinischer | Spraach erstlich beschrieben, vnd selbs Persônlich in XIII. | Jaren erfahren vnd durchwandert. | ...[Basel: Sebastian Henricpetri, 1582.] 10 p.l., 244 p. f°. Reserve 1582
Sabin 4798.
Colophon: Getruckt | Zu Basel, durch Sebastian Henricpetri. | ...
"Die Weitschweifigkeit des Originals ist etwas abgekürzt." — *G. H. Stuck, Nachtrag zu seinem Ver-*

*1582, continued*

**82A.** BENZONI, GIROLAMO, *continued*
*zeichnis von aelteren und neueren Land- und Reisebeschreibungen, Halle, 1785, p. 12, KB.*
The work consists of three parts. The first (p. 1–xcij) commences with the statement, "Under andere fürtrefflichen Gutthaten vnnd Zier, | so Gott zu vnserer zeit dem Menschlichen Geschlecht hat mitgetheilet | mögen wir billich die Offenbarung vñ erfindung der Newen Welt auch zehlen," and deals with the discovery of the new world and tells about the Spanish rule in Hispaniola, stressing the cruelties of the conquerors. The second (p. xciii–clxiiij) describes Central America. The third (p. clxv–ccxliij) treats of Peru. "Zuletst beschleusst er dieses Buoch mit erzehlung wie er widerumb auss Jndia in sein Vatterlandt kommen sey." See also the edition of Benzoni's work by W. H. Smyth, printed for the Hakluyt Society, London, 1857, *KBD (Hakluyt).*
See nos. 82, 83, 83A.

**83.** —— Another copy.   Reserve 1582
This copy does not contain the third part by Apollonius Levinus. See no. 85.

*1583*

**83A.** APOLLONIUS, LEVINUS. Dritte Theil | der Newen Welt | Des Peru- | nischen Königreichs, |... Item, | Von der Frantzosen Schiffarth in...Floridam,... M.D.LXV... Mit angehenckter | Supplication an König Carol den IX, in Franckreich, der Erschlagnen Frantzosen | Witwen, Waysen, Verwandten vnd Einwohnern in der Landtschafft Florida, | darinn sie jhr Vnschuld gegen den Spaniern vor Königlicher | May. gründtlich erkläret vnd geoffenbaret. | Alles | Durch...Levinvm Apollonivm Gandobrv- | ganvm,...beschrieben,...verteutschet, | Durch | Nicolaum Höniger... Basel: [Sebastian Henricpetri, 1583.] 6 p.l., cccxvi p., 1 l. f°. (In: G. Benzoni. Erste Theil ... Basel, 1582.)   Reserve 1582 Benzoni
Sabin 1762a.

*1585*

**84.** NEWE Zeittung auss Venedig. | Darin wirdt Confir- | mirt die gross Niderlag des Türcken | ...Daneben auch ein kurtze verzaichnuss der rei- | chen Flotta auss Terra Firme, vnd New Spanien |...Anno Dñi 1585. München [1585]. 4 l. 19 cm. (4°.)   Reserve 1585
See also Paul Roth, *Die neuen Zeitungen in Deutschland im 15. und 16. Jahrhundert,* Leipzig, 1914.

**85.** —— The same. Facsimile. Boston, 1927. 4 l. 24 cm. (Americana series; photostat reproductions by the Massachusetts Historical Society. no. 181.)   Reserve 1585

*1586*

**86.** CYSAT, RENWART. Warhafftiger Bericht, Von den New- | erfundnen Japponischen | Jnseln vnd Königreichen, auch von anderen | zuvor vnbekandten Jndianischen Landen ... Durch | Renvvardvm Cysatvm, |...auss dem Jtalienischen | in das Teutsch gebracht, vnd jetzt zum ersten- | mal im Truck aussgangen. Freyburg | in Vchtlandt [*sic!*]: bey Abraham | Gempertin, 1586. 9 p.l., 107(1) p., 9 l., 393(1) p., 3 l. 8°.   Reserve 1586
Sabin 18220.
Contains in its second part on p. 323–393: Noch ein ande- | rer Sendtbrieff H. Quiritij | Caxa,...auss | dem Collegio auff jender seydt dess Meers, in Brasilien | gelegen...im Jahr 1575. zu Latein aussgangen. | ...Jetsundt aber in die gemeine teutsche | Spraach verdolmetschet, vnd erstlich im | Truck aussgangen.

*1588*

**87.** FRICIUS, VALENTINUS. Indianischer | Religionstandt der gan- | tzen newen Welt, beider | Indien gegen Auff vnd | Nidergang der | Sonnen: | Schleinigister Form auss | gründtlichen Historien, sonder- | bar dess Hochwirdigen Vatters Franci- | sci Gonzagen Barfüsserische Ordenscroniken | vnd Didaci Vallades, geistlicher Rhetoric | zusammen gezogen, vnd aussm Latein | in hochteutsch verwendet: | Durch F. Valentinum Fricium,... Ingolstadt: durch | Wolffgang Eder. | MDLXXXVIII. 16 p.l., 199(1) p., 1 l. 8°.   Reserve 1588
Probably the earliest history of the Church in America and the Philippine Islands.
Of special interest: Das 17. Capitul (p. 157–160) narrates Columbus's voyage and continues with the founding of the first church in the new world as follows: "So bald nun dise Jnsuln eingenommen | ist F. Joannes Piretius (Welcher die Sach trewlich triben vnnd darzu jhme Columbo sehr verhuelfflich) sampt andern ansehnlichen Barfuessern das Volck zubekehren | hineingezogen | vnnd Frisch vnnd Gesund in die Jnsul kommen | vnd richteten allda ein Huettlein zu | auch darinnen sie Messen vnd Predig zu halten anfiengen vnnd das heilig Hochwirdig Sacrament auch darinnen auffbehielten | diss Huettlein ist die erste Kirch vnder allen Kirchen in disen Indien." Then are listed "Die Staett aber wo wir Cloester haben | vnd wohnen ...," p. 161–162, and "Ordens Cloester in Jndien | welche Laender von Spanniern | new Spannien genennet werden," p. 162–165. See also p. 197–198.
In part, a translation of Francesco Gonzaga's *De origine seraphicae religionis franciscanae,* and Diego Valades's *Rhetorica Christiana.*

*1589*

**88.** BIGGES, WALTER. Relation | Oder Beschreibüg der Eheiss [*sic!*] | vnd Schiffahrt auss Engellandt, in die (gegen dem | vndergang der Sonne gelegnen) Indien gethan | Durch | Einen Englischen Ritter | Franciscum Drack genant | vnd was derselbig vnderwegen mit seinem vnderha- | benden Kriegsvolck allenthalben, sonderlich aber in den Inseln | S. Jacob, S. Dominico, S. Augustin vnd in oder | vmb Carthagena, auch anderstwo dero | orten gesehen vnd auss- | gericht hat. | Sampt hiebey gefüegten, schönen, in Kupffer gestoch- | nen Charten, mit welchen, so wol die gantz Schiffart in gemein, als | auch insonderheit, ein jede für sich selbs eigentlich vnd nach | dem leben gerissen, angedeutet vnd be- | schrieben worden. [n.p.,] Gedruckt | Jm Jahr nach Christi Geburt | M.D.LXXXJX. 1 p.l., 23 [i.e., 33] p., plans. illus. 26 cm. (f°.)   *KB 1589
Sabin 20837. JCB, 1919, 1, 315.
A translation of his *A Summarie and True Discourse,* London, 1589, *KC 1589.*

## 1590

**89. BENZONI, GIROLAMO.** Novae Novi Orbis Historiae, | Das ist, | Aller Geschichten, So in der newen Welt, welche Occidentalis India, | das ist India, nach Abendwerts genent wird, vnd etwa An- | no 1492. von Christophoro Columbo gefunden worden,... Auss Hieronymi Benzonis, in Welscher Sprache beschriebe- | nem verzeichnus, Welche Vrbanus Calueto jetzt eylff Jahr | ins Latein gebracht,... Dessgleichen von der Frantzosen Meerfahrt vnnd Kriegsrůstung in | das Land Floridam, so ein stůck der newen Welt ist, Auch von derselben erbermblichen niederlage vnd schaden, so ihnen die Spanier mehr Viehischer als Mensch- | licher massen Anno 1565. zugefůget. | ... Zusambt | Kurtzer namhaffter beschreibung der Canarischen Insulen, vnd was | denckwirdiges darin gefunden werde. | Durch | Abeln Scherdigern, Pfarherrn zu Wasungen, dem gemeinen Mann | zu dienst auss dem Latein ins Deudsch gebracht, Anno 1589. | ... Helmstadt: durch Jacobum Lucium, | In Verlegung Lůdeken Brandes, Anno 1590. 15 p.l., 517 p., 6 l. 4°.

Sabin 4799. Reserve 1590
The Latin original was published in Geneva in 1518 under the title: Novae Novi | Orbis Historiae | Jd est | Rerum ab Hispanis in Jndia Occidentali hac- | tenus gestarum... (Sabin 4792.)

**90. BRY, THEODOR DE, EDITOR.** Wunderbarliche, doch Warhafftige | Erklårung, Von der Gelegenheit | vnd Sitten der Wilden in Virginia, wel- | che newlich von den Engellåndern, so im Jar 1585. | vom Herrn Reichard Greinuile, ...ist erfunden worden, Jn | verlegung H. Walter Raleigh, Ritter vnd Ober- | sten dess Zinbergwercks, ... | Erstlich in Engellåndischer Sprach beschrieben | durch Thomam Hariot, vnd newlich durch Christ. | P. in Teutsch gebracht. | ... Franckfort am Måyn: bey Johann | Wechel, in verlegung Dieterich Bry. | Anno 1590... 3 parts in 1 v. plates, map. illus. f°. Reserve Bry

Sabin, v. 3, p. 49. JCB, 1, 2, 386-387.
Part 1, First edition.
It should be noticed that the publisher is called "Dieterich Bry" on the first title of this part, but the colophon reads: Gedruckt zu Franckfurt am Maeyn | bey Johann Wechel, in verlegung Theo- | dori de Bry. | M.D.XC.
The book consists of three parts, the third entirely devoted to the Picts, and not to America. The first part (p. 7–33), entitled, "Von gelegenheit der Han- | delschafft," is dated "Hornung, im Jar | 1588." The second part, with the title, "Warhafftige Contrafacturen | Vnd Gebraeuch der Jnnwohner der | jenigen Landschafft in America, welche Virginia ist genennet | worden von den Engellaendern..." consists of 23 plates by Theodor de Bry after designs by Johann With, "welcher der Vrsach halben in diese Landschafft im Jar 1585. | vnd 1588. ist geschickt worden."
The work concludes with the following note, discriminating between the aborigines and Christian immigrants: "An den guenstigen Leser. Guenstiger Leser wisse | dass man an den orten dieser Histori | da das Wort (Jnnwohner Virginie) stehet | fuer Jnnwohner (die Wilden in Virginia) ... lesen sol. Dann dieweil verschienen Jahren ein Eynsatzung von Christen ist in gemeldte Landtschafft geschickt worden | wil es von nöten seyn | dass vnter diesen beyden ein vnterschiedt gehalten werde."
See also M. S. Giuseppi, "The work of Theodore de Bry and his sons, engravers," in Huguenot Society of London, *Proceedings*, 1916, v. 11, p. 204–226, *ARCA*.
For bibliographic details of the entire set of de Bry (the American portion of which appears in this list in chronological order), see "Catalogue of the De Bry Collection of Voyages, in The New York Public Library," in the Library's *Bulletin*, v. 8, p. 230–243. See also H. N. Stevens's "The De Bry collector's painefull peregrination along the pleasant pathway to perfection," in *Bibliographical essays; a tribute to Wilberforce Eames*, 1924, p. 269–276, * KAB.
Second edition, 1600; third edition, 1620.
See nos. 112, 149.

## 1591

**91. BRY, THEODOR DE, EDITOR.** Der ander Theyl, der Newlich erfundenen | Landtschafft Americæ, | Von dreyen Schiffahrten, so die Frantzosen in Floridam | (die gegen Nidergang gelegen) gethan...Mit Beschreibung vnd lebendiger Contrafactur, dieser Prouintze, | Gestalt, Sitten vnd Gebrauch der Wilden, Durch Jacob le Moy- | ne, sonst Morges genannt, der alles selbst gesehen... | Auss dem Frantzösischen in Latein beschrie- | ben, durch C. C. A. | Vnd jetzt auss dem Latein in Teutsch bracht, durch ... | ... H. Oseam Halen. | Auch mit schönen vnd kunstreichen Kupferstůcken, ... an Tag gegeben, durch Dieterich von Bry ... Franckfort am Mayn: bey Jo- | hann Feyerabendt, in Verlegung | Dieterich von Bry. | Anno 1591. 2 parts in 1 v. plates, map. illus. f°. Reserve Bry

Sabin, v. 3, p. 50. JCB, 1, 2, 389.
Part II, First edition.
The first part is divided into: 1. Die ander Schiffahrt der Frantzosen in Floridam | so eine Landtschafft in America ist | geschehen vnter dem Obersten Laudonniere, Anno m.d.lxiii, p. i–vi. 2. Warhafftige Beschreibung der Ersten Rheyss dess Herrn Laudonniere | in die Landtschafft | America genannt, p. vii–xxviii. 3. Warhafftige vnnd eygentliche Beschreibung der dritten Schiffahrt | der Frantzosen | in Florida, geschehen vnter dem Haeuptmann Johann Ribaldt [i.e., Jean Ribaut] | Jm Jar 1565, p. xxix–xlii.
In addition to the plates, the second part contains: Warhafftige vnnd eygentliche Beschreibung der vierdten Schiffahrt | der Frantzosen | in Americam ... geschehen unter dem Hauptmann Gourguesio [i.e., Dominique de Gourgues], Jm Jar 1567, [and] Nebenbericht von dem Authore | vnd Gelegenheyt dieser Historien.
"Also hat mich fuer gut angesehen | dir auch zu vermelden | dass ich diese Historie vnd Bilder empfangen habe von der Wittwen Iacobile Moyne | so sonsten Morgues genannt | eines fuertrefflichen Mahlers | so dem Herrn Laudonniere... in diese Landschafft | Gesellschaft geleystet..." — *Vorrede an den Leser*.
The second part is entitled, "Warhafftige Abconterfaytung der Wilden in America, | so daselbst erstlichen lebendiger weise ab- | gerissen, von Jacob le Moyne, oder | Morges genannt.
Second edition, 1603.
See *Narrative of Le Moyne, an artist who accompanied the French expeditions to Florida under Laudonnière, 1564*, Boston, 1875, †° *KF*.

## 1593

**92. BRY, THEODOR DE, EDITOR.** Dritte Buch Americæ, | Darinn | Brasilia durch Johann Staden von | Homberg auss Hessen, auss eigener erfahrung | in Teutsch beschrieben... Alles von Newem mit kůnstlichen Figuren in Kupffer | gestochen vnd an Tag geben, Durch Dieterich Bry ... [Franckfurt am Main,] 1593. 2 parts in 1 v. plates, map. f°. Reserve Bry

Sabin, v. 3, p. 51. JCB, 1, 2; p. 392–393.
Part III, First edition.
Second edition, see following title.
*Contents*: I. Von zweyen Schiffahrten | so Hans

*1593, continued*

**92. BRY, THEODOR DE,** EDITOR, *continued*
Staden in Neundthalb jaren volnbracht hat. Jst die erste Reyse aus Portugalia | die ander auss Hispania | in die neuwe Welt Americam geschehen. II. Wie er allda in der Landschafft der Wilden Leut Toppinikin genannt (so dem Koenig zu Portugal zustehen) fuer einen Buechsenschuetzen gegen die Feinde dahin gebrauchet sey. Letzlichen | von den Feinden gefangen vnd weggefuehret | zehendhalben Monat lang in der Gefahr gestanden | dass er getödt von den Feinden | vnd gefressen solt worden seyn. III. Jtem | wie Gott gnaediglichen vnd wunderlicher weise diesen Gefangenen nach vorgelessnem jar erloeset | vnnd er in sein geliebtes Vatterland wider heym kommen sey, p. 1-92.

Part 2 tells in twenty-two chapters, "Die Historia Der Schiffahrten Joannis Lerij [i.e., Jean de Léry] | nach der Landtschafft Brasilien in America," p. 93-285.

Of special interest is the xx. Capittel, "Argument. Ein Gespraech mit den Brasilianern so man die Tuppin Imbas vnd die Tuppin Ikins nennet | wenn man erstlich zu jhnen eynkehret | in Brasilianischer vnd Lateinischer Sprach beschrieben," p. 248-263.

The Library has an edition of Léry's *Reise in Brasilien*, Muenster, 1794, in * KF. "The value of this German translation is considerably enhanced by many historical notes and biographical references." — *Sabin 40156.*

For references to Hans Staden, see nos. 69, 70, 71.

**93.** —— Dritte Buch Americae, | Darinn | Brasilia durch Johann Staden von | Homberg ...auss eigener erfahrung | in Teutsch beschrieben... Alles von Newem mit künstlichen Figuren in Kupffer | gestochen vnd an Tag geben, Durch Dieterich Bry. [Frankfurt am Main,] 1593. 8 p.l., 92 p., 8 l., 93-285 p. plates, maps, illus. f°. Reserve Bry

Sabin, v. 3, p. 51. JCB, I, 2, 393.
Part III, Second edition.
First edition, see preceding title.

**1594**

**94. BRY, THEODOR DE,** EDITOR. Das vierdte Buch | Von der neuwen Welt. | oder | Neuwe vnd gründtliche Historien, von | dem Nidergängischen Jndien, so von Chri- | stophoro Columbo im Jar 1492. | erstlich erfunden. | Durch Hieronymum Bentzo von Meyland, welcher 14. | Jar dasselbig Land durchwandert, auffs fleissigst | beschrieben vnd an Tag geben. | ...Alles mit schönen vnd kunstreichen Kupfferstücken vnd deren an- | gehenckten erklärungen an Tag geben, durch Diterich | von Bry ... [Frankfurt am Main: J. Feyrabend, 1594.] 2 parts in 1 v., 24 plates, 1 map. f°. Reserve Bry

Sabin, v. 3, p. 52. JCB, I, 2, 394.
Part IV, First edition.
Colophon: Gedruckt zu Franckfort am Mayn bey Johann | Feyrabend, in verlegung Dieterichs | von Bry. M.D.XCIIII.

Separately printed title is pasted over the upper portion of the center of the original Latin edition. Title-page of the second part retains the original Latin text.

The contents of *Das vierdte Buch* are described as follows: "...nach dem Bentzo der Geschichtschreiber allhie die Vrsach vnd Lauff oder End seiner fuergenommenen Schiffart kuertzlich hat beschrieben | zeigt er deutlich vnd gruendlich an | wer sich zum ersten vnderstanden habe in dise Landschaffte zu schiffen | vnd verwirfft hiemit der Spanier falsche vnnd erdichte Fabel | die sie bissher von Erfindung der neuwen Welthaben faelschlich fuergeben. [Martin Behaim is declared the discoverer of America.] Demnach erzehlet er | wie die Spanier als sie vberhandt haben genommen | diese grosse gutthat Gottes mit Tyranney | ...vernichtet haben. Darauss denn als baldt in der Jnsel Hispaniola...der Eynwohner grosse Empoerung | vnnd der Meerraeuber vielfaltige Schiffbruech hernach seynd gefolget...Hierzwischen ist Bentzo...in die Jnsel Hispaniolam kommen (von welcher er hie im ersten Buch allein | gleich wie er im andern Buch von der Spanier Thaten vnd Handlung | so sie in der Vestung Castella aurea, Nicaragua, Guattimala, vnd andern Landschafften dess inneren Jndien begangen. Vnd im dritten von den Handlungen so sich im Koenigreich Peru haben verloffen | deren Eynwohner halsstarrige Superstition | Aberglauben | Sitten | Gebraeuch vnd wunderbarliche Fruecht | sampt der Jnsel Gelegenheit | vnd dess Erdreichs Natur vnd Eigenschafft er hie eigentlich vnd warhafft beschreibet."

Second edition, 1613.
See nos. 79, 82A, 83, 89, 97, 132, 147.

**1595**

**95. BRY, THEODOR DE,** EDITOR. Americæ | Das Fünffte Buch, | Vol schöner vnerhörter Historien, auss | dem andern Theil Ioannis [sic!] Benzonis von Mey- | landt gezogen... | Alles mit schönen vnd kunstreichen Kupfferstücken vnd deren | angehenckten Erklärungen, an Tag geben, durch | Dietherich von Bry... [Frankfurt am Main, 1595.] 2 parts in 1 v., 22 plates, 1 map. f°. Reserve Bry

Sabin, v. 3, p. 52. JCB, I, 2, 395-396.
Part V, First edition.
No colophon. The German title is printed separately and pasted over the centerpiece of the Latin original. Part 2 has the original Latin title.

For contents, see note on no. 94. Chapters of special interest: Das Sechste Capitel. Wie ettlich Teutschen der Spanier Exempel vnd Sitten nachgefolget | vnd die Jndianer auch auff mancherley weg geplaget, p. 33-35, dealing with the colonization of the Welsers in Venezuela; Das Viertzehende Capitel. Vba der Crocodillen Eyer, die gut zu essen seynd, p. 72-75; Das Sechzehende Capitel. Wie ein Jndianer der Spanier Sitten beschrieben, p. 82-89, in which an old Indian asks, "Lieber Christ, sag mir | Warzu sind die Christen nuetz..." Plate xx illustrates the scene.
Second edition, 1613.
See no. 131.

**96. QUAD, MATTHIAS.** Die Jahr Blum | Welch da begreifft vnd in sich helt | Fast alle Iahren dieser Welt. | Namhafft Personē, Stedt vnd Lant | Hieraus dir werden mit bekant. | Jn guter ordnung (auch mit fleis | Gantz kurtz gefast) vnd reimē weis | Vil mercklich thaten vnd geschicht | Durch Matthis Quaden zugericht. | ... [Cologne?] In verlegung Iohan Bussemechers | Anno | MDXCV. 39 l. illus. 4°. Engraved title page. Reserve 1595

Americus Vesputius
Mit etlich schiffen fehrt hinauss
Auffinden thut ein newes Landt |
Americam solchs hat genant
Nach Jhm: so gross ists dass mans helt
Fürs vierthe theil der gantzen Welt. — *l. 25ᵃ.*

See no. 113.

## 1597

**97.** BRY, THEODOR DE, EDITOR. Das sechste Theil | der neuwen Welt. | oder | Der Historien Hieron. Benzo von Meylandt, | Das dritte Buch. | ... Alles mit schönen Kupfferstücken vorgebildet | vnd an Tag geben | Durch Dieterich von Bry... [Frankfurt am Main: J. Feyrabendt,] M.D.XCVII. 2 parts in 1 v. plates, map. f°. Reserve Bry
Sabin, v. 3, p. 53. JCB, I, 2, 397-398.
Part VI, First edition.
Colophon: Gedruckt zu Franckfurt am Mayn | bey Johann Feyrabendt, in verlegung Dietrichs | von Bry | Anno M.D.XCVII.
German title is pasted over the centerpiece of the original Latin.
This work deals with Francisco Pizarro, in Peru.
See also note on no. 94.
Second edition, 1619.

**98.** —— Das VII. Theil America. | Warhafftige vnnd liebliche | Beschreibung etlicher fürnemmen | Jndianischen Landschafften vnd Jnsulen, | die vormals in keiner Chronicken gedacht, vnd erst- | lich in der Schiffart Vlrici Schmidts von Strau- | bingen, mit grosser gefahr erkündigt, vnd von | ihm selber auffs fleissigst beschrieben | vnd dargethan. | Vnd an Tag gebracht durch Dieterich | von Bry... [Frankfurt,] Anno M.D.XCVII. 331. illus. f°. Reserve Bry
Sabin, v. 3, p. 54. JCB, I, 2, 399-400.
Part VII, First edition.
No plates were issued with this first edition, being published at the end of the "Additamentum" to Part VIII, in 1600, and included in the second edition of Part VII, in 1617. See nos. 111, 139.
Contains the voyages of Ulrich Schmidel.
See nos. 73, 74, 139.
As to Ulrich Schmidel, see Max Pannwitz, *Deutsche Pfadfinder des 16. Jahrhunderts in Afrika, Asien und Südamerika,* Stuttgart [1912], KBD.

**99.** CASAS, BARTOLOMÉ DE LAS, BISHOP OF CHIAPA. Newe Welt. | Warhafftige Anzeigung | Der Hispanier grewli- | chen, abschewlichen vnd vnmenschlichen Ty- | ranney, von ihnen inn den Indianischen Ländern, | so gegen Nidergang der Sonnen gelegen, vnd die | Newe Welt genennet wird, begangen. | Erstlich | Castilianisch, durch Bischoff Bartholomeum de las Casas...beschrieben: Vnd | im Jahr 1552 in der Königlichen Statt Hispalis oder Sevilia in Spanien gedruckt: | Hernacher in die Frantzösische Sprach, durch Jacoben von Miggrode, den 17 | Provincien dess Niderlands, zur Warnung | vnd Beyspiel, gebracht: | Jetzt aber erst ins Hochteutsch, durch einen Liebhaber dess Vatterlands, vmb | ebenmässiger vrsachen willen, vbergesetzt. [n.p.,] Im Jahr | 1597. 8 p.l., 158 p., 6 l. 4°. Reserve 1597
Sabin 11277.
This translation into German is from the Spanish. In the same year another German translation from the French was issued in Frankfurt.
See Hans Plischke, "Westindien und Las Casas," in *Archiv für Kulturgeschichte,* Leipzig, 1928, Bd. 18, p. 309–327, *BAA;* Otto Waltz, *Fr. Bartholomé de las Casas; ein historische Skisse,* Bonn, 1905, *AN;* Alice J. Knight, *Las Casas, "the Apostle of the Indies,"* New York [cop. 1917], *AN (Casas).*
See nos. 109, 133, 185.

**100.** DRESSER, MATTHAEUS. Historien vnd Bericht | Von dem Newlicher | Zeit erfundenen Königreich China. | ... Item, Von dem auch new erfundenen | Lande Virginia. | ... In Druck verfertiget, durch | Matthævm Dresservin... Leipzig: durch Frantz Schnelboltz. | ... Anno | M.D.XCVII. 6 p.l., 297 p. 4°.
Sabin 20926. Reserve 1597
The second part is a translation from English into German of Hariot's "Virginia." A translator, Christophorus P., is mentioned.
See nos. 90, 103, 105, 112, 149.

**101.** RAUW, JOHANN. Cosmographia, | Das ist: | Ein schöne, Richtige vnd volkomliche | Beschreibung dess Göttlichen Geschöpffs, | Himmels vnd der Erden, beydes der Himmlischen vnd Jrrdischen Kugel, | Wie die Himmlische in jre Circulos vnd Sphæras, vnd die Jrrdische in jhre Theil, Europam, | Asiam vnd Aphricam, beneben Americam, ... durch | Den Ehrwirdigen vnd Wolgelährten Herrn Johann Rauwen | ... Franckfort am Mayn: durch Nicolaum Bassæum, | M.D.XCVII. 18 p.l., 1031(1) p., 6 l. incl. illus., maps, folded genealogical table, diagr. f°. †* KB 1597
Sabin 67977.
The last chapter, p. 1027–1031, is entitled: Von der Beschreibung der Newen Welt.
Rauw's *Weltbeschreibung,* Franckfort am Mayn, 1612 (Sabin 67978), is not in the Library. For an account of the work, see the *Literarische Blätter,* Nuremberg, 1803.

## 1598

**102.** ACOSTA, JOSÉ DE. Geographische vnd | Historische Beschreibung der vber- | auss grosser Landtschafft America: welche auch | West-Jndia, vnd jhrer grösse halben die New Welt genennet wirt. | Gar artig, vnd nach der kunst in xx. Mappen oder Land- | taffeln verfasset, vnd jetzt newlich in Kupffer ge- | stochen, vnd an tag gegeben. | ... Erstlich durch einen ...dess Laudes Wolerfahrnen Mann, | in Lateinischer Spraach...beschrieben. Nun aber... gar trewlich vbergesetzt, | vnd ins Teutsch bracht...Cölln: Bey Johann Christoffel, auff S. Marcellenstrass. Im jahr M.D.XCVII. 2 p.l., 51 (1) p., 20 double maps on 40 l. f°. Reserve 1598
Sabin 128.
Each map has descriptive letter press on back.
The original Latin edition was entitled: De Natvra | Novi Orbis | Libri dvo | ... Salmanticae... M.D.LXXXIX.
Consists of two parts. Of special interest is: Das Erste Buch. Das Neunzehende Capittel. Dass es dafuer zu halten sey | die Einwohner dieser Newer [sic!] Welt seyen durch Vngewitter wider ihren willen in diese Laender verworffen. Das zwantzigste Capittel. Dass es viel wahrscheinlicher | dass die erste Einwohner dieser Newen Welt sind ober Land darinn kommen. Das Ein vnd zwaentzigste Capittel. Wie die Thier vnd Vieh auss der Alten in diese Newe Welt sind kommen. Das Zwey vnd zwaentzigste Capittel. Dass das Jndische Volck nicht in America kommen sey, durch die Athlantida wie etliche meinen. Das Drey vnd zwaentzigste Capittel. Dass viele aber mit vnrecht sagen die Jndianer seyen von der Junden Geschlecht her kommen. Das Vier vnd zwaentzigste Capittel. Warumb man den ersten vrsprung der Jndianern nicht koenne gewiss wissen. Das Fuenff vnd zwaentzigste Capittel. Was die Jndianer selbst von ihrem herkommen fuergeben, p. 25–34.
See *Francisco Pizarro; der Sturz des Inkareichs; nach den Berichten des Garcilaso de la Vega vnd des Paters José de Acosta S. J.,* bearbeitet von Dr. H. G. Bonte, Leipzig, 1925 (Alte Reisen und Abenteuer), *HHK.*
See also no. 124.

*1598, continued*

103. DRESSER, MATTHAEUS. Historien vnd Bericht, | Von dem Newlicher | Zeit erfundenen Königreich China, | ... Item, Von dem auch new erfundenen | Lande Virginia. | ... In Druck verfertiget, durch | Matthævm Dresservm... | ... Leipzig: durch Frantz Schnelboltz. | ... Anno M.D.XCVIII. 6 p.l., 297 p. 4°. Sabin 20926. Reserve 1598
See nos. 90, 100, 105, 112, 149.

Describes the attempts of the Dutch to discover a North-East passage. "The account of these three[?] voyages appears to have created a general sensation throughout Europe. It was first published in Dutch in 1598 and was translated the same year into Latin, twice into German and into French — all these editions were frequently reprinted." See A. Asher, *Bibliographical essay on the collection of voyages and travels edited and published by L. Hulsius and his successors*, Berlin, 1839, p. 22-33, * *KAK (Hulsius)*.
See also *Die Reisen des Wilhelm Barents zur Entdeckung der Nordöstlichen Durchfahrt in den Jahren 1594-97*, Würzburg, 1934, KBP.

104. DER GANTZEN Wellt abcontrafetung [*sic!*] Darin Zñsehen [*sic!*] die Neuwe gefundene Indianische Schiffart Vnd was wünders man da Erfunden als die Histori meltet. Anno 98. [1598?] 11½ x 9 inches. Map Room. World 1598
Map of the world. Engraved on copper by Æ. Portraits of Columbus and Vespucci.

105. HARRIOT, THOMAS. Wunderbarlicher doch Warhaff- | tiger Bericht. | Von der Landschafft | Virginia inn der newen Welt, | welche newlich im Jahr Christi 1585. von den | Engelendern erfunden ist, | Erstlichen in Engelendischer | Sprach beschrieben, durch Thomam | Hariot, vnd hernach in Teutsch | gebracht, durch | Christophorvm P. 4°. (In: M. Dresser, Historien vnd Bericht... Leipzig, 1598. p. 171-231.) Reserve 1598
See F. V. Morley, "Thomas Hariot, 1560-1621," in *Scientific monthly*, Utica, N. Y., 1921, v. 14, p. 60-66, * *DA*; Henry Stevens, *Thomas Hariot... including biographical and bibliographical disquisitions upon the materials of history of "Ould Virginia,"* London, 1900, *AGZ p.v.29*.
See nos. 90, 100, 103, 112, 149.

106. MEER oder Seehanen Buch, | Darinn | Verzeichnet seind, die Wun- | derbare, Gedenckwürdige Reise vnd Schiffarhten, ... Auff vnd durch welche Schiffarten, ein Newe Welt gegen | Nidergang,...erfunden vnd | entdeckt seind. | ... Dise Reisen vnd Schiffahrten seind zusamen, auss ar- | dern Spraachen ins Teutsch gebracht, | Durch | Conrad Löw... Cölln: auff der Burgmauren, Bey | Bertram Buchholtz, Jm Jahr | 1598. 1 p.l., 110 p., 3 maps. f°. Reserve 1598
Short narratives of famous voyages, as those of Columbus, Cortés, Magellan, Drake.

107. VEER, GERRIT DE. Warhafftige Relation. | Der dreyen newen vner- | hörten, seltzamen Schiffart, so die Hol- | ländischen vnd Seeländischen Schiff gegen Mitternacht, | drey Jar nach einander, als Anno 1594. 1595. vnd 1596. verricht. | ...Erstlich in Niderländischen sprach beschrieben, durch Gerhart de Ver. so selb- | sten die letzten zwo Reysen hat helffen verrichten, jetzt aber ins Hochteutsch | gebracht, Durch | Levinum Hulsium. | Norimbergæ: Impensis L. Hulsij, Anno M.D.XCVIII. 11 p.l., 146 p., 34 maps and pl. 4°. Reserve Hulsius
Sabin 33655.
There is a second title page, dated 1599. This is the first issue of the first edition of the third relation in the collection of voyages of Hulsius. For the second, see no. 118.

**1599**

108. BRY, THEODOR DE, EDITOR. Americæ Achter Theil, | ... Alles mit fleiss beschrieben durch den gestrengen, Edlen vñ vesten Walthern Ralegh, | ... Zum andern, die Reyse dess Edlen vnd vesten Thomas Candisch, ... | Durch Frantzen Prettie einen Engelländer, welcher dieser Fahrt Persönlich hat | beygewohnet, von Tag zu Tag auffgezeichnet. | Vnd zum dritten die letzte Reyss der gestrengen, Edlen vnd vesten Frantzen Draeck | vnd Iohan Havckens ... Alles erstlich in Engelländischer Sprach aussgangen, jetzt aber auss der Holländischen translation | in die Hochteutsche Sprache gebracht, durch | Avgvstinvm Cassiodorvm Reinivm. | Mit etlichen schönen Kupfferstücken geziert vnd an Tag gegeben, durch Dieterichen | von Bry seligen, hinderlassene Erben. | ... Franckfurt am Mayn: durch Matthæum Becker. 1599. 3 parts in 1 v., 6 plates, 1 map. f°. Reserve Bry
Sabin, v. 3, p. 54. JCB, 1, 2, 403-405.
Part VIII, First edition.
See also "Additamentum," 1600.
Account of four voyages:
"Die erste hat verricht Walther Ralegh Ritter | vnnd Hauptman vber jhrer Majestat in Engellandt Leibsguardi [i.e., Sir Walter Raleigh], der auch die Landtschafft Virginia, die im ersten Theyl vnserer Americe beschrieben wirdt / erstlich erfunden | vnnd seiner Koenigin zu Ehren mit diesem Namen gezieret hat.
"Die andere hat der wolerfahrene Hauptman Lorentz Keymis [i.e., Lawrence Kemys] volbracht: vnd haben diese zween dieses Goldtreiche Koenigreich entdeckt | auch jhre Reysen selber beschrieben.
"Die dritte Schiffahrt ist geschehen von einem Engellaendischen vom Adel | Thomas Candisch [i.e., Thomas Cavendish] genannt | der 3 Schiff auf seinen eignen Vnkosten hat aussgerüstet | dieselbige auff 2 gantzer Jahr lang proviandirt | vnd 123 Mann besetzt | mit welchen er | als general Oberster in eigner Person gezogen | vnd sein Heyl versucht: vnd in 2 Jahren vnnd 7 Wochen mehr dann 4000 teutscher Meiln gesegelt | ...
"Zum vierdten vnd letzten haben wir auch hinzugefuegt die letzte Reyse der zween fuernembsten Meerhelden | Herrn Frantzen Draecks [i.e., Sir Francis Drake] vnd Johann Haukens [i.e., Sir John Hawkins] Rittern | welche alle beyde auff dieser Reyse jhr Leben geendet..."
See nos. 111, 154.

109. CASAS, BARTOLOMÉ DE LAS, BISHOP OF CHIAPA. Newe Welt. | Warhafftige Anzeigung | Der Hispanier grewli- | chen, abschewlichen vnd vnmenschlichen Ty- | ranney, von ihnen in den Indianischen Ländern, | ... begangen. | ... [n.p.,] Im Jahr | 1599. 7 p.l., 158 p., 6 l. 4°. Sabin 11279. Reserve 1599
See nos. 99, 133.

*1599, continued*

110. RALEIGH, SIR WALTER. Kurtze Wunderbare Beschreibung. | Dess Goldreichen König- | reichs Guianæ in America, oder newen Welt, vnter der | Linea Aequinoctiali gelegen: So newlich Anno 1594. 1595. | vnnd 1596. von dem Wolgebornen Herrn, Herrn Walthero Ra- | legh einem Englischen Ritter, besucht worden: Erstlich auss befehl seiner | Gnaden in zweyen Büchlein beschrieben, darauss Iodocus Hondius, ein | schöne Land Taffel, mit einer Niderländischen erklärung gemacht, | Jetzt aber ins Hochteutsch gebracht, vnd auss vnter- | schietlichen Authoribus erkläret. | Durch | Levinum Hulsium. Noribergæ: impensis Levini Hvlsii. | M.D.XCIX. 2 p.l., 16 p., 1 l., 6 pl., 1 map. 4°.

Sabin 33658. Reserve Hulsius
This is the first edition of part 5 of the Hulsius voyages. The original was first issued under the title: *The Discoverie of the Empyre of Guiana... Performed in the year 1595, by Sir W. Ralegh...* London: Robinson, 1596. See A. Asher, *Bibliographical essay on the collection of voyages and travels edited and published by L. Hulsius and his successors...*, Berlin, 1839, p. 38–42, \* *KAK (Hulsius)*.

## 1600

111. BRY, THEODOR DE, EDITOR. Additamentvm; | Das ist, | Zuthuung zweyer fürnemer Reysen | oder Schiffarten Herrn Francisci Draken Ritters auss Engel- | landt, Jn die West Jndien vnd Americam gethan, Neben noch etlichen | Figuren vnd Kupfferstücken, so beydes in das siebende | vnd achte Theil Americæ | gehören. | Jetzo auffs zierlichste in Kupffer gestochen, vnd an den | Tag gegeben, durch Dieterich de Bry seligen hinterlas- | sene Wittwe vnd zweene | Söhne. | ... Franckfort am Mayn: durch | Matthæum Becker. | Anno M.DC. 73 p., 15 pl. f°.

JCB, 1, 2, 404–405. Reserve Bry
Subdivided into: Kurtze Beschreibung von der Herrlichen vnd weitberuehmbten Reyse vnd Schifffahrt | so weylandt Capitein Drak in die Sudsee | vnd folgends gar vmb den gantzen Erdkreyss getan..., p. 5–45, [and] Wahrhafftige Beschreibung der Schifffahrt vnd Aussruestung der gewaltigen Armada | von den vereinigten auss Niderland | auff die West Jndien gerichtet | ..., p. 47–73. Fifteen plates follow.
Title-page before plates reads: Folgen nun die Figuren vnd Kupf- | ferstueck, deren etliche ins siebende Theil, zur beschreibung | der Reysen Vlrich Schmids von Straubingen, etliche ins achte, zur | beschreibung der Reysen Herrn Francisci Draken vnd | Herrn Thomas Candisch, gehoeren. | ...

112. —— Wunderbarliche, doch Warhafftige | Erklärung, Von der Gelegenheit | vnd Sitten der Wilden in Virginia, ... Jetzt widerumb vbersehen vnd zum andernmal | in Truck gegeben. | ... Franckfort am Mayn: bey Matthes | Becker, in verlegung Dieterich de Bry seliger | nachgelassene Wittwe, vnd beyder | Söhne. 1600. 3 parts in 1 v. plates, maps. illus. f°.

Sabin, v. 3, p. 50. Reserve Bry
Part 1, Second edition.
First edition, 1590.
See nos. 90, 149.

113. QUAD, MATTHIAS. Geographisch Handtbuch, in welchem die gelegenheit der vornembsten Lantschafften des gantzen Erdtbodems in zwej und achtzig in Kupffer geschnittenen Taffeln fürgebildt... Cöln am Rein: Bey Johan Buxemacher [1600]. 1 p.l., 82 double maps. f°. Reserve 1600
Engraved title page. Each map has descriptive letter press on verso.
Imperfect: Title page and maps 1–17, 78–82 wanting. Six maps relate to America.
Quad's *Enchiridion cosmographicum compendium universi*, 1600; *Memorabilia mundi, dass ist von namhafften und gedenckwirdigen sachen der Welt*, 1601; and *Fasciculus geographicus*, 1608, are not in the Library.

## 1601

114. BRY, THEODOR DE, EDITOR. Neundter vnd Letzter Theil | Americæ, | Dariñ gehandelt wird, von gelegen- | heit der Elementen, Natur, Art vnd eigenschafft | der Newen Welt: ... | Alles auffs trewlichste aus Niederländischer Beschreibung | Iohan. Hugen von Lintschotten, in vnser Hochteutsche Sprache | versetzet, durch Iohannem Humberger VVetteranium. | Ferner auch von der Reise der fünff Schiffe, so im Junio dess 1598. | Jahrs, in Hollandt aussgefahren,... | ...aus Niederlän- | discher Sprach beschrieben, durch | M. Gothardt Artus von Dantzig. | Alles mit schönen Kupfferstücken geziret, vnd an | Tag geben, durch | Dietrichs de Bry seligen Wittib, vnd | zween Söhne. | ... Franckfurt am Mayn: Bey Wolffgang Richter. [1601.] 2 parts in 1 v., 25 plates, 1 map. f°. Reserve Bry

Sabin, v. 3, p. 55. JCB, 1, 2, 409–411.
Part IX, First edition.
Date from title before plates.
Second edition, 1633?
"Viel Autoren haben vielerley Buecher von der newen Welt | vnd von der Hispanier Thaten geschrieben | aber keiner ist noch gefunden, der von dem Anfang oder Vrsprung der Voelcker vnnd von der Naturn vnd Eygenschafft der newen Welt gruendtlich tractieret hätte..."
Subdivided into three parts:
Part I comprises Sieben Buecher, dealing with the natural history of the new world and its aborigiues, by Jan H. van Linschoten, p. 1–327.
Part II describes the voyage of Gerrit de Veer, p. 3–72.
Part III consists of twenty-five plates, with text.
See the publications of the Linschoten Vereeniging, 's Gravenhage, 1909–1939, *KBD*.

115. RALEIGH, SIR WALTER. Kurtze Wunderbare Beschreibung, | Dess Goldreichen König- | reichs Guianæ in America oder newen Welt, vnder der Li- | nea Æquinoctiali gelegen: So neulich Anno 1594. 1595. vnd | 1596. von dem Wolgebornen Herrn, Herrn Walthero Ralegh | einem Englischen Ritter, besucht worden: Erstlich aus befehl seiner | Gnaden in zweyen Büchlein beschrieben, daraus Iodocus Hon- | dius, ein schöne Land Taffel, mit einer Niderländischen | erklärung gemacht. Jetzt aber ins Hochteutsch | gebracht, vnd auss vnterschiedlichen Au- | thoribus erkläret. Noribergæ: Impensis Levini Hvlsii. | M.DCI. 3 p.l., 19 p., 1 map, 6 plates. 4°. Reserve Hulsius

Sabin 67563.
Second edition of part 5 of the Hulsius voyages. For first edition, see no. 110.

116. —— —— Another copy. Reserve Hulsius
This copy has 26 lines on page 13 and seven lines on page 17; the preceding has 23 and 13 lines, respectively.

## 1602

**117.** BRY, THEODOR DE, EDITOR. Additamentvm, | Oder | Anhang dess neundten Theils Americæ ... | Auss Niderländischer Verzeichnuss in hochteut- | scher Sprach beschrieben | Durch | M. Gothardt Artus von Dantzigk. | Auch mit schönen Kupfferstücken gezieret, vnd an Tag geben | durch Dietrichs de Bry S. hinterlassene Wit- | tibe, vnd zween Söne.... Franckfurt am Mayn: Durch | Matthæum Becker. | M.DCII. 103 p., 14 plates. f°. . Reserve Bry
Sabin, v. 3, p. 56. JCB, I, 2, 410.
Contains the voyage around the world of Olivier van Noort, p. 3–103, and fourteen plates with accompanying text.
The Library has another German translation by Johann Schaffer, issued in Amsterdam, the same year, * *KB 1602.*

**118.** VEER, GERRIT DE. Dritte Theil, | vnd warhafftige Relation | Der dreyen newen vn- | erhörten, seltzamen Schiffart, so die Hol- | ländischen vnnd Seeländischen Schiff gegen Mitter- | nacht, drey jar nacheinander, als Anno 1594. 1595. vnd 1596. ver | richt... Auss der Niderländischen Sprach ins Hochteutsch | gebracht, Durch | Levinum Hulsium. Nürmberg: Impensis Levini Hulsii. M.DCII. 10 p.l., 147 p., 32 plates. 4°. Reserve Hulsius
First edition, second issue.
The title page and three following leaves, only, differ from the first issue, 1598.
See no. 107.

**119.** —— Dritte Theil, | Warhafftige Relation | Der dreyen newen vn- | erhörten, seltzamē Schiffart, so die Hol- | ländischen vnd Seeländischen Schiff gegen Mitter- | nacht, drey jar nacheinander, als Año 1594. 1595 vnd 1596 ver- | richt... Nürnberg: Impensis Levini Hulsii. M.DCII. 8 p.l., 121 [i.e., 122] p., 32 maps and plates. 4°. Reserve Hulsius
Second edition.
See nos. 107, 118.
Page 44 omitted in numbering.

## 1603

**120.** BRY, THEODOR DE, EDITOR. Der ander Theil, der Newlich erfundenen | Landtschafft Americae, | Von dreyen Schiffahrten, so die Frantzosen in Floridam | ...gethan... | ...Auss dem Französischen in Latein beschrie- | ben, durch C. C. A. | Vnd jetzt auss dem Latein in Teutsch bracht, durch...H. Oseam Halen. | ... jetzunder zum andern mal an Tag gegeben, durch Dieterich | de Bry. [Frankfurt am Main,] Anno 1603. 2 parts in 1 v. plates, map. illus. f°.
Sabin, v. 3, p. 51. JCB, I, 2, 389–390. Reserve Bry
Part II, Second edition.
First edition, 1591.

**121.** HULSTUS, LEVINUS, EDITOR. Sechste Theil, | Kurtze, Warhafftige | Relation vnd beschreibung der Wun- | derbarsten vier Schiffarten, so jemals verricht | worden. Als nemlich: | Ferdinandi Magellani... | Francisci Draconis ... | Thomæ Candisch | Oliuarij von Noort, ... | So alle vier vmb den gantzen Erdtkreiss gesegelt, auss vnterschie- | denen authoribus vnd sprachen zusamen getragen,... Durch, | Levinum Hulsium. Noribergæ: | Impensis Collectoris. M.D.CIIJ. 3 p.l., 54 p., 6 maps, 9 plates. 4°. Reserve Hulsius
Sabin 33660.
First edition.
Describes the circumnavigation of the earth by Magellan in 1519–1522, by Drake in 1577–1580, by Cavendish in 1586–1588, and by Noort in 1598–1601.
See A. Asher, *Bibliographical essay on the collection of voyages and travels edited and published by L. Hulsius and his successors*, Berlin, 1839, p. 43–46, * *KAK (Hulsius).*

**122.** RALEIGH, SIR WALTER. Die Fünffte | Kurtze Wunderbare Beschreibung, | Dess Goldreichen König- | reichs Guinanæ in America oder neuen Welt, | vnter der linea Æquinoctiali gelegen: So neulich Anno 1594. | 1595. vnd 1596. von dem Wolgebornen Herrn, Herrn Walthero | Ralegh einem Engelischen Ritter, besucht worden: Erstlich auss be- | fehl seiner Gnaden in zweyen Büchlein beschrieben, darauss Jodocus | Hondius, eine schöne Land Tafel, mit einer Niderländischen | erklärung gemacht. Jetzt aber ins Hochteutsch ge- | bracht, vnd auss vnterschiedlichen Av- | thoribus erkläret. Noribergæ: ...Impensis Levini Hulsii. CIƆ IƆ CIII. 2 p.l., [1]17 p., 1 l., 6 plates, map. 4°. Reserve Hulsius
Third edition.
See A. Asher, *Bibliographical essay on the collection of voyages and travels edited and published by L. Hulsius and his successors*, Berlin, 1839, p. 42, * *KAK (Hulsius).*
See no. 110.
See Gabriel Rollenhagen, *Vier Bücher Wunderbarlicher biss | daher vnerhörter, vnd vngleub|licher Indianischer Reysen...aus Griechischer | vnd Lateinischer Sprach mit fleiss ver | teutscht | durch Gabriel Rollenhagen*, Magdeburgk: J. Böttcher, 1603. (Not in the Library.) This book makes no distinction between East and West Indies. See G. Desczyk, in the Deutsch-amerikanische historische Gesellschaft von Illinois, *Jahrbuch*, Chicago, 1924/25, p. 11, *IEK*, concerning disputed authorship.

## 1604

**123.** ORTELIUS, ABRAHAM. Auszzüg auss des Abrahami Orte- | lÿ Theatro Orbis Teütsch | beschriben dürch | Levinvm Hvlsivm. Francfort am Main: | Prostant apvd Iohañem Keerbergivm et Levinvm Hvlsivm. | M.DC.IIII. 45(1) p., 134 l. (last blank) maps. obl. 4°. * *KB 1604*
Leaves are maps with accompanying text, mostly paged in duplicate.
"Die neuwe Welt oder America," map 22.

## 1605

**124.** ACOSTA, JOSÉ DE, JESUIT. America, | oder wie mans zu Teutsch nennet | Die Neuwe Welt, oder West | India. | ...in Sieben Büchern, ... Ursel: Durch Cornelium Sutorium. | Im Jahr M.DC.V. 4 p.l., 266 p., 2 l. (blank), 20 maps on 40 l. f°. †* *KB 1605*
Sabin 130.
Each map has descriptive letterpress on verso.
"The maps at the end are apparently from the 1598 Cölln edition of Acosta. They are not called for in this edition and are not mentioned in the JCB copy."
— Wilberforce Eames (pencilled note in this copy).
This German version was made by Johannes Humberger.

## GERMAN WORKS RELATING TO AMERICA 17

### 1611

125. BOTERO, GIOVANNI. Allgemeine | Historische Weltbeschreibung, | Ioannis Boteri, | ... Jn vier Bûcher abgetheilt: | Jm ersten wirdt Europa,... | dessgleichen die beschaffenheit der Newen Welt,... | beschriben. | ... Durch Ægidivm Albertinvm. | ...Auss dem Jtalianischen in die Hoch- | teutsche Sprach vbersetzt. | ... Mûnchen: durch Nicolaum Henricum, Jn | Verlegung Anthonij Hierats. | Jm Jahr. M.DC.XI. 10 p.l., 471 p., 5 maps. f°.
Sabin 6808.                                Reserve 1611
Contents of special interest: "Vierter Theil ersten Buchs handlet von der newen Welt," p. 144–153. "Fuenffter Theil ersten Buchs. Von dem Meridionalischen Theil Americae," p. 153–166. Sabin 6808 lists two more German editions of 1612 and 1661, respectively.
The Library has uncatalogued biographical material about Botero in *AN (B) n.c.7*.

125A. ROESLIN, HELISAEUS. Mitternächtige Schiffarth, von den Herrn Staden inn Niderlanden vor xv. Jaren vergebenlich fürgenommen... Oppenheim: Hieronymum Gallart, 1611. 8 l., 175 p. 8°.                Reserve 1611
Sabin 73294.

### 1612

125B. BERTIUS, PETRUS. Petri Bertii geographischer eyn oder zusammengezogener Fabeln fûnff vnterschiedliche Bûcher. In deren i. die gantze Welt in gemein. ii. Evropa. iii. Africa. iv. Asia. v. America vorgebildet vnd beschrieben wirdt. Franckfurt: Gedruckt durch M. Beckern, in Verlegung H. Lorentzen, 1612. 11 p. l., 830 p., 20 l. incl. maps. illus. 12 x 18cm.
                                                        \* KB 1612
"Engraved title-page. Maps engraved by Jodocus Hondius, Keer, Pigafetta, and Benjamin Wright." — *Phillips, Geographical atlases, 3413.*

126. RALEIGH, SIR WALTER. Die Fûnffte | Kurtze Wunderbare Beschreibung, | dess Goldreichen Kônig- | reichs Guinanæ in America oder newen Welt, | vnter der llnea Æquinoctiali gelegen: So neulich Anno | 1594. 1595. vnd 1596. von dem Wolgebornen Herrn, Herrn Wal- | thero Ralegh einem Engelischen Ritter, besucht worden: Erstlich auss | Befehl seiner Gnaden in zweyen Bûchlein beschrieben, darauss Jodocus Hondius, | eine schône Landt Tafel, mit einer Niderlåndischen Erklårung gemacht. | Jetzt aber ins Hochteutsch gebracht, vnd auss vnterschiedlichen | Authoribus erklåret. | ... Franckfurt am Mayn: bey Erasmo Kempffern, | In Verlegung Leuini Hulsij Wittibe, Im Jahr 1612. 3 p.l., 2–17 p., 1 l., map, 6 plates. 4°.
Sabin 67565.                             Reserve Hulsius
This copy of the fourth edition has the same vignette on title page as the preceding editions, but is badly cracked. See nos. 110, 115, 116, 122.
Verso of l. 3 is p. 1.
"A Synopsis of the Work and a Critique on this Edition will be found in Camus's *Mémoire* p. 97–98 and in Meusel's *Bibliotheca Historica*, v. III, part I, p. 283." — *Asher, p. 42.* See also the Lenox Library's *Contributions to a Catalogue,* no. 1, p. 9–10 for a description of this and nos. 127–129.

127. —— —— Another issue. Reserve Hulsius
Vignette on title page has been reprinted, with trees in background omitted.
Sabin 67565, annotation.

128. —— —— Another issue.
                                         Reserve Hulsius p.v.1
Vignette on title page is the same as that of no. 127.

129. —— —— Another issue. Reserve Hulsius
Vignette on title page is that of part nineteen of the Hulsius voyages: a vessel at anchor and men on the shore.
Sabin 67565, annotation.

130. VEER, GERRIT DE. Dritter Theil, | Warhafftiger Relation | Der dreyen newen vner- | hôrten, seltzamen Schiffahrt, so die Hollån- | dische vnd Seelândische Schiff gegen Mitternacht, drey | Jahr nach einander, als Anno 1594. 1595. vnd 1596. verricht. | ...Tertia editio. Franckfurt am Mayn: Jn Verlegung Leuini Hulsij Wittibe. | Jm Jahr 1612. 8 p.l., 96 p., 32 plates. 4°.                       Reserve Hulsius
Third edition. See Nos. 107, 118, 119.

### 1613

131. BRY, THEODOR DE, EDITOR. Americæ | Das Fûnffte Buch, | Vol schôner vnerhôrter Historien, auss | dem andern theil Ioannis [sic!] Benzonis von Mey- | landt gezogen... Alles mit schônen vnd kunstreichë Kupfferstûcken vñ de- | ren angehenckten erklårungen, an tag geben, durch Die- | terich von Bry... [Frankfurt am Mayn: Erasmus Kempffer, 1613.] 2 parts in 1 v. plates. f°.               Reserve Bry
Sabin, v. 3, p. 53. JCB, I, 2, 396.
Part v, Second edition.
Date from title before plates.
See no. 95.

132. —— Americae | Pars Quarta. | ... [Frankfurt am Main: M. Beckers selige Wittib, 1613.] 2 parts in 1 v. 24 plates, 1 map. f°.
Sabin v. 3, p. 52. JCB, I, 2, 394.       Reserve Bry
Part IV, Second edition.
First edition, 1594.
Has Latin title. Colophon: Gedruckt zu Frankfurt am Mayn bey Matthias Be- | ckers seligen Wittib, In Verlegung Johann Theodors | de Bry. M.DC.XIII. Second part has German title pasted over Latin title.
Another copy has laid in: German title pasted over Latin title, in Part First. "Das vierdte Buch von der neuwen Welt..." Also a map, "America sive Novvs Orbis Respectv Europaeorum Inferior Globi Terrestria Pars, 1596."

133. CASAS, BARTOLOMÉ DE LAS, BISHOP OF CHIAPA. Warhafftiger vnd gründli- | cher Bericht, | Der Hispanier grewlich: | vnd abschewlichen Tyranney | von jhnen in den West Indien, | die newe Welt genant, | begangen. | Erstlich, Castilianisch durch Bi- | schoff Bartholomæum de las Casas... Nachmals ins Hochteutsch, durch einen Liebhaber dess | Vaterlands, vbergesetzt: | Jetzunder widerumb mit schönen Figuren ge- | zieret, zur Warnung vnd Beyspiel gedruckt | ... Oppenheim: In Verlegung Ioh. | Theodori de Bry. 1613. 178 p., 17 plates. 4°.                           Reserve 1613
Sabin 11280.
See nos. 99, 109.

*1613, continued*

134. MEGISER, HIERONYMUS. Septentrio Novantiquus, | Oder | Die newe Nort Welt. | Das ist: | Gründliche vnd war- | haffte Beschreibung aller der | Mitternächtigen vnd Nortwerts gelege- | nen Landen vnd Jnsulen,... Zuvor in Teutscher Sprach nie auss- | gangen, sondern an jetzo erst alles aus vielen vnter- | schiedenen Schrifften... zusammen verfasset, verdeutschet, ...vnd in Druck | verfertiget, durch | Hieronymum Megiserum. | ... Leipzig: in verlegung Henning Grossen des Jüngern, | Anno 1613. 12 p.l., 473(1) p., 19 l. (one blank), 4 maps, 8 plates. 8°. Reserve 1613
Sabin 47383.
Although the work deals chiefly with voyages to the north, some information relative to America, especially Virginia, is included.

135. THEODORUS, JACOBUS. Neuw vollkommentlich Kreuterbuch, | mit schönen vnnd künstlichen Figuren, aller Gewächs der Bäumen, | Stauden vnd Kräutern, so in Teutschen,... Lan- | den, auch in...der Newen Welt | wachsen,... | mit sonderm Fleiss trewlich beschrieben, | Durch Iacobum Theodorum Tabernæmontanum,...Jetzt widerumb mit vielen schönen newen Figuren,...gemehret, Durch Casparum Bauhinum... Franckfurt am Mayn: Durch Nicolaum Hoffman, In verlegung Jo | hannis Bassaei vnd Johann Dreutels. | Anno M.DC.XIII. 2 v. f°. †† QEN
Second volume has title: D. Iacobi Theodori | Tabernæmontani | New vnd vollkommen | Kraeuterbuch...
On p. 633 of second volume, *Das dritte Theil dess Kraeuterbuchs* begins. The work concludes with *Zehen vnderschiedliche Register aller Namen der Kraeuter* ..., i.e., indices in the Greek, Latin, Arabic, Italian, French, Spanish, English, Moravian, German, and Dutch languages.

*1614*

136. HUDSON, HENRY. Zwölffte Schiffahrt | Oder | Kurtze Beschreibung | der Newen Schiffahrt gegen Nord Osten, | vber die Amerische Inseln in Chinam vnd Japponiam, | von einem Engellender Heinrich Hudson newlich erfunden, Bene- | ben einen Discurss an Ihr Kön. Maj. in Spanien, wegen dess fünfften | Theils der Welt, Terra Australis incognita genandt, Auch | kurtze Beschreibung der Länder der Samojeden vnd | Tingoesen in der Tartarey gelegen. | Jn Hochteutscher Sprach beschrieben durch | M. Gothardum Arthusen von Dantzig. | ... Oppenheim: bey Hieronymo Gallern, | in Vorlegung Levini Hulsii Wittib. M DC XIV. 67 p., 7 plates, incl. 5 maps. 4°.
Sabin 33666. Reserve Hulsius
The plates (three with descriptive letterpress on verso) have the title: Folgen etliche | Mappen oder Land- | Taffeln,... In Kupffer gestochen... [ Durch | Johann-Theodor de Bry.
See A. Asher, *Bibliographical essay on the collection of voyages and travels, edited and published by L. Hulsius and his successors*, Berlin, 1839, p. 65–67, * KAK (Hulsius); also Paul Dinse, *Die Anfänge der Nordpolarforschung und die Eismeerfahrten Henry Hudsons*, Berlin, 1908 (Meereskunde, Jahrg. 2, Heft 2). For non-German tracts, see the Public Catalogue of the Library.
First edition of the twelfth relation in the collection

of voyages of Hulsius, describing Hudson's search for a northwest passage in 1610–1611.

137. —— —— Another issue. Reserve Hulsius
Slight variations.

*1617*

138. BRY, THEODOR DE, EDITOR. America, | Das ist, | Erfindung vnd Offenbah- | rung der Newen Welt, deroselbigen | Völcker Gestalt, Sitten, Gebräuch, Policey | vnd Gottesdienst, in dreyssig vornemste Schifffahrten | kürtzlich vnnd ordentlich zusammen gefasset,...Durch M. Philippum Ziglerum...vnd...in Truck gegeben | Von Johan-Theodoro de Bry, | ... Franckfurt am Mayn: | Durch Nicolaum Hoffmann. | Anno M.DC.XVII. 8 p.l., 433 p. plates. illus. 33x23 cm. (f°.) Reserve 1617
Sabin 8784 (v. 3, p. 59).
This volume contains an abridgement of the first nine parts of the Great Voyages, and some other relations already published. Nohtwendiger Discurss vnd eygentliche | Beschreibung | Americæ... — p. 335.

139. BRY, THEODOR DE, EDITOR. Das VII. Theil America. | Warhafftige vnd liebliche | Beschreibung, etlicher fürnemmen, | Jndianischen keiner Chronicken gedacht, vnd | erstlich in der Schiffahrt Vlrici Schmidts von | Straubingen, mit grosser Gefahr erkündigt, | vnd von ihm selber auff das fleissigste | beschrieben vnd dargethan. | Vnd an Tag gebracht durch Dieterich | von Bry.... Jetzo zum dritten mal auffgelegt vnd gebessert | durch Johan- Theodor de Bry,... Oppenheim: Gedruckt bey Hieronymo Gallern | M DC XVII. 1 p.l., 55 p. plates. f°. Reserve Bry
Sabin, v. 3, p. 54. JCB, 1, 2, 400.
Part VII, Third edition.
See nos. 73, 74, 98.

140. HAMOR, RALPH, THE YOUNGER. Dreyzehente Schiffahrt | Darinnen | Ein Warhafftiger vnd Gründtlicher Bericht, von dem jtzigen | Zustandt der Landtschafft Virginien; Auch wie nun- | mehr der Friede mit den Indianern beschlossen; Vnd wie etliche | Stätte vnd Vestunge alda zum Schutz des Landts von den Enge- | lischen auffgebawet worden. | Sampt | Einer Relation, wie König Powhatans in Virginien | Tochter, Pocahuntas genant, Christlichen getaufft vnd mit einem | Engelischen verheurahtet worden, sehr anmütig zu lesen, &c. | Erstlichen in Engelischer Sprach durch Raphe Hamor... daselbst beschrieben, auss deren, durch einen Liebhaber der Historien, in | Teutsch vbergesetzet. | ... Hanaw: | Jn Verlegung der Hulsischen. | Anno M.DC.XVII. 76 p., 4 plates, 1 map. 4°. Reserve Hulsius
Sabin 30122.
First Hulsius edition?
This is the thirteenth relation in the collection of voyages of Hulsius. "The Events related in this Part contain valuable materials for the History of the Settlement of Virginia." See A. Asher, *Bibliographical essay on the collection of voyages and travels, edited and published by L. Hulsius and his successors*, Berlin, 1839, p. 68–71, * KAK (Hulsius).

141. —— —— Another issue. Reserve Hulsius
Differs slightly from the preceding.

# GERMAN WORKS RELATING TO AMERICA 19

*1617, continued*

142. SMITH, JOHN. Viertzehende Schiffart, | Oder | Gründliche vnd warhaffte | Beschreibung dess Neuwen Engellandts | einer Landschafft in Nordt Indien, eines Theils in Ame- | rica vnter dem Capitein Johann Schmidt, Rittern, Admiral derselben Landschafft, auch dem glücklichen Fortgang so er mit | Sechs Schiffen deren Orts gehabt. | ...Durch einen Liebhaber der Historien auss dem Eng- | lischen in Hoch Teutsch versetzt. | ...Franckfurt am Mayn: In verlegung der Hülsischen. | Im Jahr Christi 1617. 4 p.l., 64 p. map, plate. 4°.
Sabin 33667. Reserve Hulsius
The fourteenth relation in the collection of voyages of Hulsius, giving Smith's account of New England between 1614 and 1616. See A. Asher, *Bibliographical essay on the collection of voyages and travels, edited and published by L. Hulsius and his successors*, Berlin, 1839, p. 72–75, * KAK (Hulsius).

## 1618

143. BRY, THEODOR DE, EDITOR. Zehender Teil | Americæ | Darinnen zubefinden: Erstlich, zwo | Schiffarten Herrn Americi Vesputii... | Zum andern: Ein gründlicher Bericht von dem jetzigen Zustand | der Landschafft Virginien... | durch Raphe Homar...beschrieben, | in hochteutsch vbersetzt. | Zum dritten: Ein warhafftige Beschreibung dess newen Engellands, einer Landschafft | in Nord-Jndien, eines Theils in America, von Capitein Johann Schmiden,... | beschrieben,... | Alles mit schönen Kupfferstücken gezieret, vnd in Truck gegeben, in Vorlegung Johan-Theodor | de Bry... Oppenheim: bey Hieronymo Gallern, | Anno | M DC-XVIII. 73 p., 12 plates, 3 maps. f°. Reserve Bry
Sabin, v. 3, p. 37. JCB, I, 2, 412–413.
Added title page, with different vignette; also three leaves from the German edition of part XI, of the East Indies collection relating to Vespuccius's two voyages of 1501 and 1503.
Divided into three parts: I. The voyage of Amerigo Vespucci. II. Ralphe Hamor's description of Virginia (see no. 140). III. John Smith's account of New England between 1614 and 1616 (see no. 142). Twelve plates with accompanying text follow.

144. ENS, GASPAR. West- vnnd Ost Jndischer | Lustgart: | Das ist | Eyentliche Erzehlung | Wann vnd von wem die Newe Welt erfunden | besägelt, vnd eingenommen worden,... Neben Beschreibung aller derer Landschafften,... Wie auch Verfassung der fürnembsten Schiffahrten so | ...dahin,...verricht | worden. | Auss glaubwürdigen Schrifften zusamen gezogen. | ...Cöllen: | Bey Wilhelm Lützenkirchen | Anno MDCXVJJJ. 4 p.l., 436, 236 p. 4°. * KB 1618
Sabin 22657, 42742.
"A summary of the most interesting sources of American history."
*Contents:* Nohtwendiger Discurss vnd eygentliche Beschreibung Americae, darinnen | so wol die Beschaffenheit der Jnwohner | als andere Sachen | deren in folgenden Schiffarten | entweder garnicht | oder nur oben hin gedacht wirt | eygentlicher erklaeret werden, p. 1–154. Ander Theil des West Jndischen Lustgartens: Darin die Erste vnnd fuernembste Schiffarten durch welche diese Newe Welt entdecket worden...erzehlet werden, p. 155–300. Narrates the four voyages of Columbus and two voyages of Vespucci. A chapter on Brazil is followed by others on the voyages of Ulrich Schmidel, Sir Walter Raleigh, Richard Grenville, Giovanni da Verrazzano, and Jacques Cartier. The third part describes North and South America geographically and tells of the Indians, and a "Kurtzer Anhang Von der Disposition oder Anlassung der Newen Welt zum Euangelio," p. 393–436. The remaining part deals with the East Indies.

145. HULSIUS, LEVINUS. Sechste Theil, | Kurtze, Warhafftige | Relation vnd Beschreibung der Wun- | derbarsten vier Schifffahrten, so jemals ver- | richt worden. Als nemlich: | Ferdinandi Magellani... | Francisci Draconis... | Thomæ Candisch... | Oliuarii von Noort... | So alle vier vmb den gantzen Erdtkreiss gesegelt, auss vnter- | schiedenen Authoribus vnd Sprachen zusammen getragen,... Durch | Levinum Hulsium. Francofurti: | Impensis Hvlsianis, M.DCXVIII. 3 p.l., 54 p., 6 maps, 9 plates. 4°. Reserve Hulsius
Second edition. See no. 121.

## 1619

146. BRY, THEODOR DE, EDITOR. Historische Beschreibung, | Der wunderbarlichen Reyse, welche | von einem Holländer, Willhelm Schouten genandt, | neulicher Zeit ist verrichtet worden: | ... Alles von newem mit herrlichen Landtafeln, vnd schönen Kupfferstücken gezieret, | vnd ans Tage Liecht gegeben, | Durch vnd in Verlegung Johann-Dieterich von Bry. | ... Franckfurt am Mayn: | Durch Paull Jacobi: Jm Jhar | M.DC.XIX. 35 p., 9 plates. f°.
Part XI. Reserve Bry
Sabin, v. 3, p. 57. JCB, I, 2, 414–415.
Describes the voyage around the world of Willem Corneliszoon Schouten. The author of Schouten's journal is unknown.
The Library also has an edition, printed at Arnheim, in 1618, * KB 1618.

147. —— Das sechste Theil Americæ | oder | Der Historien Hieron. Benzo von Meylandt, | Das dritte Buch. | ... Alles mit schönen Kupfferstücken vorgebildet | vnd an Tag geben | Durch Dieterich von Bry... [Oppenheim: H. Galler,] M DC XIX. 2 parts in 1 v. plates, map. f°. Reserve Bry
Sabin, v. 3, p. 53. JCB, I, 2, 398.
Part VI, Second edition.
First edition, 1597.
Title of part I is printed on blank within engraved border formed by erasing engraved Latin text; title of part 2 is printed, with no engraving.

148. NICOLAI, ELIUD. Newe vnd warhaffte relation, von de- | me was sich in beederley | Das ist | Jn den West- vnd Ost- | Jndien, von der zeit an zugetragen, dass sich die Navigationes der Holl- vnnd Engelândi- | schen compagnien daselbst angefangen | abzuschneiden. | ... Alles auss gewissen Castiglianischen vnnd Portugesischen | relationen colligiert,... Durch Elivd Nicolai an tag geben. | ... München: durch Nicolaum Hen- | ricum, im Jahr | M.DC.XIX. 12 p.l., 158 p. map. 4°. * KB 1619
Sabin 55242.
Of special interest: Cap. II, Warhaffte vnnd auff leiblich geschwornen Aydt | cingezogene erfahrung | wie es dem Georg Spilberger | vnd der Hollendischen Armada ergangen..., p. 17–38. Cap. XXI, "Von etlichen Zeitungen auss China, so nit durch den Ordinari weg umb das Caput bonae Spei in Africa | sonder vber new Spanien durch Mexico gar newlich herauss kommen," p. 153–158.

### 1620

**149.** BRY, THEODOR DE, EDITOR. Wunderbarliche, doch warhafftige | Erklärung, von der Gelegenheit vnd | Sitten der Wilden in Virginia, ... | ...Jetzt widerumb vbersehen, vnd zum drittenmal | in Truck gegeben. | ... Oppenheim: bey Hieronymo Gallern, | Jn Vorlegung Johann-Theodori de Bry | M.DC.XX. 3 parts in 1 v. plates, map. illus. f°. Reserve Bry
Sabin, v. 3, p. 50. JCB, 1, 2, 387.
Part 1, Third edition.
First edition, 1590; Second edition, 1600.

**150.** —— Appendix | Dess eilfften Theils Americæ, | Das ist: Warhafftige Beschreibung der | wunderbahren Schifffahrt, so Georgius von Spielbergen, | ...1614. biss in das 1618. Jahr | verrichtet. | ...Durch | M. Gotthard Arthus von. Dantzig. ... Oppenheim: bey Hieronymo Gallern, | Jn Vorlegung Johann-Theodor de Bry. | Anno | M DC XX. 38 p., 20 plates. f°.
Part XI, 1619. Reserve Bry
Sabin, v. 3, p. 57. JCB, 1, 2, 415.
The journal of the voyage of Joris van Spilbergen, p. 5-38, kept until May 27, 1603, by Cornelis Jansz Vennip of Enkhuizen (cf. entry for June 15, 1603), and later by an unidentified member of the expedition. Twenty plates with explanatory text follow.
See Wouter Nijhoff, *Bibliographie van de reyse van Joris van Spilberghen naar Oost-Indien, 1601-1604, s' Gravenhage, 1933, KAK (Spilbergen).*

**151.** JESUITS. Auss America, das ist, auss der | Newen Welt. | Vnderschidlicher Schrei- | ben Extract, von den Jaren 1616. 1617. 1618. | Was gestalt Acht Patres Societatis, vnd zwo andere | Ordenspersonen, von dess Christlichen Glaubens wegen Jhr Blut | vergossen... Auss Frantzösischer Sprach in die Teutsche | vbergesetzt. | ...Augspurg: bey Sara Mangin | Wittib, 1620. 2 p.l., 91 p. 4°. *KB 1620
Sabin 1019.
*Contents:* Memorial. So der Kön: May: zu Hispanien im Jahr 1617. vbergeben worden | inn welchem zu finden | was gestalt inn den Occidentalischen Jndien | so man die newe Welt nennet | etliche Gaistliche wegen dess Christlichen Glaubens | im Jahr 1616. die Marter Cron empfangen, p. 1-16.
Letters of missionaries from the West Indies, Mexico, and different parts of South America follow.

### 1623

**152.** BRY, THEODOR DE, EDITOR. Zwölffter Theil | der Newen Welt, | Das ist: | Gründliche volkommene Entdeckung | aller der West Jndianischen Landschafften,... | Durch | Antonium de Herrera,...auss der | Hispanischen Sprach in die Teutsche vbergesetzet. | ... Jtem | Petri Ordonnez de Cevallos Beschreibung der West Jndia- | nischen Landschafften, samt andern Anhängen. | Alles mit schönen Landtaffeln vnd Kupfferstücken vor Au- | gen gestellt... | ... Franckfurt, in Verlegung Johann Dietherichs | de Bry, Anno 1623. 2 p.l., 131 p., 15 maps and plans. f°. Reserve Bry
Sabin, v. 3, p. 57.
*Contents:* Herrera's account of the West Indies, p. 1-74. Verzeichnuss der Praesidenten | Raehten | Secretarien | vnd Fiscalen | welche vom ersten Anfang | als die Jndien erfunden worden | biss auff heuto dato, im Koeniglichen vnd hohen Jndianischen Rath gedienet haben | vnd noch dienen, p. 74-75. Gubernatoren vnd Vice Reen oder Koenigliche Statthalter | die biss auf die gegenwertige Zeit die Koenigreiche New Hispanien vnd Peru regieret vnnd versehen haben, p. 76-77. Relation oder Bericht zweyer Caravellen | so der Koenig von Hispanien im Jahre 1618. im Octobri | von Lissabon vnter dem Capitain Herrn Johann von More abfahren lassen | den Pass dess de la Maire gegen Suden | zu besuchen vnnd zu entdecken, p. 77-79. Kurtzer Auszug Aller nach der Enge des Magellanischen Meers gethauer Reysen oder Schiff Fahrten, p. 80-91. Erklaerung Etlicher Woerter | so in der Sprache etlicher Jnsulen dieser West-Jndien gebraeuchlich seynd, p. 92-94. Sonderbare Beschreibung der West-Jndien...durch Priester Petern Ordonnez, von Cevallos [i.e., Pedro de Ordóñez de Cevallos], p. 95-131. Fifteen maps and plans follow.

**153.** HERRERA Y TORDESILLAS, ANTONIO DE. Achtzehender Theil der | Newen Welt, | Das ist: | Gründliche volkommene Entdeckung aller der | West Indianischen Landschafften, Insuln vnd Königreichen, | Secusten, fliessenden vnd stehenden Wassern, Port vnd Anlendungen, Ge- | bürgen, Grentzen, vnd Ausstheilung der Provincien, sampt eygentlicher Beschreibung der Stät- | te, Flecken vnd Dörffer, Herrschafft und Regierung,...alles nach jetziger Gestalt vnd Be- | schaffenheit von newem endeckt vnd beschrieben, | Durch | Antonium de Herrera,... Auss der Hispanischen Sprach in die Teutsche vbergesetzet. | ... Franckfurt am Mayn: durch Johann Friederich Weissen, | in Verlegung der Hulsischen, Anno 1623. 1 p.l., ii-iii f., 256 p., 14 maps. 4°. Reserve Hulsius
Sabin 33671.
This Herrera account of the West Indies is the eighteenth relation in the collection of voyages of Hulsius and the only edition in the collection. See A. Asher, *Bibliographical essay on the collection of voyages and travels edited and published by L. Hulsius and his successors,* p. 86-87, *KAK (Hulsius).*
"Herrera's account is taken almost entirely from a Sumario of the manuscript work of Juan Lopez de Velasco, since printed, in 1894, by the Geographical Society of Madrid. This description was written between 1571 and 1574, and was not up to date even at that time." — *Wagner, Spanish Southwest, p. 12.*
"Erklärung | Etlicher Wörter, so in der Sprache etlicher Insulen | dieser West Indien gebräuchlich seynd," p. 253-256.

### 1624

**154.** BRY, THEODOR DE, EDITOR. Achter Theil Americæ,... Von Newem vbersehen in ein richtiger Ordnung gebracht, vnd zum andernmahl vffgelegt, | auch mit vielen Kupfferstücken vber vorige vermehret. | Franckfurt: | Bey Caspar Rödtel: Jn Verlegung Weiland Johannis Theodori | de Bry Seeligen Erben. | M.DC.XXIV. 2 p.l., 130 p. plates, map. f°.
Sabin, v. 3, p. 55. JCB, 1, 2, 405. Reserve Bry
Part VIII., Second edition.
First edition, 1599.

### 1626

**155.** HULSIUS, LEVINUS, EDITOR. Sechste Theil, | Kurtze, Warhafftige | Relation vnnd Beschreibung der Wun- | derbarsten vier Schiffahrten, so jemals ver- | richt worden... Franckfurt: bey Hartmanno Palthenio, in Verlegung der Hulsischen Jm Jahr, 1626. 3 p.l., 54 p., 5 maps, 9 plates. 4°. Reserve Hulsius
Third edition of the sixth relation of the collection of voyages of Hulsius. See nos. 121, 145.

## 1627

156. HUDSON, HENRY. Zwölffte Schiffahrt | Oder | Kurtze Beschreibung | der Newen Schiffahrt gegen Nord Osten, | vber die Americsche Inseln in Chinam vnd Japponiam, | von einem Engellånder Heinrich Hudson newlich erfunden,... In Hochteutscher Sprach beschrieben durch | M. Gothardum Arthusen von Dantzig. | ... Oppenheim: bey Hieronymo Gallern, | In Vorlegung Levini Hvlsii Wittib. | M DC XXVII. 68 p., 3 maps, 4 plates. 4°.
Reserve Hulsius
Second edition of the twelfth relation in the collection of voyages of Hulsius. For the first, see nos. 136, 137.

## 1628

157. AUSSFÜHRLICHER Bericht, | wie es mit der | Silber Flotta hergan- | gen, wann (durch wen, wie, vnd wie viel) solche inn diesem 1628. Jahr erobert, fort vnd eingebracht | Nebenst Specificierung aller Gütter, auch | wie sie vnter die West-Jndische Compagni [sic!], | aussgetheilt worden. | Erstlich gedruckt zu Ambsterdam bey | Heinrich Mellort Jano. [n. p., 1628?] 6 l. 18½cm. (4°.) * KB 1628
Frankfurt am Main. Stadtbibliothek: Flugschriftensammlung Gustav Freytag, 1819.
The achievements of the Silber-Flotta are narrated, followed by: Absonderliche Erzehlung | aller Eroberten Gütter | wie sie vnter die West-Jndische Compania aussgetheilet.

158. BRY, THEODOR DE, EDITOR. Dreyzehender Theil Americae, | Das ist: | Fortsetzung der Historien von der | Newen Welt, oder Nidergångischen Jn- | dien, waran es auff diese Zeit noch an- | hero ermangelt. | Darinnen erstlich ein sattsame vnd gründtliche Beschreibung dess Newen | Engellandts, welches die Englische das New erfundene Landt nen- | nen, so bissher noch nicht an Tag kommen. | Zum Andern, Ein ausführlichere Erzehlung von Beschaffenheit der Landtschafften Virginia, Brasilia, Guiana, vnd Jnsul Bermuda... | ...Am Ende ist...ein... | ...Discurs, wie die Statt S. Saluator, verlohren vnd wider | gewunnen worden... | Alles mit beygefügten Kupfferstücken vnd zu gebührigen gantz newen | lustigen Landtschafften, erläutert vnd geziert, auch biss auff | das 1627. Jahr continuirt. Franckfurt: Gedruckt bey Caspar Rötel, Jn Verlegung Matthei Merian. | Anno, M.DC.XXVIII. 2 parts, 10 plates, 4 maps. f°. Reserve Bry
Sabin, v. 3, p. 58.
Contents: Der Erste Theil | Von dem Newerfundenen oder Newen Engelland. Zweyter Theil | Von der Landschafft Virginia. Der Dritte Theil | Von Bermuda oder Summers Jnsul. Der Vierdte Theil | Von Brasilien. Der Fuenffte Theil | Von Guiana. Der Sechste Theil | Von der unbewusten Mittaegischen Landschafft.

159. SMITH, JOHN. Verzehende Schiffart, | Oder | Gründliche vnd warhaff- | te Beschreibung dess Newen Engellands, | ... Franckfurt am Mayn: Jn Verlegung | Leuini Hulsii Erben. Jm Jahr 1628. 4 p.l., 64 p., 1 map, 1 plate. 4°.
Reserve Hulsius
Second edition of the fourteenth relation in the collection of voyages of Hulsius. See no. 142.

## 1629

160. WHITBOURNE, SIR RICHARD. Zwantzigste Schifffahrt, | oder Gründliche vnd sattsame Beschreibung dess Newen En- | gellands: | Wie auch | Ausführliche Erzehlung von Beschaf- | fenheit der Landschaft Virginia, vnd der Insel Bar- | muda, deren man bisshero schlechte vnnd vnvollkommene | Wissenschafft gehabt, an jetzo aber durch dero | Landt erfahrne Leuht, völ- | liglich an Tag gegeben... Franckfurt am Mayn: bey Wolffgang | Hoffmann, In Verlegung der Hulsischen Erben. | Im Jar 1629. 116 p., 1 map, 3 plates. 4°.
Sabin 33673. Reserve Hulsius
This is the twentieth relation in the collection of voyages of Hulsius. See A. Asher, *Bibliographical essay on the collection of voyages and travels edited and published by L. Hulsius and his successors*, p. 91–93. * KAK (Hulsius).

161. ——— Another copy. Reserve Hulsius
The two plates of the inhabitants of Virginia are here on one sheet, taken from Ziegler's abridgment of De Bry. The original of the plate of the men is inserted.

## 1630

162. BRY, THEODOR DE, EDITOR. Vierzehender Theil | Americanischer Historien, | Jnhaltend, | Erstlich, Warhafftige Erzehlung et- | licher West-Jndianischer Landen in dem Theil Americæ gegen Mit- | ternacht hinder Nova Hispania gelegen, Alss New Mexico... | Zum Andern, | Eine Schiffart der Holländer vnder dem Admiral Jacob Eremiten | vmb die gantze Welt, ... | Zum Dritten, | Historische Erzehlung, welcher gestalt die sehr reiche Spanische Silberflotta durch Peter | Hein,...in dem Hafen Mantanza der Jnsul Cuba... | ... ertapt vnd heim gebracht worden | ... Alles mit Zugehörigen Tafeln vnd Kupfferstücken gezieret, Verlegt | vnd an den Tag gegeben | Durch | Mattheum Merian... | ... Hanaw: bey David Aubrj, im Jahr | M DC XXX. 2 p.l., 72 p., 2 plates, 3 maps. f°. Reserve Bry
Sabin, v. 3, p. 58. JCB, 1, 2, 418–419.
"This 14th German part contains sections 8 to 15, which are in Latin in the 13th volume of the Great Voyages in that language, printed altogether only in 1634." — Sabin, v. 3, p. 59.
"...aber was die Laender | so Nordenwerts hinder Nova Hispania ligen | anlangt | sonderlich gegen Nidergang vnd dem Mare del Sur, davon hat man noch zur zeit sehr geringe wissenschafft... Vnd diss ist die Vrsach | dass bissher in vnserm grossen Americanischen Werck der Laender Novo Mexico, Cibola, Cinaloa, Tecoantepec, Quiuira, vnd deren so noch weitter gegen Septentrion ziehen | so wenig gedacht worden | da sie doch betrachtens wol werth | darumb wir auch deroselben kurtze Beschreibung diesem Theil einverleiben." — *Vorrede*.
Accounts of Jacques l'Hermite, Pieter Pieterszoon Hein, and Heinrich Cornelius Lonck (see Sabin 41850).
See also the German version of Jacques l'Hermite's *Diurnal*, Strassburg, 1629, * KB 1629.

## 1631

**163.** GOTTFRIED, JOHANN LUDWIG. Newe Welt | Vnd Americanische Historien. | Jnhaltende | Warhafftige vnd volkommene Beschreibungen Aller West-Jndianischen Landschafften,... | Alles auss verscheidenen West-Jndianischen Historien-Schreibern, vnnd mancherley | Sprachen mit sonderm fleiss zusammen getragen,... | Durch | Johan Ludwig Gottfriedt. | Mit zugehörigen Landtafeln, Contrafacturen vnd Geschichtmesigen Kupfferstücken, ... | gezieret vnd verlegt, | Durch Mattheum Merian... [Frankfurt am Main,] Anno M DC XXXI. 3 parts. plates, maps. illus. f°.

Sabin 50, annotation. Reserve 1631
*Contents:* West Jndianischer Historien Erster Theil | Von Natur und Eygenschafften der Neuen Welt, p. 1–203. West Jndianischer Historien Zweyter Theil. Von Erfindung derselben durch vnderschiedliche Schiffahrten, p. 204–562. West-Jndianischer Historien Dritter Theil | Jnhaltendt Gruendliche Beschreibung der Natur vnd Eigenschafft etlicher Landen | deren hiebevor wenig oder gar nicht gedacht worden | samt Continuation newer Schiffarten | in vnderschiedliche Provincien, 72 p.
"...also soltu merken, dass wir dasselbe in drey Theil vnderschieden haben. Im Ersten wird gehandelt von der ... Gelegenheit der Newen Welt. Jm andern Theyl werden 33 vnderschiedliche Schiffarten beschrieben | dadurch diese dess gantzen Erdklotzes helfft | nach und nach erfunden | entdeckt | vnd vor vnsern Europeischen Voelckern bewohnet worden ist ... Jm Dritten Theil dieses Wercks wird der Gunstige Leser neben Beschreibung etlicher West-Jndianischen Landtschafften in dem Nordertheil Americae, alss New Mexico, Cinalo, Quivira, vnd anderer, deren bissher weder in diesem vnserm | noch dem grossen Americanischen Werck sonderlich gedacht worden..."
— *Vorrede vnd Kurtze Erinnerung an den Leser.*
See nos. 175, 176, and note on no. 162.

## 1633

**164.** BRY, THEODOR DE, EDITOR. Neundter Theil | Americæ, | Dariñ gehandelt wird, von gelegenheit der Elementen, Natur, Art vnd eygenschafft | der newen Welt: ... | Alles mit schönen Kupfferstücken gezieret, vnd an | Tag geben, durch | Matthæum Merian von Basel ... | ... Franckfurt am Mayn: Bey Matthæo Kempffern. [1633?] 1 p.l., 206 p., 1 map. f°.

Sabin, v. 3, p. 56. Reserve Bry
Part IX, Second edition.
First edition, 1601.

**165.** ———— Another copy. Reserve Bry
Variant spelling on title page and "Gedruckt zu Franckfurt am Mayn, bey Wolffgang Hoffman."

**166.** WELPER, EBERHARD. Compendium Geographicum, | Das ist | Kurtze vñ eigentliche | Beschreibung der gantzen Erdkugel,...colligirt vnd zusammen getragen. | Durch | M. Eberhardum Welperum, | ...Strassburg: | Gedruckt vnd verlegt durch den Authorem. | Jm Jahr | M.DC.XXXIII. 6 p.l., 128 p. 4°. *KB 1633

Das XXX. Capitel. Von America, p. 82–83. The short geographical description ends with the remark, "So vil seye nun auch von America, vnnd also von der gantzen Beschreibung der Erdkugel gnug gesagt; ein mehreren vnd historischen Bericht suche bey dem Atlante Mercatoris [see no. 169], Bertio [Petrus Bertius], Cluverio [Philipp Clüver], vnd anderen..."
The Library has copies of the works of these geographers in the Reserve.

## 1639

**167.** THEATRI | Evropæi | Continuatio III. | ... Franckfurt: | Getruckt in Wolffgang Hoffmans Buchtruckerey, | Jm Jahr M.DC.XXXIX. 1 p.l., iii-iiij f., 2 l., 932 p., 11 l. maps (part folding). illus. (part folding.) † BTWA (Theatrum)
Year 1633: Privilegij vber die new angestellte Schiff-farth in beyde Jndien, p. 49–55; West Jndianische Schiff-Flotta, p. 89. Year 1634: Reich geladene Schiff [auss West Jndien] in Texel ankommen, p. 226.

## 1643

**168.** THEATRI | Europæi | Vierdter Theil, | Das ist: | Glaubwürdige Beschreibung. | Denckwürdiger Geschichten, die sich in Europa, auch zum | theil in Ost-und West-Jndien,... | ... begeben haben. | Auss vertrewlich communicirten Schrifften,... | ... zusammen getragen, ... | Beschrieben durch I. P. A. | ... Franckfurt am Mayn: in Verlegung | Matthæi Meriani ... | Anno M.DC.XXXXIII. 2 p.l., 978 p. plates (part folding), maps (part folding). illus. f°. † BTWA (Theatrum)
Year 1640: Ost- vnd West Jndische schiffe kommen mit grossem Schatz an, p. 244–245. Year 1641: Der West-Jndianischen Compagn. Actiones steigen, p. 602; Vō newer West-Jndischer Cōpagn. in Engelland remissive, p. 604.

## 1648

**169.** MERCATOR, GERARDUS. Atlas Minor, | das ist: | Eine kurtze jedoch gründliche | Beschreibung der gantzen Welt | In zwey Theile abgetheilt. | ... Mit vielen schönen newen Kupfferstücken vnd Land- | Beschreibungen vermehrt vnd verbessert. Amstelodami: | Ex officina I. Ianssonii, 1648. 2 v. in 1. illus. (maps.) 19×25 cm. (8°.) *KB 1648
The German translation by Peter Uffenbach was first published in 1609.
Sabin lists a 1631 edition, only (no. 47889).
See P. L. Phillips, *List of geographical atlases,* nos. 425 and 461, *KAB n.c.*

## 1650

**170.** MUENCKEN, JOHANN [i.e., MUNCK, JENS]. Die XXVI. Schiff-Fahrt: | Beschreibung einer | Hochst-mühseligen vnd gantz gefährlichen | Reyse, durch den See-verständigen Capitain, Herrn | Johann Müncken, inn Jahren 1619. vnd | 1620. verrichtet. | ... Franckfurt am Mayn: | Bey Christophoro Le Blon. | M DC L. 4 p.l., 64 p., 1 map, 10 plates. 4°. Reserve Hulsius Sabin 33679.
The twenty-sixth relation in the collection of voyages of Hulsius, the only Hulsius edition. See A. Asher, *Bibliographical essay on the collection of voyages and travels edited and published by L. Hulsius and his successors,* Berlin, 1839, p. 111–114, *KAK (Hulsius).*
Covers Munck's attempt to discover the North West passage.

## 1651

**171.** MERCATOR, GERARDUS. Atlas Minor, | Das ist: | Eine kurtze jedoch gründliche | Beschreibung der gantzen Weldt | ... Mit vielen schönen newen Kupfferstücken vnd Landbeschrei- | bungen vermehret vnd verbessert. Amstelodami: | Ex officina | Ioannis Ianssonii, 1651. 2 v. in 1. maps. illus. 19½ x 24½ cm. (8°.) *KB 1651
For issue of 1648, see no. 169.

## GERMAN WORKS RELATING TO AMERICA 23

### 1652

172. HEINRICH, HEINRICH. Ferdinandina | Die Mexicanische Jnsul. | Durch Beyhilff der Gottes Gebårerin Mariæ | zum Christlichen Glauben bekehrt ... Vorgestellt | Von dem Collegio der Societet Iesv,...: Durch | dess Churfürstlichen Gymnnasij Jugendt | in München. | Anno 1652. [München:] Getruckt bey Lucas Straub. [1652.] 4 l. 19 cm. (4°.)    *KB 1652
JCB, 1919, ii, 417.

Translation of the argument and synopsis only from his Neo-Latin drama, *Ferdinandina Mexicana insula Mariæ Dei parentis auxilio ad fidem conversa*. [Monachii, 1652]. *KB 1652.

"Das Stueck wurde viermal mit dem grössten Erfolg aufgeführt zu Ehren der neuen Kurfürstin Adelheid von Savoyen. Es handelt sich um die Bekehrung der von Columbus entdeckten und Cuba Ferdinandaea genannten Insel." *cf.* Johannes Mueller, *Das Jesuitendrama*, Augsburg, 1930 (Schriften zur deutschen Literatur. Bd. 7–8, *NFCA*); see especially, v. 2, p. 34–35.

173. THEATRI | Evropæi | Sechster vnd letzter Theil, | ... Auss vnzehlich vielen glaubhafften Documentis,... zusammen getragen... | Durch | Joannem Georgium Schlederum... Franckfurt am Mâyn: | Bey Weyl. Matthaei Merians Seel. Erben. | Anno M DC LII. 8 p.l., 1208 p., 17 l. maps (part folding). plates (part folding). illus. f°.    †BTWA (Theatrum)
Year 1648: Den Holländern gehets in West-Jndien ziemlich, p. 385; Ost- vnd West-Jndianischer Händel weiterer Verlauff, p. 556.- Year 1649: Portugesen halten ein genaues Aug auff West-Jndien, p. 876.

### 1654

174. LOGAU, FRIEDRICH VON. Salomons von Golaw Deutscher Sinn-Getichte Drey Tausend. Bresslaw: In verlegung C. Klossmanns [1654]. 8°. (Litterarischer Verein in Stuttgart. Bibliothek. Tübingen, 1872. 8°. [Bd.] CXIII.) NFF
This number, with separate title page, is Logau's *Sämmtliche Sinngedichte*. Tübingen, 1872. 821 p. 8°.
"Dass so viel dess göldnen Staubes hat die neue Welt gestreuet. | Drüber ist noch nichts erschienen, dass die alte Welt sich freuet;..." — *Drittes Tausend, Sechstes Hundert*, [*No.*] 62 (p. 539).

### 1655

175. GOTTFRIED, JOHANN LUDWIG, PSEUD. Newe Welt | Vnd Americanische Historien. | Inhaltende | Warhafftige und vollkommene Be- | schreibungen Aller West-Jndianischen Landschafften,... Dessgleichen | Gründlicher Bericht von der Jnnwohner Beschaffenheit,... Item, | Historische vnd Aussführliche Relation 38. Fürnembster Schiffarten vnter- | schiedlicher Völcker in West-Jndien, von der Ersten Entdeckung durch Christopho- | rum Columbum, in 150. Jahren vollbracht. | Alles auss verschiedenen West-Jndianischen Historien-Schreibern, vnnd man- | cherley Sprachen... zusammen getragen,... Durch | Johann Ludwig Gottfriedt. | ...und verlegt, | Durch Mattheum Merian, ... Franckfurt: | Bey denen Merianischen Erben. M.DC.LV. 4 p.l., 661 p., 1 l. plates, maps. illus. 33x20 cm. (f°.)    †*KB 1655
Sabin 50.
Added engraved title page, with title: *Historia antipodum oder Newe Welt*...
*Contents*: West-Jndianischer Historien Erster Theil | Von Natur vnd Eygenschafften der Newen Welt, p. 1–202. West-Jndianischer Historien Ander Theil | Von Erfindung derselben durch vnderschiedliche Schiffarthen, p. 203–559. West-Jndianischer Historien Dritter Theil. Jnhaltend gruendliche Beschreibung der Natur vnd Eigenschafft etlicher Landen | deren hiebevor wenig oder gar nicht gedacht worden | sampt Continuation newer Schiffarten in vnterschiedliche Provincien, p. 560–661.

An abridgement of parts I–XII of de Bry's German edition of the "Grand voyages," to which is added a duplicate of part XIV. This second edition contains in addition to the voyages published in the first those of Johann Müncken (see no. 170), and of H. Brawer and E. Herckemann, 1642–1643.
Authorship erroneously ascribed to J. P. Abelin. See F. Gallati, *Der königlich schwedische in Teutschland geführte Krieg*, Zürich, 1902, *EAG p.v.66, no.5*.
*See* no. 163.

176. ——— ——— Another issue.    †*KB 1655
Title page and p. 13 differ slightly.

### 1657

177. GOTTFRIED, JOHANN LUDWIG, PSEUD. Jo. Ludovici | Gottfridi | Historische | Chronica, | oder | Beschreibung der Fûrnem- | sten Geschichten, so sich von Anfang der Welt, biss auff | das Jahr Christi 1619. zugetragen: | Nach Aussheilung der viier Monarchien, vnnd beygefûg- | ter Jahrrechnung, auffs fleissigste in Ordnung gebracht, vermehret, vnd in Acht Theil abgetheilet; | Mit viel schônen Contrafaicturen, vnd Geschichtmâssigen Kupfferstû- | cken, zur Lust vnd Anweisung der Historien, gezieret, an Tag | gegeben, vnnd verlegt, | Durch | Weyland Matthæum Merianum Seel. | jetzo dessen Erben. | ... Franckfurt am Mayn: Jn W. Hoffmanns Buch-Druckerey, Jm Jahr nach Christi Geburt, | M.DC.LVII. 38 p.l., 1185(1) p., 27 l., incl. 31 plates (ports.), map, plan. illus. 31½ cm. (f°.) Sabin 50.    †*KB 1657
Preface dated: March 28, 1642.
*Contents*: I. Theil. Beschreibung der fuernehmsten Geschichten | so sich jemabls von Anfang der Welt | biss auf vnsere Zeiten zugetragen, p. 1–82. II. Theil. Jnhaltend die Geschichten der Andern oder Persianischen Monarchj. Vom Jahr der Welt 3410. biss 3620, p. 83–175. III. Theil. Jnhaltend die der Dritten oder Griechischen Monarchj. Vom Jahr der Welt 3620 biss 3902, p. 176–264. IV. Theil. Jnhaltend den Anfang der Vierdten oder Roemischen Monarchj. Von Cajo Julio Caesare biss auf Constantinum Magnum. Vom Jahr der Welt 3902 biss auf das Jahr nach Christi Geburt 306, p. 265–370. v. Theil. Von Anfang der Regierung des Grossen Constantini...biss auff das 1000. Jahr nach Christi Geburt, p. 371–498. VI. Theil. Vom Jahr vnsres HERRN 1002...biss auf...das Jahr Christi 1519, p. 499–703. VII. Theil. Von...dem Jahr 1519 biss aufs Jahr Christi 1601, p. 704–1052. VIII. Theil. Vom Jahr nach Christi Geburt 1601 biss auf ...das Jahr Christi 1618, p. 1053–1185. The discovery of America is related on p. 697.

A continuation of this work by J. P. Abelin and others was published under title *Theatrum evropæum*. See no. 179. That the *Historische Chronica* was compiled by J. L. Gottfried and not by J. P. Abelin has been proved by F. Gallati, in his *Der königlich schwedische in Teutschland geführte Krieg*, Zürich, 1902, *EAG p.v.66, no.5*.

## 1660

**178.** VEER, GERRIT DE. Dritter Theil | Warhafftiger Relation | Der dreyen newen vnerhörten, seltzamen Schifffahrt, so die Holländische vnd Seeländische Schiff gegen Mitternacht, drey | Jahr nach einander, als Anno. 1594. 1595. vnd 1596. verricht... Durch | Levinvm Hvlsivm. | Quarta Editio. | ... Franckfurt am Mayn: Jn Verlegung | Christoff le Bon. | Jm Jahr 1660. 8 p.l., 96 p., 32 plates. 4°.
Reserve Hulsius
Fourth edition. See nos. 107, 118, 119, 130.

## 1662

**179.** THEATRUM | Europæum. | Oder | Aussführliche und | Warhafftige Beschrei- | bung aller...denckwürdiger Ge- | schichten... Beschrieben durch | M. Joannem Philippum Abelinum | ... Durch | Weyland Matthaei Merians seel. Erben... Franckfurt am Mayn: bey Daniel Ficvet. Jm Jahr nach Christi Geburt M DC LXII. 2 p.l., 1147 p., 8 l. maps, plates (part folding). illus. f°. † BTWA (Theatrum)
Year 1624: Es gibt in West-Jndien zwischen dem Vice Re zu Mexico, und einen Gubernatorn eine starcke differentz, p. 800-802.

## 1663

**180.** HEMMERSAM, MICHAEL. West-Jndianische | Reissbeschreibung, | de An. 1639. biss 1645. | ... Von Michael Hemmersam,...zusammen getragen | Anietzo aber mit Kupffern gezieret, samt | einer vorrede,...und nützlichen Regi- | ster vermehret, | Durch Christoff Ludwig Dietherrn,... Nürnberg: | In Verlegung P. Fürstens,... Gedruckt daselbst bey Christoff Gerhard, 1663. 16 p.l., 116 p., 13 l., 11 plates. 15½ cm. *KB 1663
Sabin 31289. JCB, 1919, III, 88.
Also published with title: *Guineische und West-Indianische Reissbeschreibung de An. 1639 biss 1645*, Nurnberg, 1663. (Not in the Library.)
Deals particularly with Guiana and Brazil.

**181.** ROGERIUS, ABRAHAM. Abraham Rogers | Offne Thür | zu dem verborgenen | Heydenthum: | Oder, | Warhaftige Vorweisung dess | Lebens und Sittens, samt der Religion | und Gottesdienst der Bramines auf der Cust | Chormandel, und denen herumligenden | Ländern: | Mit kurtzen Anmerkungen | Aus dem Niederländischen übersetzt. | Samt | Christoph Arnolds | Auserlesenen Zugaben, | Von dem Asiatischen, Africanischen, und Ame- | ricanischen Religions-Sachen, so in XL. | Capitel verfasst. | ... Nürnberg: | In Verlegung, Johann Andreas Endter, und Wolff- | gang dess Jüng. Seel. Erben. M.DC.LXIII. 8 p.l., 998 p., 20 l. plates (part folding). 16½ cm. *KB 1663
Sabin 72603. JCB, 1919, III, 92.
The Dutch original edition was published in 1651. Translated and edited by Christoph Arnold (see Vorrede).
Pages 944-998 relate to America; also ten of the plates.

## 1664

**182.** GREAT BRITAIN. — TREATIES. Accords-Puncta, | Welcher Gestalt | Den 8. Septembr. St. N. 1664. | Neu Niederland | An die | Engländer | sonder einige Gegenwehr übergangen | Wie solches Simon Gilde von Rarop, Schiffer auff | dem Schiffe Gideon, von denen Menates oder Neu-Am- | sterdam in Neu-Niederland kommend, | mitbracht | Am 27. Augusti St. N. 1664. [n. p., 1664.] 2 l. 18 x 15 cm. (4°.)
*KB 1664
See Sabin 102876. JCB, 1919, III, 115.
Probably printed in Holland. Translation of *Artykelen, van't overgaen van Nieuw-Nederlandt*. [n.p., 1664.]
Articles of capitulation signed August 27/September 6, 1664, by six deputies commissioned by Director-general Stuyvesant and his council, and seven English commissioners, including Richard Nicolls, chief commissioner. The articles were agreed to by Stuyvesant and the council August 29/September 8.

**183.** —— Accords-Puncta, | welcher gestalt | Am 8. Septembr. st. n. 1664. | Neu-Niederland | an die | Engländer | sonder einige Hegenwehr [sic!] übergangen | Wie solches Symon Gilde von Rarop, Schif- | fer auff dem Schiffe Gideon, von denen Menates oder | Neu-Amsterdam in Neu-Niederland kommend | mitbracht | Am 27. Augusti st. v. 1664. [Amsterdam, 1664. Facsimile. Boston, 1924.] 4 l. 23½ x 19 cm. (Americana series; photostat reproductions by the Massachusetts Historical Society. no. 120.)
*KB 1664
See Sabin 102876. JCB, 1919, III, 115.
Original is the John Carter Brown Library.

**184.** WINCKELMANN, JOHANN JUST. Der | Americanischen | Neuen Welt | Beschreibung | Darinnen deren Erfindung, Lager, Natur... Beneben einer wunderbaren Schiffart... Hans von Staden, | ... Mit vielen nachdenklichen Fragen | und nothwendigen Figuren ausgezieret und zusammen getragen | durch Hans Just Wynkelmann. | ... Oldenburg: Bey Heinrich-Conrad Zimmern| im Jahr Christi 1664. 8 p.l., 228 p., 6 l., 2 ports. (1 folding). illus. 16½ x 21 cm. *KB 1664
Sabin 105680. JCB, 1919, III, 122.
Dedication: "Dem Hochwürdigen, Durchleuchtigen, Hochgebornen Fürsten und Herrn, Herrn Johann Moritzen ausgenant dem Americanern, Fürsten zu Nassau... " Signed: Hans Just Wynkelmann von Giessen aus Hessen, Oldenburg, den 14. Januar 1664.
Winckelmann's paraphrase of Staden's account of his voyage and captivity in Brazil, p. 137-223. Thirtytwo woodcuts are the same as those in the original edition of Staden, Marburg, 1557.
See nos. 69, 70, 71.

## 1665

**185.** CASAS, BARTOLOMÉ DE LAS, BISHOP OF CHIAPA. Umbständige warhafftige | Beschreibung | Der | Jndianischen Ländern, | so vor diesem von den Spa- | niern eingenommeu [sic!] und | verwüst worden, | ...Erst in Lateinischer Sprach aussgeben | Durch | Bartholomæum de las Casas, | ... Jetzt aber in das Teutsche übersetzt, und an | vielen Orten verbessert, in dieser neu- | und letztern Edition. [n. p.,] Anno M.DC.LXV. 2 p.l., 119 p., 17 illus. 20½ x 16½ cm. (4°.) *KB 1665
Sabin 11281. JCB, 1919, III, 124.
Border and engraved illustrations (several signed by Jodocus à Winghe) are printed from the copper plates first used in the de Bry edition, Frankfort, 1598. See nos. 99, 109, 131.
The Library has other copies which vary in size. For literature on this author, see note on no. 99.

## 1667

186. IRENICO-POLEMOGRAPHIÆ | Continuatio I. | Das ist, | ...dess | Theatri Europæi | Achter Theil, | ... So aussvielen...Schrifften,... zusammen getragen und beschrieben | Martin Meyer,...und verlegt | Durch | Weyl. Matthäi Merians seel. Erben | in Franckfurt am Mäyn. | Anno Christi M.DC.LXVII. 4 p.l., 1388 p., 12 l. plates (part folding), maps. f°.
 † BTWA (Theatrum)
 Year 1657: Engelländische Flott hat einen Anschlag auf die Span.-West Jndische Schiffe, p. 341.

## 1668

187. FRANCISCI, ERASMUS. Erasmi Francisci | Ost- und West-Jndischer wie auch | Sinesischer | Lust- und Stats-Garten, | Mit einem | Vorgespräch | Von mancherley lustigen Discursen; | Jn Drey Haupt-Theile unterschieden. | Der Erste Theil | Begreifft in sich die edelsten Blumen, Kräuter | Bäume, Meel- Wasser- Wein- Artzney- und Gifft-gebende | Wurtzeln, Früchte, Gewürtze, und Specereyen, in Ost Jndien | Sina und America: | Der Ander Theil | Das Temperament der Lufft und Landschafften daselbst; ... Der Dritte Theil | Das Stats-Wesen, Policey-Ordnungen ... Aus den fürnemsten, alten und neuen, Jndianischen Geschicht-Land- und Reisbeschrei- | bungen, mit Fleiss zusammengezogen... Nürnberg: | Jn Verlegung Johann Andreæ Endters, und Wolfgang | dess Jüngern Sel. Erben. | Anno M DC LXVIII. 19 p.l., 1762 p., 19 l. lxiii [i.e. lxvi] plates (incl. coat of arms). illus. 32 cm. (f°.) *KB 1668
 Sabin 25463. JCB, 1919, III, 168.
 Illustrated half-title and coat of arms signed: C. N. Schurtz, sc.
 Divided into three parts. The first and second contain the natural history of the West and East Indies, with an account of all the fabulous creatures, monstrosities, etc., which were said to live there. The third part treats at large of the various aboriginal people of America and the East Indies, their government, manners, and institutions, with many curious details.

188. ROCHEFORT, CHARLES DE. Historische | Beschreibung | Der | Antillen Inseln in | America gelegen | In sich begreiffend deroselben | Gelegenheit, darinnen befindli- | chen natürlichen Sachen, sampt deren | Einwohner Sitten und Gebräuchen mit | 45. Kupffstücken gezieret. | von | dem Herrn de Rochefort, | zum zweyten mahl in Französi- | scher Sprach an den Tag ge- | geben, nunmehr aber | in die Teutsche übersetzet. Franckfurt: | In Verlegung Wilhelm Serlins,... 1668. 10 p.l., 430 p., 6 l., 45 plates. 12°. *KB 1668
 Sabin 72321. JCB, 1919, III, 175. Pilling, Languages of the North American Indians, no. 3348 (p. 658).
 A translation of his Histoire naturelle et morale des Iles Antilles de l'Amerique, Rotterdam, 1658.
 The first volume deals with the natural history of the Antilles: Abschrifft | Etlicher Briefe die auss Ame- | rica... abgangen..., p. 409–430. The second volume, dealing with the moral history, is lacking.

## 1669

189. FRANCISCI, ERASMUS. Erasmi Francisci | Guineischer und Americanischer | Blumen-Pusch: | Welcher | Einen ergetzlichen Geruch man- | cherley merklicher Eigenschafften, wun- | derlicher Thiere, Vögel, Fische, fremder Wei- | sen, Sitten, Gebräuche selbiger Länder; u.a.m. | imgleichen aller Könige in Peru und Mexico Ge- | schichten und denckwürdigen Verrichtungen | von sich streuet. | Nebenst beygedrucktem Anhang | der, hiebey zugleich neu- auffgelegten, | Michael Hemmersams seel. Guineisch- und | West-Indianischen Reisebe- | schreibung. Nürnberg: In Verlegung Paul Fürstens, | ... Wittib und Erben... | Anno M.DC.LXIX. 4 p.l., 399(1) p., 20 l., 109 p., 13 l., 23 plates (part folding). 17 cm. *KB 1669
 Sabin 25461.
 The author describes the work as follows: "Es ist aber dieser Blumen-Pusch | in zwey Theile | unterschieden. Der erste handelt anfangs überhaupt | von der Landes-Gelegenheit | in Guinea | und America; beschreibt folgends unterschiedliche Thiere | Voegel | Fische | und dergleichen: der Zweyte von den Städten und Einwohnern. Wobey zuletzt eine grundrichtige Erzehlung der Mexicanischen und Peruanischen Könige von Anfang biss zu Ende solcher beyder Monarchien auss dem Josepho à Costa [i.e., José de Acosta, see no. 102], Petro de Cieza [i.e., Pedro de Cieza de León], Lopez de Gomara [i.e., Francisco López de Gómara], Ferdinando Cortesio [i.e., Hernando Cortés], Antonio de la Calancha, und andren beygefueget wird.
 "Diesen Blumen-Strauss aber zu binden | hat die neue Wiederaufflegung der Guineischen und West-Jndischen Reise Michael Hemmersams sel: Gelegenheit gegeben. (See no. 180.) Jn welchen Blumen-Strauss eines und andres so gemeldter Hemmersam vorbey gangen...weiter ausgeführt ist." — Vorbericht.
 "This work is divided into two parts. The first is the 'Bouquet of Flowers,' by Erasmus Franciscus. The second [the Anbang] is the voyage by Michael Hemmersam to Brazil, by Christoph Ludwig Dietherr." — Sabin.
 Imperfect: Hemmersam "Anhang" and 20 plates wanting.

## 1670

190. FRANCISCI, ERASMUS. Neu-polirter | Geschicht- Kunst- | und | Sitten-Spiegel ausländischer Völcker, | ... Dem Schau-begierigem Leser dargestellt | von | Erasmo Francisci. Nürnberg: | Jn Verlegung Johann Andreæ Endters, und Wolfgang dess Jüngern Seel. Erben. | Anno M.DC.LXX. 15 p.l., 1550 p., 15 l., xlix [i.e. li] pl. (incl. coat of arms, in port.) 33 cm. (f°.) †*KB 1670
 Sabin 25462. JCB, 1919, III, 196. Engraved half-title: Aus Ländischer Kunst- und Sitten-Spiegel, signed: Corneli Nicola Schurtz sc. Several plates signed: C. N. Schurtz, sc. Plates XVIII, XXXI, XXXIII show American aborigines or subjects relating to America. Franciscí deals with the Indians on p. 594, 632, 847, 986, 989, 1000, 1005, 1073, 1227, 1409.

## 1672

191. IRENICO-POLEMOGRAPHIÆ | Continuatio II. | Das ist: | ...dess | Theatri Europæi | Neundter Theil, | ...auss vielen... Schrifften, ...zusammengetragen | und beschrieben | Martin Meyer,... | ...verlegt durch | Weyl. Matthäi Merians seel. Erben, | ... Franckfurt am Mäyn. | Anno Christi M DC LXXII. 4 p.l., 1576 p., 32 l., plates (part folding), maps (part folding). f°. † BTWA (Theatrum)
 Year 1660: Die Flotte [Spaniens] nach America wird durch Sturm sehr ruiniret, p. 273. Year 1662: Dänemarck klaget beym Stat [i.e., Netherlands] über die West-Jndische Compagnie, p. 744–776. Year 1664: Dänemarck fordert bey dem Staat [i.e., Netherlands] von der West-Jndischen Compag. Vergügung, p. 1424.

*1672, continued*

192. KEYE, OTTO. Otto Keyens | kurtzer Entwurff | von | Neu-Niederland | Und | Guajana | Einander entgegen gesetzt, | Vmb den Vnterscheid zwischen warmen und | kalten Landen herauss zu bringen, | Und zu weisen | Welche von beyden am fûglichsten zu bewohnen, | am behendesten an zu bauen und den besten Nutzen | geben mögen. | Denen Patronen, so da Colonien an zu legen |˙gesonnen, als auch denen Personen und Familien, die | ihr Vaterland zu vergessen sich bey dergleichen Bevôlckerung | nach fremden Küsten und Reichen gebrauchen | lassen wollen. | Auss dem Hollåndischen ins Hochteutsche | versetzt | durch | T. R. C. S. C. S. Leipzig: | Jm Ritzschischen Buchlanden, | M.DC.LXXII. 10 p.l., 144 p., 4 l. 21 x 16½ cm.
\* KB 1672
Sabin 37675. JCB, 1919, III, 242. Asher 12.
Translation of his *Het waere onderschayt*... Gravenhage, 1659.
A comparison of the relative advantages for colonization offered by Surinam and New Netherlands.

193. LEDERER, JOHN. The | Discoveries | of John Lederer, | in three several Marches from | Virginia, | To the West of | Carolina, | And other parts of the Continent: | Begun in March 1669, and ended in September 1670. | Together with | A General Map of the whole Territory | which he traversed. | Collected and Translated out of Latine from his Discourse | and Writings, | By Sir William Talbot Baronet... London: Printed by J. C. for Samuel Heyrick..., 1672. 4 p.l., 27 p., folding map. 18½ x 14½ cm.
\* KC 1672
Sabin 39676. JCB, 1919, III, 242-243. Church 619. Meynen. No. 627-630 c.
Translated from the Latin. No German edition known. Lederer, a German, is characterized by Sir William Talbot as follows: "That a stranger should presume (though with Sir William Berkly's Commission) to go into these parts of the American continent where English men never had been, and whither some refused to accompany him, was, in Virginia look'd on as so great an insolence, that our traveller at his return, instead of welcom and applause met nothing but affronts and reproaches; for indeed, it was their part, that forsook him in the expedition, to procure him discredit that was a witness to theirs: therefore no industry was wanting to prepare men with a prejudice against him, and this their malice improved to such a general animosity, that he was not safe in Virginia from the outrage of the people, drawn into a perswasion that the publick levy of that year, went all to the expence of his vagaries. Forced by this storm into Maryland, he became known to me, though then ill-affected to the man by the stories that went about of him: Nevertheless finding him, contrary to my expectation, a modest ingenious person, and a pretty scholar, I thought it common justice to give him an occasion of vindicating himself from what I had heard of him..."

1673

194. MONTANUS, ARNOLDUS. Die unbekante | Neue Welt, | oder | Beschreibung | des Weltteils | Amerika, | und des | Sud-Landes: | Darinnen vom Vhrsprunge der Ameriker und Sudlån- | der, und von den gedenckwûrdigen Reysen der Europer darnach zu. | Wie auch | von derselben Festen Låndern, Jnseln, Städten, Festungen, Dôrfern | vornåhmsten Gebeuen, Bergen, Brunnen, Flûssen, und Ahrten der Tiere, | Beume, Stauden, und anderer fremden Gewåchse; Als auch von den | Gottes- und Gôtzendiensten, Sitten, Sprachen, Kleidertrachten, | wunderlichen Begåbnissen und so wohl alten als neuen | Kriegen, ausfûhrlich gehandelt wird; | Durch und durch mit vielen nach dem Leben in Ameriken selbst | entworfenen Abbildungen gezieret. | Durch D$^r$. O. D. Zu Amsterdam: | Bey J. von Meurs | ... 1673. 4 p.l., 658 p., 11 l., maps, plans, plates, ports. illus. 31½ cm. (f°.) †\* KB 1673
Sabin 50087.
"The engraved title, maps and plates are those of Meurs's *Montanus* of 1671...but the portrait of Joan Maurits, Prince of Nassau, and dedication to him found in that Dutch original are omitted from this German version." — *JCB*, *1919*, III, 260. For discussion of the view of New Amsterdam, p. 143, perhaps drawn by Augustine Herrman, see Stokes, I, 142. The map of America is signed: Per Gerardum A. Schagen. In this copy the map of America by Jacob Meurs (see Stokes, VI, 262) is tipped in. For identity of Arnoldus Montanus and Olfert Dapper, see R. R. Schuller's *Novus orbis. De A. Montanus o de O. Dapper?* [Santiago de Chile, 1907?], *H*. The translator is most probably Joh. Christoph Beer. See Joecher, pt. 2, p. 33 (Dapper).
Contents: Die Beschreibung des Weltteils Ameriken Erstes Buch. 1. Ameriken war den Alten unbekannt, p. 1-10. 2. Abkunft der Amerikaner..., p. 10-44. 3. Die ersten Entdecker der Neuen Welt..., p. 44-132. Zweites Buch von desselben Mitternaechtischer Gegend. 1. Neu Frankreich, p. 133-139. Neu-Engelland, p. 139-141. 3. Neu Niederland, p. 142-153. 4. Virginien, p. 153-163. 5. Florida, p. 164-173. 6. Die Jnsel Kuba, p. 173-178. 7. Die Jnsel Hispaniola, p. 178-186. 8. Jamaika, p. 186-188. 9. Porto Riko, p. 188-192. 10. Die Jnseln Bermudes, p. 192-194. 11. Die Jnseln der Kanibalen, p. 195-230. 12. Kalifornia und das fernere nordlichste Teil des Amerikschen Bodems, p. 231-242. 13. Neu-Mexico, p. 242-250. 14. Neu-Gallizien, p. 250-259. 15. Neu Spanien, p. 259-302. 16. Guatemala, p. 302-315. Das Dritte Buch. Die Beschreibung des Sudlichen Amerikens. 1. Terra Firma, p. 316-326. 2. Neu Granada und Popajan, p. 326-332. 3. Peru, p. 352-403. 4. Brasil, p. 403-602. 5. Guajana, p. 602-616. 6. Neu Andalusien, p. 616-620. 7. Venezuela, p. 628-644. 10. Magellanika, p. 644-649. 11. Das unbekante Sudland, p. 649-658.

1675

195. CAPELL [RUDOLF]. Vorstellungen des Norden, oder Bericht von einigen nordländern und absonderlich von dem so genandten Grünlande, aus schreibern, welche zu unterschiedenen zeiten gelebet... zusammen gezogen und... endlich umb ferner zu mehren aus D. Capel P. P. bibliothec aussgefertiget. Hamburg: Joh. Naumann und Georg. Wolff, 1675. 2 l., 236 p., frontis., map. 20 x 15½ cm. \* KB 1675
Sabin 10735.

1677

196. RICHSHOFFER, AMBROSIUS. Ambrosij Richshoffers, | Brassilianisch-und West Indianische | Reisse Beschreibung. Strassburg: | Bey Jossias Städeln, A°. 1677. 182 p., 3 l. front. (port.), 2 plates (folding), 2 maps (folding). 16½ cm. \* KB 1677
Sabin 71219. JCB, II, 454.
"The author was a native of Strassburg, who in 1629, when seventeen years of age, joined the naval expedition sent against Brazil by the Dutch West India Company under the command of Lonck and Diederik van Waerdenburch. In 1632 he returned to Holland, after a service of more than three years in Brazil and the West Indies. Many years afterwards

*1677, continued*

he wrote and published this narrative of his adventures." — *Sabin*.

There are two poems, praising the author, by Johann Joachim Bockenhoffer and Johann Heinrich Rapp respectively, added to Richshoffer's text. The following lines are quoted from Rapp:

Was die ferne Welt hoch ehret;
Wodurch wird der Ruhm vermehret
Derer in West-Jndien;
Dieses hat in jungen Jahren
Herr Richshoffer wohl erfahren
Wie auch in Brasilien.

\* \* \*

Wie die Bienen in den Feldern
Vnd in weit-entlegnen Wäldern
Suchen ihren süssen Safft;
So auch Herr Richshoffer thate;
Fleissig er wohl hielt zu rathe
Was da sey dess Reysens Krafft.

197. SPÖRRI, FELIX CHRISTIAN. Americanische | Reiss-beschreibung | Nach den Caribes Insslen, | Und, | Neu-Engelland. | Verrichtet und aufgesezt | durch | Felix-Christian Spöri, | Schnitt- und Wund-Artzet | von Zürich. | In Verlegung | Johann Wilhelm Simlers, | Und | Johann Rudolff Rhanen. | ...Zürich | Bey Michael Schauffelbergers sel. Erbin, | Durch Johannes Bachmann, 1677. 90 p. 16 cm. (In: J. W. Simler and J. R. Rahn, *compilers*, Vier Loblicher Statt Zürich Verbürgerter Reissbeschreibungen... [Zürich, 1677–78.].) \* KB 1677 Simler

Description of three voyages to the West Indies. The first (p. 3–52) starts in Amsterdam, Holland, December 28, 1660. On January 11, 1661, the ship on which Spörri is surgeon, arrives at the island of Barbados. He visits other islands in the West Indies and later New England and the Bermudas. He returns to Amsterdam on February 24, 1661. The second voyage (p. 53–61) lasts from June 10, 1661, to April 2, 1662. On the last voyage (p. 62–90), he sails on August 20, 1662, and returns to Amsterdam on February 20, 1665. He takes an examination as an Ober-Wund-Artzet [*sic!*] in Amsterdam and serves in the war between the Dutch and English on the side of the Dutch. Afterwards, he goes back to his home town, Zürich, Switzerland, as do his countrymen, Hans Georg Hegners von Winterthur and Junker Caspar Peyers von Schaffhausen. See also A. B. Faust, *Guide to the materials for American history in Swiss and Austrian archives*, Washington, D. C., 1916, 1, especially p. 4.

198. THEATRI | Europæi | Zehender Theil, | ... auss vielen...Schrifften...zusammen getragen und beschrieben | von | Wolffgang Jacob Geiger, ...aussgezieret. | Durch | Matthäi Merians Seel. Erben. | ...Franckfurt am Mäyn: bey Johann Görlin, und Joh. Bauer | [1677?]. 1 p.l., 982, 620 p. plates (part folding), maps. illus. f°. BTWA (Theatrum)

Year 1670: "West-Jndischer Commercien Tractat mit Spanien wird zu Londen ratificirt," p. 317.

199. ZELLER, HANS JACOB, AND HEINRICH HUSER. Jamaica. Neue Beschreibung | Der Insul Jamaica, in America gelegen, | samt etlichen angränzenden Orthen: | Darinnen zu gleich vermeldet wird bey | was Anlase Herr Hans Jacob Zeller, | Und | Herr Heinrich Huser, | Beyde Dienere des Göttlichen | Worts, und verburgerte zu Zürich, ihre | Reise dahin genommen, und wie diser Zeit alles daselbst beschaffen. (In: J. W. Simler and J. R. Rahn, *compilers*, Vier Loblicher Statt Zürich Verbürgerter Reissbeschreibungen... [Zürich, 1677–78.] p. 171–192.) \* KB 1677 Simler

*1678*

200. DUVAL, PIERRE. Geographiæ | universalis | pars prior. | Das ist: | Der allgemeinen | Erd-Beschreibung | Erster Theil, | Darinnen die Drey Theil der Welt, | Nemlich | America, Africa und Asia, | Samt ihren vornemsten Königreichen, | Ländern, Inseln, Städten und Schlössern, wie auch | Land Charten und Wappen, nebenst denen sich da- | selbst so wol vor langer als kurtzer Zeit zugetrage- | nen denckund noch heutiges Tages sehens- | würdigen Sachen auf das deutlichste | enthalten. | Anfangs in Französischer Sprach be- | schrieben durch P. du Val, ...Anjetzo aber ins Teutsche übersetzet, und an | unterschiedlichen Orten, wo es die Noht erfordert, | vermehret. | Nürnberg: | In Verleg. Johann Hoffmanns Kunst- | und Buchhändlers, | Gedruckt daselbst bey Christoff Gerhard. M.DC.LXXVIII. 6 p.l., 464 p., 2 l. maps, plates (coats of arms). 13½ cm. (12°.)
\* KB 1678

A translation of his: *Le Monde, ou La géographie universelle*... Paris: l'auteur, 1670. Johann Christoph Beer is the supposed translator.

*Contents:* General description of America, p. 18–36. Die Landschafft Canada, p. 37–45. Neu Holland, p. 45–49. Neu Engelland, p. 49–53. Neu Franckreich, p. 53–61. Die Landschafft Virginia, p. 61–66. Die Landschafft Florida, p. 66–73. Die Landschafft Neu Mexico, p. 73–75. Neu Hispanien, p. 75–87. Von den Antillischen Jnsulen, p. 87–103. The rest of Erster Theil (p. 103–150) covers South America.

*1679*

201. EXQUEMELIN, ALEXANDER OLIVIER. Die | Americanische | See-Räuber, | Entdeckt, | In gegenwärtiger Beschreibung | der grössesten, durch die Französisch- und | Englische Meer-Beuter, wider die Spanier | in America, verübten Rauberey und | Grausamkeit: | ... Nebst einem kurzen Bericht, | von der Cron Spanien Macht und | Reichthum in America, wie auch von allen | vornehmsten Christlichen Plätzen daselbst: | Aufgesetzt, | durch A. O. | Aller hierinn begriffenen Raubereyen Gefährten | und Genossen: | Mit schönen Figuren, Charten, und wahren | Conterfeyten, ausgeziert. | Nürnberg: | In Verlegung Christoph Riegels, | 1679. 12 p.l., 612 p., 6 plates (2 folding), 4 ports. (2 folding), maps. illus. 13½ cm.

Sabin 23470. \* KB 1679

A translation of his *De Americaensche zee-roovers*, Amsterdam, 1678, \* KB 1678.

"Perhaps no book in any language was ever the parent of so many imitations, and the source of so many fictions as this, the original of the buccaneers of America." — *Sabin*.

The "Vorbericht," signed Johann Claesz zum Horn, and dated Amsterdam | von Haus aus | den 1. Septembris | 1678, states: "Es hat aber besagtem Autori gut gedünket | sein Werk in drey unterschiedlichen Theilen zu verfassen ... Der erste Theil | verfasset den Anfang seiner Reise aus Franckreich | nach dem Westlichen Theil von America | weil er damaliger Zeit in der Franzoesisch-West Jndianischen Compagnie Dienste gewesen... Jn eben diesem Theile ist auch befindlich eine ausfuehrliche Beschreibung der Jnsulen Espagniola, Tortuga und Jamaica... [p. 1–158.] Der andere Theil | haelt in sich | den Ursprung und Aufkunft der Franzoesisch und Englischen See-Raeuber [p. 159–356]. Der dritte Theil begreiffet...in sich die Eroberung und Einaescherung der maechtigen Stadt Panama...durch die

*1679, continued*

201. EXQUEMELIN, ALEXANDRE OLIVIER, *cont'd*
Englisch und Franzoesische Räuber von Jamaica und Tortuga...[p. 357–527.]"
Kurzer Anhang und Erzehlung | von der gewaltigen Macht | Reichthum | Regierung und Einkunfften | welche die Cron Spanien gegenwärtig in America hat. Zusamt einem kurzen Begriff | der vornehmsten Plätze in America | die verschiedenen Christlichen Potentaten zugehören..., p. 528–612.

202. LA PEYRÈRE, ISAAC DE. Ausführliche | Beschreibung | des | theils bewohnt- theils unbewohnt- so genannten | Grönlands, | in zwey Theile abgetheilt: | Deren erster handelt | von des | Alt- (nunmehro verlohrnen) Grönlands Gelegenheit, Er- | findung, Inwohnern, Fruchtbarkeit, Gewächsen, | Thieren und Meerwundern. | Der andere: | von dem | Neuen (durch Suchung des alten, gefundenen) Grönland, | Eigenschafft der Wilden, und viel andern merck- | würdigen Dingen mehr. | Nebenst Einem kurtzem Begriff der seltsamen Reisen, so M. Forbeisser, Gotzke | Lindenau, Christian Richard, und die Koppenhagen-Grönländische Gesell- | schafft, alt Grönland wieder zu finden, in unterschiedlichen Jahren gethan. | Mit | Anfügung des Tagbuchs eines die Durchfahrt zwischen Grönland und | America suchenden Dänischen Schiffes... Beschrieben, und mit verschiedenen Historischen Anhängen | durchgehends erklärt und erweitert | durch | S von V. [Simon de Vries.] | Nürnberg: in Verlegung Christof Riegels, 1679. 4 p.l., 131 p. folding maps. 20½ x 16½ cm.  *KB 1679
Sabin 25997, 38972, 38974. JCB, II, 460.
Listed here because of its mention of efforts to find the Northwest Passage. The earlier work, *Bericht von Gröhnland,* Hamburg, 1674 (*KB 1674*), is omitted because it describes only Greenland.

203. LATOMUS, SIGISMUND, FIRM, PUBLISHERS, FRANKFURT AM MAIN. Relationis Historicæ | Semestralis Autumnalis Continuatio. | Jacobi Franci | Historische Beschrei | bung der denckwürdigsten Geschichten, so sich in Hoch- | und Nieder-Teutschland, ...Wie nicht weniger in Ost- und West-Indien, &c. Vor- und zwischen jüngst verflossener Frankfurter | Oster- biss an- und in die Herbst-Mess dieses lauffenden 1679. Jahrs, hin und wider in der | Welt, zu Land und Wasser, glaubhafftig zugetragen. | Alles auss überschickten Lateinischen, Italiänischen, Spanischen, Frantzösischen, | Hoch- und Nider-Teutschen Documentis, brieflichen Urkunden und Geschichtreichen Schriff- | ten ...Durch Sigismundi Latomi, sonsten Mäurers genannt | Seel. Erben, fortgeführt, und verlegt ...Franckfurt am Mayn...bey den Latom. Erben zu finden, 1679. 96 p. plates. 20 x 16 cm. (4°.)  *KB 1679
Of special interest: Zehender Haupt-Titul. Von Englaendischen | Schott- und Irrlaendischen Geschichten, p. 54–59, an account of the quarrel between the king of England and his brother, the Duke of York. Eilffter Haupt-Titul. Von Niederlaendischen Geschichten. See nos. 208, 215.

**1681**

204. BOS, LAMBERT VAN DEN. Leben | und | Tapffere Thaten | der aller-berühmtesten| See-Helden, | Admiralen und Land-Erfinder | un-serer Zeiten, | angefangen mit | Cristoforo Colombo | Entdeckern der Neuen Welt, | und geendigt mit dem | Welt-berühmten Admiral | M. A. de Ruyter, Rittern | &c. | Worinnen | Viel seltsame Geschichten, Ritterliche Verrichtungen, klüglich-tapffere | Anschläge, und blutige See-Treffen, aus beglaubten Schrifften und Originalien | beurkundet, und mit schönen Kupffer-Figuren beleuchtet, zur finden sind: | Unlängst in Nider-Teutscher Sprache aufgesetzt, | durch V. D. B. | Anjetzo aber in unsere Hoch-Teutsche reinlich überbracht, | Von | Matthia Krämern, ...Samt einem Anhange, | Vieler Denckwürdigkeiten, welche der Niderländische Author den | Helden-Thaten Almeyda, Albuquerque, und Acuniæ, entweder ausge- | lassen, oder nur kürtzlich gerühret, beygetragen und erstattet, | Durch | Erasmum Francisci. | Nürnberg: | In Verlegung Christoph Endters Seel. Handlungs-Erben. | Anno M DC LXXXI. 6 p.l., 1090 p., 9 l. plates (part folding), ports., folding map. 19 x 16 cm. *KB 1681
Sabin 6441, 7407. JCB, II, 472–473.
A translation of his *Leeven en daden der doorluchtighste see-helden,* Amsterdam, 1676, *KB, 1676.
The work is divided into two parts. Of special interest are biographies of Columbus, Amerigo Vespucci, Francis Drake, Thomas Cavendish (as Candish), Oliver van Noort, Sebastian Cabot, Martin Frobisher, John Davis, Jacob van Wassenaer, and Michiel Adriaensz de Ruyter.
In Part II, is an account of the cession of New Netherland to the English and the treaty then made, p. 826–830 (see nos. 181, 183). On p. 983 is an account by de Ruyter of the recapture of New Amsterdam by the Dutch.

205. —— Leben und Thaten | Der | Durchläuchtigsten | See-Helden | Und | Erfinder der Länder dieser Zeiten, | Anfahend | Mit | Christoph Columbus | Dem | Erfinder der neuen Welt, | Und sich endend mit dem höchstberühmten | Admiral | M. A. de Ruyter, | Rittern u.s.f. | Worinnen viel seltzame Fälle, tapffere Verrich- | tungen, Grossmüthige Verwaltungen, und harte | See-Treffen u.s.w. vorgestellet wer- | den. | Mit grossem Fleiss, aus vielen glaubwürdigen Schrifften, | und gewissen bewährten Urkünden, in Holländischer Sprache, | zusammen gebracht, und beschrieben, | Durch | V. D. B. | Nunmehr aber | In die hochteutsche Sprache übersetzt und heraus | gegeben. | ...Sulzbach: | In Verlegung Johann Hofmanns, Kunst- und Buch-Händlers | in Nürnberg. [1681.] 2 v. in 1. map, plates, ports. 20½ x 17 cm. (4°.)  *KB 1681
JCB, II, 473.
The portraits have legends in Dutch; one plate is signed: C. Karsch fe. *See* no. 204.

**1682**

206. THEATRI | Europæi | Eilffter Theil, | ... verlegt | Durch | Matthäi Merians sel. Erben. | Franckfurt am Mäyn, | Gedruckt bey Johann Philipp Andreä. | Jm Jahr Christi M DC LXXXII. 3 p.l., 1300 p., 16 l. plates, maps (part folding.) illus. f°. † BTWA (Theatrum)
Year 1674: "Was ausserhalb Europa, insonderheit aber in Ost- und West-Jndien...vorgegangen," p. 650–652. Year 1675: "Indianer in Neu-Engeland empören sich wider die Englische," p. 774.

## 1683

**207.** PENN, WILLIAM. Eine | Nachricht | Wegen der Landschafft | Pennsilvania | in | America. | Welche | Jüngstens unter dem grossen Siegel | in | Engelland | an | William Penn, &c. | Samt den Freiheiten und der Macht, so zu behöriger | guten Regierung derselben nöthig, | übergeben worden, | und | Zum Unterricht derer, so etwan bereits bewogen, oder noch bewogen | werden möchten, um sich selbsten darhin zu begeben, oder einige Bediente und Gesinde an diesen Ort zu senden, hiemit | kund gethan wird, | Aus dem in London gedrucktem, und aldar bey Benjamin | Clark, Buchhåndlern in George-Yard Lombardstreet befindlichem Englischen übersetzet. | Nebenst beygefügtem ehemaligen im 1675. Jahr gedrucktem | Schreiben des oberwehnten Will. Penns. | Franckfurth, | Im Jahr, Christi 1683. 1 p.l., p. [275]–304, 1 l. 4°.     *KB 1683
Sabin 59719.
p. 278–289 wrongly numbered 178–188, 186.
Running title: Appendix. The Library has a second copy in the set of the publication from which this title is extracted: *Diarii Europæi*, continuatio XLIV, Franckfurt am Mayn, 1683, *BTW*. The appendices are continuously paged. The added leaf of the independent copy listed here, the "Verzeichnüss der jinigen Acten, denckwürdigen Handelungen und anderer Schrifften, welche in dem Appendice...zu finden sind," is not present in the set.
This is a German translation of Penn's *Some account of the provinces of Pennsylvania*, London, 1681, * KC 1681.
Included is an abstract of the patent granted by the king to William Penn, &c: VI. und letzliche, ein Ausszug auss dem offenen, Brief vom König, in Erwegung vergnüglich geschehener Ursachen (upon valuable considerationes) an William Penn, &c. übergeben den 4. Martii, 1681, *p. 188–192 [i.e., 288–292]*.
See also "A German translation of William Penn's letter to the Free Society of Merchants in London, 1683," in *German American annals*, Philadelphia, 1910, new series, v. 8, p. 51–75, *NFCA*, and Emil Heuser, *Pennsylvanien im 17. Jahrhundert und die ausgewanderten Pfälzer in England*, Neustadt a. d. Hardt, 1910.

## 1684

**208.** LATOMUS, SIGISMUND, FIRM, PUBLISHERS, FRANKFURT AM MAIN. Relationis Historicæ | Semestralis Vernalis Continuatio. | Jacobi Franci | Historischen Beschrei | bung der denckwürdigsten Geschichten, so sich in Hoch- | und Nieder-Teutschland, ...Wie nicht weniger in Ost- und West-Indien, &c. Vor- und zwischen jüngst verflossener Franckfurter | Herbst-Mess 1683. biss an- und in die Oster-Mess dieses lauffenden 1684. Jahrs, hin und wieder | in der Welt, zu Land und Wasser, glaubhafftig zugetragen. | Alles auss überschickten Lateinischen, Italiånischen, Spanischen, Frantzösischen, | Hoch- und Nider-Teutschen Documentis, brieflichen Urkunden und Geschichtreichen Schriff- | ten...Durch Sigismundo Latomi, ... | sel. Erben, fortgeführt, und verlegt. | ...Franckfurt am Mayn: ...bey den Latom. Erben zu finden, 1684. 96 p. plates. 20 x 16 cm. (4°.)     *KB 1684
*See* nos. 203, 215.

**209.** PASTORIUS, FRANCIS DANIEL. Copia, eines von einem Sohn an seine Eltern auss America abgelassenen Brieffes, | sub dato Philadelphia, den 7. Martii, 1684. 1 p. 12°. (In: M. D. Learned, The Life of Francis Daniel Pastorius, Philadelphia, 1908. Plate between p. 124 and 125.)     AN (Pastorius)
A photographic reproduction of a printed document in the Zentralbibliothek zu Zürich.

**210.** —— Sichere Nachricht auss America, wegen der Landschafft | Pennsylvania, | von einem dorthin gereissten Teutschen, | de dato Philadelphia, den 7. Martii 1684. 8 p. 12°. (In: M. D. Learned, The Life of Francis Daniel Pastorius, Philadelphia, 1908. Plates between p. 128 and 129.)     AN (Pastorius)
A photographic reproduction; the original is in the Zentralbibliothek zu Zürich.

**211.** PENN, WILLIAM. Beschreibung | Der in America neu-erfundenen | Provinz | Pensylvanien. | Derer Jnwohner, Gesetz, Arth, Sitten und Gebrauch: | Auch såmtlicher Reviren des Landes, | Sonderlich der Haupt-Stadt Philadelphia | Alles glaubwurdigst | Auss des Gouverneurs darinnen erstatteten | Nachricht. [Hamburg:] Jn Verlegung bey Henrich Heuss an der Banco, Im Jahr 1684. 1 p.l., 47 p. 20 x 16 cm. (4°.)     * KB 1684
JCB, II, 493.
Caption-title on page 1: Schreiben vom William Penn ...geschrieben an die Commissarien der freyen Societåt der Kauffleute auf selbiger Provintz, welche sich in London auffhalten. Dated: Philadelphia 18 des 8ten Monats Augustus genand, 1683.
As to the difference between the English and Dutch editions: Preface is signed, "Benjamin Furlij;" "Auss der Holländischen in der Hochdeutschen Sprache übergesetzt. durch J. W. Hamburg. Bey Heinrich Heusch im Jahr 1684."—p. 1. "Eine kurtze Erzehlung der Situation und grösse der Stadt Philadelphia," by Thomas Holme, p. 28–29; "Extract eines Brieffes auss Pensylvania, geschrieben von Thomas Paskell, an J. J. von Chippenham, in Engelland de dato den 15. February 1683. Hollåndischen Styli," p. 29–32.

## 1685

**212.** IRENICO-POLEMOGRAPHIA, | Sive | Theatri Europæi | Continuati | Septennium: | ...So | Auss vielen glaubhafften Scripturen, ...zusammen getragen, und...beschrieben | Johannes Georgius Schlederus, | ...Und verlegt | Durch | Weyl. Matthåi Merians seel. Erben, in Franckfurt am Mayn: | Getruckt bey Johann Görlin. | M DC LXXXV. 2 p.l., 1100 p. 18 l. plates, maps. illus. f°.     †BTWA (Theatrum)
Year 1655: "Hülffe nach America zu schicken im Werck," p. 818. Year 1656: "Beschaffenheit der Americanischen Jnsul Neu-Schwedē genannt," p. 904. Year 1656: "Englische zwacken um Cadix der Spanischen-West Jndianischen Silber Flotta 2. köstliche Schiff ab," p. 1001.

## 1687

**213.** HAPPEL, EBERHARD WERNER. Everhardi Gverneri Happelii | Mundus Mirabilis | Tripartitus, | Oder | Wünderbare Welt, | in einer kurtzen | Cosmographia | fürgestellet...Ulm druckts und verlegts Matthaeus Wagner: druckts und verlegts Matthæus Wagner, 1687 [-1689]. 3 v. diagrs., fronts. (incl. port.). maps, plates. illus. 4°.     KAY
Sabin 30278; *see also* Sabin 30277.
Contains a description of America, an account of the manners, customs, etc., of the inhabitants of

*1687, continued*

213. HAPPEL, EBERHARD WERNER, *continued*
Canada, Virginia, Florida, and elsewhere, and treats of American languages.
See nos. 210, 225, 226; also Maynen, nos. 223-226.
Note also his *Der insularische Mandorell*, Frankfurt, 1682 (not in the Library). "Dieser Roman macht den Leser an Hand einer abenteuerlichen Darstellung mit allen Inseln auf der ganzen Welt bekannt; aber von 772 Seiten sind nur 11 Amerika gewidmet. Ost- und Westindien werden hier wohl auseinandergehalten; auch als Festland ist 'Terra Firma' (Südamerika) erkannt, nicht so jedoch der Norden..." — *Gerhard Deczryk, in Deutsch-amerikanische historische Gesellschaft von Illinois, Jahrbuch, Chicago, 1924-25, p. 12, IEK.*

**1688**

214. HAPPEL, EBERHARD WERNER. Thesaurus Exoticorum. | Oder eine mit Ausslåndischen | Raritäten und Geschichten | Wohlversehene | Schatz-Kammer | Fürstellend | Die Asiatische, Africanische und | Americanische | Nationes | Der...Canadenser, Virgenier, Floridaner, Mexicaner, ...Alles...aus den berühmtesten Scribenten zusammen | getragen...Von Everhardo Gvernero Happelio. Hamburg: | Gedruckt und Verlegt durch Thomas von Wiering,...Jm Jahr 1688. 8 p.l., 875 p., 7 l., 4 maps, 21 plates. f°.  †† BAP
Sabin 30279.
Of special interest are the chapters: Einwohner von neu Frankreich, p. 89-90; Einwohner in Neu Niederland, p. 91-92; Einwohner von Virginia, p. 93-94; Der König von Florida, p. 95-96; Einwohner auf der Jnsul California, p. 97-98, etc. (with curious illustrations of the aborigines of these countries); and Der neuen Welt Entdeckung, p. 119-120.

215. LATOMUS, SIGISMUND, FIRM, PUBLISHERS, FRANKFURT AM MAIN. Relationis Historicæ | Semestralis Vernalis Continuatio. | Jacobi Franci | Historische Beschrei | bung der denckwürdigsten Geschichten, so sich in Hoch- | und Nieder-Teutschland,...Wie nicht weniger | in Ost- und West-Indien, &c. vor und zwischen jüngst-verflossener Franckfurter Herbst-Mess 1687. | biss an- und in die Oster-Mess dieses lauffenden 1688. Jahrs, hin und wieder in der Welt, | zu Land und Wasser, glaubhafftig zugetragen. | Alles auss überschikten Lateinischen, Italiänischen, Spanischen, Französischen, | Hoch- und Nieder-Teutschen Documentis, brieflichen Urkunden und Geschichtreichen Schrifften: | ...Durch Sigismundi Latomi...sel. Erben, Und Johann Steindeckern fortgeführt und verlegt. | Franckfurt am Mayn: bey den Latom. Erben und Steindeckern zu finden. | M DC LXXXVIII. 104 p. 19½ x 15½ cm. (4°.) *KB 1688
Of special interest: Zwoellfter Haupt-Titul. Von allerhand denckwuerdigen Begebenheiten, p. 93-98.
See nos. 203, 208.

216. MOCQUET, JEAN. Wunderbare | Jedoch | Gründlich- und warhaffte Geschichte | und | Reise Begebnisse | In Africa, Asia, Ost- und | West-Indien | von Jan Mocquet...aus dem Französichen [*sic!*] in Hochteutsche Sprache übersetzet und entdecket | durch | Johann Georg Schochen. Lüneburg: | In Verlegung Johann Georg Lippers [1688]. 30 p.l., 632 p., front., 10 plates, folding plan. 21 x 18 cm.
Sabin 49793. JCB, II, 515. *KB 1688
Some of the engravings by Peter Schenk, Amsterdam, have Dutch texts.
Consists of the same sheets as the edition (following) published at Nürnberg. This copy is extra-illustrated with 22 plates and 12 portraits.
A translation of Mocquet's *Voyages en Afrique, Asie, Indes orientales & occidentales,* Paris, 1616. The Library has the Paris, 1617, edition, * *KB 1617*.
Of special interest is the second Buch, p. 25-88, which has a separate title-page: Wunder-Geschichte und Reise-Begebnuessen nach West-Jndien | als dem Strom der Amazonen | die Lande der Caripousen und Caribanen | nebenst andern Landschafften und Jnsulen in Westen | von Jan Mocquet, aus Frankreich | Das Andere Buch. Plates II, III, IV (not signed) represent Indian life.

217. —— Wunderbare | Jedoch | Gründlich- und warhaffte Geschichte | und | Reise Begebnisse | In Africa, Asia, Ost- und | West-Indien | von Jan Mocquet...aus dem Französichen [*sic!*] | in Hochteutsche Sprache übersetzet und entdecket | durch | Johann Georg Schochen. | Nürnberg: In Verlegung Christoff Riegels, 1688. 30 p.l., 632 p., front., 10 plates, folding plan. 21 x 17½ cm. *KB 1688
Consists of the same sheets as the edition published at Lüneburg, preceding.

**1689**

218. HENNEPIN, LOUIS. Beschreibung | Der Landschafft | Lovisiana | Welche, Auf Befehl des Königs in Frank- | reich, neulich gegen Sudwesten | Neu-Frankreichs | In America | entdecket worden. | Nebenst einer Land-Carten, | und Bericht von den Sitten und | Lebens-Art der Wilden in sel- | biger Landschafft. | In Französischer Sprache heraus | gegeben durch P. Ludwig Hennepin...Nun aber ins Teutsche übersetzet. | Nürnberg: In Verlag Andreā Otto, 1689. 425 p., 3 l., 2 folding maps. 13½ x 8 cm. *KB 1689
Sabin 31364. JCB, II, 520. V. H. Paltsits, *Hennepin,* p. LII.
Sabin mentions an edition of 1692.
Hennepin's text is divided into: Beschreibung der Landschafft Louisiana. Welche neulich auf Befehl Jhro Koenigl. Majestät in Frankreich | gegen Sud-Westen in Neu-Frankreich ist entdecket worden, p. 3-262. Sitten und Gebraeuche derer Wilden. I. Von der Fruchtbarkeit des Landes derer Wilden, p. 263-268. II. Von der Wilden Ursprung, p. 269-274. III. Von der Wilden Leibs-Beschaffenheit, p. 274-278. IV. Von der Wilden Arzney-Mitteln, p. 279-283. V. Von der Wilden Kleidung, p. 283-287. VI. Von der Wilden Heyrathen, p. 287-296. VII. Von der Wilden Gastereyen, p. 296-301. VIII. Von der Wilden Spielen, p. 301-305. IX. Von der Wilden Unhoeflichkeit, p. 305-309. X. Von der Wilden Hoeflichkeit, p. 309-311. XI. Von der Wilden Art zu kriegen, p. 312-315. XII. Von der Wilden Policey und Regierungs-Art, p. 322-324, XIV. Von der Wilden Art zu jagen, p. 324-331. XV. Von der Wilden Manier zu fischen, p. 331-334. XVI. Von der Wilden Hausrath, p. 334-337. XVII. Von der Wilden Manier zu begraben, p. 337-338. XVIII. Von der Wilden Aberglauben, p. 338-339. XIX. Von der Wilden laecherlichen Meinungen, p. 339-345. XX. Von denen Hindernissen un deren willen die Wilden so uebel zu bekehren sind, p. 345-348. XXI. Von der Wilden Unpartheilichkeit, p. 348-352.
To the text of Hennepin is appended (p. 353-425) Marquette's narrative, with half-title: Beschreibung Einer sonderbaren Reise Etlicher bisher noch unbekannter Länder und Völcker im Mitternächtigen America. Welche im Jahr 1673. Durch P. Marquette S.J. und Herrn Jolliet verrichtet worden..."

## 1690

219. FUNCK, DAVID, EDITOR. Der in | Europa und America | verehrliche | Thron und Kron | Gross-Britanniens | Oder | Des Königreichs Engel- | Schod- und Irrlands gründ- | liche Abschilderung. | Worinnen entworffen und | abgehandelt dieser Königreiche alte und | neue Namen, Einwohner, Könige, Reichs- | Satzungen, Provintzen, Städte, Lands-Frucht- | barkeit- und Eigenschafften...Hervorgegeben und verlegt | Von David Funcken, Kunst und Buchhändler | in Nürnberg. [Nürnberg: D. Funck, 169–.] 2 p.l., 3–285 p. plates, ports. 13 cm. (12°.) *KB 169–
The first eight chapters (p. 3-209) treat of England, Scotland, and Ireland. Only Das IX. Capitel (p. 209-215) deals with America. Das X. und letzte Capitel (p. 216-285) is devoted to contemporary history.

## 1691

220. THEATRI | Europæi | Continuati | Zwölffter Theil, | ...verlegt. | Durch | Matthäi Merians Sel. Erben. | ...Franckfurt am Mäyn. | Gedruckt bey Johann Görlin. | Jm Jahr M DC XCI. 1 p.l., 1146 p., 18 l., plates (part folding), maps (part folding). illus. f°.
† BTWA (Theatrum)
Year 1683: "Zeitung aus West-Jndien," p. 617.

## 1693

221. GAGE, THOMAS. Thomas Gage | Neue merckwürdige Reise-Beschreibung | Nach | Neu Spanien, | Was ihm daselbst seltsames begegnet, und | wie er durch die Provintz Nicaragua wider zurück | nach der Havana gekehret: | ...Ingleichen | Eine vollkommene Beschreibung aller Län- | der und Provinzen, welche die Spanier in gantz Ame- | rica besitzen; ...wie auch von...der...Indianer und Schwartzen, Sitten | und Lebens-Art. | ...Aus dem Frantzöschen ins Deutsche übersetzt. | Leipzig: | Verlegts Johann Herbordt Kloss, Buchhändl. | Anno M.DC.XCIII. 4 p.l., 471 p. incl. front. 20½ x 17½ cm. (4°.) *KB 1693
Sabin 26309.
The author "belonged to the Dominican order, originally, but joined the English Church before he wrote his travels. He appears to have been a believer in witchcraft and sorcery, and admits into his work many curious relations on those subjects." — Sabin.
Part I. Neuer Bericht von denen West-Jndien | und von denen Verschickungen der Geistlichen in Jndien, p. 1-130. Parts II, III, IV. Neuer Bericht von denen Occidentalischen Jadien, p. 131-248, 249-400, 401-456. Appendix: Kurtzer Unterricht, die Jndianische Sprache | die man Poconchi oder Pocoman nennet | und in der Gegend umb Gvatimala, und an etlichen Orthen der Honduras gebraeuchlich ist | zu erletnen, p. 457-471.

## 1698

222. HENNEPIN, LOUIS. Neue | Reise-Beschreibung | Durch viele Länder, weit grösser, als | gantz | Europa, | Die neulichst zwischen Neu-Mexico und | dem Eiss-Meer in America entdecket | worden. | Worinn enthalten eine besondere | Beschreibung der Länder, Sitten und Ge- | wohnheiten der wilden Völcker in dem Süd- und | Norder-Theil der neuen Welt ...In Frantzösischer Sprache beschrieben...von R. P. Ludovico Hennepin | ...Ins Teutsche übersetzet von | M. J. G. Langen ...Bremen: | In Verlegung Phil. Gottfr. Saurmans, | 1698. 24 p.l., 288 p. front., map, plates. 14 x 8½ cm. (12°.) *KB 1698
Sabin 31366. JCB, II, 574.
See no. 224.

223. THEATRI | Europæi | Continuati | Dreyzehender Theil, | ...verlegt | Durch | Matthäi Merians Sel. Erben. Franckfurt am Mayn: | gedruckt bey Johann Görlin. | Jm Jahr M DC XCVIII. 3 p.l., 1363 p. 24 l. plates, maps (part folding). illus. f°. † BTWA (Theatrum) und Spaniern in America," p. 237. Year 1689: "Americanische Geschichte," p. 994–997; year 1690, p. 1352.

## 1699

224. HENNEPIN, LOUIS. Neue | Entdeckung | vieler sehr grossen | Landschafften | In | America | Zwischen Neu-Mexico und dem Eyss- | Meer gelegen, welche bisshero denen Europäern | noch unbekant gewesen, und an Grösse gantz | Europa übertreffen. | Wie auch eine völlige Beschreibung des | erschrecklichen Wasser-Falles von Niagara, ...Sr. Gross-Brittannis. Maj. Wilhelm | dem III. in Frantzösis. Sprache überreichet | und beschrieben von | R. P. Ludovv. Hennepin ...Ins Teutsche übersetzet durch | M. J. G. Langen ...Bremen: | In Verlegung Philip Gottfr. Saurmans, Buchh. 1699. 24 p.l., 382 p., 1 l., front., map, 2 plates. 13½ cm. (12°.) *KB 1699
Sabin 31367. JCB, II, 585.
See no. 222.
For a later edition, Bremen, 1742, see Sabin 31369.

## 1700

225. PASTORIUS, FRANCIS DANIEL. Franz Daniel Pastorius' Beschreibung von Pennsylvanien. Nachbildung der in Frankfurt a./M. im Jahre 1700 erschienenen Original-Ausgabe. Herausgegeben vom Crefelder Verein für wissenschaftliche Vorträge. Mit einer Einleitung von Friedrich Kapp. Crefeld: Druck von Kramer & Baum, 1884. 3 p.l., xxiii p., 6 l., 140 p. 17½ cm. ISC
According to Meynen no. 223, the Beschreibung was published first in W. E. Tenzel's Monatliche Unterredungen einiger guten Freunde von allerhand Büchern und andern annehmlichen Geschichten, Leipzig, Aprilis 1691, p. 278-288.
See nos. 209, 210, 226.

226. —— Umständige Geographische Beschreibung Der zu allerletzt erfundenen Provintz Pensylvaniæ, In denen End-Gräntzen Americæ In der West-Welt gelegen, durch Franciscum Danielem Pastorium, J. V. Lic. und Friedens-Richtern daselbsten. Worbey angehencket sind einige notable Begebenheiten, und Bericht-Schreiben an dessen Herrn Vattern Melchiorem Adamum Pastorium, und andere gute Freunde. Franckfurt und Leipzig: Zufinden bey Andreas Otto, 1700. 6 p.l., 140 p. 16½ cm. *KB 1700
Sabin 59028.
"Dieses empfieng der Verleger aus der Hand Melchioris Adami Pastorii J. V. D. Hoch Fürstl. Brandenb.

*1700, continued*

**226. PASTORIUS, FRANCIS DANIEL,** *continued*
Raths und Historici. Dessen Sohn noch würcklich in Pensylvania wohnhafft lebet." "William Penns eigene Beschreibung Pensylvaniä an seine Freunde nacher Londen." — *p. 123-135.*
An excerpt was published in *Monatlicher Auszug aus allerhand neu-herausgegebenen, nützlichen und artigen Büchern, December,* m.d.cc, Hannover, 1700, p. 895-902. See Meynen 228. An excerpt was also published as late as 1792: Geographisch-statistische Beschreibung der Provinz Pensylvanien v. Fr. Dan. Pastorius im Auszuge mit Anmerkung. Memmingen: Bei Seyler, 1792. See *Allgemeine Literatur Zeitung,* Jahr 1796, Bd. 2, p. 224, *NAA.*
See also Friedrich Kapp's introduction to his edition of the work, Crefeld, 1884, *ISC;* also "Zwei unbekannte Briefe von Pastorius. Herausgegeben von Julius Goebel," in *German American annals,* Philadelphia, 1904, new series, v. 2, p. 492-503, *NFCA.*

1702

**227.** ALTE und Neue Schwarm-Geister-Bruth, und Quåcker-Greuel, Das ist Gründliche Vorstellung und Glaubwürdige Erzehlung Von denen Alten Quackern und Neuen Frey-Geistern... [Frankfurt a. M.?] Im Jahre Christi, 1702. 9 p.l., 367 p. plates, ports. 33 cm. (f°.)
†\* KB p.v.26
"Bericht von Wiedereinnehmung der Juden in Engelland. Sammt Der Indianer Bekehrung in Neu-Engelland," p. 234-243.

**228.** [MÜLLER, JOHANN ULRICH.] Neu-aussgefertigter Kleiner Atlas. Oder Umständliche Beschreibung dess gantzen Erden-Cråyses, Nach seinen Verschiedenen Theilen, ...Dergestalten entworffen, dass Darinnen nicht nur jeden Landes Gränzen Grösse, Abtheilung, wunderbare Natur-Seltenheiten...zu finden; Sondern über dieses Auch jeder Erd-Theil in 163. kleinen Land-Cårtlein absonderlich zu beschauen vor Augen gestellet wird...Ulm: bey Georg Wilhelm Kühnen...Anno 1702. 2 v. maps. 16°. KAM
Description of America in second volume.

1704

**229.** FALCKNER, DANIEL. Curieuse Nachricht Von Pensylvania in Norden-America, welche, auf Begehren guter Freunde, Uber vorgelegte 103. Fragen, bey seiner Abreiss aus Teutschland nach obigem Lande Anno 1700. ertheilet, und nun Anno 1702 in den Druck gegeben worden. Von Daniel Falknern, Professore, Burgern und Pilgrim allda. Franckfurt und Leipzig: Zu finden bey Andreas Otto, Buchhåndlern, Im Jahre Christi 1702. 3 p.l., 8 [i.e. 58] p. 17 cm. (8°.) (In: Gabriel Thomas, Continuatio der Beschreibung der Landschafft Pensylvaniæ, Franckfurt und Leipzig, 1702. Bound with: F. D. Pastorius, Umständige Geographische Beschreibung... Franckfurt und Leipzig, 1704.) \*KB 1704
Written in answer to 103 questions "propounded by Rev. August Hermann Francke to Daniel Falckner upon his return from Pennsylvania to Germany in the year 1699." See Meynen no. 234.
*See* nos. 230, 231.

**230.** PASTORIUS, FRANCIS DANIEL. Umständige Geographische Beschreibung Der zu allerletzt erfundenen Provintz Pensylvaniæ, In denen End-Gräntzen Americæ In der West-Welt gelegen, durch Franciscum Danielem Pastorium ...Franckfurt und Leipzig: Zufinden bey Andreas Otto, 1704. 6 p.l., 140 p., 2 l., front. (map.) 17 cm. \*KB 1704
See Meynen nos. 228, 237, 267.
For an earlier edition see nos. 225, 226.

**231.** THOMAS, GABRIEL. Continuatio der Beschreibung der Landschafft Pensylvaniæ An denen End-Gräntzen Americæ. Uber vorige des Herrn Pastorii Relationes. In sich haltend: Die Situation, und Fruchtbarkeit des Erdbodens. Die Schiffreiche und andere Flüsse. Die Anzahl derer bisshero gebauten Städte. Die seltsame Creaturen an Thieren, Vögeln und Fischen. Die Mineralien und Edelgesteine. Deren eingebohrnen wilden Völcker Sprachen, Religion und Gebräuche. Und die ersten Christlichen Pflantzer und Anbauer dieses Landes. Beschrieben von Gabriel Thomas 15. Jährigen Inwohner dieses Landes. Welchem Tractätlein noch beygefüget sind: Des Hn. Daniel Falckners Burgers und Pilgrims in Pensylvania 193. [*sic!*] Beantwortungen uff vorgelegte Fragen von guten Freunden. Franckfurt und Leipzig: Zu finden bey Andreas Otto, Buchhändlern, Im Jahre Christi 1704. 2 p.l., 40 p., 3 l., 8 [i.e. 58] p. 17 cm. (8°.) \*KB 1704
Bound with F. D. Pastorius, Umständige geographische Beschreibung der zu allerletzt erfundenen Provintz Pensylvaniæ, Franckfurt und Leipzig, 1704. *See* no. 230.
The "Continuatio" is a translation, slightly condensed, of the part relating to Pennsylvania in Thomas's *An historical and geographical account of the Province and country of Pensilvania...,* first published in London, 1698.

1705

**232.** KIMAYER, THOMAS. Neu-Eröffnetes Raritäten-Cabinet, Ost- West-Indianischer und ausländischer Sachen. Darinnen allerhand rare Denck- und Seltsahme Merckwürdigkeiten, So sich in China, Japan, Choromandel, Peru, Guina &c. Tartarien und andern Ländern finden. Darinnen auch nicht weniger Die Heyraths-Ceremonien, Leichen-Begängnissen, Fischen- und Jägereyen, auch andere Sitten und Gewohnheiten etlicher dieser Heydnischen Länder und Völcker enthalten. Dem solche Sachen-liebenden Leser dargestellet [*sic!*] und aus den besten Scribenten und berühmtesten Reise-Beschreibungen zusammen getragen von Thomas Kimayer. Hamburg: Verlegts Christian Liebezeit. Druckts Philipp Ludwig Stromer, 1705. 4 p.l., 256 p. 4 l. 17½ cm. (8°.)
Sabin 37746. \*KB 1705
In the *Vorrede,* the works of Erasmus Francisci (see nos. 187, 189, 190) and of Eberhard Werner Happel (see no. 214) are praised. But as these are expensive books, this cheaper collection of rare things in the West Indies may also be welcome.
"Register," 4 l., at end.

## GERMAN WORKS RELATING TO AMERICA 33

### 1706

233. Von Engel- und Holland. (Die Europäische Fama. [Leipzig,] 1706. 16°. Theil 55, p. 530–533.) BTA
The French attack the English colonies in the West Indies, p. 530.

### 1707

234. THEATRI Europæi Continuati Funffzehender Theil, ...Franckfurt am Mayn: Gedruckt bey Johann Philipp Andreä. Jm Jahr M D CCVII. 3 p.l., 876 p. 14 l. plates (part folding), maps (part folding). illus. f°.
† BTWA (Theatrum)
Year 1697: "Ankunft der Virginischen und Barbados Flotte," p. 350. Year 1700: "African- und Americanische Geschichte," p. 871–872.

### 1708

234A. DAS AELTESTE deutsch-amerikanische Kirchenbuch. 1708–1719. (Jahrbuch für auslanddeutsche Sippenkunde. Herausgegeben... vom Deutschen Ausland Jnstitut. Stuttgart, 1936. 12°. [Jahrg. 1,] p. 56–60.) ATA
Meynen no. 478a.
Incorporated in an article by Otto Lohr on the oldest German-American church register.

235. BELLEGARDE, JEAN BAPTISTE MORVAN DE. Allgemeine historische Einleitung, zu allen bissher ans Licht getretenen Reisen zu Wasser und Land, in die Alte und Neue Welt. Durchgehends mit besondern, so geographischen als andern curieusen Anmerckungen, und schönen Kupffern. Von ...Hn. von Bellegarde... Verteutscht durch M. V**. Hamburg: Thomas von Wierings seel. Erben, 1708. 27 p.l., 272 p., 4 l. plates. 16½ cm. (8°.) *KB 1708
French original published at Paris in 1701 with title: Histoire universelle des voyages. (Sabin 4508.)
Aside from the introduction the work relates wholly to America.
Ludwig F. Vischer is the translator. See Allgemeine deutsche Bibliographie, Bd. 40, p. 65; Bd. 45, p. 675, NAA.
"Jnhalt | Der in diesem Tractat enthaltenen Merckwuerdigkeiten," 4 l. at end.

### 1709

236. LA HONTAN, LOUIS ARMAND DE LOM D'ARCE, BARON DE. Des berühmten Herrn Baron De Lahontan Neueste Reisen nach Nord-Indien, Oder dem Mitternächtischen America, Mit vielen besondern und bey keinem Scribenten befindlichen Curiositæten. Aus dem Frantzösischen übersetzet Von M. Vischer. Hamburg und Leipzig: Im Reumannischen Verlag, MDCCIX. 6 p.l., 459 p. map. 13½ x 8½ cm.
Sabin 38647. Paltsits, p. LXXIV. † KB 1709
Preface signed MV***.
A translation, somewhat abridged, of vols. 1 and 2 of his *Nouveaux voyages*..., first published in 1703, 3 v., *KC (1703).
Vol. 2 contains "Anhang eines Wörterbuchs von der wilden Sprache."
For later edition (1711), see no. 241.

236A. THÖRIGTEN Abzug einiger Untertanen nach Pensilvaniam betreffend. Anno 1709. (Deutsch-amerikanische historische Gesellschaft von Illinois. Jahrbuch. Chicago, Ill., 1912. 12°. v. 12, p. 129–189.) IEK
Incorporated in an article by Julius Goebel, "Briefe deutscher Auswanderer aus dem Jahre 1709." The emigrants come from the duchy of Nassau-Dillenburg.

### 1710

237. GOTTFRIED, JOHANN LUDWIG, PSEUD. Joh. Ludov. Gottfridi Historische Chronica, oder Beschreibung der fürnehmsten Geschichten, so sich von Anfang der Welt, biss auf das Jahr Christi 1619. zugetragen. ..Durch Matthæum Merianum. [Franckfurt am Mayn:] Auffs neue getruckt im Jahr nach Christi Geburt M DCC X. 38 p.l., incl. 31 plates (ports.), 1185 p., 27 l., folding map, folding plan. illus. 32 cm. † BA
For an earlier edition see no. 177.

238. VON Gross-Britannien. (Die Europäische Fama. [Leipzig,] 1710. 16°. Theil 101, p. 414–420; Theil 102, p. 502–510.) BTA
Indian chiefs of Canada visit London, p. 414, 502–504. William Penn acts as host, p. 504.

### 1711

239. [BERCKENMEYER, PAUL LUDOLPH.] Fortsetzung des Curieusen Antiqvarii, Das ist: Allerhand ausserlesene Geographische und Historische Merckwürdigkeiten, So in Asia, Africa und America zu finden, Aus Berühmter Männer Reisen zusammen getragen, und mit einen zweyfachen Register versehen. Hamburg: Bey Benjamin Schillern, Buchh. im Dom, 1711.
Contents of special interest: KAT
Des Curieusen Antiqvarii Dritten Abtheilung. Erstes Capitel. Von America insgemein | und dessen Geographischen und Politischen Eintheilung, p. 347–355. Das II. Capitel. Von Canada, p. 356–357. Das III. Capitel. Von Neu-Holland, p. 357–360. Das IV. Capitel. Von Neu-Engeland, p. 360. Das V. Capitel. Von der Landschafft Virginia, p. 360–362. Das VI. Capitel. Von der Landschafft Florida, p. 363–364. Das VII. Capitel. Von Neu-Mexico, p. 365. Das VIII. Capitel. Von Neu-Spanien oder den eigentlich so genannten Mexico, p. 366–370. Das IX. Capitel. Von der in America Meridionali oben an den Isthmo gelegenen grossen Landschafft, p. 370–375. Das X. [–XIV.] Capitel: [South America,] p. 376–396. Das XVII. Capitel. Von denen um America liegenden Jnsulen, p. 397–408. Two of the plates relate to America: Perienfang [and] Masaus Thier mit dessen jagd. Die Blase darinnen der Bisem ist.
"Es ist der erste Theil des Antiqvarii...mit so geneigten Augen angesehen worden, dass man innerhalb zwey Jahres-Frist zu drey neuen Auflagen schreiten, und...selbige um ein ziemliches vermehren müssen." — *Vorrede*.

240. BOEHME, ANTON WILHELM. Das verlangte, nicht erlangte Canaan bey den Lust-Gräbern; Oder Ausführliche Beschreibung Von der unglücklichen Reise derer jüngsthin in Teutschland nach dem Engelländischen in America gelegenen Carolina und Pensylvanien wallenden Pilgrim, absonderlich dem einseitigen übelgegründeten Kochenthalerischen Bericht wohlbedächtig entgegen gesetzet. In I. Einem Beantwortungs-Schreiben etlicher diese Sach angehenden Fragen; nebst einer Vorrede Moritz Wilhelm Höens. II. Ermahnungs-Schreiben an die bereits dahin verreisste Teutsche, Anthon Wilhelm Böhmens. III. Der Berg-Predigt Christi, und Gebettern vor die noch dahin auf

## 1711, continued

**240. BOEHME, ANTON WILHELM,** continued
dem Weg begriffenen &c. IV. Königl. Englischen deswegen nach Teutschland erlassenen Abmahnung. V. Kurtzen Relation, jener dabey erlittenen Elendes und Schicksals. VI. Noch einer andern Relation davon. VII. Einem Stück der Warnungs-Predigt von Hn. Johann Tribecko, &c. den zuruckreisenden in London gehalten. Alles aus Liebe zur Warheit und Patriotischem Wohlmeinen zusammen verfasset. Franckfurt und Leipzig: [Andreä] MDCCXI. 8 p.l., 127 p. 16 cm. *KB 1711
Sabin 2390, 32377, 98990. Meynen 240.
The "Beantwortungs-Schreiben" is signed: Anton Wilhelm Böhme.
The report on Carolina by Josua von Kocherthal (Sabin 2391, 4867, 10959) is not in the Library. See Meynen nos. 239, 240; also W. A. Knittel, *Early eighteenth-century Palatine emigration,* Philadelphia, 1937, *IEK.*

**241. LA HONTAN, LOUIS ARMAND DE LOM D'ARCE, BARON DE.** Des berühmten Herrn Baron De Lahontan Neueste Reisen nach Nord-Indien, Oder dem Mitternächtischen America Mit vielen besondern und bey keinem Scribenten befindlichen Curiositäten. Auch bey dieser andern Auflage mit Seiner Reise nach Portugall, Dennemarck und Spanien, vermehret. Aus dem Frantzösischen übersetzet Von M. Vischer. Hamburg und Leipzig: Im Reumannischen Verlag MDCCXI. 12 p.l., 753 p. map, 14 cm. (12°.)
*See* no. 236. *KB 1711
Bookplate by C. W. G. V(on) N(ostitz).

**242. VON Engelland.** (Die Europäische Fama. [Leipzig,] 1711. 16°. Theil 122, p. 142–153.)
References to Canada, p. 151. BTA

**243. VON Gross-Britannien.** (Die Europäische Fama. [Leipzig,] 1711. 16°. Theil 123, p. 242–254.) BTA
References to the English attack on Canada, p. 245.

## 1712

**244. [LAWSON, JOHN.]** Allerneuste Beschreibung der Provintz Carolina In West-Indien. Samt einem Reise-Journal von mehr als Tausend Meilen unter allerhand Indianischen Nationen. Auch einer Accuraten Land-Carte und andern Kupfer-Stichen. Aus dem Englischen übersetzet durch M. Vischer. Hamburg: Gedruckt und verlegt, durch seel. Thomas von Wierings Erben bey der Börse im güldnen A, B, C, Anno 1712. 7 p.l., 365 p. 2 l. front., folding map. 17 cm.
See Meynen, no. 242. *KB 1712
Translation of Lawson's *A new voyage to Carolina,* London, 1709, by M. [i.e. Magister] Ludwig Friedrich Vischer.

**245. VON Engelland.** (Die Europäische Fama. [Leipzig,] 1712. 16°. Theil 129, p. 779–789.) BTA
References to America, p. 784–789. "Man hat eine fliegende Nachricht, als ob Engelland heuer 120, Holland aber 80 Krieges-Schiffe in See stellen und eine starcke Flotte nach West-Jndien zu Ausführung eines geheimen Desseins abgeschickt werden sollte. Nun ist gewiss West-Jndien noch der Mühe werth, eine Farth dahin anzustellen; alleine mit Macht dörffte wenig auszurichten seyn."

## 1714

**246. VOM Heil. Röm. Reiche.** (Die Europäische Fama. [Leipzig,] 1714. 16°. Theil 157, p. 10–44.) BTA
References to Iroquois visiting London, p. 35.

## 1715

**247. VON Engel-und Holland.** (Die Europäische Fama. [Leipzig,] 1715. 16°. Theil 175, p. 559–564.) BTA
Letter from Charleston, June 8, 1715, referring to a rebellion of the Indians in Carolina.

## 1717

**248. DAPPER, OLFERT.** Dappervs Exoticvs Cvriosvs, Das ist, des viel-belesenen Hn. Odoardi Dapperi Africa- America- und Asiatische Curiositäten, So in den Drey Haupt-Theilen der Welt verwundernd vorkommen; Den Begierigen zur Lust, Den Armen zum Heyl, Den Gelehrten zum Gebrauch, Den Studirenden zum Nutz, Allen aber zur Vergnügung. Auffs kürtzeste zusammen getragen Von M. J. C. Männling ...Franckfurt und Leipzig: Bey Michael Rohrlachs sel. Wittben und Erben, von Liegnitz, 1717. 7 p.l., 536 p., 36 l., 184 p., 18 l., 174 p., 14 l. front. 17½ cm. *KB 1717
Sabin 18523–4.
The fourth part has colophon: Jena: bedruckt bey Paul Ehrichen. Following the first part is a title-page: Dapperi Exotici curiosi continuatio. Oder des vielbelesenen Hn. Odoardi Dapperi Americanische Curiositäten, So in diesen Haupt-Theile der Welt verwundernd vorkommen, Auffs kürtzeste zusammen getragen Von M, J. C, Männling... Franckfurt und Leipzig: Bey Michael Rohrlachs sel. Wittib und Erben in Liegnitz, 1718.
Description of America, p. [1]–184.

**249. SIMMENDINGER, ULRICH.** Warhaffte und glaubwürdige Verzeichnüss, Jeniger, durch die Gnade Gottes, annoch im Leben sich befindenden Personen. Welche sich Anno 1709. unter des Herren wunderbarer Führung aus Teutschland In Americam oder Neue Welt gezogen, und allda an verschiedenen Orten ihr Stücklein Brods suchen. Allen Liebhabern, insonderheit aber deroselben Familien und nahen Freunden zur freudigen Nachricht gestellet. Von Ulrich Simmendinger, Siebenjährigen Nord-Americanern, in der Provintz Neu-Yorck, anjetzo aber wieder in seiner Vatter-Stadt Reuttlingen... [Reuttlingen:] Joh. G. Füsing [1717?]. 12 l. 16 cm. (8°.) *KB 1717
See Meynen 486, 486a, 817, 817a.
An account by one of the Palatine Germans.
The Library has an English translation of the tract in *APR (New York).* As to Simmendinger, see W. A. Knittel, *Early eighteenth-century Palatine emigration,* Philadelphia, 1937, *IEK.*

## 1719

**250. VON Franckreich.** (Die Europäische Fama. [Leipzig,] 1719. 16°. Theil 227, p. 601–678.) BTA
Refers to Law's West-Indian Company and describes the Mississippi district, p. 640–677. See also note on no. 254.

## 1720

251. AUSFÜHRLICHE Historische und Geographische Beschreibung Des an dem grossen Flusse Mississipi in Nord-America gelegenen herrlichen Landes Louisiana; In welches die neu-aufgerichtete Frantzösische grosse Indianische Compagnie Colonien zu schicken angefangen; Worbey zugleich einige Reflexionen über die weit-hinaus sehende Desseins gedachter Compagnie, Und des darüber entstandenen Actien-Handels eröffnet werden. Andere Auflage. Mit neuen Beylagen und Anmerckungen vermehret. Leipzig: Bey J. Fried. Gleditschens seel. Sohn, 1720. 3 p.l., 102 p. front. (map). 8°. Sabin 32104. \*KB 1720
Originally published with title, *Historische und geographische Beschreibung*... [Leipzig:] Leipziger Neu-Jahrs-Messe, 1720.
See no. 253; also note on no. 254.

252. ——— Dritte Auflage. Mit neuen Beylagen und Anmerckungen vermehret. Leipzig: Bey J. Friedr. Gleditschens seel. Sohn, 1720. 3 p.l., 102 p. map. 16½ cm. \*KB 1720
Third edition of no. 251. No variations in title.

253. HISTORISCHE und Geographische Beschreibung des an dem grossen Flusse Mississipi in Nord-America gelegenen herrlichen Landes Louisiana; In welches die neu-aufgerichtete Frantzösische grosse Indianische Compagnie Colonien zu schicken angefangen; Worbey zugleich einige Reflexionen über die weithinaus sehende Desseins gedachter Compagnie, Und des darüber entstandenen Actien-Handels eröffnet; Auch über dieses noch einige curiöse Beylagen, So zu der Historie dieser Angelegenheit gehören, mitgetheilet werden. [Leipzig:] Leipziger Neu-Jahrs-Messe, 1720. 4 p.l., 84 p. map. 16½ cm. (8°.) \*KB 1720
Sabin 32104.
"Anhang, worinnen die sogenannte Isle Royale, auff welcher der Herr de la Bourlardiere eine Colonie auffrichten wollen, beschrieben," p. 75-79.
"La compagnie de Mississipi," in verse, p. 80-84.
See nos. 251, 252; also note on 254.
See also *A full and impartial account of the Company of Mississippi*, London, 1720, \* *KC 1720;* also Georges Oudard, *John Law: a fantastic financier*, 1671-1729, London, 1928, *AN (Law).*
An evaluative bibliography of the works on Louisiana that were known to the geographers of the eighteenth century is in T. F. Ehrmann's introduction to "Schilderung von Louisiana. Aus dem Französischen des von Duvallon herausgegebenen Werkes zweckmässig abgekürzt," in M. C. Sprengel, editor, *Bibliothek der neuesten und wichtigsten Reisebeschreibungen*, Weimar, 1804, Bd. 10, *KBD*.
See also *Allgemeine geographische Ephemeriden*, Weimar, 1803, Bd. 12, p. 586, *KAA*.

254. KURTZE Remarqves über den ietziger Zeit Welt-beruffenen Missisippischen Actien-Handel in Paris, und andere grosse Unternehmungen des Herrn Laws, Welche derselbe zum Profit seiner neu-errichteten Indianischen Compagnie, Vornehmlich aber zu Verbesserung der Königl. Financien und des Frantzösischen Commercii, biss hierher ziemlich fortgeführet; Wobey zugleich von der Natur der Actien insgemein und was es mit solchen in der gleichen grossen Compagnien vor eine Bewandniss habe, auch welches die festen Länder, Insuln, Festungen und See-Porten seyn, welche in America Septentrionali der Frantzösischen neuen Ost-Indianischen Compagnie zu ihrem Handels-Gebrauch und Nutzen zugeeignet worden, gehandelt wird, entworffen von P. J. M. Cum censura. Leipzig: im Durchgange des Rathhauses, 1720. 4 l. 4°. \*KB 1720
Possibly by Paul Jakob Marperger.
A thorough contemporary German account of Law's enterprise can be found in *Die Europäische Fama*, 1720. See also J. H. Dieler, *The settlement of the German coast of Louisiana and the Creoles of German descent*, Philadelphia, 1909, *ITP*, and his *Die ersten Deutschen am unteren Mississippi und die Creolen deutscher Abstammung. Vortrag gehalten am 16. September 1904 vor dem "Germanistischen Congress" in der Congresshalle der St. Louiser Weltausstellung*, New Orleans, La., 1904, *IEK p.v.4, no.5*.

255. THEATRI Europæi Achtzehender Theil... Franckfurth am Mayn: gedruckt bey Anton Heinscheidt. Im Jahr Christi 1720. 1 p.l., 322, 294, 392 p., 30 l. plates (part folding), maps (part folding). illus. f°. †BTWA (Theatrum)
Year 1708: "Project eines Handels Vergl. nach West-Jndien zwischen Franckr. u. Span," p. 248.

256. VON Franckreich. (Die Europäische Fama. [Leipzig,] 1720. 16°. Theil 232, p. 279-335.) BTA
Refers to West-Indian Company, p. 289, 308.

257. VON Gross-Britannien und Irrland. (Die Europäische Fama. [Leipzig,] 1720. 16°. Theil 237, p. 745-809.) BTA
Description of the Palatine Germans in North America, p. 773-775.

258. WARHAFFTE Nachricht von einer Hochteutschen Evangelischen Colonie zu Germantown, in Nord-Virginien in America, und derselben Dringendliches Ansuchen an Ihre Glaubens-Genossen in Europa. [n. p.,] Anno 1720. 4 l. 4°. \*KB 1720
See Sabin 27160.
This appeal was also "printed in the *Extraordinaire Kayserliche Reichs-Post-Zeitung*, Anno 1720, den 15. See *Historical notes relating to the Pennsylvania Reformed Church*, v. 1, no. 1, May, 1899, p. 8-10, *ZXBA*.
For an account of the colonization of Germanna, and the sending of Jacob Zollickoffer to England and Germany to secure funds for the erection of a church, see J. W. Hinke's "The first German Reformed Colony in Virginia: 1714-1750," in the *Journal of the Department of History of the Presbyterian Church of the U. S. A.*, v. 2, nos. 1-3, 1903, *IAA*.

## 1721

259. ANALECTA historico - litterario - curiosa. Oder vermischte und gesammlete Anmerckungen, aus der Historie, Litteratur, und curieusen Wissenschafften...publiciret Von Poliandern. Fasciculus I. So in 9 Gängen bestehend. Erffurt: Druckts und verlegts Joh. Michael Funcke, 1721. 441(1) p., 12 l. illus. 16°. \*DF
Continuously paged.
No. 1. "Von der Chocolate," p. 9-14. No. XLIII. "Von Zucker," p. 42-43.

260. VON Franckreich. (Die Europäische Fama. [Leipzig,] 1721. 16°. Theil 243, p. 195-247; Theil 251, p. 833-911.) BTA
Refers to the re-conditioning of the West-Indian Company, p. 205-221, and to John Law's imprisonment, p. 893.

## 1722

**261.** HISTORISCH- und Geographischer Calender, Nach dem verbesserten Stylo, Auf das Jahr nach Christi Geburt, M DCC XXIII. Welches ein gemeines Jahr ist, Auf Seiner Königlichen Majestät in Preussen, Chur-Märckische und übrige Reichs-auch benachbarte Lande gerichtet, Und herausgegeben unter Approbation Der Von Seiner Königl. Majestat in Preussen, in Dero Residentz Berlin gestiffteten Societät der Wissenschafften. [Berlin? 1722?] *KB 1722

Map has title "America Septentrionalis et Meridionalis Nova." Text is entitled: Fortsetzung. Des geographischen Unterrichts von Amerika.
A concise geography of both North and South America.

**262–63.** VESPUCCI, AMERIGO. Allerälteste Nachricht von der Neuen Welt Welche Deren Erfinder Americus Vesputius Florentinus ehemahls ertheilet Voritzo aus einem alten und raren Exemplar Zum Neuen Abdruck befördert von Mart. Frider. Vossio Pastore in Tauche. Berlin: Bey Christoph Gottlieb Nicolai, 1722. 8 p.l., 63 p. 8°. *KB 1722

Sabin 910.
Signed: Americus Vesputius in Lisbona.
Reprinted from the translation by Michael Herr which first appeared in the German edition of the "Novus Orbis Regionum" — *Die New Welt* (for full entry, see no. 57), Strassburg, 1534; see also no. 536.

## 1723

**264.** MARTINI, JOHANN CHRISTIAN. Kurtze und deutliche Anweisung zur neuen Staats-Geographie... Franckfurth und Leipzig: Zu finden bei Paul Lochner, 1723. 854 p. front., plates (part col'd). 16°. KAM
Nord America, p. 840-851.

## 1724

**265.** DER AMERICANISCHE Robinson, In Drey unterschiedenen, curieusen, seltsamen und angenehmen Begebenheiten vorgestellet, und Seiner Vortrefflichkeit wegen aus dem Frantzösischen ins Teutsche übersetzet. Cölln [i. e. Dresden: Zimmermann], 1724. 219 p. 17 cm. (8°).
*KB 1724
Authority for imprint: Hermann Ullrich's "Robinson und Robinsonaden," Teil 1, p. 115 (Literarhistorische Forschungen. Weimar, 1819. 8°. Heft 7. NABM).
For German "Robinsonaden" relating to America, but not in the Library, see Sabin 72220, 72221, 72225, 72227, 72229, 72231, 72232, 72234, 72236.
The Library has K. F. Tröltsch, *Der fränkische Robinson,* in *KL.

**266.** GRÜNDLICHE Erweisung, dass Ihro Römisch-Kayserl. Majest. in Dero Oesterreichischen Niederlanden, nach allerhöchsten Belieben Commercia zu stabiliren, und zu Aufrichtung einer Ost-und West-Indischen Compagnie behörige Allergnädigste Privilegia zu ertheilen, berechtiget. Entworffen von Friedrich Ludewig, Edlen Herrn von Berger 1723. (Europäische Staats-Cantzley. Nürnberg, 1724. 16°. Theil 43, p. 515–608.) BTA
Published in book form: Regensburg und Leipzig, 1723. Sabin 4847a. Not in the Library.

## 1725

**267.** VON Gross-Britannien. (Die Europäische Fama. [Leipzig,] 1725. 16°. Theil 280, p. 255–346.) BTA
A description of Carolina, p. 326–333. Excerpt from J. P. Purry, *Mémoire presenté à Sa Gr. Mylord Duc de Newcastle... sur l'état present de la Caroline & sur les moyens de l'ameliorer,* Londres, 1724. Sabin 66725.

## 1726

**268.** [CROUCH, NATHANIEL.] Der Englische Held und Ritter Franciscus Dracke, In einer ausführlichen Beschreibung von dessen Leben, Thaten und See-Reisen, darunter besonders die Reise um die Welt sehr merckwürdig, Vormahls von Roberto Brown [pseud.] in Englischer Sprache entworffen; anitzo aber ins Teutsche übersetzet, Welcher ein Anhang beygefüget von dem erstaunens-würdigen Schiffbruch des Ost-Indischen Jagdt-Schiffes, der Schelling genannt. Leipzig: Verlegts Wolffgang Deer, unter Schwabens Haus in der Grimmischen Gasse [1726?]. 472 p. incl. front. (port.) 8°. *KB 1726
Sabin 8547.
"Erstaunens-würdige Beschreibung des unerhörtgefährlichen Schiff-Bruchs, von dem Ost-Indischen Jagt-Schiff der Schelling genannt... von Frantz Janss von der Heyde," 1 l., p. [329-]472.
Concerning the pseudonyms, Robert Brown and (as the English editions have) Robert Burton, see Sabin 5969–5971, 8547, 9500, 9501, 17686.

**269.** JESUITS. LETTERS FROM MISSIONS. Allerhand so lehr- als geist-reiche Brief, Schrifften und Reis-Beschreibungen, welche von denen Missionariis der Gesellschafft Jesu aus beyden Indien, und andern über Meer gelegenen Ländern, seit An. 1642. biss auf das Jahr 1726. in Europa angelangt seynd. Jetzt zum erstenmal theils aus handschrifftlichen Urkunden, theils aus denen französischen Lettres edifiantes verteutscht und zusammen getragen von Joseph Stöcklein, gedachter Societät Jesu Priester... Augspurg und Grätz: In Verlag P., M., und J. Veith seel. Erben, Buchhändlern, 1726-58. 36 parts in 5 v. (bound in 10). front. (v. 3), maps, plans, plates, ports., tables. illus. 32½ cm. (f°.) †*KB 1726
Sabin 52376.
The work is divided into 36 parts and also five "Bünde." Theil 1 and Bund 2 have added engraved title-pages: "Der neüwe Welt- Bott mit allerhand Nachrichten deren Missionarien Soc. Iesu."
"Mostly taken from unpublished manuscripts. Only the smaller part has been translated from the 'Lettres edifiantes.'" Completed after Stöcklein's death by Peter Probst and Franciscus Keller.
For the second edition *see* no. 272.
"Brief aus denen Philippinischen Insuln und deroselben Gegend," Briefe 10–12.
"Brief aus Nord-America," Briefe 28–33, 52–56, 71–74, 139–140, 171–174, 187, 211–212, 320–321, 528–529, 532–538, 567–568, 571, 608–619, 652–665.
"Brief aus West-Indien...," Briefe 309-311.

**270.** VON denen zu Wien und Hannover verbundnen Staaten. (Die Europäische Fama. [Leipzig,] 1726. 16°. Theil 293, p. 335–538.) BTA
Refers to Spanish infringements on the English colonies in America, p. 406–411.

## GERMAN WORKS RELATING TO AMERICA

### 1727

271. THEATRI Europæi Neunzehender Theil... Franckfurth am Mayn: gedruckt bey Anton Heinscheidt [1727?]. 2 p.l., 808, 560 p. plates. illus. f°. † BTWA (Theatrum)
Year 1710: "Printzen aus Canada in Engelland. Sprechen die Königin an. Reisen wieder nach ihrem Land ab," p. 227–228. Year 1711: "Engelland schafft arme Pfältzer fort," p. 674. Year 1711: "Englischer Anschlag auff Quebec misslungen," p. 698. Year 1712: "Abbildung der Wunderschönen Americanischē Aloe." Illustration by Busch," between p. 212 and 213. Year 1712: "Frantzösisches umständliches Friedens-Erbitten in Ansehung Engellands. (Acadie will Franckreich an Engelland abtreten)," p. 334, 337, 347. Year 1712: "Spanier wollen Engell. Handlung in America nicht zustehen," p. 453.

### 1728

272. JESUITS. LETTERS FROM MISSIONS. Allerhand so lehr- als geist-reiche Brief, Schrifften und Reis-Beschreibungen, welche von denen Missionariis der Gesellschafft Jesu aus beyden Indien, und andern uber Meer gelegenen Ländern, seit An. 1642. biss auf das Jahr 1726. in Europa angelangt seynd. Jetzt zum erstenmal theils aus handschrifftlichen Urkunden, theils aus denen französischen Lettres edifiantes verteutscht und zusammen getragen von Joseph Stöcklein, gedachter Societät Jesu Priester... Anderte Edition... Augspurg und Grätz: In Verlag P., M., und J. Veith seel. Erben, 1728–1761. 38 parts in 5 v. fronts. (v. 2–3), maps, plans, plates, ports., tables. illus. 33½ cm. (f°.)
See also no. 269. †* KB 1728

273. VON Gros-Britannien. (Die Europäische Fama. [Leipzig,] 1728. 16°. Theil 311, p. 893–968.) BTA
The English fight the Spanish trade in America, p. 954–959.

### 1729

274. HUEBNER, JOHANN. [Johann Hübners Kurtze Einleitung zur politischen Historia... Leipzig? J. F. Gleditsch's Sohn? 1729.] 1,032 p. front. 12°. * KB 1729
Binder's title: J. Hübners Historische Fragen. 10. Theil.
Issued as Theil 10 of his *Kurtze Fragen aus der politischen Historia bis auf gegenwärtige Zeit*, in Theil I–IX of which the "Einleitungen" originally appeared.
Comprises the "Einleitung zum ersten [-neunten] Theile der Historischen Fragen. Neue Auflage 1729."
Only pages 108–120 of part IX deals with America.
"Verzeichniss einiger historischen und politischen Bücher, welche Joh. Fried. Gleditschens seel. Sohn in Leipzig verlegt hat," p. [1030–1032.]
As to the use of a school book by Johann Hübner in the schools of Pennsylvania, see J. M. Cavell, "Religious education among people of Germanic origin in colonial Pennsylvania," in Pennsylvania German Society, *Proceedings and addresses*, Lancaster, Pa., 1929, v. 36, p. 29–45, IEK.

### 1730

274A. DOPPELMAYR, JOHANN GABRIEL. Historische Nachricht Von den Nürnbergischen Mathematicis und Künstlern,... Jn Zweyen Theilen an das Licht gestellet, Auch mit vielen nütz-lichen Anmerckungen und verschiedenen Kupffern versehen von Johann Gabriel Doppelmayer... Nürnberg: P. C. Monath, 1730. 14 p.l., 314 p., 9 l., 15 plates, incl. map. 36½ cm.
* KB 1730
Contains, on p. 28–31, a valuable survey of the authors who believe that Martin Behaim was the discoverer of America. Ample quotations from Hartmann Schedel (see no. 1), Johannes Schoener, Michael Friedrich Lochner, Johann Christoph Wagenseil, and others. Note especially Wagenseil's "Memoria Behaimia," contained in Caspar Hagen, *Memoriae philosophorum, oratorum, poetarum, historicorum et philologorum, nostrae aetatis clarissimorum renovatae*, Francofurti et Lipsiae, 1710. — cf. British Museum catalogue.
The first to state that Martin Behaim discovered America and knew the Strait of Magelhaens were most probably Martinus Cellarius and Wilhelm Postell. See Martinus Cellarius [i.e., Martin Borrhaus], *Elementale cosmographicum*, 1539, * KB, and Wilhelm Postell, *Cosmographia disciplina*, 1561 (not in the Library).
G. Benzoni (see nos. 79, 83, 84) accepts the theory in his *La storia del mondo nuovo*, Venetia, 1564, as do Antonio Herrara (no. 153) and Giovanni Battista Riccioli in his *Geographiae...libri duodecim*, Venetiis, 1672, * KB 1672. Cellarius and Riccioli both say that Behaim visited the American continent and the Strait of Magelhaens, but Stuvenius appears to have been the first to give great importance to this statement by asserting in his treatise, *De vero Novi Orbis Inventori*, Francofurti ad Moenum, 1714, * KB 1714, that Behaim had accurately traced on his globe preserved at Nürnberg the Islands of America and even the Strait of Magelhaens. Professor Toze combated this assertion (see nos. 385, 386, 393). The discussion was carried on by Christoph Gottlieb Murr (see no. 580). In 1786, the *Transactions* of the American Philosophical Society, v. 2, p. 263–284, * EA, printed *A Letter from Mr. Otto [i.e. Louis Guillaume Otto, Count de Mosley] to Dr. Francklin with a memoir on the discovery of America*. The tract was opposed by Christobal Claders in his *Investigationes historicas, HAI* and * KF.
Note also F. W. Ghillany, *Geschichte des Seefahrers Ritter Martin Behaim*, Nürnberg, 1853, † AN (Behaim). See also notes on 382, 1019.

### 1732

275. AUSFÜHRLICHE Historie Derer Emigranten Oder Vertriebenen Lutheraner Aus dem Ertz-Bissthum Saltzburg, Worinnen man findet I. Eine Geographische Beschreibung, nebst einer accuraten Land-Charte dieses Ertz-Bissthums. II. Eine Historische Erzehlung von dessen Ursprunge, und denen remarquabelsten Ertz-Bischöffen. III. Eine gründliche Ausführung der dortigen Religions-Händel, die so wohl nach der Reformation bis auf unsere Zeiten, als vornehmlich jetzo in diesen Jahren darinn vorgegangen. IV. Was sich vor, bey und nach der jetzigen grossen Vertreibung daselbst zugetragen. Alles aus glaubwürdigen Historien-Schreibern und denen zu Regensburg gedruckten Acten heraus gezogen, Auch aus denen Friedens-Schlüssen mit Fleiss erläutert. Andere Auflage. Leipzig: Zu finden in Teubners Buchladen, 1732 [–34]. 4 parts in 1 v. fronts., col'd maps. plate. 4°. * KB 1732
See De Renne, 1931, I, 11–14.
"Verzeichniss derer Schrifften, welche bey Gelegenheit dieser saltzburgischen Emigration ans Licht getreten seyn," 8 l., in Theil 4. Chapter VI of Theil 4 entitled: Von denen, so nach Georgien in America abgegangen.
Engravings by Uhlich and J. G. Schreiber.
As to German tracts relating to the Salzburgers in America that are not in the Library, see Sabin 10975, 27555, 33622, 38041.

*1732, continued*

275. Ausführliche Historie..., *continued*

See E. Dannappel, *Die Literatur über die Salzburger Emigration, 1731–1735* [Berlin, 1886]. \* *KAB*; Gottfried Hecking, *De praestantia coloniae georgico-anglicanae prae coloniis aliis,* Avgvstae Vindel. litteris Brinhav serianis [1747], \* *KB 1747* (dissertation); G. G. Goecking, *Vollkommene Emigrations Geschichte von denen aus den Ertz-Bissthum Saltzburg vertriebenen und grosstentheils nach Preussen gegangenen Lutheranern,* Frankfurt und Leipzig, 1734–37 (not in the Library; see British Museum catalogue); C. F. Arnold, *Die Vertreibung der Salzburger Protestanten,* Leipzig, 1900 (not in the Library); J. J. Mayr, *Die Emigration der Salzburger Protestanten von 1731–1732,* Salzburg, 1931 (originally published in Gesellschaft für Salzburger Landeskunde, *Mitteilungen,* Salzburg. 1929–1931, Vereinsjahr 69, 70, 71, *FHN*); A. Prinzinger, "Die Ansiedlung der Salzburger im Staate Georgien in Nordamerika," in Gesellschaft für Salzburger Landeskunde, *Mitteilungen,* 1882, Vereinsjahr 22, p. 1–36, *FHN*; P. A. Stroebel, *The Salzburgers and their descendants,* Baltimore, 1855, *ITK (Ebenezer);* Hildegard Binder-Johnson, "Die Haltung der Salzburger in Georgia zur Sklaverei 1734–1750," in Gesellschaft für Salzburger Landeskunde, *Mitteilungen,* Salzburg, 1939, Vereinsjahr 78, p. 183–196, *FHN*; M. Hofer, "The Georgia Salzburgers," in *Georgia historical quarterly,* Savannah, Ga., 1934, v. 18, p. 99–118, *IAA*; H. W. Newton, "Agricultural activities of the Salzburgers in colonial Georgia," in *Georgia historical quarterly,* Savannah, Ga., 1934, v. 18, p. 248–263, *IAA,* also her "Industrial and social influences of the Salzburgers in colonial Georgia," in *Georgia historical quarterly,* Savannah, Ga., 1934, v. 18, p. 335–354, *IAA*.

276. Besonderes Gespräche In dem Reiche der Lebendigen, Zwischen einem Römisch-Catholischen Und Evangelisch-Lutherischen, Von Derer Evangelischen Saltzburger Emigranten Lehre, und wie sie dazu gekommen, ingleichen von ihrem Lebens-Wandel ausgestandener Verfolgungs-Emigration, March Route wie auch freundlichen Empfang und Aufnehmung bey denen Evangelischen gehandelt wird, Alles aus authentischen Memorialien und Schreiben entweder in Forma oder per Extractum genommen und in Form eines Gespräches abgefasset. Franckfurt am Mayn, 1732. 24 l. incl. front. 4°.
\* KB 1732
E. Dannappel, Die Literatur über die Salzburger Emigration. (Neuer Anzeiger für Bibliographie und Bibliothekswissenschaft. Berlin, 1886. 8°. Jahrg. 47, p. 38–39, \* *GAA [Petsholt]*.)

277–78. Copia Desjenigen Brieffes, Welchen Ihro Päbstl. Heiligkeit Clemens xii. An den Teuffel geschrieben, Und denselben ein Stück vom Fege-Feuer Zum Verkauff anbietet. [n. p., 1732.] 4 l. 4°. \* KB 1732
Contains several references to the Salzburgers.

279. Die freundliche Bewillkommung der Saltzburgischen Emigranten in Leipzig, Anno 1732... Leipzig: Zu finden bey Böcklin, Kupferstecher [1732]. broadside. illus. 16¾ x 12½ in. folding f°. \* KVB 1732
In verse. Engraving colored by hand.

280. Die Göttliche Allmacht In der Wunderthätigen Ausbreitung seines heiligen allein seligmachenden Wortes und Erhaltung der wahren Evangelischen Religion, Bey Betrachtung Derer in dem Ertz-Bisstumb Saltzburg viele Jahre her sehr bedrängten Nachfolger Christi, und über Zwantzig Tausend Seelen desshalber aus diesen Landen sich wegbegebenen Emigranten, In Einer Erbaulichen und hierzu dienlichen Nachricht vorgestellet. Franckfurth und Leipzig, 1732. 32 l. incl. front. 4°. \* KB 1732
Dannappel, p. 34 (full entry, no. 275: note).

281. Hunnius, Christoph Friedrich. Der gläubige Emigrant, Das ist, Eine Emigranten Predigt, Aus dem nten Cap. der Epistel an die Hebräer, Von mehr als 500. Saltzburgischen Emigranten, Und sonsten darzu gekommenen grossen Menge Volcks, Den ii. Julii 1732. in der Kirche zu Cranichfeld, gehalten, Und mit einigen Historischen Umständen versehen, In Druck gegeben Von Christoph Friedrich Hunnio, P. P. Superintend. und Consistoriali daselbst. Jena: Verlegts Johann Friedrich Ritter [1732]. 39 p. 4°. \* KB 1732

282. Koelling, Johann Friedrich. Die Thränen derer standhafften Bekenner des Evangelischen Glaubens wie selbige vor Saltzburg häuffig vergossen, von dem jetzigen Bischoffe Leopoldo, höhnisch verlachet, aber von den Grossen Monarchen in den Heil. Römischen Reiche Herrn Friederich Wilhelm, Könige in Preussen...angenommen wurden, wolte...nach Möglichkeit sammlen und daselbst ausgiessen M. Joann Friedrich Kölling, Nordhusanus. Nordhausen: Gedruckt bey des seel. Cölers Erben [1732?]. 2 l. f°. \* KV 1732
In verse. Slightly mutilated.

283. Die Krafft und Wahrheit des Göttlichen Wortes, Wie solche sich an denen Saltzburgischen Emigranten erwiesen, Indem viele Tausend derselben dadurch erleuchtet, und zum Erkänntniss des Heyls gelanget sind, auch die tröstlichen Verheissungen Gottes darinnen an ihnen wahr geworden; Nebst Zuverlässiger Nachricht, Von ihrem Zustand, und sonderbahren speciellen Umständen von ihrer Verfolgung und Verjagung, auch wie sie hie und da aufgenommen und empfangen worden, Zu Verherrlichung des Nahmens Gottes, Erbauung des Nächsten, und kräfftiger Überzeugung der Bibel-Verächter, ans Licht gegeben. Mit beygefügtem Kupffer, von Derselben Ankunfft, Einzug und Bewirthung in Magdeburg. Magdeburg, 1732. 4 p.l., 44 p. front. 21 cm. \* KB 1732
De Renne, 1931, i. 23.
Frontispiece signed: Brühl. delin. et sc. Lips.

284. Küttner, Johann David. Der Allervortheilhaffteste und Seeligste Verlust Derer Nachfolger Jesu, wurde Aus Matth. xix. v. 29. Bey Anwesenheit einiger Saltzburgischen Emigranten in Leipzig, Am Sonnabend vor dem i. p. Trinitatis 1732. der Christlichen Gemeine zur Erweckung und Trost vorgestellet von M. Joh. David Küttner, Sonnabends-Predigern zu St. Thomä. Leipzig: Zu finden in Teubners Buchladen [1732]. 3 p.l., 14 p. 4°.
De Renne, 1931, i, 25. \* KB 1732 Umständliche
Bound with: Umständliche Nachricht. Stolberg am Hartz [1732].

*1732, continued*

285. LESSER, FRIEDRICH CHRISTIAN. Friedrich Christian Lessers... Umständliche Nachrichten von denenjenigen 2790. Evangelisch-Saltzburgischen Emigranten, welche zu Zweymahlen nemlich den 26. August und 23. September 1732. In der Kåyserl. Freyen Reichs-Stadt Nordhausen ankommen, Wie solche von denen Evangelischen Einwohnern mit grosser Begierde aufgenommen, mit hertzlicher Liebe so geistlich als leiblich bewirthet, und mit vielen Seegens-Wünschen dimittiret worden, deme in behöriger Ordnung noch beygefüget, I) die gantzen An- und Abzugs-Reden; II) die Dispositiones derer Predigten, so bey der erstern Ankunfft in der angestellten Beth-Stunde gehalten worden; III) eine curieuse Remarque über eine Propheceyunge Pauli Sperati; und IV) ein Brief D. Lutheri an Mart. Lodingern, einem Saltzburgischen Prediger geschrieben. Nordhausen: Verlegts Johann Heinrich Grosse, 1732. 1 p.l., 77 p. 4°.     *KB 1732

Dannappel, p. 60 (full entry, no. 275: note).

286. MEMORIALE oder Rechtliche Ansuchungs-Schreiben Wegen der bedruckten Saltzburgischen Emigranten, Welche Verschiedene Protestantische Puissancen Durch Dero Hohe Gesandte An Ihro Röm. Kayserl. Majeståt, Nach Innhalt Des Westphålischen Friedens, haben ergehen lassen. Franckfurt am Mayn, 1732. 16 p. 4°.     *KB 1732

Dannappel, p. 67 (full entry, no. 275: note).

287. NOVELLARIUS, PSEUD. Das über die Glückliche Ankunfft etlicher hundert Saltzburger Emigranten Sich Höchsterfreute Meissen, Bestehend in einem Send-Schreiben Wie solche Leute am 10. Augusti 1732. allda sind eingeholet, freudig aufgenommen, reichlich beschencket und am 12. ejusd. darauf wieder dimittiret worden. [Meissen?] Gedruckt, 1732. 4 l. 4°.     *KB 1732

Dannappel, p. 67 (full entry, no. 275: note).
Signed and dated: Novellarius, Meissen, d. 12. August 1732.

288. DIE SEUFFTZENDE Saltzburger, Oder Besondere Unterredung Im Reiche der Lebendigen, Zwischen einem der Religion halben aus dem Lande emigrirenden Saltzburger Und einem gleichfalls wegen des Glaubens aus dem [sic!] Italiånischen und Frantzösischen Grentzen vertriebenen Waldenser, Darinnen beyder Schicksale und Verfolgungen, insonderheit aber die Historie der emigrirenden Saltzburger vollståndig beschrieben wird. Magdeburg: Gedruckt und zufinden bey sel. Joh. Siegelers Wittwe, Anno MDCCXXXII. 3 parts in 1 v. fronts. (parts 1-2), port. 21 cm.     *KB 1732

De Renne, 1931, I, p. 36.
Engraved frontispieces and portrait of Leopold, archbishop of Salzburg. Frontispiece to part 2 signed: Brühl del. et sc. Lips. Parts 2-3 have title: Die zweyte [-dritte] Unterredung im Reiche der Lebendigen...

289. STUSS, JOHANN HEINRICH. Schrifftmåssige Anrede an die Saltzburgischen Religions-Exulanten, als deren bey Fünff hundert den 28. Julii 1732. zu Gotha ankommen, und liebreich aufgenommen und bewirthet worden, verfasset von Johann Heinrich Stuss... Gotha: gedruckt mit Reyherischen Schrifften [1732]. 6 l. 4°.     *KB 1732

Dannappel, p. 100 (full entry, no. 275: note).

290. THEATRI Europæi Zwantzigster Theil... Franckfurth am Mayn: gedruckt bey Johann Benjamin Andreå [1732?]. 3 p.l., 704, 442, 419 p., 49 l. plates, maps. illus. f°.
    † BTWA (Theatrum)
Year 1713: "Reiche Flotte aus West-Jndien kommt in Spanien an," p. 523.

291. DIE TREUEN Bekenner Christi Das ist gründliche Beschreibung derer mehr als 20000. Vertriebene Saltzburger, Aus dem Ertz-Bissthum Saltzburg In welchen auch enthalten der Ursprung der Verfolgung und der Kern derer jenigen Briefe so die in Ketten gefangen an das Evangeliischr [sic!] Corpus in Regenspurg abgehen lassen. Nach dem Regenspurger Exemplar. Eissleben: zu finden bey Johann Friedrich Hillern, 1732. 8 l. 4°.     *KB 1732

Illustrated title-page.
Includes words of "Ich bin ein armer Exulant," by Joseph Schaitberger, and another hymn composed by the emigrants in their wanderings. (See P. A. Strobel, "The Salzburgers and their descendants." Baltimore, 1855. p. 38, *ITK*.)

292. DIE UM das [sic!] Evangelii willen vertribene Saltzburger. Leipzig: Zu finden bey D. V. Böcklin Kupferstecher [1732?]. broadside. 11¾ x 8¼ in.     *KVB 1732

Engraving, colored by hand. In verse.

293. DIE UM des Evangelii Willen verjagte nach Preussen eilende Saltzburger... Halle: Zu verkaufen bey C. G. Lieben, Universitäts Kupferstecher in Mons. Dans Hause auf der grossen Ulrichs Strasse wohnhaft [1732?]. broadside. 13⅝ x 8¼ in.     *KVB 1732

Engraving, colored by hand. In verse.

294. UMSTÅNDLICHE NACHRICHT, Welchergestallt ein, in 600 Seelen bestehender Troup Saltzburgischer Emigranten in der Hoch-Gråfl. Residentz-Stadt Stolberg am Hartz den 2ten, 3ten u. 4ten Aug. 1732. eingeholt, empfangen, geistlicher und leiblicher Weise verpflegt, nachhero auf die vorhabende fernere Reise geleitet worden. Pro Memoria: VVIr StoLberger haben VertrIebene SaLtzbVrgIsche EXVlanten beVVIrthet. Den ZVVeyten, DrItten VnD VIerten AVgVstI. Stolberg am Hartz: Zu finden bey dem Verfasser der wöchentlichen Stolbergischen Sammlung &c., und gedruckt bey Johann Christoph Ehrhart Gråfl. priv. Hof-Buchdr. [1732.] 8 l. 4°.
    *KB 1732

*1732, continued*

295. UMSTÄNDLICHE Und Wahrhafftige Nachrichten, Von denen Saltzburgischen Emigranten, Was dieselben vor Leute sind: Wie und warum sie genöthiget worden ihr Vaterland, und alle das Ihrige zu verlassen; Wie man mit ihnen vor und bey der Austreibung verfahren; Was sie vor Gefahr und Ungemach bisher ausgestanden, und noch ausstehen müssen; Wie sie sich gegen ihre Feinde verhalten; und wie sie bey allen ihrem Elende dennoch freudig, gutes Muths und getrost sind. Mit Einer Neuen Vorrede, Von dem Anfang und Fortgang Des Saltzburgischen Reformations-Wesens, Von Lutheri Zeiten an, biss hieher. Nach dem Berlinischen Exemplar gedruckt, und mit verschiedenen Sammlungen einiger hieher gehöriger Urkunden, vermehret. Hildesheim: Gedruckt und verlegt durch Just Henning Matthäi, 1732. 72 p. 21 cm. *KB 1732
Second issue.
"Urkunden," p. 25–46; "Verfolg Der Urkunden Wegen der Saltzburgischen Emigranten, Welche Neulich herausgekommen." Zweyte Auflage. Nach dem Berlinischen Exemplar gedruckt. 1732," p. [49]–72. Zweyter Verfolg... (not in the Library). Dritter Verfolg Derer Urkunden...[n. p.,] anno 1732. 79(1) p. 21 cm.

296. VETERES Migrate Coloni, Oder: Poetischer Zuruff an die Saltzburgischen Emigranten Welche um der Evangelischen Wahrheit willen aus ihrem Vaterlande verjaget worden, und dadurch ein ausnehmend Exempel Christlicher Standhafftigkeit bewiesen, andern zur Erweckung also entworffen von einem, der sich hertzlich erfreuet über solche Christi Getreue Glieder. [n. p., 1732?] 2 l. f°. *KVB 1732
In verse.

297. VOPELIUS, GEORG CHRISTOPH. Das Hochzupreisende Werck des Herrn, An denen Saltzburgischen Emigranten, Wolte, Als den 14ten Augusti Anno 1732. Achthundert und 40. von diesen verjagten Evangelischen Glaubens-Genossen in Quedlinburg ankamen, und mit Freuden bis den 16. Aug. bewirthet wurden, Nebst der, an dem damahls einfallenden Monatlichen Buss-Tage über Ps. 49, 15 gehaltenen Buss- und Erweckungs- Rede, Auch einer kurtzen Relation Von der Ankunft, Aufnahme, Verhaltung, und Abzuge der Emigranten, vorstellen, und Auf Verlangen dem Druck übergeben M. Georg Christoph Vopelius, P. ad. Div. Blasii Halberstadt: Gedruckt bey Nicolaus Martin Langen, 1732. 64 p. 4°. *KB 1732
Contains a bibliography, p. 3–4, 58–60; and the famous "Reise-Lied der Emigranten," p. 64.

298. WALCH, JOHANN GEORG. Erweckungs-Rede, Welche An die in Jena angekommene Saltzburgische Emigranten, Auf Verordnung Einer hochlöblichen Academie in der Collegen-Kirche Den 3. Julii MDCCXXXII. gehalten und auf vieler Verlangen herausgegeben Johann Georg Walch, Der H. Schrift D. und P. P. Zweyte Auflage. Jena: druckts und verlegts Joh. Friederich Ritter [1732]. 24 p. 21 cm.
*KB 1732
Dannappel, p. 106 (full entry, no. 275: note).

*1733*

299. HUNNIUS, CHRISTOPH FRIEDRICH. Das aufgemunterte Crannichfeldt, Wie es sich sonderlich Durch die Saltzburgische Emigrations-Geschichte lassen erwecket finden, Und die in dieser Tagen, Davon allda gehaltene Emigrations-Predigt fleissig erwogen, Alles vorgestellet Durch den jetzigen Superintendenten in Crannichfeldt, Christoph Friedrich Hunnio, P. P. Sup. und Consistoriali daselbst. Jena: Verlegts Johann Friedrich Ritter, 1733. 26 l. 4°. *KB 1733
*Contents:* "Vorrede," l. 2–4. Additamentum! (including words of two hymns composed by the emigrants in their wanderings), l. 4–6.
Dannappel, p. 41 (full entry, no. 275: note).

300. NAAS, JOHANNES. Reisetagebuch des Johannes Naas aus Crefeld, von Rotterdam bis Germantown in Pennsylvanien. 1733. (Der Deutsche Pionier. Cincinnati, O., 1880. 8°. Bd. 12, p. 341–349.) IEK

301. VON Gross-Britannien. (Die Europäische Fama. [Leipzig,] 1733. 16°. Theil 343, p. 602–614.) BTA
Colonization of Georgia and other references to America, p. 611–612.

302. ZEDLER, JOHANN HEINRICH. Grosses vollständiges Universal Lexicon Aller Wissenschafften und Künste... [mit Supplementen]. Halle und Leipzig, 1733–1764. 68 v. f°. †*AM
Various references to America.

*1734*

303. FISCHER, JOHANN GOTTLOB. Reise-Beschreibung Der Saltzburg-Dürnberger Emigranten, Die um des Bekänntnisses des Christlichen Evangelii willen ihr Vaterland verlassen, Haab und Güter, Hauss und Hoff, viele auch Eltern, Geschwister und Freunde mit dem Rücken angesehen, und ihre beschwerliche Winter-Reise unter mancherley Verfolgung und Schmach mit Göttl. Beystand nach Holland angetreten, Zu Regenspurg, Nürnberg, Franckfurth und andern vielen Orten geistlich und leiblich erquicket, auch von denen Hochmögenden Herren General-Staaten in die Flandrische Insel Cadsand gnädig aufgenommen worden, Von Dero vocirten und ordinirten Prediger und Seelsorger Johann Gottlob Fischern, Kürtzlich aufgezeichnet übersendet, und auf Begehren zum öffentlichen Preiss Gottes nebst einigen Anmerckungen dem Druck überlassen durch dessen Vater Johann Gottfried Fischern...Pfarrern zu Grieffstädt in Thüringen. Leipzig, 1734. 40 p. 21 cm. (4°.) *KB 1734
Sabin 24422.

303A. FRANCKENSTEIN, JACOB AUGUST. D. Jacob August Franckensteins Unmassgebliche Gedancken über das Emigrations-Recht wegen der Religion, so bey Gelegenheit der starcken Emigration derer Saltzburgischen Protestanten, entworffen, Und Nach denen Reichs-Grund-Gesetzen, auch andern in Teutschland üblichen Rechten erwogen, Und mit nöthiger Anführung bewährter Autorum versehen worden. Leipzig, 1734. 60 p. 4°. (In: Ausführliche Historie derer Emigranten. Theil 4. 60 p. at end.)
*KB 1732 Ausführliche

## 1735

**304. TÜBINGEN.** — UNIVERSITÆT: ENGELISCH-THEOLOGISCHE FACULTÆT. Der Theologischen Facultæt zu Tübingen Bedencken über die Frage: Ob die Mährische Brüder-Gemeine in Herrnhut supposito in doctrinam Evangelicam Consensu, bey ihren seit 300. Jahren her gehabten Einrichtungen und bekanter Disciplina Ecclesiastica verbleiben, und dennoch ihre Connexion mit der Evangelischen Kirchen behaupten könne und solle? Neue und ächte Auflage. sammt einigen Beylagen. Tübingen: Bey Christoph Heinrich Berger, 1735. 128 p., 4 l. 22 cm. (4°.) *KB 1735

See also: "The last responsorical Letters of the Theological Faculty at the University of Tübingen, to his Most Serene Highness the Duke of Würtemberg, against Count Zinzendorf. Translated from the original German. Dated: Tuebingen, May 8, 1747," in Henry Rimius, *A candid narrative of the rise and progress of the Herrnhuters*... Second edition, London, 1753, p. 105–120, *ZXHC*.
For literature on the Moravian Brethren, see the bibliography in J. T. Hamilton, *A history of the church known as the Moravian Church...during the eighteenth and nineteenth centuries*, Bethlehem, Pa., 1900, *ZXHC*.
Of special interest: Paul De Schweinitz, "The German Moravian settlements in Pennsylvania, 1735–1800," in Pennsylvania-German Society, *Proceedings*, Lancaster, Pa., 1894, v. 4, p. 54–72, *IEK;* Abraham Reincke, "A register of members of the Moravian Church and of persons attached to said church in this country and abroad, between 1727 and 1754," in Moravian Historical Society, *Transactions*, Nazareth, Pa., 1885, v. 1, p. 283–426, *IAA;* A. Grindely, *Geschichte der Böhmischen Brüder, 2. Aufl.*, Prag, 1861–62, *ZXHC; Quellen und Untersuchungen zur Geschichte der Böhmischen Brüder*, hrsg. von J. Goll, Prag, 1878–82, *ZXHC;* J. T. Mueller, *Geschichte der Böhmischen Brüder*, Herrnhut, 1922–31, *ZXHC;* E. A. De Schweinitz, "Some of the fathers of the American Moravian Church; a series of brief biographies," in Moravian Historical Society, *Transactions*, Nazareth, 1886, v. 2, p. 145–269, *IAA;* and "The autobiography of Abraham Luckenbach; translated from the German by H. E. Stocker," in Moravian Historical Society, *Transactions*, Nazareth, Pa., 1917, v. 10, p. 359–408, *IAA*.

**305. URLSPERGER, SAMUEL.** Der Ausführlichen Nachrichten Von der Königlich-Gross-Britannischen Colonie Saltzburgischer Emigranten in America. Erster [bis dritter] Theil. Worin Von der Gelegenheit und andern Umständen ihrer Aufnahme, ihrem dreyfachen Transport aus Teutschland nach Georgien in America, Beschaffenheit dieses Landes, Auskunft darin, erstem Anbau in Eben-Ezer, überstandenen mannigfaltigen Schwierigkeiten, schönem Zustand im geistlichen, auch nach und nach immer besser erfolgten äusserlichen Einrichtung, und andern dahin gehörigen Merckwürdigkeiten, ein umständlicher und bis auf das Ende des Jahres 1738. sich erstreckender Bericht ertheilet wird, Von der ersten ausführlichen Nachricht an bis zu der fünften Continuation derselben. Nebst einem vollständigen Register herausgegeben von Samuel Urlsperger... Halle: In Verlegung des Waysenhauses, MDCCXXXXI. [1735]–1752. 20 parts in 3 v. front. (port.), 2 folding maps, folding plan, folding table. illus. (music.) 21 x 17 cm. *KB 1735
De Renne, 1931, t. p. 57–68.
The "Nachricht," 1735, and 18 continuations, 1738–1752, were originally issued separately. Each has special title-page and "Vorrede" by Urlsperger. Some of the earlier continuations were reprinted in 1744. For continuation, 1754–1767, see his *Amerikanisches Ackerwerk Gottes (see* no. 350). The 13th–18th continuations have imprint "Halle und Augsburg. In Verlegung des Hallischen Waysenhauses."
For detailed collation of this work, see Library of Congress card.

*Contents:*

Appleton, N. Predigt...bey der Ordination des... Herrn Johann Sargent...1735, zu Deerfield. v. 1, 1st cont.
Belcher, J. ...Extract eines Briefes an den Editorem, aus Boston vom 26. mart. 1736. Aus dem Lateinischen... v. 1, 2nd cont.
Boltzius, J. M. Briefe und Extracte derselben... an den Editorem [1743–1751]. v. 3, 13th, 14th, 15th, 16th, 17th cont. (Ein gründliches Bedencken von der Schädligkeit Mohrensclaven in eine Colonie einzuführen. v. 3, 13th cont., 1st part.)
—— Nebendiarium, oder einige Anmerkungen aus dem Reiche der Natur... August, 1748. v. 3, 14th cont.
—— Zweyte Probe einiger aus dem Reiche der Natur im...Sept. 1748...gemachten Anmerkungen. v. 3, 15th cont.
—— ...Reise-Diarium...von Eben Ezer bis Charles-Town, und wieder zurück... [1734–1742.] v. 1, Ausführliche nachricht; v. 2, 11th cont.
—— Tageregister...[1747–1751.] v. 3, 13th cont., 2nd pt.-18th cont.
—— Zuverlässige Antwort auf einige vorbelegte Fragen die Landschaft Carolina betreffend, in welcher ...zugleich auf die Beschaffenheit der Colonie Georgien gesehen wird. v. 3, 18th cont.
Boltzius, J. M. Beschreibung des in Eben Ezer gefeyerten jährlichen Dankfestes, den 10. mart. 1744. v. 3, 13th cont., 2nd pt.
Boltzius, J. M., and I. C. Gronau. Einige merckwürdige hieher gehörige Briefe. [1733–1734.] v. 1. Ausführliche Nachricht.
—— Einige Briefe der Herrn Prediger in Eben Ezer. [1734–1741.] v. 1, 1st cont.–v. 2, 8th cont.
—— Auszüge einiger Schreiben...der...Prediger als auch etlicher Glieder der Gemeine... [1743.] v. 2, 10th cont.
—— Nachricht vom Einfall der Spanier in Carolina und Georgien...1742. v. 2, 9th cont.
—— Herrn Boltzii und...Gronau Reise-Diarium ...von Halle...nach Georgien. v. 1, Ausf. Nachr.
—— Tage-register...[1734–1743.] v. 1, 1st cont.; v. 2, 12th cont.
Colman, B. Schreiben des Herrn Collmanns...an den Editorem vom 22. mart. 1736. v. 1, 2nd cont.
Einige Briefe aus Eben Ezer von Anno 1742. v. 2, 9th cont.
Einiger Saltzburger ihre Briefe aus Eben Ezer... 1735, 1737 und 1738. v. 1, 2nd cont.
Extracte einiger aus London und Kensington an den Editorem...1749, erlassener Briefe. v. 3, 14th cont.
—— Kurze und gründliche Nachricht vom Evangelischen Armenhaus in Georgien anno 1752. v. 3, 18th cont.
Lemke, H. H. [Briefe und Extracte derselben...an den Editorem.] [1745–1751.] v. 3, 13th cont., 1st pt.-17th cont.
Massachusetts. Relation von der Conferentz...zu Deerfield...27. August...1735...zwischen...J. Belcher...und...Ountaussogor...v. 1, 1st cont.
Müller, J. G. ...Extract aus dem Reise-Diario vom 12. Iunii 1741... Ausmarsch des 4. Transports aus Augspurg bis den 17. Sept. einsd. a...v. 2, 9th cont.
Reck, P. G. F. von. Diarium von seiner Reise nach Georgien mit dem dritten Transport einiger...1735 dahin abgegangenen Emigranten...und Nachricht von den Indianern in America. v. 1, 2nd cont.
—— Eine...kurtze Nachricht von Georgien und denen dasigen Indianern. v. 1. Ausführl. Nachricht, 4. Stück.
Reck, P. G. F. von. Reise-Diarium...von Eben-Ezer ...nach denen Nord-Ländern von America, und von dar...nach England, Holland und Teutschland... [1734.] v. 1. Ausführl. Nachricht, 3. Stück.
Sanftleben, G. Extract aus dem... Reise-Diario, von Augspurg bis Eben Ezer. [1739.] v. 1, 4th cont.

*1735, continued*

**305. URLSPERGER, SAMUEL,** *continued*

Urlsperger, S. Copien von den Vocationen der Herren Prediger [Boltzius, Gronau und Lemke] in Eben Ezer. v. 3, 13th cont., 2nd pt.

—— ...Die den 17. may 1751. an dem Tage der Trauung des Editoris jüngsten Tochter Maria Magdalena Urlspergerin, mit Marx Friederich Kraus... gehaltene Rede. v. 3, 18th cont.

—— Eine Erinnerung der vor 20. Jahren geschehenen grossen Salzburgischen Emigration. v. 3, 17th cont.

—— Eine kurtze Aufmunterung zu einer...Liebes-Steuer für Eben Ezer...v. 1, 3rd cont.

Urlsperger, S. Eine schriftmässige Ermunterungsrede an die Ebenezerische Gemeine...statt einer... Vorrede... v. 3, 16th cont.

—— [Umständliche Nachricht von dem 4. Transport saltzburgischer Emigranten. 1741.] v. 2, 7th cont.

—— Umständlicher Vorbericht dessen, was bey der Aufnahme und Abschickung einiger Saltzburgischen Emigranten nach Georgien in America vorgegangen. v. 1. Ausführliche Nachricht, 4. Stück.

Vigera, ——. Diarium...von London bis Eben Ezer ...1741. v. 2, 9th cont.

Zuverlässige Nachricht von den preussischen Saltzburgern in Litthauen... [1741-1742.] v. 2, 8th cont.

Zwey Schreiben der zu Eben-Ezer in...Georgien etablirten ...saltzburgischen Emigranten.... I. Ein dancksagungs-schreiben an alle bisherige Wohlthäter ... II. Ein Ermahnungs-Schreiben an ihre...Lands-Leute in und ausser dem Reich...v. 1, 5th cont.

See also *An extract of the journals of Mr. Commissary Von Reck who conducted the first transport of Saltzburgers to Georgia: and of the Reverend Mr. Bolzius, one of their ministers,* London, 1734, \* KC 1734.
See also no. 668.

**306.** —— Second copy. 1735-1752. 20 parts in 17 v. 20½ cm. \*KB 1735
Some variations from preceding. See Public Catalogue for details.

**307.** —— Die Sammlung und Führung des rvten Transports saltzburgischer Emigranten und nach Eben-Ezer in dem americanischen Georgien von den Hn. Hn. Trustees in London gnädig beruffenen gross-brittannischen Colonisten: das ist: Eine ausführliche Nachricht: wie sie zu diesem Beruff gekommen, was ihnen bey ihrem Aufbruch, auf dem March bis nach Canstatt, und vor, bey und nach ihrer Embarquirung daselbst auf dem Nekkar, vor vieles Gute, sonderlich von dem Hertzogthum Würtemberg wiederfahren; als ein Beweiss des noch lebenden alten guten Gottes, zu seinem Preis, und zur Stärckung des Glaubens in diesen Zeiten, auch aus Danckbarkeit gegen die respective höchste, hohe, und andere Christliche Wohlthäter dieses Transports und der eben-ezerischen Gemeine, besonders ediret von Samuel Urlsperger... Halle: In Verlegung des Waysenhauses, 1741. 52 p. table. 4°. \*KB 1735
De Renne, 1931, I, 97-98.
A reprint of the "Vorrede" to the "Siebente Continuation der ausführlichen Nachricht von den Saltzburgischen Emigranten," Halle, 1741.
Bound with his: Der Ausführlichen Nachrichten... Halle, 1741 [1735]-1752. 7th continuation, 2nd copy. *See* no. 306.

**308.** —— Zuverlässiges Sendschreiben von den geist- und leiblichen Umständen der Saltzburgischen Emigranten, die sich in America niedergelassen haben, wie sich solche bis den 1sten September 1735. befunden, und von denen Herren Predigern in Eber Ezer und einigen Saltzburgern selbst nach Teutschland überschrieben worden... Halle: In Verlegung des Waysenhauses, 1736. 14 p. 20½ cm. \*KB 1735 Urlsperger
With his: Der Ausführlichen Nachrichten... Halle, 1741 [1735]-1752. Ausführliche Nachricht [copy 1]. *See* no. 305.
See De Renne, 1931, I, 69.
There is a second copy of this in copy 2. *See* no. 306.

**309. VOLLSTÄNDIGE** So wohl Historisch- als Theologische Nachricht Von der Herrnhuthischen Brüderschafft, Wie solche einige Jahre daher in der Ober-Lausitz hat wollen überhand nehmen, und sich von dannen hie und da durch gantz Teutschland, Schweitz, Holland, Dännemarck, Pensylvanien, besonders aber und vornemlich unter denen Normännern und Lappländern ausgebreitet, Durch eine nach Herrenhuth angestellte Reise persönlich eingeholet, Und allen denenjenigen So die reine Evangel. Wahrheit in der Krafft der wahren Gottseligkeit lieb haben, zu genauerer Prüfung und höchst-nöthigen Vorsicht, Mit vielen selbst erkannten Specialibus entdecket, Und mit nützlichen und Lehr-reichen Supplementis erläutert, Uber dieses auch mit einer zwar kurtzen doch deutlich- und gründlichen Refutation des Tübingischen Bedenckens über die Mährische Brüderschafft zu Herrenhuth versehen Von einem Liebhaber reiner und unverfälschter Wahrheit die zur wahren und ungeheuchelten Gottseligkeit führet, der zum Wahlspruch hat: Prüfet alles, und das Gute behaltet, 1 Thess. v, 21. Auf Kosten des Autoris. Franckfurt und Leipzig, 1735. 4 p.l., 163 p. 21 cm. (4°.) \*KB 1735
See also nos. 304, 313A, 314, 323, 365.

**1738**

**310. JUBILÆUM** Theatri Europæi, Das ist, Der die Geschichts-Erzehlung von Einhundert Jahren beschliessende Ein und Zwantzigste Theil Desselbigen... Franckfurth am Mayn: gedruckt im Jahr Christi 1738. 7 p.l., 500, 467, 502 p., 15 l., plates, maps. illus. f°.
† BTWA (Theatrum)
Year, 1716: "West-Indische Flotte kommt an," p. 350.

**311. NEU-EINGERICHTETE** und vermehrte Bilder-Geographie, Von Europa, Asia, Africa und America, Worinnen Alle Nationen nach ihrem Habit in saubern Figuren, Anbey die Länder nach ihrer Lage, Flüssen, Climate, Fruchtbarkeit, Beschaffenheit der Einwohner, Religion, vornehmsten Städten, Commercien Macht, Regiment und Merckwürdigkeiten vorgestellet werden! Nebst einem vollständigen Register. Erffurth: Verlegt von Johann Michael Funcken, Buchh, und Universitäts-Buchdrucker, 1738. 8 p.l., 592 p., 28 l. incl. front. illus, 8°. \*KB 1738
"Vorrede" signed: Joh. Jacob Martini.
A new edition, with additional woodcuts, of "Neueröffnetes Amphi-theatrum, worinnen...alle Nationen nach ihrem Habit, in saubern Figuren repräsentiret," issued by the same publisher, 1723 [-1728].
See F. J. Lipperheide, *Katalog der Freiherrlich von Lipperheide'schen Kostümbibliothek,* Berlin, 1896-1905, no. 36, † MMB.

## 1740

312. EGEDE, HANS POULSEN. Ausführliche und wahrhafte Nachricht vom Anfange und Fortgange der Gronländischen Mission, wobey die Beschaffenheit des Landes sowohl, als auch die Gebräuche und Lebens-Arten der Einwohner beschrieben werden, getreulich angemerckt und aufgezeichnet von Hans Egede, Ehemahligen Lehrer...bey der Gemeine zu Wogen in Norwegen, und nachmahligen Königl. Dänischen Missionario in Gronland. Hamburg: Bey Christian Wilhelm Brandt, 1740. 8 p.l., 288 p. 4°. \*KB 1740
Sabin 22023.

## 1741

313. WALDO, SAMUEL. Kurtze Beschreibung derer Landschafft Massachusetts-Bay in Neu-Engellandt, Absonderlich dess Landstrichs an der Breyton Bay, so dem Königlichen Britischen Obristen, Samuel Waldo, Erbherrn der Breyten Bay, zugehörig, sampt denen Hauptbedingungen nacher welchen sich fremde Portestanten daselbsten ansiedlen mögen. Speyer, getruckt und zu haben in der Götselschen Truckerey-Anstalt, 1741. (Der Deutsche Pionier. Cincinnati, Ohio, 1882. 8°. Bd. 14, p. 10–13.)   IEK
The text is copied from an original in the records of 1784 of the Court of Massachusetts.
See Meynen, no. 255.

## 1742

313A. BÜDINGISCHE Sammlung Einiger In die Kirchen-Historie Einschlagender Sonderlich neuerer Schriften. Erster [-zweiter] Band... Büdingen: Gedruckt bey J. C. Stöhr, 1742–1743. 2 v. 8°.   \*KB 1742
A collection of letters and papers relating to the Moravian Brethren, including many by Zinzendorf. Three volumes were issued, of the projected twelve. Meynen (p. 155–157) gives a detailed summary.
The British Museum catalogue mentions, under Budingen Collection: *Etliche zu dieser Zeit nicht unnütze Fragen über einige Schrifft-Stellen, welche von den Liebhabern der lautern Wahrheit deutlich erörtert zu werden gewünschet hat ein Wahrheit-Forschender in America, im Jahr 1742* [etc.], [and] *Diarium der Heyden-Boten unter den Indianern in Schecomeko*, 1742, Stueck 14.
See also nos. 304, 309, 314, 323, 365.

314. ZINZENDORF, NICOLAUS LUDWIG, GRAF VON. Des Herrn Grafen Ludwig von Zinzendorff Sieben Letzte Reden So Er In der Gemeine, Vor seiner am 7. Aug. erfolgten abermahligen Abreise nach America, gehalten. Büdingen: Gedruckt bey Johann Christoph Stöhr, 1742. 79 p. 8°.   \*KB 1742
A few of Count Zinzendorff's poems relating to America are not in the Library.
In 1742, an anonymous pamphlet, *A compendious extract containing the chiefest articles of doctrine and most remarkable transactions of Count Lewis of Zinzendorff and the Moravians*, Philadelphia [1742], was published. It was answered by Zinzendorf in his *The remarks which the author of the Compendious extract, &c. in the preface to his book, has friendly desired of the Rev. of Thurenstein* [pseud.] *for the time pastor of the Lutheran congregation of J. C. in Philadelphia*, Philadelphia, 1742, \* KD 1742.

315. ——— Pennsylvanische Nachrichten Von dem Reiche Christi, anno 1742. [Büdingen: Johann Christoph Stöhr, 1742?] 191 p. 18 cm.
See Seidenstricker, p. 16–18.   \*KB 1742
*Contents:* B. Ludewigs wahrer Bericht, de dato Germantovu, den 20. Febr. 1741½ an seine liebe Teutsche, und wem es sonst nützlich zu wissen ist, wegen sein und seiner Brüder Zusammenhanges mit Pennsylvania, zu Prüfung der Zeit und Umstände ausgefertiget; nebst einem p. s. de dato Philadelphia, den 5. martii. und einigen unsre Lehre überhaupt, und dieses Schrifftgen insonderheit, erläuteruden Beylagen, p. [3]–47.

## 1743

316. BOCK, FRIEDRICH SAMUEL. Kurz gefasste Missions Geschicht, oder merkwürdige Nachrichten von den in neuern Zeiten angewandten Bemühungen die Heyden zum Christlichen Glauben zu bekehren. Auss den eigenen Schriften dieser Lehrer zur Erbauung der Gemeine Jesu ans Licht gestellet von Friedrich Samuel Bock... Königsberg: Druck und Verlag Johann Heinrich Hartungs, 1743. 23(1), 336 p., 6 1. 17½ cm. (8°.)   \*KB 1743
*Contents:* I. Von dem Heydenthum überhaupt, p. 1–30. II. Von den Anstalten der paebstischen Kirche zur Bekehrung der Heyden, p. 31–82. III. Von den Bemuehungen der Evangelischen, die Heyden zu bekehren überhaupt, und den deshalb gestifteten Gesellschaften, p. 83–102. IV. Von den daenischen Missionen in den Landschaften der Heyden, p. 102–204. V. Von den Missionen der Engelaender in Ost- und Westindien, p. 205–242. VI. Von den Bemuehungen der Hollaender die Heyden zum christlichen Glauben zu bringen, p. 242–257. VII. Von den schwedischen Missionen, insonderheit in Lappland, p. 257–270. VIII. Von der russischen Mission unter den Ostiaken, p. 271–281. X. Von einigen Mitteln, welche dieselbe befoerdern koennten, p. 323–336.
p. 177–202 describes Hans Poulsen Egede's missionary activities. See no. 312. Of special interest are p. 26–30, describing the religion of the Indians, and p. 236–242, dealing with Daniel Weissiger's report in the *Sammlungen auserlesener Materien zum Bau des Reiches Gottes*, Stück. 24, p. 973 (see no. 317), which describes the religious situation in Pennsylvania.
His *Einleitung in die Kenntniss der Reiche und Staaten der Welt*, Koenigsberg, 1745 (Sabin 6104), is not in the Library.

## 1744

317. KURTZE Nachricht von einigen evangelischen Gemeinen in America. Halle: In Verlegung des Wäysenhauses, 1744. 24 p. 4°. Sabin 51694, 60185, 78013.   \*KB 1744
First edition of the first of the so-called "Hallische Nachrichten."
Daniel Weissiger whose *Kurtze Nachricht aus America*, published in Hildesheim, in 1734 (p. 5) is quoted as follows: "Wir leben in einem Lande voller Ketzerey und Secten, stehen in äusserstem Mangel und Armuth unserer Seelen, und sind nicht im Stande mit unsern eigenen Mitteln uns daraus zu erretten, wo uns GOtt nicht anderwärtige Hülfe und Mittel zeiget, und ist jämmerlich zu-beweinen dass die grosse Haufe der heranwachsenden Jugend, welche nicht weiss, was linck [sic!] oder recht ist, und ist wegen Ermangelung von Kirchen und Schulen, wo nicht bald Hülfe geschicht, zu befürchten, dass die meisten auf schwere Irrwege verleitet werden mögten." On p. 3–4, a Nachricht of similar contents is quoted to have appeared in the *Sammlungen auserlesener Materien zum Bau des Reiches Gottes*, Stück 24, p. 973. See note on 316. The departure of Henry Melchior Mühlenberg (see no. 1482) is related on p. 6.
See Charles Lewis Maurer, *Early Lutheran education in Pennsylvania*, Philadelphia, 1932, *SSL*; also

## 1744, continued

**317. KURTZE Nachricht..., continued**

Johann Caspar Stöver, *Kurtze Nachricht von einer Evangelisch-Lutherischen Deutschen Gemeinde in dem Americanischen Virginien,* Hannover, 1737. Sabin 91984. Not in the Library. "Stoever was the first Lutheran pastor in Virginia." — *cf.* Cassell, *Finck and Henkel's history of the Lutheran Church in Virginia,* 1930, p. 36.
Contains several references to the Salzburgers.
Review: *Allgemeine deutsche Bibliothek.* Jahrg. 25, Anhang 5, p. 2668-2673, *NAA.*

**318. URLSPERGER, SAMUEL.** Ausführliche Nachricht Von den Saltzburgischen Emigranten, Die sich in America niedergelassen haben. Worin, Nebst einem Historischen Vorbericht von dem ersten und andern Transport derselben, Die Reise-Diaria Des Königlichen Gross-Britannischen Commissarii und der beyden Saltzburgischen Prediger, wie auch eine Beschreibung von Georgien imgleichen verschiedene hierzu gehörige Briefe enthalten. Herausgegeben von Samuel Urlsperger... Halle: In Verlegung des Wäysenhauses, 1744. 7 p.l., 242 p., front. (ports.), folding map. 20½ cm. *KB 1744
First published 1735, afterwards re-issued as first part of "Der Ausführlichen Nachrichten...erster [bis dritter] Theil..." Halle, 1741-1752. 3 v. 21 cm.
*See* nos. 305, 306.

**319. WEISER, CONRAD.** Conrad Weiser's Tagebuch. Herausgegeben von I. D. Rupp (Der Deutsche Pionier. Cincinnati, O., 1870. 8°. Bd. 2, p. 182-186, 216-221.) IEK
Written about 1744.
An English translation was published in *Early western travels, 1748-1846,* Cleveland, 1904, v. 1, p. 15-44, *IW.* For several tracts on the author, see the Public Catalogue. Of special interest is: Pennsylvania (colony). — Treaties, *Minutes of conferences, held with the Indians, at Harris's Ferry, and at Lancaster, in March, April, and May, 1757,* Philadelphia, 1757, †* *KD 1757;* it contains "The report of Conrad Weiser, the Indian interpreter of his journey to Shamokin on the affairs of Virginia and Maryland; his mediation for adjusting the differences between the Indians of the Six Nations and these provinces, delivered to the Governor in Council, the 21st day of April 1743," p. 20-22.
As to Conrad Weiser, see Friedrich Kapp, "Die Deutschen im Staate New York während des achtzehnten Jahrhunderts," in *Geschichtsblätter, Bilder und Mittheilungen aus dem Leben der Deutschen in Amerika,* 1884, Bd. 1, IEK.

## 1746

**320. ANDERSON, JOHANN.** Herrn Johann Anderson... Nachrichten von Island, Grönland und der Strasse Davis, zum wahren Nutzen der Wissenschaften und der Handlung. Mit Kupfern, und einer nach den neuesten und in diesem Werke angegebenen Entdeckungen, genau eingerichteten Landcharte. Nebst einem Vorberichte von den Lebensumständen des Herrn Verfassers... Hamburg: Verlegts Georg Christian Grund, 1746. 15 p.l., 328 p., 6 l. front., plates, folding map. 20 cm. *KB 1746
Sabin 1405.
Based on Hans Egede's work. "Vorbericht" signed: Z * * * [i. e. J. G. Winckler].
Anhang: Dictionariolvm (Danish-German-Eskimo); Appendix formularum loquendi usitatissimarum [etc.], p. 285-328.
For a later edition, see no. 324.

**321. FRESENIUS, JOHANN PHILIP.**...Bewährte Nachrichten von Herrnhutischen Sachen. Sammlung 1 [-8]. Franckfurt am Mayn: J. L. Buchner, 1746-1751. 8 v. in 1. 12°. ZXHC
Bd. 3, Stück 3 contains: Americanische Nachrichten Von Herrnhutischen Sachen, p. 87-872.
*See* Meynen, p. 157-160, in which a summary of Fresenius's Pastoral-Sammlungen is given. The 12th part of the Sammlungen containing several articles on America is not in the Library.
See also the English version of 1762, *ZXHP.*

**322. [KRAMER, JOHANN MATTHIAS.]** Neueste und richtigste Nachricht von der Landschaft Georgia in dem Engelländischen Amerika. Worinnen enthalten 1. Die Original-Berichte, welche die Königlichen Commissarien über die Beschaffenheit dieser Landschaft eingeschicket haben. 2. Ein zuverlässiger Bericht derer vornehmsten Privilegien, Freyheiten und Wohlthaten, so alle diejenigen zu geniessen haben, die sich in dieser fruchtbaren Provinz häusslich niederlassen; Nebst einem Unterricht für selbige zu ihrer Dahinreise. Durchaus mit Anmerkungen der Uebersetzer bey seinem vieljährigen Aufenthalt in Amerika angestellet hat, begleitet von J. M. K. Göttingen: Aus der Universitäts Buchdruckerei, Verlegts Johann Peter Schmid, 1746. 88 p. 18 cm. (8°.)
Sabin 56848. *KB 1746
Entered under Kramer in Meusel's *Lexikon,* v. 7, p. 314.
*Contents:* Erste Abtheilung. Von der Lage und Beskerung oder Bepflanzung; Gesetze und Regierung, deren Sicherheit, Luft, Fruchtbarkeit, Handlung und anders überhaupt. Contains a list of prices for victuals. Zweyte Abtheilung. Von den Freiheiten und Privilegien, so Se. Königliche Gross-Britannische Majestät der Provinz Georgia allergnädigst verliehen...und auf was Weise Erlaubnis gegeben wird, sich daselbst häusslich nieder zu lassen und solcher Freiheiten zu geniessen. Dritte Abtheilung. Von denen verschiedenen Wohlthaten und Vortheilen, die die Provinz Georgia vor vielen andern Ländern von Europa, und selbst einigen der übrigen americanischen Provinzen hat; So alle um der Protestantisch-Evangelischen Religion und Wahrheit willen verjagt oder sonsten in ihrem Vaterlande nicht fortkommen könnende nahrungslose Menschen bewegen können, vor andern Oertern ihre Zuflucht dahin zu nehmen. Vierte und lezte Abtheilung. Von der nötigen Beschaffenheit und Tüchtigkeit, so alle diejenigen haben müssen, welchen Erlaubniss gegeben...sich in der Provinz Georgia häusslich niederzulassen. Promotion literature.
Note: *Neu-Gefundenes Eden. Oder ausführlicher Bericht von Süd und Nord Carolina, Pensilphania, Mary Land & Virginia,* 1737 (Sabin 52362), is not in the Library.
"This new-found Eden, or a detailed account of South and North Carolina, Pennsylvania, Maryland, and Virginia is the result of two journeys made through these provinces, and includes considerable correspondence, which bears on the condition of the country, contains also full information concerning its resources, evidently intended to influence emigration." — *Sabin.*

**323. PHILORTHODOXO, CHRISTIAN, pseud.** Ungeheuchelte Theologische Unterredung welche in Philadelphia zwischen dem Grafen Haubold Xaverius von Bourignon und dem Grafen Ludwig Heinrich von Guion von des Grafen Nicol. Ludwigs von Zinzendorfs Leben, Hochmuth, Indifferentisterey, Staats-Maximen und Mährischen Brüdern 1745. gehalten und der Wahrheit zum Besten ans Licht gestellet worden von Christian Philorthodoxo. Jena und Leipzig: verlegts Christian Friedrich Gollner, 1746. 1 p.l., 46 p. sq. 4°. *KB 1746
A defence of Zinzendorf and the doctrine of the Moravian Brethren.

## 1747

**324.** ANDERSON, JOHANN. Herrn Johann Anderson... Nachrichten von Island, Grönland und der Strasse Davis, zum wahren Nutzen der Wissenschaften und der Handlung. Mit Kupfern, und einer nach den neuesten und in diesem Werke angegebenen Entdeckungen, genau eingerichteten Landcharte. Nebst einem Vorberichte von den Lebensumständen des Herrn Verfassers. Frankfurt und Leipzig, 1747. 15 p.l., 368 p., 4 l., frontis., 1 folding map, 4 folding plates. 8°. *KB 1747
Sabin 1405.
For an earlier issue, see no. 320.

## 1748

**325.** BANDINI, ANGELO MARIA. Americus Vespucci, eines florenzischen Edelmannes, Leben und nachgelassene Briefe, worinnen dessen Entdeckungen der neuen Welt und die Merckwürdigkeiten seiner Reisen historisch und geographisch beschrieben werden. Aus dem Italienischen des Herrn Abts Angelus Maria Bandini übersetzet, und mit Anmerkungen erläutert. Hamburg: bey Georg Christian Grund, und in Leipzig, bey Adam Heinrich Holle, 1748. 5 p.l., 299(1) p., 4 l., frontis. illus. 8°.
Sabin 3150. *KB 1748
Frontispiece signed: F. Rolffsen Hamburg, 1747.
*Contents:* 1. Von dem Ursprunge des Geschlechts Vespucci und den berühmten Männern desselben. 2. Von Americus Geburt, Auferziehung und Studien. 3. Von seinen Reisen. 4. Kurze Ausschweifung, darinnen untersuchet wird, wem eigentlich Americus die Nachricht von seinen Seereisen zugeschrieben habe. 5. Es werden darinnen die Verrichtungen Americus nach Vollendung seiner vier Reisen angemerket, und zugleich wird von der Zeit seines Todes gehandelt. 6. Man zeiget hieselbst, dass Americus der wahre Erfinder der neuen Welt gewesen sey. 7. Von den Bildnissen, die man von Americus gemacht hat, und den Schriftstellern, die desselben mit Ruhm erwähnet haben. Then follows: Americus Vespucci Brief von den Eylaendern, die er auf seinen vier Seereisen entdecket hat. Die erste Reise, p. 155-195. Die zweyte Reise, p. 195-209. Die dritte Reise, p. 209-221. Die vierte Reise, p. 222-229.
Three letters by Vespucci follow: 1. Brief gerichtet an Lorenz, Peter Franciscus von Medici Sohn, darinnen eine umständliche Erzählung von seiner zweyten Reise enthalten ist, die derselbe auf Befehl des Königs in Spanien unternommen hat; itzo zum erstenmale aus Licht gestellt, p. 230-257. 2. Eine noch ungedruckte Nachricht von der Ausschickung eines Geschwaders, die der König in Portugall nach dem Vorgebirge der guten Hoffnung und der Stadt Calicut veranstaltet hat; gerichtet an den hochansehnlichen Herrn Lorenz, Peter Franciscus von Medici Sohn, von Americus Vespucci, p. 258-274. 3. Americus Vespucci Brief, von seiner dritten Reise, die derselbe auf Befehl des Königes in Portugall nach Brasilien gethan hat. Von diesem glaubte man bisher, dass er an Peter Soderini gerichtet gewesen; itzo aber hat man befunden, mittelst einer alten lateinischen Uebersetzung desselben, dass er an Lorenz, Peter Franciscus von Medici Sohn, abgelassen worden, p. 275-299.
Note: Emil Sarnow und Kurt Trübenbach, *Drucke und Holzschnitte des 15. und 16. Jahrhunderts in getreuer Nachbildung*, Strassburg, 1903, is not in the Library.

**325A.** EINE KRONE Georgs I. Königs von Grossbritannien u.s.w. von A. 1723. (Köhlers [Johann David] im Jahr 1748... Historischen Müntz-Belustigung, Nürnberg [1748]. 8°. Theil 20, p. 233-240.) MHA
This is also Stück 30, dated: 24 Jul. 1748.
New American coins, p. 240.

**326.** NACHRICHT von dem Zustand der Saltzburgischen Emigranten in Georgien. (Europäische Staats-Cantzley. Nürnberg, 1748. 8°. [Theil 93,] p. 757-763.) BTA
Dated: Eben Ezer in Georgien Febr. 10th, 1746.
Signed: Sämmtliche Saltzburgische Einwohner zu Eben-Ezer in Georgien.

**327.** [SCHULTZE, BENJAMIN.] Orientalisch- und occidentalischer Sprachmeister, welcher nicht allein hundert Alphabete nebst ihrer Aussprache, So bey denen meisten Europäisch-Asiatisch- Africanisch- und Americanischen Völckern und Nationen gebräuchlich sind, Auch einigen Tabulis Polyglottis verschiedener Sprachen und Zahlen vor Augen leget, Sondern auch das Gebet des Herrn, In 200 Sprachen und Mund-Arten mit dererselben Characteren und Lesung, nach einer Geographischen Ordnung mittheilet. Aus glaubwürdigen Auctoribus zusammen getragen, und mit darzu nöthigen Kupfern versehen. Leipzig: Zu finden bey Christian Friedrich Gessnern, 1748. 12 p.l., 4-219(1) p., 3 l., 4-128 p., 7 l. plates, tables. illus. 8°. *KB 1748
Dedication signed: Benj. Schultze. Preface signed: Johann Friedrich Fritz.
*Contents:* I. Alphabete derer Europäisch-Asiatisch-Africanisch- und Americanischen Völcker, p. 1-172. II. Von denen Ziffern oder Zahlen Europäisch-Asiatisch-Africanisch- und Americanischer Völcker, p. 173-219. III. Orationis Dominicae Versiones Plurium Linguarum Europaearum, Asiaticarum, Africanarum et Americanarum. Appendix, p. 4-128.
"The prefatory epistle is by B. Schultze, but the compilation of the text is mainly the work of J. F. Fritz, under whose name it properly belongs. Pages 124-127 of the second part contain specimens of the Lord's Prayer in eight American languages, namely Mexicana, Poconchia, Caraibia, Savanahica, Mohogica, Karivica, and Guaranica sive Brasilica." — *Sabin*. See also Sabin 78008 for another edition: Naumburg und Zeitz, 1769.

## 1750

**328.** ELLIS, HENRY. Reise nach Hudsons Meerbusen, welche von zweyen Englischen Schiffen, der Dobbs-Galley und California, in den Jahren 1746 und 1747. wegen Entdeckung einer nordwestlichen Durchfahrt in die Süds-See verrichtet worden, nebst einer richtigen Abzeichnung der Küste, und einer kurzen Naturgeschichte des Landes, Beschreibung der Einwohner, auch einer wahren Vorstellung der Umstände und Gründe, welche die künftige Erfindung einer solchen Durchfahrt wahrscheinlich machen, beschrieben von Heinrich Ellis... aus dem Englischen übersetzt, und mit Anmerkungen aus andern hieher gehörigen Schriftstellern versehen. Mit Kupfertafeln und zwoen neuen Karten von Hudsons Meerbusen und den angränzenden Ländern. Göttingen: Verlegts Abram Vandenhoeck, 1750. 12 p.l., 364 p., 5 l., 2 maps, 9 plates. 8°. (Sammlung neuer und merkwürdiger Reisen zu Wasser und zu Lande. Theil 1.) *KB 1750
Sabin 22314.
The English original appeared in London in 1748 under the title, *A voyage to Hudson's-Bay...*, *KC 1748.

*1750, continued*

329. HISTORISCHE Anmerkungen was sich von Anno 1750 an, folgentlich bisz 1775 mit den Schwenkfeldern, merkliches Verlauffen; [and] Historische Anmerkungen was sich von Anno 1775 an folgentl mit den Schwenckfeldern merkliches zugetragen; worin auch einige Begebenheiten in vorigen Jahren sich ereignet, mit angeführt werden, um die Sachen einiger Massen in ihrem Zusammenhang vorstellig Zumachen. (Americana Germanica. New York, etc., 1898. 4°. v. 2, no. 1, p. 47–69.)
NFCA (German)
Title of periodical changed to German American annals.
See H. W. Kriebel, *Die Schwenckfelders in Pennsylvania, a historical sketch*, Lancaster, 1904 (Pennsylvania German Society, Proceedings and addresses, v. 13, *IEK*).
See also no. 461.

330. HISTORISCHE und Geographische Beschreibung von Neu-Schottland, darinnen von der Lage, Grösse, Beschaffenheit, Fruchtbarkeit und besondern Eigenschaften des Landes, wie auch von den Sitten und Gewohnheiten der Indianer, und von den merckwürdigsten Begebenheiten, so sich zwischen denen Cronen Franckreich und England seit deren Besitznehmung zugetragen, hinlängliche Nachrichtertheilet wird. Auf Befehl Seiner Grossbrittanischen Majestät Georg II. und des Parlements in Englischer Sprache verfasset, Nunmehro aber ins teutsche übersetzet. Franckfurt und Leipzig: Bey Heinrich Ludwig Brönner, 1750. 2 p.l., 216 p., frontis. (folding map.) 8°. *KB 1750
Sabin 56138.
Translated from *A geographical history of Nova Scotia*, London, 1749, * KC 1749.
Meynen (no. 256) mentions as the translator "den Agenten Köhler."

331. EIN SCHREIBEN aus Carolina an einen guten Freund in London von der Klapperschlange. (Sammlung kleiner Ausführungen... Hannover, 1750. 8°. Bd. 1, p. 47–48.) *DF
Signed: A.

332. ZORGDRAGER, CORNELIUS GIJSBERTSZ. Cornelius Gisbert Zorgdragers Beschreibung des Grönländischen Wallfischfangs und Fischerey, nebst einer gründlichen Abhandlung von dem Bakkeljau- und Stockfischfang bey Terreneuf, und einer kurzen Abhandlung von Grönland, Island, Spitzbergen, Nova Zembla, Jan Mayen Eiland, der Strasse Davids u. a. Aus dem Holländischen übersezt, und mit accuraten Kupfern und Land-Charten gezieret. Nürnberg: Bey Georg Peter Monath, 1750. 3 p.l., 370 p. 5 l., frontis., maps, plates. 4°. *KB 1750
The Dutch original was published in Amsterdam in 1720 under the title, *C: G: Zorgdragers Bloeyende opkomst der aloude en hedendaagsche Groenlandsche visschery*, * KB 1720.

**1751**

333. ACHENWALL, GOTTFRIED. Entwurf einer politischen Betrachtung über die Zunahme des Goldes und Abnahme des Silbers in Europa. (Sammlung kleiner Ausführungen... Hannover, 1752–1753. 8°. Bd. 1, p. 343–351; Bd. 2, p. 170–183.) *DF
Second installment has different title: Anmerkungen über die den 93ten Stücke des vergangen Jahres...
Achenwall defends his opinion against an attack, made by Herr S*** in *Sammlung kleiner Ausführungen*, Hannover, 1751, Stück 17.
Export of American gold to Europe and its effect on the European monetary system.

334. CRESPEL, EMMANUEL. Des Ehrwürdigen Pater Emanuel Crespels merkwürdige Reisen nach Canada, daselbst gehabte Begebenheiten, und erlittener Schifbruch bey seiner Heimreise nach Franckreich; der bewunderswürdigen Vorfälle wegen aus dem Französischen übersezt. Franckfurt und Leipzig: Bey Georg Peter Monath, 1751. 4 p.l., 112 p. 8°. *KF 1751
Sabin 17478.
Preface signed: Ludwig Crespel.
Interleaved with English translation in manuscript, by L. E. Chittenden.

335. VON dem zwischen der Cron Spanien und Gross-Brittannien getroffenen Compensations-Tractat den Assiento der Negers, und das jährliche Schiff nach West-Indien betreffend. Num. 1[–II]. (Europäische Staats-Cantzley. Franckfurt und Leipzig [1751]. 8°. Theil 100, p. 221–228.) BTA
Num. II has sub-title: Compensations-Tractat wegen des Neger-Handels und des Permiss-Schiffes nach America, wie solcher zwischen Spanien und Gross-Brittannien am 5. Octobr. 1750. errichtet worden.
This treaty concerning slave-trade is a substitute for article XVI in the treaty of Aachen. See *Europäische Staats Cantzley*, Theil 99, Capitel VIII, BTA.

336. DES ZU Wasser und Lande weit und breit herumreisenden und weltberühmten Leonhardi Mirifici, eines Americanischen Passagiers, seltsame und sehr merckwürdige Begebenheiten, Worinnen nicht allein dessen wunderliche von vornehmen Frauenzimmer gespielte Liebes-Händel angemercket, sondern auch dessen ausgeübte Heldenthaten ausführlich zu lesen sind, Welche der curieusen Welt zum Vergnügen entworffen D. N. H. Franckfurt und Leipzig, 1751. 1 p.l., 188 p., frontis. 8°. *KL
Running title: Begebenheiten eines americanischen Passagiers. Fiction.

**1752**

337. ABSCHRIFT einer Vollmacht, welche Kapitain Heerbrand an seine Unterwerber ausstellte. [Heilbronn am Neckar: 1752.] (Der Deutsche Pionier. Cincinnati, O., 1882. 8°. Bd. 14, p. 357.) IEK
See also Meynen, nos. 125–144, this chapter being entitled "Die Auswanderung aus der Heimat."

338. ABSCHRIFT eines Beschlusses des Rathes der kaiserlichen Stadt Nürnberg, in Angelegenheiten Romingers. [1752?] (Der Deutsche Pionier. Cincinnati, O., 1882. 8°. Bd. 14, p. 357.) IEK
Persons who want to emigrate from Nürnberg to New England must get permission to do so from the "Rath."

*1752, continued*

339. FORMULAR eines Kontrakts, welchen Kapt. Jakob Friedrich Heerbrand von den durch seine Leute Angeworbenen unterzeichnen liess. [1752?] (Der Deutsche Pionier. Cincinnati, O., 1882. 8°. Bd. 14, p. 356–357.)   IEK
The original is said to be printed on a folio sheet. The following postscriptum is added: N. B. Drey Exemplare der anbey letzt genannten Contract-Articuln, unterschrieben von unterscheidliche Leuthen in unterscheidlichen Provintzen des Reichs, absonderlich Franken und Nürnberg, seynd an Herrn Crell zu Cölln, (Mai 31. Juny 1.) gesandt worden. Rominger, ein Helfer des Heerbrand, welcher genöthigt worden, den 25ten letztverwichenen May auss Nürnberg sich zu verbergen, allwo er gedachte Leuthe am 26ten May sich zu versammlen bestimmete, hat selbige zu Frankfurt zurückgelassen, sammt denen Stücken gezeichnet No. 32 und 33, sowie alle übrige Briefschaften des Heerbrand.

340. LE BEAU, CLAUDE. Des Hrn. Claudii Le Beau... neue Reise unter die Wilden in Nord-America; oder merkwürdige Nachricht von den alten und neuen Gebräuchen und Sitten samt der Lebensart dieser Völker, nebst der Beschreibung seiner sonderbaren Begebenheiten: mit Kupfern und einer Landkarte. In das Deutsche übersetzt von Johann Bernhard Nack... Frankfurt und Leipzig: Bey den Gebrüdern van Düren, 1752. 2 v. in 1. map, plates. 8°.   *KF 1752
Sabin 39584.
"Was mich angehet, so habe ich den Vortheil gehabt, mit diesen Völkern, welche wir Barbaren nennen umzugehen." — *Vorrede des Verfassers.*
*Contents:* I. Der Verfasser zeiget die Ursachen an, welche ihn veranlasset haben, nach America zu reisen. II. Wie der Verfasser an den Bord des Elephanten aufgenommen worden... III. Abreise des Schiffes Taufe an der grossen Bank von Neuland, mit der Beschreibung des Flusses St. Laurentii. IV. Schiffbruch des Verfassers. Sitten und Aufführung der Einwohner von Canada. v. Ankunft des Verfassers zu Quebec... VI. Kurze Beschreibung der Städte Trois Riviers und Montreal, und der Handlung der Wilden. VII. Abreise des Verfassers mit Wilden... VIII. Beschwerlichkeit des Verfassers bey dem ersten Lasttragen. IX. Der Verfasser wird von sieben Canadiern und acht Wilden überfallen. X. Die Art, wie die Wilden ihre Nachen tragen. XI. Unbegreifliche Beschwerlichkeit des Verfassers... XII. Seltsame Begebenheit,...mit den Iroquoisen. XIII. Wie die Wilden...zu Kriegsdiensten angenommen werden. XIV. Die Iroquoisen noethigen den Verfasser, dass er seine Briefe an der Spitze einer Stange tragen soll. XV. Der Verfasser trifft...einen Vater einer wilden Familie mit seinen drey Kindern an. XVI. Einfalt der Wilden in Religionssachen. XVII. Fortsetzung der Kriegsergötzlichkeit. XVIII. Die Wilden noethigen den Verfasser zum Tanzen. XIX. Beschreibung des Bibers. XX. Vortreffliche Meinung der Huronen über die Unsterblichkeit der Seelen. Zweyter Theil. XXI. Ankunft des Verfassers zu Naranzouac. XXII. Beschreibung von Naranzouac. XXIII. Alte und neue Kleidungen der wilden Manns- und Weibspersonen. XXIV. Von der Kinderzucht. Von denen Glücksspielen der Wilden. XXV. Der Verfasser nimmt Abschied von seinen Huronen. XXVI. Gewöhnliche Krankheiten der Wilden. XXVII. Eine Mahlzeit von Menschenfleisch. XXVIII. Gültige Entschuldigung für die Mörder unter den Wilden. XXIX. Der Verfasser wird gefährlich krank. XXX. Was das Tödenlied der Wilden ist. XXXI. Ursachen, warum die Wilden vermeynen, dass sie nicht so grausam seyen als wir. XXXII. Der Verfasser wird bey den Tsonnontouanern entführt. XXXIII. Dem Verfasser wird von seiner Liebsten übel begegnet. XXXIV. Bürgerliches und peinliches Verfahren der Wilden. XXXV. Auf was Weise der Adel unter den Wilden üblich ist. XXXVI. Letzte Pflicht, welche alle Wilden...ihren Toden erweisen. XXXVII. Trauer der Wilden; ihr Todenfest. XXXVIII. Der Verfasser wird von seiner Liebsten betrogen. XXXIX. Ankunft des Verfassers in einem neuen Dorf. Auf was Weise die Wilden die Clystiere geben. XL. List des Maskikik, den Verfasser zu verderben. XLI. Wie der Verfasser an dem Gaukler gerächet wird. Er verlässt seine Wildin und kommt zu den Engelländern.
See J. E. Roy, "Des fils de famille envoyés au Canada: Claude Le Beau," in Royal Society of Canada, *Proceedings and transactions,* Ottawa, 1901, series 2, v. 7, Mém. sec. 1, p. 7–33, * *EC.*
See also no. 1250.
"Kurzer Entwurf von der Nuzbarkeit der Neuen Sammlung merkwürdiger Reisegeschichten," v. 2, p. [478–]504.
Another German translation by Wilhelm Ernst Burkhard Rosler, published in Erfurth in 1751 is not in the Library.

341. [SCHRÖTER, JOHANN FRIEDRICH.] Algemeine Geschichte der Länder und Völker von America... Nebst einer Vorrede Siegmund Jacob Baumgartens, der h. Schrift Doctors und öffentl. Lehrers, auch des theologischen Seminarii Directors auf der königl. preussl. Friedrichs-universität in Halle. Mit vielen Kupfern. Halle: Bey Johann Justinus Gebauer, 1752-1753. 2 v. frontis., plates (part folding), maps (part folding). 25½ x 20½ cm.   *KF 1752
Sabin 38595, 77989.
Dedication signed: J. F. S.
The first part, comprising most of v. 1, is a translation of J. F. Lafitau's *Mœurs des sauvages amériquains comparées aux mœurs des premiers temps,* Paris, 1724, * *KB 1724.* Part 2 is compiled from various sources, and includes "Das chronologische Verzeichnis der Entdeckungen der Newen Welt," translated from Charlevoix's *Histoire et description generale de la Nouvelle France,* 1745 (i. e. 1744), * *KB 1744.*
Baumgarten's "Vorrede" contains a bibliography of the New World.
See obituary of Schröter in *Allgemeine Literatur Zeitung,* 1788, Bd. III, p. 800, *NAA.*

*1753*

342. GARCILASO DE LA VEGA, EL INCA. Geschichte der Eroberung von Florida. Aus dem Spanischen Les [sic!] Ynca Garcilasso de la Vega in die Französische, und aus dieser in die Teutsche Sprache übersetzet von Heinrich Ludwig Meier. Zelle, Franckfurt und Leipzig: In Verlag George Conrad Gsellius, 1753. 52, 456 p. 18 cm.   *KF 1753
Sabin 98746.
A translation of *La Florida del Inca,* 1605, * *KB 1605.*
Reissued under title: Authentische Geschichte der Eroberung von Florida durch Ferdinand von Soto, Aus dem Spanischen des Garcilasso de la Vega, Deutsch von H. Leipzig, 1794. See also no. 869.
See C. Justi, "Ein Bildnis des Dichters Garcilaso de la Vega," in *Jahrbuch der Königlich preussischen Kunstsammlungen,* Berlin, 1893, Bd. 14, p. 177-190, *MAA*; Julia Fitzmaurice-Kelly, *El Inca Garcilasso de la Vega,* London, 1921 (Hispanic notes and monographs, [v.] 2), *AN (Vega)*; Hayward Keniston, *Garcilaso de la Vega,* New York, 1922 (Hispanic notes and monographs, Peninsular series [v. 6]), *NPBC (Vega),* bibliography, p. 439–453; *Francisco Pizzarro: der Sturz des Incareichs nach dem Berichten des Garcilaso de la Vega und des Paters José de Acosta, bearbeitet von Dr. H. G. Bonte,* Leipzig, 1925 (Alte Reisen und Abenteuer. no. 14), *HHK.*

*1753, continued*

343. [NACHRICHTEN von Christlob Mylius' Reise nach America.] (Göttingische Anzeigen von gelehrten Sachen. Göttingen, 1853. 12°. Jahr 1753, Bd. 1, p. 51, 606; Bd. 2, p. 873-883.) *DF

Consists of paragraphs without titles; title adapted from entry in index, v. 2.

His *Beschreibung einer grönländischen Thierpflanze*, London, 1753 (Sabin 51647) is not in the Library.

344. DIARIUM einer Reise von Bethlehem, Pa., nach Bethabara, N. C. Von October 8 his November 23, 1753. Herausgegeben Von Prof. Wm. J. Hinke. (German American annals. New York, etc., 1905–1906. 4°. new series v. 3, p. 342–356, 369–379; new series v. 4, p. 16–32.) NFCA

345. *Review*: Dissertation sur l'origine de la Maladie Vénerienne, pour prouver que le mal n'est pas venu de l'Amérique mais qu'il a commencé en Europe par une Epidemie, par Antonio Ribeiro Sanchéz. Paris: Durand et Pissot, 1752. 110 p. 12°. (Göttingische Anzeigen von gelehrten Sachen. Göttingen [1753], 12°. Jahr 1753, Bd. 1, p. 421–423, *DF.)

Title quoted in review varies slightly from the form adopted.

As to the author, see António Ferrão, "Ribeiro Sanches e Soares de Barros," in Academia das ciencias de Lisboa, *Boletim da segunda classe*, Coimbra, 1939, v. 20, parte 2, p. 5–99, *ES.

## 1754

346. EINIGE Physicalisch-Oeconomische Sätze der Theorie von der Natur, sowohl der Halm- und Stroh- als weichlaubigten Pflantzen, nebst einem Anhang von wilden Bäumen oder Holtz-Pflantzen. (In: [G. H. Zincke.] Leipziger Sammlungen von Wirthschafftlichen, Policy-Cammer- und Finantz- Sachen... Leipzig, 1754. 12°. Bd. 10, p. 249–276, 358-373.) *AM

Refers to American trees, p. 370–372.

"Es ist aber kein Zweifel, dass unter denen in dem Nordischen America, sonderlich wachsenden vielen schoenen Baeumen, verschiedene sehr nuetzlich bey uns angepflantzet werden koenten und fortkommen wuerden."

Note: M. Catesby, *Die naturhistorische Beschreibung von Carolina, Florida und den Bahamischen Inseln...*, Nürnberg [1755]. Not in the Library. "Georgi gives the date 1756." — *Sabin 11510*.

Note also: M. Catesby, *Abbildung verschiedener Fische Schlangen Insecten...*, Nürnberg, 1750; continued, 1755, 1757. Not in the Library. "Title from Georgi." — *Sabin 11512*.

347. KALM, PEHR. Des Herren Peter Kalms Professor der Haushaltungskunst in Aobo, und Mitgliedes der königlichen schwedischen Akademie der Wissenschaften Beschreibung der Reise die er nach dem nördlichen Amerika auf den Befehl gedachter Akademie und öffentliche Kosten unternommen hat... Eine Uebersetzung... Göttingen: Wittwe Abrams Vandenhoek, 1754–1764. 3 v. 8 plates. (1 folding). 21½ cm. (Sammlung neuer und merkwürdiger Reisen zu Wasser und zu Lande. Theil 9–11.) *KF 1754

Sabin 36987.

The original was published in Stockholm, 1753, under the title, *En resa til Nova America...*, *KF 1753*. This translation by J. F. Murray and J. A. Murray includes the portion relating to England, omitted in the English, Dutch, and French translations.

"Peter Kalm was a professor of economy in the university of Abo, Swedish Finland. He set out from Sweden in February 1748, accompanied by a gardener well skilled in the knowledge of plants, first studied husbandry and botany in England, and arrived at Philadelphia in September. He made a tour through the middle colonies, going as far west as Niagara, and returned to Stockholm in 1751." — *Thelma Evans, European impressions of America, Madison, 1903, † I.*

Related works are Peter Loefling's *Reise nach den Spanischen Ländern in den Jahren 1751 bis 1756...*, Berlin und Stralsund, 1766, and *Zweite Auflage... Reisebeschreibung...*, Berlin, 1776 (Sabin 41773), which are not in the Library.

348. PHILADELPHIA. (Göttingische Anzeigen von gelehrten Sachen. Göttingen [1754–1755]. 12°. Jahr 1754, Bd. 1, p. 248; Jahr 1755, Bd. 2, p. 779–780.) *DF

Relates on the establishment of the Academy. "Wir würden dergleichen von einer deutschen Schule freilich nicht anführen, allein was man in einem so entlegenen Welt-Theil weniger vermuthet, wird doch manchen nicht unangenehm... seyn."

349. ROHR, JULIUS BERNHARD VON. Julius Bernhards von Rohr Physikalische Bibliothek, worinnen die vornehmsten Schriften, die zur Naturlehre gehören, angezeiget werden, mit vielen Zusätzen und Verbesserungen herausgegeben von Abraham Gotthelf Kästner... Leipzig: Bey Johann Wendler, 1754. 15 p.l., 694 p., 15 l., 1 plate. 12°. OAG

Essential bibliography of publications relating to America, p. 302, 633–642.

350. URLSPERGER, SAMUEL. Americanisches Ackerwerk Gottes; oder zuverlässige Nachrichten, den Zustand der americanisch englischen und von salzburgischen Emigranten erbauten Pflanzstadt Ebenezer in Georgien betreffend, aus dorther eingeschickten glaubwürdigen Diarien genommen, und mit Briefen der dasigen Herren Prediger noch weiter bestättiget. Erstes [-viertes] Stück, herausgegeben von Samuel Urlsperger... Augsburg, 1754–1767. 5 pt. in 5 v. front. (port.) 22 x 18½ cm. *KF 1754

De Renne, 1931, I, p. 131–133.

Frontispiece engraved by Joh. Jacob Haid, after Jeremiah Theüs, head-pieces in 2. and 3. Stücke, engraved by Christian de Mechel.

A continuation of the author's *Ausführliche Nachrichten...*, Halle, 1735–52. See no. 305.

v. 1, 1754; v. 2, 1755; v. 3, 1756 are styled Erstes, Zweytes and Drittes Stück, respectively. There follows a supplementary volume, 1760, not numbered, intended as an introductory part of v. 4. v. 4 has title *Samuel Urlspergers in seinem 82sten Jahre durch Gottes Gnade noch lebenden resignirten Senioris eines evangelischen Predigiamts in Augsburg Amerikanisches Ackerwerk Gottes...Viertes Stück...*Augsburg, 1767.

*Contents*:

Vol. 1. Vorrede. Tageregister vom Jahre 1751 [Apr. 1, 1751 – Febr. 28, 1752; von J. M. Boltzius] Briefe und Extracte derselben, von Herrn J. M. Bolzius [u. a.] an den Editorem. Rede bey der Ordinations-

*1754, continued*

handlung des tit. Herrn Christian Rabenhorst, dritten ebenezerischen Predigers [von S. Widemann].
Vol. 2. Vorrede [etc.] Tageregister vom Jahre 1752 [March 1, 1752 – Febr. 28, 1753; von J. M. Boltzius]. Briefe und Extracte derselben von denen Herren Predigern in Ebenezer an den Editorem [von J. M. Boltzius u. a.] Erbauliche Briefe von einigen Preussisch-Lithauen zu Rastenberg und Krausendorf wohnenden salzburgischen Emigranten vom Jahr 1753, an ihre Landsleute zu Ebenezer in Georgien...
Vol. 3. Vorrede [etc.] Tageregister vom Jahre 1753 [March 1, 1753 – Dec. 29, 1754; von J. M. Boltzius] Briefe und Extracte derselben von Herrn J. M. Boltzius [u. a.] an den Editoren [*sic!*].
Vol. 3a. Vorbericht [etc.] Amtsdiarium vom Januar [-may] 1759 [von J. M. Boltzius] Briefe und Extracte derselben von Herrn J. M. Boltzius [u. a.] an den Editorem. Observation des Wetters... zu Ebenezer 1759... nach dem baselischen thermom.
Vol. 4. Vorrede [von J. A. Urlsperger] Briefe und Extracte derselben, aus Ebenezer und Londen [von J. M. Boltzius u. a.] Amts-diarium Herrn Prediger Rabenhorsts vom ersten jun. 1759 bis an das Ende eben selbigen Jahres. Besonderes Amts-Diarium Herrn Pastor Boltzius...1759 [–1760] Herrn.Pastor Boltzius ordentliches Amts Diarium... 1760.
Review in *Göttingische Anzeigen von gelehrten Sachen*, Jahr 1770, Bd. 1, p. 187 ff., * DF.

### 1755

351. [BUTEL-DUMONT, GEORGES MARIE.] Der Engländischen Pflanzstädte in Nord-America Geschichte und Handlung nebst einer zuverlässigen Nachricht von der gegenwärtigen Anzahl der dasigen Einwohner, und einer umständlichen Beschreibung der Landesverfassung, absonderlich was Neu-England, Pensylvanien, Carolina und Georgien betrifft. Aus dem Französischen übersetzt. Stuttgard: Jm Verlag Johann Benedict Metzlers, 1755. 8 p.l., 216 p. 17 cm.   *KF 1755
Sabin 22598; *see also* Sabin 27215.
A translation of the author's *Histoire et commerce des colonies angloises*, Paris, 1755, * *KF 1755*.
"Obgleich aber die Werke der Herren Oldmixon und Blome von dem Grossbritannischen Reiche in der neuen Welt, ingleichen des Herrn Salmons Buch von America eben dieselbige Materie als das meinige abhandeln, ja ohnerachtet auch die nurbesagten Verfasser alle drey mir manche schöne Nachricht geliefert haben; so ist doch die gegenwärtige Ausgabe der englandischen Pflanzlande weder eine Uebersetzung, noch ein Auszug ihrer Schriften." — *Vorbericht*.
Jnnhalt der Kapitel. Einleitung. Erstes Kapitel. Von der Hudsons-Bay. Errichtung einer Pflanzstadt an dieser Bay. Jhr Zustand. Was sie hervorbringe. Handlung und Nutzen. Zweytes Kapitel. I. Von der Jnsel Neuland. Jhre Entdeckung. Was für Waaren sie liefere. Jhre Bevölkerung. Zustand dieser Pflanzstadt. II. Vom Stockfischfange, und von dem Handel, der damit getrieben wird. [See no. 801.] Drittes Kapitel. Von Acadia oder Neu-Schottland. Bevölkerung des Landes. Seine Gränzen. Sein Zustand. Seine Waaren. Seine Handlung. Was für Leute dahin geschickt wurden. Viertes Kapitel. Von Neu-England. Fünftes Kapitel. I. Neu-York. II. Ausführlichen Nachricht vom Rauchhandel. III. Neu-Jersey. Sechstes Kapitel. Pensylvanien. Siebendes Kapitel. Von Virginien und Maryland. Achtes Kapitel. Von Carolina und Neu-Georgien.
For another translation by "A. G. U.," published by J. B. Andrea in Frankfourt on Mayn in 1755, see Sabin 27215, 22598. For an edition, Frankfourt on Mayn, 1758, see Sabin 9604.
Note also: *Die Geschichte der Errichtung und des Handels der Englischen Colonien im mitternächtlichen Amerika. Aus dem Französischen*, Rostock, 1756. Sabin 27211. Not in the Library.

352. HUSKE, JOHN, SUPPOSED AUTHOR. Allgemeine Amerikanische Kriegsgeschichte, an den Flüssen Ohio, St. Laurenz, St. Johann, &c. Oder: Gründliche Nachricht von den Angelegenheiten der Grosbrittanischen und Französischen Kronen, in Ansehung des gegenwärtigen Krieges in Nordamerika. Aus dem Englischen übersetzt. Mit einer dazu gehörigen Landkarte und Kupferstich begleitet, und herausgegeben von H. V. W. Frankfurt und Leipzig, 1755. xviii, 121(1) p., 1 l. front., map, plate. 8°.   *KF 1755
The map, engraved by I. M. Eben of Frankfurt, is undated and has title: Karte von Canada und von dem englischen [*sic!*] Colonien am Ohio und St. Johan Fluss.
Frontispiece, representing Fischerey und Dörrung der Stockfische auf den Küsten des Neu-Lands in America, signed: I. C. Back, Sc. Plate, representing Hinrichtung eines Kriegsgefangenen bey den Wilden is unsigned.

353. PRÉVOST D'EXILES, ANTOINE FRANÇOIS. [...Erste Reisen, Entdeckungen, und Niederlassungen der Europaer in America.] Leipzig: bey Arkstee und Merkus, 1755. xxi(i) p., 1 l., 696 p., 16 l. plates (part folding), maps (part folding), plans. 25 cm. (Allgemeine Historie der Reisen zu Wasser und zu Lande; oder Sammlung aller Reisebeschreibungen. Bd. 13.)   KBC
Caption title used, which commences: Allgemeine Sammlung von Reisebeschreibungen. III Theil, Das v Buch... Title page is devoted to series title.
This is a German translation of the fifth book of Prévost d'Exiles and others' *Histoire générale des voyages*, Paris, 1746–1789, * *KB 1746*.
Translators of the whole *Allgemeine Historie* include J. J. Schwabe, editor, A. G. Kästner, F. W. Beer, M. C. C. Woog, J. G. Müller, F. J. Bierling. — *cf.* "Vorbericht" in vol. 21.

354. WELSCH, GEORG HIERONYMUS. Von dreyen Amerikanischen Früchten, welche noch von niemand beschrieben worden. (Leopoldinisch-Carolinische deutsche Akademie der Naturforscher. Der Römischen Kaiserlichen Akademie der Naturforscher auserlesene... Abhandlungen. Nürnberg, 1755. 8°. Theil 1, p. 290–291.) 3–* EE
"Dr. Welsch in einem Briefe an D. Sachsen." — *Editor's note.* As Dr. Welsch had died in 1677, this was a rather antiquated account.

### 1756

355. CHARLEVOIX, PIERRE FRANÇOIS XAVIER DE. [Allgemeine Geschichte und Beschreibung von Neu-Frankreich; worinnen alles dasjenige enthalten ist, was die Entdeckung und Eroberungen der Franzosen in den nordlichen America betrifft...] Leipzig: bey Arkstee und Merkus, 1756. vii(i), 648 p., 20 l. plates (part folding), maps (part folding). 25 cm. (Allgemeine Historie der Reisen zu Wasser und Lande; oder Sammlung aller Reisebeschreibungen. Bd. 14.)   KBC
Sabin 12138.
Caption title used. Title page is devoted to series title.
Translation of the author's *Histoire et description générale de la Nouvelle France, avec le Journal historique d'un voyage fait par ordre du roi dans l'Amérique Septentrionnale*, Paris, 1744, * *KB 1744*.
See no. 367, 378.

*1756, continued*

356. GEDANCKEN über die Aufgabe und Frage: Woher kömmt es überhaupt, dass diejenigen Gegenden, wo Gold- Silber- und Kupfer-Berg- und Hütten-wercke getrieben werden, ärmer, als die andern sind? (In: [G. H. Zincke.] Leipziger Sammlungen von Wirtschafftlichen, Policey- Cammer- und Finantz- Sachen.... Leipzig, 1757. 12°. Bd. 12, p. 672-686.) *AM
References to America.
"Es ist aber wenigstens unstreitig, dass z. E. America in einigen Gegenden, was die Klüffte der Erde be- trifft, vor und nach seiner Entdeckung reich, was seine eingebornen Einwohner aber anlanget, vorher und darnach arm gewesen, die Europäer aber, so Ein- kömmlinge waren, und auch hernach die Ein- wohner in Europa selbst, erst daraus bereichert wor- den, die doch nur erst durch viele Hände die ameri- canischen Reichthümer erlangen." — *p. 673.* See also § 10, p. 684.

357. GESCHICHTE und Handlung der franzö- sischen Pflanzstädte in Nordamerika, Nebst einer zuverlässigen Nachricht von deren Be- völkerung, ihren Einwohnern und der natür- lichen Beschaffenheit des Landes, wie auch einer kurzen Einleitung in die jezige Strittig- keiten der Engländer und Franzosen wegen Akadien; und den Ansprüchen der erstern auf einen grossen Theil von Canada und Louisiana. Mit einer Landcharte. Stuttgart: Bey Johann Benedict Mezler, 1756. 4 p.l., 376 p., folding map. 17½ cm. *KF 1756
Sabin 27216.
*Contents:* Einleitung. (Erster Abschnitt. Von den Strittigkeiten der Engländer und Franzosen über die Gränzen von Neuschottland oder Akadien. Zweyter Abschnitt. Von den Strittigkeiten beyder Nationen in Ansehung der übrigen Nordamerikanischen Länder.) Erstes Capitel. Chronologisches Verzeichniss der Ent- deckungen und Niederlassungen in Nordamerika. Zweytes Capitel. Bank bey Neufundland, und St. Lorenzbay. Drittes Capitel. Von Cap Breton und Neuschottland oder Akadien. Viertes Capitel. Canada von der Mündung des Lorenzflusses bis Montreal. Fünftes Capitel. Canada, von Montreal an bis an Louisiana. Sechstes Capitel. Von Louisiana.
The following titles which are supplementary to nos. 351 and 357 are not in the Library: *Geschichte der europäischen Pflanzstäde auf den Antillischen Inseln ...,* Stuttgart, 1760 (Sabin 27212) and *Das Spanische Reich in Amerika...,* Sorau, 1763 (Sabin 88938).

358. LISTE der Schiffe und Negern...welche vom Jahre 1706 bis 1739. zu Charlestown in Südcarolina angekommen. (Bremisches Maga- zin zur Ausbreitung der Wissenschaften Künste und Tugend. Hannover, 1756. 8°. Bd. 1, p. 357-358.) *DF
Taken from *Gentleman's magazine,* 1755, Aug., p. 344, *DA.

359. MITTELBERGER, GOTTLIEB. Gottlieb Mittel- bergers Reise nach Pennsylvanien im Jahre 1750. und Rückreise nach Teutschland im Jahre 1754. Enthaltend nicht nur eine Beschreibung des Landes nach seinem gegenwärtigen Zu- stande, sondern auch eine ausführliche Nach- richt von den unglückseligen und betrübten Um- ständen der meisten Teutschen, die in dieses Land gezogen sind, und dahin ziehen. Frank- furth und Leipzig, 1756. 4 p.l., 120 p. 17 cm. Sabin 49761. *KF 1756
English translation by C. T. Eben, *Journey to Pennsylvania,* Philadelphia: McVey, 1898, *ISC.*
See W. A. Knittel, *Early eighteenth century Palatine emigration,* Philadelphia, 1937, *IEK;* it contains an excellent bibliography.
See Meynen nos. 259, 260.

360. ...NACHRICHT von einer Amerikanischen Wespe der Mäurer genannt. (Bremisches Magazin zur Ausbreitung der Wissenschaften Künste und Tugend. Hannover, 1756. 8°. Bd. 1, p. 129-131.) *DF
Taken from *Gentleman's magazine,* July, 1754, p. 330, *DA.*
Describes a wasp observed on Barbados and other islands of the Caribbean Sea.

361. ...NACHRICHT von einer der Unter- weisung der deutschen Protestanten in Pen- sylvanien gemachten Anstalt. (Bremisches Magazin zur Ausbreitung der Wissenschaften Künste und Tugend. Hannover, 1756. 8°. Bd. 1, p. 202-205.) *DF
Taken from *Gentleman's magazine,* March, 1755, p. 103 seq., *DA.*
Calls for support of churches and schools of Ger- man Protestants in Pennsylvania. The following will be the regulations for the schools: "1. Sie sollen nur protestantische Kinder, aber von allen Bekenntnissen, annehmen. 2. Die Knaben lernen die engelländische und hochdeutsche Sprache, Schreiben, Rechnen, Singen, und die Grundwahrheiten des Christenthums; die Mädgen werden im Lesen und Nähen unterrichtet. 3. Man lässt ein jedes Kind den Catechismus lernen, welche seine Eltern verlangen, ohne Zwang und Partheilichkeit, wegen verschiedner Meinungen, die nicht zum Wesen der wahren Gottseligkeit und Tugend gehören. 4. Es sollen Bibeln und andere gute Bücher unter ihnen ausgetheilet werden. 5. Es sollen eigene Aufseher ernennet werden, die alle Vierteljahr eine Visitation halten. 6. Am Ende jedes Jahres werden die Rechnungen nachgesehen und geschlossen, und die- jenigen, welche vor andern fleissig gewesen, beschen- ket." — *p. 204.*
See C. L. Maurer, *Early Lutheran education in Pennsylvania,* Philadelphia [1932], *SSL.*

362. VON dem Kriege zwischen Gross-Britan- nien und Frankreich. (Europäische Staats- Cantzley. Nürnberg, 1756. 12°. Theil 110, p. 580- 656.) BTA
"Unterricht von den zwischen den Cronen Frank- reich und Grossbrittanien entstandenen Streitigkeiten, über die Grenzen des Landes Acadien in Nord- America," p. 580-610.
"Discussion sommaire sur les anciennes Limites de l'Acadie," p. 611-640.
An extract from *Memoires des Commissaires de S. H. Très-Chrétienne & des ceux de M. Brittanique sur les possessions & droits respectifs des ceux couron- nes en Amérique avec les actes publics & pieces justi- ficatives,* A Copenhague [1755]. *cf.* Sabin [18503]. The extract had appeared previously in *Hannöverische nützliche Sammlungen,* Stück 86. It intends to show the difference in the interpretation of the treaty of Utrecht by the British and the French.

363. *Review:* A Concise description of the Eng- lish and French Possessions in North-America for the better explaining of the Map published with that Title. By I. Palairet... The second edition improved. London: Haberkorn, 1755. 69(1) p. 8°. (Göttingische Anzeigen von ge- lehrten Sachen. Göttingen [1756]. 12°. Jahr 1756, p. 10-11, *DF.)
Sabin 57308.
The reviewer blames I. Palairet for not mentioning the Salzburgers and their settlements in Georgia.
The Library has the first, but not the second, edition of this work, also the French edition, *KF 1755.

## 1757

**364.** ABBILDUNG Nordamericanischer Länder und Eingebohrner Wilden, dabey die Erd-Beschreibung und Natur-Seltenheiten der dortigen Gegenden, auch die sonderbahren Gebräuche der Landes Einwohner, die Handlung, Policey und Regiments-Verfassung, vorgestellet werden. Zugleich kommet ein Unterricht von den Irrungen zwischen Grossbritannien und Franckreich und eine Beschreibung des zeither dort geführten Krieges. Erfurt: Bey Joh. Heinr. Nonnens sel. Wittib, 1757. 6 p.l., 360 p., double front. 17½ cm. *KF 1757
Sabin 55453.
Illustration shows North America and aboriginal savages.
"Das Krieges-Feuer, welches in den dortigen Gegenden ausgebrochen ist, hat die Neubegierigen lüstern gemacht, nähere Nachrichten von diesen weitschichtigen Provintzien zu empfangen." — *Vorrede*.
Entwurf dieser Abhandlung. I. Von der Entdeckung der neuen Welt überhaupt. II. Von der Entdeckung der nördlichen Theile West-Jndiens. III. Von den Ländern der Nordamericanischen Gegenden Grossbritannischer Hoheit. IV. Von Pensilvanien, Neu-Yorck und Neu-Jersey. V. Von Neu-England, Neu-Schottland und Neuland. VI. Von den Ländern der Nordamericanischen Gegenden unter Frantzösischer Bothmässigkeit. VII. Von der Beschaffenheit der Frantzösischen Nord-americanischen Ländern, und den dortigen Einwohnern. VIII. Von den Nordamericanischen Wilden. IX. Unterricht von den zwischen den Cronen Grossbritanien und Franckreich entstandenen Streitigkeiten, über die Grentzen des Landes Acadien in Nordamerica. X. Beschreibung des Krieges, so zeither in Nordamerica zwischen den Engelländern und Frantzosen ist geführet worden.
See no. 362.

**365-66.** KURZE, zuverlässige Nachricht Von der, unter dem Namen der Böhmisch-Mährischen Brüder bekanten, Kirche Unitas Fratrum Herkommen, Lehr-Begrif, äussern und innern Kirchen-Verfassung und Gebräuchen, aus richtigen Urkunden und Erzehlungen von einem Ihrer Christlich Unpartheiischen Freunde heraus gegeben und mit sechzehn Vorstellungen in Kupfer erläutert. [n. p.,] M DCC LVII. 64 p., 16 double plates. 8°. *KF 1757
Sabin 97851.
"Eine Act zur Einladung des unter dem Namen Unitas Fratrum oder Vereinigte Brüder, bekannten Volkes, sich in Sr. Majestät Colonien in America niederzulassen," p. 59–64.
Interesting plates by J. Rud. Holzhalb.
See Henry Rimius, *A candid narrative of the rise and progress of the Herrnhuters, commonly called Moravians, or, Unitas Fratrum*, London, 1750, ZXHC; second edition, in which the Latin appendix is rendered into English, 1753, ZXHC. The book has a supplement (London, 1755) which contains "Animadversions on sundry flagrant untruths advanced by Mr. Zinzendorf," p. 1–90.
See note on no. 304.

## 1758

**367-68.** [CHARLEVOIX, PIERRE FRANÇOIS XAVIER, AND OTHERS.] ...Reisen und Niederlassungen in dem nordlichen America. (Allgemeine Historie der Reisen zu Wasser und Lande, oder Sammlung aller Reisebeschreibungen. Leipzig, 1758. 4°. Bd. 16, p. 394–736.) KBC
This pagination includes Cap. XI-XIII.

Title page of this volume is devoted to a full description of the whole work; title of this volume is the main caption title: ...Fortsetzung der Reisen, Entdeckungen und Niederlassungen in dem südlichen America. [Imprint and collation:] Leipzig: Arkstee und Merkus, 1758. 6 p.l., 736 p., 17 l. plates (part folding), maps (part folding), plans (part folding). 25 cm.
Charlevoix's contributions are a continuation of his *Allgemeine Geschichte und Beschreibung vom Neu-Frankreich*, Leipzig, 1756, which is Bd. 14 of the "Allgemeine Historie"; *see* no. 355.

**369.** FRANKLIN, BENJAMIN. Des Herrn Benjamin Franklins Esq. Briefe von der Elektricität. Aus dem Engländischen übersetzet, nebst Anmerkungen von J. C. Wilcke. Leipzig: Gottfried Kiesewetter, 1758. 13 p.l., 354 p. diagr. 8°.
*KF 1758
Anmerkungen zu den Briefen des Hrn. Benjamin Franklins von der Elektricität [von J. C. Wilcke], p. [215–]354.

**370.** NACHRICHT von dem Lande, welches itzo der Sitz des Krieges in Nord-Amerika ist, und den ursprünglichen Einwohnern desselben, gemeiniglich die Indianer genannt. (Bremisches Magazin zur Ausbreitung der Wissenschaften Künste und Tugend. Bremen, 1758. 12°. Bd. 2, p. 335–373.) *DF
From *Universal magazine*, May, 1757, p. 193.
Deals exclusively with the Indians.

**371.** *Notice:* The history of new Jork from its first discovery to the 1752. by Wm Smith, M.A. of New Jork. Historie von Neu Jork, von dessen ersten Entdeckung bis auf 1752. durch Wm. Smith etc. (Bremisches Magazin zur Ausbreitung der Wissenschaften Künste und Tugend. Bremen, 1758. 12°. Bd. 3, p. 234–235, *DF.)
This is William Smith's *The history of the province of New-York from the first discovery to the year* M.DCC.XXXII... London, 1757, *KF 1757.
Mentioned among "Neue Bücher," vom May, 1757.

**372.** *Review:* Account of the European Settlements in America. [By Edmund Burke.] London, 1757. 2 v. 8°. (Göttingische Anzeigen von gelehrten Sachen. Göttingen [1758]. 12°. Jahr 1758, p. 1416, *DF.)
The Library's class mark for this work: *KF 1757.
"Der erste Band enthält die Geschichte der Entdeckung dieses Welttheils von Christopher Columbus an, eine Beschreibung der Sitten und Gewohnheiten der ursprünglichen Einwohner desselben, wie auch des spanischen und portugiesischen Antheils an America. Der zweyte Band beschreibt das Antheil, welches die Franzosen, Niederländer, Dänen, und insonderheit die Engländer daran haben..." The two maps are by Emanuel Bowen.

**373.** *Review:* The Contest in America between Great Britain and France, with its consequences and Importance. 7 Bogen in 8° ohne die Vorrede, welche 6 Bogen stark ist. (Göttingische Anzeigen von gelehrten Sachen. Göttingen [1758]. 12°. Jahr 1758, p. 1416, *DF.)
For full information about this work by John Mitchell, *see* no. 368.

1759

374-75. ANMERKUNGEN über drey Lieder der Iroquoisen. (Hannoverische Beyträge zum Nutzen und Vergnügen. Hannover, 1759. 4°. Theil 1, col. 561-568.) *DF
"Uebersetzt aus dem *Journal Etranger Mens.* May 1754. p. 229."
With music.
*See also* no. 383.

376. EIN AUSSERORDENTLICHER Nebel. Auszug eines Briefes von Kensington in Connecticut, 1758. den 20 Jänner. (Bremisches Magazin zur Ausbreitung der Wissenschaften Künste und Tugend. Bremen, 1759. 12°. Bd. 3, p. 634.) *DF
Taken from *London magazine*, April, 1758, p. 212.

376A. AUSZUG aus den Philosophisch. Transactions. [Art. XXXIII-LVII.] (Bremisches Magazin zur Ausbreitung der Wissenschaften Künste und Tugend. Bremen und Leipzig, 1759. 8°. Bd. 3, p. 49-70.) *DF
Supplement to *Gentleman's magazine*, 1756, p. 616, and January, 1757, * DA.
Sections of interest:
Art. LI. Elektrische Versuche, welche nach der Vorschrift des Herrn Cantons gemacht worden, am J. Christm. 1753. mit Erläuterungen von Herrn Benj. Franklin, p. 67.
Art. LII. Auszug aus einem Briefe, betreffend die Elektricität, von B. Franklin an Herrn Dalibard, p. 68.
Art. LV. Nachricht von dem grossen Vortheile des Ventilators, bey vielen Gelegenheiten, zur Erhaltung der Gesundheit und des Lebens der Menschen, in Sclaven- und andern Transportschiffen; von Stephan Hales, p. 70.

377. AUSZUG der Artikeln des zweyten Theils des XLIX. Bandes der Philosophical-Transactions [der K. G. der Wissenschaften in London]. (Bremisches Magazin zur Ausbreitung der Wissenschaften Künste und Tugend. Bremen, 1759. 12°. Bd. 3, p. 254-272, 421-445, 539-551.) *DF
Contents of interest to America:
Art. LXXIV. Eine Nachricht, welche bemerket, dass 1755. im Anfange des Weinmonats, der See Ontario in Amerika, zu dreyen verschiedenen malen, binnen einer halben Stunde, fünf und einen halben Fuss gestiegen und gefallen ist, p. 266.
Art. LXXXII. Beobachtungen, welche auf dem Schwefelberge der Jnsel Guadelupa gemacht worden, von Herrn Peysonelle, Königl. Arzte und Botanisten auf bemeldeter Jnsel. Guadelupa... ist eine von den Jnseln in Amerika, welche die Antillischen genannt werden, und hat, wie die mehresten derselben, einen feuerspeyenden Berg und Schwefelminen. Art. XCII. Beobachtungen bey den antillischen Juseln in Amerika; von Dr. Peysonelle. Art. XCVII. Nachricht von der neulich in Pennsylvanien entdeckten Kupferquelle.
Taken from *Gentleman's magazine*, 1757, May, p. 222b; August, p. 353; September, p. 409; October, p. 445; November, p. 506; December, p. 548.

378. [CHARLEVOIX, PIERRE FRANÇOIS XAVIER DE. ...Fortsetzung der Reisen, Entdeckungen und Niederlassungen in Nord-America.] Leipzig: bey Arkstée und Merkus, 1759. 4 p.l., 726 p., 21 l. plates, maps (part folding). 25 cm. (Allgemeine Historie der Reisen zu Wasser und zu Lande, oder Sammlung aller Reisebeschreibungen. Bd. 17.) KBC
Title is caption title, commencing: Allgemeine Sammlung Reisebeschreibungen. Dritter Theil...
Title page is devoted to the series title: Allgemeine Historie...
This continues the author's contributions listed under no. 367.

379. HISTORIE des letzten Parlaments in Grossbritannien, welches 1757. den 1 Christm. den Anfang genommen; worin eine ausführliche Nachricht gegeben wird, sowol von allen wichtigen Sachen, die darin abgethan worden, als auch von den Betrachtungen, welche die Staatskundige darüber gemachet haben. (Bremisches Magazin zur Ausbreitung der Wissenschaften Künste und Tugend. Bremen, 1759. 12°. Bd. 3, p. 635-652.) *DF
Taken from *London magazine*, August, 1758.
Expenditure for the British army in the American colonies.
The announced continuation did not appear.

379A. *Notice:* The contest in America between Great Britain and France. Die Streitigkeit in Amerika Zwischen England und Frankreich. (Bremisches Magazin zur Ausbreitung der Wissenschaften Künste und Tugend. Bremen, 1759. 12°. Bd. 3, p. 236, *DF.)
This is John Mitchell's *The contest in America between Great Britain and France... By an Impartial Hand.* London: Millar, 1757, * KF 1757.
Mentioned among "Neue Bücher" vom May 1757. *See also* no. 373.

379B. *Notice:* A letter from new Iersey in America, giving some account and description of that province. (Bremisches Magazin zur Ausbreitung der Wissenschaften Künste und Tugend. Bremen, 1759. 12°. Bd. 2, p. 709, *DF.)
Listed among "Neue Bücher des Herbstmonaths," 1756.

380. SCHLESISCHE privilegirte Staats-Kriegsu. Friedens-Zeitungen. No. 26-37, 3.-28. Mart. Breslau, 1759. p. 137-202. 12°. EBY
Reports on events during the Seven Years' War, 1756-1763.
Various references to America.

381. VON dem Kriege zwischen Gross-Brittanien und Frankreich. Nachricht von der Insel Cap-Breton und den Vortheilen welche Engeland durch den Besitz derselben zufliessen können. (Europäische Staats-Cantzley. Nürnberg, 1759. 12°. Theil 114, p. 560-591.) BTA
"Bey dem gegenwärtigen Kriege haben wir Deutschen Ursache, nicht allein auf dasjenige aufmerksam zu seyn, was in unserm Weltheile vorgehet; die Begebenheit, die in Amerika sich zugetragen, sind mit unsern Angelegenheiten allzu sehr verwandt als dass wir uns nicht nach ihnen mit starker Neugier erkundigen sollen," p. 561. Erster Abschnitt, welcher eine kurze topographische Nachricht von der Jnsel Cap-Breton mittheilet. Zweyter Abschnitt, Von den Vortheilen, welche den Franzosen durch den Besitz des Cap-Breton zufliessen. Dritter Abschnitt, Von dem Schaden, welchen die Franzosen durch die von den Engelländern geschehene Eroberung von Cap Breton erlitten haben. The first chapter contains a recipe for spruce beer in a note on p. 568-569.
The essay, based mainly on Charlevoix (see nos. 355, 367), is taken from the *Hannöverische nützliche Sammlungen 1758*, Stück 84 (not in the Library). The author is Johann Franz Wagener. The *Bremisches Magazin zur Ausbreitung der Wissenschaften, Künste und Tugend,* Bremen, 1759, Bd. 3, p. 664, *DF, mentions under the heading of *Neue Bücher* "An account of the customs and manners of the Micmakis and Moricheets, savage nations, now dependent on the government of Cape Breton," but indicates neither year nor place of publication.

## 1760

**382.** AMERICANISCHE Urquelle derer innerlichen Kriege des bedrängten Teutschlands, nach denen wahrhaftesten Umständen und mit der genauesten Unpartheylichkeit nebst allen zur Erläuterung einschlagenden Nachrichten des Verhåltnůsses der Englisch- und Französischen Handlung historisch verfasset durch L. F. v. d. H. Augsburg: Georg Christoph Kilian, 1760. 354 p., 9 l., 36 maps, 21 plans, 2 plates. 8°. *KF 1760
One plan wanting.
"Hier komme ich auf denjenigen Grundsaz, welcher meine Leser ueberfuehren wird, was sich in dem Vorbericht dieser Geschichte behauptet. Nemlich, dass unser ungluecklisches Vaterland durch die Americanische Unruhen in den gegenwaertigen Krieg verwickelt worden." — *p. 53.*
This work, listed neither by Sabin nor Kayser nor in the catalogue of the British Museum, is a history of America from its discovery to the Peace of Hubertusburg, 1763. Chapter II is entitled, "Die Entdeckung von America, erstlich durch die Deutschen denen hernach andere Völker gefolget." It attributes the discovery of America to Martin Behaim. This opinion is based on Johann Friedrich Stüven, *De vero Novi orbis inventore*, Francofurti ad Moenum, 1714, * KB 1714.
See nos. 274A, 385, 386, 393, 580, 1019.

**383.** ANMERKUNGEN über drey Lieder der Jrokesen. (Historisch-Kritische Beyträge zur Aufnahme der Musik. Berlin, 1760. 12°. Bd. 5, p. 341–346.) *MA
Reprinted from *Journal étranger*, May, 1754, p. 229. (This number not in the Library.)
With music.
See also no. 375.

**384.** BESCHREIBUNG des Fichtenbieres der Americaner. (Hannoverische Beyträge zum Nutzen und Vernügen, vom Jahre 1760. Hannover, 1761. 4°. Theil 2, col. 1079–1084.) *DF
Title page dated 1761; contents, 1760.
"Unter den Getränken, die in den europäischen Pflanzorten in Nordamerica gewöhnlich getrunken werden, gibt es eine Art Bier, welches allgemeiner bekannt gemacht zu werden verdienet... Dieses Fichtenbier ist vornehmlich bey den Franzosen in Canada sehr im Gebrauche..."
See nos. 381, 402.

**385.** TOZE, EOBALD. Beweis, dass dem berühmten Seefahrer Martin Behaim die erste Entdeckung der neuen Welt nicht zugeschrieben werden könne. (Hannoverische Beyträge zum Nutzen und Vergnügen, vom Jahre 1760. Hannover, 1761. 4°. Theil 2, col. 689–732.)
Title page dated 1761; contents, 1760. *DF
E. Toze also published *Der gegenwärtige Zustand von Europa...*, Bützow, 1767, a remodeled edition of which appeared under the title, *Einleitung zur allgemeinen und besondern Staatskunde*, at Bützow, 1779, for the first; in 1790, for the fourth time. The Library has an English version of the work, *The present state of Europe: exhibiting a view of the natural and civil history of the several countries and kingdoms*, London, 1770, BTX. References to Spanish America, v. 1; British and French colonies, v. 2; Danish and Swedish colonies, v. 3. Detailed index, v. 1.
E. T. Toze was also the translator of Johanna Campbell's *Leben und Thaten der Admirale und anderer berühmten brittanischen Seeleute aus dem Englischen*, Göttingen, 1755; see *Hannoverische Beyträge zum Nutzen und Vergnügen vom Jahre 1762*, Hannover, 1763, Theil 4, col. 1122–1123, *DF.
See nos. 386, 393.

**386.** —— Von den Betrůgereyen des Americus Vespucci, wodurch er sich die Ehre der Entdeckung des festen Landes in der neuen Welt zugeschrieben, und dieselbe dem ersten Erfinder Christoph Colon entzogen hat. (Hannoverische Beyträge zum Nutzen und Vergnügen, vom Jahre 1760. Hannover, 1761. 4°. Theil 2, col. 193–230.) *DF
Title page dated 1761; contents, 1760.
See nos. 382, 385, 393.

**387.** VERSUCHE, die nordwestliche Fahrt nach Indien zu entdecken. (Hannoverische Beyträge zum Nutzen und Vergnügen, vom Jahre 1761. Hannover, 1761. 4°. Theil 2, col. 1177–1182.)
"Aus dem Englischen." *DF
Title page dated 1761; contents, 1760.

**388.** [ZINZENDORF, NICOLAUS LUDWIG, GRAF VON.] Des Ordinarii Fratrum. Öffentliche Reden, von dem Herrn, der Unsere Seligkeit ist, und über die Materie Von Seiner Marter, die Derselbe als vocirter Pastor bey der einzigen damals zu Philadelphia in Pennsylvanien bekanten Evangelisch-Lutherischen Gemeine in ihrer Kirche daselbst Im Jahr 1742. gehalten hat, Nebst einem Anhang zweyer andern dergleichen Predigten, und einiger Lieder Von Ihm selbst revidirt und ausgefertigt. Herausgegeben von Gottfried Clemens,... Schlossprediger zu Barby. 3te Edition. London und Barby: Zu finden bey dem Seminario Theologico, 1760. 8 p.l., 3–256 p., 1 l. 8°. *KF 1760
See A. L. Fries, *Some Moravian heroes*, Bethlehem, Pa., 1936, ZAE p.v.699, and W. C. Reichel, *Memorials of the Moravian Church*, Philadelphia, 1870, v. 1.

**389.** *Review:* A natural and civil history of California containing an accurate description of the country translated from the Original spanish of Miguel Venegas... London: Rivington and Fletcher, 1759. 2 v. 8°. (Göttingische Anzeigen von gelehrten Sachen. Göttingen [1760]. 12°. Jahr 1760, p. 874–880, *DF.)
The Library's copies of this English edition are in class mark * KF 1759.
See nos. 445, 454.

## 1761

**390.** BESCHREIBUNG der Insel Martinike. (Hannoverische Beyträge zum Nutzen und Vergnügen, vom Jahre 1761. Hannover, 1762. 4°. Theil 3, col. 909–935.) *DF
Signed: Heise.
Title page dated 1762; contents, 1761.
See no. 403.

**391.** HÜBNER, JOHANN. Johann Hübners Neuvermehrtes und verbessertes Reales, Staats-Zeitungs- und Conversations-Lexicon, Darinnen sowohl Die Religionen und geistlichen Orden, die Reiche und Staaten... deutlich beschrieben werden. Die allerneueste Auflage, Darinnen alles, was sich in Publicis, Geographicis, Genealogicis und andern Stücken verändert, bis auf gegenwärtige Zeit fleissig verändert zu finden... Regensburg und Wien: In Verlegung Emerich Felix Baders...1761. 13 p.l., 1280 p., 28 l., 9 pl. table. 8°. *AM
Reviews: *Göttingische Anzeigen von Gelehrten Sachen*, Jahr 1760, p. 689 ff., *DF; *Allgemeine deutsche Bibliothek*, Bd. 3, p. 111, NAA.

*1761, continued*

392. EIN SCHREIBEN aus Ludewigsburg an den H * * * * von den Sitten der Wilden. (Hannoverische Beyträge zum Nutzen und Vergnügen, vom Jahre 1761. 4°. Theil 3, col. 185–204.) *DF
Title page dated 1762; contents, 1761.
"Aus dem Englischen übersetzt."

393. TOZE, EOBALD. Der wahre und erste Entdecker der neuen Welt Christoph Colon, gegen die ungegründeten Ansprüche, welche Americus Vespucci und Martin Behaim auf diese Ehre machen, vertheidigt von E. Tozen, Universitäts-Secretär zu Göttingen. Göttingen: Verlegts Victorin Bossigel, 1761. 5 p.l., (1) 4–128 p. 18 cm. (4°.) *KF 1761
Sabin 96406. JCB, III², 336.
Reprint of augmented articles originally published in the *Hannoverische Beyträge*: see nos. 385, 386.

394. WEDEKIND, E. C. Aufgabe [von einer Krankheit der americanischen Hunde]. (Hannoverische Beyträge zum Nutzen und Vergnügen, vom Jahre 1761. Hannover, 1762. 4°. Theil 3, col. 663–664.) *DF
Title page dated 1762; contents, 1762.
Deals with rabies and smallpox of dogs. Taken from Don Antonio de Ulloa, "Reise nach Südamerika," in *Allgemeine Historie der Reisen zu Wasser und zu Lande*, Bd. 9, p. 217, KBC.

395. *Review*: History of the origin and progress of the present War. London Magazin, 1761. In installments. (Göttingische Anzeigen von gelehrten Sachen. Göttingen [1762]. 12°. Jahr 1761/1762, p. 170–172, * DF.)
This series, the full title of which is "An impartial and succinct History of the Origin and Progress of the present war," commences in the *London magazine*, v. 28, p. 227, May, 1759, * DA.
"Von diesem [i.e. French and Indian war] giebt sie wirklich manches, so einem Deutschen aus den Zeitungen nicht bekannt seyn kann, erläutert ihn durch Nachrichten von der Lage, Interesse und Gesinnungen der dortigen Pflanzstätte..."

## 1762

396. BESCHREIBUNG der Grossbritannischen Insel New-Land, New-Found-Land, oder Newland im nordlichen Amerika. (Hannoverische Beyträge zum Nutzen und Vergnügen, vom Jahre 1762. Hannover, 1763. 4°. Theil 4, col. 1121–1158.) *DF
Title page dated 1763; contents, 1762.
Contains a bibliography of the sources for this article. See col. 1121–1123. Among other works are mentioned: a German version by Theodor Arnold of John Oldmixon's *The British Empire in America*, Lemgo, 1741 (Sabin 57161 date, 1744), and *Geographische und historisch-politische Nachrichten von demjenigen Theil des nordlichen Amerika...*, Frankfurt und Leipzig, 1756 (not in Sabin or British Museum catalogue).

397. HISTORISCH-GEOGRAPHISCHE Beschreibung der in diesem Krieg von den Engländern eroberten französischen Antillischen Inseln, besonders von Guadaloupe und Martinique &c. Zur Erläuterung der gegenwärtigen Kriegs-Staats- und Handlungs-Geschichte. Stutgart: Bey Johann Benedict Mezler, 1762. 4 p.l., 264 p. 8°.
Sabin 32101. *KF 1762

398. KÖHLER, JOHANN TOBIAS. Beschreibung der Insel Cuba, und ihrer Hauptstadt Havana, nebst einer kurzen Nachricht von dem Handel aus Spanien nach Amerika, und dem daselbst von verschiedenen Völkern getriebenen Schleichhandel. (Hannoverische Beyträge zum Nutzen und Vergnügen vom Jahre 1762. Hannover, 1763. 4°. Theil 4, col. 1409–1446.) *DF
Title page dated 1763; contents, 1762.
Contains a bibliography of the works from which the material for this article is taken. See also note on no. 400.
Note also his *Sammlung neuer Reisebeschreibungen aus fremden Sprachen, besonders der Englischen*, Erster Band, Göttingen und Gotha, 1767–69 (Sabin 38223), which is not in the Library.
See also no. 407.

399. —— Kurze Beschreibung der von der Grossbritannischen Seemacht in America ohnlängst eroberten Inseln Grenada, St. Vincent und St. Lucia. (Hannoverische Beyträge zum Nutzen und Vergnügen vom Jahre 1762. Hannover, 1763. 4°. Theil 4, col. 817–848.) * DF
Title page dated 1763; contents, 1762.
The works from which the information for this article is taken are mentioned in col. 818.

400. —— Von dem Handel der Spanier nach Westindien, und von dem Schleichhandel, wodurch auch andere europäische Völker an den dortigen Schätzen Theil nehmen. (Hannoverische Beyträge zum Nutzen und Vergnügen vom Jahre 1762. Hannover, 1763. 4°. Theil 4, col. 1473–1496, 1505–1516.) *DF
Title page dated 1763; contents, 1762.
"Ich finde für nöthig anzuzeigen, dass ich die gegenwärtigen Nachrichten aus den bey der Beschreibung von Cuba im 89ten Stücke [see no. 398] angezeigten Büchern, vornehmlich aber aus der *History of Spanish America* genommen, deren eigener Worte ich mich meistentheils, besonders bey Dingen, die die Engländer betreffen, bedienet habe." — *Author's note*.

401. KURZE Beschreibung der schönen Stadt Philadelphia. (Hannoverische Beyträge zum Nutzen und Vergnügen vom Jahre 1762. Hannover, 1763. 4°. Theil 4, col. 235–240.) * DF
Taken from the *London magazine*, October, 1761, p. 575, * DA.
Title page dated 1763; contents, 1762.

402. NACHRICHT von dem Biere aus hiesigen Fichten, zur Nachahmung dessen, so die Engländer in America brauen. (Hannoverische Beyträge zum Nutzen und Vergnügen vom Jahre 1762. Hannover, 1763. 4°. Theil 4, col. 625–636.) *DF
Signed: A.F.E.J.
Title page dated 1763; contents, 1762.
See no. 384.

403. NACHRICHT von der Insel Martinique. (Hannoverische Beyträge zum Nutzen und Vergnügen vom Jahre 1762. Hannover, 1763. 4°. Theil 4, col. 417–436.) *DF
Title page dated 1763; contents, 1762.
Surveys maps of the island of Martinique.
See no. 390.

404. NACHRICHT von Neu-York. (Hannoverische Beyträge zum Nutzen und Vergnügen vom Jahre 1762. Hannover, 1763. 4°. Theil 4, col. 205–220.) *DF
From *London magazine*, August, 1761, p. 399, * DA.
Title page dated 1763; contents, 1762.

## 1763

**405.** BESCHREIBUNG von Mobile, welches den Engländern im Frieden abgetreten ist. (Hannoverisches Magazin...vom Jahre 1763. Hannover, 1764. 4°. Jahrgang 1, col. 647–650.) *DF
From *Lloyd's evening-post*, 1763, p. 354.
Title page dated 1764; contents, 1763.

**406.** BESCHREIBUNG von Neu-Orleans, welches den Franzosen im Frieden verbleibet. (Hannoverisches Magazin...vom Jahre 1763. Hannover, 1764. 4°. Jahrgang 1, col. 649–654.) *DF
From *Lloyd's evening-post*, 1763, p. 354.
Title page dated 1764; contents, 1763.

**407.** KÖHLER, JOHANN TOBIAS. Beschreibung des Landes Florida in dem nördlichen Amerika, welches durch den neulichen glorreichen Frieden von Spanien an Grossbritannien abgetreten worden. (Hannoverisches Magazin...vom Jahre 1763. Hannover, 1764. 4°. Jahrgang 1, col. 417–460.) *DF
Title page dated 1764; contents, 1763.
"Es ist ... kein Wunder, dass einige missvergnügte Britten, deren besonderer Eigennutz der glorreiche Friede zuwider ist, aus Verdruss darüber in die bittersten Satyren gegen die Eroberung von Florida ausbrechen, deren Erdreich lauter Torf ist." Contains a bibliography of works on Florida, col. 419.
See also 398.

**408.** MORAVIAN BRETHREN. Das Kleine Brüder-Gesang-Buch in einer Harmonischen Sammlung von kurzen Liedern, Versen, Gebeten und Seufzern bestehend. Dritte Auflage. Gedrukt zu Barby, 1763. 8 p.l., 488 p., 32 l. 8°. *KF 1763
"Des kleinen Brüder-Gesangbuchs erster Theil enthaltend die Hirten-Lieder von Bethlehem... Nach der Germantowner Edition von 1742. und der Londner im Brüder-Hofe von 1754..." p. 1–88.
See R. R. Drummond, *Early German music in Philadelphia: University of Pennsylvania*, New York, 1910, *MF; R. H. Scott, *Music among the Moravians, Bethlehem, Pa., 1741–1816* [n. p., 1938?], *MF. (Bibliography, f. 254–259.)

**408A.** SCHREIBEN an Büffon, von dem Geschmacke der Engländer an dem Gartenbaue und Anpflanzen der Bäume; von den vielen vortreflichen Büchern, die sie über diese Materie haben, und von dem glücklichen Fortgange, mit welchem die königliche Societät zu London die natürliche und Experimentalphilosophie getrieben. (Hannoverische Beyträge zum Nutzen und Vergnügen vom Jahre 1762. Hannover, 1763. 4°. Theil 4, col. 1495–1504.) *DF
"Noch kürzlich hat man in Carolina einen Versuch mit Thee gemacht, und er soll recht gut fortgekommen seyn."— *col. 1503*.

**409.** *Review:* Voyages from Asia to America, for compleating the discoveries of the Northwest coast of America...a summary of the voyages of the Russians on the frozen Sea. Translation from the German of S. Müller. London: Thomas Jefferies, 1761. 119 p. 4°. (Göttingische Anzeigen von gelehrten Sachen. Göttingen [1763]. 12°. Jahr 1763, p. 237–240. *DF.)
Sabin 51285.
This is G. F. Müller's *Voyages from Asia...*, *KF 1761.

## 1764

**410.** HAGER, JOHANN GEORG. M. Johann Georg Hagers... Geographischer Büchersaal, zum Nutzen und Vergnügen der Liebhaber der Geographie eröfnet... Chemnitz: Bey Johann David Stössels Erben [1764–1778]. 3 v. 12°.
KA
"Issued periodically (irreg., 10 parts per volume), 1764–78."— *L. C. card*.
In this periodical the following reviews are of special interest: v. 1, p. 155, *Das Brittische und Spanische Reich in Amerika. Dritte Auflage*, Sorau, 1764; p. 473, *Christopher Columbus*; v. 2, p. 474–480, *Neue Geographische Spielcharte von Asia, Africa und America*..., Nürnberg, 1696; p. 563–589, *Descriptionis Ptolemaicae Augmentum*..., Louanii, 1598; v. 3, p. 218–233, *Neueste Geographie zum Gebrauche der Jugend*..., Breslau, 1775; p. 644–698, 771–778, *Geographische Belustigungen*..., Leipzig, 1776. See no. 513.
J. G. Hager's erroneous opinion on America is criticized in *Goettingische Anzeigen von gelehrten Sachen*, Goettingen [1755], Jahr 1755, Bd. 1, p. 664, *DF.
Reviews: *Allgemeine deutsche Bibliothek*, Anhang zu Bd. 1–12, p. 805–806, *NAA;* Anhang zu Bd. 25–36, p. 1398–1399, *NAA; Allgemeine deutsche Bibliothek*, Bd. 3, Stück 2, p. 288–290, *NAA*.

## 1765

**411.** AUSZUG eines Privatschreibens aus Edinburg, vom 9ten März: Nord-Amerika betreffend. (Hannoverisches Magazin...vom Jahre 1765. Hannover, 1766. 4°. Jahrgang 3, col. 713–718.) *DF
"Aus dem *London Chronicle* Nr. 1288. vom Jahr 1765."
About Indians, plants, and animals.
Title page dated 1766; contents, 1765.

**412.** CRANZ, DAVID. Historie von Grönland enthaltend Die Beschreibung des Landes und der Einwohner &c., insbesondere die Geschichte der dortigen Mission der Evangelischen Brüder zu Neu-Herrnhut und Lichtenfels. Mit acht Kupfertafeln und einem Register. Barby: Bey Heinrich Detlef Ebers, und in Leipzig in Commission bey Weidmanns Erben und Reich, 1765. 19 p.l., 5–1132 p., 14 l., 2 maps. 6 plates. 8°.
Sabin 17413. *KF 1765
Review: *Allgemeine deutsche Bibliothek*, 1767, Bd. 4, p. 213, *NAA*.
First edition.
Second edition, 1770; see no. 449.

**413.** FRAGEN, welche erst nach einigen Jahrhunderten können aufgelöst werden. (Hannoverisches Magazin...vom Jahre 1765. Hannover, 1766. 4°. Jahrgang 3, col. 1441–1448.)
Title page dated 1766; contents, 1765.
"Aus dem patriotischen Zuschauer, 251 St."
"Vielleicht werden einmal die Wissenschaften und Künste, der Handel, die Staatskunst nach America versetzt? das ist sehr möglich."— *col. 1448*.
Signed: C. D. E. [i.e. C. D. Ebeling.]

**414.** EIN KLEINER Versuch mit dem sibirischen Buchweizen und americanischen Flachs- oder Leinsaamen. (Hannoverisches Magazin...vom Jahre 1765. Hannover, 1766. 4°. Jahrgang 3, col. 391–396.) *DF
Signed: P. B. z. S. & E.
Title page dated 1766; contents, 1765.

*1765, continued*

415. VON der Indianischen oder Mohren-Hirse. (Hannoverisches Magazin...vom Jahre 1765. Hannover, 1766. 4°. Jahrgang 3, p. 509–512.)
See no. 421, 430. *DF
Title page dated 1766; contents, 1765.
See also Johann Beckmann, *Beytraege zur Geschichte der Erfindungen*, Leipzig, 1786, v. 2, p. 533–547, V.

416. *Review:* The ancient right of the English Nation to the American fishery and its various diminutions examined and Stated. London: Backer, 1764. 105 p. 4°. (Göttingische Anzeigen von gelehrten Sachen. Göttingen [1765]. 12°. Jahr 1765, p. 437–438, * DF.)
William Bollan is the author of this English work; the Library's copies are in * KF 1764.
"Der letzte Friede setzte Engelland in Besitz von ganz Canada, und die Nordamericanische Fischerey beschäftigte nunmehr bey 20000 Englische Seeleute. Nur soll die Menge an Fischen abgenommen haben."
Another work by William Bollan was rendered into German and published under the title, *Die Wichtigkeit und Vortheil des Kap-Breton*, Leipzig, 1747. Sabin 6217; only the English original is in the Library, * KC 1746.

417. *Review:* Coloniæ Anglicæ illustratæ, or the acquest of Dominion and the plantation of the Colonies made by the English in America. P. I. London: Backer, 1762. 141 p. 4°. (Göttingische Anzeigen von gelehrten Sachen. Göttingen [1765]. 12°. Jahr 1765, p. 436–437, * DF.)
William Bollan is the author of this English work, of which part I only was published; the Library's copies are in * KF 1762.
"...nur dass kein Buchstabe dem Titel entspricht, und von den Englischen Colonien in demselben kein Wort vorkommt."

**1766**

418. BEGEBENHEIT eines jungen Englischen Officiers unter den Abenakies. (Hannoverisches Magazin...vom Jahre 1766. Hannover, 1767. 4°. Jahrgang 4, col. 9–14.) *DF
"Aus dem *Gentleman's Magazine*, 1765."
Signed: C. C. K.
Title page dated 1767; contents, 1766.
See note on no. 603.

419. MEISTER, ALBERT LUDWIG FRIEDRICH. Nachricht von einem neuen musikalischen Instrumente, Harmonica genant. (Hannoverisches Magazin...vom Jahre 1766. Hannover, 1767. 4°. Jahrgang 4, col. 929–938.) *DF
Refers to Benjamin Franklin.
Title page dated 1767; contents, 1766.
"Der Erfinder des, unter dem Namen Harmonica, in England und Frankreich mit grossem Beyfall aufgenommenen, und in der Art, wie die Töne hervorgebracht werden, völlig neuen musikalischen Instrumentes, ist der berümte Franklin."
See B. M. Victory, *Benjamin Franklin and Germany*, [Philadelphia,] 1915 (Americana Germanica, no. 21), AN (*Franklin*).

420. NACHRICHT von den Proben und Ceremonien, bey der Aufnahme der Aerzte unter den Indianischen Caraiben, von Guyana in America erfodert werden, wie auch von der Art und Weise, wie diese Aerzte ihre Kunst treiben. (Hannoverisches Magazin...vom Jahre 1766. Hannover, 1767. 4°. Jahrgang 4, col. 513–524.) *DF
"Aus der *Gazette salutaire*, 1766. Nr. 7, 8."
Title page dated 1767; contents, 1766.

421. VON der Indianischen Hirse... (Hannoverisches Magazin...vom Jahre 1766. Hannover, 1767. 4°. Jahrgang 4, col. 455–460.) *DF
See nos. 415, 430.
Title page dated 1767; contents, 1766.

422. WESTFELD, C. F. G. Von dem Coffee. (Hannoverisches Magazin...vom Jahre 1766. Hannover, 1767. 4°. Jahrgang 4, col. 1475–1482.) *DF
Title page dated 1767; contents, 1766.
Describes experiments with coffee imported from the island of Martinique.
Author's full name: Christian Friedrich Gotthold Westfeld.

423. *Review:* Benjamin Franklin's book, entitled the interest of Great-Britain consider'd with regard to her Colonies and the acquisitions of Canada and Guadaloupe. 2nd edition. London: Th. Becket, 1761. (Neue Bibliothek der schönen Wissenschaften und der freyen Künste. Leipzig, 1766. 12°. Bd. 3, p. 125–127, *NAA.)
This is considered by the best authorities to have been jointly produced by Benjamin Franklin and Richard Jackson, under whose names it is catalogued in this Library; class mark, * KF 1761. Copies of the first edition are in * KF 1760.

424. *Review:* Cortes von Friedrich Wilhelm Zachariae Erster Band. Braunschweig: In Commission der Fürstl. Waisenhaus Buchhandlung, 1766. 14 v. kl. 8°. (Neue Bibliothek der schönen Wissenschaften und der freyen Künste. Leipzig, 1766. 12°. Bd. 3, p. 77–93, *NAA.)
Sabin 106241.
See no. 447.

425. *Review:* Die Junge Amerikanerin oder Verkürzung müssiger Stunden auf dem Meere, aus verschiedenen Sprachen übersetzt. Zwey Theile. Ulm: Bey Bartholomäi, 1765. 43 Bogen. 8°. (Allgemeine deutsche Bibliothek. Berlin, 1766. 12°. Bd. 2, Stück 2, p. 271, *NAA.)
Generally ascribed to Gabrielle Villeneuve. See *Gesamtkatalog der preussischen Bibliotheken*, v. 3, p. 927 ("see reference," only), listing an edition published 1765–1768. Sabin (99738) lists the French edition, published at The Hague, 1740–1741, 5 vols., but not the German.
"Feenmährchen zur Verkürzung der Reise erzählt."

426. *Review:* Der Nutzen und Gebrauch des Tobakrauchclystieres nebst zwoen dazu bequemen Maschinen beschrieben, und bey dieser zweyten Auflage vermehrt von Johann Gottlieb Schäffer... Regenspurg: verlegts Johann Leopold Montag, 1766. 12 Bogen. 4°. (Allgemeine deutsche Bibliothek. Berlin, 1767. 12°. Bd. 5, Stück 1, p. 276, *NAA.)
According to Kayser, v. 5, p. 54B, this is the second edition of an identical title which first appeared in Regensburg, 1757. A third edition followed in 1772.

## 1767

**427.** [ACHENWALL, GOTTFRIED.] Einige Anmerkungen über Nordamerika, und über dasige Grosbritannische Colonien. (Aus mündlichen Nachrichten des Hrn. Dr. Franklins.) (Hannoverisches Magazin...vom Jahre 1767. Hannover, 1768. 4°. Jahrgang 5, col. 257-296, 481-508.) *DF

Title page dated 1768; contents, 1767.
The author's report of what Benjamin Franklin told him.
According to Sabin (107), this was subsequently published in book form, with title, *Einige Anmerkungen über Nord-Amerika und über dasige Grossbrittannische Colonien. Aus mündlichen Nachrichten des Herrn D. Franklins verfasst. Nebst...John Wesleys Schrift von den Streitigkeiten mit den Colonien in Amerika*, Stuttgart, 1769, and, Helmstedt, 1777. (Title corrected according to *Gesamtkatalog der preussischen Bibliotheken*, v. 1, p. 507.)
According to the *Gesamtkatalog* (v. 1, p. 506), the first appearance was with the title, *Achenwalls Anmerkungen über Nord Amerika und über dasige grossbritannische Colonien aus mündlichen Nachrichten des Herrn Dr. Franklins*, and published at Frankfurt and Leipzig, 1769.
L. C. card shows further slight variations in spelling for the later appearance.
See Achenwall's *Observations on North America.* 1767. *Translated by J. G. Rosengarten*, Philadelphia, 1903, *IF p.v.4;* B. M. Victory, *Benjamin Franklin and Germany*, [Philadelphia,] 1915 (Americana Germanica, no. 21), *AN (Franklin)*.
Translation by J. G. Rosengarten in *Pennsylvania magazine of history and biography*, 1903: "Inexcusable treatment of a historical document; whole sentences omitted and translation is very careless." — B. Q. Morgan, *A critical bibliography of German literature in English translations*, 1938, p. 31, *RB-NFB*.

**428.** BESCHREIBUNG der Armonica des Hrn. Franklins. (Neue Bibliothek der schönen Wissenschaften und der freyen Künste. Leipzig, 1767. 12°. Bd. 4, p. 116-127.) NAA

Dated: H * * * den 26. Febr. 1767.
Description of the musical instrument called Armonica, and praise of Benjamin Franklin in general.
At end: "Written during his sojourn in Germany by one of his acquaintances."
See B. M. Victory, *Benjamin Franklin and Germany*, [Philadelphia,] 1915 (Americana Germanica, no. 21), *AN (Franklin)*.
One of the first accordion concerts in Germany is described in *Allgemeine Literatur-Zeitung*, Jahr 1788, Bd. 2, col. 215-216, 639-640, *NAA*.

**429.** CAMERARIUS, RUDOLF JACOB. Von dem Gebrauch der Beere des Americanischen traubentragenden und zur Fårberey dienlichen Nachtschattens, zu der Alkermes Confection. (Leopoldinisch-Carolinische deutsche Akademie Naturforscher. Der Römisch-Kaiserlichen Akademie der Naturforscher auserlesene ... Abhandlungen. Nürnberg, 1767. 4°. Theil 16, p. 173-176.) 3-* EE

"Geschrieben an D. Wepfer den älteren, welcher auch zu dieser fernern Untersuchung eingeladen worden." — *p. 176.*
See no. 443.

**430.** ETWAS, den Bau der Indianischen- oder Mohrenhirse, (Holcus Sorghum Linn.) betreffend. (Hannoverisches Magazin...vom Jahre 1767. Hannover, 1768. 4°. Jahrgang 5, col. 445-448.) *DF

Title page dated 1768; contents, 1767.
"Jn dem Jntelligenz-Comtoir ist Saamen für die Liebhaber zu bekommen."
See nos. 415, 421.

**431.** NACHRICHT von Versteinerungen, die in Amerika gefunden sind. (Hannoverisches Magazin...vom Jahre 1767. Hannover, 1768. 4°. Jahrgang 5, col. 287-288.) *DF

From *Journal des sçavans*, June, 1766, 3-OA.
Title page dated 1768; contents, 1767.
Don Ulloa, governor of Louisiana, reports about petrified shells found in Guancavelica, near Lima, South America. His letter is dated: Havanna, Dec. 30th, 1765.

**432.** *Review:* L'Espion américain en Europe, ou Lettres Ilinoises [Printed in Frankfurt]. 332 p. 8°. (Göttingische Anzeigen von gelehrten Sachen. Göttingen [1767]. 12°. Jahr 1767, p. 278-279, * *DF*.)

Sabin (2296) has the entry, *L'Espion Américain in Europe...suivies d'un poème intitulé la Religion Raisonnable. Par M. de V\*\*\**. London: aux dépens de la compagnie, 1766.
"Dieses ist wieder eine der vielen Nachahmungen des *l'Espion Turc.*" — *p. 278.*
This work has been recently acquired by the Library.

**433.** *Review:* Etrennes aux des oeuvrés ou Letre d'un Quaker à ses frères et a un grand Docteur. Iverdun [1767?]. 70 p. 8°. (Göttingische Anzeigen von gelehrten Sachen. Göttingen [1767]. 12°. Jahr 1767, p. 423-424, * *DF*.)

"Man hat wider die Hrn. Hume und Voltaire eben die Waffen brauchen wollen, die der letztere öfters glücklich gebraucht hat. Man lässt ziemlich unwahrscheinlich über einen so unerheblichen Streit, einen Pen. aus Pensylvanien schreiben..." *See no. 434.*

**434.** *Review:* Etrennes aux desoeuvrés [*sic!*], ou lettre d'un Quaker à ses freres [*sic!*] et à un grand docteur. London. 48 p. 8°. (Göttingische Anzeigen von gelehrten Sachen. Göttingen [1767]. 12°. Jahr 1767, p. 1120, * *DF*.)

London is fictitious for Haag.
"Es sind zwey Briefe, unter Ludw.[!] Penns Nahmen gedichtet, welche Rousseaus Streitigkeiten mit Hume ...und Voltairen betreffen... Der erste den Penn an die Quaker in Pensilvanien schreiben..." *See no.* 433.

## 1768

**435.** ADELUNG, JOHANN CHRISTOPH. Geschichte der Schiffahrten und Versuche welche zur Entdeckung des Nordöstlichen Weges nach Japan und China von verschiedenen Nationen unternommen worden. Zum Behufe der Erdbeschreibung und Naturgeschichte dieser Gegenden entworfen von Johann Christoph Adelung ... Halle: bey Joh. J. Gebauer, 1768. 4 p.l., 740 p., 29 plates (incl. maps). 25½ x 20½ cm. KBP

"Ich liefere in dem Werke nur diejenigen (Reisen), welche zum Behuf der nordöstlichen Durchfahrt unternommen worden."
There are discussions about the American aborigines, their manners, their language, etc., in the sixth book. Hudson's voyage is on page 63 et seq.

**436.** VON dem ersten Anbau der Cartuffeln in Deutschland. (Hannoverisches Magazin...vom Jahre 1768. Hannover, 1769. 4°. Jahrgang 6, col. 685-688.) *DF

Title page dated 1769; contents, 1768.
In *Hannoverisches Magazin...vom Jahre 1767*, Hannover, 1768, Jahrg. 5, col. 1643-1646 ("Von den Erdtoffeln") the question was raised as to when the potato had been brought to Germany. An answer is given in the above essay, concluding: "Weiss man doch jetzo noch Gegenden, wo die Cartuffeln noch nicht eingeführet, und noch...in Verachtung sind..."

*1768, continued*

437. *Review:* Gli Americani, Tragedia. In Firenze: appresso Gio. Batista Stecchi, e Anton Giuseppe Pagani, 1768. 99 p. 8°. (Neue Bibliothek der schönen Wissenschaften und der freyen Künste. Leipzig, 1768. 12°. Bd. 7, p. 159–160, *NAA.*)
"Der Verfasser hat sich nicht genennet; doch weiss man, dass er sich schon durch andre dramatische Werke viel Ruhm erworben. Das gegenwärtige befestigt denselben. Er scheint darinnen den Menschen im Stande der Natur schildern zu wollen..." The Library's copy of this work is in * *KL.*

438. *Review:* Histoire naturelle et politique de la Pensylvanie, et de l'établissement des Quakers dans cetté contrée, traduit de l'allemand par P. M. D. S. Censeur Royal. Paris: Ganeau, 1768. 376 p. (Göttingische Anzeigen von gelehrten Sachen. Göttingen [1768]. 12°. Jahr 1768, p. 1151–1152, * *DF.*)
This work, compiled by J. P. Rouselot de Surgy, is based mainly on P. Kalm's *Resa till Norra Amerika,* 1753–61 (* *KF 1753*), and G. Mittelberger's *Reise nach Pennsylvanien im Jahr 1750,* 1756 (* *KF 1756*), among other contemporary accounts. Its class mark is * *KF 1768.*
Various errors in quotation of title in review.

439. *Review:* Inkle und Yariko, ein prosaisches Trauerspiel in drey Handlungen, 1768. 5 Bogen 8°. (Neue Bibliothek der schönen Wissenschaften und der freyen Künste. Leipzig, 1768. 12°. Bd. 7, p. 344–345, *NAA.*)
The original, *Incle and Yarico; a tragedy in three acts...,* was published in London in 1742. It was written by a journeyman printer, Wedderburn, according to Halkett and Laing's *Dictionary of anonymous and pseudonyms,* v. 3, p. 146. See also L. M. Price, *Inkle and Yarico album,* 1937, *NABX.*
Bibliographical notes by Gerhard Desczyk, in Deutsch-amerikanische historische Gesellschaft von Illinois, *Jahrbuch 1924–25,* p. 115, *IEK.*
Note also Dorat, *Barnewell im Gefängniss und Yariko in der Sklaverei. Aus dem Französischen* [von *H. W. D. Brässl*], Braunschweig, 1766. Sabin 20617. Not in the Library.

440. *Review:* Voyage d'un Philosophe ou observations sur les moeurs et les arts des peuples de l'Amerique, de l'Asie et de l'Afrique par Poivre. Yverdun, 1768. 142 p. 12°. (Göttingische Anzeigen von gelehrten Sachen. Göttingen [1768]. 12°. Jahr 1768, p. 707–710, * *DF.*)
The author is Pierre Poivre; the class mark, *KBI.*
"Originally read before the Royal Society of Agriculture at Lyons... For the benefit of the American farmers and legislators it is now printed.."—*Preface.*
Sabin (63720) mentions a German version: *Reisen eines Philosophen, oder Bemerkungen über die Sitten und Künste der Einwohner von Afrika, Asien und Amerika,* Salzburg, 1783, which is not in the Library.

*1769*

441. [ADELUNG, JOHANN CHRISTOPH.] Versuch einer kurzen Geschichte des Jesuiter-Ordens von dessen ersten Stiftung an bis auf die gegenwärtigen Zeiten... Berlin und Halle, 1769–1770. 3 v. in 2. 8°. ZMTK
Many references to America.
Note also *Kurtze Nachricht von der Republique, so von denen R. R. P. P. der Gesellschaft Jesu der Portugiesisch- und Spanischen Provinzen,* Lissabon, 1760 (Sabin 38355); *Sammlung der neuesten Schrifften, welche die Jesuiten in Portugal betreffen,* Franckfurt und Leipzig, 1760–62 (Sabin 75904); *Charles de Brosses, Vollständige Geschichte der Schiffarthen nach den... Südlandern,* Halle, 1767. These are not in the Library. The last work "contains voyages of Vespucci, Magellan, Drake, Sarmiento, Hawkins, De Nort, Spilberg, Nodal, Schouten, the Buccaneers, etc..."— *Sabin 8389.* See also Sabin 9731, 9736, 17317, 29590.

442. [FRANKLIN, BENJAMIN.] The Triumph of the Arts (ode). (Neue Bibliothek der schönen Wissenschaften und der freyen Künste. Leipzig, 1769. 12°. Bd. 8, p. 181–185.) NAA
English text with German translation.
It is stated (p. 181) that the ode is printed from Benjamin Franklin's own manuscript, and that it was sung at the occasion of the institution of the Royal Academy of Arts in London, January 1st, 1769.
See B. M. Victory, *Benjamin Franklin in Germany,* [Philadelphia,] 1915 (Americana Germanica, no. 21), *AN (Franklin).* Bibliographical notes, p. 160–180.

443. SCHULZ, GOTTFRIED. Vom Americanischen traubentragenden und zur Färbung dienlichen Nachtschatten. (Leopoldinisch-Carolinische deutsche Akademie Naturforscher. Der Römisch-Kaiserlichen Akademie der Naturforscher auserlesene... Abhandlungen. Nürnberg, 1769. 4°. Theil 18, p. 285.) 3–* EE
The experiment described in this work was undertaken as early as 1689.

444. SPEELHOVEN, MARTIN. Die Glücks- und Unglücksfälle Martin Speelhovens, eines Kaufmanns, aus dem Clevischen gebürtig, welche ihm sowohl in seiner Jugend, als auch auf Reisen nach America begegnet, nebst Dessen Gefangennehmung und Flucht wie auch achtzehnjährigen Aufenthalte auf einer damals noch nie besuchten Jnsel und endlichen Befreyung von ihm selbst beschrieben. Dressden und Leipzig: Bey Joh. Nicolaus Gerlachs Wittwe und Sohn, 1769. x, 460 p., frontis. 12°. * KF 1769
Sabin 89243.
First edition, 1763.

445. [VENEGAS, MIGUEL.] Natürliche und bürgerliche Geschichte von Californien nebst einer neuen Charte dieses Landes und der benachbarten Meere. Aus dem Englischen übersetzt und herausgegeben von Johan Christoph Adelung... Lemgo: In den Meyerschen Buchhandlung, 1769–1770. 3 v. in 1. frontis. (map.) 24 cm. * KF 1769
Sabin 98846.
Original: *Noticia de la California...,* Madrid, 1757, * *KF 1757.*
Review: *Göttingische Anzeigen von gelehrten Sachen,* Jabr 1770, p. 130; Zugabe, p. 360, * *DF.* See nos. 389, 454.
Another German version, *Nachricht von Californien und seiner Einnahme bis aufs Jahr 1752,* Thal-Ehrenbreitstein [n. d.] (Sabin 98844; Kayser, v. 4, p. 196A), is not in the Library.

446. *Review:* The American Traveller or Observations on the present State, Culture and Commerce of the British Colonies in America and the further Improvements of which they are capable. London, 1769. 122 p. 4°. (Göttingische Anzeigen von gelehrten Sachen. Göttingen [1768]. 12°. Jahr 1768, p. 1354–1357, * *DF.*)
The Library's copies of this work by Alexander Cluny are in * *KF 1769.*
Sabin (69142) mentions a German version: *Reisen durch Amerika,* Leipzig, 1783, which is not in the Library.

## GERMAN WORKS RELATING TO AMERICA 59

### 1769, continued

**447.** *Review:* Cortes, von Friedrich Wilhelm Zachariä. Erster Band. Braunschweig: In Commission der Waisenhausbuchhandlung, 1766. 14 Bogen. 8°. ohne Vorrede. (Allgemeine deutsche Bibliothek. Berlin, 1769. 8°. Bd. 9, Stück 1, p. 323–328, *NAA*.)
See no. 424.

### 1770

**448.** Büsch, Johann Georg. Allgemeine Anmerkungen über den Zustand der Handlung in den europäischen Staaten, und über einige Vorurtheile der neuern Handlungspolitik. (Hannoverisches Magazin...vom Jahre 1770. Hannover, 1771. 4°. Jahrgang 8, col. 1153–1216.) *DF
Title page dated 1771; contents, 1770.
German exports to America, col. 1202.
"...mit den nordamerikanischen [Kolonien] hat England weit mehr Mühe. Denn da diese einen dem englischen so sehr ähnlichen Boden und Witterung haben, so fällt es freylich schwer für England, sie auf immer zu hindern, dass sie nicht auf diesem Boden die Produkten, die ihnen England bisher geliefert, selbst ziehen..."

**449.** Cranz, David. ...Historie von Grönland, enthaltend Die Beschreibung des Landes und der Einwohner &c., insbesondere die Geschichte der dortigen Mission der Evangelischen Brüder zu Neu-Herrnhut und Lichtenfels. Zweyte Auflage. Mit acht Kupfertafeln und einem Register. Barby: Bey Heinrich Detlef Ebers; und in Leipzig..., 1770. 18 p.l., 5–1132 p., 13 l., folding plates, 2 folding maps. 18 cm. *KF 1770
Second edition.
For first edition, *see* no. 412.

**450.** [Heise, H.N.] Von der Nation der Caraiben in America. (Hannoverisches Magazin ...vom Jahre 1770. Hannover, 1771. 4°. Jahrgang 8, col. 865–888.) *DF
Title page dated 1771; contents, 1770.
Attribution of authorship from index.
Author's full name: Johann Christoph Friedrich Heise.
Information in this article taken from various sources: *Allgemeine Historie der Reisen zu Wasser und zu Lande*, v. 7 (see no. 378); Father Raymond's *The Carribian vocabulary*, 1666 (see British Museum catalogue); and Father Labat's work (see nos. 874, 921).

**451.** Nach dem jezigen Staat eingerichtete Bilder-Geographie, darinnen von den vier Haupttheilen des Erdbodens Europa, Asia, Afrika und Amerika Nachricht gegeben, alle Nationen nach ihrer Kleidung in saubern Figuren vorgestellet, und die Länder nach ihrer Lage, Flüssen, Clima, Fruchtbarkeit, Einwohnern, Handlung, Macht, Regierungsform, vornehmsten Städten und Merkwürdigkeiten beschrieben werden; als ein bequemes Handbuch zum Gebrauch der neuesten geographischen Charten eingerichtet, und mit doppeltem Register versehen. Nürnberg: Zu finden bey Christoph Riegels seel. Wittib, 1770. 40 p.l., 5–834 p., 25 l. incl. engraved frontis., folding map. illus. 8°. *KF 1770
For sources of this book, see note on the Library's Public Catalogue card.

**452.** Von Ableitung der Donnerstrahlen. (Hannoverisches Magazin...vom Jahre 1770. Hannover, 1771. 4°. Jahrgang 8, col. 321–336.) *DF
Title page dated 1771; contents, 1770.
Refers to Benjamin Franklin.
"Ob ich gleich im folgenden erweisen werde, dass die Mittel welche der Herr D. Franklin zu Ableitung der Donnerstrahlen vorgeschlagen hat, nicht die bequemsten sind, so werde ich dennoch aus seinem Systeme selbst sowohl die Gründe dazu nehmen, als auch in Vorschlag bringen, wie sie auf eine sichere Art eingerichtet werden können."

**453.** Von den Schicksalen einer englischen Colonie. (Hannoverisches Magazin...vom Jahre 1770. Hannover, 1771. 4°. Jahrgang 8, col. 1089–1098.) *DF
Title page dated 1771; contents, 1770.
Relates to Newfoundland.

**454.** *Review:* Noticia de la California y de sa conquista. En Madrid: En la Imprenta de la Viuda de Manuel Fernandez, 1757. 3 v. 4°. (Göttingische Anzeigen von gelehrten Sachen. Göttingen [1770]. 12°. Jahr 1770, Zugabe, p. 360, *DF.)
See nos. 389, 445.

**455.** *Review:* Philosophische Untersuchungen über die Amerikaner, oder wichtige Beyträge zur Geschichte des menschlichen Geschlechts. Aus dem Franz. des Hrn. von P.** [Paw]. Berlin: Bey Decker und Winter, 1769. (Allgemeine deutsche Bibliothek. Berlin, 1770. 12°. Bd. 12, Stück 1, p. 114–139, *NAA*.)
Sabin 59248.
Translation of *Recherches philosophiques sur les Américains*, by Corneille de Pauw (various editions in *KF*).
See nos. 456, 457, 491.

**456.** *Review:* Philosophische Untersuchungen über die Americaner. Berlin: 1769. 2 v. (Göttingische Anzeigen von gelehrten Sachen. Göttingen [1770]. 12°. Jahr 1770, p. 177–182, *DF.)
See nos. 455, 457, 491.

**457.** *Review:* Recherches philosophiques sur les Americains ou Memoires interessants pour servir a l'histoire de l'espéce humaine par M. de P** ... A Berlin: Chéz George Jacques Decker, 1768. 8°. (Allgemeine deutsche Bibliothek. Berlin, 1770. 8°. Bd. 12, Stück 1, p. 114–139, *NAA*.)
See nos. 455, 456, 491.

### 1771

**458.** Amerikanisches Mittel wider den Rheumatismus oder die Gicht. (Hannoverisches Magazin...vom Jahre 1771. Hannover, 1772. 4°. Jahrgang 9, col. 1663–1664.) *DF
"Aus dem hamburg. Adrescomtoir-Nachrichten."
Title page dated 1772; contents, 1771.

**459.** Die Ananas. (Hannoverisches Magazin ...vom Jahre 1771. Hannover, 1772. 4°. Jahrgang 9, col. 465–478.) *DF
"Aus der Encyclopédie œconomique Tome II, a Yverdun 1770."
Compares pineapples grown in Europe with those of the West Indies.
Title page dated 1772; contents, 1771.
For the history of the use of pineapples in Germany, see Johann Beckmann, in *Beytraege zur Geschichte der Erfindungen*, Leipzig, 1786, v. 1, p. 435–446, *V*.

*1771, continued*

**460.** CRANZ, DAVID. Alte und Neue Brüder-Historie oder kurz gefasste Geschichte der Evangelischen Brüder-Unität in den ältern Zeiten und insonderheit in dem gegenwärtigen Jahrhundert. Von David Cranz... Barby: Bey Heinrich Detlef Ebers, und in Leipzig: Bey H. D. Ebers...1771. 8 p.l., 868 p., 29 l. 8°.
*See* Sabin 17410.                     *KF 1771
Deals with the colonization of the Moravian Brethren in Pennsylvania, Georgia, Surinam, and the West Indies. The work is dated: Amerika, St. Jans in West Jndien den 2ten Sept. 1743.

**461.** ERLÄUTERUNG für Herrn Caspar Schwenckfeld, und die Zugethanen, seiner Lehre, wegen vieler Stücke, beydes aus der Historie und Theologie, welche insgemein unrichtig vorgestellet, oder gar übergangen werden. Worinnen Deroselben Historie bis 1740. kürtzlich entworffen... Alles aus bewährten glaubhaften und vielen noch niemahls an Tag gekommenen, richtigen Documenten, und eigener Erfahrung, treulich und einfältig beschrieben...durch Etliche der ehemahligen Emigranten aus Schlesien, und nunmehro eingesessene Innwohner in Pensylvanien in Nord-America... Breslau und Leipzig: In Commission bey Gottfr. Wilh. Seidel, Buchhändler; Jauer: Gedruckt bey Heinrich Christian Müllern, 1771. 8 p.l., 464 p., 2 l. 19 cm. *KF 1771
See also C. G. Jaehne, *Dankbare Erinnerung an die Gemeinde der Schwenkfelder zu Philadelphia in Nordamerika*, Görlitz, 1816, *ZXP*; S. K. Brecht, *The genealogical record of the Schwenkfelder families*, New York and Chicago, 1923, *APR*; *Corpus Schwenckfeldianorum*... *Published under the auspices of the Schwenckfelder Church, Pennsylvania*, v. 1-13, Leipzig, 1907-35, *ZXP*. Contains bibliographies; H. W. Kriebel, *Die Schwenkfelders in Pennsylvania; a historical sketch*, Lancaster, 1904 (Pennsylvania German Society, Proceedings and addresses, v. 13), *IEK*. It may be noted here that in 1762 the Schwenckfelders published their *Neueingerichtetes Gesangbuch;* see A. A. Seipt, *Schwenkfelder hymnology and the sources of the first Schwenkfelder hymn-book printed in America*, Philadelphia, 1909 (Americana Germanica, new series, monographs, v. 7), *ZHT*.
See no. 329.

**462.** GREGOR, CHRISTIAN. Meiner Tochter Christiane Gregorin zu ihrem eilften Geburtstage den 13. October 1771. aus Bethlehem nach Herrnhut. (In: J. W. von Goethe. Goethes Werke, herausgegeben im Auftrage der Grossherzogin Sophie von Sachsen. Weimar, 1887-1919. 4°. Bd. 5, Abtheilung 2, p. 140-144.)
Dated Bethlehem, im Juny 1771.       NFGK
The rhymed letter influenced Goethe's poem, "An Silvie von Ziegesar. Karlsbad, zum 21. Juni 1808," beginning "Nicht am Susquehanna, der durch Wüsten fliesst..."
See C. F. Schreiber, *Goethe — Herrnhut — America*, in Deutsch-amerikanische historische Gesellschaft von Illinois, *Jahrbuch*, Chicago, Ill., 1920-21, v. 20-21, p. 305-313, *IEK*.
This volume dated 1910.

**463.** MORALISCHER Artikel aus dem Pensylvanischen Haushaltscalender, vom Jahre 1770. (Hannoverisches Magazin...vom Jahr 1771. Hannover, 1772. 4°. Jahrgang 9, col. 609-624.)
Dated: Philadelphia, 1769.             *DF

Signed: Joh. Pet. Celler, deutscher Calendermacher. Contains an interesting annotation by the editor concerning Pennsylvania.
Title page dated 1772; contents, 1771.
Concerning German almanacs in the United States, see Pennsylvania German Society, *Proceedings*, Lancaster, Pa., 1935, v. 45, p. 257-287, *IEK*.
Joh. Pet. Celler is most probably identical with Johan Peter Keller who, aged 35, arrived on the *Patience and Margaret*, John Govan, captain, from Rotterdam in 1748. See List 123A in R. B. Strassburger and W. M. Hinke, *Pennsylvania German pioneers; a publication of the original lists of arrivals in the port of Philadelphia from 1727 to 1808*, Norristown, Pa., 1934, v. 1, p. 387, *IEK (Pennsylvania)*.

**464.** NACHRICHT von der Insel Jamaica. (Aus den Briefen eines daselbst wohnenden Deutschen.) (Hannoverisches Magazin...vom Jahre 1771. Hannover, 1772. 4°. Jahrgang 9, col. 145-164.)                      *DF
"Aus den Manheimischen Beyträgen."
Title page dated 1772; contents, 1771.
*Contents:* Von der natürlichen Beschaffenheit der Jnsel. Von den Einwohnern dieser Jnsel und zwar erstlich von den Europäern oder Weissen. Von den Schwarzen.
See no. 466.

**465.** ZIMMERMANN, PETER CARL. Peter Carl Zimmermann Reise nach Ost- und West-Indien. Hamburg: bey Buchenröder und Ritter, 1771. 40 p. 8°.                             *KF p.v.12

**466.** *Review:* Beyträge zur Sittenlehre, Oekonomie, Arzneywissenschaft, Naturlehre und Geschichte in ihrem allgemeinen Umfange aus den westlichen Gegenden Deutschlandes. Erstes Stück. Manheim: Schwan, 1770. 127 p. 8°. (Göttingische Anzeigen von gelehrten Sachen. Göttingen [1771]. 12°. Jahr 1771, p. 784, *DF.)
The fifth "Abhandlung" of the *Beyträge* is entitled "Eines Ungenannten, der aber auf der Jnsel gewesen ist, Nachrichten von Jamaica."
See no. 464.

---

*1772*

**467.** [BAEGERT, JACOB.] Nachrichten von der Amerikanischen Halbinsel Californien: mit einem zweyfachen Anhang falscher Nachrichten. Geschrieben von einem Priester der Gesellschaft Jesu, welcher lang darinn diese letztere Zeit gelebt hat... Mannheim: Churfürstl. Hof- und Academie-Buchdruckerey, 1772. 8 p.l., 358 p., 1 l. plates, folding map. 17½ x 10 cm.                         *KF 1772
Sabin 4363.
Kayser, v. 4, p. 196A notes a cheaper edition of Baegert's work: "bei Franz in München," n. d.
Chapt. 20 relates to the language of the Indians of California. There is a translation of the ethnological portions, by Charles Rau, in the "Smithsonian report," 1863, p. 352-369, and 1864, p. 378-399.
See *Georg Christoph Lichtenbergs Aphorismen. Viertes Heft, 1789-1793. Nach den Handschriften herausgegeben von Albert Leitzmann*, Berlin, 1908 (Deutsche Litteraturdenkmale des 18. und 19. Jahrhunderts, 3. Folge, No. 20, *NFF*). Aphorism no. 125 (p. 28) reads: "Nach Begerts Erzaehlung binden die Californier Stücke Fleisch an Bindfaden und verschlucken sie, ziehn sie alsdann wieder heraus, und so sehr ofttmal, um es offt zu schmecken."
*Review: Göttingische Anzeigen von gelehrten Sachen*, 1772, p. 1256-1260, *DF*.
See no. 477.

1772, continued

468. ENGEL, SAMUEL. ...Geographische und Kritische Nachrichten und Anmerkungen über die Lage der nördlichen Gegenden von Asien und Amerika...welchen noch ein Versuch über einen Weg durch Norden nach Indien, und über die Errichtung eines...Handels in die Südsee beygefüget ist...Nebst zwo...Karten. Aus dem Französischen übersetzet, von dem herrn verfasser...durchgesehen verb. und mit vielen neuen zusätzen bereichert... Mietau [etc.]: bey Jacob Friedrich Hinz, 1772-1777. 2 v. 5 folding maps. 25½ cm.   *KF 1772
The Library has volume 2, only.
v. 2 has title page: ...Neuer Versuch über die Lage der nördlichen Gegenden von Asia und Amerika, und dem Versuch eines Wegs durch die Nordsee nach Indien; nebst denen Schriften so Hr. Daines Barrington in London zu Behauptung eben dieses herausgegeben. Mit drey Charten. Basel: Bey C. A. Serini, 1777.
v. 2 has added title page: ...Nachrichten und Anmerkungen über die Lage der nördlichen Gegenden von Asia und Amerika, und dem Versuch eines Wegs durch die Nordsee nach Indien. Zweyter Theil... Basel: Bey Carl August Serini, 1777.
Reviews: *Allgemeine deutsche Bibliothek*, 1777, Anhang zu Bd. 13/24, p. 677-681; 1780, Anhang zu Bd. 25/36, Abth. 3, p. 1468-1472, *NAA*.
Note also his *Anmerkungen über den Theil von Cap. Cooks Reise-relation, so die Meerenge zwischen Asia und Amerika ansiehet*, [n. p.,] 1780. Sabin 22567. Not in the Library. See also no. 728.

469. NACHRICHT von der Provinz Virginien in Nord-America, nebst ausführlichen Beschreibung der entsetzlichen Wasser-Fluth so gedachte Provinz im Jahre 1771. Monaths May erlitten. Als auch Beschreibung von der Schlacht und gänzlichen Ausrottung der Regulatorn in Nord-Carolina in America. Deme annoch beygefüget eine ausführliche und accurate Geographische Beschreibung der Provinz Pennsylvanien in Nord-America. Frankfurt am Mayn: In Joh. Georg Fleischers Buchhandlung, 1772. 16 p. 4°.   *KF 1772
Sabin 51690. Meynen 261.
Review: *Büschings wöchentliche Nachricht*, 1773, p. 421.
Not in the Library.

470. *Review*: Flora Americae Septentrionalis; or a Catalogue of the Plants of North America. Containing an Enumeration of the known Herbs, Shrubs and Trees, many of which are but lately discovered. By John Reinhold Forster. London. 8 v. (Deutsche Litteraturdenkmale des 18. Jahrhunderts. Heilbronn, 1883. 8°. [Nr.] 7/8, p. 246-247, *NFF*.)
This volume is a reprint of *Frankfurter gelehrte Anzeigen vom Jahr 1772*, in which the review originally appeared.
"Hr. Forster, der Uebersetzer von Kalms Reisen und der Verf. einer Nordamericanischen Zoologie, liefert hier nach D. Gronov Flora Virginica alle Nordamericanische Pflanzen mit englischen Namen."

471. *Review*: A general history of the British Empire in America: Including all the countries in North America and the Westindies, ceded by the peace of Paris. By Mr. Wynne. 2 Vols. 10 S. Boards. 8°. London: Richardson and Urquhart, 1770. (Deutsche Litteraturdenkmale des 18. Jahrhunderts. Heilbronn, 1883. 8°. [Nr.] 7/8, p. 286-291, *NFF*.)
This volume is a reprint of *Frankfurter gelehrte Anzeigen vom Jahr 1772*, in which the review originally appeared.
The Library's copy of this English work by J. H. Wynne is in *KF 1770. See Sabin 67675.

472. *Review*: An historical Essay on the English Constitution; or an impartial Inquiry into the elective Power of the People, from the first Establishment of the Saxons in this Kingdom, wherein the Right of Parliament to tax our distant Provinces is explained and justified, upon such constitutional Principles as will afford an equal Security to the Colonists as to their Brethren at home. London: Dilly, 1771. 4 p. 8°. (Deutsche Litteraturdenkmale des 18. Jahrhunderts. Heilbronn, 1883. 8°. [Nr.] 7/8, p. 161-165, *NFF*.)
This volume is a reprint of *Frankfurter gelehrte Anzeigen vom Jahr 1772*, in which this review originally appeared.
The author of the work is Allan Ramsay. See Sabin no. 67675.

473. *Review*: The present State of the European Settlements on the Missisippi, with a geographical Description of that River; illustrated by Plans and Draughts. By Captain Philipp Pittmann. Nourse, 1770. 6 S. sewed. 4°. (Deutsche Litteraturdenkmale des 18. Jahrhunderts. Heilbronn, 1883. 8°. [Nr.] 7/8, p. 39-40, *NFF*.)
This volume is a reprint of *Frankfurter gelehrte Anzeigen vom Jahr 1772*, in which this review originally appeared.
The Library's copy is in *KF 1770. For further details see Sabin 63103.
"Die Europäische Pflanzstädte an dem Fluss Missisippi begreifen Louisiana, einen Theil von Westflorida, und das Land der Jndianer, die man unter dem Namen der Illinois kennt. Es ist eine Art von Staatsschrift, die von dem Minister, der die Angelegenheiten der Colonien besorgt, von dem Verfasser verlangt wurde."

474. *Review*: Transactions of the American Philosophical Society, held at Philadelphia, for promoting useful Knowledge. Vol. 1. from January 1st, 1769 to Jan. 1, 1771. Printed at Philadelphia, 1771. 4°. (Deutsche Litteraturdenkmale des 18. Jahrhunderts. Heilbronn, 1883. 8°. [Nr.] 7/8, p. 40-41, *NFF*.)
This volume is a reprint of *Frankfurter gelehrte Anzeigen vom Jahr 1772*, in which this review originally appeared.
The Library's copy of the *Transactions*, in *KD 1771*, has the following dedication: "The American Philosophical Society held at Philadelphia, humbly desirous to co-operate with the Royal Society of Göttingen in the laudable Endeavors for the Advancement of useful knowledge, request that Learned and respectable Body, to accept this Volume, as the first Fruits of their Labors in this new World. By Order of the Society, signed: William Smith, Robert Strettell Jones, secretaries." By mistake, apparently, another copy was sent to Germany.
Contains articles on astronomy, meteorology, machines, agriculture, making of wine, volcanos, analysis of well water, medicine. The contributors are: Edward Antill, Samuel Bard, Isaac Bartram, Moses Bartram, Owen Biddle, Thomas Bond, John Bradley, Landon Carter, Thomas Coombe, John De Normandie, John Ellis, John Ewing, Archibald Gloster, William Henry, Henry Hollingworth, John Jones, Dr. John Lorimer, Nevil Maskelyne, John Morel, John Morgan, Peter Mueller, Lewis Nicola, Bodo Otto, David Rittenhouse, Benjamin Rush, Robert Smith, William Smith, Benjamin West, Richard Wells, Hugh Williamson.
The *Transactions* also contain, "A Letter from Bethlehem, on making currant wine."
See no. 492.

*1772, continued*

475. *Review:* Der Westindier, ein Lustspiel in fünf Handlungen, aus dem Englischen des Hrn. Cumberland. Hamburg, 1772. 186 p. 8°. (Deutsche Litteraturdenkmale des 18. Jahrhunderts. Heilbronn, 1883. 8°. [Nr.] 7/8, p. 265-266, *NFF.*)
This volume is a reprint of *Frankfurter gelehrte Anzeigen vom Jahr 1772*, in which this review originally appeared.
For a later German version (Marburg, 1838), see Sabin 17878.
"Da unsere Natur zur Bewunderung zu klein, und zum Lachen zu schlecht geworden ist, so können wir's dramatischen Dichtern nicht übel nehmen, dass sie sich Naturen aus fremden Welttheilen holen."
In 1792, the famous actor, F. L. Schroeder, took over the part of the Westindier and scored a great and long success. See Gerhard Desczyk, in *Deutsch-amerikanische historische Gesellschaft von Illinois, Jahrbuch*, Chicago, 1924-25, p. 37, *IEK.*
*See* no. 476.

476. *Review:* Der West-Indier, ein Lustspiel aus dem Englischen des Hrn. Richard Cumberland, von Johann Joachim Christoph Bode. Hamburg, 1772. 186 p. 8°. (Göttingische Anzeigen von gelehrten Sachen. Göttingen [1772]. 12°. Jahr 1772, Zugabe, p. 320, *\* DF.*)
*See* no. 475.

**1773**

477. [BAEGERT, JACOB.] Nachrichten von der Amerikanischen Halbinsel Californien: mit einem zweyfachen Anhang falscher Nachrichten. Geschrieben von einem Priester der Gesellschaft Jesu, welcher lang darinn diese letztere Jahr gelebet hat. ...Mannheim: Churfürstliche Hof- und Academie Buchdruckerey, 1773. 8 p.l., 358 p., plates, folding map. 17½ x 10 cm.  *\* KF 1773
Sabin 4363.
First published in 1772.
Plates by E. Verelst.
*See* no. 467.

478. EIN NEUES Lied von Amerika. [1773?] (In: F. W. Freiherr von Ditfurth. Historische Volkslieder der Zeit von 1756 bis 1871... Aus fliegenden Blättern, handschriftlichen Quellen und dem Volksmunde... Berlin, 1871-1872. 8°. Bd. 1 [Theil 2], p. 4-5.)  NFL
Called Theil 2 on main title page; has separate title: Die Historischen Volkslieder vom Ende des siebenjährigen Kriegs, 1763, bis zum Brande von Moskau, 1812... Berlin: Lipperheide, 1872.

479. POLITISCHE Nachrichten. (Der Deutsche Merkur. Weimar, 1773. 12°. Bd. 1, Stück 3, p. 276-283.)  *\* DF (Neue)
Predicts the American revolution, p. 279.
For Chr. M. Wieland's attitude towards America, see H. S. King, in University of California, *Publications in modern philology*, Berkeley, 1929, v. 14, p. 129-134, *STG*, and Hans Wahl, *Geschichte des Teutschen Merkur*, Berlin, 1914, *NAC p.v.136*. As to the stand of the *Teutscher Merkur* on the American Revolution, see J. A. Walz, in *Modern language notes*, Baltimore, 1901, v. 16, p. 225, *RAA*, and H. P. Gallinger, *Die Haltung der deutschen Publizistik zu dem amerikanischen Unabhängigkeitskriege 1775-1783*, Leipzig, 1900, *IG*.
See nos. 497, 523, 546, 712.
This periodical subsequently called *Der Neue teutsche Merkur*, under which it is shelved.

480. SPANGENBERG, AUGUST GOTTLIEB. Leben des Herrn Nicolaus Ludwig Grafen und Herrn von Zinzendorf und Pottendorf, beschrieben von August Gottlieb Spangenberg. Theil 1-2. [Barby:] Zu finden in den Brudergemeinen [1773]. 2 parts in 1. 8°.  AN (Zinzendorf)
Theil 3-8 lacking.
An English translation by Samuel Jackson is in *AN (Zinzendorf)*. See also A. L. Fries, *Some Moravian heroes*, Bethlehem, Pa., *ZAE p.v. 699*, and W. C. Reichel, *Memorials of the Moravian Church*, Philadelphia, 1870, v. 1.
*See* no. 486.

480A. *Review:* Die Harbkesche wilde Baumzucht, theils nordamerikanischer und anderer fremden... Bäume, Sträucher und strauchartigen Pflanzen, ... beschrieben von Dr. Johann Philipp du Roi. Braunschweig: Im Waysenhause, 1772. 8°. (Allgemeine deutsche Bibliothek. Berlin, 1773. 12°. v. 19, p. 418-428, *NAA.*)
"Der Rittersitz des Hrn. Hofrichters von Veltheim, Harbke, enthält die Pflanzungen, die hier beschrieben werden, und liegt an der Gränze des magdeburgischen und Braunschweigischen Gebiets. Seitdem man in Pflanzungen nordamerikanischer Bäume Geschmack gefunden (d.i. seit 20 Jahren etwa, wie Hr. du Roi bemerkt) haben wir doch kein Buch das so genau eine pflanzenreiche beschriebe als das gegenwärtige, so sehr wir auch die im 5ten Th. des Hausvaters vom Hrn. v. Münchhausen mitgetheilten Abhandlungen des Hrn. Jacobi schätzen."
The British Museum catalogue mentions Otto von Muenchhausen, *Der Hausvater*, 6 Theile, Hannover, 1766, 1765-73.
A supplement to du Roi's work is T. M. Hennert, *Bemerkungen auf einer Reise nach Harbke*, Berlin, 1792.

481. *Review:* Histoire philosophique & politique des établissemens & du Commerce des Européens dans les deux Indes. 6 v. 8°. (Der Deutsche Merkur. Weimar, 1773. Bd. 1, Stück 3, p. 259-260, *\* DF [Neue].*)
This periodical subsequently called *Der Neue teutsche Merkur*, under which it is shelved.

**1774**

482. CLAUDIUS, MATTHIAS. Asmus omnia sua Secum portans, oder Sämmtliche Werke des Wandsbecker Bothen. Wandsbeck: Beym Verfasser, 1774 [-1812]. 8 v. 8°.  NFG
Of special interest: "Der Schwarze in der Zuckerplantage," v. 1, p. 8; "Billet doux von Görgel an seinen Herrn, den 10. Jan.," v. 3, p. 31; and "Urians Reise um die Welt, mit Anmerkungen," v. 5, p. 113.

483. REFORMED CHURCH IN THE UNITED STATES. Neuvermehrt- und vollständiges Gesang-Buch, Worinnen sowohl die Psalmen Davids, Nach D. Ambrosii Lobwassers Uebersetzung hin und wieder verbessert, Als auch 750. auserlesener alter und neuer Geistreichen Liedern begriffen sind, Welche anjetzo sämtlich in denen Reformirten Kirchen der Hessisch - Hanauisch - Pfältzisch - Pensylvanischen und mehreren anderen angränzenden Landen zu singen gebräuchlich, in nützlicher Ordnung eingetheilt, Auch Mit den Heydelbergischen Catechismo und erbaulichen Gebätern versehen. Vierte Auflage. Philadelphia: Zu finden bey E. L. Baisch, 1774. 190 p., 2 l., 3-480 p., 6 l., 72 p. incl. front. 12°.  *\* KF 1774
Hildeburn 3023.
Printed in Germany.
German words with tunes.
"Kern alter und neuer, in 750 bestehender, geistreicher Lieder...nebst Joachimi Neandri Bundesliedern... Vierte Auflage. Philadelphia: Zu finden bey E. L. Baisch, 1774," 1 l., 3-480 p.

## 1774, continued

**484.** SCHUBART, CHRISTIAN FRIEDRICH DANIEL. [Excerpts from contributions to the *Deutsche Chronik*, 1774–1777.] (German American annals. Philadelphia, 1903. 4°. new series, v. 1, p. 209–224, 257–274, 346–356, 406–419, 593–600.) NFCA

These excerpts are incorporated in an essay by J. A. Walz, "Three Swabian journalists and the American Revolution," of which part III is devoted to Schubart.

See Rudolf Krauss, "Zur Geschichte der Schubartschen Chronik. Beschwerden und Widerrufe, Zensurfreiheit und Zensur," in *Württembergische Vierteljahrshefte für Landesgeschichte*, Stuttgart, 1902, Neue Folge, Jahrg. 11, p. 78–94, *EMN*; G. S. Ford, "Two German publicists on the American Revolution," in *Journal of English and Germanic philology*, Urbana, Ill., 1909, v. 8, p. 145–176, *RKA*; Chr. Fr. D. Schubart, "Schubarts Leben und Gesinnungen von ihm selbst im Kerker aufgesetzt," in *Deutsche Literatur... in Entwicklungsreihen. Reihe 25, Deutsche Selbstzeugnisse*, Leipzig, 1936, Bd. 9, p. 214–253, *AGK*.

**485.** —— Der sterbende Indianer an seinen Sohn. (In his: Sämmtliche Gedichte. Frankfurt am Main, 1825. 16°. Bd. 2, p. 226–227.)
"Nach dem Englischen." NFW

Appeared originally in *Deutsche Chronik*, Augsburg, 1774.

See P. A. Barba, "The American Indian in German fiction," in *German American annals*, Philadelphia, 1913, v. 15 (new series, v. 11), p. 143–174, *NFCA*.

**486.** SPANGENBERG, AUGUST GOTTLIEB. Leben des Herrn Nicolaus Ludwig, Grafen und Herrn von Zinzendorf und Pottendorf, beschrieben von August Gottlieb Spangenberg... Theil 5–8. [Barby:] Zu finden in den Brudergemeinen, 1774–1775. 4 v. in 1. 8°. *KF 1774
See no. 480.

**487.** STOLBERG, FRIEDRICH LEOPOLD. Mein Vaterland. An Klopstock. [1774.] (In his: Gesammelte Werke. Hamburg, 1820–25. 12°. Bd. 1, p. 53–55.) NFG

Praises the efficiency of German farmers in "Columbia" (i.e., America).

Kolumbia, du weintest, gehüllt
In Trauerschleyer, über den Fluch
Welchen der lachende Mörder
Oeden Fluren zum Erbe liess;

Da sandte Deutschland Segen und Volk:
Der Schoss der Jammererde gebar,
Staunte der schwellenden Aehren,
Und der schaffende Fremdlinge!

**488.** VOM Lord Howe. (Der Teutsche Merkur. Weimar, 1774. 8°. Bd. 7, p. 254.) * DF (Neue)
War anecdote.
This periodical subsequently called *Der Neue teutsche Merkur*, under which it is shelved.

**489.** VON dem Aufstande der Amerikaner und Schwarzen in einigen Ländern von Amerika. (Hannoverisches Magazin... vom Jahre 1774. Hannover, 1775. 4°. Jahrgang 12, col. 1217–1240.) *DF
Signed: H. (i.e. Johann Christoph Friedrich Heise.)
Title page dated 1775; contents, 1774.

**490.** *Review:* Der bekannte Wasserfall zu Niagara in Nordamerika, mit umliegender Gegend. Eine prächtige Aussicht, von Richard Wilson nach der Natur gemalet, und von Wilhelm Byrne wohl gestochen. (Neue Bibliothek der schönen Wissenschaften und der freyen Künste. Leipzig, 1774. 12°. Bd. 16, p. 311, *NAA*.)

**491.** *Reviews:* 1) Recherches Philosophiques sur les Américains... par Mr. de P * *. A Berlin, 1772. 2) Dissertation sur l'Amérique... Contre les Recherches philosophiques de Mr. de P * * par Dom Pernety... A Berlin: chez Samuel Pitra, Libraire, n. d. 3) Defense des Recherches Philosophiques sur les Americains... Par Mr. de P * *. Berlin, 1772. 4) Examen des Recherches Philosophiques sur l'Amérique. I. et II. Part. A Berlin: Chez G. I. Decker, 1773. (Allgemeine deutsche Bibliothek. Berlin, 1774. 12°. Bd. 22, Stück 1, p. 366–382, *NAA*.)

"Mr. de P**, i.e., Cornelius de Pauw. The third volume of Pauw's work is the defence of the first two, against the Abbé Pernety, in 1770. The author endeavors to show the inferior character of everything American, especially of the inhabitants; his work evoked considerable controversy. It contains a curious account of the 'Hermaphrodites de la Floride,' and the custom of 'Circoncision' and 'Infibulation.' " — *Sabin 59241*. A German edition (see no. 455) was published in 1769.

The publication, *De l'Amérique et des Américains*, Berlin, 1771, *KF 1771*, and Berlin, 1774 (Kayser v. 1, p. 52A), incorrectly attributed to A. J. Pernety, is by C. de Bonneville, i.e., Zacharie de Pazzi de Bonneville. See Sabin 1292, 6327.
See nos. 455, 456, 457.

**492.** *Review:* Transactions for promoting useful knowledge. Vol. I. from Jan. 1, 1769 to Jan. 1, 1771. Philadelphia: Bradford, 1771. 504 p., 7 plates. 4°. (Göttingische Anzeigen von gelehrten Sachen. Göttingen [1774]. 12°. Jahr 1774, Zugabe, p. 25–31. * DF.)
The Library's copy of *Transactions*, v. 1, is in * KD. See detailed note on no. 474.

**493.** *Review:* Zuverlässiger Briefwechsel über die merkwürdige Geschichte eines zweyten Josephs, in der Person des sächs. Amerikaners, welcher bisher in Döbeln gewesen ist. Erstes bis viertes Stück. Amsterdam, 1772. 247 S. in 8°. (Allgemeine deutsche Bibliothek. Berlin, 1774. 12°. Bd. 21, p. 206, *NAA*.)

"Wie ein Tuchmacher aus Döbeln vorzeiten einmal auf die Wanderschaft gegangen, nach Surinam geschifft, daselbst zu grossem Vermögen gelangt, endlich aber mit Schätzen beladen in sein Vaterland zurückgekehrt ist, gegen seine armen Anverwandeten sich wohltätig erwiesen, auch unter seine guten Freunde ein paar Centner Coffe ausgetheilet...;" forty fictitious letters with lengthy moralistic discourses.

## 1775

**494.** ETAT vom Brittischen Amerika. I. The staff of the army in America. II. Civil establishment of America. III. Governments in America. (In: A. L. Schlözer. Briefwechsel meist statistischen Inhalts. Göttingen, 1775. 8°. p. 219–224.) BAC

"Aus dem diesjährigen Royal Kalender, der bis zum 20. Jan. 1775 corrigirt ist."
See "August Ludwig Schlözers öffentliches und Privatleben von ihm selbst beschrieben," in *Deutsche Literatur, Reihe* [25] : *Deutsche Selbstzeugnisse*, Leipzig, 1934, Bd. 8, p. 121–188, *AGK*; F. Frensdorff, "Von und über Schlözer," in Königliche Gesellschaft der Wissenschaften zu Göttingen, *Abhandlungen: Philosophisch-historische Klasse*, Berlin, 1909, Neue Folge, Bd. No. 4, * *EE* (*Gesellschaft*).
See G. S. Ford, "Two German publicists on the American Revolution," in *Journal of English and Germanic philology*, Urbana, Ill., 1909, v. 8, p. 145–176, *RKA*.

**1775,** *continued*

**494A. ETAT** vom Spanischen Amerika, zu Ende des J. 1773. a. Arzobispos y Obispos en la America. b. Tribunales que tiene S. M. en las provincias. c. Gobernadores de las principales Plazas y Puertos de las provincias. (In: A. L. Schlözer, Briefwechsel meist statistischen Inhalts. Göttingen, 1775. 8°. p. 92-94.) BAC
The article refers to all the then Spanish parts of the American continent, including Mexico, Panama, the West Indies, etc.

**495. ETWAS** von den Nordamerikanischen Indianern oder sogenannten Wilden. (Hannoverisches Magazin...vom Jahre 1775. Hannover, 1776. 4°. Jahrgang 13, col. 1473-1504.) *DF
Excerpt from James Adair's *History of the American Indians*. London, 1775, * *KF 1775*.
Title page dated 1776; contents, 1775.
See no. 699.
"Der Verfasser ist also der Meynung, dass die amerikanischen Jndianer von den Hebräern abstammen." — *Anm. des Uebers., col. 1491-1492.*
See note to no. 466.

**496. LIED** eines jungen Engländers in Amerika. (Der Teutsche Merkur. Weimar [1775]. 8°. Jahr 1775, Vierteljahr 4 [Bd. 12], p. 105.)
*DF (Neue)
This periodical subsequently called *Der Neue teutsche Merkur*, under which it is shelved.
Reprinted from *Neue Hamburger Zeitung*, 1775, no. 152. "Aus einem Schreiben von Neuyork."
An English boy under 18 complains of not being allowed to fight the American rebels.
"Jn dem unglücklichen, zwischen den [*sic!*] Engländischen Ministerio und den amerikanischen Colonien entstandenen Kriege ward im Monath Julius des 1775. Jahres den von letzteren abgeschickten Werbeofficiren befohlen, niemanden in ihre Dienste aufzunehmen, der sich unter 18 Jahren befände."

**497. POLITISCHE** Neuigkeiten. (Der Teutsche Merkur. Weimar [1775]. 8°. Jahr 1775, Vierteljahr 4 [Bd. 12], p. 86-90, 185-191, 292-295.)
*DF (Neue)
This periodical subsequently called *Der Neue teutsche Merkur*, under which it is shelved.
See no. 479.

**498. PROBE** von der Beredtsamkeit eines amerikanischen Wilden. (Hannoverisches Magazin ...vom Jahr 1775. Hannover, 1776. 4°. Jahrgang 13, col. 687-688.) *DF
Taken from *London chronicle*, 1775, no. 2856.
Title page dated 1776; contents, 1775.

**499. SCHUBART, CHRISTIAN FRIEDRICH DANIEL.** Die Freiheit. Ein Mährchen. 1775. (In his: Sämmtliche Gedichte. Frankfurt am Main, 1825. 12°. Bd. 2, p. 237-238.) NFW
Ending: "Seitdem vernimmt man, dass sich die Göttin [i.e. Liberty] in Columbus Welt niedergelassen."

**499A. ———** Freiheitslied eines Kolonisten. 1775. (Reprinted in: Deutsche National-Litteratur...herausgegeben von Joseph Kürschner. Berlin und Stuttgart, n. d. 12°. Bd. 81, p. 349-350.) NFF
This poem was first printed in *Deutsche Chronik*, Bd. 64, Stück 10, August, 1775.

"Hinaus! Hinaus ins Ehrenfeld
Mit blinkendem Gewehr!
Columbus, deine ganze Welt
Tritt mutig daher.
   *  *  *
Da seht Europens Sklaven an,
in Ketten rasseln sie!
Sie braucht ein Treiber, ein Tyrann
Für würgbares Vieh."

**500. STOLBERG, FRIEDRICH LEOPOLD.** Lied eines deutschen Soldaten in der Fremde. 1775. (In: Christian, Graf zu Stolberg. Gesammelte Werke. Hamburg, 1820-1825. 12°. Bd. 1, p. 73-76.) NFG
The song is thought to have been sung by one of the German auxiliaries in America.
See J. A. Walz, in *Modern language notes*, Baltimore, 1901, v. 16, p. 174, note, *RAA*.

**500A. [STURZ, HELFERICH PETER.]** Ueber den Vaterlandsstolz. (Deutsches Museum. Leipzig, 1776. 8°. [Jahr] 1776, Bd. 1, p. 408-409.) *DF
Signed: Ue.
"Wenn die Abenakis und die Mikimakis, die Chawanesen und die Cherokesen bey jedem Krieg ihrer Nachbarn die Axt gegen ihre Brüder erheben, kämpfen sie für's Vaterland?" See H. S. King, "Echoes of the American Revolution in German literature," in University of California, *Publications in modern philology*, Berkeley, 1929, v. 14, p. 44-45, *STG*.

**501. UNTERREDUNGEN** zwischen W * * und dem Pfarrer zu * * *. (Der Teutsche Merkur. Weimar [1775]. 8°. Jahr 1775, Vierteljahr 2 [Bd. 10], p. 70-96, 243-268; Vierteljahr 3 [Bd. 11], p. 251-268; Vierteljahr 4 [Bd. 12], p. 61-74, 263-271.) *DF (Neue)
Signed: W (i.e., Wieland).
This periodical subsequently called *Der Neue teutsche Merkur*, under which it is shelved.
"Die guten Sitten cirkulieren in der Welt herum, wie alles andre. Ict sehen wir sie in den Kolonien von Nordamerika. Es ist ein labender Anblick für die Menschenverstand, ein tugendhaftes Volk zu sehen! — Hundert Tausende, von einem durch die alle hinströmenden Geiste belebt, die mit hohem Muthe, standhaft und unerschütterlich, die unverlierbaren Rechte der Menschheit behaupten, ihre Privatvortheile dem Gemeinen Besten aufopfern; wo Alte und Junge, Männer und Weiber, denken und handeln, wie die besten Helden und Heldinnen im Plutarch."
See no. 479.

**502.** *Review*: Geschichte der Englischen Colonien in Nord America, bis 1763, aus d. Engl. von der ersten Entdeckung dieser Länder durch Sebastian Cabot bis auf den Frieden 1763. In zwey Theilen. [Leipzig: bey Caspar Fritsch, 1775.] 8°. (Göttingische Anzeigen von gelehrten Sachen. Göttingen [1775-1777]. 12°. Jahr 1775, p. 1158; Jahr 1777, p. 730-735, *DF*.)
Sabin 9288.
The English original, *History of the British dominions in North-America*, London, 1773, is in * *KF 1773*.
According to Kayser, v. 2, p. 357A, the translator is K. E. Klausing.
*See* no. 535.

### 1776

**503. ANEKDOTE** über die ware Ursache der NAmerikanischen Empörung. (In: A. L. Schlözer. Briefwechsel meist historischen und politischen Inhalts. Göttingen, 1776. 8°. Theil 1, p. 381-384.) BAC
"Aus Pinto's *Réponse* p. 40-42" (i.e. Isaac de Pinto. Réponse. La Haye, 1776, * *KF p.v.3, no.3*).

**503A. AUSSICHT** in die Zukunft. (Taschenbuch für Dichter und Dichterfreunde. Leipzig, 1776. 8°. Abtheilung 6, p. 143-145.) NFK
Signed R-r.
A poem praising the Quakers and lauding William Penn.

*1776, continued*

504. AUSSÖHNUNGS-PLAN zwischen Grossbritannien und Nord-Amerika. (In: A. L. Schlözer. Briefwechsel meist historischen und politischen Inhalts. Göttingen, 1776. 8°. Theil 1, p. 257–267.)
BAC

"Vorgelegt von dem Verfasser der *Remarks on the Principal Acts of the xiiith Parliament of Great Britain (London, 1775. v. I, containing Remarks on the Acts relating to the Colonies, with a Plan of Reconciliation*) pag. 483–500."
The Library's copies of this English work by John Lind are in CK and * *KF 1775*.
A German version was issued with title: Anmerkungen über die vornehmsten Acten des dreyzehnten Parlements von Groszbritannien. Braunschweig, 1778. Sabin. 41285. Not in the Library.

505. AUSZUG [eines] Schreibens aus H., vom 11 Novemb. 1776, zur Berichtigung von oben Num. 56, Heft v. (In: A. L. Schlözer. Briefwechsel meist historischen und politischen Inhalts. Göttingen, 1776. 8°. Theil 1, p. 373–381.)
BAC

"Indessen ist noch keine Sache so allgemein populär gewesen, als die amerikanische, und also auch von keiner noch so viel, als von dieser, geschrieben worden." The letter contains a valuable list of twenty-four English publications concerning the quarrel between Great Britain and her American colonies.
"Wundern möchte man sich, warum kein patriotischer, d.i. auf gute Verlags-Artikel speculirender deutscher Buchführer, auf eine Sammlung aller dieser Pièces du tems gefallen ist." — *Schlöser.*
See nos. 526, 542.

505A. AUSZÜGE aus Tagebüchern und Aufzeichnungen hessischer Offiziere und Regiments-Chroniken im amerikanischen Befreiungskrieg [1776–1783]. (Deutsch-amerikanische historische Gesellschaft von Illinois. Jahrbuch. Chicago, Ill., 1920–21. v. 20–21, p. 251–279.)
IEK

See also "Hessians in America. Papers relating to the service of the Hessian troops in America, comprising returns, lists and other official papers, letters of officers, journals and extracts from journals of various campaigns, including the journal of Captain Cleve while in captivity, with plans of battles [etc.]." f°. In German. 27 transcripts. [1862?] Bancroft Collection. Lettered: Brunswick Papers, v. 2. In Manuscript Division.

505B. BARDELEBEN, HEINRICH VON. Tagebuch des Hessischen Offiziers Heinrich von Bardeleben, 29 Februar 1776 bis 22. Juni 1777. (Deutschamerikanische historische Gesellschaft von Illinois. Jahrbuch. Chicago, Ill., 1928. 8°. v. 27–28, p. 7–119.)
IEK
Meynen 2947.
Introduction signed J. G. [i.e., Julius Goebel.]
*Contents*: 1. Abmarsch der Truppen nach Bremen. 2. Einschiffung und Abfahrt nach England. 3. Von England nach Amerika. 4. Ankunft im Hafen von New York. 5. Landung auf Long Island. Schlacht bei Flatbush. 6. Flucht der Amerikaner. 7. Eroberung von New York. Schlacht bei Harlem Heights. 8. Die Kämpfe bei White Plains. 9. Eroberung von Fort Washington und Fort Lee. 10. Winterquartier in New York. 11. Der Überfall vor Trenton. 12. Winterquartier in New York. 13. Vorbereitungen zum neuen Feldzug. 14. Feldzug in New Jersey.

506. BRIEFE von deutschen evangelischen Geistlichen in Pensylvanien, an Hrn. Prof. Freylinghausen in Halle. (In: A. L. Schlözer. Briefwechsel meist historischen und politischen Inhalts. Göttingen, 1776. 8°. Theil 1, p. 152–156.)
BAC

First letter dated, Philadelphia, den 18. Juli 1775; signed by Pastor Kunze. The second, Lancaster, den 25. August 1775, by Pastor Helmuth. "Der Leser wähnt doch nicht, dass diese Briefe bloss wegen der darin enthaltenen, theils längst bekannten, teils falschen Nachrichten, hier stehen?" — *Schlöser.*

507. BURNABY, ANDREW. Reisen durch die Mittlern Kolonien der Engländer in Nord-Amerika, nebst Anmerkungen über den Zustand der Kolonien. Von M. Andreas Burnaby, Vicar zu Greenwich. Aus dem Englischen übersetzt mit Anmerkungen und Zusätzen. Hamburg und Kiel: Bey Carl Ernst Bohn, 1776. 8 p.l., 192 p., 7 l. 17 cm.
* *KF 1776*
Sabin 9361.
English original is this author's *Travels through the middle settlements in North-America*, London, 1775, * *KF 1775*.
"Vorrede" signed: C. D. Ebeling.
"Franziskus Faquiers Wetterbeobachtungen in Virginien vom Jahre 1760," 6 l. at end. Review: *Allgemeine deutsche Bibliothek*, Bd. 28, p. 535–539, *NAA.*

508. DIE DEUTSCHEN Hülfstruppen nach Amerika. 1776. (In: F. W. von Ditfurth. Historische Volkslieder der Zeit von 1756–1871... Aus fliegenden Blättern, handschriftlichen Quellen und dem Volksmunde... Berlin: Franz Lipperheide, 1871–1872. 8°. Bd. 1 [Theil 2], p. 5–7.)
NFL

Called Theil 2 on main title page; has separate title: Die Historischen Volkslieder vom Ende des siebenjährigen Kriegs, 1763 bis zum Brande von Moskau, 1812. Berlin: Lipperheide, 1872.
"Wer will mit nach Amerika?
Die Hannoveraner sind schon da,
Die Hessen werben mit Gewalt,
Kommen die Braunschweiger auch alsbald.
Wer will mit nach Amerika?
Alles was man wünscht ja,
Findt man in Amerika!"

509. DOHM, CHRISTIAN WILHELM VON. Etwas Apologetisches wegen der englisch-amerikanischen Handlung. (Deutsches Museum. Leipzig, 1776. 8°. [Jahr] 1776, Bd. 2, p. 835–851.)
* *DF*

Contradicts Pinto's remark in A. L. Schlözer, *Briefwechsel meist historischen und politischen Inhalts*, Göttingen, 1776, Theil 1, p. 114, *BAC*; see no. 526.
This argument is described in Walther Hofstaetter's *Das Deutsche Museum*... (Leipzig. Universität: Deutsches Seminar. *Probefahrten*. Leipzig, 1908. 4°. Bd. 12, p. 67–68. *STN.*)

510. —— Geschichte des fünften Weltheils im Kleinen. (Deutsches Museum. Leipzig, 1776. 8°. [Jahr] 1776, Bd. 1, p. 49–62, 372–381.)
* *DF*

Review: *Allgemeine deutsche Bibliothek*, Anhang zu Bd. 25/36, Abth. 4, p. 2297, *NAA.*

511. —— Nordamerikanische Handlung. (Deutsches Museum. Leipzig, 1776. 8°. [Jahr] 1777, Bd. 1, p. 307–313.)
* *DF*

"The tobacco trade of Virginia is discussed in this article which considers the value of American trade to Great Britain." — *J. T. Hatfield and E. Hochbaum, The Influence of the American Revolution upon German literature*, New York [1900?], *p. 3, NFC p.v.4.* The statistical material is taken from John Entick, *The present state of the British Empire*, London, 1774, v. 4, p. 451, and Thomas Pennant, *A tour in Scotland*, Chester, 1774, p. 131. The Library has only a German translation of Entick's work, *Der*

*1776, continued*

**511.** DOHM, CHRISTIAN WILHELM VON, *cont'd*
*gegenwärtige Zustand des brittischen Reichs*, Berlin, 1778–81, *CBD.* Copies of Pennant's book are in * *KBD* and *CPW.*

This article belongs to a series by Dohm, entitled "Miscellanien statistischen und historischen Jnhalts," in which references to America occur frequently. Topics treated include: Influence of quarrel between Grt. Britain and America on commerce and mail, p. 307; Whaling, p. 317; Export of German linen to North America via Great Britain, p. 323. Published in book form as, *Materialien zur Statistik der neuesten Staatengeschichte. 5 Lief. mit Anhang*, Lemgo: Meyer, 1777–85. Not in the Library.

See no. 834.

**511A.** DONOP, CARL EMIL CURT VON. [Letters. 1776-1777.] (The Pennsylvania magazine of history and biography. Philadelphia, 1938. 8°. v. 62, p. 488–501.) IAA

The letters, dated January 25, 1776, January 6, 1777, and September 2, 1777, are incorporated in an article by Hans Huth, "Letters from a Hessian mercenary." Colonel Donop was mortally wounded in an unsuccessful attack upon Fort Mercer, on the New Jersey side of the Delaware below Philadelphia, made in connection with General Howe's campaign of 1777. François Jean, Marquis de Chastellux, in his *Voyage dans l'Amérique*, v. 1, p. 227 (see no. 840), quotes the Colonel as having said while dying, "It is an early end of a fine career, but I die a victim of my ambitions and of the avarice of my sovereign." But Max von Eelking, *Die deutschen Hülfstruppen im nordamerikanischen Befreiungskriege, 1776 bis 1783*, Hannover, 1863, *IG*, and E. J. Lowell, *The Hessians and the other German auxiliaries of Great Britain in the Revolutionary War*, New York, 1884, *IG*, question the statement.

**511B.** DU ROI, THE ELDER. Journal of Du Roi the Elder, lieutenant and adjutant in the service of the Duke of Brunswick. 1776-1777. (German American annals. Philadelphia, 1911. 4°. new series, v. 9, p. 40–64, 77–129, 131–244.) NFCA

Translated from the original manuscript in the Library of Congress, by Charlotte S. J. Epping.

**511C.** FREDERICK II, THE GREAT, KING OF PRUSSIA. Mémoires depuis la paix de Hubertsbourgh jusqu'à la paix de Teschen. 1775. (In his: Oeuvres. Berlin: Chez Rodolphe Decker, 1846–57. 4°. v. 6, p. 1–208.) † EHR

"Le général Washington, qu'à Londres on appelait le chef des rebelles, remporta, dès les premières hostilités, quelques avantages sur les royalistes assemblés près de Boston... Il était évident que le nombre des troupes en Amérique était trop faible pour remplir le dessein qu'on voulait exécuter... Ils trouvèrent en Allemagne des princes avides ou obérés qui prirent leur argent; ce qui leur valut douze mille Hessois, quatre mille Brunswicois, douze cent hommes d'Ansbach, autant de Hanau, sans compter quelques centaines d'hommes que leur fournit le prince de Waldeck..." *— p. 116.*

Frederick exacted the same toll for soldiers marched through his dominions bound for America as for cattle. *cf.* J. A. Walz, in *Modern language notes*, Baltimore, 1901, v. 16, p. 175, *RAA*.

See also Johannes von Müller, "Vier und zwanzig Buecher allgemeiner Geschichten besonders der europäischen Menschheit," in his *Sämmtliche Werke*, Berlin, 1810–18, Bd. 3, Buch 23, p. 325–450, the chapter, "Theresia, Friedrich und Nordamerica;" also F. Kapp, *Friedrich der Grosse und die Vereinigten Staaten von Amerika*, Leipzig, 1871, *IG*; and G. M. Fisk, *Die handelspolitischen und sonstigen Beziehungen zwischen Deutschland und den Vereinigten Staaten*

*von Amerika*, Stuttgart, 1897, *TB*, especially the chapters: Preussen und die amerikanischen Kolonien, Der Vertrag von 1785, [and] Der Vertrag von 1799; see also C. St., "Friedrich der Grosse und George Washington; ein Gedenkblatt aus der Weltgeschichte," in *Staats-Zeitung, Sonntagsblatt*, New York, 1902, v. 54, no. 7, p. 13, * *A;* J. G. Rosengarten, *Frederick the Great and the United States*, Lancaster, Pa., 1906, *IGA*, also his *The German soldier in the wars of the United States*, Philadelphia, 1886, *IEK;* P. L. Haworth, "Frederick the Great and the American Revolution," in *American historical review*, New York, 1904, v. 9, p. 460–478, * *R-IAA;* F. F. Schrader, "Prussia and the United States, Frederick the Great's influence on the American Revolution," in Concord Society, *Historical bulletin*, [New York,] 1923, no. 2, *IEK.*

For numerous articles on Frederick the Great and translations of his works that appeared in American magazines of those days, see "List of translations of German prose," and "List of articles on the German countries," in E. Z. Davis, *Translations of German poetry in American magazines, 1741–1810*, Philadelphia, 1905, p. 191–214 (Americana Germanica press, new series, v. 1), *NFK*.

Note also *Das Leben und die heroischen Thaten des Königs Friedrich II von Preussen*, Philadelphia, 1761. *cf.* F. Kapp, in *Deutsche Rundschau*, Berlin, 1880, v. 25, p. 93, * *DF*.

**512.** GEDANKEN über den Aufstand der englischen Colonien in dem nördlichen Amerika. Göttingen: Bey Johann Christian Dietrich, 1776. 40 p. 18 cm.     * KF 1776

**513.** GEOGRAPHISCHE Belustigungen zur Erläuterung der neuesten Weltgeschichte. Mit Landkarten, Planen und Kupfern nach den neuesten und besten Originalen. (Zum Besten einer Freyschule in Sachsen.) Erstes [-Zweytes] Stück. Leipzig: In der Johann Carl Müllerischen Buch- und Kunsthandlung, 1776. 2 v. in 1. 3 maps. 4°.     * KF 1776
Sabin 26980.

*Contents:* Stück 1. Allgemeine Beschreibung der engländischen Colonien in Nord-Amerika, nebst einem Plane von Boston. Stück 2. Allgemeine Beschreibung der engländischen Colonien in Nord-Amerika, nebst der einer Karte von denselben und einer Karte von Long-Island.

Reviews: *Allgemeine deutsche Bibliothek*, Anhang zu Bd. 25/36, Abth. 3, p. 1367–1369; Bd. 34, Stück 1, p. 235–241, *NAA;* J. G. Hager, *Geographischer Büchersaal*, Chemnitz [1754–1778], v. 3, p. 674–698, 771–788, *KA.* See no. 410.

**514.** GOETHE, JOHANN WOLFGANG. Stella. Ein Schauspiel für Liebende in fünf Akten...von J. W. Göthe. Berlin: Bey August Mylius..., 1776. (Reprinted in his: Werke. Herausgegeben im Auftrage der Grossherzogin Sophie von Sachsen. Weimar: Hermann Böhlau, 1887–1919. 8°. Bd. 11, p. 125–196.)     NFGK
Reference to America in Act I (p. 136).

See F. H. Reinsch, "Goethe's political interests prior to 1787," in University of California, *Publications in modern philology*, Berkeley, 1923, v. 10, p. 183–278, *STG.*

Note also Goethe's remark in *Aus meinem Leben; Dichtung und Wahrheit*, Theil 4, Buch 19: "Wohlwollende hatten mir vertraut, Lili habe geäussert, indem alle die Hindernisse unserer Verbindung ihr vorgetragen worden: sie unternehme wohl aus Neigung zu mir alle dermaligen Zustände und Verhältnisse aufzugeben und mit nach Amerika zu gehen. Amerika war damals [i.e. cr. 1775] vielleicht mehr noch als jetzt [i.e. cr. 1820] das Eldorado derjenigen, die in ihrer augenblicklichen Lage sich bedrängt fanden." *— Bd. 29, p. 156.*

*1776, continued*

515. GREAT BRITAIN. — TREATIES. Die drey vollståndigen Subsidien-Tractaten, welche zwischen Sr. Grossbritannischen Majeståt einer Seits, und dem Durchlauchtigsten Landgrafen von Hessel-Cassel, dem Durchlauchtigsten Herzoge von Braunschweig und Lûneburg, und dem Durchlauchtigsten Erb-Prinzen von Hessen-Cassel, als regierenden Grafen von Hanau, andrer Seits, geschlossen sind. Englisch und Teutsch. Frankfurt und Leipzig, 1776. 31 p. 4°.
  \*KF 1776
Text in English and German on opposite pages.
Other titles of interest include:
Brunswick. — Army. Returns of the Brunswick troops in British pay, showing their strength at embarkation and at other periods, 1776, 1777, 1779; and general orders of Gen. Riedesel, Sept. 15, 1782. 10 documents, in English, French and German. Unbound. Bancroft Manuscripts. Manuscript Division.
Brunswick Papers. Letters and documents relating to the service of the Brunswick troops in America, 1776–1777, comprising letters of Gen. Riedesel to the Duke of Brunswick, his journal of the northern campaign of 1776 and 1777, letters of other officers, and a journal of the voyage, with lists of troops, and several maps, plans and tables. 39 transcripts, the greater part in German. 1862? f°. Bancroft Manuscripts. Manuscript Division.
See also 1484A, 1485.
"Copy of the treaty between His Majesty & the Margrave of Brandenbourg Anspach, February 1, 1777 and Copy of a treaty between His Majesty & the hereditary Prince of Hesse concluded and signed at Hanau, February 10, 1777," in Charles Rainsford, "Transactions as commissary for embarking foreign troops in the English service from Germany; with copies of letters relative to it...1776–1777," in New York Historical Society, *Collections: Publication Fund series*, New York, 1879, p. 313–543, *IAA*.
Hans Droysen, "Die Braunschweigischen Truppen im nordamerikanischen Unabhängigkeitskriege," in Braunschweiger Geschichtsverein, *Jahrbuch*, Wolfenbüttel, 1914, Folge 1, Bd. 13, p. 145–159, *EOT*.
Max von Eelking, *Die deutschen Hülfstruppen im nordamerikanischen Befreiungskriege, 1776–1783*, Hannover, 1863, *IG*; abridged translation, *IAG*.
G. W. Greene, *The German element in the War of American Independence*, New York, 1876, *IG*.
Friedrich Kapp, *Der Soldatenhandel deutscher Fürsten nach Amerika...2. ed.*, Berlin, 1874, *IG*.
E. J. Lowell, *The Hessians and the other German auxiliaries of Great Britain in the Revolutionary War*, New York, 1884, *IG*; historical background in chapter II (The Treaties) and III (The Treaties before Parliament).
Julien Mauveaux, *Une figure militaire montbéliardaise à la fin du XVIIIe siècle...(Campagnes d'Amérique: 1776–1781)*, Montbéliard, 1925 (Société d'émulation de Montbéliard, *Mémoires*, v. 48, \* *EN*).
E. E. Slafter, "The landing of the Hessians," in Massachusetts Historical Society, *Proceedings*, Boston, 1905, series 2, v. 18, p. 243–250, *IAA*.
A. H. T., Freiherr von Werthern, *Die hessischen Hülfstruppen im nordamerikanischen Unabhängigkeitskriege 1776–1783*, Cassel, 1895, *IG*.
Paul Zimmermann, "Beiträge zum Verständnis des zwischen Braunschweig und England am 9. Januar 1776 geschlossenen Subsidienvertrages," in Braunschweiger Geschichtsverein, *Jahrbuch*, Wolfenbüttel, 1914, Folge 1, Bd. 13, p. 160–176, *EOT*.
Note also Albert Pfister, *Die amerikanische Revolution, 1775–1783*, Stuttgart u. Berlin [n. d.], which is not in the Library.

516. [HEERINGEN, VON.] Auszug eines Schreibens aus Amerika an Sr. [*sic!*] Excellenz den Herrn Generallieutenant von \* \* \* [Darmstadt?] 1776. 23 p. 16½ cm. \*KF 1776
Photostat reproduction.
Dated and signed: Long Island den 1ten Sept. 1776. v. H.
"This printed extract of a letter from America is from the original letter addressed to Lieutenant General von Lossberg by Colonel von Heeringen of the Fusilier Regiment von Lossberg, dated Sept. 1, 1776 on Long Island, when Lieut. Gen. von Lossberg was on Staten Island, where he had remained with the convalescents and guard on Staten Island when General von Heister, who had the general command of the Hessians, had brought his regiments over to Long Island on August 25th." — *V. H. Paltsits, Aus dem Reisejournal des Herrn Generaladjutanten von D... an einen Freund in L., p. 21–23*.
See Max von Eelking, *The German allied troops in the North-American War of Independence, 1776–1783*, Albany, 1893 (Munsell's historical series, no. 19), *IG*.
See no. 641.

516A. HEISTER, VON. Auszüge aus dem Tagebuche eines vormaligen kurhessischen Offiziers über den Nordamerikanischen Freiheitskrieg 1776 und 1777. Mitgetheilt durch den Lieut. von Heister I., im ersten Garde-Regiment zu Fuss. (Zeitschrift für Kunst, Wissenschaft und Geschichte des Krieges. Berlin [etc.], 1828. 12°. Bd. 12, p. 223–270.) VWA
Meynen 2950.

517. KLINGER, FRIEDRICH MAXIMILIAN VON. Sturm und Drang. Ein Schauspiel von Klinger. n. p., 1776. 115 p. 8°. (Reprinted in: F. M. Klinger. Dramatische Jugendwerke. [Leipzig, 1912–1913.] 8°. Bd. 2, p. 261–355.) NGC
"Die Scene Amerika."
"Ha! lass mich's nur recht fühlen auf amerikanischem Boden zu stehen, wo alles neu, alles bedeutend ist." — Erster Akt. Zweite Scene.
"Ich will die Campagne hier mitmachen, als Volontär, da kann sich meine Seele ausrecken..." — *Erster Akt. Zweite Scene, p. 68*. See also M. Rieger, *Klinger in der Sturm- und Drangperiode*, Darmstadt, 1880.
"Der ruehelose Dichter selbst wollte seinem Tatendrange in Amerika Luft machen und mit aller Gewalt im Lande seiner Sehnsucht wirken; doch konnte er seinen beissen Wunsch, zu dessen Erfüllung Franklin in Paris und die Herzogin Amalie in Weimar aufgeboten wurden, nicht verwirklichen." — *Broffka, — p. 4*.
As to Klinger's desire to enlist in the American military service, see Kurz, in *Geschichte der deutschen Literatur*, v. 3, p. 423. "Franklin repeatedly complains in his letters about the numerous applications for appointments in the American army which he receives from all parts of Europe and which he cannot possibly endorse." — *John Bigelow, in Benjamin Franklin's Works, v. 6, p. 99*.

517A. KOBLENZ, G. VON. Gebeugter Vaterlandsstolz. 1776. (University of California. Publications in modern philology. Berkeley, Cal., 1929. 4°. v. 14, p. 158–159.) STG
"Zum Dienst der reichen Britten schwimmt
Der Teutsche auf dem Meer!
Nimmt von dem stolzen Krämer Geld,
Schwimmt hin in eine neue Welt
Und würgt ein freyes Heer."
Appeared originally in *Deutsche Chronik*, Augsburg, 1776, p. 374. See no. 484.

518. [KORN, CHRISTOPH HEINRICH.] Geschichte der Kriege in und ausser Europa. Nürnberg: G. N. Raspe, 1776–1784. 30 parts in 4 v. folding plates (part col'd), plans (part folding), folding maps, folding tables. 20 cm. \*KF 1776
Sabin 27213. See also C. H. Heartman's "Geschichte der Kriege in und ausser Europa...," New York, 1916. 7 p. (Bibliographical leaflet, no. 1.) *IG p.v.12, no.6*.
In parts 1–6, the title reads: Geschichte der Kriege in und ausser Europa vom Anfange des Aufstandes der brittischen Kolonien in Nordamerika; in parts 7–8: Vom Anfange des Aufstandes der brittischen

*1776, continued*

518. [KORN, CHRISTOPH HEINRICH], *continued*
Kolonien in Amerika an; part 21:... Vom Aufstande der brittischen Kolonien in Nordamerika an; parts 22–23:... Vom Anfange des amerikanischen Aufstandes an.
Reviews: *Allgemeine deutsche Bibliothek*, Bd. 34, p. 282–284; Bd. 36, p. 584–589; Anhang zu Bd. 25/36, Abth. 4, p. 3329–3330, *NAA*.

518A. KRAFFT, JOHN CHARLES PHILIP VON. Journal... 1776–1784. With six illustrations reproduced by artotype process and biographical sketch and index by T. H. Edsall. New York: Printed for private distribution only, 1888. 2 p.l., 4, 217 p., 5 l., 6 plates. 8°. IG
J. C. P. von Krafft was a lieutenant in the Hessian regiment von Bose.

519. KRAUSENECK, JOHANN CHRISTOPH. Columbus. (Taschenbuch für Dichter und Dichterfreunde. Leipzig, 1776. 8°. Abtheilung 6, p. 2.)
"Es flog ein Täubchen über Flut, NFK
Und prophezeihte, fromm und gut,
Das Ende vom Gericht und Sterben.
Es schwamm ein Täubchen über Meer,
Und brachte Tausenden und mehr
Tod, Untergang und das Verderben."

See Ernst Wetzel, *Der Kolumbusstoff im deutschen Geistesleben*, Breslau, 1936. (Reviewed by P. H. Baginsky in *German quarterly*, Lancaster, Pa., 1937, v. 10, p. 203–204, *RLA*.)
His other poems relating to America, e.g. "Lied eines Wilden," "Lied eines Negersklaven," "Zween Neger," first published in *Almanach der deutschen Musen*, 1776, 1778, respectively, are not in the Library.
Goedeke (1915, v. IV, 1, p. 104) mentions a publication of Krauseneck's, *Feldgesang eines teutschen Grenadiers in Nordamerika*, Bayreuth, 1778, 8°, which is verified by Kayser, v. 2, p. 199 b.

520. LENZ, JAKOB MICHAEL REINHOLD. Henriette von Waldeck oder Die Laube. 1776. (In his: Gesammelte Schriften. München und Leipzig, 1909–1913. 8°. Bd. 3, p. 209–234.) NFG
First published in the author's *Dramatischer Nachlass*... Frankfurt a. Main, 1828, which is not in the Library.
"Um einen Rang zu gewinnen, will in Lenz' Fragment gebliebenem Drama 'Die Laube' der unglücklich verliebte Konstantin nach Amerika gehen." — *Gerhard Descryh, in Deutsch-amerikanische historische Gesellschaft von Illinois, Jahrbuch, 1924–1925, p. 42, IEK.*
"Lenz, all his life connected with military affairs, in 'Die Laube', a fragment of a drama which is very closely connected with his own life, represents the hero as departing with the Hessians for America." — *J. T. Hatfield and E. Hochbaum, The influence of the American Revolution upon German literature, New York [1900?], p. 28, NFC p.v.4.* As to how far this fact is autobiographical, see H. S. King, in University of California, *Publications in modern philology*, Berkeley, 1929, v. 10, p. 56–57, *STG*.
Note also J. M. R. Lenz's correspondence with and in behalf of the poet, Heinrich Julius von Lindau, who went to America in 1776; see also L. Geiger in *Blätter für literarische Unterhaltung*, 1898, No. 10 (this volume not in the Library), and *Goethe-Jahrbuch*, Frankfurt a.M., 1911, Bd. 32, p. 24, *NFGG*.

521. LETTSOM, JOHN COAKLEY, AND J. ELLIS. Geschichte des Thees und Koffees. Aus dem Englischen der Herren John Coackley Lettsom und John Ellis übersetzt und mit einigen Zusätzen vermehrt. Mit Kupfern. Leipzig: Verlegts die Dyckische Buchhandlung, 1776. 243 p. plates. 12°. *KF 1776
"Verzeichniss derer Artikel und Waaren, die aus England nach den americanischen Inseln ausgeführet werden," p. 238–243.

521A. LICHTENBERG, GEORG CHRISTOPH. Briefe aus England. (Deutsches Museum. Leipzig, 1776–78. 8°. [Jahr] 1776, Bd. 1, p. 562–574; Bd. 2, p. 982–992; [Jahr] 1778, Bd. 1, p. 11–25, 434–444.) *DF
There are several references to America and Americans, e.g., Benjamin Franklin.
"Wie wenn nun unsere Pflanzen erst gar die Sonne hätten, die sie in England haben, wo sie noch ausserdem vor dem Strahl sicher sind, für den bis jetzt in Deutschland noch kein Franklin einen Ableiter gefunden hat." — [*Jahr*] 1776, Bd. 1, p. 574. See also a few references to the American Revolution in "Briefe aus G. Chr. Lichtenbergs englischem Freundeskreis, herausgegeben von Hans Hecht," in Universitaetsbund, Goettingen, *Vorarbeiten zur Geschichte*, No. 2, Goettingen, 1925, *STN (Goettingen)*. See also note to no. 936A.

521B. PAUSCH [GEORG]. Journal of Captain Pausch, chief of the Hanau artillery during the Burgoyne campaign. [May 15, 1776 – Oct. 7th, 1777.] Translated and annotated by W. L. Stone. Introduction by E. J. Lowell. Albany, N. Y., 1886. (Munsell's historical series, no. 14, *IAG*.)
This is a translation of a German manuscript in the Ständische Landesbibliothek at Cassel, Germany.
"The Journal is most copious in describing the three battles in which Pausch and his battery took an active part, viz: the naval action against Arnold on Lake Champlain, and the battles on the 19th of September, and the 7th of October... The Journal also dwells freely on the personal experiences of its author and his men, while in Canada." — *Preface*.

522. [PINTO, ISAAC DE.] Schreiben über die Empörung der Nord-Amerikaner. (In: A. L. Schlözer. Briefwechsel meist historischen und politischen Inhalts. Göttingen, 1776. 8°. Theil 1, p. 29–53.) BAC
Translation of his *Lettre de Mr. ***** à Mr. S. B. ...au sujet des troubles qui agitent actuellement toute l'Amérique Septentrionale*, La Haye, 1776, * *KF p.v.3*, no.1.
"Hr. Pinto soll der Verfasser seyn," *p. 29*.
Pinto gives excerpts from Dalrymple's *Great Britain asserted against the claims of America* (see Sabin 18347), and *Remarks upon the principal acts of the 13th Parliament of Great Britain* (see no. 599). He tries to prove that Great Britain has the right to tax her American colonies. He refutes the *Précis des differends survenus entre la Grande-Brétagne et ses colonies*. Finally, the author turns the reader's attention to the fact that Benjamin Franklin's declaration before Congress in February, 1766, concerning the Stamp Act, is added in a German version as a supplement to *Reise des Herrn Olof Toree nach Surate und China, nebst einer Nachricht von dem gegenwärtigen Zustand der englischen Colonien in dem Nördlichen Amerika von Th. Blackford*, Leipzig, 1772 (see Sabin 96191).

523. POLITISCHE Neuigkeiten. (Der Teutsche Merkur. Weimar [1776]. 8°. Jahr 1776, Vierteljahr 1 [Bd. 13], p. 96–98, 198–202, 284–289; Vierteljahr 2 [Bd. 14], p. 114–120, 214–216, 306–310; Vierteljahr 3 [Bd. 15], p. 91–96, 188–192; Vierteljahr 4 [Bd. 16], p. 93–96, 188–192, 282–287.) *DF (Neue)
This periodical subsequently called *Der Neue teutsche Merkur*, under which it is shelved.
See nos. 479, 497, 546, 712.

# GERMAN WORKS RELATING TO AMERICA 69

*1776, continued*

524. POLITISCHE Weissagungen des Hrn. von Pinto über Nord-Amerika. (In: A. L. Schlözer. Briefwechsel meist historischen und politischen Inhalts. Göttingen, 1776. 8°. Theil 1, p. 103–110.) BAC
Isaac de Pinto asks why the American colonies do not yet become independent of Great Britain.

525. PREDIGTEN von einem Bostonschen Geistlichen bey verschiedenen Gelegenheiten gehalten. Boston: Bey J. J. Simon, 1776. (Bern: Typographische Societät.] 117 p. 16°. *KF 1776
According to Weller, the imprint, Boston, is fictitious, the book having been actually printed at Bern.
No references to America.

526. RECHNUNG zwischen Grossbritannien und Nord-Amerika. (In: A. L. Schlözer. Briefwechsel meist historischen und politischen Inhalts. Göttingen, 1776. 8°. Theil 1, p. 110, 116, 312–320.) BAC
Short-title used; title commences: Zur Erläuterung der oben Heft II, Num. 21, S. 110, aus den *Rights of Great-Britain ausgezogenen...Rechnung* (i.e., *The rights of Great Britain [asserted] against the claims of America*, by Dalrymple). See Sabin 18347.
Contents: 1. Etat der Subsidien, welche das Brittische Parlement...zur Beschützung von Amerika bewilligt hat. 2. Etat der Summen, die den verschiedenen Provinzen von Nord Amerika...bewilliget worden. 3. Summen, die das Parlement den Nord Amerikanischen Provinzen für ihre im letztern Kriege geleistete Dienste ...verwilliget hat. 4. Kosten der beiden leztern Kriege. 5. Gegen-Rechnung der Amerikaner.
See also no. 509, 522.

527. RUSH, BENJAMIN. Untersuchung der Arzneykunde unter den Indiern in Nordamerika, und Vergleichung ihrer Krankheiten und Heilungsmittel mit denen, die bey gesitteten Völkern gewöhnlich sind. (Hannoverisches Magazin...vom Jahre 1776. Hannover, 1777. 4°. Jahrgang 14, col. 1457–1470, 1473–1507, 1553–1584.) *DF
"Aus dem Englischen des Prof. Rusch zu Philadelphia übersetzt von Hn. Cand. Med. J. P. Ebeling.
Eine Rede vor der amerikanischen Gesellschaft gehalten von Benjamin Rush, Professor der Chemie auf der Universität zu Philadelphia."
Vieles, was von der Naturgeschichte der Medicin unter den Jndiern in dieser Rede angeführt wird, ist aus La Hontan [see no. 236] und Charlevoix Geschichte von Canada [see no. 355] hergenommen. Aber das wesentlichste hat der Verfasser Männern zu verdanken, die unter den Jndiern herumreisten. Unter diesen beobachtete hauptsächlich Herr Eduard Hand, Wundarzt des achtzehnten Regiments, etliche Jahre hindurch, die er sich zu Fort Pitt aufhielt, die Gebräuche, Krankheiten und Heilungsmittel der Jndier mit einem Erfolge, der seiner Beurtheilungskraft und seinem Fleisse gleich viel Ehre bringt."
Title page dated 1777; contents, 1776.

528. SCHUBART, CHRISTIAN FRIEDRICH DANIEL. Der Britte an Howe nach der Schlacht bey Flatland. (German American annals. Philadelphia, 1903. 4°. new series, v. 1, p. 222–223.) NFCA
These excerpts are incorporated in an essay by J. A. Walz, "Three Swabian journalists and the American Revolution," of which part III is devoted to Schubart.

528A. SENDEN, ERNST JOHANN FRIEDRICH SCHÜLER VON. Denkwürdigkeiten aus den hinterlassenen Papieren E. Schüler's von Senden.

[1776–81.] (Zeitschrift für Wissenschaft des Krieges. Berlin, 1839–40. 8°. Bd. 47, p. 137–189; Bd. 48, p. 70–92, 142–185.) VWA
The author was a member of the infantry regiment von Specht. A short biography is given as an introduction to Senden's account of the American Revolution. See also the transcript of the *Denkwürdigkeiten* in the Manuscript Division.

529. SPRICKMANN, ANTON MATTHIAS. Nachrichten aus Amerika. (Deutsches Museum. Leipzig, 1776. 8°. [Jahr] 1776, Bd. 2, p. 992–1007.) *DF
Belletristic narrative about a young couple who elope and find happiness by emigrating to America.
In his introduction to *Stürmer und Dränger*, Erster Teil (Deutsche National Literatur, v. 79, NFF), A. Sauer quotes the author as having stated: "Alles ist verdreht und nirgends Genuss für den ganzen Menschen, wenn nicht in Amerika Friede mit Freiheit kömmt — freier Bürger auf eignem Acker, das ist das einzigel ist Beschäftigung für Körper, für Gefühl und Verstand zugleich — alles andre, Wissenschaft und Ehre und was wir sonst noch für schöne Raritäten haben, ist alles einseitig und barer Quark." — p. 28. For many more references to America (even for a plan to emigrate there with friends), see H. Jansen, *Aus dem Göttinger Hainbund; Overbeck und Sprickmann; ungedruckte Briefe Overbecks*, Münster, 1933, NGR, and A. M. Sprickmann, "Meine Geschichte in Deutsche Literatur," in *Entwicklungsreihen... Reihe [25], Deutsche Selbstzeugnisse*, Leipzig, 1936, v. 9, p. 254–284, AGK.
Review: *Allgemeine deutsche Bibliothek*, Anhang zu Bd. 25/36, Abth. 4, p. 2302, NAA.

530. TAGEBUCH der Seereise von Stade nach Quebec in Amerika durch die zweyte Division Herzoglicher Braunschweigischer Hülfsvölker. Von einem Officier unter des Herrn Obersten Specht Regimente. Frankfurth und Leipzig, 1776. 48 p. 18 cm. *KF 1776
Wrongly attributed to F. V. Melsheimer, chaplain of a regiment of dragoons. For an English translation, see New York State Historical Association, *Quarterly journal*, Geneva, 1927, v. 8, p. 323–351, IAA.
Review: *Allgemeine deutsche Bibliothek*, Bd. 35, p. 526, NAA.
The diary of the chaplain of the Third Waldeck Regiment, started May 20, 1776 and continued till December 31, 1780, was not printed before 1907; see M. D. Learned, *Philipp Waldeck's Diary of the American Revolution*, Philadelphia, 1907, IGE (Waldeck). See also no. 615.
Note also "Journal of the voyage of the Brunswick auxiliaries from Wolfenbüttel to Quebec... Minden, 1776 [Translated from the German by W. Wood and W. L. Stone]," in Literary and Historical Society of Quebec, *Transactions*, Quebec, 1891, no. 20, p. 133–178, HWA.

531. VOM Deutschen-Handel in NAmerika. (In: A. L. Schlözer. Briefwechsel meist historischen und politischen Inhalts. Göttingen, 1776. 8°. Theil 1, p. 217–226.) BAC
I. Aus der xiten Fortsetzung der Nachricht von einigen Evangelischen Gemeinden in Amerika, absonderlich in Pensylvanien, Halle, 1769, p. 997–1000. II. Aus Dominicus Blackford's kurzer Nachricht von dem gegenwärtigen Zustande der Englischen Kolonien in Nordamerika.
Both chapters deal with the custom of ships' captains taking indigent emigrants to America, upon receipt of a pledge to work in the New World without remuneration until the fare was paid in full.
The Library's copy of Dominique de Blackford's *Précis de l'état actuel des colonies angloises dans l'Amérique Septentrionale*, Milan, 1771, is in *KF 1771.
See no. 317.

1776, *continued*

**532.** VON der bei den Deutschen in Philadelphia angelegten lateinischen Schule: ein Schreiben des Hrn. Pastor Kunze, vom 16 Maj 1773. (In: A. L. Schlözer. Briefwechsel meist historischen und politischen Inhalts. Göttingen, 1776. 8°. Theil 1, p. 206–217.) BAC
Pastor Kunze organizes in Philadelphia, Pa., in 1773, the Gesellschaft zur Befoerderung des Christenthums und aller nützlichen Erkenntnis unter den Deutschen in Amerika and a school in connection with it. He asks for German support, but A. L. Schloezer comments upon the Germans in Pennsylvania as follows: "[Sie] sind keine Deutsche mer, sie haben freiwillig sich von uns getrennt, und sind brittische Untertanen." He pleads for spending the money on Germans in Germany, and blames the German emigrants. "Vielleicht wären sie nicht arm, wenn sie im Lande geblieben, und sich redlich ernäret hätten."
See C. F. Haussmann, *Kunze's Seminarium and the Society for Propagation of Christianity and Useful Knowledge among the Germans in America*, Philadelphia, 1917 (University of Pennsylvania, Americana Germanica monographs, no. 27, *STG*).

**533.** WAGNER, HEINRICH LEOPOLD. Die Kindermörderin. Ein Trauerspiel. Leipzig: Im Schwickartschen Verlage, 1776. (Reprinted in: Deutsche National-Litteratur...herausgegeben von Joseph Kürschner. Berlin und Stuttgart, n. d. 12°. Bd. 80, p. 283–357.) NFF
This volume has individual title: Stürmer und Dränger. Zweiter Teil. Lenz und Wagner...
Evchen: "O wenn ich ein Mann wäre!"
Frau Humbrecht: "Was wär's?"
Evchen: "Noch heute macht' ich mich auf den Weg nach Amerika; und hälf' für die Freiheit streiten."
—*Act 4, Scene 1.*

**533A.** WIEDERHOLDT, CAPTAIN. Tagebuch des Capt. Wiederholdt, vom 7 Oktober 1776 bis 7 December 1780. (German American annals. Philadelphia, 1901. 4°. v. 4, p. iii–xvii, 19–93.) NFCA
Introduction by M. D. Learned. Translation by C. Grosse. See E. J. Lowell, *The Hessians and the other German auxiliaries of Great Britain in the Revolutionary War*, New York, 1884, *1G*. Chapt. iv. Wiederhold's voyage — an episode — September 1779.

**534.** *Review:* Geschichte der Engländischen Handelschaft, Manufakturen, Colonien und Schiffarth in den alten, mittlern und neuern Zeiten, bis auf das lauffende Jahr 1776. von Fr. Wilh. Taube... Leipzig: Bey Paul Kraus, 1776. (Der Teutsche Merkur. Weimar, 1776. 8°. Jahr 1776, Vierteljahr 3 [Bd. 15], p. 262–263, *DF, Neue.*)
This periodical subsequently called *Der Neue teutsche Merkur*, under which it is shelved.
Kayser, *Vollständiges Bücherlexicon*, v. 5, p. 404, *R-GDH*, mentions also F. W. von Taube, *Thoughts on the present state of our colonies in North America, on their behaviour to their Mother Country*, London, 1766. No further record found.
See no. 663, especially the note.

**535.** *Review:* Geschichte der englischen Colonien in Nordamerika, von der Entdeckung bis 1763. Zwey Theile. Aus dem Englischen. Leipzig: Bey Caspar Fritsch, 1775. 8°. (Allgemeine deutsche Bibliothek. Berlin, 1776. 8°. Bd. 28, p. 534–535, *NAA.*)
See no. 502.

1777

**536.** ALLERERSTE Nachrichten von der Entdeckung von Amerika: aus Privatbriefen des Petrus Martyr, eines Freundes und Correspondenten von Christoph Colon, zwischen den Jaren 1493–1496. (In: A. L. Schlözer. Briefwechsel meist historischen und politischen Inhalts. Göttingen, 1777. 8°. Theil 2, p. 207–227.) BAC
In Latin. Excerpts from *Opus Epistolarum Petri Martyris...*, first printed in Alcala in 1530.
"Vossius gab zu Berlin 1722 eine Allerälteste Nachricht von der Neuen Welt heraus: allein diese allerälteste Nachricht ist nichts als ein Brief von dem Windbeutel Americo Vespucci, der erst nach dem J. 1500 im Publico erschien, und 1534 in Augsburg deutsch gedruckt worden ist. Martyrs Nachrichten aber sind weit älter..." — *Editor.*
See no. 262.

**537.** AUS einem Schreiben vom 1sten Januar 1777. aus dem Lager bey Fort Knyphausen. (Deutsches Museum. Leipzig, 1777. 8°. [Jahr] 1777, Bd. 2, p. 188–191.) *DF
Description of Long Island, etc., by a Hessian.
This volume called Bd. 4 on spine.

**538.** AUSZUG aus Cooks Reise um die Welt in den Jahren 1772, 1773, 1774, 1775. (Hannoverisches Magazin...vom Jahre 1777. Hannover, 1778. 4°. Jahrgang 15, col. 1281–1360.) *DF
Title page dated 1778; contents, 1777.
The Library's copies of Cook's "Voyages" are in † *KBF* and †* *KF 1777.*

**539.** BRIEFE vom J. 1757 aus Amerika, worinnen der jetzige Aufrur dasselbst vorausgesagt worden. (In: A. L. Schlözer. Briefwechsel meist historischen und politischen Inhalts. Göttingen, 1777. 8°. Theil 2, p. 197–206.) BAC
Reprinted from the *London chronicle*, April 22nd–24th, 1777, p. 889.
Letters from the Marquis de Montcalm, Governor General of Canada to Mess. de Berryer and de la Molé, in the years 1757–1759, with an English translation. 28 p. 8°. (Library's catalogue entry: P. J. A. Roubaud, supposed author. Lettres... London, 1777. * *KF 1777.*)
"Ich setze nämlich voraus, dass diese Briefe nicht erdichtet sind; sonst wären sie freilich des Drucks nicht werth. Was hier von der Grund-Ursache des NAmerikanischen Aufstandes gesagt wird; ist nicht unbekannt, aber meines Wissens nirgends so umständlich erklärt." — *Editor.*

**540.** CITATION von Horchheim nach NAmerika, Worms, den 25 Febr. 1777. (In: A. L. Schlözer. Briefwechsel meist historischen und politischen Inhalts. Göttingen, 1777. 8°. Theil 2, p. 111–112.) BAC
Caspar Schoenebrugh of Marbrunch (?), in North America, is called upon to make 124 Gulden as balance of a debt contracted by Heinrich Fetter, who died on his return to his homeland from St. Croix aboard the frigate *Adrian und Jean.*

**541.** DEUTSCHE Hülfstruppen nach Amerika. 1777. (In: F. W. von Ditfurth. Historische Volkslieder der Zeit von 1756 bis 1871... Aus fliegenden Blättern, handschriftlichen Quellen und dem Volksmunde... Berlin: Franz Lipperheide, 1871–1872. 8°. Bd. 1 [Theil 2], p. 7–8.) NFL
Called Theil 2 on main title page; has separate title: Die Historischen Volkslieder vom Ende des siebenjährigen Kriegs, 1763 bis zum Brande vom Moskau, 1812. Berlin: Lipperheide, 1872.

## 1777, continued

**541A.** DOEHLA, JOHANN KONRAD. Tagebuch eines Bayreuther Soldaten aus dem Nordamerikanischen Freiheitskrieg 1777-1783... (Archiv für Geschichte und Altertumskunde von Oberfranken. Bayreuth, 1912. 8°. Bd. 25, Heft 1, p. 81-201; Heft 2, p. 107-224.)    ELS
Vorwort by W. Frhr. von Waldenfels. Also printed in Deutsch-amerikanische historische Gesellschaft von Illinois, *Jahrbuch*, Chicago, Ill., 1918, v. 17, p. 9-358, *IEK*, in which several poems were added: 1. An die aus America zurückgekommenen ruhmvollen bayreuthischen Krieger und Freunde. Gesprochen bey ihrem Einzug in Culmbach den 16. November 1783 von Friedrich Wilhelm Philipp Ernst Freiherrn von Reitzenstein. 2. Ein anderes, welches in Bayreuth verfertigt wurde und wir daselbst gedruckt bekamen. Auf unsere Zurückkunft aus Amerika und Einmarsch in Bayreuth, den 20. November im Jahre 1783. 3. Ein Lied, welches in unsern Winter-Quartier in Philadelphia auf die Rebellen gemacht worden ist. Von einem Anspacher Mousquetier, namens Thormann. 4. Ein Lied, welches auf die Bestürmung und Einnahme des Forts Mont-Gommery d. 6. Octobris Anno 1777 von einem Anspacher Grenadier, namens Braun poesiert wurde. 5. Ein Lied, welches auf die Ein- und Ausfahrt der französischen Flotte zu New-Port und des Attacts mit den Rebellen auf der Insel Rhode-Island, den 29ten August, im Jahre 1778 vorgefallen ist, von dem Mousquetier Apel von Capitaine von Eyb-Compagnie verfertigt. 6. Aus einer Rebellen-Zeitung von Boston, den 18. Februar 1779 [prose]. 7. Ein Danck-Gebeth [prose]. 8. Danck Gebeth [prose]. 9. Groser und erhabener Gott! [prose]. 10. Nun folget das Lied darauf. 11. Ein Schreiben eines Geistlichen an sein Beichtkind, einem in das Feld, nach America gehenden Soldaten. 12. Ein Lied über die herzogl. Braunschw. Trouppen nach America, in engl. Sold gehend, vom Jahre 1776 bis 1777... 13. Fortsetzung des Liedes vom Feld-Zuge in 2ten Jahr, oder 1777. 14. Nachtrag.
See also "Amerikanische Feldzüge, 1777-1783: Tagebuch von Johann Konrad Döhla," in *Deutsch-amerikanisches Magazin*, Cincinnati, O., 1887, Bd. 1, p. 57-86, 239-269, 373-402, 546-567, *IEK*.

**542.** DOHM, CHRISTIAN WILHELM VON. Briefe nordamerikanischen Inhalts. (Deutsches Museum. Leipzig, 1777. 8°. [Jahr] 1777, Bd. 1, p. 159-186.)    *DF
Signed: Kassel den 9ten Jänner 1777.
Reply to Schlözer's attack in his *Briefwechsel meist historischen und politischen Inhalts*, Göttingen, 1776, Theil 1, p. 312-320, and on remarks of an anonymous writer in the same magazine, Theil 1, p. 373, *BAC*.
Review: *Allgemeine deutsche Bibliothek*, Anhang zu Bd. 25/36, Abth. 4, p. 2304-2305, *NAA*.
See nos. 505, 526.

**543.** ⸻ Einige der neuesten politischen Gerüchte gesammelt von Christ. Wilhelm Dohm. (Der Teutsche Merkur. Weimar, 1777. 8°. Jahr 1777, Vierteljahr 1 [Bd. 17], p. 75-91.)
   *DF (Neue)
"Das grösste politische Eräugnis des siebenten Decenniums unsers Jahrhunderts (und vielleicht bey der Nachwelt des ganzen Sekulums) ist ohne Zweifel der noch immer fortdaurende Prozess zwischen Mutter und Tochter, Grossbrittanien und seinen Kolonien..."
This periodical subsequently called *Der Neue teutsche Merkur*, under which it is shelved.

**544.** ⸻ Ueber die Kaffeegesetzgebung. (Deutsches Museum. Leipzig, 1777. 8°. [Jahr] 1777, Bd. 2, p. 123-145.)    *DF

**545.** [FENNING, DANIEL.] Neue Erdbeschreibung von ganz Amerika... Aus dem Englischen. Herausgegeben von August Ludwig Schlözer, Professor in Göttingen. Göttingen und Leipzig: In der Weygandschen Buchhandlung, 1777. 2 parts in 1 v. 4 folding pl., 3 folding maps. 18 cm.    *KF 1777
Sabin 77659.
A translation chiefly by G. C. H. List and W. J. K. Henneman of book IV (Americas) of the 4th edition of *A new system of geography*, by Daniel Fenning, Joseph Collyer and others. See "Vorrede." Published also Bern, 1777.
Contents: 1. Theil, Eine allgemeine Einleitung, und das brittische Amerika. 2. Theil. Das französische, holländische, dänische, portugiesische, und spanische Amerika... Nebst einem Anhange vom fünften Welttheile.
Plates by G. G. Endner, sculp.
Review: *Allgemeine deutsche Bibliothek*, Anhang zu Bd. 25/36, Abth. 3, p. 1511-1513, *NAA*.

**546.** FORTSETZUNG der Neuesten Politischen Gerüchte. (Der Teutsche Merkur. Weimar, 1777. 8°. [Jahr] 1777, Vierteljahr 2 [Bd. 18], p. 62-84, 136-153; Vierteljahr 3 [Bd. 19], p. 259-273; Vierteljahr 4 [Bd. 20], p. 3-22, 221-246.)    *DF (Neue)
The last two continuations do not deal with America.
This periodical subsequently called *Der Neue teutsche Merkur*, under which it is shelved.
See nos. 479, 497, 523, 712.

**547.** GESANG [Bey Dem Abmarsch Der Hochfürstlich Brandenburg-Anspach-Baireuthischen Auxiliartruppen] Nach Amerika Anno 1777. (Americana Germanica. New York, 1897. 4°. v. 1, no. 3, p. 84-89.)    NFCA (German)
Edited by M. D. Learned after a copy of the original in Bayreuth.
Periodical subsequently called *German American annals*, under which it is shelved.
For a discussion of this work, see J. T. Hatfield and E. Hochbaum, *The influence of the American Revolution upon German literature*, New York [1900?], p. 43, *NFC p.v.4*.

**548.** GESCHICHTE des Compasses. (Hannoverisches Magazin... vom Jahre 1777. Hannover, 1788. 4°. Jahrgang 15, col. 401-420.)    *DF
References to Columbus.
Signed: H...g in H.

**549.** DIE HESSEN nach Amerika. 1777. (In: F. W. von Ditfurth. Historische Volkslieder der Zeit von 1756 bis 1871... Aus fliegenden Blättern, handschriftlichen Quellen und dem Volksmunde... Berlin: Franz Lipperheide, 1871-1872. 8°. Bd. 1 [Theil 2], p. 9.)    NFL
Called Theil 2 on main title page; has separate title: *Die Historischen Volkslieder vom Ende des siebenjährigen Kriegs, 1763 bis zum Brande von Moskau, 1812*. Berlin: Lipperheide, 1872.
"Frisch auf, ihr Brüder ins Gewehr,
'S geht nach Amerika!
Versammelt ist schon unser Heer,
Vivat, Viktoria!
Das rothe Gold, das rothe Gold,
Das kömmt man nur so hergerollt,
Da giebt's auch, da giebt's auch, da giebts auch bessern Sold."
"Mündlich 1829 von einem alten Soldaten, namens Mirbach, zu Kassel, der den Feldzug mitgemacht hatte, nun aber betteln musste." — Ditfurth.

*1777, continued*

550. LANDMACHT von Grossbritannien zu Anfang des J. 1777. (In: A. L. Schlözer. Briefwechsel meist historischen und politischen Inhalts. Göttingen, 1777. 8°. Theil 2, p. 347-355.) BAC
Garrisons in North America were: 1. Nova Scotia: Annapolis Royal, Halifax. 2. Newfoundland: Placentia, St. John's. 3. Louisburgh. 4. Isl. of St. John. 5. Quebec. 6. Montreal. 7. East Florida: St. Augustin. 8. West-Florida: Pensacola. 9. Mobile. 10. South Carolina. 11. Providence. 12. Bermudas. There were additional garrisons in the West Indies, the Southern Caribbee Islands, Grenada and the Grenadines, St. Vincent, Tobago, Dominica.
Under the heading Officers of the Hospitals for the Forces in North-America are listed: "6 physicians, 8 surgeons, 8 apothecarys, 3 purveyors, 1 chaplain." (See p. 351.)

550A. LETTRE du Landgrave de Hesse, au commandant de ses troupes en Amerique. [n. p., 1777.] 8 p. 8°. *KF 1777
Sabin 40679.

551. LIED eines Deutschen in fremden Kriegsdiensten. (Musenalmanach für 1777. Herausgegeben von Joh. Heinr. Voss. Hamburg: Bey L. E. Bohn [1777]. 24°. p. 108-111.) NFA
Title page of this volume reads: Poetische Blumenlese für das Jahr 1777.

"O wehe dem, der mich mit Trug
In dieses Land gebracht!
Mein Leid verwandle sich in Fluch
Und quäl ihn Tag und Nacht."

The poem, signed F. S., is by F. L. Graf zu Stolberg. (See Goedeke, v. 4, p. 365, 394, *RS-NFB.)

551A. [MIRABEAU, HONORÉ GABRIEL RIQUETTI, COMTE DE.] Avis aux Hessois et autres peuples de l'Allemagne vendus par leur princes à l'Angleterre. A Clèves [i.e., Cleve]: Chez Bertol, 1777. 16 p. 8°. *KF 1777
Sabin 2496.
See also "Warning to Hessians (Mirabeau, Avis aux Hessois) [in 1777]," in *German American annals*, Philadelphia, 1914, new series, v. 12, p. 228-232, NFCA.
See also no. 896.

552. MULGRAVE, CONSTANTINE JOHN PHIPPS, 2ND BARON. Reise nach dem Nordpol. Auf Befehl Ihro Königl. Grossbrittannischen Majestät. Unternommen im Jahre 1773. Von C. J. Phips, aus dem Englischen, Mit Zusätzen und Anmerkungen von Herrn Landvogt Engel... Mit Kupfern. Bern: Bey der typographischen Gesellschaft, 1777. 3 p.l., x, 122, 304 p., 3 l. maps, plates. 4°. *KF 1777
Sabin 62575.
Review: *Allgemeine deutsche Bibliothek*, Anhang zu Bd. 25/36, Abth. 3, p. 1468-1472, NAA.

553. NEW YORKS ISLAND, im Gebiete Harlem, 5 engl. Meilen von der Stadt Neujork, und 100 Yards von Hornhuck am East-River, den 18 Sept 1776. (In: A. L. Schlözer. Briefwechsel meist historischen und politischen Inhalts. Göttingen, 1777. 8°. Theil 2, p. 99-108.) BAC
"Von dem seel. Hrn. Lieut. Hinricks, an den Herausgeber." Reports on Revolutionary war. "1. Von Bremerlehe über Portsmouth und Halifax nach Staten Island. 11. Aufenthalt auf Staten-, Long-, und New York's Island."
See note to no. 575B.

554. DAS NORD-AMERIKA Historisch und Geographisch beschrieben... Hamburg: F. C. Ritter, 1777-1778. 4 v. in 2. front. (port., v. 4), map. 17½ cm. *KF 1777
Sabin 55454.
Vol. 3, p. 87-179 and v. 4 wanting.
Vol. 4 has imprint: Hamburg: In der Möllerschen Buchhandlung, 1778.
History and description of the British colonies in America, with an account of the American revolution.
Attributed to J. N. C. Buchenröder by Otto Lange in his *Catalogue 61*.
Review: *Allgemeine deutsche Bibliothek*, Bd. 34, p. 235; Bd. 41, p. 240, NAA.

555. OLDENDORP, CHRISTIAN GEORG ANDREAS. C. G. A. Oldendorps Geschichte der Mission der evangelischen Brüder auf den caraibischen Inseln S. Thomas, S. Croix und S. Jan. Herausgegeben durch Johann Jakob Bossart... Barby: Bey C. F. Laux, 1777. 2 v. maps, plates. 8°. *KF 1777
Sabin 57152.
First plate signed: C. G. A. Oldendorp del. J. G. Sturm sc. Nbg; the second: C. G. A. O. 1768. 15. Apr., G. F. Nussbiegel sc. Nor.; the third: C. G. A. O. pinx., G. P. Nussbiegel sc. Nor.
Review: *Neueste Litteratur der Geschichtskunde*, Theil 2, p. 168-171, BAA.

556. PERIODEN der Geschichte von Amerika. (In: A. L. Schlözer. Briefwechsel meist historischen und politischen Inhalts. Göttingen, 1777. 8°. Theil 2, p. 227-231.) BAC
The following periods of American history are suggested: Die Vorgeschichte von Amerika. — Seine Geschichte; 1. Entdeckung und Besetzung von Westindien und Süd-Amerika durch Spanier und Portugiesen, bis etwa 1584. 11. Anfang der Brittischen und Französischen Colonien in NAmerika und Westindien, von etwa 1584-1660. 111. Befestigte Teilung von Amerika zwischen Spaniern, Portugiesen, Britten, Franzosen und Holländern, von etwa 1660-1762. iv. Alleinherrschaft der Britten im vorderen NAmerika, 1762-1775.

556A. PFEFFEL, GOTTLIEB KONRAD. Recept wider den Krieg. 1777. (In his: Poetische Versuche. Wien: Bey F. A. Schraembl, 1791-92. 8°. Theil 1, p. 27-28.) NFF

"Die fernen Zonen
Der Tobolakiten und Huronen
Verstärkten des Czaar Bären Macht."

This is "Sammlung der vorzüglichsten Werke Deutscher Dichter und Prosaisten," XXI. Band.

556B. POPP [STEPHAN]. Popp's journal. 1777-1783. By Joseph G. Rosengarten. map. (Pennsylvania magazine of history and biography. Philadelphia, 1902. 4°. v. 26, p. 25-41, 245-254.) IAA
"Not without interest is Popp's diary — he was a soldier in the Bayreuth Anspach regiment — who came to this country in his twenty second year, an illiterate young fellow. He began his diary on June 26, 1777, and carried it on after his return home, adding some curious verses [e.g. "Das Lied vom Ausmarsch"]. It closes with some notes as late as 1796, and has some good maps of the operations on the Hudson, on the Delaware and around Philadelphia." — *J. G. Rosengarten, American history from German archives, n. p.* [1900], *IG p.v.5*.

*1777, continued*

557. [PURMANN, JOHANN GEORG.] Sitten und Meinungen der Wilden in America. Mit Kupfern. Frankfurth am Mayn: Bey Johann Gottlieb Garbe, 1777-1778. 4 v. folding plates. 17½ cm. *KF 1777
Sabin 66712.
Several of the copper engravings are by Zell.
For a later edition, Wien, 1790, see Sabin 81476.
"An account of the manners and customs of the Indian natives of North and South America, and of the South Sea Islands. The second and third volumes are dated respectively 1778 and 1779." — *Sabin*.
See Jacob Minor in *Göttingische Anzeigen von gelehrten Sachen*, Jahr 1896, p. 662, **DF*, who draws a parallel between it and Herder's "Volksliedersammlung" (1778).
Review: *Allgemeine deutsche Bibliothek*, Anhang zu Bd. 25/36, Abth. 3, p. 1490; Bd. 50, p. 514, *NAA*.

558. DIE QUAKER. (Musenalmanach für 1777. Herausgegeben von Joh. Heinr. Voss. Hamburg: Bey L. E. Bohn [1777]. 24°. p. 90.) NFA
Signed: R.
Title of this volume reads: Poetische Blumenlese für das Jahr 1777.

Jost: Gevatter, hört! Hier steht im Zeitungsblatt, Dass in Amerika, wo England Händel hat, Ein Völklein Quaker sey. Sinds Menschen oder Affen?
Jorg: Ja, Menschen! Bald so gut, als wie sie Gott erschaffen!
 * * *
Jost: Poz, Sapperlot! möcht doch 'n Quäker sehen!

559. ROBERTSON, WILLIAM. Wilhelm Robertson's...Geschichte von Amerika. Aus dem Englischen übersetzt von Johann Friedrich Schiller... Leipzig: Weidmannsche Erben und Reich, 1777. 2 v. in 1. front. (port.), folding plates, folding maps. 20 cm. HAB
A third volume, which is not in the Library, appeared in Leipzig in 1797, according to *Nürnbergische gelehrte Zeitung*, 1799, p. 21-24.
Johann Friedrich Schiller, the poet's godfather and distant relative, was an agent in Hesse and Württemberg for the purpose of obtaining troops for Holland's foreign possessions. Later, he went to England, where he seems to have served the British government in a similar capacity. Here he translated Robertson's *History of America*, 1777. He dedicated his translation to Queen Charlotte. His translation was sent to Zollikofer for improvement of language. See *Briefwechsel zwischen Christian Garve und Georg Joachim Zollikofer*, Breslau, 1804, p. 252.
Several then famous personalities wished to translate Robertson's successful work. Christian Garve, the well-known "Popularphilosoph," writes to Christian Felix Weisse, from Breslau on March 12, 1774: "Wenn Robertson's Geschichte von Amerika herauskommen wird, das wäre etwas für mich zu übersetzen." On March 11, 1775, he writes: "Ich weiss nicht, was ich so gern übersetzt hätte, als den Robertson. Ich schätze ihn so hoch—ich denke, ich würde es erträglich gut machen — und weg ist er. Das wäre das Buch, dass ich übersetzt hätte, ohne es zu kennen, weil ich nicht glaube, dass er etwas Mittelmaessiges schreiben kann. Und Amerika ist jetzt ein so wichtiger Vorteil! Wie in 200 Jahren sich die Gestalt der Dinge verändert hat!" See *Briefe von Christian Garve an Chr. F. Weisse*, Breslau, 1803, v. 1, p. 59 and 85.
Kayser, v. 4, p. 526, knows of a French version, published in Frankfurt am Main, in 1778, and a German edition of the English text with the imprint, Frankfurt am Main: Brönner, 1828, in addition to the editions listed as nos. 912 and 1060 of this list. See also no. 735A.
Reviews: *Neueste Litteratur der Geschichtskunde*, Theil 1, p. 14-28, *BAA*; *Allgemeine deutsche Bibliothek*, Anhang zu Bd. 25/36, Abth. 3, p. 1531-1532, *NAA*.
See nos. 735C, 912, 1060.

560. SCHREIBEN an einen guten Freund über die Gedanken vom Ursprunge der amerikanischen Völker so im danziger Geschichtscalender stehen. Thorun, 1777. 24 p. 16½ cm.
Sabin 77971. *KF 1777
Note also L. J. Ubland, *Rede vom Ursprunge der Bevölkerung in Amerika*, Tübingen, 1767. Sabin 97676. Not in the Library.

561. UEBER den amerikanischen Krieg. (Deutsches Museum. Leipzig, 1777. 8°. [Jahr] 1777, Bd. 1, p. 186-190.) *DF
Signed: U.
This volume called Bd. 3 on spine.
"Wenn der Himmel Cäsars Parthey nimmt, so halten wir es immer mit Kato, und der Kongress hat wichtige Freunde unter unsern Schriftstellern und Dichtern, die es alle nur mühsam begreifen, wie es zugeht, dass ein gedungenes Heer diese Söhne der Freyheit bändigen kann."
Review: *Allgemeine deutsche Bibliothek*, Anhang zu Bd. 25/36, Abth. 4, p. 2305.

562. VON den Niederlanden, Lower oder Delaware Counties, der 13ten rebellischen Kolonie in NAmerika. (In: A. L. Schlözer. Briefwechsel meist historischen und politischen Inhalts. Göttingen, 1777. 8°. Theil 2, p. 108-111.) BAC

563. VON Walter Raleigh, dem Hauptstiffter der Brittischen Colonien in Amerika, 1584. (In: A. L. Schlözer. Briefwechsel meist historischen und politischen Inhalts. Göttingen, 1777. 8°. Theil 2, p. 231-237.) BAC
Excerpts from Hakluyt's edition of *De Orbe Novo Petri Martyris...*
See no. 82.

564. *Review:* Briefe, den gegenwärtigen Zustand von Nordamerika betreffend. 1. Sammlung. Göttingen: Bey Dietrich, 1777. 8 Bogen. 8°. (Göttingische Anzeigen von gelehrten Sachen. Göttingen [1777]. 12°. Jahr 1777, p. 499-500, *DF*.)
Sabin 89756.
The author of the *Briefe* is Matthias Christian Sprengel, who sympathizes here with Great Britain. See also no. 823.

564A. *Review:* Die Werbung für England. Ein Lustspiel in einem Aufzuge, von J. C. Krausneck. Bayreuth: Bey Lübeck, 1776. 8°. (Allgemeine deutsche Bibliothek. Berlin, 1777. 8°. Bd. 31, p. 497-498, *NAA*.)
Signed Fm.
"Der alte Brawe, vormaliger Grenadier, muss bey dem Englischen Subsidientraktat seines Fürsten, im 45sten Jahre wieder die Muskete tragen; er hinterlässt ein Weib und zwo Töchter in grösster Armuth, die älteste wird von dem jungen Knaut geliebt. Zum Glück verirrt sich der Hauptmann Stromberg, unter dem Brawe ehemals gedient, in dessen Hütte, der beyde befreyt, und dafür zween andere von seiner Werbung stellt... Der Stoff... könnte bey jetzigen Zeitläuften vortrefflich behandelt werden, da jedem deutschen Patrioten das Herz wehe thun muss über den Verlust so mancher seiner Brüder, die das Schwerdt ...in einem so entfernten Lande fressen wird, da gewiss der hundertste Theil von dessen Existenz vorher etwas gewusst hat."

*1777, continued*

565. Review: Historisch statistisch Notiz der Grossbritanischen Colonien in Nordamerika [von Glob. Bd. Schirach]. Frankfurt und Leipzig, 1776. 96 p. 8°. (Göttingische Anzeigen von gelehrten Sachen. Göttingen [1777–1783]. 12°. Jahr 1777, p. 1152; Jahr 1783, p. 363, *DF.)
Sabin 77635.
"It was upon information such as is contained in this rare book, that the Princes were induced to sell their Hessians to serve under Burgoyne and others in America in 1777." — *Stevens*. See Sabin 32103, 77635.
Note also his *Politisches Journal nebst Anzeige von gelehrten und andern Sachen. Herausgegeben von einer Gesellschaft von Gelehrten* [ed. Gottlob Ben. v. Schirach], Hamburg, 1781–1840. Not in the Library. The first volume (p. 307) contains an article on Vermont.
See nos. 595, 764.

566. Review: Kurze Schilderung der Grossbrittannischen Colonieen in Nordamerica. Zwey Bogen in Folio... Göttingen: Bey J. Chr. Dietrich, 1776. (Allgemeine deutsche Bibliothek. Berlin, 1777. 8°. Bd. 32, p. 169–170, *NAA.*)
Sabin (38362) gives imprint as Göttingen, 1777.
The author is Matthias Christian Sprengel.
See no. 567.

567. Review: Kurze Schilderung der Grossbrittannischen Colonien in Nord America. Göttingen: J. Chr. Dietrich, 1776. (Göttingische Anzeigen von gelehrten Sachen. Göttingen [1777]. 12°. Jahr 1777, p. 497–499, *DF.)
The author of this work is Matthias Christian Sprengel.
See no. 566.

568. Review: Neue Nachrichten von denen neuentdeckten Insuln in der See zwischen Asien und Amerika; ...verfasset von J. L. S. ** Hamburg und Leipzig: Bey Gleditsch, 1776. 11 Bogen in 8°. (Allgemeine deutsche Bibliothek. Berlin, 1777. 8°. Bd. 32, p. 183–185, *NAA.*)
Sabin 52367.
Review signed: Pe.

569. Review: Das von den Russen in den Jahren 1765, 66, 67 entdeckte nordliche Inselmeer, zwischen Kamtschatka und Nordamerika, beschrieben vom Herrn von Stählin... Stuttgart: Bey Cotta, 1774. 3 Bogen in 8°. (Allgemeine deutsche Bibliothek. Berlin, 1777. 8°. Bd. 32, p. 183–185, *NAA.*)
According to the review, J. Stählin von Stocksburg's "Nachrichten" were previously published as a supplement to the *Petersburgischer geographischer Kalendar vom Jahre 1774.*

1778

570. Auszüge aus Hrn. D. Johann Reinhold Forsters...Reise um die Welt, während den Jahren 1772–75. (Der Teutsche Merkur. Weimar, 1778. 8°. [Jahr] 1778, Vierteljahr 3 [Bd. 23], p. 59–75, 144–164; Vierteljahr 4 [Bd. 24], p. 137–155.) *DF (Neue)
See no. 575.
This periodical subsequently called *Der Neue teutsche Merkur*, under which it is shelved.

571. [BABO, FRANZ JOSEPH MARIUS.] Das Winterquartier in Amerika. Ein Originallustspiel in einem Aufzug. Aufgeführt im k. k. Nationaltheater. Wien: zu finden beym Logenmeister, 1778. 35 p. 16°. NGB p.v.115
"Der Schauplatz ist zu Whern-ye-will in Amerika." There is no American atmosphere otherwise in this comedy, although the time is the American Revolution.

572. BEI Philadelphia, on the Neck, 18. Jan. 1778 vom Hrn. Hauptmann H. (In: A. L. Schlözer. Briefwechsel meist historischen und politischen Inhalts. Göttingen, 1778. 8°. Theil 3, p. 149–153.) BAC

573. BRIEFE aus NAmerika. I. Rhode-Island, vom 24. Jun. 1777, Von einem Hessischen an seinen Bruder. — II. Aus dem Lager bei Duar House, den 31 Aug. 1777, von einem Braunschweigischen...in der Burgoynischen Armee. (In: A. L. Schlözer. Briefwechsel meist historischen und politischen Inhalts. Göttingen, 1778. 8°. Theil 3, p. 27–42.) BAC
Compare this narrative of war events with the description in *Büttner, der Amerikaner. Eine Selbstbiographie..., Zweite Auflage*, Camenz, 1828, * KF *1828.* The author, born in 1754 at Lauta (near Senftenberg, Silesia), served during the American Revolution, first in the American army and later in the British army. He died as a surgeon in Senftenberg. For an English translation, see *Heartman's historical series*, no. 1, * KP *(Heartman).*

574. ETWAS von dem Gymnotus electricus, oder elektrischen Aal. (Hannoverisches Magazin... vom Jahre 1778. Hannover, 1779. 4°. Jahrgang 16, col. 87–94.) *DF
"Aus einem Briefe aus Charlestown in Südcarolina."
"Aus den Philosophical Transactions."
Signed: D.
Title page dated 1779; contents, 1778.

575. FORSTER, GEORG. Johann Reinhold Forster's...Reise um die Welt während den Jahren 1772 bis 1775 in dem von Seiner itztregierenden Grossbrittannischen Majestät auf Entdeckungen ausgeschickten und durch den Capitain Cook geführten Schiffe the Resolution unternommen. Beschrieben und herausgegeben von dessen Sohn und Reisegefährten George Forster... Vom Verfasser selbst aus dem Englischen übersetzt, mit den Wesentlichsten aus des Capitain Cooks Tagebüchern und andern Zusätzen für den deutschen Leser vermehrt und durch Kupfer erläutert... Berlin: Bey Haude und Spener, 1778–1780. 2 v. map, 12 plates. 26 cm. (4°.)
Sabin 25131. * KF 1778
"Forster who at the age of 18 with his father accompanied Captain Cook on his journey round the world, was the first of the great German circumnavigators of the globe. It was he who gave to the German public the first intimate knowledge of the Northern regions of North America." — *P. C. Weber, America in imaginative German literature, NFCX.*
Review: *Der teutsche Merkur*, [Jahr] 1780, Vierteljahr 2 [Bd. 22], p. 77–78, * DF *(Neue).*
Note also J. R. Forster, *Bemerkungen auf seiner Reise um die Welt*, Berlin, 1783 (Sabin 25132. Not in the Library), and G. C. Lichtenberg, "Einige Lebensumstände von Capt. Cook, grösstentheils en schriftlichen Nachrichten einiger seiner Bekannten gezogen, nebst dessen Bildnisse," in his *Vermischte Schriften*, Göttingen, 1844–67, v. 4, p. 138–185, *NFG.* First published in *Göttingisches Magazin der Wissenschaften und Literatur*, Jahr 1780, Stück 2, p. 243.

## GERMAN WORKS RELATING TO AMERICA

*1778, continued*

575A. HERMES, JOHANN TIMOTHEUS. Sophiens Reise von Memel nach Sachsen. Schaffhausen: Bey Benedict Hurter und Sohn, 1778. 6 v. in 3. 12°. NGK
"Deutschland hat Volk genug! wie könnte es sonst mit seinem gesündesten Blut die amerikanischen Aecker düngen." — *Fuenfter Theil.*
See also A. Henneberger, "Deutsche Literaturbilder des 18. Jahrhundert," in *Zeitschrift für deutsche Kulturgeschichte,* Nürnberg, 1858, Jahrg. 3, p. 577–601, *BAA,* especially p. 598.

575B. HINRICHS, JOHANN. Extracts from the letter-book of Captain Johann Heinrichs of the Hessian Jäger Corps, 1778–1780. Translated by Julius F. Sachse. [Philadelphia: The Historical Society of Pennsylvania, 1898.] 34 p. 8°. IGE
"The Historical Society of Pennsylvania has secured in Germany one of the letter-books of Captain Heinrichs [*sic!*]." — *Introduction.*
A "Diary of Captain Johann Hinrichs" also appears in B. A. Uhlendorf's *The siege of Charleston* (University of Michigan, Publications, History and political science, v. 13, *IGE*), in which also appear: "Letter and diary of Captain Johann Ewald"; "Diary of Major General Johann Christoph von Huyn"; "Letters to Baron von Jungkenn."

576. KURZE Lebensgeschichte des Columbus. (Hannoverisches Magazin...vom Jahre 1778. Hannover, 1779. 4°. Jahrgang 16, col. 1441–1488.) *DF
Title page dated 1779; contents, 1778.

577. LEISTE, CHRISTIAN. Beschreibung des Brittischen Amerika zur Ersparung der englischen Karten. Nebst einer Special-karte der mittlern Brittischen Colonien von Christian Leiste, Corrector an der Herzoglichen grossen Schule zu Wolfenbüttel. [Wolfenbüttel:] Gedruckt mit Bindseilschen Schriften, 1778. 29 (i.e. 20), 571(1) p., folding map. 12°. *KF 1778
Sabin 39937.
Reviews: *Allgemeine deutsche Bibliothek,* Bd. 41, p. 239–240, *NAA; Neueste Litteratur der Geschichtskunde,* Theil 5, p. 323–325, *BAA.*

578. —— Beschreibung des brittischen Amerika zur Ersparung der englischen Karten. Nebst einer Special-Karte der mittlern brittischen Colonien. Von Christian Leiste... Braunschweig: In der Fürstl. Waysenhaus-Buchhandlung, 1778. 29 (i.e. 20), 571(1) p. map. 8°. *KF 1778
Sabin 39937.

578A. MALSBURG. Vor 100 Jahren. Blätter aus dem während des Nordamerikanischen Unabhängigkeitskriegs geführten Tagebuch eines Kurhessischen Offiziers. [April - May, 1778.] [Darmstadt, 1878.] p. 126–127, 133–134, 142–143, 149–150, 157–159, 167. 4°. †IG
Extract from *Allgemeine Militär-Zeitung,* Jahrg. 53, No. 16–21, 1878.

579. MEISSNER, AUGUST GOTTLIEB. Anrede einiger Indianer an den Cortes; nach Montagne. (Taschenbuch für Dichter und Dichterfreunde. Leipzig: In der Dykischen Buchhandlung, 1778. 8°. Abtheilung 8, p. 142.) NFK

580. MURR, CHRISTOPH GOTTLIEB. Diplomatische Geschichte des portugesischen berühmten Ritters Martin Behaims. Aus Originalurkunden. Von Christoph Gottlieb von Murr... Nebst einer Kupfertafel. Nürnberg: Bey Joh. Eberhard Zeh, 1778. 144 p. map. 8°. *KF 1778
Sabin 51478.
The Library also has three copies of the second edition, published by Perthes in Gotha, 1778 (*KF 1778; AN*). For translations into several languages, consult the Public Catalogue.
As to whether Christopher Columbus or Martin Behaim discovered America, see nos. 274A, 382, 385, 386, 393.
Sabin (51480) says of C. G. Murr: He "was not only a ripe scholar, but an accomplished linguist. In regard to matters connected with the Indian languages, and among them of the Amaran, the Chilian, the Brazilian, the Paraguyan, Californian, Quichen, and Yungan tribes, spread at the time chiefly over South and Western America, from which the German Jesuit Fathers had just been expelled on the suppression of their Order in 1773 by Pope Ganganelli." In this connection see Murr's *Journal zur Kunstgeschichte und zur allgemeinen Litteratur,* Nürnberg, 1775–79, 17 v., followed by *Neues Journal,* 2 v. (Sabin 51480); see also his *Reisen einiger Missionarien der Gesellschaft Jesu in Amerika. Aus ihren eigenen Aufsätzen herausgegeben,* Nürnberg, 1785, *KF 1785 (Sabin 51481), and his *Nachrichten von verschiedenen Ländern des Spanischen Amerika. Aus eigenhändigen Aufsätzen einiger Missionare, der Gesellschaft Jesu herausgegeben,* Halle, 1809–11, Sabin 51481. Not in the Library. Finally, Wolfgang Bayer, *Herrn P. Wolfgang Bayers, ehemaligen americanischen Glaubenspredigers der Gesellschaft Jesu, Reise nach Peru. Von ihm selbst beschrieben. Herausgegeben von C. G. von Murr,* Nürnberg, 1776, *KF 1776. Sabin 4043.
Review: *Neue Bibliothek der schönen Wissenschaften und freyen Künste,* Bd. 23, p. 117–125, *NAA.*

580A. NEUESTE Litteratur der Geschichtkunde. Herausgegeben und größtentheils verfertiget von Johann Georg Meusel... Theil 1–6. Erfurt: Im Verlag der Keyserschen Buchhandlung, 1778–80. 3 v. 12°. BAA
Edited by Johann Georg Meusel.
Contains reviews of Robertson's *Geschichte von Amerika,* Theil 1, p. 14–28 [see no. 564]; [Sprengel's] *Briefe, den gegenwärtigen Zustand von Nordamerika betreffend,* Theil 2, p. 91–96 [see no. 619]; [Soame Jenyns's] *Beschreibung der europäischen Kolonien in Amerika,* Theil 2, p. 155–157 [see no. 626]; Leiste's *Beschreibung des brittischen Amerika,* Theil 5, p. 323–325 [see no. 577]; Russell's *Geschichte von Amerika,* Theil 6, p. 131–151 [see note to no. 649].

581. SCHREIBEN aus Stockholm, 16 Dec. 1777. (In: A. L. Schlözer. Briefwechsel meist historischen und politischen Inhalts. Göttingen, 1778. 8°. Theil 3, p. 43–51.) BAC
North America's trade with Sweden, p. 46.

582. VERMISCHTE Briefe. I. Philadelphia, 7 Maj 1778. II. Boston, le 5 Fevr. 1778... IV. Castle Town in New Hampshire, 20 Jul. 1777... (In: A. L. Schlözer. Briefwechsel meist historischen und politischen Inhalts. Göttingen, 1778. 8°. Theil 3, p. 259–290.) BAC

583. VERMISCHTE Nachrichten. (I. New York, 7 Decemb. 1777, von einem Feldprediger.) (In: A. L. Schlözer. Briefwechsel meist historischen und politischen Inhalts. Göttingen, 1778. 8°. Theil 3, p. 127–135.) BAC
Letter relating to action at Fort Mud-Island, Red Banc [i.e. at Forts Mifflin and Mercer] on the Delaware River and to Philadelphia.

*1778, continued*

584. VOLKSMENGE von Connecticut in N Amerika. (In: A. L. Schlözer. Briefwechsel meist historischen und politischen Inhalts. Göttingen, 1778. 8°. Theil 3, p. 290-291.) BAC
"Handschriftlich eingesandt an den Herausgeber, aus Philadelphia unter dem 4. März 1778, und eingelaufen in Göttingen den 19 Maj."

585. VON Kanada, aus Briefen eines deutschen Stabs-Officiers, dat. Batiscamp (einer Paroisse in Kanada) den 2. Novemb. 1776. (In: A. L. Schlözer. Briefwechsel meist historischen und politischen Inhalts. Göttingen, 1778. 8°. Theil 3, p. 320-340.) BAC
See no. 606.

586. WEPPEN, JOHANN AUGUST. Klage einer Hessin bey dem Abschiede ihres Geliebten. (Musenalmanach für 1778. Herausgegeben von Joh. Heinr. Voss. Hamburg: Bey C. E. Bohn [1778]. 32°. p. 189-192.) NFA
His comedy, *Der Hessische Officier in Amerika*, 1783, is not in the Library.
"Der Hessische Officier in Amerika, a comedy, Goettingen, 1783, has no great literary value, but some local interest, as the scene is laid in Philadelphia during the occupancy by the British, and Indians, Quakers, British und German soldiers and native citizens are among the dramatis personae. If it was not written by some one who had been here, it shows at least considerable familiarity with the conflicting parties during the Revolution." — *J. G. Rosengarten, in American history from German archives* [n. p.], 1900, *IG p.v.S.*

587. *Review:* Amerikanische Bibliothek, hg. v. C. D. Ebeling. Erstes Stück. Leipzig: In der Weygandischen Hdlg. 1777. 9 Bogen. 8°. Zweytes Stück 8 Bogen. Drittes Stück 16 Bogen. (Allgemeine deutsche Bibliothek. Berlin, 1778. 8°. Bd. 35, p. 212-215, *NAA.*)
Sabin 21747.
See no. 655.

588. *Review:* Amerikanisches Archiv, herausgegeben von J. A. Remer... 2ter Band. Braunschweig: In der Waisenhaus-Buchhandlung, 1777. (Der Teutsche Merkur. Weimar [1778]. 8°. Jahr 1778, Vierteljahr 2 [Bd. 22], p. 78, *\*DF, Neue.*)
This periodical subsequently called *Der Neue teutsche Merkur*, under which it is shelved.
The *Amerikanisches Archiv* of 1777 contains translations of Richard Price's *Observations on civil liberty and the justice and policy of the war with America*, 1776; Edmund Burke's *Speech on conciliation of the colonies*, 1775; letters from generals Lee and Burgoyne ("bey Gelegenheit der Ankunft des Letzteren in Boston" [see Sabin 9259]); Johnson's *Taxation no tyranny*; Josiah Tucker's productions advocating the recognition of the independence of America; and *Beruhfung auf die Gerechtigkeit und den Vortheil der Grossbritannischen Nation in den gegenwärtigen Streitigkeiten mit Amerika, von einem alten Mitgliede des Parlements, aus dem Englischen übersetzt*.
See no. 655.

589. *Review:* Briefe, den gegenwärtigen Zustand von Nordamerika betreffend. Erste Sammlung. Göttingen: Bey Dietrich, 1777. 8 Bogen. 8°. (Allgemeine deutsche Bibliothek. Berlin, 1778. 8°. Bd. 35, p. 208-212, *NAA.*)
See no. 564, 627.

590. *Review:* Briefe über die jetzige Uneinigkeit zwischen den Amerikanischen Colonien und dem Englischen Parlament. Aus dem Englischen. Hannover, 1776. 7 Bogen in 8°. (Allgemeine deutsche Bibliothek. Berlin, 1778. 8°. Bd. 35, p. 527, *NAA.*)
"Kayser gives the imprint: Berlin: Himburg, 1777." — *Sabin 7930.*
"...Diese Schrift sieht mehr einer Abhandlung als Briefen ähnlich; sie ist eine beleidigende und unverschämte Vertheidigung der Colonien. Der zügellose Verf. verlangt, der König soll ohne Umschweif für wahnwitzig erklärt, und ihm, bis alles wieder hergestellt ist, die Regierung abgenommen werden." See no. 660.

591. *Review:* Edmund Burkes Jahrbücher der neuern Geschichte der Englischen Pflanzungen in Nordamerika. Aus dem Englischen. Des Zweyten Bandes Erste Abtheilung. Danzig: Bey Flörke, 1777. 16 Bogen. 8°. (Allgemeine deutsche Bibliothek. Berlin, 1778. 8°. Bd. 35, p. 215-216, 539-540. *NAA.*)
Incorrectly attributed to Edmund Burke; see Library of Congress card and Sabin 9287.
See no. 592.

592. *Review:* Edmund Burkes Jahrbücher der neuern Geschichte der Englischen Pflanzungen in Nordamerika seit 1755 bis zu unsern Zeiten, übersetzt und ergänzt, oder abgekürzt. 2 v. Danzig: Flörke, 1777. (Göttingische Anzeigen von gelehrten Sachen. Göttingen [1778]. 12°. Jahr 1778, Zugabe, p. 369-372, *\*DF.*)
See no. 591.

593. *Review:* Ephemeriden der Menschheit. Basel, 1777. (Göttingische Anzeigen von gelehrten Sachen. Göttingen [1778]. 12°. Jahr 1778, p. 635-639, *\*DF.*)
Includes a discussion of Philadelphia's regulations concerning the indigent.
"Ein vortrefflicher Aufsatz."
The attitude of the *Ephemeriden* towards the American Revolution is discussed circumstantially in H. P. Gallinger, *Die Haltung der deutschen Publizistik zu dem amerikanischen Unabhängigkeitskriege 1775-1783*, Leipzig, 1900, *IG.*

594. *Review:* Historische und geographische Beschreibung der zwölf vereinigten Colonien von Nordamerika. Nebst einer Abschilderung des gegenwärtigen Zustandes von Grossbrittannien. Bunzlau: Im Waisenhause [1777]. (Allgemeine deutsche Bibliothek. Berlin, 1778. 8°. Bd. 35, p. 555-556, *NAA.*)
The "Beschreibung" is by Andreas Friedrich Löwe.
"Erd- und Geschichtsschreiber sollten doch wohl erst einen Friedensschluss abwarten, ehe sie mit dem Titel der vereinigten Colonien so freygebig sind..."

595. *Review:* Historisch-statistische Notiz der Grossbrittanischen Colonien in Amerika, mit politischen Anmerkungen die gegenwärtigen Unruhen betreffend. Frankfurt, 1776. 6 Bogen. 8°. (Allgemeine deutsche Bibliothek. Berlin, 1778. 8°. Bd. 35, p. 538-539, *NAA.*)
See nos. 565, 764 (note).

596. *Review:* Letters and Essays on several deseases of the West Indies — by different Practitioners. London: John Murray, 1778. [xl,] 320 p. ... (Göttingische Anzeigen von gelehrten Sachen. Göttingen [1778]. 12°. Jahr 1778, p. 1105-1110, *\*DF.*)
For full, correct entry, see the "Surgeon General's Catalogue," v. 8, p. 71, *Ref. Cat. 1239.*
"Die Vorrede enthält kürzlich eine natürliche Geschichte von Jamaica, besonders viel vom Clima."

# GERMAN WORKS RELATING TO AMERICA

*1778, continued*

597. *Review:* Medical advice for the use of the Army and Navy in the present American Expedition; intended for the perusal of private Gentlemen as well as medical Practitioners, by W. Rowley. London, 1776. 47 p. 8°. (Göttingische Anzeigen von gelehrten Sachen. Göttingen [1778]. 12°. Jahr 1778, p. 470-471, * *DF.*)

598. *Review:* Practical Remarks on Westindia diseases. London: Newbery, 1776. 127 p. 8°. (Göttingische Anzeigen von gelehrten Sachen. Göttingen [1778]. 12°. Jahr 1778, p. 471, * *DF.*)
"Der Verf. lebt auf den Westindischen Inseln, und verspricht noch in einem zweyten Theile die langwierigen Krankheiten abzuhandeln."

599. *Review:* Remarks upon the principal acts of the 13th Parliament of Great Britain, by the Author of Letters concerning the state of Poland. (Göttingische Anzeigen von gelehrten Sachen. Göttingen [1778]. 12°. Jahr 1778, Zugabe, p. 358-367, **DF.*)
The Library's copy of this work by John Lind is in * *KF.*

600. *Review:* Sechs Blätter von Aussichten merkwürdiger Gegenden in der Insel Jamaika, an Ort und Stelle von George Robertson gezeichnet und sehr wohl gestochen von D. Lerpiniere, T. Vivares und J. Mason. (Neue Bibliothek der schönen Wissenschaften und der freyen Künste. Leipzig, 1778. 8°. Bd. 22, p. 183, *NAA.*)
"Romantische Landschaften, etwas über 13 Zoll Höbe zu 19 Zoll Breite."

601. *Review:* Ueber den Aufstand der englischen Colonien in Amerika. Frankfurt, 1776. 24 p. in 8°. (Allgemeine deutsche Bibliothek. Berlin, 1778. 8°. Bd. 35, p. 526-527, *NAA.*) Sabin 97665.
"Der Verfasser eifert wider die Colonien, denen er vorwirft, dass sie ihren blühenden Zustand (der freilich einige Einschränkungen leidet)...der väterlichen Regierung ihres mütterlichen Landes und der Grossmuth ihrer Mitbürger in Europa zu verdanken haben."

## 1779

602. Aus Cambridge, bei Boston in Neu-England, den 10 Oktober 1778. (Von einem Braunschweiger Officier). (In: A. L. Schlözer. Briefwechsel meist historischen und politischen Inhalts. Göttingen, 1779. 8°. Theil 4, p. 278-280.) BAC

603. Begebenheit eines jungen Engländers unter den wilden Abenakis in Nordamerika. (Hannoverisches Magazin...vom Jahre 1779. Hannover, 1780. 4°. Jahrgang 17, col. 785-790.)
*See* no. 418.                                        * DF
Title page dated 1780; contents, 1779.
A young English soldier, taken prisoner by the Indians, is released for moral reasons when he refuses to fight his own people together with the Indians.

604. Cortés, Hernando. Briefe des Ferdinand Cortes an Kayser Carl den 5ten über die Eroberung von Mexico, nebst einer Einleitung und Anmerkungen herausgegeben von J. J. Stapfern... Heidelberg: Bey den Gebrüdern Pfähler, 1779. 2 v. in 1. 8°.        * KF 1779
Sabin 16953.
v. 2 has title-page: Briefe des Ferdinand Cortes an Kaiser Carl den Fünften über die Eroberung von Mexiko. Mit einer Einleitung und Anmerkungen... Heydelberg: Bey den Gebrüdern Pfähler, 1779.

605. —— Briefe des Ferdinand Cortes an Kaiser Carl den Fünften über die Eroberung von Mexiko. Mit einer Einleitung und Anmerkungen herausgegeben von J. J. Stapfer... Bern: Bey der typographischen Gesellschaft, 1779. 2 v. 16½ cm.           * KF 1779
Sabin 16953.
The second volume has imprint: Heydelberg, bey den Gebrüdern Pfähler, 1779.

605A. Doernberg, Karl Ludwig von, Freiherr. Journal d'un voyage en Amérique l'an 1779[-1781]. (Königliches Bismarck-Gymnasium zu Pyritz. Program. Pyritz, 1899-1900. 4°. Beilage zum Program, No. 149, 151.)                                                IG
In French. Edited under the title *Tagebuchblätter eines hessischen Offiziers aus der Zeit des nordamerikanischen Unabhängigkeitskrieges von Gotthold Marseille.*

606. Erster Feldzug der Braunschweiger in Kanada im J. 1776. (In: A. L. Schlözer. Briefwechsel meist historischen und politischen Inhalts. Göttingen, 1779. 8°. Theil 5, p. 267-279.)
Dated: Batiscamp, 2 Nov. 1776.                           BAC
"Ein vollständiges Tagebuch über den Marsch dieser Truppen vom 24. Sept. bis zum 2. Novemb. 1776 von dem Verfasser der vertraulichen Briefe aus Kanada: mit untermischten vielen andern kleinen, aber charakteristischen Nachrichten, besonders einer genauen Topographie des ganzen Strichs von Kanada zwischen Quebec und Lac Champlain..." — *Schlözer.*
See Max von Eelking, *The German allied troops in the North American War of Independence, 1776-1783,* Albany, 1893 (Munsell's historical series, no. 19), *IG.*
*See* no. 585.

607. Gleditsch, Johann Gottlieb. Neu vermehrte Erläuterung über die schädlichen Wirkungsfolgen eines bey uns sichere Kenntniss und sonderlichen Verdacht lange Zeit unterhaltenen nordamerikanischen Giftrebenstrauchs. (Berlinische Gesellschaft naturforschender Freunde. Beschäftigungen. Berlin, 1779. 12°. Bd. 4, p. 263-313.)
3-* EE (Gesellschaft)
A paper on the same subject was previously read before the Kgl. Akademie der Wissenschaften. Gleditsch refers to the "Giftbaum" (Toxicodendron).
The society was subsequently known as Gesellschaft naturforschender Freunde, under which its publications are archived.

608. [Hilliard d'Auberteuil, Michel René.] Betrachtungen über den gegenwärtigen Zustand der französischen Colonie zu San Domingo. Aus dem Französischen übersetzt und mit einigen Anmerkungen versehen... Leipzig: Bey Johann Friedrich Junius. 1779. 2 v. in 1. 8°.                                                  * KF 1779
Sabin 31898.
Translated by J. A. Engelbrecht.
The original is *Considérations sur l'état present de la colonie française de Saint-Domingue,* Paris, 1776-1777, * KF 1776.

*1779, continued*

609. HISTORISCHE und politische Betrachtungen über die Colonien besonders in Rücksicht auf die Englisch-Amerikanischen. Bern: in der Hallerschen Buchhandlung, 1779. 2 p.l., 152 p. illus. 8°. *KF 1779

Sabin 32105 (title incorrect).
*Contents:* 1. Beweggründe der Völker, die Colonien angelegt haben. 2. Ursachen der Wohlfahrt der neuen Colonien. 3. Anwachs der Englischen Colonien. 4. Vortheile, die Europa aus dem Amerikanischen Handel gezogen hat. 5. Vorschläge zur Aussöhnung der Colonien mit dem Mutterland. 6. Von der Handlung mit Indien. Fehler, die von den ausschliessenden Gesellschaften unzertrennbar sind.

610. ISELIN, ISAAK. Jsaak Jselin über die Geschichte der Menschheit... Basel: Bey J. Schweighauser, 1779. 2 v. in 1. 16°. BAP

This is the fourth edition. The first edition was published 1764-1770.
References to America.

611. LIED einer Amerikanerin. (In: H. P. Gallinger. Die Haltung der deutschen Publizistik zu dem amerikanischen Unabhängigkeitskriege 1775-1783. Leipzig, 1900. 8°. p. 65-66.) IG

An American girl, wooed by two youths, vows not to marry any suitor who has not fought for his fatherland for at least two summers. She is imitated by other girls, and thousands of warriors leave for war to gain both glory and the girls they love.
Originally appeared in: Neueste Mannigfaltigkeiten. Berlin: Wang, 1779, p. 347.
Periodical first called *Mannigfaltigkeiten,* Jahrg. 1-4, Berlin, 1770-73; continued as *Neue Mannigfaltigkeiten,* Berlin, 1774-77, *Neueste Mannigfaltigkeiten,* Berlin, 1778-81, and *Allerneueste Mannigfaltigkeiten,* Berlin, 1782-85. The series contains several articles relating to America. Not in the Library.

612. LISTE der Generals Personen, die in der Armee der Rebellen dienen, vom Monat Maj 1778. (In: A. L. Schlözer. Briefwechsel meist historischen und politischen Inhalts. Göttingen, 1779. 8°. Theil 5, p. 195.) BAC

613. OBSERVATIONS sur la situation présente des Affaires entre l'Angleterre et la Hollande. (In: A. L. Schlözer. Briefwechsel meist historischen und politischen Inhalts. Göttingen, 1779. 8°. Theil 4, p. 213-230.) BAC

"Verhalten gegen Gross-Britannien im Americanischen Kriege."
In French.

614. ON the neck bei Philadelphia, 2 Jun. 1778. Von Hrn. Hauptmann H —. (In: A. L. Schlözer. Briefwechsel meist historischen und politischen Inhalts. Göttingen, 1779. 8°. Theil 4, p. 115-117.) BAC

615. PENSACOLA in West Florida, 18. März 1779. Von dem Waldeckschen Feld Prediger, Hrn. Waldeck. (In: A. L. Schlözer. Briefwechsel meist historischen und politischen Inhalts. Göttingen, 1779. 8°. Theil 5, p. 112-113.) BAC

See also Philipp Waldeck's *Diary of the American Revolution. Printed from the original manuscript, with introduction and photographic reproduction of the list of officers. By M. M. Learned.* Philadelphia, 1907 (Americana Germanica. new series, v. 6, IGE).
See no. 624.

616. PFEFFEL, GOTTLIEB KONRAD. Lied eines Negersklaven. (Musenalmanach für 1779. Herausgegeben von Joh. Heinr. Voss. Hamburg: Bey L. E. Bohn, 1779. 32°. p. 41-43.) NFA

"Wohl dir, liebes Afrika!
Nun behälst du deine Kinder;
Schon verkauft Germania
Seine Helden, wie die Rinder.

* * *

Trotzig wirft das Sklavenjoch
Washington vom Löwennacken.

* * *

Dann schliesst einen ehrnen Kreis
Um des Quakers fette Saaten,
Welcher nichts von Sklaven weiss,
Nichts von Pfaffen und Soldaten!
Er nur ist der Freiheit werth!
Brüder, wenn wir für ihn siegen,
Wollen wir mit Howens Schwert
Pens geweihte Felder pflügen!"

617. SAVANNAH in Georgien, 16. Jan. 1779. (In: A. L. Schlözer. Briefwechsel meist historischen und politischen Inhalts. Göttingen, 1779. 8°. Theil 5, p. 1-8.) BAC

618. SCHLÖZER, AUGUST LUDWIG. Vertrauliche Briefe aus Kanada und Neu England vom J. 1777. und 1778. Aus Hrn. Prof. Schlözers Briefwechsel, Heft XXIII und XXIV. Göttingen: Im Verlag der Wittwe Vandenhoeck, 1779. 84 p. 8°. *KF 1779

Sabin (77658) lists a work of 10 vols., published 1777-1781.
The book comprises nos. 622 and 623.
An English translation appears in *Letters of Brunswick and Hessian officers during the American Revolution,* Albany, N. Y., 1891 (Munsell's historical series, no. 18, IG).
As to Schloezer's attitude towards the Revolution, see J. A. Walz, in *Modern language notes,* Baltimore, Md., 1901, v. 16, p. 208-209, RAA.
See also C. S. Blue, "The Canadian legion in Canada," in *Canadian magazine,* Toronto, 1915, v. 44, p. 229-238, *DA; E. J. Lowell, The Hessians and the other German auxiliaries of Great Britain in the Revolutionary War,* New York, 1884, IG (especially Ch. 10: The Brunswickers in Canada, 1776); R. B. Mowat, "Fresh light on the War of Independence," in *Discovery,* London, 1929, v. 10, p. 252-254, *DA; R. W. Pettengill, *Letters from America, 1776-1779; being letters of Brunswick, Hessian, and Waldeck officers with the British armies during the Revolution,* Boston and New York, 1924, IG.
Note also "Auszug einiger Briefe eines Braunschweigischen Offiziers an seinen Freund," in *Journal von und für Deutschland,* Eilrich, 1789 (not in the Library), which is rich in articles relating to America. See also H. S. King, in University of California, *Publications in modern philology,* Berkeley, 1929, v. 14, STG; also the letters from Canada, in *Gelehrte Beyträge von den Braunschweigischen Anzeigen* [ed. J. J. Eschenburg], Jahr 1776, p. 437, and a description of New York elsewhere in the volume. Not in the Library.

619. SPRENGEL, MATTHIAS CHRISTIAN. Vom Ursprung des Negerhandels. Halle: J. C. Hendel, 1779. 4 p.l., 71 p. 8°. *KF 1779

Sabin 89763.
"Sprengel was the compiler of several collections of voyages, containing items of American interest. Copies of these have been located as follows: *Auswahl der besten ausländischen geographischen und statistischen Nachrichten,* 1794-1800; *Bibliothek der neusten und wichtigsten Reisebeschreibungen,* 1800-1814. In cooperation with J. R. Forster, *Beiträge zur Völker- und Länderkunde,* 1787-1790; in cooperation with Georg Forster, *Neue Beiträge zur Völker- und Länderkunde.* 1790-1793." — Sabin.

## GERMAN WORKS RELATING TO AMERICA

*1779, continued*

620. STAUNTON in Virginien, 1 Jun. 1779. (In: A. L. Schlözer. Briefwechsel meist historischen und politischen Inhalts. Göttingen, 1779. 8°. Theil 5, p. 413–420.) BAC
Captain Edmonstone, former aide of General von Riedesel, takes this letter personally to Brunswick, where he had studied at the "Collegio Carolino."

620A. STOLBERG, FRIEDRICH LEOPOLD. Die Zukunft. 1779–1782. (Archiv für Litteraturgeschichte. Leipzig, 1885. 8°. Bd. 13, p. 84–115, 251–272.) NAA
References to America, especially verses i, 57, 206–209, v, 178–184, 187–192. See also *Musen Almanach für 1800. Von J. H. Voss*, Neustrelitz, 1800, p. 54–58, *NFA*, and H. S. King in University of California, *Publications in modern philology*, Berkeley, 1929, v. 14, p. 32–37, *STG*.

621. VERTRAULICHE Briefe aus Jamaika vom 31 Okt. – 23. Dec. 1778. (In: A. L. Schlözer. Briefwechsel meist historischen und politischen Inhalts. Göttingen, 1779. 8°. Theil 5, p. 313–329.) BAC
Dated: 1. An Bord des Transport Schiffes Crawford, 31. Okt. 1778. 11. An Bord vom Crawford auf dem atlantischen Meere, unter 27° Lat. gegen Florida über: 17 Novemb. 1778. 111. In See, an Bord Crawford, Sonntags den 29. Nov. 1778, unter 20° 10' Nördl. Br. und zwischen 74–75° Westl. Länge: rechts die Insel Cuba, und links die Insel Hispaniola. IV. Crawford Transport Schiff im Hafen von Kingston, auf der Insel Jamaica, in West-Indien. Montags den 14 Dec. 1778. V. Mitwochs, den 16 Decemb. 1778. VI. Montags, den 21 Dec. 1778, im Hafen vom Kingston, Jamaica. VII. Mittwochs, den 23 Dec. 1778.
Note also *Historisches Journal von Mitgliedern des Kgl. Historischen Instituts zu Göttingen* [ed. *J. C. Gatterer*], Theil 1–16, Göttingen, 1772–81 (not in the Library), which contains articles on Jamaica (Theil 5) and on Carolina (Theil 7, 9).

622. VERTRAULICHE Briefe aus Kanada. St. Anne, 9 März – 20 April 1777. (In: A. L. Schlözer. Briefwechsel meist historischen und politischen Inhalts. Göttingen, 1779. 8°. Theil 4, p. 288–323.) BAC
War reports. Meynen (no. 2974 i) names Du Roy as editor.
Note "Urkunden von einem Anspacher," in *Historische Litteratur für das Jahr 1781* [ed. *J. G. Meusel*], Erlangen, 1781 (not in the Library).

623. VERTRAULICHE Briefe aus Neu England Cambridge, vom 15 Nov. 1777 – 10 Okt. 1778. (In: A. L. Schlözer. Briefwechsel meist historischen und politischen Inhalts. Göttingen, 1779. 8°. Theil 4, p. 341–387.) BAC
"Burgoynes Niederlage bei Saratoga ist das...an Folgen reichste, was bisher in dem ganzen NAmerikanischen Kriege vorgefallen..." — *Schlözer*.
Nos. 622 and 623 are included in no. 618. For an English translation, see note to no. 618.

624. VON den Wilden auf Long Island bei Neu York in Amerika. Aus einem Schreiben eines Waldeckschen Feld-Predigers...vom Junius 1777. (In: A. L. Schlözer. Briefwechsel meist historischen und politischen Inhalts. Göttingen, 1779. 8°. Theil 5, p. 31–34.) BAC

625. WEKHRLIN, WILHELM LUDWIG. Chronologen. Ein periodisches Werk von Wekhrlin. Frankfurt und Leipzig: Felssecker, 1779–1781

[1784]. 12 v. (Americana Germanica. Philadelphia, 1902. 4°. v. 4, p. 267–291.) NFCA (German)
The excerpts are incorporated in an essay by J. A. Walz, "Three Swabian journalists and the American Revolution," of which part 11 is devoted to Wekhrlin. Periodical subsequently called *German American annals*, under which it is shelved.
Note H. P. Gallinger, *Die Haltung der deutschen Publizistik zu dem amerikanischen Unabhängigkeitskriege 1775–1783*, Leipzig, 1900.
Wekhrlin is also the author of *Chronologische Briefe* [n. p., n. d.] (Kayser, v. 1, p. 347B). Not in the Library.
The following quotation is from a review on "Circularschreiben des Congresses vom 13. September 1779," which appeared in *Chronologen*, v. 4, p. 181: "Niemals ist die Lage eines Staats, die Nachtheile und die Hilfsquellen desselben offenherziger an Tag gestellt: niemals sind Data, welche man in allen übrigen europäischen Regierungen für Staatsgeheimnisse hält, freymüthiger behandelt worden. Sie ist eine seltsame Acte in ihrer Art. Und sie verdient die Aufmerksamkeit aller Geschichtsschreiber." — *cf.* H. S. King in University of California, *Publications in modern philology*, Berkeley, 1929, v. 14, p. 123, *STG*.

625A. *Review*: Abhandlungen zur Naturgeschichte, Physik und Oekonomie, aus den philosophischen Transactionen und Sammlungen, gesammelt und mit einigen Anmerkungen übersetzt. Ersten Bandes erster Theil. Mit Kupfern. Leipzig: Bey Weygand, 1779. 292 Seiten. 4°. (Allgemeine deutsche Bibliothek. Berlin, 1779. 8°. Bd. 39, p. 203–206, *NAA*.)
Contents: 19. Edward Lyson, Zergliederung des mexikanischen Bisamschweines. 24. Von dem neuen amerikanischen Walfischfange bey den bermudischen Inseln. 29. Edward Lyson, Beschreibung einer Klapperschlage. 36. Villermont, Von einer besonderen Art Bienen in Westindien. 51. H. Sloane, Von dem Pfefferbaume aus Jamaica. 54. H. Sloane, Von einer Art Mistel (Tillandsia) aus Jamaica. 56. H. Sloane, Vom Kaffeebaume. J. P. Gamelli, Von dem wahren Amomum oder Lupus von den philippinischen Inseln.

626. *Review*: Beschreibung der Europäischen Kolonien in Amerika; nach der sechsten verbesserten Ausgabe aus dem Englischen übersetzt von J. Reinhold Bey Weidmanns Erben und Reich, 1778...Nebst 2 Landkärtchen, worauf Süd- und Nordamerika abgebildet ist. (Neueste Litteratur der Geschichtskunde. Erfurt, 1779. 8°. Theil 2, p. 155–156, *BAA*.)
According to the review, the author of the book, first published in 1757, is Soame Jenning, i.e., Soame Jenyns. "Erst auf Robertson's Empfehlung — in seiner Geschichte von Amerika — hat man es übersetzt... Es enthält nicht nur die Geschichte der Entdeckung des vierten Erdtheils und aller neuern Kolonien im Kleinen, so auch von dem Zustand der Verfassung dieses ganzen grossen Landes, als man zum bessern Verständnis der dortigen...Händel braucht. Das vornehmste Augenwerk des Verfassers...giebt auf die Geschichte der Handlung in den amerikanischen Kolonien der Europäer; wir sehen auch, dass Raynal dieses Werk tapfer geplündert hat."
See no. 558. Sabin (9288) attributes this work to William Bourke (Burke), friend of Edmund Burke. The first German edition has the imprint: Leipzig: Caspar Fritsch, 1775.

627. *Review*: Briefe, den gegenwärtigen Zustand von Nordamerika betreffend. Göttingen: Bey Dietrich. 8 Bogen. 8°. (Neueste Litteratur der Geschichtskunde. Erfurt, 1779. 8°. Theil 2, p. 91–96, *BAA*.)
*See* no. 564, 589.

1779, continued

628. *Review:* Charaktere, oder unpartheyische Musterung des öffentlichen Betragens und der Fähigkeiten der vornehmsten Personen im Parlemente von Grosbritannien. Aus dem Englischen. Altona, 1778. 12½ Bogen. 8°. (Allgemeine deutsche Bibliothek. Berlin, 1779. 8°. Bd. 39, p. 226–227, *NAA.*)

629. *Review:* Grundriss von Nordamerika, entworfen von J. N. C. B. [i.e. Buchenröder]. Hamburg: in der Möllerschen Buchhandlg., 1778. 3 Bogen in 8°. (Allgemeine deutsche Bibliothek. Berlin, 1779. 8°. Bd. 39, p. 226–227, *NAA.*)
Sabin 29012.
According to the reviewer, the author dedicates his work to his uncle and calls himself, "Buchenroeder."
See no. 544.

630. *Review:* Historischer Beweis der in Nordamerika vorgefallenen Staatsveränderung. Vom Anfange des Jahres 1774 bis 1sten Jenner 1778 von M. an einen Amerikaner. Aus dem Französischen. Bern: Haller, 1779. 8°. (Allgemeine deutsche Bibliothek. Berlin, 1779. 8°. Bd. 39, p. 206–209, *NAA.*)
Sabin 32106 (slight variation in title).
In favor of the American Revolution.
See no. 654.

631. *Review:* History of the Colonization of the free States of Antiquity, applied to the present Contest between Great Britain and her American Colonies. London: Cadell, 1777. 151 p. 4°. (Göttingische Anzeigen von gelehrten Sachen. Göttingen [1779]. 12°. Jahr 1779, Zugabe, p. 59–62, * *DF.*)
The Library's copies of this English work by William Barron are in * *KF 1777*.
A French translation by A. M. Cerisier, *Histoire de la fondation des colonies*, Utrecht, 1778 (* *KF 1778*), has an appendix defending the colonies.

632. *Review:* Philosophische und politische Geschichte der Besitzungen und des Handels der Europäer in beyden Indien. Aus dem Französischen übersetzt und mit Anmerkungen versehen von J. Mauvillon. Hannover: Helwig, 1778. 7 Th. 8°. (Allgemeine deutsche Bibliothek. Berlin, 1779. 8°. Bd. 39, p. 276–281, *NAA.*)
Sabin 68095.
See nos. 633, 692.

633. *Review:* Philosophische und politische Geschichte der europäischen Handlung und Pflanzörter in beyden Indien. Aus dem Französischen mit Anmerkungen. Kopenhagen und Leipzig: bey Heinek und Faber. 7 Theile. 8°. (Allgemeine deutsche Bibliothek. Berlin, 1779. 8°. Bd. 39, p. 276–281, *NAA.*)
Sabin (68115) lists: *Wilhelm Thomas Raynals philosophische und politische Geschichte der Besitzungen und Handlung der Europäer in beyden Indien*, Kempten, 1784. Not in the Library.
See nos. 632, 692.

634. *Review:* Die Säugthiere in Abbildungen nach der Natur, mit Beschreibungen. Dritter Theil. Erlangen, 1778. (Der Teutsche Merkur. Weimar, 1779. 12°. Jahr 1779, Vierteljahr 1 [Bd. 24], p. 81–82, * *DF* [*Neue*].)
References to North American mammals.
This periodical subsequently called *Der Neue teutsche Merkur*, under which it is shelved.

1780

635. ABENDFANTASIEN eines Hessen in Amerika. plate. (Musen Almanach. Göttingen [1780]. 32°. Jahr 1780, p. 86–88.) NFA
Signed: J. N. B–ff.
With music on accompanying plate.
Title of this volume: *Poetische Blumenlese auf das Jahr 1780...*

636. ANFRAGE über den Kanadischen Zuckerbaum. (Hannoverisches Magazin...vom Jahre 1780. Hannover, 1781. 4°. Jahrgang 18, col. 79–80.) * *DF*
Title page dated 1781; contents, 1780.
See no. 637.

637. ANTWORT auf die...gethane Anfrage "Ueber den Canadischen Zuckerbaum." (Hannoverisches Magazin...vom Jahre 1780. Hannover, 1781. 4°. Jahrgang 18, col. 175–176.) * *DF*
See no. 636.
Excerpt from A. L. Schloezer, *Briefwechsel meist historischen und politischen Inhalts*, Göttingen, 1779, Theil 4, Heft 23, p. 312.
Deals with maple sugar.
See no. 622.
According to the index, the answer was given by J. Ch. Bock, in Hannover.
Title page dated 1781; contents, 1780.
The article states that J. G. Gleditsch [see no. 607] in his *Systematische Einleitung in die neuere aus ihren eigenthümlichen physikalisch-ökonomischen Gründen hergeleitete Forstwissenschaft*, Berlin 1774–75, v. 1, p. 296–297, does not recommend the making of maple sugar in Germany, and that more about American maple trees can be found in J. P. du Roi, *Die Harbkesche wilde Baumsucht, theils nordamerikanischer, theils einheimischer Bäume, Sträucher und Pflanzen*, Braunschweig, 1771–72. Another edition, "Mit Vermerkungen und Veränderungen, herausgegeben von Johann Friedrich Pott, 2 v. Mit Kupfern," Braunschweig, 1795–1800.

638. AUF welche Art und Weise der Stockfisch zum Verkauf zubereitet wird. (Hannoverisches Magazin...vom Jahre 1780. Hannover, 1781. 4°. Jahrgang 18, col. 157–158.) * *DF*
Title page dated 1781; contents, 1780.
"Neu-Foundland und Neu-Schottland nebst den dazu gehörigen Inseln sind in Nordamerika die einzigen Länder, wo der Stockfischhandel in einiger Vollkommenheit getrieben wird."

639. AUSZÜGE aus Briefen eines reisenden Engländers, nach seiner eigenen deutschen Uebersezung. (Deutsches Museum. Leipzig, 1780. 8°. [Jahr 1780], Bd. 1, p. 76–97, 148–165, 212–227.) References to the American Revolution. * *DF*

640. BILANZ der Literatur des verwichnen Jahres. (Der Teutsche Merkur. Weimar [1780]. 12°. Jahr 1780, Vierteljahr 2, p. 18–51.) * *DF* (Neue)
References to the Moravian Brethren, p. 24, and to Carver's travels, p. 30.
This periodical subsequently called *Der Neue teutsche Merkur*, under which it is shelved.
See no. 642.

641. BROOKLAND, bei Neu York, 7 Sept 1776. Von einem Hessischen Feld Prediger. (In: A. L. Schlözer. Briefwechsel meist historischen und politischen Inhalts. Göttingen, 1780. 8°. Theil 7, p. 362–363.) BAC
Reprint from *Auszug eines Schreibens aus Amerika an Se. Exc. den Hrn. Gen. Lieut. von ° ° ° [i.e. Losberg], 1776. 24 p. 8°.*
See no. 516.

*1780, continued*

642. CARVER, JONATHAN. ...Johann Carvers Reisen durch die innern Gegenden von Nord-Amerika in den Jahren 1766, 1767 und 1768, mit einer Landkarte. Aus dem Englischen. Hamburg: Bey Carl Ernst Bohn, 1780. xxiv, 456 p., folding map. 18½ cm. (Neue Sammlung von Reisebeschreibungen. Theil 1.)     *KF 1780
Sabin 11187.
"Vorbericht" signed: C. D. Ebeling.
Review: *Der Teutsche Merkur*, Jahr 1780, Vierteljahr 3, p. 77-78, * *DF (Neue)*.
For a discussion of authorship of this work, see E. G. Bourne's "The travels of Jonathan Carver," in the *American historical review*, v. 11, p. 287-302, * *R-IAA;* and J. T. Lee's *A bibliography of Carver's travels and Captain Jonathan Carver, additional data*, 1910, * *KAK (Carver)*.
See no. 640.

643. COPIA eines Schreibens von dem General Major von Steuben, an den Geheimen Rat... in Heckingen: im Lager zu Neu Windsor am Nord Fluss, den 4 Jul. 1779. (In: A. L. Schlőzer. Briefwechsel meist historischen und politischen Inhalts. Gőttingen, 1780. 8°. Theil 7, p. 327-337.)    BAC
"Mitgeteilt von Höchster Hand." — *Schlözer*.

See also Steuben's letter to George Washington, in which he offered his services, December 6th, 1777: "I could say, moreover, were it not for the fear of offending your modesty, that your Excellency is the only person under whom, after having served under the King of Prussia, I could wish to pursue an art, to which I have wholly given up myself. I intend to go to Boston in a few days, where I shall present my letters to Mr. Hancock, member of Congress, and there I shall wait for your Excellency's orders, according to which I shall take convenient measures." This letter and a letter of introduction by Benjamin Franklin will be found in George Washington, *Writings, ed. by Jared Sparks*, Boston, 1855, v. 5, p. 526-529, *IAW (Washington)*.

Note also the following quotations from the "Journal of the United States Congress assembled.... Proceedings," Philadelphia [1788], v. 13, p. 114-116: "In January 1778, Congress received a letter from the Baron de Steuben dated Portsmouth, December 6, 1777, in the words following, viz., 'Honourable gentlemen, The honour of serving a respectable nation, engaged in the noble enterprize of defending its rights and liberty, is the only motive, that brought me over to this continent. I ask neither riches nor titles. I am come here from the remotest end of Germany at my own expence, and have given up an honourable and lucrative rank. I have made no condition with your deputies in France, nor shall I make any with you. — My only ambition is to serve you as a volunteer to deserve the confidence of your General in Chief, and to follow him in all his operations, as I have done during seven campaigns with the King of Prussia; two and twenty years past at such a school, seem to give me a right of thinking myself in the number of experienced officers; and if I am possessor of some talents in the art of war, they should be much dearer to me, if I could employ them in the service of a republic such as I hope soon to see America. I should willingly purchase at my whole blood's experience the honour of seeing one day my name, after those of the defenders of your liberty. Your gracious acceptance will be sufficient for me, and I ask no other favour than to be received among your officers. I dare hope you will agree this my request, and that you will be so good as to send me your orders to Boston, where I shall expect for them, and accordingly take convenient measures. — I have the honour to be with respect, honourable Gentlemen, your most obedient and very humble servant, (signed) Steuben.' " "Your committee further report, that in December, 1782, the Baron addressed a letter to the President of Congress requesting a committee to enquire into and report his situation and pretensions; which being granted, he stated his pretensions in the words following, viz., 'My demands were these, to join the army as a volunteer — that I wished to be known by the commander in chief, and to leave it to the officers of the army if my capacity entitled me to hold a commission in it — that the General would employ me in such a branch where he thought my service the most useful — that I was determined not to ask a favor or a reward previous of having deserved it. — That however I expected from the generosity of Congress, that in imitation of all European powers, they would defray my expences, although a volunteer, according to the rank which I held in Europe, as well for myself, as my aids and servants.' "

A biography of Steuben appeared in *Journal von und für Deutschland* [ed. Bibra], Ellrich, 1784, Stück 8 (not in the Library). See H. S. King, in University of California, *Publications in modern philology*, Berkeley, 1929, v. 14, p. 143, *STG;* also Friedrich Kapp, *Leben des amerikanischen General Friedrich Wilhelm von Steuben*, Berlin, 1858, *AN (Steuben)*.

644. ETAT der erfoderlichen Zalung für das hochlöbl. Hessische Leib-Infanterie-Regiment in Amerika, pro Febr. 1776. (In: A. L. Schlőzer. Briefwechsel meist historischen und politischen Inhalts. Gőttingen, 1780. 8°. Theil 6, p. 342-344.)    BAC

645. FRANKLIN, BENJAMIN. Des Herrn D. Benjamin Franklin's...sämmtliche Werke. Aus dem Englischen und Französischen übersetzt. Nebst des französischen Uebersetzers, des Herrn Barbey[!] Dubourg, Zusätzen, und mit einigen Anmerkungen versehen von G. T. Wenzel... Dresden: In der Waltherischen Hofbuchhandlung, 1780. 3 v. diagrs., front. (v. 1, port.) tables. 20½ cm. (8°.)     *KL 1780
Sabin 25581.
"A union of Dubourg's and Vaughan's editions."
— *P. L. Ford, Franklin bibliography, 344°*.
Illustration by Carl Gottfried Nestler.

A translation by G. T. Wenzel, of another work relating to America is S. W. Prenties, *Seereise eines jungen Officiers, oder Geschichte eines Schiffbruchs, auf der Königs-Insel, sonst Cap Breton genannt*, Strassburg, 1786. Sabin 65080. Not in the Library.

645A. [GOECKINGK, LEOPOLD FRIEDRICH GÜNTHER VON.] Kriegeslied eines Provinzjalen. (Musen Almanach für 1780. Herausgegeben von Voss und Goeckingk. Hamburg: Bey Carl Ernst Bohn, 1780. 32°. p. 102-104.)    NFA
This poem is also incorporated in an essay by J. T. Hatfield and E. Hochbaum, "The influence of the American Revolution upon German literature," in *Americana Germanica*, Philadelphia, 1899-1900, v. 3, p. 368-370, *NFCA (German)*: "The poem invites Germans to join the American battle for freedom, instead of taking sides with the oppressor."
The Americans address the mercenaries as follows:

"Was gehn dich unsre Händel an?
Was that dir unser Land,
Wo schon so mancher deutscher Mann,
Glück, die er sucht', auch fand?"

Hatfield and Hochbaum quote several more poems by Goeckingk, dealing with the German mercenaries sent to America. One of them is entitled "Antwort eines deutschen Soldaten," representing an answer to the above quoted lines, which "satirizes the mechanical willingness of the stolid German soldier to follow blindly the orders of his tyrant."

"Nichts gehn mich eure Händel an!
Weiss, traun! davon nicht viel,
Auch spiel ich, wenn ich's ändern kann
Nicht gern ein Trauerspiel."

*1780, continued*

**645A.** [GOECKINGK, L. F. G. VON], *continued*
Another of the poems, "Epistle an Herrn** in P*" (p. 377), contains the satirical lines:

"Fällst du zurück, so trag die Schande
Für dich! Aus deinem Vaterlande
Flücht hin ins Land des Wilhelm Penn,
Und werd' ein Ziel der Rifflemen."

Note also the poem "Golddurst, 1782" (p. 376–377), scorning the soldier traffic and "Der gute Fürst" (1787). See also H. S. King, "Echoes of the American Revolution in German literature," in *University of California, Publications in modern philology*, Berkeley, 1929, v. 14, p. 40–42, *STG*.

**645B.** HERDER, JOHANN GOTTFRIED VON. Dissertation sur l'influence des Sciences sur le Gouvernement et du Gouvernement sur les Sciences... A Berlin: Chez George Jacques Decker, 1780. (Reprinted in his: Sämmtliche Werke. Herausgegeben von Bernhard Suphan. Berlin: Weidmannsche Buchhandlung, 1877–1913. 8°. Bd. 9, p. 307–408.) NFG

The tract received the reward of the Berliner Akademie on June 1, 1780. The established German title is *Vom Einfluss der Regierungen auf die Wissenschaften, und der Wissenschaften auf die Regierung*. Of special interest: "Die einzigen Kolonien der Engländer machen eine ewigrühmliche Ausnahme. Vielleicht wenn die Wissenschaften in Europa verfallen seyn werden, werden sie dort aufgehn, mit neuer Blüthe, mit neuen Früchten," p. 363.
See no. 1132.

**645C.** LESSING, GOTTHOLD EPHRAIM. Ernst und Falk. Gespräche für Freymäurer. Fortsetzung. 1780. (Reprinted in his: Sämtliche Schriften. Herausgegeben von Karl Lachmann. Dritte... Auflage, besorgt durch Franz Muncker. Leipzig: G. J. Göschensche Verlagshandlung, 1886–1924. 8°. Bd. 13, p. 387–411.) NFG
Published first by H. L. Brönner at Frankfurt am Main, in 1780.
Falk: Er ist von denen, die in Europa für die Americaner fechten —
Ernst: Das wäre nicht das Schlimmste an ihm.

**645D.** LESSING, KARL GOTTHELF. Die Mätresse. Ein Lustspiel in fünf Aufzügen. Berlin: Bey Christian Friedrich Voss und Sohn, 1780. (Reprinted in: Deutsche Litteraturdenkmale des 18. und 19. Jahrhunderts in Neudrucken herausgegeben von Bernard Seuffert. Stuttgart: Göschen, 1887, v. 28.) NFF
Act ii, scene 8.
"The drama is a product of the Storm and Stress. Its theme is Back to nature, and the political phase of the subject is presented in a dialogue between the two brothers Hans and Otto von Krefeld, of whom the latter has lived in America. Though lacking in European culture, he has gained practical experience; when his pedantic brother asserts that the superiority of the paternistic régime prevalent in Europe is an apodictic truth, Otto derides him, points to the greater freedom and prosperity under the English system of government, and expresses his preference for life in America. The dialogue represents the radicals of the Storm and Stress; the tendency is, if anything, pro-American." See H. S. King, University of California, *Publications in modern philology*, Berkeley, 1929, v. 14, *STG*.

**646.** MÉMOIRE sur les productions, commerce, etc. de Louisiane. 1763. (Magazin für die neue Historie und Geographie. Halle, 1780. 4°. Bd. 14, p. [109–] 122.) BAA
In French.
"Der zweyte Abschnitt, von den Producten und von dem Handel der nord-amerikanischen Provinz Louisi-

ane, ist mir aus Hamburg geschenkt, und dabey versichert worden, dass er aus der Feder eines Mannes geflossen sey, der dieses Land und desselben Verwaltung sehr genau kenne. Er deckt viele Fehler in der Regierung dieses Landes auf." — *Editor's "Vorrede,"* f. [2b.]

**647.** MISCELLANEA. (In: A. L. Schlözer. Briefwechsel meist historischen und politischen Inhalts. Göttingen, 1780. 8°. Theil 6, p. 364–370.)
BAC
An account of a German-American farmer on p. 369.

**648.** PHILADELPHIA, 16 Febr. 1779. (In: A. L. Schlözer. Briefwechsel meist historischen und politischen Inhalts. Göttingen, 1780. 8°. Theil 6, p. 298–300.) BAC

**649.** RUSSELL, WILLIAM. Geschichte des Ursprungs und des Fortganges des gegenwärtigen Streites zwischen England und seinen Colonien. Aus dem Englischen übersetzt. Mit einer Charte von Nord-Amerika. Leipzig: Im Schwickertschen Verlage, 1780. xiv, 480 p., front. (port.) folding map. 19 cm. *KF 1780
A George Washington portrait is by Liebe.
Also published as v. 4 of Russell's *Geschichte von Amerika. Aus dem Englischen*. Leipzig: Schwickert, 1779–1780. 4 v. — *cf.* Sabin 74384.
Reviews: *Allgemeine deutsche Bibliothek*, Bd. 40, p. 531–532; Bd. 44, p. 491–492, *NAA; Neueste Litteratur der Geschichtskunde*, Theil 4, p. 131–150, *BAA*.
The same author's *Geschichte des älteren Europa*, Berlin, 1794–97 (Kayser, v. 4, p. 575B), contains some references to American affairs.
See no. 735C.

**650.** UEBER den Schleichhandel und dessen mancherlei Arten. Ein Schreiben des amerikanischen Weltweisen Benjamin Fränklins. (Hannoverisches Magazin... vom Jahre 1780. Hannover, 1781. 4°. Jahrgang 18, col. 1333–1342.) *DF
From the *London chronicle*, November, 1767.
Title page dated 1781; contents, 1780.

**651.** WAREN Preis, für welchen ohnlängst Amerikanische Waren in Gotenburg durch öffentliche Versteigerung verkauft worden. (In: A. L. Schlözer. Briefwechsel meist historischen und politischen Inhalts. Göttingen, 1780. 12°. Theil 7, p. 370–371.) BAC
Signed: Lorents Jenssen.
From Götheborgs "Allehanda," No. 65, Aug. 15th, 1780.
"Die Veranlassung zu dieser Publication war, weil sich von Marstrand her ein Gerücht verbreitet hatte, als wäre die Auction für die Amerikanischen Verkäufer sehr nachtheilig ausgefallen." — *Editor's note*.

**652.** WEKHRLIN, WILHELM LUDWIG. Über die Insurgenten. [1780.] (Americana Germanica. New York, 1902. 4°. v. 4, p. 280–283.)
NFCA (German)
Immer möge das Glück,
Diese eigensinnige und inconsequente Göttin,
Noch so schmeichelhafte Palmen in America ausstreuen:
Lasst mich einen Teutschen seyn!
In this poem Wekhrlin's prejudice against the Americans finds strong expression; not even the gentle Quaker of Philadelphia is spared. He presents the fiction of going to America himself with high hopes, as a result of reading Raynal; what he sees brings disillusionment. The Americans appear sober because far removed from city life; their virtues are trumpeted in the newspapers, but vice nestles in their homes, and he concludes with a not very convincing eulogy of Germany.

*1780, continued*

See Gottfried, Ritter von Böhm, *Ludwig Wekhrlin (1739–1792)*, München, 1893, *AN (Wekhrlin)*.
Appeared originally in *Chronologen. Ein periodisches Werk von Wekhrlin*. Frankfurt und Leipzig: Felsecker, 1780. Bd. 8.
This poem is incorporated in an essay by J. A. Walz, "Three Swabian journalists and the American Revolution," of which this is part 11, devoted to Ludwig Wekhrlin.
This periodical subsequently called *German American annals*, under which it is shelved.

**653.** *Review*: Abhandlung über die Kolonien überhaupt, und die amerikanischen besonders. Bern: Bey Walthard, 1779. 152 S. 8°. (Allgemeine deutsche Bibliothek. Berlin, 1780. 12°. Bd. 41, p. 570–572, *NAA*.)
Suggests declaring the American colonies independent and making commercial treaties with them.
"The author predicted that in one hundred years the seat of the English government would be in America."
— *Sabin 38231*.

**654.** *Review*: Abrégé de la révolution de l'Amérique angloise, depuis le commencement de l'année 1774, jusqu'au premier Janvier 1778. Par M<sup>xxx</sup>, Américain. Yverdon, M.DCC.LXXIX. 15 Bogen. 12°. (Neueste Litteratur der Geschichtskunde. Erfurt, 1780. 8°. Theil 5, p. 222–223, *BAA*.)
See no. 630.

**655.** *Review*: Amerikanisches Archiv, hg. v. J. A. Remer. Erster bis Dritter Band. Braunschweig: Waisenhaus Buchhandlung, 1777. in 8°. (Allgemeine deutsche Bibliothek. Berlin, 1780. 12°. Anhang zu Bd. 25/36, p. 1474, 1503–1506, *NAA*.)
See nos. 588, 599, 656.

**656.** *Review*: Anmerkungen über die vornehmsten Acten des dreyzehnten Parlements von Grossbritannien, von dem Verfasser der Briefe über den jetzigen Zustand von Polen. Nach der ersten Ausgabe von 1775 aus dem Engl. übersetzt. Braunschweig [n. d.]. (Allgemeine deutsche Bibliothek. Berlin, 1780. 12°. Anhang zu Bd. 25/36, p. 1503–1506, * *DF*.)
This is the third volume of Remer's *Amerikanisches Archiv*.
Sabin 41285. Translation of John Lind's *Remarks on the principal acts of the Thirteenth Parliament of Great Britain*, London, 1775.
See nos. 588, 599, 655.

**657.** *Review*: Bericht eines englischen Amerikaners von Philadelphia, an seinen Freund in Engelland über den dermaligen Krieg Gross-Britanniens mit seinen Amerikanischen Kolonien... Nach dem Englischen Original. Frankfurt: 1777. 3 Bogen in 8°. (Allgemeine deutsche Bibliothek. Berlin, 1780. 12°. Anhang zu Bd. 25/36, p. 1510–1511, *NAA*.)
Sabin 4864.
In favor of the American revolutionary war.

**658.** *Review*: Beschreibung der europäischen Kolonien in Amerika, nach der sechsten verbesserten Ausgabe aus dem Englischen übersetzt, von J. Erster Band 311 S., Zweyter Band 304 S. Leipzig: Bey Weidmanns Erben u. Reich, 1778. 8°. (Allgemeine deutsche Bibliothek. Berlin, 1780. 12°. Bd. 41, p. 240–241, *NAA*.)
"Das englische Original trat, wie man aus der Vorrede sieht, schon im Jahre 1761 an das Licht; daher findet man darin kein Wort von den nachher erfolgten amerikanischen Begebenheiten... Es werden darin [jedoch] von der Entdeckung der amerikanischen Länder, ihrer Lage, Geschichte, den dasigen Naturprodukten, Sitten, Regierungs- und Staatsverfassungen, sonderlich dem Handel, allerley gute Nachrichten mitgetheilt..."
See no. 626.

**659.** *Review*: Briefe über den gegenwärtigen Zustand von Amerika, besonders in Ansehung der Politik, der Künste, der Sitten und der schönen Wissenschaften. Aus dem Englischen übersetzt. Zweyter Theil. Leipzig: Bey Kummer, 1777. 224 S. 8°. (Allgemeine deutsche Bibliothek. Berlin, 1780. 12°. Anhang zu Bd. 25/36, p. 1507–1508, *NAA*.)
"Das Original scheint etliche Jahre vor dem Ausbruch des jetzigen Kriegs geschrieben zu seyn. Der Uebersetzer hat das Jahr nicht angezeigt, und der Rezensent das Original nicht zu Gesicht bekommen... Es kommen darinn Gedanken vor, die Erwägung verdienen, z. B. von Nationalschuld, öffentlichen Einkünften, und vom Krieg zur See..."

**660.** *Review*: Briefe über die jezige Uneinigkeit zwischen den amerikanischen Kolonien und dem englischen Parlament. Aus dem Engl. Hannover, 1776. 7 Bog. in 8°. (Allgemeine deutsche Bibliothek. Berlin, 1780. 12°. Anhang zu Bd. 25/36, p. 1510–1511, *NAA*.)
One of the few reports which support the colonies.
See no. 590.

**661.** *Review*: Edmund Burkes Jahrbücher der neuern Geschichte der englischen Pflanzungen in Nordamerika. Des zweyten Bandes zweyte Abtheilung. Danzig: Bey Flörke, 1778. 238 S. 8°. (Allgemeine deutsche Bibliothek. Berlin, 1780. 12°. Anhang zu Bd. 25/36, p. 1502–1506, *NAA*.)
For attribution of this work to Edmund Burke, see note on Library of Congress card, which cites the *Dictionary of national biography*.
See no. 591.

**662.** *Review*: Gesammelte Nachrichten von den Englischen Kolonien in Nordamerika, bis auf jetzige Zeiten. Hamburg: Bey Buchenröder und Ritter, 1776. 2½ Bogen in 8°. (Allgemeine deutsche Bibliothek. Berlin, 1780. 12°. Anhang zu Bd. 25/36, p. 1503–1506.)
Sabin 27205.
"...eine periodische Schrift, darinn historische und geographische Beschreibungen nebst Zeitungs-Nachrichten geliefert werden..."

**663.** *Review*: 1. Geschichte der Englischen Handelschaft, Manufakturen, Colonien und Schiffarth in den alten, mittlern und neuern Zeiten bis auf das laufende Jahr 1776. Im Grundrisse entworfen von Friedrich Wilhelm Taube. Mit einer zuverlässigen Nachricht von den wahren Ursachen des jetzigen Krieges in Nordamerika, und andern dergleichen Dingen. Leipzig: Bei Kraus, 1776. 10 Bogen 8°. 2. Abschilderung der Englischen Handlung, Schiffarth und Colonien, nach ihrer jetzigen Einrichtung und Beschaffenheit. Theils aus eigener Erfahrung, theils aus zuverlässigen und glaubwürdigen Nachrichten entworfen von Fr. Wilhelm von Taube. Theil 1 [n. p.] 1777; Theil II. n. p., 1778. (Allgemeine deutsche Bibliothek. Berlin, 1780. 12°. Anhang zu Bd. 25/36, p. 2212–2213, *NAA*.)
As to Friedrich Wilhelm von Taube, see *Allgemeine Literatur Zeitung*, 1787, v. 2, p. 407–408, *NAA*.
See also no. 534.

*1780, continued*

664. *Review:* Geschichte der Kolonisirung der freyen Staaten des Alterthums, angewandt auf den gegenwärtigen Streit zwischen Grossbritannien und seinen amerikanischen Kolonien. Aus dem Englischen. Leipzig: Weygandsche Buchhandlung, 1778. 13 Bogen. 8°. (Allgemeine deutsche Bibliothek. Berlin, 1780. 12°. Bd. 41, p. 241–243, *NAA.*)
Sabin 27217.
See nos. 631, 665.

665. *Review:* [1.] History of the Colonization on the free states of Antiquity, applied of the present Contest between Great Britain and her American Colonies. With Reflexions concerning the future Settlement of these Colonies. London, 1774. 4°. [2.] Geschichte der Kolonisirung der freyen Staaten des Alterthums, angewandt auf den gegenwärtigen Streit zwischen Grossbritannien und seinen amerikanischen Kolonien; mit Betrachtungen über die künftige Einrichtung dieser Kolonien. Aus dem Engl. Leipzig: In der Weygandschen Handlung, 1778. 13 Bogen. 8°. (Neueste Litteratur der Geschichtskunde. Erfurt, 1780. 12°. Theil 5, p. 345–348, *BAA.*)
See nos. 631, 664.

666. *Review:* J. Mauvillon's Sammlung von Aufsätzen über Gegenstände aus der Staatskunst... Leipzig: Weygandsche Buchhandlung. Erster Theil 1776, Zweyter Theil 1777. (Allgemeine deutsche Bibliothek. Berlin, 1780. 12°. Anhang zu Bd. 25/36, p. 2217, *NAA.*)
J. Mauvillon, professor at the Carolinum in Cassel, attacks Schloezer's position on the American Revolution. See J. A. Walz in *Modern language notes*, Baltimore, 1901, v. 16, p. 209, *RAA.*
The collection contains essays, such as: "Das wahre Beste Grossbritanniens in Rücksicht auf seine Kolonien," Theil 1, 2; "Anmerkungen über der Herren Pinto und Schlözer sophistische Vertheidigung des englischen Ministeriums gegen die Colonien," Theil 1, 3; "Erläuterungen der Nordamerikanischen Angelegenheiten, aus Staatsschriften und andern authentischen Papieren," Theil 3.
"England solle sich gänzlich von seinen nordamerikanischen Colonien trennen, sie für ein freyes und unabhängiges Volk erklären, und sich erbieten, diese Freyheit und Unabhängigkeit gegen alle und jede ausländische Feinde zu garantieren."
See Alfred Stern, "Jakob Mauvillon als Dichter und Publizist," in *Preussische Jahrbücher*, Berlin, 1932, Bd. 230, p. 239–252, * DF.

667. *Review:* Kurzgefasste Geschichte des Christoph Columbus, ersten Entdeckers von Amerika. Frankfurt am Mayn: Bey den Eichenbergischen Erben. 36 S. in 8°. (Allgemeine deutsche Bibliothek. Berlin, 1780. 12°. Bd. 40, p. 193–194, *NAA.*)

668. *Review:* Kurz gefasste Nachricht von dem Etablissement derer Salzburgischen Emigranten zu Ebenezer, in der Provinz Georgien in Nordamerica, wie solche auf Verlangen von dem Hrn. Regierungsrath von Reck... mitgetheilt worden. Hamburg: Bey Ritter, 1777. 44 S. in 8°. (Allgemeine deutsche Bibliothek. Berlin, 1780. 12°. Anhang zu Bd. 25/36, p. 1467–1468, *NAA.*)
Sabin 38365.
An English edition of 1734 is in * *KC 1734*.
See no. 305.

669. *Review:* L. A. Baumanns...Abriss der Staatsverfassung der vornehmsten Länder in Amerika... Brandenburg: Bey den Gebrüdern Halle, 1776. 700 S. in 8°. (Allgemeine deutsche Bibliothek. Berlin, 1780. 12°. Anhang zu Bd. 25/36, p. 1507, *NAA.*)
Sabin 3987.

670. *Review:* A Poetical Epistle to his Excellency George Washington etc. from an Inhabitant of the State of Maryland,...Annapolis, 1779; London: Reprinted for Dilly, 1780. (Neue Bibliothek der schönen Wissenschaften und der freyen Künste. Leipzig, 1780. 12°. Bd. 25, p. 169–170, *NAA.*)
The author is Charles Henry Wharton. The book is in * *KGW*.
"...Eine Probe amerikanischer Poesie voller Wärme und Kraft... Auch ist das beygefügte Leben des Amerikanischen Feldherrn interessant und wohlgeschrieben..."

671. *Review:* Eine Rede die auf dem Staatshause zu Philadelphia vor einer grossen Versammlung Donnerstags den 1. Aug. 1776 von Samuel Adams...gehalten worden. Aus dem Englischen. n. p., 1778. (Allgemeine deutsche Bibliothek. Berlin, 1780. 12°. Bd. 42, p. 628–629, *NAA.*)
"Wir wagen es nicht, den grossen Zwist zu beurtheilen, der jetzt die halbe Welt in Erwartung hält... Das bindet uns aber nicht von der Klugheit, Thätigkeit, Beredsamkeit und Unerschrockenheit verschiedener Anführer der neuen vereinigten Provinzen die grössten Begriffe zu unterhalten... Wir wundern uns daher nicht, dass wir solche Meisterstücke der Beredsaamkeit von daher erhalten, wie die gegenwärtige Rede ist, voll wichtiger und kräftiger, kühner Gedanken, Ausdrucks und hohen Gesinnungen."

## 1781

672. AMERIKANISCHE Generale und Stabs Officiere. (In: A. L. Schlözer. Briefwechsel meist historischen und politischen Inhalts. Göttingen, 1781. 12°. Theil 8, p. 3–6.) BAC
"Einige Namen mögen nicht richtig geschrieben seyn; aber sonst ist der Aufsatz aus sichern Händen." — *Schlözer.*
See Max von Eelking, *The German allied troops in the North American War of Independence, 1776–1783*, Albany, 1893 (Munsell's historical series, no. 19, *IG*).

673. BRIEF von Herrn O. an Herrn Bl. in Str. über die Oneidas. (Deutsches Museum. Leipzig, 1781. 4°. Bd. 1, p. 508–515.) * DF
Dated: Philadelphia, 1780. About the Indian tribe mentioned.

674–76. COLUMBUS und der Abendwind. (Musen Almanach. Göttingen [1781]. 32°. Jahr 1781, p. 92–93.) NFA
Signed: Kr.
This volume of the series is called: Poetische Blumenlese auf das Jahr 1781.

677. GENERAL Washington, nach einem Gemälde von J. Trumbull aus Connecticut,...von V. Green in schwarzer Kunst. (Neue Bibliothek der schönen Wissenschaften und der freyen Künste. Leipzig, 1781. 12°. Bd. 26, p. 364.)
Description of the etching. NAA

1781, continued

677A. GOETHE, JOHANN WOLFGANG. Das Neueste von Plundersweilern. 1781. (Reprinted in his: Werke... Herausgegeben im Auftrage der Grosshrzg. Sophie von Sachsen. Weimar: Hermann Böhlau, 1887-1919. 8°. Bd. 16, p. 41-55.) NFGK
Goethe's reference to the mercenaries, written down when the troops left Germany for America (1781), although printed not before 1817, cannot be withheld.

"Und zwar mag es nicht etwa sein
Wie zwischen Cassel und Weissenstein,
Als wo man emsig und zu Hauf
Macht Vogelbauer auf den Kauf
Und sendet gegen fremdes Geld
Die Vöglein in die weite Welt."
— lines 7–12.

The point of the figure is that the sale of soldiers is depopulating Hesse, which is contrasted with the flourishing community of Plundersweiler.
See W. A. Fritsch, "Stimmen deutscher Zeitgenossen über den Soldatenhandel deutscher Fürsten nach Amerika," in *Deutsch-amerikanisches Magazin*, Cincinnati, O., 1886/87, v. 1, p. 589-593, *IEK*; and J. T. Hatfield and E. Hochbaum, *The influence of the American Revolution upon German literature*, New York [1900?], *NCF p.v.4*.

678. JUNG-STILLING, JOHANN HEINRICH. Die Geschichte Florentins v. Fahlendorn. Eine lehrreiche und anmuthige Begebenheit. Von Heinrich Stilling. Mannheim, 1781-83. 8°. (Reprinted in his: Sämmtliche Schriften... Stuttgart: J. Scheible's Buchhandlung, 1835-1838. 8°. Bd. 9, p. [5-]300.) YLE
The Library also has an American edition, with title: Die sieben Lezten Posaunen oder Wehen... Reading: C. M'Williams, 1820, * *KF*.
"Jung-Stilling leiht dem Karaiben unbedenklich das majestätische Wesen des Huronen." "Als eine Heilanstalt der Vorsehung erscheint das Westland dem frommen Jung-Stilling." — G. Descsyk, Deutsch-amerikanische historische Gesellschaft von Illinois, Jahrbuch, 1924-1925, p. 23, IEK.

679. KOCH, JOHANN GOTTLIEB FRANZ FRIEDRICH. Versuch eines Kriegs-Rechts der Negern in Afrika und Indianer in Amerika. Oder Sitten, Gebräuche, und Gewohnheiten, deren sich dieselbe bei ihren Kriegen gewöhnlich bedienen aus ächten Quellen zusammen getragen und herausgegeben von J. G. F. Koch, Jur. Cand. Tübingen: Bei Johann Georg Cotta, 1781. 86 p. 17 cm. *KF 1781
Sabin 38204.
"Eine um so minder erhebliche Compilation, als die ächten Quellen nicht angezeigt sind." Review: *Allgemeine deutsche Bibliothek*, Bd. 44, p. 92, *NAA*.

680. KURZGEFASSTE Geschichte des Ferdinand Cortez Eroberers von Mexiko und Franz Pizarro ersten Entdeckers und Eroberers von Peru. Frankfurt am Mayn: Bey den Eichenbergischen Erben, 1781. 7 p.l., 128 p. illus. 8°.
*KF 1781

681. MERCK, JOHANN HEINRICH. Herr Oheim der Jüngere, eine wahre Geschichte. (Der Teutsche Merkur. Weimar, 1781-1782. 12°. Jahr 1781, Vierteljahr 4 [Bd. 36], p. 144-166; Jahr 1782, Vierteljahr 1 [Bd. 37], p. 123-138.)
*DF (Neue)
This periodical subsequently called *Der Neue teutsche Merkur*, under which it is shelved.
"Besitzer, die, durch Missgeschick gezwungen, Haus und Hof verkauft haben, um drüben neu anzufangen, werden von Merck in der Geschichte 'Herrn Oheims des Jüngeren'... erwähnt." — G. Descsyk *in Deutsche amerikanische Gesellschaft von Illinois. Jahrbuch, 1924–1925, p. 43, IEK*.
"Haben Sie über Gewaltthätigkeiten, oder Drükungen zu klagen, fieng der Oberschultheiss an... Werden unsre Kinder nach Amerika verkauft, und mit unserm eignen Gelde montirt und armirt, damit sie recht hoch können verkauft werden?"
See Hermann Braenning, "Johann Heinrich Merck als Mitarbeiter an Wielands Teutschen Merkur in den Jahren 1773–1791," in *Archiv für das Studium der neueren Sprachen und Literaturen*, Braunschweig, 1913, Bd. 131 [Neue Serie, Bd. 31], p. 24–29, 285–304, *RAA*.

682. [NACHRICHTEN zum Nuzen und Vergnügen. Stuttgart: Mäntler, 1781.] (Americana Germanica. New York, 1902. 4°. v. 4, p. 95–129.) NFCA
Excerpts from the *Nachrichten* are incorporated in a series of essays by J. A. Walz, "Three Swabian journalists and the American Revolution," of which this is no. II, devoted to Johann Friedrich Schiller. Walz discusses Schiller's contribution to the *Vermischte Neuigkeiten und Nachrichten zum Nuzen und Vergnügen*.
Periodical subsequently called *German American annals*, under which it is shelved.
Schiller's journalistic talent to criticize the soldier traffic without being curbed by the censor may be seen from the following lines: "Am 4. März [1781] wurden aus Ansbach die nach Amerika bestimmten Truppen eingeschifft. Kurz vor dem Ausmarsch hatte die Residenz das wonnevolle Entrücken, ihren angebeteten Landesvater und Regenten im besten Wohlsein von der Reise nach der Schweiz zurückkommen zu sehen."
See W. H. Carruth, "Schiller and America," in *German American annals*, Philadelphia, 1906, v. 8, p. 131–146, *IEK*; W. W. Florer, "Schiller's conception of liberty and the spirit of '76," in *German American annals*, Philadelphia, 1906, v. 8, p. 99-115, *IEK*; Jacob Minor, "Der junge Schiller als Journalist," in *Vierteljahrschrift für Litteraturgeschichte*, 1889, Bd. 2, p. 346–394, *NFCA*.

683. NEU JORK, 11 Sept. 1780 (von einem deutschen Officier). (In: A. L. Schlözer. Briefwechsel meist historischen und politischen Inhalts. Göttingen, 1781. 12°. Theil 9, p. 383-387.) BAC
War accounts and criticism on the American population.

683A. SCHILLER, JOHANN CHRISTOPH FRIEDRICH VON. Der Venuswagen... [n. p., n. d.] 24 p. 8°. NFGW
First issued, without imprint, by J. B. Metzler in Stuttgart in 1781; see J. Minor, in *Zeitschrift für deutsche Philologie*, Halle, 1888, v. 20, p. 75, *RKA*.
"So gebot der weise Venusrichter.
Wie der weise Venusrichter hiess?
Wo er wohnte? Wünscht ihr von dem Dichter
Zu vernehmen — so vernehmet diss:
Wo noch kein Europersegel brauste,
Kein Kolumb noch steuerte, noch kein
Kortez siegte, kein Pizarro hausste,
Wohnt auf einem Eiland — Er allein." — p. 23.

684. ULLOA, ANTONIO DE. ...Physikalische und historische Nachrichten vom südlichen und nordöstlichen America. Aus dem Spanischen übersetzt von Johann Andreas Dieze, Prof. der gelehrten Geschichte zu Göttingen. Mit Zusätzen. Leipzig: Bey Weidmanns Erben und Reich, 1781. 2 v. 8°. *KF 1781

## 1781, continued

685. ...VERSUCH einer Beschreibung u. Geschichte der Antillischen Inseln. Erstes [-sechstes] Stück... (Johann Bernoulli's Sammlung kurzer Reisebeschreibungen. Berlin, 1781-1784. 12°. Bd. 1, p. 335-406; Bd. 2, p. 333-384; Bd. 5, p. 293-388; Bd. 8, p. 329-360; Bd. 15, p. 401-432.) KBC (Bernoulli)
Section-title; installments are numbered, except the last.

686. VON dem Zuckerahorn... Ob, und unter welchem Namen etwa ein canadischer Zuckerbaum in Deutschland bekant, oder in England unter den mancherlei dort verpflanzten amerikanischen Bäumen zu haben sey? (Hannoverisches Magazin...vom Jahre 1781. Hannover, 1782. 4°. Jahrgang 19, col. 433-448.) *DF
Title page dated 1782; contents, 1781.

687. VON Jamaica. Eingesandt aus NAmerika, im Decemb. 1780. (In: A. L. Schlözer. Briefwechsel meist historischen und politischen Inhalts. Göttingen, 1781. 12°. Theil 8, p. 143-145.) BAC
An "Account of Stock and Negroes" in the island of Jamaica, as entered in the Roll at the Receiver General's Office the 31st December 1778.

688. WANGENHEIM, FRIEDRICH ADAM JULIUS VON. Beschreibung einiger Nordamericanischen Holz- und Buscharten, mit Anwendung auf teutsche Forsten; zum Gebrauch für Holzgerechte Jäger und Anpflanzer fremder Holzarten, von Friedrich Adam Julius von Wangenheim, Capitain beym Hochfürstl. Hessen-Casselischen Feldjäger Corps in Nordamerica, aus den in dortigen Provinzen seit den Jahren 1777. bis 1780. gemachten Bemerkungen. Göttingen: Bey Johann Christian Dietrich, 1781. 4 p.l., 151 p., 9 l. 18 cm. *KF 1781
"During the Revolutionary War the author distinguished himself in the engagements at Brandywine and Charleston. He devoted his spare time to the study of the immense American forests. After his return to Europe (1781) he published his treatise, in which he gives detailed information about the various kinds of trees in the forests of America, mainly in the States of New York, New Jersey, and Pennsylvania. He also points out to what extent these trees and shrubs could be utilized in German forests." — P. C. Weber, America in imaginative literature, New York, 1926, NFCX.
Reviews: Allgemeine Literatur Zeitung, Bd. 4, p. 190-192, NAA; Göttingische Anzeigen von gelehrten Sachen, Jahr 1783, p. 1217 ff., *DF; Neues Forst Archiv, Bd. 1, p. 126, 165, VQN.

689. ZIMMERMANN, HEINRICH. Heinrich Zimmermanns von Wissloch in der Pfalz, Reise um die Welt mit Capitain Cook. Mannheim: Bei C. F. Schwan, kuhrfürstl. Hofbuchhändler, 1781. 110 p. 8°. *KF 1781
Account of a German sailor. See the English translation by Michaelis and French: Zimmermann's Captain Cook, Toronto, 1930, KBF.

690. Review: Beyträge zur Völker- und Länder-Kunde, herausgegeben von J. R. Forster und M. C. Sprengel. Erster Theil... Leipzig: Weygandsche Buchhandlung, 1781. (Göttingische Anzeigen von gelehrten Sachen. Göttingen [1781]. 12°. Jahr 1781, p. 1172-1174, *DF.)
This issue of the Beyträgs contains an article by M. C. Sprengel on the northern part of North America, then being discovered by the Russians.

691. Notice: Collection des Portraits des Hommes, qui se sont rendus célebres dans la révolution des treize Etat Unis de l'Amerique Septentrionale, par Prevot nach Zeichnungen, die Du Similier nach dem Leben gemacht. (Neue Bibliothek der schönen Wissenschaften und der freyen Künste. Leipzig, 1781. 12°. Bd. 26, p. 344, NAA.)
See no. 838.

692. Review: Europens Handel mit beyden Indien. Ein Auszug aus Raynal's Geschichte; von M. Chr. Lorenz Karsten. Rostock: bey Koppe, 1780. 716 S. 8°. (Allgemeine deutsche Bibliothek. Berlin, 1781. 12°. Bd. 48, p. 493-494, NAA.)
See nos. 632, 633.

693. Review: Historical Account of the Rise and Progress of the Colonies of Carolina and Georgia. London: Alexander Donaldson, 1779. 2 v. 8°. (Göttingische Anzeigen von gelehrten Sachen. Göttingen [1781]. 12°. Jahr 1781, p. 283-288, *DF.)

694. Review: Historische Litteratur für das Jahr 1781. Stck. 1-3. Erlangen: Palm, 1781. (Göttingische Anzeigen von gelehrten Sachen. Göttingen [1781]. 12°. Jahr 1781, p. 479-480, *DF.)
The reviewed magazine contains an essay on "die Verfasserin der widerspenstigen Amerikaner."
See note on 700, 734.

695. Review: The history of the Civil War in America, vol. I comprehending the Campaigns of 1775. 1776. and 1778. by an Officir of the army. The second Edition. London: Th. Paine and J. Sewel, 1780. 467 p. 8°. (Göttingische Anzeigen von gelehrten Sachen. Göttingen [1781]. 12°. Jahr 1781, p. 1222-1223, *DF.)

696. Review: Neue Nordische Beyträge zur physikalischen und geographischen Erd- und Völkerbeschreibung, Naturgeschichte und Oekonomie. St. Petersburg, 1781-1782. 8°. (Göttingische Anzeigen von gelehrten Sachen. Göttingen [1781]. 12°. Jahr 1781, p. 1035-1039, *DF.)
Contains: "Reisebericht des russischen Steuermanns Saikof über eine bis an das feste Land von Amerika im Jahre 1772/73 geschehene Schiffahrt."
In Bd. 3, No. 11, is an essay by Fischer on "Gedanken vom Ursprunge der Amerikaner."

697. Review: Philosophical Transactions of the Royal Society of London, v. LXX for the year 1780. London, 1780. (Göttingische Anzeigen von gelehrten Sachen. Göttingen [1781]. 12°. Jahr 1781. Zugabe, p. 497-503, *DF.)
"Hr. F. Fontana über das amerikanische Gift Ticunas," p. 499.

GERMAN WORKS RELATING TO AMERICA 87

1782

698. ABRISS der Begebenheiten des Jahres 1781. (Historisches Portefeuille zur Kenntnis der gegenwärtigen und vergangenen Zeit. Wien [1782]. 12°. Jahrgang 1, p. 40–93, 197–241, 304–347, 500–544, 626–650, 772–794, 917–943, 1036–1056, 1158–1191, 1326–1336, 1472–1488, 1566–1592.) BAA
Many references to America.

699. ADAIR, JAMES. Geschichte der Amerikanischen Indianer; besonders der am Missisippi, an Ost- und Westflorida, Georgien, Süd- und Nord-Karolina und Virginien angrenzenden Nationen, nebst einem Anhange, von James Adair... Aus dem Englischen übersetzt. Bresslau: Verlegts Johann Ernst Meyer, 1782. 4 p.l., 419(1) p. 21½ cm. *KF 1782
Sabin 156.
Translated by Schack Hermann Ewald. See Meusel.
Review: *Historisches Portefeuille zur Kenntnis der gegenwärtigen und vergangenen Zeit*, Bd. 1, p. 1157–1158, BAA.

700. DER AKADEMIE der Wissenschaften, Litteratur und Künste zu Lyon Anzeige einer von dem Herrn Abbé Reynal gestifteten Preisaufgabe. (Der Teutsche Merkur. Weimar [1782]. 12°. Jahr 1784, Vierteljahr 3 [Bd. 39], p. 93–96.) *DF (Neue)
This periodical subsequently called *Der Neue teutsche Merkur* under which it is shelved.
Argument on the topic "Ist die Entdeckung von Amerika dem Menschlichen Geschlechte nüzlich oder schädlich gewesen? Wenn Vortheil daher entstanden sind, welches sind die Mittel sie zu erhalten, und zu vermehren? Wenn sie böse Folgen hervorgebracht hat, welches sind die Mittel, solchen abzuhelfen?"
See also the announcement of the contest in *Historische Litteratur für das Jahr 1781* [ed. J. G. Meusel], Erlangen, 1781, Jahrg. 1, Stück 1, p. 74.

701. AUS Nord Amerika. (In: A. L. Schlözer. Stats-Anzeigen. Göttingen, 1782. 12°. Bd. 2, p. 3–15.) BAC
War account, dated May 3rd, 4th, and the middle of August.

702. BETRACHTUNGEN über die jetzige Beschaffenheit des öffentlichen Credits von Grossbritannien. (Historisches Portefeuille zur Kenntnis der gegenwärtigen und vergangenen Zeit. Wien [1782]. 12°. Jahrgang 1, p. 1391–1418.) BAA

703. DEANE, SILAS. Betrachtungen über den künftigen Handel der unabhängigen Vierzehn vereinigten Staaten von Nordamerika. (Historisches Portefeuille zur Kenntnis der gegenwärtigen und vergangenen Zeit. Wien [1782]. 12°. Jahrgang 1, p. 1193–1218.) BAA
Dated: June 14th, 1781.
Letter sent by Silas Deane from Paris to Robert Morris in Philadelphia.

703A. —— Schreiben Silas Deane aus Paris an den Obersten Duner[!] zu Philadelphia, welches in einem Amerikanischen Packetboot aufgefangen worden. (Historisches Portefeuille zur Kenntnis der gegenwärtigen und vergangenen Zeit. Wien, 1782. 12°. Jahrgang 1, p. 979–986.) BAA
Letter is dated: Paris, den 14. Juny, 1781.

703B. —— Schreiben Silas Deane aus Paris an Jeremias Wadsworth zu Hartford in Connecticut, welches in einem Amerikanischen Packetboot aufgefangen worden. (Historisches Portefeuille zur Kenntnis der gegenwärtigen und vergangenen Zeit. Wien, 1782. 12°. Jahrgang 1, p. 970–979.) BAA
Letter is dated: June 13th, 1781.
Note of the translator: "Silas Deane war in Paris von Seiten des Congresses in öffentlichen Angelegenheiten."

704. —— Ein vertrauter Brief des Silas Deane, Mitunterhändlers des Herrn Fränklin zu Paris an Sam H. Parsons Esq., General Brigadier in Diensten der vereinigten Staaten von Amerika, gefunden in einem neulich erwischten rebellischen Felleisen. (Historisches Portefeuille zur Kenntnis der gegenwärtigen und vergangenen Zeit. Wien [1782]. 12°. Jahrgang 1, p. 1092–1104.) BAA
Note of the translator: "Aus dem Political Magazine übersetzt. Die Parthey der Amerikaner in England zweifelt an der Aechtheit dieser Briefe, da die Parthey des Hofes sie fur authentisch behauptet. Dem sey wie ihm wolle: so liefern diese Briefe doch die vollständigsten und deutlichsten Nachrichten von Amerikas vorigem und jetzigem Zustande, und von dessen Aussichten, wenn Amerika seine Unabhängigkeit behauptet."
Dated: Paris, May 14th, 1781.

705. ENGELSCHALL, JOSEPH FRIEDRICH. Malchens Loblied auf den Zucker. (Musen Almanach. Göttingen: Bey Johann Christian Dieterich [1782]. 32°. Jahr 1782, p. 125–126.) NFA
Volume has title: Poetische Blumenlese auf das Jahr 1782.
"Da war im Land Amerika
Einmal der Zucker theuer:
Was thaten sie? sie sandten, ha!
Flugs Volk mit Schwert und Feuer.
O, hätte man doch kurz und gut
Nur Zucker hingesendet;
Vergossen wär kein Menschenblut,
Und aller Zwist geendet!"

706. ETWAS von den Schlangen in Nordamerika. (Hannoverisches Magazin vom Jahre 1782. Hannover, 1783. 4°. Jahrgang 20, col. 1297–1310.) *DF
Taken from *Letters from an American farmer*. See no. 782.

707. ETWAS von der Volksmenge in den vereinigten Nordamerikanischen Staaten, verglichen mit ihrer Ausfuhr. (Historisches Portefeuille zur Kenntnis der gegenwärtigen und vergangenen Zeit. Wien [1782]. 12°. Jahrgang 1, p. 1509–1513.) BAA
From *Essais historiques et politiques sur les Anglo-Americains*, by M. R. Hilliard d'Auberteuil (Library's copies are in *KF 1781). "Von diesem brauchbaren Buche wird nächstens eine Uebersetzung im Bohnschen Verlage zu Hamburg erscheinen."
See no. 763, 764.

708. FELDZUG der vereinigten Franzosen und Nordamerikaner in Virginien im Jahre 1781, nebst einer Karte des Kriegstheaters und sieben Original Beylagen. Wien: J. T. edl. v. Trattnern [1782?]. 1 p.l., 122 p., 2 l., map. 12° in eights. *KF 1782

*1782, continued*

709. FRANKLIN, BENJAMIN. Ein Brif die Rechtschreibung betreffend, aus des berümten Benjamin Franklins Political, miscellaneous and philosophical pieces (p. 473) übersezt. (Deutsches Museum. Leipzig, 1782. 8°. Bd. 2, p. 307-311.) *DF
Dated: London, 1768, Sept. 28.
Relates to phonetic spelling.
"Wär kan anders über di Ortografi denken, als Franklin und ich?" *cf.* Klopstock's letter to Johann Andreas Cramer from Hamburg, December 10, 1782, in Klopstock's *Briefe*, Braunschweig, 1867, p. 308, *NFD*.

710. FREYMÜTHIGE Betrachtungen über den Zustand von Europa in dem Jahre 1781. (Historisches Portefeuille zur Kenntnis der gegenwärtigen und vergangenen Zeit. Wien [1782]. 12°. Jahrgang 1, p. 1-40.) BAA
References to the American Revolution.

711. GEDANKEN über die jetzige Administration an die Königl. Grossbritannischen Staatsminister. (Historisches Portefeuille zur Kenntnis der gegenwärtigen und vergangenen Zeit. Wien [1782]. 12°. Jahrgang 1, p. 1258-1280.)
References to America. BAA

712. GESPRÄCHE über einige neueste Weltbegebenheiten. (Der Teutsche Merkur. Weimar [1782]. Jahr 1782, Vierteljahr 2 [Bd. 38], p. 19-46.) *DF (Neue)
Numerous references to America.
This periodical subsequently called *Der Neue teutsche Merkur*, under which it is shelved.
See nos. 479, 497, 523, 546.

713. HERRN D. Weiss Beantwortung der zwoten Preisfrage über das Anstecken der Viehseuche, welche von der Gesellschaft Naturforschender Freunde gekrönt worden ist. (Berlinische Gesellschaft naturforschender Freunde. Schriften. Berlin, 1782. 8°. Bd. 3, p. 1-19.)
3-* EE (Gesellschaft)
Refers to the "Yaws," an illness among the Negro slaves, on p. 22.
Organization subsequently called Gesellschaft naturforschender Freunde zu Berlin, under which its publications are shelved.

714. IST es gut, dass die engländischen nordamerikanischen Kolonien unabhängig werden? beantwortet von einem Europäer. (Deutsches Museum. Leipzig, 1782. 8°. [Jahr] 1782, Bd. 2, p. 440-469.) *DF
Signed: U — t in B. Upholds point of view of the American colonies.
See *Göttingisches Magazin der Wissenschaften und Literatur* [ed. G. C. Lichtenberg and G. Forster], Jahrg. 1-4, Göttingen, 1780-85 (not in the Library), especially Jahr 1783, Theil 2, p. 685-734.

715. IWAN Al...z, eines russischen Edelmanns Besuch bei dem Quaker John Bertram, einem berühmten Pensylvanischen Botanisten. (Hannoverisches Magazin...vom Jahre 1782. Hannover, 1783. 4°. Jahrgang 82, col. 1361-1384.)
*DF
From *Letters from an American farmer*, by Hector St. John de Crèvecoeur (Michel Guillaume St. John de Crèvecoeur); the Library's copies of the English original are in * *KF 1782*.
Title page dated 1783; contents, 1782.
See no. 782.

716. KLINGER, FRIEDRICH MAXIMILIAN VON. Die Falschen Spieler. Ein Lustspiel. Wien: Bey Joseph Edlen v. Kurzbeck, 1782. 102 p. 8°. (Reprinted in his: Werke. Leipzig, 1832. 8°. v. 1, p. 91-192.) NFG
References in Act 2, Scene 1.

717. KLOPSTOCK, FRIEDRICH GOTTLIEB. Der jezige Krieg. (Musen Almanach für 1782. Herausgegeben von Voss und Goeking [*sic*]. Hamburg: Bey Carl Ernst Bohn, 1782. 24°. p. 125-128.) NFA
"Du bist die Morgenröthe.
"Eines nahenden grossen Tags!" — *p. 125.*
"The ode *Der jezige Krieg* cannot be called a glorification of the American Revolution. Though it refers to the great war between England on the one hand, and France, Spain, Holland and the American colonies on the other, it treats only of the European theatre of war. Klopstock does not praise the war because one side is fighting for liberty, but because both sides seem to hesitate about shedding blood. That is to him a sign that the spirit of humanity is modifying the cruel warfare of former times. From the modern point of view, the ode may be called naïve, but Herder who had dreamed of an era of universal peace, called it 'eine Prophetenstimme der Zukunft'." — J. A. Walz, in *Modern language notes*, Baltimore, 1901, v. 16, p. 170, *RAA*.
"Of the poets of Germany, the veteran Klopstock beheld in the American war the inspiration of humanity and the dawn of an approaching great day. He loved the terrible spirit which emboldens the peoples to grow conscious of their power..." — George Bancroft, *History of the United States*, Boston, 1861-75, v. 10, p. 90, † *IAE*.
For Herder's opinion on the ode, see no. 1169.

718. MORRIS, ROBERT. Authentischer Bericht von den Finanzen der Amerikaner, und der Unterstützung in Gelde, welche sie von Frankreich, Holland und Spanien erhalten haben. (Historisches Portefeuille zur Kenntnis der gegenwärtigen und vergangenen Zeit. Wien [1782]. 12°. Jahrgang 1, p. 1430-1437.) BAA
"Der Amerikanische Generalfinanzier, Robert Morris, stellt den Zustand der Finanzen der dreyzehn vereinigten Staaten von Nordamerika in einem Circularschreiben, wovon dieses...an den Amerikanischen Gouverneur der Provinz Neuyork gerichtet ist, selbst folgendermassen vor." — *Note of the translator.*

719. PORTRAIT des Generals Washington. (Historisches Portefeuille zur Kenntnis der gegenwärtigen und vergangenen Zeit. Wien [1782]. 12°. Jahrgang 1, p. 1381-1383.) BAA
The anonymous author describes his personal impression of George Washington.

720. [SCHMOHL, JOHANN CHRISTOPH.] Ueber Nordamerika und Demokratie. Ein Brief aus England... Koppenhagen, 1782. 212 p., 1 l. 18 cm. (8°.) *KF 1782
The place of printing is not Koppenhagen but Königsberg. See E. O. Weller's *Die falschen und fingirten Druckorte*, 1864, v. 1, p. 120, * *KAB*.
"It might be called the classic of German response to the American Revolution. It reveals the only known case of a German writer thinking out the American ideas, and going to America to fight for them." — *cf.* H. S. King, "Echoes of the American Revolution in German literature," in University of California, *Publications in modern philology*, Berkeley, 1929, v. 14, p. 90-93, 95-96, *STG*. The author was drowned near the Bermuda Islands upon his arrival. See also *Allgemeine deutsche Bibliothek*, Berlin, 1782, Bd. 49, p. 237, *NAA*.

*1782, continued*

721. SCHREIBEN eines deutschen Patrioten über die Veränderung im Brittischen Ministerio, und über die Charaktere der alten und neuen Minister. (Historisches Portefeuille zur Kenntnis der gegenwårtigen und vergangenen Zeit. Wien [1782]. 12°. Jahrgang 1, p. 715–745, 1297–1318.) BAA
First letter is dated: London, May 18th, 1782; the second: Birmingham, Aug. 21st, 1782.

722. SONDERBARER französischer Wechsel, gezogen in NAmerika auf Paris 1781. (In: A. L. Schlözer. Briefwechsel meist historischen und politischen Inhalts. Göttingen, 1782. 12°. Theil 10, p. 366–367.) BAC

723. SPRENGEL, MATTHIAS CHRISTIAN. Geschichte der Europäer in Nordamerica. Von Matthias Christian Sprengel... Bd. 1. Leipzig: In der Weygandschen Buchhandlung, 1782. 7 p.l., (1)4–243(1) p. 8°.  *KF 1782
Sabin 89757.
No more published.
Review: *Historisches Portefeuille*, Jahrg. 2, p. 399–402, *BAA*.

724. UNTERSUCHUNG der Frage: ob die Unabhängigkeit von Nord Amerika, und ein Bündniss mit demselben vorteilhaft für die Republik Holland sei? Im Juni 1781. (In: A. L. Schlözer. Briefwechsel meist historischen und politischen Inhalts. Göttingen, 1782. 12°. Theil 10, p. 130–154.) BAC
Uebersetzung von: Consideration op de Memorie aan H. H. M. M. geadresseerd door John Adams, en geteekend Leiden, den 19 April 1781. "Beigehende Abhandlung schien mir über diese Materie so gründlich geschrieben zu seyn, dass ich sie einer deutschen Uebersetzung und mereren Bekanntwerdung wert hielt. Sie ist von dem geschickten Advocaten Luzac in Leiden." — *Editor*.

725. VERZEICHNISS der Englischen Linienschiffe im September 1782. nebst ihren bekannten Befehlshabern... (Historisches Portefeuille zur Kenntnis der gegenwårtigen und vergangenen Zeit. Wien [1782]. 12°. Jahrgang 1, p. 1438–1446.) BAA
Note of the editor: P. N. zeigt diejenigen Schiffe an, welche mit Admiral Piyot von Jamaika, Ende Julius, nach Neuyork segelten.

726. VOLKSMENGE in den vereinigten Niederlanden; in Frankreich; in Spanien; in den vereinigten Staaten von Nordamerika; und in Grosbritannien. (Historisches Portefeuille zur Kenntnis der gegenwårtigen und vergangenen Zeit. Wien [1782]. 12°. Jahrgang 1, p. 374.) BAA
"Ein augenscheinlicher Beweis von der Richtigkeit der Bemerkung jenes grossen Staatsmanns [i.e. Franklin]: dass die Macht der Staaten nicht in der Menge ihrer Quadratmeilen und in der Anzahl der Köpfe bestehe." — *Footnote*.

727. ZINNER, JOHANN, EDITOR. Merkwürdige Briefe und Schriften der berühmtesten Generäle in Amerika, nebst derselben beygefügten Lebensbeschreibungen. Herausgegeben von Johann Zinner, Professor der Philosophie und Statistik auf der Kaiserl. Akademie in Kaschau. Augsburg: Bey Eberhard Kletts sel.

Wittwe und Franck, 1782. 8 p.l., 352 p. 16° in eights. *KF 1782
Sabin 106349.
"... aus öffentlichen Schriften und aus dem Briefwechsel der beyderseitigen Generäle und Personen von Wichtigkeit, die von Seiten Englands, oder von Seiten des Congresses, gebraucht worden sind..."
Also published under title: Beiträge zur Geschichte des amerikanischen Krieges. 1. Theil, 1775–1780. Philadelphia und Leipzig, 1788.
See Max von Eelking, *The German allied troops in the North American war of independence, 1776–1783*, Albany, 1893 (Munsell's historical series, no. 19, IG).

728. *Review:* Anführung des Capitains Cook, Clerke, Gore und King mit einer neuen verbesserten Karte und Kupfer nach der originellen Handschrift getreulich beschrieben. Eine Uebersetzung nebst Anmerkungen von Johann Reinhold Forster, Berlin, 1781. S. 357. (Historisches Portefeuille zur Kenntnis der gegenwärtigen und vergangenen Zeit. Wien [1782]. 12°. Jahrgang 1, p. 134, *BAA*.)

729. *Review:* Beyträge zur Länder- und Völkerkunde von J. R. Forster und M. C. Sprengel. Zweyter Band. Leipzig: Weygand, 1782. 302 S. 8°. (Göttingische Anzeigen von gelehrten Sachen. Göttingen [1782]. 12°. Jahr 1782, p. 899–902, * *DF*.)
There is an article on Connecticut by M. C. Sprengel, as well as several other articles pertaining to America, in this issue of the *Beyträge*.
"Spanier besegeln ungeachtet des Tractats von Tordesillas schon 1542 die Philippinen von America aus," p. 900.

730. *Review:* Briefe an einen vornehmen Herrn und Pair von Grossbritannien, über den in den mittlern Colonien in Amerika geführten Krieg... Aus dem Englischen des Herrn Joseph Galloway. Hamburg: Bey Bohn, 1780. 7½ Bogen. 8°. (Allgemeine deutsche Bibliothek. Berlin, 1782. 8°. Bd. 52, p. 277–278, *NAA*.)
The Library's copies of the English original, *Letters to a nobleman*... — first edition, 1779, and subsequent editions — are in *KF.

731. *Review:* A concise account of voyages for the discovery of a north-west passage undertaken for finding a new way to the East-Indies, etc. by a Sea-Officer. London, 1782. xxviii, 69 p. 8°. (Göttingische Anzeigen von gelehrten Sachen. Göttingen [1782]. 12°. Jahr 1782, p. 1110, **DF*.)
The reviewer supposes that Lieutenant Richard Pickersgill is the author; The British Museum "Catalogue" (old series), "Halkett and Laing," and others confirm this.

732. *Review:* Elogj Storici di Cristoforo Colombo e di Andrea d'Oria. Parma: In der königl. Druckerey, 1782. 337 S. 4°. (Göttingische Anzeigen von gelehrten Sachen. Göttingen [1782]. 12°. Jahr 1782, p. 1188–1189, **DF*.)

733. *Review:* General History of Connecticut from its first Settlement under George Fenwick to its latest Period of Amity with Great Britain. By a Gentleman of the Province. London: J. Bew, 1781. 424 S. 8°. (Göttingische Anzeigen von gelehrten Sachen. Göttingen [1782]. 12°. Jahr 1782, p. 417–422, **DF*.)

*1782, continued*

733A. *Review:* Geschichte der neuesten Weltbegebenheiten im Grossen. Zweyter Band, welcher die Geschichte des J. 1782 einschliesst. Leipzig: Weygand, 1787. 566 S. 8°. (Allgemeine Literatur-Zeitung. Jena, 1787. 4°. Jahr 1787, Bd. 3, col. 190, *NAA*.)
Surveys the events of 1781 and 1782 in the thirteen states and the West Indies.

734. *Review:* Historische Litteratur für das Jahr 1781, Stck. 4–12 und für das Jahr 1782, Stck. 1–3. Erlangen: Palm, 1781–1782. (Göttingische Anzeigen von gelehrten Sachen. Göttingen [1782]. 12°. Jahr 1782, p. 648, *DF*.)
According to the reviewer, the magazine contains "viele Briefe von den in Nordamerica fechtenden deutschen Kriegsbedienten."

735. *Review:* Litteratur und Völkerkunde... (Der Teutsche Merkur. Weimar, 1782. 12°. Jahr 1782, Vierteljahr 4 [Bd. 40], p. 285–287, *DF, Neue.*)
Stück 1, 5. Beschreibung des berühmten Wasserfalls von Niagara in Nordamerika.
Stück 1, 6. Fragment einer Parlamentsrede des Grafen von Chatam [*sic!*], beym Anfange des jetzigen amerikanischen Krieges.
Stück 1, 7. Bemerkungen über die Religion, Gebräuche, Diät und Medicin der Negern.
Stück III, 7. Bemerkungen über die Akensas ein Nordamerikanisches Volk.
This periodical subsequently called *Der Neue teutsche Merkur,* under which it is shelved.

735A. *Review:* Neue Nordische Beyträge von Pallas. II. Band. St. Petersburg, 1781. (Göttingische Anzeigen von gelehrten Sachen. Göttingen [1782]. 12°. Jahr 1782, Stück 21, p. 165–167, *DF.*)
"...enthält u.a. Bericht von einer im Jahre 1772 angetretenen vierjährigen Seereise zu den zwischen Kamtschatka u. Amerika liegenden Inseln."

735B. *Review* — III. Band. St. Petersburg, 1782. (Göttingische Anzeigen von gelehrten Sachen. Göttingen [1782]. 12°. Jahr 1782, Stück 128, p. 1035–1039, *DF.*)
"...enthält 15 merkwürdige Aufsätze naturwissenschaftlicher Art, auch ein Tagebuch einer im Jahre 1775 zur Untersuchung der nördlich von Californien fortgesetzten Küsten geschehenen Reise durch den Steuermann der spanischen Flotte, Don Francisco Antonio Maurelle."

735C. *Review:* Neueste Reisen durch England, vorzüglich in Absicht auf die Kunstsammlungen, Naturgeschichte, Oeconomie, Manufakturen und Landsitze der Grossen, aus den besten neuern Schriften zusammengetragen von D. J. J. Volckmann. Leipzig: Bey Fritsch, 1781. 449 p. 8°. (Allgemeine deutsche Bibliothek. Berlin, 1782. 12°. Bd. 49, p. 172–177, *NNA*.)
"Aber Hrn. Verfassers Empfehlungen ist überhaupt nicht zu trauen, denn wer...Russels Werk über America, (das ein lichtscheuer Tagelöhner in einer Buchmanufactur zusammengestoppelt hat, denn ein wirklicher Schriftsteller dieses Namens existirt eben so wenig, als Harvey, oder Marschall) einem Robertson vorziehen kann, der muss doch ganz erst lernen, von nützlichen und unterrichtenden Büchern zu urtheilen," *p. 174.* As to Russel and Robertson, see nos. 649, 559 respectively. J. J. Volkmann translated Johann Barrow's *Sammlungen von Reisen und Entdeckungen in chronologischer Ordnung,* Leipzig, 1767.

736. *Review:* Portrait du Général Wasinghton [*sic!*] nach einem Gemälde von Trumbull, von Leroy gestochen. (Neue Bibliothek der schönen Wissenschaften und der freyen Künste. Leipzig, 1782. 8°. Bd. 27, p. 363–364, *NAA*.)
"Diess Blatt machet einen Theil der Kupferblätter zu den Essais historiques et politiques sur les Anglo-Americains par M. d'Auberteuil."

737. *Review:* Revolution de l'Amerique. Par M. L'Abbé Raynal a Londres. M.DCCLXXXI, 183 S. 8°. (Historisches Portefeuille zur Kenntnis der gegenwärtigen und vergangenen Zeit. Wien [1782]. 12°. Jahrgang 1, p. 130–131, *BAA.*)

738. *Review:* Traité sur le vénin de la vipere, sur les poisons americains, sur le Laurier-Cerise, et sur quelques autres poisons vegetaux ...par Fel. Fontana... Florence, 1781. 2 v. 4°. (Göttingische Anzeigen von gelehrten Sachen. Göttingen [1782]. 12°. Jahr 1782, Zugabe, p. 417–431, *DF.*)
"Giftbaum" (Rhus Toxicodendr.), p. 425.
See no. 607.

739. *Review:* Ueber den jetzigen Nordamerikanischen Krieg und dessen Folgen für England und Frankreich. Von Matthias Christian Sprengel... Leipzig: bei Weigand, 1782. 8 Bogen. 8°. (Historisches Portefeuille zur Kenntnis der gegenwärtigen und vergangenen Zeit. Wien [1782]. 12°. Jahrgang 1, p. 1565–1566, *BAA.*)
Sabin 89761.

740. *Review:* Von der Wirkung des Mohnsaftes in der Lustseuche, nebst andern zur Arzneygelahrtheit und Naturlehre gehörigen Beobachtungen, Nordamerika betreffend, von D. J. J. Schöpf. Erlangen, 1781. 48 S. 8°. (Allgemeine deutsche Bibliothek. Berlin, 1782. 8°. Bd. 50, p. 417–418, *NAA.*)
This work deals with syphilis and mumps.

1783

741. ABRISS der Begebenheiten. (Historisches Portefeuille zur Kenntnis der gegenwärtigen und vergangenen Zeit. Wien, 1783. 12°. Jahrg. 2, Bd. 1, p. 112–125, 271–287, 409–420, 548–559, 734–747, 848–860; Bd. 2, p. 121–137, 248–264, 350–376, 485–511, 641–668, 764–786.) BAA
Many references to America.

742. ANMERKUNGEN über die neuerlich versuchte Fahrt durch Norden nach Ostindien. (Historisches Portefeuille zur Kenntnis der gegenwärtigen und vergangenen Zeit. Wien, 1783. 12°. Jahrg. 2, Bd. 1, p. 321–339; Bd. 2, p. [517–518.]) BAA
"Erklärung der Zeichen und einiger Ausdrücke, welche auf der Charte, von der Durchfahrt und den neuen Entdeckungen zwischen Asia und Nordamerika vorkommen," p. 517–518.
Map, following, is paged in; wrongly called "S. 321." Inscription: Dies Stück ist aus Hrn. Forsters Karte.

**1783,** *continued*

**742A.** Auszüge aus Briefen. (Deutsches Museum. Leipzig, 1784. 8°. [Jahr] 1784, Bd. 1, p. 75–94, 479–480, 567–570.) *DF
"Ganz Hessen ist jezt mit Gesprächen über die Truppen beschäftigt, welche nun nächstens aus Amerika zurückerwartet werden, und zum Theil schon da sind. Sie sollen bis auf den gemeinen Mann grosse Summen Geldes mitbringen..." p. 88. Survey on French subsidies sent to America, p. 479, 480. See also H. S. King in University of California, *Publications in modern philology*, Berkeley, 1929, v. 14, p. 139–140, *STG*.

**743.** Beschreibung eines bisher unbekannt gewesenen amerikanischen Frosches, welcher sich in der Naturaliensammlung des Herrn Hofraths Beireis in Helmstädt befindet. (Berlinische Gesellschaft naturforschender Freunde. Schriften. Berlin, 1783. 8°. Bd. 4, p. 178–182.)
3–* EE (Gesellschaft)
Organization subsequently called Gesellschaft naturforschender Freunde zu Berlin, under which its publications are shelved.

**743A.** Claudius, Matthias. Erdäpfellied. (Deutsches Museum. Leipzig, 1784. 8°. [Jahr] 1784, Bd. 1, p. [571].) *DF
Music by K. in K.
"Schön rötlich die Kartoffeln sind,
Und weiss, wie Alabaster,
Sie daun sich lieblich und geschwind,
Und sind für Mann und Frau und Kind
Ein rechtes Magenpflaster."

**744.** Die Freiheit Amerika's: eine Ode. Auszugs Weise, aus der Berlinischen Monats-Schrift April 1783, S. 386. (In: A. L. Schlözer. Stats-Anzeigen. Göttingen, 1783. 12°. Bd. 4, p. 140–144.) BAC
The ode is signed J. F. H-l. According to H. S. King, this stands for Johann Friedrich Häberlin, brother of Karl Friedrich Häberlin, a professor at Helmstaedt. See H. S. King in University of California, *Publications in modern philology*, Berkeley, 1929, v. 14, p. 155, 179, *STG*.
Reprinted in "Berliner Gedichte, 1763–1806" [collected by Ludwig Geiger], in *Berliner Neudrucks*, Serie 2, Bd. 3 (not in the Library).
See also Karl Biedermann, "Die nordamerikanische und die französische Revolution in ihren Rückwirkungen auf Deutschland," in *Zeitschrift für deutsche Kulturgeschichte*, Nürnberg, 1858, Jahrg. 3, p. 483–495, 654–668, *BAA*.
The *Berlinische Monatschrift* [ed. F. Gedike und J. E. Biester], Bd. 1–28, Berlin, 1783–96 (not in the Library) contains a number of articles relating to America, e.g., in Jahr 1794, v. 23, p. 408–437 (Jefferson) and Jahr 1795, v. 25, p. 222–261, 281–307. Of less importance, the *Berlinisches Journal für Aufklärung* [ed. G. N. Fischer, A. Riem], Bd. 1–8, Berlin, 1788–90 (not in the Library), has an article on the freedom of religion in the United States in v. 2, and an essay on general conditions in this country in v. 3 and 4. Moreover, *Wissenschaftliches Magazin für Aufklärung* [ed. E. L. Posselt], Bd. 1–3, Kehl, 1785–88 (not in the Library), contains "Ueber den Frieden und das freye Amerika," v. 2, and F. X. Jellenz, "Fragment einer Rede eines amerikanischen Richters bey der Aufnahme zweyer Hessen zu Bürgern," v. 3.
See no. 798.

**745.** Gespräch derer europäischen Mächte und der freien Staaten von Amerika über den jetzigen Friedensschluss. 3. Sept. 1783. (In: F. W. Freiherr von Ditfurth. Historische Volkslieder der Zeit von 1756 bis 1871... Aus fliegenden Blättern, handschriftlichen Quellen und dem Volksmunde... Berlin, 1871–1872. 8°. Bd. 1 [Theil 2], p. 32–36.) NFL
Called Theil 2 on main title page; has separate title: Die Historischen Volkslieder vom Ende des siebenjährigen Kriegs, 1763, bis zum Brande von Moskau, 1812... Berlin: Lipperheide, 1872.
1. England. Was hab ich denn jetzt gewonnen
In dem letzten Kriege da?
All mein Glücke ist verronnen,
Fort ist halb Amerika.
Billiger hätt ich's können haben,
Wann ich nicht auf Krieg gedacht,
Mehr den edlen Friedensgaben,
Als dem Streite nachgetracht.
15. Oesterreich. Zwar das Republikanerwesen
Passet nicht in unsern Kram,
Ist niemalen gut gewesen,
Doch wird's schon von selbsten zahm;
Es kann nicht sehr lange währen,
Republiken dauern nie —
Also giebt's uns kein Beschweren —
Letztlich kommt doch Monarchie.

**746.** Goethe, Johann Wolfgang. Liebes Lied eines Amerikanischen Wilden. Das Journal von Tiefurt. 1783. (Goethe-Gesellschaft. Schriften. Weimar, 1892. 8°. Bd. 7, p. 303.) NFGG
Goethe found the material for this poem in Montaigne's *Essais*, chapter 30. As he adds "brasilianisch" to the title, it concerns South America.
For additional history of this poem see Herder's *Sämmtliche Werke*, Berlin, 1885, v. 25, p. 685, *NFG*.
See no. 747.

**747.** —— Todeslied eines Gefangenen. Das Journal von Tiefurt. 1783. (Goethe-Gesellschaft. Schriften. Weimar, 1892. 8°. Bd. 7, p. 296–297.) NFGG
Goethe found the material for this poem in Montaigne's *Essais*, chapter 30. As he adds "brasilianisch" to the title, it concerns South America.
See no. 746.

**748.** Handelsnachrichten. (Historisches Portefeuille zur Kenntnis der gegenwärtigen und vergangenen Zeit. Wien, 1783. 12°. Jahrg. 2, Bd. 1, p. 420–424; Bd. 2, p. 669–671.) BAA
Refers to the ships of the State of Maryland and the trade from Bordeaux to North America.

**749.** Kunz und Hinz 1776. (Musen Almanach für 1783. Herausgegeben von Voss und Goeking [sic!]. Hamburg: Bey Carl Ernst Bohn [1783]. 24°. p. 217.) NFA
Signed: X.
K: Hinz, möchtet ihr im Monde leben?
Es sollen dort auch Leute sein.
H: Denn doch wenn sie dort Streit erheben,
Schickt uns der Prinz für Geld hinein.
K: Jo Mond? Was schert der Krieg uns da?
H: Denkt doch nur an Amerika!
The author is Heinrich Christian Boie. See the same author's poem, "In des Königs Namen," which treats of the life of a mercenary, but does not refer to America, in *Musen Almanach für 1784*, p. 43.
See no. 775.

**750.** Liebe und Tugend. (Magazin für Frauenzimmer. Strasburg, 1783. 12°. Jahrg. 2, Bd. 3, p. 279–282.) *DF
Anecdote of the Revolutionary War.

**751.** Miscellaneen. (Historisches Portefeuille zur Kenntnis der gegenwärtigen und vergangenen Zeit. Wien, 1783. 12°. Jahrg. 2, Bd. 2, p. 229–235.) BAA
Includes "Volksverlust der Engländer durch den Nordamerikanischen Krieg vom 1776 bis 1780," p. 231–234; Berechnung der Summen, welche England zur Vertheidigung von Canada und zur Führung des Krieges mit den Colonien vom 1. Jun. 1776. bis zum 24. Oct. 1782. verwandt hat," p. 234–235.

1783, *continued*

752. NOTHZUCHT und Brudermord. (Magazin für Frauenzimmer. Strasburg, 1783. 12°. Jahrg. 2, Bd. 3, p. 284–285.) *DF
Anecdote of the Revolutionary War. The scene is Charleston.

753. PRÄLIMINAIR-FRIEDENSARTIKEL zwischen Sr. Grossbrittannischen Majestät und den Generalstaaten. (Historisches Portefeuille zur Kenntnis der gegenwärtigen und vergangenen Zeit. Wien, 1783. 12°. Jahrg. 2, Bd. 2, p. 619–629.) BAA
References to America.

754. SCHILLER, JOHANN FRIEDRICH. An Henriette von Wolzogen. Hannover den 8. Jenn. 1783. (In his: Briefe. Herausgegeben und mit Anmerkungen versehen von Fritz Jonas. Stuttgart [1892–1896]. 8°. Bd. 1, p. 89–91.)
NFGT (Jonas)
"Ich habe eine Hauptveränderung in meinem Plane gemacht, und da ich anfangs nach Berlin wollte, wend ich mich jezt vielleicht gar nach England. Doch gewis ist es noch nicht, so grosse Lust ich habe, die Neue Welt zu sehen. Wenn Nordamerika frei wird, so ist es ausgemacht, dass ich hingehe." — *p. 90–91.*
Schiller's use of America in his letters should not be construed as an indication of interest in the struggle; it was merely a feint. *cf.* H. S. King, "Echoes of the American Revolution in German literature," in University of California, *Publications in modern philology*, Berkeley, 1929, v. 14, p. 82, STG.

754A. —— An einen Stuttgarter Freund (Lempp?). Frankfurt am Main d. 19. Juni <Donnerstag> 1783. (In his: Briefe. Herausgegeben und mit Anmerkungen versehen von Fritz Jonas. Stuttgart [1892–1896]. 8°. Bd. 1, p. 135–136.) NFGT (Jonas)
"Überall finde ich zwar immer manche trefliche Leute, und vielleicht könnte ich noch wohl mich an einem Orte niederlassen, aber ich mus fort, ich will nach America und dies soll mein Abschiedsbrief seyn." — p. 136.
See also his letter to Reinwald, July 22, 1783, from Bauerbach.
The following fragmentary verses by Schiller are of uncertain date:
"Nach dem fernen Westen wollt'ich steuern,
Auf der Strasse, die Columbus fand.
Und mit seinen Kähnen * * *
Die Columb mit seinem Wanderschiffe
An die alte Erde * * * band.
Dort vielleicht ist Freiheit.
Ach, dort ist sie nicht.
Flieh! * * *
Liegt sie jenseits dem Atlantenmeere,
Die Columb, mit wandernder Galeere * * *."
See also H. Carruth, "Schiller and America," in *German American annals*, Philadelphia, 1906, new series, v. 4, p. 131–146, NFCA, and W. W. Florer, "Schiller's conception of liberty and the Spirit of '76," in the same, p. 99–115.

755. SCHNEIDER, JOHANN GOTTLIEB. Allgemeine Naturgeschichte der Schildkröten, nebst einem systematischen Verzeichnisse der einzelnen Arten und zwey Kupfern. Von Johann Gottlob Schneider... Leipzig: In der Johan Gotfried Müllerschen Buchhandlung, 1783. xlviii, 364 p., 1 l., 3 plates. 8°. QLV

756. SCHREIBEN eines deutschen Juden an den Präsidenten des Kongresses der vereinigten Staaten von Amerika. (Deutsches Museum.

Leipzig, 1783. 8°. [Jahr] 1783, Bd. 1, p. 558–566.) *DF
With an introduction by L. F. G. Gökingk. The letter asks for virgin land in America on which to settle Jews.

757. SCHREIBEN eines deutschen Patrioten über die politischen Neuigkeiten und die Regierungsverfassung von Grossbritannien. (Historisches Portefeuille zur Kenntnis der gegenwärtigen und vergangenen Zeit. Wien, 1783. 12°. Jahrg. 2, Bd. 1, p. 501–516, 642–661.) BAA
Dated: London, Febr. 27th, 1783.
Signed: Teutelieb (pseud.).
Refers to Great Britain's profit from the Floridas on p. 508.

757A. STOLBERG, FRIEDRICH LEOPOLD. Der Prüfstein. (Deutsches Museum. Leipzig, 1783. 8°. [Jahr] 1783, Bd. 2, p. 385–388.) *DF
"Wer spricht von Chatam [*sic!*] der im Leben gross
Und grösser noch in seinem Tode war?
Wer vom bescheidnen Helden Washington?
* * *
Führ ungerechten Krieg, und werde reich
Durch Kirchenraub; dein Pöhel staunt dich an!
Nicht lange! die gerechte Nachwelt nimmt
Den Prüfstein in die Hand......"
See H. S. King, "Echoes of the American Revolution in German literature," in University of California, *Publications in modern philology*, Berkeley, 1929, v. 14, p. 32–37, STG.

758. VERZEICHNIS der, von der königlich Grossbrittanischen Flotte, während des jetzigen Krieges, den Feinden abgenommenen Schiffe. (Historisches Portefeuille zur Kenntnis der gegenwärtigen und vergangenen Zeit. Wien, 1783. 12°. Jahrg. 2, Bd. 2, p. 252–256.) BAA
"Diese Liste wurde im November 1782 angefertiget, sollten nach der Zeit einige von den letzten Kriegsschiffen zum Vorschein gekommen seyn, oder sich noch finden; so werden wir es unsern Lesern anzeigen."

759. VON der Art, wie sich verschiedene Völker um Liebe bewerben. (Magazin für Frauenzimmer. Strasburg, 1783. 12°. Jahrg. 2, Bd. 1, p. 37–45.) *DF
Refers to customs in Massachusetts. Taken from William Alexander's *Geschichte des weiblichen Geschlechts...*, Leipzig, 1780–1781, v. 2, p. 181 et seq. (German translation of Alexander's *History of women* not in the Library.)

760. WASHINGTON, GEORGE. Circularschreiben des Generals George Washington, Oberbefehlshabers der Armeen der vereinigten Nordamerikanischen Staaten. (Historisches Portefeuille zur Kenntnis der gegenwärtigen und vergangenen Zeit. Wien, 1783. 12°. Jahrg. 2, Bd. 2, p. 385–404.) BAA
Signed: Washington.
Dated: Im Hauptquartiere zu Newburgh, den 18. Jun. 1783.
"Dieses Schreiben ist in manchem Betracht wichtig und zur Beurteilung der inneren Verfassung des neuen Freistaats sehr brauchbar."

761. *Review:* Almanach Americain ou etat physique, politique, ecclesiastique et militaire de l'Amerique par M. D. L. R. C. A. L. T. de M. Paris: Chez Lamy, 1783. 12°. (Göttingische Anzeigen von gelehrten Sachen. Göttingen [1783]. 12°. Jahr 1783, p. 1182–1183, *DF.)
The Library's copy of this four-volume series by J. C. Poncelin de La Roche-Tilhac, 1783–86, is in *KSD.
See nos. 829A, 908.

## GERMAN WORKS RELATING TO AMERICA 93

*1783, continued*

762. *Review:* Die Entdekkung von Amerika, ein angenehmes und nüzliches Lesebuch für Kinder und junge Leute von J. G.[!] Campe. Zweyter Theil. Hamburg: Bey Carl Ernst Bohn, 1782. (Allgemeine deutsche Bibliothek. Berlin, 1783. 12°. Bd. 53, p. 506, *NAA.*)

Sabin 10293.
This original German edition appeared in 1780–81. The Library has various early German editions, other than the first; see the Public Catalogue.
For the first American edition, see F. H. Wilkens, in *German American annals*, Philadelphia, 1899, v. 3, p. 199–200, *NFCA.*
See nos. 850, 1079, 1304, 1309.

762A. *Review:* Dr. Christoph Gottwaldts physikalisch-anatomische Bemerkungen über den Biber. Aus dem Lateinischen übersetzt, mit 7 Kupfertafeln. Nürnberg: Bey G. N. Raspe, 1782. Der Text 4 Bogen in gross 4. (Allgemeine deutsche Bibliothek. Berlin, 1783. 12°. Bd. 53, p. 430–432, *NAA.*)

Anatomy of a Canadian beaver mentioned on p. 430.
Verified by Kayser, v. 2, p. 411A.

763. *Review:* Essays [*sic!*] historiques et politiques sur les Anglo Americains par Hilliard d'Auberteuil. Brüssels, 1781–1783. 198 p. (Gôttingische Anzeigen von gelehrten Sachen. Gôttingen [1783]. 12°. Jahr 1783, p. 362–366, * *DF.*)

The Library's copies of this French work by M. R. Hilliard d'Auberteuil are in * *KF 1781.*
Title of the German version: Historischer und politischer Versuch über die Anglo-Amerikaner und die Staatsveränderung in Nordamerika. In zwölf Büchern. Aus dem Französischen des Herrn Hilliard d'Auberteuil übersetzt [von A. Wittenberg], Hamburg und Kiel, 1783. Sabin 31902. Not in the Library.
See nos. 707, 764.

764. *Review:* Essays [*sic!*] historiques et politiques sur les Anglo-Americains par Mr. Hilliard d'Auberteuil. T. I. II. A Bruxelles, 1781. 8°. (Historisches Portefeuille zur Kenntnis der gegenwärtigen und vergangenen Zeit. Wien, 1783. 12°. Jahrg. 2, Bd. 1, p. 541–544, *BAA.*)

The review compares the first part of the book with a description of North America, published under the title, *Historisch-litterarische Notiz der englischen Colonien*, Frankfurt und Leipzig, 1776. The latter title is listed neither by Kayser nor in the British Museum catalogue. It may be assumed that the reviewer means *Historisch statistische Notiz;* see nos. 565, 595.
See nos. 707, 763.

765. *Review:* Reisen, Entdeckungen u. Unternehmungen des Schifscapitains Johann Smiths grösstentheils aus dessen eigenen Schriften beschrieben von Carl Friedrich Scheibler. Berlin: Hesse, 1782. 232 S. 8°. (Gôttingische Anzeigen von gelehrten Sachen. Gôttingen [1783]. 12°. Jahr 1783, p. 1286–1288, * *DF.*)

For earlier and later editions, see Sabin 77538.
F. C. Scheibler is also the author of *Geschichte derer von den Evangelischen in Frankreich unternommenen Seereisen und Colonieanstalten in Südamerika*, Dessau und Leipzig, 1783. Sabin 77537. Not in the Library.
See also his drama *Pocahuntas.* "Hier ist eine richtige Nordamerikanerin Heldin." — G. *Descxyk, in Deutschamerikanische historische Gesellschaft von Illinois, Jahrbuch, 1924–1925, IEK.*

766. *Review:* Ueber den jetzigen Nordamerikanischen Krieg und dessen Folgen für England und Frankreich, von Matthias Christ. Sprengel. Leipzig: Bey Weygand [1782]. 126 S. 12°. (Allgemeine deutsche Bibliothek. Berlin, 1783. 8°. Bd. 53, p. 273–275, *NAA.*)

767. *Review:* Ueber den Nordamerikanischen Krieg und dessen Folgen für England und Frankreich von M. C. Sprengel. Leipzig: Weigand, 1781. 126 S. 8°. (Gôttingische Anzeigen von gelehrten Sachen. Gôttingen [1783]. 12°. Jahr 1783, p. 1251–1254, * *DF.*)

"Der Schmutztitel: Etwas über die Kosten des jetzigen Nordamerikanischen Krieges und die Vermehrung der englischen und französischen Nationalschulden, bezeichnet den Inhalt dieser Schrift genauer..."

768. *Review:* Ueber die Grösse, Volksmenge, Clima und Fruchtbarkeit des nordamerikanischen Freistaats; von A. F. W. Crome. Dessau und Leipzig: in der Buchhandlung der Gelehrten, 1783. 4½ Bogen. 8°. (Historisches Portefeuille zur Kenntnis der gegenwärtigen und vergangenen Zeit. Wien, 1783. 12°. Jahrg. 2, Bd. 2, p. 236–238, *BAA.*)

Sabin 17599.

769. *Review:* Voyage dans l'Amérique septentrionale en l'année 1781. et Campagne de l'armée de M. le Comte de Rochambeau, par Mr. l'Abbé Robin. A Philadelphie [Paris], 1782. 222 S. 8°. (Gôttingische Anzeigen von gelehrten Sachen. Gôttingen [1783]. 12°. Jahr 1783, p. 689–691, * *DF.*)

The Library's copy of this work is in * *KF 1782.*
Sabin (72037) mentions a German version, *Neue Reise durch Nordamerika in dem Jahre 1781, nebst dem Feldzuge der Armee des Hrn. Grafen Rochambeau. Aus dem Französischen übersetzt,* Nürnberg, 1783. Not in the Library.

770. *Review:* Le Voyageur Americain ou Observations sur l'Etat actuel, la Culture, le Commerce des Colonies Britanniques en Amerique, traduit de l'Anglois et augmenté d'un Précis sur l'Amerique Septentrionale, et la Republique des treize Etats unis. Amsterdam: chez Schuring, 1782. 362 S. 8°. (Historisches Portefeuille zur Kenntnis der gegenwärtigen und vergangenen Zeit. Wien, 1783. 12°. Jahrg. 2, Bd. 1, p. 539–541, *BAA.*)

The Library's copies of this French work are in * *KF 1782.*

1784

771. ABRISS der Begebenheiten. (Historisches Portefeuille zur Kenntnis der gegenwärtigen und vergangenen Zeit. Wien, 1784. 12°. Jahrg. 3, Bd. 1, p. 114–148, 283–294, 432–443, 570–580, 777–797; Bd. 2, p. 113–129, 237–254, 345–367, 477–498, 626–644, 756–778.) BAA

Many references to America.

772. "ADVERTISSEMENT." Formular eines holländischen Seelen Verkäufers-Lock Zettels nach NAmerika. (In: A. L. Schlözer. Stats-Anzeigen. Gôttingen, 1784. 12°. Bd. 6, p. 217–219.)

Dated: Amsterdam, July 1783. BAC
Soliciting emigration.

*1784, continued*

773. ALLERHAND Briefe und Anzeigen... (In: A. L. Schlözer. Stats-Anzeigen. Göttingen, 1784. 12°. Bd 5, p. 59–60.) BAC
v. Von dem NAmerikan. General von Steuben.

774. ALLERHAND Briefe und Anzeigen. (In: A. L. Schlözer. Stats-Anzeigen. Göttingen, 1784. 12°. Bd. 6, p. 131–132.) BAC
1. London, 2. Mai 1784, von dem gewesenen Attorney-General zu New York, John Tabor Kempe, Esq., an Hrn Leib Medicus D. Michaelis.
Relates to a rumored war between New York and Vermont. Corrected by A. L. Schlözer's *Stats-Anzeigen*, Bd. 16, p. 126.

775. AMERIKA. (Musen Almanach für 1784. Herausgegeben von Voss und Göcking. Hamburg: Bey Carl Ernst Bohn [1784]. 24°. p. 59.)
Signed: X. NFA
"Sei froh! bist frei! bist frei
"Von deiner Mutter Tirannei!
"Nun wird das Recht dir niemand disputieren,
"Dich selber zu tirannisiren."
This poem is by Heinrich Christian Boie. See H. S. King, "Echoes of the American Revolution, in German literature," in University of California, *Publications in modern philology*, Berkeley, 1929, v. 14, p. 42, STG.

776. ANEKDOTE. (Deutsches Museum. Leipzig, 1784. 12°. [Jahr] 1784, Bd. 2, p. 563.) *DF
Alludes to the American Revolution.

777. AUSWANDERUNGEN aus Deutschland. (In: A. L. Schlözer. Stats-Anzeigen. Göttingen, 1784. 12°. Bd. 6, p. 214–217.) BAC
Law forbidding emigration.
Signed: Joseph [11]. Dated: July 7th, 1768.
See also: Committee for Relieving the Poor Germans Who Were Brought to London in 1764, *Proceedings*, London, 1765, †* KF 1765. The committee was appointed "to provide for the immediate support and maintenance of these poor emigrants...and...for their commodious transportation to Charles-Town South Carolina." — *cf.* p. xii.

778. AZAKIA. Eine canadische Erzählung. (Hannoverisches Magazin...vom Jahr 1784. Hannover, 1785. 4°. Jahrg. 22, col. 321–336.)
*DF
"Aus dem *Universal Magasine* February 1783."
Translated by V. in H.
Title page dated 1785; contents, 1784.
See no. 1444.

779. BERECHNUNG des Verlusts deutscher Truppen bei dem Amerikanischen Kriege. (In: A. L. Schlözer. Stats-Anzeigen. Göttingen, 1784. 12°. Bd. 6, p. 521–522.) BAC

780. BETRACHTUNGEN über den jetzigen Zustand des Gewerbes zwischen Sr. Grossbrittanischen Majestät Zucker-Kolonien und dem Gebiete der vereinigten Staaten von Amerika. (Historisches Portefeuille zur Kenntnis der gegenwärtigen und vergangenen Zeit. Wien, 1784. 12°. Jahrg. 3, Bd. 2, p. 455-460, 574-589.)
BAA

781. BRIEFE über Amerika. (Der Teutsche Merkur. Weimar, 1784. 12°. Jahr 1784, Vierteljahr 3 [Bd. 47], p. 97–108.) *DF (Neue)
Description of Canada.
The announced continuation did not appear.
This periodical subsequently called *Der Neue teutsche Merkur*, under which it is shelved.
See no. 479 (note).

782. CRÈVECŒUR, MICHEL GUILLAUME ST. JEAN DE. Sittliche Schilderungen von Amerika, in Briefen eines Amerikanischen Guthsbesitzers an einen Freund in England. Von J. Hektor St. John. Aus dem Englischen. Liegnitz und Leipzig: Bey David Siegert, 1784. 10, 462 p., 2 folding maps. 17 cm. *KF 1784
Sabin 17500.
The original was published under title: Letters from an American farmer... London, 1782.
According to Brissot de Warville, the letters were addressed to William Seton, of the Bank in New York.
Note also his "Reise in Ober-Pennsylvanien und im Staate Neu-York, von einem adoptirten Mitgliede der Oneida-Nation," in *Magazin von merkwürdigen neuen Reisebeschreibungen*, Berlin, 1802, Bd. 23, p. 1–472, KBC. An earlier edition with the imprint, Leipzig: Crusius, 1788, is not in the Library.
See the chapter entitled "Hector St. John De Crèvecoeur goes among the Nantucket whalers," Book ii, chapt. 7, in Mark Van Doren, *An Autobiography of America*, New York, 1929, AGZ.
Review: *Allgemeine deutsche Bibliothek*, Bd. 63, p. 493–494, NAA.

783. [DU BUISSON, PAUL ULRIC.] Vorstellung der Staatsveränderung in Nordamerika, von den ersten Unruhen im Jahr 1774 bis zu dem Bündniss der Krone Frankreichs mit den Kolonien. Von einem Amerikaner. Zweyte Auflage, vermehrt mit den Reflexionen eines Engländers. Bern: In der Hallerschen Buchhandlung, 1784. viii, 374 p. 8°. *KF 1784
The French original, *Abrégé de la Révolution de l'Amérique angloise, depuis le commencement de l'anné 1774 jusqu' au 1ᵉʳ janvier 1778, par M***, Américain*, Paris, 1778, is in *KF 1778.
The first German edition, *Historischer Abriss...* was issued in Berlin, in 1779. See JCB, Catalogue, no. 257.
The "Reflexionen eines Engländers" are entitled, "John Wesley's Schrift von den Streitigkeiten mit den Colonien in Nord Amerika in einem Auszuge," p. 152–174 [i.e., 353–374].

784. EINSCHRÄNKUNG der Statute des Cincinnatusordens in Amerika. (Historisches Portefeuille zur Kenntnis der gegenwärtigen und vergangenen Zeit. Wien, 1784. 12°. Jahrg. 3, Bd. 2, p. 451–454.) BAA

785. ETWAS von dem Verlust der Provinz Virginien im letzten Kriege. (Historisches Portefeuille zur Kenntnis der gegenwärtigen und vergangenen Zeit. Wien, 1784. 12°. Jahrg. 3, Bd. 1, p. 55–58.) BAA
Deals especially with Virginian tobacco and the history of its growth in Virginia from 1616 to 1781.

786. FRANKLIN, BENJAMIN. Anecdoten, die Sitten der Wilden in Nordamerika betreffend. (Historisches Portefeuille zur Kenntnis der gegenwärtigen und vergangenen Zeit. Wien, 1784. 12°. Jahrg. 3, Bd. 2, p. 217–226.) BAA

787. GEISLER, ADAM FRIEDRICH. Adam Friedrich Geisler's, des jüngern, Geschichte und Zustand der Königl. Grosbrittannischen Kriegsmacht zu Wasser und zu Lande von den frühesten Zeiten bis an's Jahr 1784. Nebst einem Abris des lezten amerikanischen Krieges, und anhangweise: Schilderungen einiger in diesem Kriege sich vorzüglich ausgezeichneter brittischer Offiziere, wie auch Verzeichnisse einiger deutscher in diesem Kriege rühmlichst zur Hülfe gewesener Offiziere. Mit ausgemalten

## GERMAN WORKS RELATING TO AMERICA

*1784, continued*

Kupfern... Dessau und Leipzig: In der Buchhandlung der Gelehrten, und beim Verfasser, 1784. xcviii, 604 p. incl. tables. 2 folding plates. 8°. *KF 1784

Also published under the title: Kurze Karakter- und Thatenschilderung von hundert und siebenfunfzig sich in lextern amerikanischen Kriege vorzüglich ausgezeichneter brittischer Offiziere wie auch einiger Offiziere von den deutschen Hülfstruppen, Dresden und Leipzig, 1784. Sabin 26843. Not in the Library. "Among the sketches are the characters of André, Arnold, Asgill, Burgoyne, Carleton, Clinton, Cornwallis, Gage, Howe, Sir William Howe, Governor Hutchinson, Johnstone, Kempenfeld, Keppel, Prescott, Rodney, Tarleton, etc." — *Sabin.*

788. HANDLUNGSNACHRICHTEN. (Historisches Portefeuille zur Kenntnis der gegenwårtigen und vergangenen Zeit. Wien, 1784. 12°. Jahrg. 3, Bd. 1, p. 797–799; Bd. 2, p. 253–254, 645.)
Contains references to America. BAA

789. HENNINGS, AUGUST ADOLF FRIEDRICH. Sammlung von Staatsschriften, die, während des Seekrieges von 1776 bis 1783, sowol von den kriegführenden, als auch von den neutralen Mächten, öffentlich bekannt gemacht worden sind; in so weit solche die Freiheit des Handels und der Schiffahrt betreffen. Herausgegeben, und mit einer Abhandlung über die Neutralität und ihre Rechte, insonderheit bey einem Seekriege, begleitet von August Hennings... Altona: Gedruckt und verlegt von Johann David Adam Eckhardt...in Commission bey Benj. Gottl. Hoffmann in Hamburg, 1784[–85]. 2 v. in l. 8°. *KF 1784
Includes the most important state papers relating to the American Revolution.
Review: *Allgemeine deutsche Bibliothek*, Bd. 69, p. 472, NAA.

790. HERDER, JOHANN GOTTFRIED. Ideen zur Philosophie der Geschichte der Menschheit von Johann Gottfried Herder... Riga und Leipzig: Bei Johann Friedrich Hartknoch, 1784–1791. (Reprinted in his: Sämmtliche Werke. Herausgegeben von Bernhard Suphan. Berlin, 1877–1913. 12°. Bd. 13, 14.) NFG
Of especial interest: Buch 6, VI; Organisation der Amerikaner.
See P. C. Weber, *America in German imaginative literature*, 1926, p. 20, NFCX.

791. JUDE. [Berlin, 1784.] p. 293–618, 1 plate, 1 table. 12°. *PBZ
Extract from *Oeconomische Encyclopädie*, Theil 31. Relates to the Jews in North America.

792. LIED eines Negersklaven in Amerika. (Musen Almanach. A. MDCCLXXXIV. Göttingen: Bey J. C. Dietrich [1784]. 32°. p. 88–89.) NFA
Signed: A. E.
Ends with the admonition, "Weisse! gebt mich frey."

793. LINDEMANN, JOHANN GOTTLIEB. Geschichte der Meinungen älterer und neuerer Völker, im Stande der Roheit und Cultur, von Gott, Religion, und Priesterthum, nebst einer besondern Religionsgeschichte der Aegypter, Perser, Chaldåer, Chinesen, Indianer, Phönicier, Griechen und Römer etc. wie auch von der Religion der wilden Völker, als Brasilianer, Mexicaner, Peruaner etc... Erster [–Siebenter] Theil. Stendal: Bey Franzen und Grosse, 1784–1795. 7 v. in 4. 8°. *KF 1784
Sabin 41289.

793A. LINGEN, VON. Contrast alter und neuer Zeit. (Musen Almanach. Göttingen: Bey J. C. Dietrich, 1784. 32°. [Jahrg.] 1784, p. 155–156.) NFA
"Als jüngst ein teutscher Held dem Rufe folgen musste,
Der für der Britten Recht zu streiten ihm befahl;
So nahm das treue Weib, die kaum die Nachricht wusste
Den Degen selbst zur Hand -und reicht' ihn dem Gemahl
"Geh!" — sprach sie, — sey ein Mann und fürchte nicht zu sterben
Nur mich verlässest du! — Wir sind ja ohne Erben."

794. MENNONISTEN in Holland. (In: A. L. Schlözer. Stats-Anzeigen. Göttingen, 1784. 12°. Bd. 5, p. 447.) BAC
States that the Mennonites are insurgents. See no. 803.

795. MOSER, JOHANN JACOB. Nord-America nach den Friedensschlüssen vom Jahr 1783. Nebst 1. Einem Vorbericht von America überhaupt, 2. einigen Charten, und 3. einem hinlänglichen Register. Von Johann Jacob Moser... Leipzig: Bey Johann Friedrich Junius, 1784–1793. 3 v. folding maps. 8°. *KF 1784
Sabin 51055.
"Johann Jacob Moser, professor of German political science in Tübingen, later chancellor of the university in Frankfurt a. O. Like Schubart, he fell a victim to ducal tyranny in Würtemberg and was from 1759 to 1764 a political prisoner at the Hohentwiel... The author begins this first fundamental comprehensive work on America as a republic with a discussion of the various stages of the conclusion of peace in 1783. In regard to the British-American controversy he reserves his own opinion and simply states the views of others. He takes up the climate and physical features, the inhabitants and their religion, treating each State separately. Special sections of the work refer to the American landscape, to charts and publications about the country, and to international European law in its bearing on America." — *P. C. Weber, America in imaginative literature*, 1926, NFCX.
Reviews: *Allgemeine Literatur Zeitung*, Jahr 1785, Bd. 2, p. 138, NAA; *Allgemeine deutsche Bibliothek*, Bd. 66, p. 184, NAA; *Göttingische Anzeigen von gelehrten Sachen*, Jahr 1785, p. 1182, * DF; *Tübinger gelehrte Anzeigen*, Jahr 1785, p. 761; also *Allgemeine Literatur-Zeitung*, Jahr 1785, Bd. 4, col. 189, NAA.

796. REDE eines Amerikanischen Wilden, an Lord Dunmore, Gouverneur von Virginien. (Der Teutsche Merkur. Weimar, 1784. 12°. Jahr 1784, Vierteljahr 3, p. 95–96.)
*DF (Neue)
This periodical subsequently called *Der Neue teutsche Merkur*, under which it is shelved.

797. SCHILLER, JOHANN FRIEDRICH. Kabale und Liebe, ein bürgerliches Trauerspiel in fünf Aufzügen von Fridrich Schiller. Mannheim: In der Schwanischen Hofbuchhandlung, 1784. 167 p. 8°. 8–NFGX
Of especial interest: Act II, Scene 2.
"[The scene]...is so drastic that the words referring directly to America had to be omitted in the first performances, in order to give no offense to the representatives of the princes engaged in the traffic, and to

*1784, continued*

797. SCHILLER, JOHANN FRIEDRICH, *cont'd*
assure the continuance of the play upon the boards." — *Alexander Gleichen-Russwurm.*
Note the book notice on "Cabal and Love, a tragedy, translated from the German of F. Schiller, author of The Robbers, Don Carlos, The Conspiracy of Fiesco, &c.," in *The American monthly review, or literary journal*, Philadelphia, 1795, v. 3, p. 184, * DE.
The earliest American appearance was in *Select plays, from celebrated authors*, Baltimore, 1802, v. 2 (not in the Library). For later editions, see F. H. Wilkens, *Early influence of German literature in America* [with bibliography], New York, 1899, *NFC*; also E. C. Parry, "Friedrich Schiller in America," in *Americana Germanica*, Philadelphia, 1905, new series, v. 3, *NFGX (German)*.

798. SCHLÖZER, AUGUST LUDWIG. An die Hrn. Herausgeber der Berlinischen Monatschrift (Jun. 1784, S. 574 folgg.). (In: A. L. Schlözer. Stats-Anzeigen. Göttingen, 1784. 12°. Bd. 6, p. 512-515.) BAC
Conclusion of the argument concerning the ode entitled "Die Freiheit Amerika's."
*See no. 744.*

798A. SCHUBART, CHRISTIAN FRIEDRICH DANIEL. Ein Gespräch auf dem Schiffe. (In his: Sämmtliche Gedichte. Frankfurt am Main, 1825. 16°. Bd. 2, p. 121-123.) NFW
A discussion aboard a ship between a mercenary and the chaplain of the ship concerning the expedition to America. The poem was published in his *Gedichte aus dem Kerker*, Zürich, 1785. See also S. Nestriepke, *Schubart als Dichter*, Pössneck i. Thür., 1910, p. 184, *NFD*; on p. 192 a poem entitled "Drohender Kampf in Amerika," printed first in his *Chronik 1788*, Stück 17 (see no. 487) is mentioned. See also H. S. King, in *University of California, Publications in modern philology*, Berkeley, 1929, v. 14, p. 112-121, *STG*.

799. SPRENGEL, MATTHIAS CHRISTIAN. Allgemeines historisches Taschenbuch oder Abriss der merkwürdigsten neuen Welt-Begebenheiten enthaltend für 1784 die Geschichte der Revolution von Nord-America von C. M. Sprengel ... Mit 18 Kupfern und einer illuminirt. Landcharte. Berlin: Bey Haude und Spener [1784]. 1 p.l., 74 p., 3 l., 182 p. plates. 12°. *KF 1784
First edition, with the genealogies and the Leipzig colophon on p. 182. *See also no. 800.*
The illustrations, probably by Daniel Chodowiecki, are of great beauty. See Wilhelm Engelmann's *Daniel Chodowiecki's Sämmtliche Kupferstiche*, Leipzig, 1857-60, *MDG (Chodowiecki)*. Portraits of Washington, Gates, Franklin, Laurens, and Paul Jones. Etchings represent some of the principal events connected with the American Revolution.
Subjects treated: Beschreibung der 13 Provinzen. Entwurf einer Zeitrechnung von Amerika. Geschichte der Nord-Amerikanischen Independence. Präsidenten des Congresses seit 1774. Bevölkerung der 13 Nord-Amerikanischen Staaten. Grossbrittanischer Handel in den 13 Nord-Amerikanischen Staaten seit dem ersten Pariser Frieden, 1763. Einfluss des Krieges auf den Virginischen Tabacks-Bau. Ungefähre Rechnung wie viel jede Provinz zu den allgemeinen Ausgaben beyträgt.
J. T. Hatfield and E. Hochbaum mention: Historisch-genealogischer Calender oder Jahrbuch der merkwürdigsten Weltbegebenheiten für 1784, Berlin: Bey Haude und Spener 1784; see *Americana Germanica*, Philadelphia, 1899-1900, v. 3, p. 352 and 384, *NFGA (German)*. This is the engraved title of the above work. Sabin (89755) gives the year of publication as 1783.
Reviews: *Historisches Portefeuille*, Jahrg. 2, Bd. 1, unnumbered pages following p. 671, *BAA*; *Göttingische Anzeigen von gelehrten Sachen*, Jahr 1784, p. 621-622, * DF.

800. —— Allgemeines historisches Taschenbuch oder Abriss der merkwürdigsten neuen Welt-Begebenheiten enthaltend für 1784 die Geschichte der Revolution von Nord-America von C. M. Sprengel, Professor der Geschichte auf der Universität zu Halle. Mit 18 Kupfern und einer illuminirt. Landcharte. Berlin: Bey Haude und Spener [1784]. 4 p.l., 182 p., map, plates. 12°. *KF 1784
Second edition. Lacks the genealogies and colophon of first edition; *see no. 799.*

801. STOCKFISCHFANG der Franzosen und Britten bei Neufundland und bei den lezten Nordamerikanischen Kriege. (Historisches Portefeuille zur Kenntnis der gegenwärtigen und vergangenen Zeit. Wien, 1784. 12°. Jahrg. 3, Bd. 2, p. 536-549.) BAA

802. STUCK, GOTTLIEB HEINRICH. Verzeichnis von aeltern und neuern Land- und Reisebeschreibungen. Ein Versuch eines Hauptstücks der geographischen Litteratur mit einem vollstaendigen Realregister und einer Vorrede von M. Iohann Ernst Fabri... Halle: In Iohann Christian Hendels Verlage, 1784. xvi, 504 p. 8°. KB
This index of the then known publications relating to America (and other countries) is invaluable.
Reviews: *Allgemeine deutsche Bibliothek*, Bd. 70, p. 225, *NAA*; *Göttingische Anzeigen von gelehrten Sachen*, Jahr 1785, Bd. 1, p. 479, * *DF*; *Allgemeine Literatur-Zeitung*, Jahr 1785, Bd. 1, col. 35, *NAA*.
*See no. 825.*

803. VERTEIDIGUNG der Mennonisten in NAmerika. (In: A. L. Schlözer. Stats-Anzeigen. Göttingen, 1784. 12°. Bd. 4, p. 373-376.) BAC
Controversy as to whether the Mennonites are insurgents or not.
Signed: Barby, 4. März 1784.
*See no. 794.*

804. VOM Wallfisch, dessen Fange und Benutzung. (Historisches Portefeuille zur Kenntnis der gegenwärtigen und vergangenen Zeit. Wien, 1784. 12°. Jahrg. 3, Bd. 2, p. 186-210, 346-374, 591-619.) BAA
References to North America, p. 614.
Signed: J. G. Schneider.

805. WEPPEN, JOHANN AUGUST. Eine Parabel am 20sten Januar 1783. als am Tage des Friedensschlusses zu Versailles. (Musen Almanach. A. MDCCLXXXIV. Göttingen: Bey J. C. Dietrich [1784]. 32°. p. 183-188.) NFA
"It treats the war in deliciously humorous fashion and is notable for the question it raises as to whether the Spanish colonies in South America will follow the example of England's North American colonies. It also prophesies a future friendship between America and England." — H. S. King, "Echoes of the American Revolution in German literature," in *University of California, Publications in modern philology, Berkeley, 1929, v. 14, p. 157, STG.*
*See no. 586.*

805A. ZIMMERMANN, JOHANN GEORG. Ueber die Einsamkeit. Theil 1-4. Carlsruhe: C. G. Schmieder, 1784-90. 4 v. 12°. YFH
..."Ein vortrefflicher deutscher Schriftsteller hat in einem meisterhaften Aufsatze über Fränklins Leben gesagt: Fränklins Vortrag habe nie einen Anschein von Gelehrsamkeit, nirgends die Mine eines Compendiums. Alles seyen einzelne Bemerkungen... Dieser feine Geist des Weltmanns, dieser gesunde Natursinn des unpedantischen Weisen lebe und webe überall in Fränklin's Schriften. — *v. 2, p. 32.*

*1784, continued*

**806.** *Review:* The Constitutions of the several Independent States of America, the Declaration of Independence, and the Articles of Consideration [sic] between the said states, the whole arranged by Wil. Jackson. London: J. Stockdale, 1783. 471 S. 8°. (Göttingische Anzeigen von gelehrten Sachen. Göttingen [1784]. 12°. Jahr 1784, p. 249-253, * *DF*.)
The Library's copies of this English compilation are in * *KF 1783 (Constitutions)*.

**806A.** *Review:* Faustin, oder das philosophische Jahrhundert. Ohne Druckort und Verleger, 1783. 381 p. 8°. (Allgemeine deutsche Bibliothek. Berlin, 1784. 12°. Bd. 58, p. 134-136, *NAA*.)
Published in Zürich, in 1783. The author is Johann Pezzl. See *Allgemeine deutsche Biographie*, v. 25, p. 578-579, * *RR-AGV*.
"Faustin...brachte den Glauben an schon geschehene allgemeine Aufklärung und Eifer für deren Ausbreitung mit in die grosse Welt. Letzterer stürzte ihn in mancherley Unfälle, wodurch er von Bayern nach Italien, Spanien, Frankreich, Engelland, zuletzt auch nach Amerika verschlagen wurde... Er sieht... den Negerhandel und die Behandlung der Negern in Westindien... Gegen das Ende...findet Faustin seinen durch Verfolgungen verjagten Bonifaz [his teacher] in Amerika wieder, wo er nach dortigem Brauche sollte verkauft werden zur Bezahlung der Fracht..."
Also references to soldier traffic.

**807.** *Review:* Geschichte der Entdeckungen und Schiffahrten im Norden... von Johann Reinhold Forster. Frankfurt a. d. Oder: Bey Strauss, 1784. 39 Bogen. 8°. (Historisches Portefeuille zur Kenntnis der gegenwärtigen und vergangenen Zeit. Wien, 1784. 12°. Jahrg. 3, Bd. 2, p. 233-237, *BAA*.)

**807A.** *Review:* Johann Ingenhouss, Vermischte Schriften physisch-medicinischen Innhalts. Uebersetzt und herausgegeben von Nicolaus Carl Molitor. Zweyte, verbesserte und mit ganz neuen Abhandlungen vermehrte Auflage. Erster Band. Wien: Wappler, 1784. 452 S. mit Kupfern. 8°. (Allgemeine Literatur-Zeitung. Jena, 1785. 4°. Jahr 1785, Bd. 2, p. 158-160, *NAA*.)
"...ein kurzer Begriff des Franklinschen Systems von der Elektricität."

**808.** *Review:* Der Naturforscher. Halle, 1784. 322 S. 3 Kupferplatten. (Göttingische Anzeigen von gelehrten Sachen. Göttingen [1784]. 12°. Jahr 1784, p. 1926, * *DF*.)
Contains "Beschreibung des Amerikanischen Barschings," by Schöpf.

**809.** *Review:* Observations on the Commerce of the American States by John Lord Sheffield, a new edition much enlarged with an Appendix. London: De Brett, 1784. 287 p. (Göttingische Anzeigen von gelehrten Sachen. Göttingen [1784]. 12°. Jahr 1784, p. 1265-1273, * *DF*.)
The Library's various copies of this and the earlier editions are in * *KF*.

**810.** *Review:* Das politische Journal. Hamburg, 1783. (Göttingische Anzeigen von gelehrten Sachen. Göttingen [1784]. 12°. Jahr 1784, p. 246-247, * *DF*.)
Contains: Hasenclever. Bemerkungen über Amerika. See no. 1222.

**810A.** *Review:* Psalm Boek voor die tot die evangelische Broeer-Kerk behoorende Neger Gemeenten na S. Croix, S. Thomas en S. Jan. Barby und in Commission bey Kummer in Leipzig, 1784. 368 S. 8°. (Allgemeine Literaturzeitung. Jena, 1785. 4°. Jahr 1785, Bd. 3, p. 354-355, *NAA*.)
"So wenig diese westindischen Producte eigentlich für die Literatur besonders Deutschlands bestimmt zu seyn scheinen mögen, so sehr verdienen sie doch wirklich die Aufmerksamkeit des Beobachters..."

**810B.** *Review:* Reisen durch Amerika; oder Beobachtungen über den gegenwärtigen Zustand, Cultur und Handel der Brittischen Colonien in Amerika, deren Aus- und Einfuhr mit Grossbritannien, und Uebersicht der Einkünfte, welche letzteres daraus zieht. Von einem erfahrenen Kaufmann, in Briefen an den Grafen von Chatham gerichtet. Aus dem Englischen. Nebst einem Abriss von Nord-Amerika, und der Republik der dreyzehn vereinigten Staaten. Aus dem Französischen. Leipzig: Schneider, 1783. 238 p. 8°. (Allgemeine deutsche Bibliothek. Berlin, 1784. 12°. Bd. 59, p. 174-175, *NAA*.)
According to this review the *Abriss* was written in Holland and praises the Netherlands for having recognized the independence of the United States. "Tabellen, welche Preise von Waaren, Verkaufsrechnungen, den Gehalt von Münzen u. dgl. m. in sich fassen." The letters "zeigen die Wichtigkeit der Vortheile, welche England aus seinen Amerikanischen Colonien zog, so einleuchtend, dass man auch hieraus sehen kann, wie vergeblich sich manche jetzt, nach dem Verluste dieser Colonien bemühen, zu demonstrieren, sie wären von geringer Erheblichkeit für das Mutterland gewesen."

**810C.** *Review:* Zur Kunde fremder Völker und Länder. Aus französischen Missionsberichten, mit Kupfern und Karten. Leipzig: In der Weygandschen Buchhandlung. 8°. Erster Band 1781. 349 p. und 2 Blatt Inhalt, auch 1 Kupfer und Karte. Zweyter Band 1782. 216 p. 1 Karte. Dritter Band 1782. 438 p., 2 Kupfer. Vierter Band 1783. 352 p. 1 Karte. (Allgemeine deutsche Bibliothek. Berlin, 1784. 12°. Bd. 57, p. 178-182, *NAA*.)
"Unter diesem Titel liefert Hr. Bibliothekarius Reichard in Gotha einen Auszug von den bekannten und allgemein geschätzten lettres édifiantes et curieuses écrites des missions étrangères..." Of special interest in v. 2: "Auch findet man Nachrichten von einigen Völkern am Mississippi"; v. 3: Missionary activities in Mexico.

## 1785

**811.** ABRISS der Begebenheiten. (Historisches Portefeuille zur Kenntnis der gegenwärtigen und vergangenen Zeit. Wien, 1785. 12°. Jahrg. 4, Bd. 1, p. 221-240; Bd. 2, p. 124-145, 657-679.) *BAA*
Many references to America.

**812.** AUS Nord Amerika, an einen Frei Herrn in Franken. (In: A. L. Schlözer. Stats-Anzeigen. Göttingen, 1785. 12°. Bd. 7, p. 3-54.) *BAC*
First letter dated: Nazareth, Aug. 23rd, 1783; the second: Baltimore, Oct. 27th, 1783; the third: Philadelphia, Nov. 10th, 1783; the fourth: Philadelphia, Nov. 13th, 1783.
The anonymous writer is Johann David Schöpf. The letters were accompanied by a copy of *An introductory Discourse to an Argument in support of the*

*1785, continued*

812. Aus Nord Amerika, ... *continued*
*payments made of British debts into the Treasury of Maryland during the late war, by John Francis Mercer, Annapolis, 1789.* See also *Allgemeine Literatur-Zeitung,* Jena, 1785, Jahr 1785, Bd. 2, col. 121-123, *NAA.*
An argument against the letters appears in this periodical, Bd. 13, p. 527-528.
See no. 984.

813. Auszug aus Cooks lezter Reise. (Historisches Portefeuille zur Kenntnis der gegenwärtigen und vergangenen Zeit. Wien, 1785. 12°. Jahrg. 4, Bd. 2, p. 92-102, 202-219, 292-301, 333-341, 467-475, 529-538.) BAA

814. Baltimore-County in Maryland, 3. Okt. 1785. (In: A. L. Schlözer. Stats-Anzeigen. Göttingen, 1785. 12°. Bd. 8, p. 511-512.) BAC
"N-Amerikanische Bank, ihrer Freiheit Briefe 1785 beraubt." — *Index.*

815. Begebenheiten des Obersten Daniel Boon, eines der ersten Kolonisten in Kentuke; worinn eine Nachricht von den Kriegen mit den Indianern am Ohio von 1769 bis auf jetzige Zeiten, und von der ersten Einrichtung und dem Fortgang der Niederlassungen an selbigen Flusse enthalten ist. (Historisches Portefeuille zur Kenntnis der gegenwärtigen und vergangenen Zeit. Wien, 1785. 12°. Jahrg. 4, Bd. 2, p. 31-53.) BAA
"Vom dem Obersten selbst verfasset. In der Grafschaft Fayette in Kentuke..."
"Die Nachrichten schienen uns aus mehr als einer Ursache der Uebersetzung werth. Wir sehen erstlich daraus, wie wenig wir noch das Innere jenes Landes kennen, und zweitens, mit welchen Beschwerlichkeiten und Gefahren die Engl. Anbauer zu kämpfen haben, wovon wir uns hier in unsern friedlichen civilisirten Gegenden keinen Begriff machen können."
See nos. 871, 872.

816. Etwas von den Tänzen der fremden und wilden Völker. (Historisches Portefeuille zur Kenntnis der gegenwärtigen und vergangenen Zeit. Wien, 1785. 12°. Jahrg. 4, Bd. 1, p. 87-91.) BAA
"Zur Erklärung des Kupferstichs, der einen Otaheitischen Tanz vorstellt." The etching is not signed.

817. Handlungsnachrichten. (Historisches Portefeuille zur Kenntnis der gegenwärtigen und vergangenen Zeit. Wien, 1785. 12°. Jahrg. 4, Bd. 2, p. 146-149.) BAA
Refers to the rice crops in South Carolina and the English trade with Jamaica.

818. Iffland, August Wilhelm. Die Jäger. Ein ländliches Sittengemählde in fünf Aufzügen von Wilhelm August Iffland. Berlin: Bei George Jacob Decker, 1785. (Reprinted in: Adolf Hauffen. Das Drama der klassischen Periode... Stuttgart [1891]. 8°. Teil 1, Abt. 1, p. 213-313.) NGB
Added title page: Deutsche National-Litteratur, Bd. 139.
"Besitzer, die, durch Missgeschick gezwungen, Haus und Hof verkauft haben, um drüben neu anzufangen, werden von...Iffland in den 'Jägern' (Akt 3, Szene 13) erwähnt." — *Gerhard Descsyk, in Deutsch-amerikanische historische Gesellschaft von Illinois, Jahrbuch, 1924-1925, p. 43, IEK.*

819. [Jacquin, Nikolaus Joseph, Freiherr von.] Dreyhundert auserlesene amerikanische Gewächse nach Linneischer Ordnung... Nürnberg: Auf Kosten der Raspischen Buchhandlung, 1785-1788. 6 v. in 3. 300 col'd plates. 8°. Sabin 35519. *KF 1785
Edited by Johann Zorn.
v. 2-6 have title: Amerikanische Gewächse nach Linneischer Ordnung.
Composed chiefly of reduced copies of the plates of Jacquin's *Selectarum stirpium Americarum historia,* Vindobonae, 1763, with explanations.
Reviews: Erstes Hundert, 1. Hälfte: *Allgemeine Literatur-Zeitung,* Jahr 1787, Bd. 2, col. 57-58, *NAA; Allgemeine deutsche Bibliothek,* Anhang zu Bd. 53-86, p. 744, *NAA; Gothaische gelehrte Zeitungen,* Jahr 1787, Bd. 1, p. 36 (not in the Library); *Leipziger gelehrte Anzeigen,* Jahr 1785, Bd. 4, p. 2284 (not in the Library). 2. Hälfte: *Allgemeine Literatur-Zeitung,* Jahr 1787, Bd. 2, col. 57-58, *NAA; Allgemeine deutsche Bibliothek,* Anhang zu Bd. 53/86, p. 744, *NAA; Gothaische gelehrte Zeitungen,* Jahr 1787, Bd. 1, p. 36 (not in the Library); *Leipziger gelehrte Anzeigen,* Jahr 1786, Bd. 3, p. 1311 (not in the Library). Zweites Hundert, 1. Hälfte: *Allgemeine Literatur-Zeitung,* Jahr 1787, Bd. 1, col. 51-52, *NAA; Allgemeine deutsche Bibliothek,* Anhang zu Bd. 53/86, p. 744, *NAA.* 2. Hälfte: *Allgemeine Literatur-Zeitung,* Jahr 1787, Bd. 4, col. 237-238, *NAA; Allgemeine deutsche Bibliothek,* Anhang zu Bd. 53/86, p. 744, *NAA.* Drittes Hundert, 1. Hälfte: *Allgemeine Literatur-Zeitung,* Jahr 1788, Bd. 1, col. 67, *NAA.*

820. Moritz, Karl Philipp. Anton Reiser. Ein psychologischer Roman von Karl Philipp Moritz. Berlin: Bei Friedrich Maurer, 1785 [-1790]. 4 Theile. (Reprinted: Leipzig: Verlag von Philipp Reclam jun. [pref. 1906]. 476 p. frontispiece. (port.) 15 cm. NGK
Reclams Universal-Bibliothek. Nr. 4813-4816.
Of especial interest is the song in Theil 3, p. 312, addressing the English: "Doch du getreues Volk deinem König, verhülls nur dein Antlitz, und weine! Siehe nicht wie dein Bruder im fernen Lande sich auflehnt gegen seinen König."

821. [Neue Mitglieder der Societät der Wissenschaften zu Philadelphia.] (Allgemeine Literatur Zeitung. Jena, 1785. 4°. Jahr 1785, Bd. 4, p. 128.) NAA
Under headings: Kurze Nachrichten: Beförderungen.

822. Schreiben des Christoph Columbus an den König von Spanien. (Historisches Portefeuille zur Kenntnis der gegenwärtigen und vergangenen Zeit. Wien, 1785. 12°. Jahrg. 4, Bd. 2, p. 489-497.) BAA
The letter, published for the first time in the *Gentleman's magazine,* June, 1785, is dated: Jamaica, 1503. The explanatory note of the editor, also translated, precedes the letter.
"Kolumbus, nach der Wahrheit geschildert," in *Archiv für den Menschen und Bürger in allen Verhältnissen* [ed. *J. A. Schlettwein*], Bd. 3, Leipzig, 1781. This periodical which contains several more articles relating to America is not in the Library.

823. Sprengel, Matthias Christian. M. C. Sprengel, ordentlichen Lehrers der Geschichte in Halle, Geschichte der Revolution von Nord-America. Mit einer illuminirten accuraten Charte von diesem neuen Freystaate, Frankenthal: Bey L. B. F. Gegel, 1785. 5 p., col'd, folding map (col'd). 8°. *KF 1785
Sabin 89758.
"This work, based on extensive bibliographical sources, which are, to be sure, mostly English, is divided into two main parts. The first gives an account

*1785, continued*

of the historical development of each state, including its political constitution. In the second part, which treats the History of American Independence, the author discusses at length the British-American controversy, taking sides here with the Americans. A special chapter is devoted to a characterization of American military and naval leaders." — *P. C. Weber, America in imaginative German literature*, 1926, *NFCX*.
See nos. 799, 800.

824. —— Geschichte der Revolution von Nord-Amerika von M. C. Sprengel... Mit einer illuminirten Charte. Speyer: Bey der typographischen Gesellschaft, 1785. 5 p.l., 196 p., 1 l. map. 8°. \*KF 1785
See note on preceding entry.
Reviews: *Allgemeine Literatur-Zeitung*, Jahr 1785, Bd. 5, col. 278, *NAA*; *Allgemeine deutsche Bibliothek*, Bd. 65, p. 302, *NAA*.

825. STUCK, GOTTLIEB HEINRICH. Gottlieb Heinrich Stuck's Nachtrag zu seinem Verzeichnis von aeltern und neuern Land- und Reisebeschreibungen... Halle: In Iohann Christian Hendels Verlage, 1785. 80 p. 8°. KB
See no. 802.
Reviews: *Allgemeine Literatur-Zeitung*, Jahr 1785, Bd. 2, col. 205, *NAA*; *Allgemeine deutsche Bibliothek*, Bd. 70, p. 232, *NAA*.
See 802.

826. TOBAKRAUCHEN. (Deutsches Museum. Leipzig, 1785. 8°. [Jahr] 1785, Bd. 1, p. 376.)
\*DF
"Wenn dem Franzosen Jacob Cortier im Jahre 1534 das Tobakrauchen am Lorenzflusse sehr wunderbar vorgekommen ist, so ist es den Bewohnern der Marschländer an der Elbe bei dem Einfall der Schweden unter Torstensohn nicht besser gegangen. Man glaubte, die Schweden wären vom Teufel besessen, und spieen Feuer bei lebendigem Leibe. Jetzt raucht in eben diesen Gegenden nicht allein das männliche, sondern auch das weibliche Geschlecht Tobak."

827. UEBER die Einrichtung der 7 Freihäfen in dem französischen West Indien. Aus Austrasien, im Febr. 1786. (In: A. L. Schlözer. Stats-Anzeigen. Göttingen, 1785. 12°. Bd. 8, p. 385–400.) BAC

828. WALBAUM, JOHANN JULIUS. Verzeichniss einiger ausländischen Frösche. (Berlinische Gesellschaft naturforschender Freunde. Schriften. Berlin, 1785. 8°. Bd. 6, p. 158–184.)
Refers to American frogs, 3–\*EE (Gesellschaft)
Organization subsequently called Gesellschaft naturforschender Freunde zu Berlin, under which its publications are shelved.

829. ZUVERLÄSSIGE Nachrichten von dem Geschlecht und Herkommen des Nordamerikanischen Generals Friederich Wilhelm Ludolf Gerhard Augustin von Steuben. (Historisches Portefeuille zur Kenntnis der gegenwärtigen und vergangenen Zeit. Wien, 1785. 12°. Jahrg. 4, Bd. 1, p. 447–453.) BAA
See nos. 643, 1097.

829A. *Review:* Almanach Américain, Asiatique et Africain ou état physique, politique, ecclésiastique et militaire des Colonies d'Europe en Asie, en Afrique et en Amérique... Paris:

Beym Verfasser und bey Lamy, Merigot &c., 1785. 390 S. und das Recueil diplomatique. 132 S. (Allgemeine Literatur-Zeitung. Jena, 1785. 4°. Jahr 1785, Bd. 3, col. 35–36, *NAA*.)
The Recueil is Roche-Tilhac. This is the third edition. For others see nos. 761 and 908.
This edition is "bescheiden geworden," since it treats only the European colonies in America and does not promise any longer to be an "Adresskalender der ganzen Welt." "Das angehängte Recueil diplomatique enthält verschiedne öffentlichen Tractate, besonders aber französische Edicte, grösstentheils die Handlung betreffend von 1784."

830. *Review:* Briefe über Amerika, nach der neuesten Ausgabe aus dem Italiänischen des Hrn. Carlo Carli übersetzt und mit einigen Anmerkungen versehen von Chr. Gfr. Hennig. Erster [-Dritter] Theil. Gera: Chr. Fr. Beckmann, 1785. 3 Alph. 18 Bogen. 8°. (Göttingische Anzeigen von gelehrten Anzeigen. Göttingen [1785]. 12°. Jahr 1785, p. 399–400, 1269, \**DF*.)
Sabin 10914, 31914.
"These letters originated in a correspondence of Carli with his cousin, the Marquis Gravisi, in 1777 and 1779. The author describes the manners and customs of the Americans before their country was discovered by the Europeans. Count Carli's object is to confute the assertions of M. de Pauw [see no. 455] and to show that the Americans were descended from the ancient Atlantides." — *Rich, v. 1, p. 292, 351; quoted in Sabin*.
See no. 831, 867.

831. *Review:* Briefe über Amerika nach der neuesten, verbesserten und mit dem 3ten Theile vermehrten Ausgabe, aus dem Italiänischen des Herrn Grafen Carlo Carli übersetzt und mit einigen Anmerkungen versehen von Christian Gottfried Hennig. Erster [-dritter] Theil. Gera: Bey Christoph Friedrich Beckmann, 1785. 3 Alph. 18 Bogen. 8°. (Allgemeine Literatur-Zeitung. Jena, 1785. 4°. Jahr 1785, Bd. 3, p. 225–228, 233–236, 237–238; Jahr 1790, Intelligenz Blatt, p. 1209, *NAA*.)
See no. 830, 867.

831A. *Review:* Défense de l'inoculation et relation des progrès qu'elle a faits à Philadelphie en 1758. Par Thomas Bond, Vicepresident de la Société philosophique en Amérique et médecin de l'hospital de Pensylvanie. Strassburg: Buchhandlung der Universität, 1784. 80 S. 8°. (Allgemeine Literatur-Zeitung. Jena, 1785. 4°. Jahr 1785, Bd. 2, col. 265–266, *NAA*.)
"...in Rücksicht auf die Geschichte des stufenweisen Fortganges der Pockeneinpfropfung in Amerika ein in manchem Betracht erhebliches Buch... In Philadelphia ist die Einpfropfung im Jahre 1758 erst mit Glück ausgeübt worden."

832. *Review:* Drury's Abbildungen und Beschreibungen exotischer Insekten, mit fein illuminirten Kupfertafeln. Aus dem Englischen übersetzt... von Georg Wolfgang Franz Panzer. Nürnberg: In der Adam Wolfg. Winterschmidtschen Kunsthandlung, 1785. 1. Heft. 6 Bogen in 4°. 7 Kupfertafeln. (Allgemeine Literatur-Zeitung. Jena, 1785. 4°. Jahr 1785, Bd. 4, p. 312–313.)
Tafel III: Die amerikanische Odoraphaläne.

*1785, continued*

832A. *Review:* Die Entdeckungen des fünften Welttheils, oder Reisen um die Welt. Ein Lesebuch für die Jugend von M. Joh. Georg Friedr. Pabst, Nürnberg, 1784, 21 Bogen. 8°. (Allgemeine deutsche Bibliothek. Berlin, 1785. 8°. Bd. 61, p. 212–214, *NAA.*)
"Sollte wirklich in dem Kabinet der Brüdergemeinde zu Barby eine so grosse Menge Otahitischer und Neuseeländischer Producte und Manufakturarbeiten befindlich seyn, als hier...aus einem Brief von daher versichert wird?"

833. *Review:* An Essay on the Treatment and Conversion of African Slaves in the British Sugar Colonies. By James Ramsay. London: Philipps, 1784. (Göttingische Anzeigen von gelehrten Sachen. Göttingen [1785]. 12°. Jahr 1785, p. 1397–1403, * *DF.*)

833A. *Review:* F. L. Walther von Menschenfressenden Völkern und Menschenopfern. Hof: Vierling, 1785. 84 p. 8°. (Allgemeine Literatur-Zeitung. Jena, 1785. 4°. Jahr 1785, Bd. 4, col. 247–248, *NAA.*)
Cannibals in North and South America.

833B. *Review:* Friedrich Ludwig Walther, Von menschenfressenden Völkern und Menschenopfern. Hof: In der Vierlingischen Buchhandlung. 84 S. (Allgemeine Literatur-Zeitung. Jena, 1785. 4°. Jahr 1785, Bd. 3, col. 212, *NAA.*)
Cannibals in North and South America.

834. *Review:* Die fünfte Lieferung der Materialien für die Statistik und neuere Staatengeschichte gesammlet von Hrn. geh. Rath Dohm. Lemgo, 1785. (Göttingische Anzeigen von gelehrten Sachen. Göttingen [1785]. 12°. Jahr 1785, p. 1414–1415, * *DF.*)
Contains a German translation of an essay by Thomas Paine, "Berichtigung dessen, was der Abbt Raynal über die nordamerikanische Revolution gesagt hat," p. 555–672; see no. 860.
See also nos. 509, 510, 511.

834A. *Review:* Geographische Tabellen für die Jugend zur Vorbereitung und Wiederholung. Erster Theil von Europa... Zweyter Theil enthält Asien, Afrika, Amerika und einen Anhang. Friedrichstadt: Gedruckt bey G. A. Gerlach [n. d.]. 8 Bogen. (Allgemeine Literatur-Zeitung. Jena, 1785. 4°. Jahr 1785, Bd. 5, col. 47–49, *NAA.*)
"Bey Kalifornien wird auch Quivira (ein Land der Einbildung) genannt, wo die Menschenfresser das Blut trinken, sich in Viehhäute kleiden, die Hörner statt Trompeten gebrauchen und den Mist statt Holz brennen. Florida wird unter die Engländer, Franzosen und Wilden getheilt. Jenen gehört noch Carolina, Georgien, die Halbinsel Tegeste und das östliche Louisiana... Das übrige von Nordamerika nennt er Kanada, welches er in das ehemals Französische und Neuengland eintheilt... Zu Neuengland rechnet er ausser den Freystaaten auch Neuschottland und Labrador."
The author's name is Lipsius.

834B. *Review:* Geschichte der neuesten Weltbegebenheiten im Grossen aus dem Englischen in einem Auszuge. Achter Bd., welcher die Geschichte der Jahre 1778 u. 1779 einschliesst. Leipzig: Bey Weigand, 1784. 540 p. 8°. (Allgemeine Literatur-Zeitung. Jena, 1785. 4°. Jahr 1785, Bd. 1, col. 50–51, *NAA.*)
"In dem VIII. und neuesten Band findet man die Begebenheiten Grossbrittaniens und seiner ehemaligen Colonien in den Jahren 1778 und 1779."
See no. 869C.

834C. *Review:* Geschichte der Weltbegebenheiten im Grossen. Zehnter Band. Leipzig, 1785. 526 S. 8°. (Allgemeine Literatur-Zeitung. Jena, 1786. 4°. Jahr 1786, Bd. 1, col. 538–539, *NAA.*)
History of the American Revolution.

835. *Review:* Herrn Friedr. Osterwalds Historische Erdbeschreibung, zum Nutzen deutscher Jugend eingerichtet... Vierte verbesserte Ausgabe. Strassburg: in Treuttels Buchhandlung, 1785. 4 Bog. Vorrede, 594 S. und Register, ½ Bogen Statistische Tabellen. 8°. (Allgemeine Literatur-Zeitung. Jena, 1785. 4°. Jahr 1785, Bd. 4, p. 183–184, *NAA.*)
"In Amerika ist die Grösse der Nordamerikanischen Freystaaten aus dem Leiste häufig sehr falsch abgeschrieben... Harkarts Collegium zu Cambridge soll heissen Harvards Collegium... Das dürre armselige Kalifornien wird als ein angenehmes und fruchtbares Land beschrieben..."

835A. *Review:* Histoire impartiale des evenements militaires et politiques de la dernière guerre dans les quatre parties du monde par M. de L. Tom. I. II. et III. 1785 Paris. gr. Duodez, jeder Theil ungefähr ein Alphabet stark. (Göttingische Anzeigen von gelehrten Sachen. Göttingen [1785]. 12°. Jahr 1785, p. 2046–2048, * *DF.*)

836. *Review:* Kurzgefasste Geschichte der drey ersten Entdecker von Amerika. Frankfurt: Eichenb. Erben, 1781. 154 S. in 8°. (Allgemeine deutsche Bibliothek. Berlin, 1785. Anhang zu Bd. 37/52, p. 546–547, *NAA.*)
The author is Friedrich Dominik Ring. *cf.* Sabin 38363, 71422; Kayser, v. 4, p. 357B.
"Dieses ist für Ungelehrte ein hinlänglicher Auszug aus Robertson." See no. 559.
Ring also edited *Fragment einer Reise nach Domingo* [n. p., n. d.]; see Kayser. v. 4, col. 519B.

837. *Review:* Lettres d'un cultivateur Américain écrites à W. S. écuyer, depuis l'année 1770 jusqu'à 1781. Traduites de l'anglois par * * * Paris: Bey Cuchet, 1784. 2 v. 8°. (Allgemeine Literatur-Zeitung. Jena, 1785. 4°. Jahr 1785, Bd. 1, p. 297–299, *NAA.*)

837A. *Review:* Neuere Beobachtungen über fremde Länder und Sitten. Grösstentheils nach englischen, russischen und französischen Journalen verdeutscht. Basel: Flick, 1785. 436 S. 8°. (Allgemeine deutsche Bibliothek. Berlin, 1786. 8°. Bd. 65, p. 463–464, *NAA.*)
Contains excerpts from Sprengel's *Geschichte der Revolution von Nord-Amerika* (see nos. 823, 824).

837B. *Review:* Neueste Erdkunde, welche Asien, Afrika, Europa, Amerika...nebst einem Anhange von der natürlichen und wissenschaftlichen Erdkunde aus den neuesten und zuverlässigsten Reisebeschreibungen, historischen Zeitund andern Schriften enthält, nebst einer neuen Weltkarte, worauf Cooks und andrer Reisen befindlich. Nürnberg und Altdorf: b. Monath [n. d.]. 391 S. 8°. (Allgemeine Literatur-Zeitung. Jena, 1785. 4°. Jahr 1785, Bd. 2, col. 193–195, *NAA.*)
The reviewer names as the author, Herr Walthers, Hofmeister in Hof, and claims that the map shows only one American town, Philadelphia.

## GERMAN WORKS RELATING TO AMERICA   101

*1785, continued*

837C. *Review:* Des Pater Labat Reisen nach Westindien im amerikanischen Meer liegenden Inseln. Nach der neuesten Pariser Ausgabe übersetzt...von G. Friedr. Cas. Schad. IV. Band. Nürnberg: Bey G. N. Raspe, 1784. 24 Bogen. 8°. (Allgemeine deutsche Bibliothek. Berlin, 1785. 8°. Bd. 63, p. 218–219, *NAA*.)

838. *Review:* Sammlung von Bildnissen der im amerikanischen Kriege berühmt gewordenen Männer, nach Gemälden von M. Dusimitier in Philadelphia. Philadelphia: Bey R. Wilkinson [1785?]. 4°. (Neue Bibliothek der schönen Wissenschaften und freyen Künste. Leipzig, 1785. 12°. Bd. 30, p. 157, *NAA*.)
Etchings by B. B. C. after Du Simitière's paintings, representing Silas Deane, J. Dickinson, W. H. Drayton, General Gates, S. Huntington, John Jay, H. Laurens, Gouverneur Morris, General Reed, General Steuben, E. Thomson, and General Washington.
See no. 691.

839. *Review:* Unterricht vom Blitz und den Blitz- oder Wetterableitern, zur Belehrung und Beruhigung, sonderlich der Ungelehrten und des gemeinen Mannes. Mit einer Kupfertafel. Von Johann Friedrich Lutz, Ober-Caplan zu Gunzenhausen. Frankfurt und Leipzig: Bey Weigel und Schneider. 11 Bogen. 8°. (Allgemeine deutsche Bibliothek. Berlin, 1785. 12°. Bd. 60, p. 170–172, *NAA*.)
"Zuerst giebt der Verfasser eine zwar kurze, aber genaue Geschichte der Blitzableiter [Benjamin Franklin]..."

840. *Review:* Voyage de Mr. le Chevalier de Castellux en Amerique. [n. p.] 1785. 228 S. 8°. (Göttingische Anzeigen von gelehrten Sachen. Göttingen [1785]. 12°. Jahr 1785, p. 663–664, \**DF*.)
This work by the Marquis de Chastellux was published first in the *Cahiers de Lecture* in Gotha, then under the titles *Voyage en Amérique*, Leipzig, 1785, and *Voyage de Mr. le chevalier de Castellux en Amérique*, Cassel, 1785 (a surreptitious edition; see Library of Congress card). The first German translation has the title, *Des Ritters von Chastellüx Reisebeobachtungen über Amerika*, Hamburg, 1785 (Sabin 12231). In 1786, the following German versions were published: 1. *Reisebeobachtungen über Amerika*, Hamburg: Chaidron (Sabin 12232); and 2. *Reisen durch Amerika; aus dem Französischen*, Wien: Schaumburg. Hildegard Meyer lists an edition, *Reise durch Amerika. Aus dem Französischen*, Frankfurt und Leipzig, 1786 (see *Uebersee-Geschichte*, v. 3, p. 164, *BAA*). Sabin 12232.
Chastellux, a member of the French Academy, traveled in America; he gives a detailed geographical description of North America as well as his impressions of the American people, *cf.* Thelma Evans, *European impressions of America*, Madison, Wisconsin, June, 1925, t I.
Note also his *Abhandlung über die Vortheile und Nachtheile, die für Europa aus der Entdeckung von Amerika entstehen*, Halle, 1788. Not in the Library.

840A. *Review:* Voyage de Mr. le Chevalier Chastellux en Amérique. n. p. 1785. 228 S. 8°. (Allgemeine Literatur-Zeitung. Jena, 1785. 4°. Jahr 1785, Bd. 2, p. 42–43, *NAA*.)

841. *Review:* A Voyage to the Pacific Ocean. Undertaken... To termine [*sic!*] the Position and Extent in the West Side of Nord [*sic!*] America... Performed under... Captain Cook, Clerke, and Gore... London: T. Cadell, 1784. 3 v. 4°; 1 v. f°. (Neue Bibliothek der schönen Wissenschaften und der freyen Künste. Leipzig, 1785. 12°. Bd. 30, p. 165–166, *NAA*.)
The Library's copies of this edition of Cook's "Voyages" are in †† *KF* and ††† *KF*.

841A. *Review:* A voyage to the Pacific Ocean. Undertaken... To determine The Position and Extent of the West Side of North America... Performed under... Captain Cook, Clerk and Gore... London, n. d. 4°. 3 v. (Allgemeine Literatur-Zeitung. Jena, 1785. 4°. Jahr 1785, Bd. 4, p. 329–344, 365–368, 381–382, *NAA*.)

841B. *Review:* Zusammenkünfte am Atlas zu Kenntniss der Länder, Völker und ihrer Sitten herausgegeben für die Jugend. Erster Theil. Gotha: Bey Ettinger, 1785. 199 S. 8°. (Allgemeine Literatur-Zeitung. Jena, 1786. 4°. Jahr 1786, Bd. 1, col. 108–109, *NAA*.)

1786

842. ABRISS der Begebenheiten. (Historisches Portefeuille zur Kenntnis der gegenwärtigen und vergangenen Zeit. Wien, 1786. 12°. Jahrg. 5, Bd. 1, p. 100–115, 241–261, 756–780; Bd. 2, p. 100–126, 648–668.) BAA
Many references to America.

843. AKTE zur Befestigung und Erhaltung der Religionsfreyheit, errichtet in der Versammlung des Staats von Virginien zu Anfange des Jahres 1786. (Historisches Portefeuille zur Kenntnis der gegenwärtigen und vergangenen Zeit. Wien, 1786. 12°. Jahrg. 5, Bd. 2, p. 659–663.) BAA
Note articles on Virginia [and the Bahamas] in *Physikalische Arbeiten der einträchtigen Freunde in Wien*, Wien, 1783–86. Not in the Library.
See no. 875.

843A. [ANDERSON, JAMES.] Beschreibung des Berges Morne-Garou auf der Jnsel St. Vincent, und des Feuerberges auf seinem Gipfel. Jn einem Briefe von Hrn. James Anderson... illus. (Historisches Portefeuille zur Kenntnis der gegenwärtigen und vergangenen Zeit. Wien, 1786. 12°. Jahrg. 5, Bd. 2, p. 583–608.) BAA
West Indies.
The illustration is missing in the Library's copy.

844. ANKÜNDIGUNG einiger Schriften für die deutsche Jugend in Nord Carolina, von einer Gesellschaft Helmstädtischen Professoren. (In: A. L. Schlözer. Stats-Anzeigen. Göttingen, 1786. 12°. Bd. 9, p. 494–496.) BAC

845. ANMERKUNGEN aus der neuen und alten Welt bey Gelegenheit der Beschreibung des Siebenjährigen Seekrieges zwischen England und den amerikanischen Staaten, in Briefen abgefasset, für Leser, die darüber denken wollen. Berlin, 1786. 482 p., 1 l. 19 cm. BAC
"Vorbericht" signed: R\*\*\*.
Reviews: *Allgemeine Literatur-Zeitung*, Jahr 1789, Bd. 1, col. 737–740, *NAA*; *Allgemeine deutsche Bibliothek*, Anhang zu Bd. 53–86, p. 929, *NAA*.

*1786, continued*

846. DIE ART der Indianer in Nordamerika, Krieg zu führen. (Historisches Portefeuille zur Kenntnis der gegenwärtigen und vergangenen Zeit. Wien, 1786. 12°. Jahrg. 5, Bd. 1, p. 701-706.) BAA
From Jeremy Belknap's *The history of New-Hampshire*, London & Philadelphia, 1784, * KD.
See no. 872A.

847. AUSMESSUNGEN in den Amerikanischen Staaten. (Der Teutsche Merkur. Weimar, 1786. 12°. Jahr 1786, Vierteljahr 3 [Bd. 55], p. 82-84.) *DF (Neue)
"Diese Ausmessungen wurden auf Befehl des Congresses unternommen, und demselben im August 1785 vorgelegt."
This periodical subsequently called *Der Neue teutsche Merkur*, under which it is shelved.

848. BESCHREIBUNG des berühmten Wasserfalls von Niagara in Nordamerika. (Auswahl kleiner Reisebeschreibungen und anderer statistischen und geographischen Nachrichten. Leipzig, 1786. 12°. Theil 4, p. 958-965.) KBC

849. BRETZNER, CHRISTIAN FRIEDRICH. Das Räuschgen. Ein Lustspiel in vier Akten von C. F. Bretzner. Leipzig: Bei Friedrich Gotthold Jacobäer, 1786. (Reprinted in: Adolph Hauffen. Das Drama der klassischen Periode... Stuttgart [1891]. 8°. Teil 1, p. 315-398.) NGB
Added title page: Deutsche National-Litteratur, Bd. 138.
"Einen deutschen Offizier mit seiner amerikanischen Frau auf deutschem Boden zeigt Bretzners Lustspiel; 'Das Räuschgen.'" — G. Descayk, in *Deutsch-amerikanische historische Gesellschaft von Illinois, Jahrbuch, 1924-1925, p. 39, IEK.*
See also J. A. Walz, in *Modern language notes*, Baltimore, 1901, v. 16, p. 227-229, *RAA*, who analyzes the references to America occurring in the play.

850. CAMPE, JOACHIM HEINRICH. Sammlung interessanter und durchgängig zweckmässig abgefasster Reisebeschreibungen für die Jugend von J. H. Campe. Erster [-Zwölfter] Theil. Reutlingen: Gedruckt bey Johannes Grözinger, 1786-1796. 12 v. in 7. map, plate. 8°. *KF 1786
The narratives are all abridged. Of special interest: v. 3. Beschreibung einer Reise um die Erdkugel, angestellt von dem englischen Commodore Byron im Jahre 1764 und vollendet im Jahr 1766. Beschreibung einer Reise um die Erdkugel, angestellt von dem brittischen Schifskapitain Samuel Wallis in dem Jahre 1766 und vollendet im Jahre 1768. Beschreibung einer Reise um die Erdkugel, angestellt von dem brittischen Schifskapitain Philipp Carteret, in dem Jahre 1766 und vollendet im Jahre 1669 [i.e. 1769]. v. 4 Das Interessanteste aus Johann Carver's Reisen, durch die innern Gegenden von Nordamerika (see no. 642 and Sabin 10303; J. H. Campe, *Das Interessanteste aus Joh. Carver's Reisen durch Nordamerika*, Braunschweig, 1788, not in the Library), v. 5. Beschreibung einer Reise um die Erdkugel, angestellt von dem englischen Schifskapitain Cook, und den Gelehrten Banks und Salander in den Jahren 1768-1771 (see no. 962). v. 6. Beschreibung einer Reise um die Erdkugel. The Wolfenbüttelsche Schul-Buchhandlung, "welche den... Zweck hat... die bisherigen Campischen Erziehungs-Schriften und Kinder-Bücher... zu einem Preise zu verbreiten, welcher ohne ein besonders buchhändlerisches Institut dieser Art nicht gehalten werden könnte" (quoted from *Nachricht*, p. 294) edited the *Sammlung* in 1786, in "Almanachs-Format" and in a so-called second edition both on Holländ Papier and Druckpapier. The Library has two volumes of the Wolfenbüttel (second) edition in *NAS*. Note also the edition published at Wien, 1807-08, 11 v., 9-*NASZ*.

851. CLAUDIUS, MATTHIAS. Urians Reise um die Welt... (Musen Almanach für 1786. Herausgegeben von Voss und Gocking [*sic!*]. Hamburg: Bey Carl Ernst Bohn [1786]. 24°. p. 166-171.) NFA
"Nun war ich in Amerika;
Da sagt'ich zu mir: "Lieber!
Nordwestpassage ist doch da;
Mach dich einmal darüber!"

"Von hier ging ich nach Mexico,
Ist weiter als nach Bremen,
Da, dacht ich, liegt das Gold wie Stroh,
Du sollst 'n Sack voll nehmen."

852. CLAVIJERO, FRANCISCO-JAVIER. Des Herrn Abts Clavigero Abhandlung von der natürlichen Beschaffenheit des Königreichs Mexico und der neuen Welt überhaupt. (Der Teutsche Merkur. Weimar, 1786. 12°. Jahr 1786, Vierteljahr 3 [Bd. 55], p. 3-52, 154-181; Vierteljahr 4 [Bd. 56], p. 30-43.) *DF (Neue)
Discusses the animals of North America.
This periodical subsequently called *Der Neue teutsche Merkur*, under which it is shelved.

853. COOK, JAMES. Neueste Reisebeschreibungen, oder Jacob Cook's dritte und letzte Reise, welche auf Befehl des Königs von England nach den Südinseln des stillen Meers und dann weiter nach den nordamerikanischen und asiatischen Küsten, um die Möglichkeit einer nördlichen Durchfahrt nach Europa zu entscheiden, in den Jahren 1776 bis 1780 unternommen worden. Erster [-Anderer] Band. Mit Kupfern. Nürnberg und Leipzig: Bey C. Weigel und Schneider, 1786. 2 v. in 1. 3 maps, 24 plates. 8°. *KF 1786
Sabin 16263.

853A. FORSTER, GEORG. Noch etwas über die Menschenrassen. (Der Teutsche Merkur. Weimar, 1786. 12°. Jahr 1786, Vierteljahr 4 [Bd. 56], p. 57-86, 150-166.) *DF (Neue)
Indians.
This periodical was subsequently called *Der Neue teutsche Merkur*, under which it is shelved.
See no. 1164A.

854. FRANKLIN, BENJAMIN. Dr. Benjamin Franklin über die Verfassung und das Interesse von Nordamerika. (Historisches Portefeuille zur Kenntnis der gegenwärtigen und vergangenen Zeit. Wien, 1786. 12°. Jahrg. 5, Bd. 2, p. 428-437.) BAA
Taken from *Gentleman's magazine*, July, 1786.
According to Kayser, v. 4, p. 96, Johann Jacob Meyen published *Franklin, der Philosoph und Staatsmann. In fuenf Gesaengen*, Alt-Stettin, 1787. The work is not in the Library. Verified through *Allgemeine deutsche Biographie*, v. 21, p. 553, * RR-AGK.
Note also Benjamin Franklin, *Freyer Wille, ein Werk für denkende Menschen, über die Macht des Zufalls*, Leipzig, 1787 (2te Auflage 1811). Kayser, v. 2, p. 252B.

854A. JONES. Ueber die physischen Merkwürdigkeiten des Sumpfs Diomal Swamp in Nordamerika. Vom Hrn. Jones, einem Einwohner der dortigen Gegend. (Magazin für das Neueste aus der Physik und Naturgeschichte. Gotha, 1786. 8°. Bd. 3, Stück 4, p. 56-65.) 3-OA

# GERMAN WORKS RELATING TO AMERICA 103

*1786, continued*

855. NACHRICHT von einem neuen Kirchenbuche der Amerikaner in Neuengland. (Historisches Portefeuille zur Kenntnis der gegenwärtigen und vergangenen Zeit. Wien, 1786. 12°. Jahrg. 5, Bd. 2, p. 98–100.) BAA
Translated from the *Political magasine* for May, 1786.
This article deals with *A Book of Common Prayer for the use of the first Episcopal Church established in America*, published after the American Revolution and using the suggestions of Mr. Lindsey, an English theologian.

856. NACHRICHT von einigen Merkwürdigkeiten in den Sitten der Nordamerikaner von den sechs vereinigten Nationen. (Historisches Portefeuille zu Kenntnis der gegenwärtigen und vergangenen Zeit. Wien, 1786. 12°. Jahrg. 5, Bd. 2, p. 271–277.) BAA
Excerpts from an essay in the "Philosophical Transactions," v. 76.

857. NACHRICHTEN von der Nation der Akensas in Nordamerika. (Auswahl kleiner Reisebeschreibungen und anderer statistischen und geographischen Nachrichten. Leipzig, 1786. 12°. Theil 4, p. 965–973.) KBC

858. NORDAMERIKANISCHE Nationalbank. Bedenklichkeiten gegen das Handlungsunternehmen nach Nordamerika. (Göttingische Anzeigen von gelehrten Sachen. Göttingen [1786]. 12°. Jahr 1786, p. 2035 et seq.) *DF
These pages are missing from the Library's copy.

859. PHYSIKALISCHE Beschaffenheit, Produkte, Regierungsform, Zustand der Sklaven und Handlung auf der Insel St. Domingue. (Historische Portefeuille zur Kenntnis der gegenwärtigen und vergangenen Zeit. Wien, 1786. 12°. Jahrg. 5, Bd. 2, p. 354–372.) BAA
"Ein Auszug aus *Voyage d'un Suisse dans différens Colonies d'Amerique*. 8. Neuchatel 1785."
The Library's copy of this work, ascribed to Justin Girod-Chantrans, is in * KF.

860. RAYNAL, GUILLAUME THOMAS FRANÇOIS. Geschichte der Revolution von Nord-America vom Abt Raynal. Nebst Anmerkungen über diese Geschichte von Thomas Payne, Staatssecretair des americanischen Congresses in dem Departement der auswärtigen Affairen. Aus dem Französischen übersetzt. Berlin: Im Verlage der Rellstabschen Buchdruckerey, 1786. 8 p.l., 368 p. 8°. *KF 1786
Vorbericht des Uebersetzers signed: F. H. Wernitz.
Following: "Vorerinnerung des Hn. Geh. Rath Dohm zu der Schrift des Hrn. Payne." See no. 834.
Note also an excerpt with the following title: *Raynals philosophische Beschreibung des Handels und der Besitzungen der Europäer in Asien und Amerika... Aus dem Französichen, Zweyte unveränderte Auflage,* Strassburg: Akademisches Buchhandlung, 1788.
At the end of the text by Raynal: Philadelphia den 21ten August, 1782.
See the following note in *Der Teutsche Merkur*, Anzeiger, Weimar, May, 1785, Bd. 50, p. LXXXXIV: "In meinem Verlage wird nächstens eine Uebersetzung der Revolution in Amerika vom Abt Raynal, nebst einer Berichtigung dieser Schrift vom Herrn Payne, Minister des Congresses in Amerika, erscheinen. Berlin, den 17. April 1785. C. F. Rellstab, Buchdrucker und Musikhändler."
Review: *Allgemeine Literatur-Zeitung*, Jahr 1786, Bd. 5, col. 225, *NAA*.
Note also Raynal's *Staatsveränderung von Amerika*.

*Aus dem Französischen*, Frankfurt und Leipzig, 1782. Sabin 68108. Not in the Library.
See no. 737.

861. SCHMIDT, CLAMOR EBERHARD KARL. An den Biber, aus dessen Haar Wisens Hut gemacht ist. (Musen Almanach. A. MDCCLXXXVI. Goettingen: Bey Joh. Christ. Dietrich [1786]. 32°. p. 116–117.) NFA
"Glücklich bist du, edler Biber,
"Aus dem fernen Kanada,
"Dessen Haar der Huterschäffer
"Sich zu diesem Hut ersah."

861A. SCHUBART, CHRISTIAN FRIEDRICH DANIEL. Der kalte Michel. Erzählung, 1786. (Reprinted in: Deutsche National-Litteratur... herausgegeben von Joseph Kürschner. Berlin und Stuttgart, n.d. 12°. Bd. 81, p. 405–408.) NFF
First printed in *Ch. F. D. Schubarts sämmtliche Gedichte. Von ihm selbst herausgegeben*, Stuttgart, 1786, Bd. 2, 247 ff. A humorous poem, "representing a nobleman who, having lost relatives and property, is on the brink of despair, but is cheered by the advice of his servant, who tells him to go to America." The last stanza follows:
"Und mir nichts, dir nichts, plötzlich
Floh er mit ihm davon!
Europa bleibt zurücke,
Sie machten bald ihr Glücke
Beim grossen Washington."
See J. T. Hatfield and E. Hochbaum, *The Influence of the American Revolution upon German literature*, New York [1900?], *NFC p.v.4*.

862. UEBER das Papiergeld in den Nordamerikanischen Freystaaten. (Historisches Portefeuille zur Kenntnis der gegenwärtigen und vergangenen Zeit. Wien, 1786. 12°. Jahrg. 5, Bd. 2, p. 641–644.) BAA
Excerpts from *A short address to the public on the pay of the British army, by an Officer, 1786*.

863. UEBERSICHT des gegenwärtigen Zustandes der Schiffart und des Handels von Neuschottland. (Historisches Portefeuille zur Kenntnis der gegenwärtigen und vergangenen Zeit. Wien, 1786. 12°. Jahrg. 5, Bd. 2, p. 397–419.) BAA
From *An account of the present State of Nova Scotia*, Edinburgh and London, 1786. See no. 907.
Two other excerpts from the same work appeared in *Niederelbisches historisch-politisch-literarisches Magazin*, 1787, Bd. 1, Stück 1, and in *Beyträge zur Völker und Länderkunde*, Theil 7. Neither is in the Library.

864. VELTHUSEN, JOHANN CASPAR. Einige Nachricht von der evangelischen Kirchenverfassung in Nordcarolina; insonderheit von den Schicksalen und Bemühungen des im J. 1773 ...dahin abgesandten Predigers, Herrn Adolph Nüssmann... (Hannoverisches Magazin... vom Jahre 1786, 1788. Hannover, 1787–89. Jahrg. 24, col. 1441–1456; Jahrg. 26, col. 773–780.) *DF
Title pages dated 1787, 1789; contents, 1786, 1788.

864A. *Review:* Der Americaner. Ein Lustspiel in einem Aufzuge nach dem Inhalte des le Sauvage, von Pleissner, Schauspieler. Frankfurt bey Fleischer, 1783. 5 Bogen. 8°. (Allgemeine deutsche Bibliothek. Berlin, 1786. 8°. Bd. 69, p. 102–103, *NAA*.)
"In dem Americaner sind wohl noch hie und da leidliche Gedanken, obgleich das Sujet nicht neu (das Sujet ist ja auch im Huron bearbeitet), Dialog und Bearbeitung aber sind unbeschreiblich schlecht."

**1786,** *continued*

**865.** *Review:* Bericht für diejenigen, welche nach Nord-Amerika sich begeben und alldort ansiedeln wollen. A. d. Engl. des berühmten Doktors Benjamin Franklin. Hamburg: Bey Albers, 1786. 48 S. 8°. (Allgemeine Literatur-Zeitung. Jena, 1786. 4°. Jahr 1786, Bd. 5, col. 632, *NAA.*)
Sabin 25515.
Paragraph, under "Literarische Nachrichten," commences: Kleine geogr. Schriften.
Translation of Benjamin Franklin's *Remarks for the information of those who wish to become settlers.*

**866.** *Review:* Beyträge zur Völker- und Länderkunde. Herausgegeben von M. C. Sprengel. Leipzig: In der Weygandschen Buchhandlung, 1786. Fünfter Theil, 300 p. 8°. Sechster Theil, 296 p. 8°. (Allgemeine Literatur-Zeitung. Jena, 1786. 4°. Jahr 1786, Bd. 5, col. 307–308, *NAA.*)
Part v contains: no. 1. Ramsay's Versuch über die Behandlung der Negersklaven in den Westindischen Zuckerinseln. No. 3: Unangebaute Gegenden des Nordamerikanischen Freystaates. No. 4: Entgegnung zu No. 1.

**867.** *Review:* Briefe über Amerika; nach der neuesten, verbesserten und mit dem dritten Theile vermehrte Ausgabe aus dem Italienischen des Grafen Carlo Carli übersetzt und mit einigen Anmerkungen versehen von Christi. Gottfr. Hennig. I. Theil. Gera 1785... 2. Thl. eb. 1785...3. Thl. eb. 1785. 8°. (Litterarische Annalen der Geschichtskunde. Bayreuth, 1786. 8°. Jahr 1786, p. 355, *BAA.*)
*See* no. 830, 831.

**867A.** *Review:* Briefe über Amerika, nach der neuesten, verbesserten und mit dem dritten Theile vermehrten Ausgabe, aus dem Italiänischen des Grafen Carlo Carli übersetzt, und mit einigen Anmerkungen versehen von Christian Gottfried Hennig. Erster [-Dritter] Theil. Gera: Beckmann, 1785. 8°. (Allgemeine deutsche Bibliothek. Berlin, 1786. 12°. Bd. 68, p. 187–190, *NAA.*)

**867B.** *Review:* De La France et des Etats unis par Etienne Claviere et J. P. Brissot de Warville. London [i.e., Paris], 1786. 344 p. 8°. (Allgemeine Literatur-Zeitung. Jena, 1788. 4°. Jahr 1788, Bd. 3, col. 26–29, *NAA.*)
"Dies Werk ist ein Gegenstück zu Lord Sheffields bekannten Schriften über den Handel der americanischen Staaten und ihre Verfasser suchen darinn die Vortheile auseinander zu setzen, die Frankreich und die neue Republik von einem genauern Handelsverkehr künftig haben werden..."

**868.** *Review:* Des Moyens de conserver la Santé des Blancs et des Nègres, aux Antilles ou climats chauds et humides de l'Amérique. S. Domingo et Paris: Méquignon, 1786. 126 p. 8°. (Göttingische Anzeigen von gelehrten Sachen. Göttingen [1786]. 12°. Jahr 1786, p. 1193–1198, *DF.*)

**869.** *Review:* Ferdinand von Soto, oder Erster Kriegszug der Spanier durch Florida, aus dem Spanischen des Ynka Garcilasso de la Vega, ins französ. und daraus ins deutsche übersetzt von Gottfr. Konr. Böttger. Nordhausen: Bey Gross, 1785. 1ter Theil, 304 S., 2ter Theil 255 S. 8°. (Allgemeine Literatur-Zeitung. Jena, 1786. 4°. Jahr 1786, Bd. 3, col. 283–284, *NAA.*)
Sabin 98744.
According to Kayser, a second edition was published in 1796. For a reissue under the title, *Der tapfere Spanier während des Feldzuges in Florida,* Nordhausen, 1810, see Sabin 98761.
G. C. Böttger also translated Vega's *Primera parte de los Commentarios Reales* under the title *Geschichte der Ynkas, Könige von Peru. Von der Entstehung dieses Reichs bis zur Regierung seines letzten Königs Atahualpa,* Nordhausen, 1787[-88]; *Neue Auflage,* 1798. See Sabin 98747.
See no. 342.

**869A.** *Review:* Geographie zum Gebrauch der Schulen in den evangelischen Brüdergemeinen. ister Theil: Europa. 236 S. iiter Theil: die übrigen Erdtheile. 237–432 S. Barby und Leipzig: In Commission bey Kummer [n. d.]. (Allgemeine Literatur-Zeitung. Jena, 1786. 4°. Jahr 1786, Bd. 1, col. 77–78, *NAA.*)
"Aus der Vorrede ersehen wir, dass Hr. Carl Gotthold Reichel Verfasser von dieser neuen Erdbeschreibung ist, welcher, wie wir vernehmen, seit einiger Zeit als Inspector und Prediger der Brüdergemeinde in Nazareth in Pensylvanien vorsteht..."

**869B.** *Review:* Geographisches Spiel die Jugend von S. L. Hegard. Wien: Bey Hertel [n. d.]. 124 S. (Allgemeine Literatur-Zeitung. Jena, 1785. 4°. Jahr 1785, Bd. 3, col. 280, *NAA.*)

**869C.** *Review:* Geschichte der neuesten Weltbegebenheiten im Grossen. Aus dem Engl. Elfter Band. Leipzig: In der Weygandschen Buchhandlung, 1789. 534 p. 8°. (Allgemeine Literatur-Zeitung. Jena, 1786. 4°. Jahr 1786, Bd. 4, col. 324–326, *NAA.*)
"Die Kriegsvorfälle in America zwischen den Engländern und ihren ehemaligen Colonien...machen den Anfang... Bittschrift der Stadt London an den König, wider die Fortsetzung des americanischen Krieges..."
See no. 834B, 834C.

**869D.** *Review:* Herrn Friedrich Osterwalds historische Erdbeschreibung, zum Nutzen deutscher Jugend eingerichtet. Vierte verbesserte Ausgabe... Strassburg: In Treutels Buchhandlung, 1785. 544 S. 8°. (Allgemeine deutsche Bibliothek. Berlin, 1786. 4°. Bd. 69, p. 189–193, *NAA.*)
The reviewer states: "Neuyork ist 2463, nicht 2663 Quadratmeilen... Die Hauptstadt in Neujersey heisst Perth Amboy, nicht Port Amyboy. Süd-Karolina hat 1160, nicht 1600 Quadratmeilen."

**870.** *Review:* Des Herrn Ritters von Chastellux Reise durch Amerika. Aus dem Französischen. Frankfurt und Leipzig: B. Stahel, 1786. 213 Seiten. 8°. (Allgemeine Literatur-Zeitung. Jena, 1786. 4°. Jahr 1786, Bd. 5, col. 535–536, *NAA.*)
"Diese Reise is zuerst in den Gothaischen *Cahiers de Lecture* erschienen," edited by H. A. O. Reichard and published at Gotha, 1784–94. This production, previously published under the title, *Journal de Lecture,* v. 1–8, Dessau and Gotha, 1782–83, contains many articles relating to America. It is not in the Library.
See no. 840.

# GERMAN WORKS RELATING TO AMERICA

*1786, continued*

871. *Review:* Histoire de Kentucke, nouvelle colonie à l'ouest de la Virginie;...ouvrage pour servir de suite aux lettres d'un cultivateur Américain. Traduit de l'anglois de M. John Filson, par M. Parraud. Paris: Bey Buisson, 1785. 232 S. 8°. (Allgemeine Literatur-Zeitung. Jena, 1786. 4°. Jahr 1786, Bd. 1, col. 553-554, *NAA.*)
Sabin 24338. A German version is mentioned by Sabin (24339): J. Filson, *Reise nach Kentucke und Nachrichten von dieser neu angebaueten Landschaft in Nordamerika. Aus dem Englischen übersetzt,* Leipzig, 1790. Another translation appeared in *Bibliothek der neuesten Reisebeschreibungen,* Nürnberg, 1790, Bd. 12, Abt. 2. Not in the Library.
"...die Entdeckung und erste Besitznehmung dieser schoenen Gegend war dem Obristen Boon im Jahre 1769 aufbehalten: die Geschichte seiner Abentheuer, und der Pflanzer, die er dahin führte, machen eine eigne hier mitgetheilte Erzählung aus, die sehr unterhaltend, und in den Reichardschen Cahiers de lecture von diesem Jahre abgedruckt ist... Der Uebersetzer hat verschiedene Zusätze hinzugefügt, die seiner Uebersetzung einen Vorzug vor dem Original geben..."
See also no. 815.

872. *Review:* Histoire de Kentucke, nouvelle colonie à l'ouest de la Virginie; avec une Carte: ouvrage pour servir de suite aux Lettre d'un cultivateur Americain. Traduit de l'Anglois de M. Joh. Filson, par M. Parraud. A Paris, 1785. 8°. (Litterarische Annalen der Geschichtskunde. Bayreuth, 1786. 12°. Jahr 1786, p. 357-358, *BAA.*)
*See* no. 871.

872A. *Review:* The History of New Hampshire. v. 1. By Ieremy [*sic!*] Belknap. 1785. 8°. (Litterarische Annalen der Geschichtskunde. Bayreuth, 1786. 12°. Jahr 1786, p. 163, *BAA.*)
"Der Verfasser lebt zu Philadelphia und ist Mitglied der dortigen philosophischen Gesellschaft. Das Werk ist mit Einsicht und Unparteylichkeit geschrieben..."
The Library has copies of this work.
See also no. 846.

872B. *Review:* J. H. Campe geographisches Kartenspiel: ein Weihnachtsgeschenk für Kinder und junge Leute, nebst 300 geogr. Spielkärtchen u.e. geogr. Umriss von Deutschland. Hamburg [Bohn], 1784. 8°. (Allgemeine Literatur-Zeitung. Jena, 1785. 4°. Jahr 1785, Bd. 4, col. 62, *NAA.*)

872C. *Review:* Joh. Leonhard Neusingers... Erdbeschreibung für Kinder, enthaltend Asien, Afrika, Amerika und die neuentdeckten Länder ...zum Gebrauche auch auf Schulen. Nürnberg: Bey Grattenauer [n.d.]. 16 Bogen. 8°. (Allgemeine Literatur-Zeitung. Jena, 1786. 4°. Jahr 1786, Bd. 1, col. 98-99, *NAA.*)
Has a special chapter called Russisch Amerika.

872D. *Review:* Konge Vetenskaps Academiens Nya Handlingar. Tom. vii. för Ar 1786. Stockholm: J. G. Lange, 1786. 323 S. 8°. (Allgemeine Literatur-Zeitung. Jena, 1787. 4°. Jahr 1787, Bd. 3, col. 14-15, *NAA.*)
Conclusion of Fahlberg's notes on St. Bartholomy. See no. 913B.

873. *Review:* Medical Commentaries; for the year 1781-1782; exhibiting a concise view of the latest and most important Discoveries in Medicine and Medical Philosophy. Collected and published by A. Duncan. London: C. Dilly & J. Murray, 1783. v. VIII. 457 p. (Göttingische Anzeigen von gelehrten Sachen. Göttingen [1786]. 12°. Jahr 1786, p. 1801-1807, * *DF.*)
Contains an essay, entitled: Ueber die Vorbereitung und Lebensordnung bey der Einimpfung und über die Behandlung der natürlichen Blattern in Westindien, by J. Makittrick Adair.

873A. *Review:* Neuere Beobachtungen über fremde Länder und Sitten. Grössentheils nach englischen, russischen und französischen Journalen verdeutscht. Basel: Bey Flick, 1786. 436 S. 8°. (Allgemeine Literatur-Zeitung. Jena, 1786. 4°. 1786, Bd. 4, col. 456, *NAA.*)

873B. *Review:* Neueste Erdbeschreibung aller vier Theile der Welt und der wenig bekannten Länder nebst einer mathematischen Beschreibung der Erdkugel. Vorzüglich zum Unterricht der Jugend aufgesetzt...von H. A. Kunstmann. Berlin: Bey dem Verfasser und in Commission der Hessischen Buchhandlung, 1786. 649 S. 8°. (Allgemeine Literatur-Zeitung. Jena, 1786. 4°. Jahr 1786, Bd. 5, col. 221-222, *NAA.*)
"Weit besser ist verhältnissmässig Amerika gerathen, ob es gleich auch sehr viele Fehler hat."

873C. *Review:* Neueste Erdkunde, welche Asien, Afrika, Europa, Amerika, die Südländer oder den fünften Welttheil...enthält... Nürnberg und Altdorf: Bey Monath, 1785. 8°. (Allgemeine deutsche Bibliothek. Berlin, 1786. 8°. Bd. 66, p. 172-174, *NAA.*)
The author is F. L. Walther.

874. *Review:* Des Paters Labat Reisen nach Westindien nach der neuesten Pariser Ausgabe übersetzt von G. Fr. Casimir Schad. Erster Band. Nürnberg: Im Raspenschen Verlage, 1786. 1 Alph. 4½ B., 2 B. Kupfer. (Allgemeine Literatur-Zeitung. Jena, 1786. 4°. Jahr 1786, Bd. 5, col. 347-348, *NAA.*)
Note also *Des Paters Labats Abhandlung vom Zucker, dessen Bau, Zubereitung und mancherley Gattungen,* Nürnberg: Bey Raspe, 1785. 1 Alph., 6 Bogen. 8°. Not in the Library. Authority: *Litterarische Annalen der Geschichtskunde...für das Jahr 1786,* Beyreuth und Leipzig, 1786, p. 73-74, *BAA.*

875. *Review:* Physikalische Arbeiten der einträchtigen Freunde in Wien: aufgesammlet von Ignaz, Edlen von Born. Des zweyten Jahrganges erstes Quartal. Mit Kupfern. Wien: Bey Christian Fridrich Wapler, 1786. 128 S. 4°. (Allgemeine Literatur-Zeitung. Jena, 1786. 4°. Jahr 1786, Bd. 5, col. 62, *NAA.*)
Contains as No. 5: Hrn Prof. Märters Nachrichten von den Bahamischen Inseln. See note on 843.

876. *Review:* Reise eines Schweitzers in verschiedene Colonien in America während dem letzten Krieg nebst einer kurzen Relation von dem Seetreffen vom 12ten April 1782. Aus dem Französischen. Leipzig, 1786. 19 Bogen. 8°. (Allgemeine Literatur-Zeitung. Jena, 1786. 4°. Jahr 1786, Bd. 5, col. 257-259, *NAA.*)
Sabin 69145; verified from Kayser, v. 4, p. 479A. Translation of Sabin 27510 and 100812. See also note on no. 859 of this list.

*1786, continued*

**876A.** *Review:* Reise nach dem stillen Ocean auf Befehl des Königs von Grossbrittanien unternommen, Entdeckungen in der nördlichen Halbkugel zu machen etc. In einigen Auszügen aus dem Englischen übersetzt. Mit einer Reisekarte und Kupfer. Frankfurt an der Oder: Straus, 1785. 208 S. 8°. (Allgemeine Literatur-Zeitung. Jena, 1786. 4°. Jahr 1786, Bd. 1, col. 207-208, *NAA*.)
One of the illustrations represents a dance in Haiti.

**876B.** *Review:* Reisecorrespondenz in, durch und aus allen fünf Theilen der Welt. Erster Band. Quedlinburg: Bey Ernst, 1786. 213 S. 8°. (Allgemeine Literatur-Zeitung. Jena, 1786. 4°. Jahr 1786, Bd. 5, col. 350, *NAA*.)
A collection of articles which appeared previously in German magazines.

**876C.** *Review:* A Sketch of the history of Jamaica... London, 1785. 8°. (Litterarische Annalen der Geschichtskunde. Bayreuth, 1786. 12°. Jahr 1786, p. 162, *BAA*.)
"Alte und neue Geschichte dieser Jnsel von einem Manne, der dort geboren worden, Plantagen daselbst besitzt und lange dort gelebt hat."

**877.** *Review:* Staatsgesetze der dreyzehn vereinigten amerikanischen Staaten; aus dem Franz. übersetzt. Dessau und Leipzig, 1785. (Litterarische Annalen der Geschichtskunde. Bayreuth, 1786. 12°. Jahr 1786, p. 76, *BAA*.)

**877A.** *Review:* Statistische Uebersicht der vornehmsten deutschen und sämtlichen europäischen Staaten, in Ansehung ihrer Grösse und Bevölkerung ihres Finanz- und Kriegszustandes; mit einem Anhange gleichen Inhalts über den Nordamerikanischen Freystaat. [n. p.,] 1786. 8°. (Allgemeine Literatur-Zeitung. Jena, 1786. 4°. Jahr 1786, Bd. 3, col. 339-343, *NAA*.)
"S. 136 folgt der Nordamerikanische Freystaat, der auf 40 bis 45000 Q.M., mithin um mehrere Tausend gevierte Meilen zu gross angegeben wird. Die Volkszahl aber ist jetzt wahrscheinlich viel grösser als 2.363.300 Seelen... Wahrscheinlich ist der einsichtsvolle Verf[asser] ein Mann, der in einem praktischen Amte steht, und deshalb seines Namens nicht nennen durfte."
The anonymous author is J. A. F. Randel.

**877B.** *Review:* Statistische Uebersicht der vornehmsten Deutschen und sämmtlichen Europäischen Staaten, in Ansehung ihrer Grösse, Bevölkerung, ihres Finanz- und Kriegszustandes. Mit einem Anhange gleichen Inhalts über den Nordamerikanischen Frey-Staat. [n. p.,] 1786. 162 S. f°. (Göttingische Anzeigen von gelehrten Sachen. Göttingen [1786]. 12°. Jahr 1786, p. 1710-1711, \**DF*.)

**877C.** *Review:* Voyage d'un Suisse dans différentes colonies d'Amérique, pendant la dernière guerre avec une table d'observations météorologiques faites à Saint-Dominique. Neufchâtel: Bey der typographischen Gesellschaft, 1785. 416 S. 8°. (Allgemeine Literatur-Zeitung. Jena, 1786. 4°. Jahr 1786, Bd. 1, col. 154-157, *NAA*.)

*1787*

**878.** ABRISS der Begebenheiten. (Historisches Portefeuille zur Kenntnis der gegenwärtigen und vergangenen Zeit. Wien, 1787. 12°. Jahrg. 6, Bd. 1, p. 108-136.) BAA
Many references to America.
The Library does not have Jahrg. 7 (1788) of this periodical, which contains a "Beytrag zur Statistik von Neu York."

**878A.** ARCHENHOLZ, JOHANN WILHELM VON. Anzeiger des Teutschen Merkur, Julius 1787. Theil 5. (Der Teutsche Merkur. Weimar [1787]. 8°. Jahr 1787, Vierteljahr. 3 [Bd. 59], p. xcii-xcviii, \**DF, Neue.*)
This periodical subsequently called *Der Neue teutsche Merkur*, under which it is shelved.
In a letter, dated Hamburg, June 9, 1787, Archenholz announces his plan to translate the *British Mercury*. Several references to America.

**879.** AUSZUG aus einem Briefe. (Auswahl kleiner Reisebeschreibungen und anderer statistischen und geographischen Nachrichten. Leipzig, 1787. 12°. Theil 5, p. 213-231.) KBC
Dated: Mainz June 10th, 1782.
Contains a poem, entitled "Auf Amerika" by Isaak Mauss, 1748-1833, a farmer of Badenheim, a village in the Palatine.
"Amerika ficht tapfer für die Rechte,
Für Freiheit, ein zu edles Gut!
Es badet sich in Heldenblut,
Und nicht in Thränen feiger Knechte.
Bellona sieht's, und schwingt die Freiheitsfahne,
Hoch über ihre Scheitel her:
Der Neid stürzt sich ins wilde Meer,
Und rast im wütenden Orkane."
As to Isaac Mauss, see *Deutsches Museum*, Leipzig, 1784, [Jahr 1784,] Bd. 1, p. 23-29, \**DF*.

**880.** AUTHENTISCHER Beweis von dem unglücklichen Zustande einiger Nordamerikanischen Provinzen. (Historisches Portefeuille zur Kenntnis der gegenwärtigen und vergangenen Zeit. Wien, 1787. 12°. Jahrg. 6, Bd. 1, p. 545-558.) BAA
"Rede des Oberrichters Pendleton, an die grosse Jury von Georgetown, Cherawa, und Camden in Carolina, im November 1786."
"Wenn die Erzählungen von Nordamerica's jetzigem unglücklichen Zustand bloss durch englische Zeitungs-Nachrichten, und durch wahre oder erdichtete Briefe misvergnügter, in ihren Speculationen hintergangener Kaufleute belegt werden, so verdiente sie keine Aufmerksamkeit. Aber diese Rede auf einer provinzial Versammlung ist mehr, und ihr Zutrauen versagen wollen, würde entweder Parteylichkeit seyn, oder es hiesse den historischen Scepticismus zu weit treiben."
*— Editor's note.*

**881.** BEMERKUNGEN über die Religion, Gebräuche, Diät und Medicin der Negern. (Auswahl kleiner Reisebeschreibungen und anderer statistischen und geographischen Nachrichten. Leipzig, 1787. 12°. Theil 5, p. 46-51.) KBC

**882.** BESCHREIBUNG der afrikanischen Küste, wo man mit Sklaven handelt; imgleichen des Charakters, der Sitten und Neigungen der Neger-Sklaven, welche man aus Afrika bringt. (Hannoversches Magazin... vom Jahre 1787. Hannover, 1788. 4°. Jahrg. 25, col. 785-814, 817-826.) \**DF*
Translation from the French.
Title page dated 1788; contents, 1787.
"Die Neger sind nicht, wie man's in Amerika faelschlich sagt, der Vernunft und der Tugend beraubt ...Alle Negern, welche aus Guinea oder aus den Jnseln sind, Maenner und Weiber, haben einmal in ihrem Leben die venerische Krankheit."

*1787, continued*

883. BESCHREIBUNG der Insel Amat, von ihren Einwohnern Otahiti genannt. (Auswahl kleiner Reisebeschreibungen und anderer statistischen und geographischen Nachrichten. Leipzig, 1787. 12°. Theil 5, p. 248-268.) KBC
Treats Haiti.
Bibliographical notes, p. 264-268.

884. BESCHREIBUNG der Schwedischen Insel St. Barthelemy in Westindien...mit einer Charte. (Historisches Portefeuille zur Kenntnis der gegenwärtigen und vergangenen Zeit. Wien, 1787. 12°. Jahrg. 6, Bd. 1, p. 673-711.) BAA
Translated by M.
Taken from Sven Dahlmann's account, edited by the Erziehungsgesellschaft in Stockholm.
This is a translation of *Bescrifning om S. Barthelemy, swensk O uti Westindien, författad af Sv. Dahlmann*, Stockholm, 1786. The translator is J. G. Peter Möller.
Note also "Account of the Swedish Island of St. Bartholomew, in the West Indies," *Monthly magazine and American review*, New York, 1800, v. 3, p. 68, *DA*, and Amandus Johnson, *The Swedes in America*, 1638-1900, Philadelphia, 1914, *IEP*.

885. BETRACHTUNGEN über die Månner-Wochen, und über die freywilligen Verstümmelungen unter verschiedenen Völkern. (Göttingisches historisches Magazin. Hannover, 1787. 8°. Bd. 1, p. 26-39.) BAA (Neues)
Signed: M (i.e., Christoph Meiners, 1747-1810).
Periodical subsequently called *Neues göttingisches historisches Magazin*, under which it is shelved.

886. BÜRGSDORF, FRIEDRICH AUGUST LUDWIG VON. Ueber die in den Waldungen der Kurmark-Brandenburg befindlichen einheimischen und in etlichen Gegenden eingebrachten fremden Holzarten. (Gesellschaft naturforschende Freunde zu Berlin. Schriften. Berlin, 1787. 8°. Bd. 7, p. 236-266.) 3-*EE
Discusses trees and plants imported from North America.
Review: *Forst Archiv*, Bd. 2, p. 24-25, *VQN*.

887. CHARAKTER, Zustand und Anzahl der Indianer in Nordamerika. (Historisches Portefeuille zur Kenntnis der gegenwärtigen und vergangenen Zeit. Wien, 1787. 12°. Jahrg. 6, Bd. 2, p. 144-154.) BAA
Taken from J. F. D. Smyth's *Tour in the United States of America*, London, 1784, v. 2.
With an explanatory note by the translator.
Note also several articles on the Indian tribes in *Magasin für die Naturgeschichte des Menschen* [ed. Karl Grosse], Bd. 1-3, Zittau und Leipzig, 1788-1791, which is not in the Library.

887A. COOK, JAMES. Capitain Cooks dritte und letzte Reise, oder Geschichte einer Entdeckungsreise nach dem stillen Ocean, welche auf Befehl Sr. Grossbritannischen Majestät, zu genauerer Erforschung der nördlichen Halbkugel unternommen, und unter Anführung der Capitaine Cook, Clerke und Gore...während den Jahren 1776, 1777, 1778, 1779, und 1780 ausgeführt worden ist. Aus den Tagebüchern der Capitaine James Cook...James King... Eine Uebersetzung nach der zwoten grossen englischen Ausgabe...mit einigen Anmerkungen von Johann Ludwig Wetzel... Anspach: Auf Kosten des Uebersetzers gedruckt mit Messerischen Schriften, 1787-1812. 5 v. frontis., maps, plates, ports., table. 8°. *KF 1787
Note also an edition with the imprint: Frankfurt an der Oder: Bey Strauss, 1785; Sabin 16264, also, Andreas Kippis, *Leben des Capitäns James Cook, aus dem Engl. von Wittenberg*, Hamburg, 1789. Neither is in the Library.

888. EINIGE Anmerkungen über die Aufbringung der öffentlichen Gelder in den Nordamerikanischen Freystaaten. (Historisches Portefeuille zur Kenntnis der gegenwärtigen und vergangenen Zeit. Wien, 1787. 12°. Jahrg. 6, Bd. 1, p. 45-49.) BAA
Excerpt from Gisbert Karl v. Hagendorp's doctoral thesis, *De acquabili descriptione subsidiorum inter Gentes foederatas*.
Hagendorp had been in America for seven months. On his return he took the degree of Doctor Iuris at the University of Leiden. Later, he was in the army of the Erbprinz von Nassau-Oranien.
"...das Verfahren in Hebung dieser Auflagen ist so fehlerhaft, so aeusserst willkuerlich und partheyisch, dass die Amerikaner dergleichen gewiss nicht ausgesezt gewesen sind, so lange sie unter Englands Herrschaft befindlich waren. Zu gleicher Zeit ist es ein Beweis, wie weit die Anarchie in diesen Staaten gegangen ist."

889. EINIGE Bemerkungen über das zwischen Grossbritannien und der Republik Holland im Jahr 1678 geschlossene Bündniss. (Historisches Portefeuille zur Kenntnis der gegenwärtigen und vergangenen Zeit. Wien, 1787. 12°. Jahrg. 6, Bd. 1, p. 635-672.) BAA
Refers to the American revolutionary war.

890. ERKLÄRUNG des hieroglyphischen Berichts, den ein Iroquoise von einem Feldzuge gegen die Englischen Colonien im Bündnisse mit Frankreich abgestattet hat. illus. (Historisches Portefeuille zur Kenntnis der gegenwärtigen und vergangenen Zeit. Wien, 1787. 12°. Jahrg. 6, Bd. 2, p. 53-55.) BAA
Accompanied by an etching representing symbols incorrectly called hieroglyphs; between p. 52-53.

891. ETWAS über eine Kolonie Måhrischer Brüder, oder: sogenannte Herrnhuter. Dann die eigentliche, ursprüngliche Bewohner der Eylande, Karaiben. (Auswahl kleiner Reisebeschreibungen und anderer statistischen und geographischen Nachrichten. Leipzig, 1787. 12°. Theil 5, p. 107-112.) KBC

892. GOETHE, JOHANN WOLFGANG. Die Mitschuldigen. Ein Lustspiel in Versen und drei Acten. (In his: Werke. Herausgegeben im Auftrage der Grossherzogin Sophie von Sachsen. Weimar: H. Böhlau, 1887-1919. 8°. Bd. 9, p. 39-115.) NFGK
This play is reprinted from Goethe's *Schriften*, Leipzig, 1787, Bd. 2, p. 1-80, in which edition he inserted two references to America. See p. 44 and 89.
See F. P. Reinsch, "Goethe's political interest prior to 1787," in *University of California, Publications in modern philology*, Berkeley, 1923, v. 10, p. 183-278, *STG*, Walter Wadepuhl, *Goethe's interest in the New World*, Jena, 1934, *NFF* p.v.107, for list of books on America and by Americans with which Goethe had come in contact (books in Goethe's private library, and books that he drew from the Grand-Ducal Library); also in H. S. White, "Goethe in Amerika,"

*1787, continued*

892. GOETHE, JOHANN WOLFGANG, *continued*
in *Goethe-Jahrbuch*, Frankfurt a. M., 1884, v. 5, p. 219–256, *NFGG*.

"Söller:
Ach, apropos, Papa! Man sagt mir heute früh,
In Deutschland gäb's ein Chor von braven jungen Leuten,
Die für Amerika Succurs und Geld bereiten.
Man sagt, es wären viel und hätten Muth genug,
Und wie das Frühjahr käm, so geh der ganze Zug."

893. HANDLUNGSNACHRICHTEN. (Historisches Portefeuille zur Kenntnis der gegenwärtigen und vergangenen Zeit. Wien, 1787. 12°. Jahrg. 6, Bd. 1, p. 62–81, 729–734.) BAA
References to the newly built free-port of the U. S. A. on the island of St. Mauritius, and to several matters concerning the West Indies, p. 79–80. Mention of a trade treaty between U. S. A. and Portugal, p. 730.

894. KURZE Geschichte der Meynungen roher Völker, von der Natur des Himmels, der Gestirne, der Erde, und der vornehmsten Natur-Erscheinungen am Himmel und auf der Erde. (Göttingisches historisches Magazin. Hannover, 1787. 12°. Bd. 1, p. 106–124.) BAA (Neues)
Periodical subsequently called *Neues göttingisches historisches Magazin*, under which it is shelved.

895. KURZE Geschichte des Adels unter den verschiedenen Völkern der Erde. (Göttingisches historisches Magazin. Hannover, 1787. 12°. Bd. 1, p. 385–441.) BAA (Neues)
Periodical subsequently called *Neues göttingisches historisches Magazin*, under which it is shelved.

896. MIRABEAU, HONORÉ GABRIEL RIQUETTI, COMTE DE. Des Grafen von Mirabeau Sammlung einiger philosophischen und politischen Schriften, die vereinigten Staaten von Nordamerica betreffend. Nebst einem Schreiben von demselben an den Uebersetzer. Aus dem Französischen. Berlin und Libau: Bei Lagarde und Friedrich, 1787. vi, 324 p., 1 l., frontis. 8°.
Sabin 49396.                                              * KF 1787
Caption-title: Betrachtungen über den Cincinnatusorden.
Translator's preface signed: Johann Brahl.
*Contents:* Betrachtungen über den Cincinnatusorden-Schreiben des Herrn Turgot, Staatsministers in Frankreich, an den Herrn Dr. Price. Bemerkungen über die Wichtigkeit der americanischen Revolution, und über die Mittel selbige der Welt nützlich zu machen. Von Richard Price... Betrachtungen über die vorstehende Schrift. Einzelne Anmerkungen zu dem Werke des Herrn Dr. Price. Schreiben des Verfassers an den Uebersetzer. The French original appeared in London, 1784, under the title, *Considérations sur l'ordre de Cincinnatus, ou Imitation d'un pamphlet anglo-américain,* * KF 1784. For further details, see Library of Congress card.
See A. B. Gardiner, *The institution of the Order of the Cincinnati and the connection with the order of the officers of the army and navy of France who took part in the War for American Independence* [n. p.], 1902, *IG p.v.5.*
See also Gustav Hägermann, *Die Erklärungen der Menschen- und Bürgerrechte in den ersten amerikanischen Staatsverfassungen,* Berlin, 1910 (Historische Studien, Heft 78), *BAC;* Justus Heshagen, "Zur Entstehungsgeschichte der nordamerikanischen Erklärungen der Menschenrechte," in *Zeitschrift für die gesammte Staatswissenschaft,* Tuebingen, 1924, Jahrg. 78, p. 461 ff, *TAA;* Georg Jellinek, "Die Erklärung der Menschen- und Bürgerrechte," in *Staats- und völkerrechtliche Abhandlungen,* Leipzig, 1895, v. 1, No. 3, *SEB;* Fritz Klövekorn, "Die Entstehung der Erklärung der Menschen- und Bürgerrechte," in *Historische Studien,* Berlin, 1911, Heft 90, p. 88–92, *BAC.*
Note Richard Price, *Anmerkungen über die Natur der bürgerlichen Freyheit, über die Grundsätze der Regierung und über die Rechtmässigkeit und Politik des Krieges mit Amerika,* Braunschweig, 1777. Sabin 65454. Not in the Library.
K. H. Gildemeister, in his *Johann Georg Hamann's, des Magus im Norden, Leben und Schriften,* Gotha, 1857–73 *(AN [Hamann])*, quotes the following judgment of Hamann on the "Considérations": "Das englische Pamphlet ist im vorigen Jahre [1784] zu Philadelphia auskommen unter dem Namen eines Andreas Burke, der zuerst über die Errichtung des neu errichteten Ordens Lärm geblasen, der als ein erblicher Adel oder Patriciat das ganze demokratische Gebäude zu Grunde gerichtet haben würde." — *v. 3, p. 156 and 235.*

897. NACHRICHTEN von den vereinigten Deutschen Evangelisch-Lutherischen Gemeinen in Nord-America, absonderlich in Pensylvanien. Erster Band. Mit einer Vorrede von D. Johann Ludewig Schulze... Halle: In Verlegung des Waisenhauses, 1787. 1 v. in 2. 4°.
No more published.                                        * KF 1787
First collected edition of the so-called "Hallische Nachrichten," comprising the second (1750) edition of the "Kurtze Nachricht" (first published in 1744), and sixteen "Fortsetzungen" which appeared between 1745 and 1787, the general title page, preface and index being issued with the sixteenth Fortsetzung.
See no. 317, 531.
Note G. A. Freylinghausen and J. L. Schulze, *Neuere Geschichte der Evangelischen Missions-Anstalter zu Belehrung der Heiden in Ostindien* [etc.], Halle, 1784–99. Sabin 25919. Not in the Library.
"Periodical missionary accounts from the United States, relating chiefly to the history of Germans, memoirs of eminent Lutheran divines in the United States, etc." — *Sabin.*
See also Sabin 51694, 78013, 78014, 78015.

898. SCHOEPF, JOHANN DAVID. Beschreibungen einiger Nord-Amerikanischer Fische, vorzüglich aus den Neu-Yorkischen Gewässern. (Gesellschaft naturforschender Freunde zu Berlin. Schriften. Berlin, 1787. 8°. Bd. 8, Stück 3, p. 138-194.)                                         3–* EE
Review: *Göttingische Anzeigen von gelehrten Sachen,* Jahr 1789, p. 1396–1400, * *DF.*

899. —— Beytrage zur mineralogischen Kenntniss des östlichen Theils von Nordamerika, seiner Gebürge von D. Johann David Schöpf... Erlangen: Verlegt von Joh. Jacob Palm, 1787. 6 p.l., 194 p., 1 l. 8°.                               * KF 1787
The introduction is a letter by D. Schoepf to Hofrath Schreber.
Reviews: *Allgemeine deutsche Bibliothek,* Bd. 84, p. 161, *NAA; Göttingische Anzeigen von gelehrten Sachen,* Jahr 1788, p. 414–416, * *DF.*

900. SCHREIBEN eines deutschen Patrioten an seinen Freund in Deutschland, über den jetzigen Zustand von Grossbrittanien, in Ansehung seiner Macht, Reichthümer und Resourcen. (Auswahl kleiner Reisebeschreibungen und anderer statistischen und geographischen Nachrichten. Leipzig, 1787. 12°. Theil 5, p. 156–212; Theil 6, p. 269–290, 291–320.) KBC
References to America, p. 164, 178.
Pagination continuous in Theil 5, 6.

## GERMAN WORKS RELATING TO AMERICA 109

*1787, continued*

901. UEBER den Hang verschiedener Völker zur Völlerey. (Gôttingisches historisches Magazin. Hannover, 1787. 12°. Bd. 1, p. 251–262.) BAA (Neues)
Periodical subsequently called *Neues göttingisches historisches Magasin*, under which it is shelved.

902. UEBER den Hang vieler Völker zu fetten Speisen und Getränken. (Gôttingisches historisches Magazin. Hannover, 1787. 12°. Bd. 1, p. 247–250.) BAA (Neues)
Periodical subsequently called *Neues göttingisches historisches Magasin*, under which it is shelved.

903. UEBER den Religionszustand unter den Deutschen in Nordamerika. (Historisches Portefeuille zur Kenntnis der gegenwårtigen und vergangenen Zeit. Wien, 1787. 12°. Jahrg. 6, Bd. 2, p. 21–28.) BAA
Taken from "Vom gebahnten Lebenswege" by Joh. Christoph Kunze, who was a Prediger in New York.

904. UEBER die Begriffe verschiedener Völker von dem Werthe der Jungfrauschafft. (Gôttingisches historisches Magazin. Hannover, 1787. 12°. Bd. 1, p. [5]–25.) BAA (Neues)
Signed: M (i.e., Christoph Meiners, 1747–1810).
Periodical subsequently called *Neues göttingisches historisches Magasin*, under which it is shelved.

905. UEBER die grosse Verschiedenheit der Biegsamkeit und Unbiegsamkeit, der Hårte und Weichheit der verschiedehen Ståmme, und Raçen der Menschen. (Gôttingisches historisches Magazin. Hannover, 1787. 12°. Bd. 1, p. 210–246.) BAA (Neues)
Periodical subsequently called *Neues göttingisches historisches Magasin*, under which it is shelved.

906. VON den Måhrischen Brüdern in Nord-Carolina. (Historisches Portefeuille zur Kenntnis der gegenwårtigen und vergangenen Zeit. Wien, 1787. 12°. Jahrg. 6, Bd. 2, p. 290–293.) BAA
Taken from J. F. D. Smyth's *Tour in the United States of America*, London, 1784, v. 1, p. 213 et sq.

907. *Review*: An account of the present State of Nova Scotia. Edinburg: Creech, 1786. 157 p. 8°. (Gôttingische Anzeigen von gelehrten Sachen. Gôttingen [1787]. 12°. Jahr 1787, p. 857–860, *DF.)

907A. *Review*: Allgemeines Archiv für die Länder-, Völker- und Staaten-Kunde, deren Literatur und Hülfsmittel aufs Jahr 1786; herausgegeben von Friedrich Gottlieb Canzler. Göttingen: Bey Dietrich, 1787. 160 S. 8°. (Allgemeine Literatur-Zeitung. Jena, 1787. 4°. Jahr 1787, Bd. 4, col. 710–712, *NAA.)

908. *Review*: Almanach Américain, Asiatique et Africain ou état physique, politique, ecclesiastique et militaire de l'Asie, de Afrique [*sic!*] et de l'Amérique. Theil VII. Paris: Beym Verfasser und Leroy, 1787. 442 p. 12°. (Allgemeine Literatur-Zeitung. Jena, 1787. 4°. Jahr 1787, Bd. 3, col. 167, *NAA.)
See nos. 761, 829A.

908A. *Review*: Arctic Zoology. v. i. Introduction. Class i. Quadrupeds. London: Hughs, 1784. v. ii. Class ii. Birds. 1785. CC. 586 p. Nebst 23 Kupfertafeln. 4°. (Allgemeine Literatur-Zeitung. Jena, 1787. 4°. Jahr 1787, Bd. 2, col. 289–296, 314–320, 353–355, *NAA.)
Many references to the natural history of America.

908B. *Review*: Avis aux habitans des Colonies, particulièrement à ceux de l'Isle St. Dominique sur les principales causes des maladies... Par J. F. Lafosse... Paris: Royez, 1787. 8, 235 p. 8°. (Allgemeine Literatur-Zeitung. Jena, 1788. 4°. Jahr 1788, Bd. 4, col. 537–539, *NAA.)
"Ein zehnjähriger Aufenthalt des Verf. auf der Insel St. Domingo, wo er als Arzt practicirte, musste ihn allerdings in den Stand setzen, den physischen Zustand dieses Eilands und seiner Einwohner genau kennen zu lernen."

909. *Review*: Beytrag zur deutschen holzgerechten Forstwissenschaft, die Anpflanzung nordamerikanischer Holzarten, mit Anwendung auf deutsche Forste, betreffend, von Friedrich Adam Julius von Wangenheim... Göttingen: Bey Dietrich, 1787. 45 Bogen. 30 Kupfertafeln. f°. (Allgemeine Literatur-Zeitung. Jena, 1787. 4°. Jahr 1787, Bd. 4, col. 190–192, *NAA.)

910. *Review*: D. Jo. Davidis Schöpf Materia medica americana potissimum regni vegetabilis. Erlangen: Bey Palm, 1787. 170 S. 8°. (Allgemeine Literatur-Zeitung. Jena, 1787. 4°. Jahr 1787, Bd. 1, col. 617–619, *NAA.)
See no. 918.

911. *Review*: Einige Nachricht von der Evangelischen Kirchenverfassung in Nordcarolina. [Stade?] (Göttingische Anzeigen von gelehrten Sachen. Göttingen [1787]. 12°. Jahr 1787, p. 101–103, *DF.)

911A. *Review*: Einige Nachrichten von der evangelischen Kirchenverfassung in Nordcarolina, von Abbt Velthusen, Helmstädt 1786. (Göttingische Anzeigen von gelehrten Sachen. Göttingen [1787]. 12°. Jahr 1787, p. 101–102, *DF.)
"...schildert den in hilflosem Zustande befindlichen Gottisdienst und Religionsunterricht Nord- und Südcarolinas."

911B. *Review*: Friedrich August Ludwig von Burgsdorf Versuch einer vollständigen Geschichte vorzüglicher Holzarten in systematischen Abhandlungen zur Erweiterung der Naturkunde und Forsthaushaltungswissenschaft. Zweyter Theil. Die einheimischen und fremden Eichenarten. Erster Band, physikalische Geschichte. Berlin: Bey Pauli, 1787. Mit 9 illum. Kupfertafeln in folio. 234 S. 4°. (Allgemeine Literatur-Zeitung. Jena, 1787. 4°. Jahr 1787, Bd. 3, col. 715–717, *NAA.)
"How to grow American oak trees in Germany. "Bey der Anzucht der einheimischen Eichen empfiehlt der Vf. die Herbstsaat als die naturgemässeste, inzwischen muss noch bis jetzt bey den Nordamerikanischen die Frühlingssaat gewählt werden, da sie bey uns noch keine Saamen zeitigen, und solcher aus Amerika erst im März zu erhalten steht."
See nos. 886, 1036.

*1787, continued*

911C. *Review:* Geschichte der Seereisen und Entdeckungen welche auf Befehl Sr. Grosbrittanischen Majestät des Dritten unternommen sind... Sechster Band. Aus dem Englischen übersetzt von Hn. Georg Forster... Berlin: Haude und Spener, 1787. (Allgemeine Literatur-Zeitung. Jena, 1788. 4°. Jahr 1788, Bd. 1, col. 129-136, *NAA.*)

911D. *Review:* Grefve Grasses Sjö-Batailler och Kriegsoperationerne uti Westindien, Stockholm: Holmberg, 1787. 8 Bogen. 8°. (Allgemeine Literatur-Zeitung. Jena, 1788. 4°. Jahr 1788, Bd. 1, col. 617-618, *NAA.*)

The author was a Swedish officer who observed the naval war between France and Great Britain from the fleet of Count Grasse, describing naval actions between April 29, 1781, and April 12, 1782.

912. *Review:* The History of Amerika by William Robertson. Leipzig: Bey Schwickert, 1786. 3 v. 8°. (Allgemeine Literatur-Zeitung. Jena, 1787. 4°. Jahr 1787, Bd. 1, col. 268-269, *NAA.*)

913. *Review:* Instructions for the treatment of Negroes. London: Bey Shepperson und Reinolds, 1786. 30 Seiten. 8°, (Allgemeine Literatur-Zeitung. Jena, 1787. 4°. Jahr 1787, Bd. 2, col. 56, *NAA.*)

913A. *Review:* Johann Leonhard Nensingers ... Erdbeschreibung für Kinder, enthaltend Asien, Afrika, Amerika und die neu entdeckten Länder oder den fünften Welttheil zum Gebrauch auf Schulen. Nürnberg: Bey Grattenauer, 1785. 250 S. 8°. (Allgemeine deutsche Bibliothek. Berlin, 1787. 8°. Bd. 77, p. 194-198, *NAA.*)

"In Nordamerika macht das Russische Amerika schon einen sehr grossen Theil von vielen hundert Meilen aus." The author is criticised by the reviewer for the statement that Annapolis is the largest place in Nova Scotia.

913B. *Review:* Köngl. Vetenskaps Academiens Nya Handlingar För Manaderne Julius, Augustus, Septembr. Mit Kupf. Stockholm: Bey I. G. Lange, 1787. (Allgemeine Literatur-Zeitung. Jena, 1787. 4°. Jahr 1787, Bd. 3, col. 7-8, *NAA.*)

"Den Schluss machen eine Menge zur Naturhistorie der jetzigen schwedischen Insel St. Barthelemy dienende Nachrichten, von Hr. Fahlberg, der selbst an Ort und Stelle gewesen ist..."
See nos. 872D, 884.

914. *Review:* Lehrbücher für die Jugend in Nordcarolina, entworfen von einer Gesellschaft Helmstädtischer Professoren. Erste Lieferung: Catechismus und Fragebuch. Leipzig, 1787. 8°. (Göttingische Anzeigen von gelehrten Sachen. Göttingen [1787]. 12°. Jahr 1787, p. 2096, **DF.*)

"Aus gutthätiger Absicht ist es zugleich als Helmstädtischer Catechismus gedruckt, als Lehrbuch für das unter Hrn. D. Velthusen stehende Catechistische Institut und den damit verbundenen wöchentlichen Unterricht der Catechumenen."
In *Allgemeine Literatur-Zeitung,* Jena, 1788, Jahr 1788, Bd. 1, col. 78-80, *NAA,* the following is stated: "Von dem daraus zu erwartenden Gewinne wollen sie [the publishers] die Ueberfahrt für zwey bis drey evangelische Prediger mit einem guten Vorrathe geschenkter Bücher bis Charlestown bezahlen... Die Jugend in Nordcarolina ist sehr verwildert, wie Hr. Nüssmann klagt, und wie man ohnehin leicht denken kann."

915. *Review:* Lettres d'un Cultivateur Américain depuis l'année 1770 jusqu'en 1786 par Mr. St. John de Crevecoeur; traduites de l'anglois. Paris: Bey Cuchet, 1787. 3 v. 8°. (Allgemeine Literatur-Zeitung. Jena, 1787. 4°. Jahr 1787, Bd. 4, col. 73-79, *NAA.*)

916. *Review:* Literatur und Völkerkunde. Vierter Jahrgang oder VIIter u. VIIIter Band. Göschen, 1785-1786. (Allgemeine Literatur-Zeitung. Jena, 1787. 4°. Jahr 1787, Bd. 2, col. 188-189, *NAA.*)

Oct. 1785: No. 1. Nachricht von einer sonderbaren Societät in Pensilvanien, die man Dunkers nennt. No. 6. Charakteristische Beobachtungen über Virginien und Amerika überhaupt. Fragment aus dem Voyage de Mr. le Chevalier de Castellux en Amerique.
Nov. 1785: No. 6. Das wiedergefundene Kind. Eine amerikanische Anekdote, aus den Lettres d'un Cultivateur américain. No. 7: Schreiben eines Engländers aus Virginien an seinen Freund in London, vom 6ten März 1785.
Jan. 1786: No. 4. Ueber die Sitten und Gebräuche der wilden Völker in Nordamerika. Ein Auszug aus des Berühmten Engländers, Major Roberts Nachrichten.
Februar 1786; No. 8. Fragment einer philosophischen Rede, gehalten in Philadelphia. (Mit dieser schönen Rede beschloss den 20. Jul. 1785, Doctor Moyes ein philosophisches Collegium, wobey er die vornehmsten Einwohner beyderlei Geschlechts zu Zuhörern hatte. So weit also ist es gekommen, dass wir der vornehmsten Welt in Europa die vornehme Welt in America zum Muster vorstellen müssen!) März 1786: No. 5. Das jetzige Zeitalter. Ein Fragment aus dem *Politischen Herold.* Das spanische America wird nicht lange zaudern, dem englischen Nordamerica zu folgen. No. 9. Die Pressfreyheit in America im Jahre 1785. (Sie ist ganz unumschränkt. Freyheit, Cultur und Aufklärung scheinen sich aus Europa nach America, wie vormals aus Asien nach Europa zu wenden. In den entferntesten Regionen von Kentucky soll die grosse Entdeckung des Perpetuum mobile gemacht worden seyn.)

917-18. *Review:* Literatur und Völkerkunde. IX. Bd. 1786. (Allgemeine Literatur-Zeitung. Jena, 1787. 4°. Jahr 1787, Bd. 2, col. 596-600, *NAA.*)

Julius 1786: No. 5. Ueber die Indianer in Nordamerica.
August 1786: No. 2. Apologie des Grafen von Zinzendorf. No. 4. Friedenscongress der Piankaschawa, einer nordamericanischen Völkerschaft und der Americaner der vereinigten Staaten, gehalten zu St. Vincent, den 15ten April 1784. No. 7. Connatonto. Eine americanische Geschichte aus dem letzten Kriege. Heroische Liebe und römischer Nationalstolz bey einer wilden Americanerin.
November 1786: No. 7. Ueber das Interesse und die Politik der vereinigten Staaten. Von Doctor Franklin, jetzigen Präsidenten des Staats von Pensilvanien. (Der Ackerbau und die Fischereyen werden als die ergiebigsten Hülfsquellen der vereinigten Staaten gepriesen.)

919. *Review:* Memoirs of the literary and philosophical Society of Manchester. 1785. 2 v. plates. 8°. (Göttingische Anzeigen von gelehrten Sachen. Göttingen [1787]. 12°. Jahr 1787, p. 998-1004, **DF.*)

The reviewer describes essay no. 24 in v. 2 as follows: "D. B. Rush [i.e. Doctor Benjamin Rush]...theilt gedrängte Resultate seiner Beobachtungen mit, die er während des letzten americanischen Kriegs, wo er den Posten als erster Arzt aller Lazarethe der vereinigten Staaten bekleidete, zu machen Gelegenheit gehabt haitte."
The Library's file of the *Memoirs* is in * EC.

*1787, continued*

919A. *Review:* Neue Reisen eines Deutschen nach und in England im Jahr 1783. Ein Pendant zu des Hrn. Professor Moritz Reisen. Berlin: Bey Maurer, 1784. 254 Seiten. 8°. (Allgemeine deutsche Bibliothek. Berlin, 1787. 12°. Bd. 71, p. 172-174, *NAA.*)

"Der damalige Erbprinz, jetzt Landgraf von Hessen Cassel, den politische Verhältnisse, die der Privatmann eben nicht immer kennt, vielleicht nöthigten, wider seine Neigung Truppen nach America zu schicken, legte die Englischen Subsidien zu Wilhelmsbad dann doch wenigstens patriotisch an...
"*The rights of Great Britain against the claims of America* [see no. 526], dies so belehrende Werk, las der Verf[asser] wohl nie; sonst hätte er sich des Deklamierens wider diejenigen, welche die Americaner in letzten Kriege mit dem Namen Rebellen belegten, vielleicht enthalten." — *p. 173.*
As to K. P. Moritz, *Reisen eines Deutschen in England im Jahr 1782,* see *Deutsche Litteraturdenkmale des 18. Jahrhunderts in Neudrucken,* Heilbronn, 1903, no. 26, *NFF.*

920. *Review:* Niederelbisches historisch-politisch-literarisches Magazin, nebst literarischem Anhange. Bd. 1. Stck. 1-4. 352 p. + 64 p. litterarischer Anhang. 8°. (Allgemeine Literatur-Zeitung. Jena, 1787. 4°. Jahr 1787, Bd. 3, col. 349-352, *NAA.*)

The volume contains: Heft I: Nachricht von dem jetzigen Zustande von Neuschottland... Heft III: Anmerkungen über die Quäker in Pensylvanien.

921. *Review:* Des P. Labats Reisen nach Westindien. Sechster Band. Mit Kart. und vielen Kupf. Nürnberg: Bey Raspe, 1787. 516 p. 8°. (Allgemeine Literatur-Zeitung. Jena, 1787. 4°. Jahr 1787, Bd. 5, col. 15, *NAA.*)

921A. *Review:* Des Pater Labats. Reisen nach Westindien, oder den im amerikanischen Meere liegenden Inseln. Nach der neuesten Pariser Ausgabe übersetzt...von Georg Friedr. Casim. Schad... v. Band. Nürnberg: Bey Raspe, 1786. 4½ Bogen. 8°. (Allgemeine deutsche Bibliothek. Berlin, 1787. 8°. Bd. 75, p. 553-556, *NAA.*)

921B. *Review:* Des Pater Labats Reisen nach Westindien, oder den im Amerikanischen Meere liegenden Inseln. Nach der neuesten Pariser Ausgabe übersetzt...von G. Fr. Cas. Schad. Bd. 4. Nürnberg: Raspe, 1787. 12 Bogen. 8°. (Allgemeine deutsche Bibliothek. Berlin, 1788. 8°. Bd. 84, p. 528-530, *NAA.*)

921C. *Review:* Ferdinand von Soto, oder erster Kriegszug der Spanier durch Florida, aus dem Spanischen des Ynca Garcilasso de la Vega ins Französich und aus diesem ins Deutsche übersetzt von Gottfr. Böttger. Nordhausen: Bei Gross, 1783. 8°. 2 Theile. (Allgemeine deutsche Bibliothek. Berlin, 1787. 8°. Bd. 77, p. 191-192, *NAA.*)

921D. *Review:* Publicistische Uebersicht aller Regierungsarten sämmtlicher Staaten und Völkerschaften auf der Welt, von J. T. Plant. Berlin: Bey Vierweg dem Aelteren, 1787. 15 S. klein Folio. (Allgemeine Literatur-Zeitung. Jena, 1787. 4°. Jahr 1787, Bd. 4, col. 770-772, *NAA.*)
Kayser, v. 4, p. 356A.
Treats among others the government of the United States and the "anarchy" of Indian tribes in America.

921E. *Review:* Schätzung der verhältnismässigen Stärke von Grossbritannien während der gegenwärtigen und der vier vorhergehenden Regierungen und des Verlustes seines Handels in jeden [*sic!*] Krieg seit der Staatsveränderung von George Chalmers. Aus dem Englischen... von Valentin August Heinze. Berlin und Stettin, 1786. 320 S. 8°. (Allgemeine deutsche Bibliothek. Berlin, 1787. 8°. Bd. 77, p. 274-277, *NNA.*)

This is a translation of George Chalmers, *An estimate of the comparative strength of Britain during the present and four preceding reigns,* London, 1782.

921F. *Review:* Statistisch-historisch-geographisches Handbuch zur Grundlegung der Kenntniss der Staaten und Länder und ihrer Geschichte, von A. A. Watermeyer. Zweyte verbesserte Auflage. Hamburg: Bey Hofmann, 1786. 560 S. 8°. (Allgemeine Literatur-Zeitung. Jena, 1787. 4°. Jahr 1787, Bd. 2, col. 454-456, *NAA.*)

"Der geographische Theil enthält das merkwürdigste von den europäischen Reichen, auch von Nordamerika..."

921G. *Review:* Statistische Uebersicht der vornehmensten Deutschen und sämmtlichen Europäischen Staaten in Anschauung ihrer Grösse, Bevölkerung ihres Finanz- und Kriegszustandes mit einem Anhang gleichen Inhalts über den Nordamerikanischen Freystaat, [n. p.], 1786. 21 Bogen. f°. (Allgemeine deutsche Bibliothek. Berlin, 1787. 8°. Bd. 75, p. 29-34, *NAA.*)

921H. *Review:* Tableau general du commerce de l'Europe avec Afrique, les Indes Orientales et l'Amérique, fondé sur les traités de 1763 et 1787. Paris: Bey Desennes. [n. d.] 416 S. 8°. (Allgemeine Literatur-Zeitung. Jena, 1787. 4°. Jahr 1787. Bd. 4, col. 158-159, *NAA.*)

Mostly excerpts from Abbé Raynal's work.
The Library's copy of this work is in * KF 1787.

921I. *Review:* Tableau général du commerce de l'Europe avec l'Afrique, les Indes orientales et l'Amérique. Fondé sur les traités de 1763 et 1783. Paris: Desenne. [n. d.] 2 Bogen. 8°. (Göttingische Anzeigen von gelehrten Sachen. Göttingen [1787]. 12°. Jahr 1787, p. 1457-1458, **DF.*)

"Der ungenannte Verfasser sagt, er schreibe für Kaufleute, welche einige allgemeine Nachrichten von den Ländern, wohin die Europäer ausser Europa handeln, haben möchten, aber weder Lust noch Zeit hätten, den weitschweifigen und unzuverlässigen Raynal zu lesen... Vom neuesten Zustande von Florida, seitdem es, seit 1783, wieder den Spaniern gehört, weiss der Verfasser nichts."

921J. *Review:* Therese Westen, die Geschichte unglücklicher grossmütiger Treue, Berlin u. Leipzig, 1786. 8°. 156 S. (Allgemeine Literatur-Zeitung. Jena, 1787. 4°. Jahr 1787, Bd. 5, p. 28, *NAA.*)

"...schildert die Liebe eines jungen Mädchens, dessen Liebhaber nach Amerika geht und später zu ihr zurückkehrt."

*1787, continued*

922. *Review:* Transactions of the american philosophical Society, held at Philadelphia, for promoting useful knowledge. Philadelphia: Bey Aitken, 1786. v. 2. (Göttingische Anzeigen von gelehrten Sachen. Göttingen [1787]. 12°. Jahr 1787, p. 1760-1768, * *DF.*)

The Transactions contain among other articles Benjamin Rush's discourse "Warum in Pensylvanien gallichte und Wechselfieber zunehmen," and "Schreiben Hrn. Franklin an Hrn. Ingenhouss über den Bau der Camine."

About another essay by Benjamin Franklin, it is said: "Herr Franklin meldet Hrn Nairne, dass Behältnisse zu Magneten und Taschenperspectiven von Mahoganyholze, die in England zulänglich weit waren, in Amerika viel zu enge geworden sind, sich in England und Frankreich wiederum erweitert haben, also die amerikanische Luft viel trockener seyn muss."

922A. *Review:* Ueber die Anpflanzung ausländischer Holzarten zum Nutzen der Forsten in den königl. Preussischen Staaten, von Georg Heinrich Borowski, Prof. der Oekonomie und Naturgeschichte zu Frankfurt. Berlin: Bey Baum, 1787. 6 Bogen. 8°. (Allgemeine Literatur-Zeitung. Jena, 1787. 4°. Jahr 1787, Bd. 4, col. 270, *NAA.*)

How to grow American trees, such as Quercus virginiana, Ulmus americana, Fraxinus caroliniana, Juglans nigra, Populus canadensis, Populus Carolinensis, Pinus canadensis, Juniperus virginiana etc., in Prussia. "Endlich noch eine kurze Betrachtung über die Vortheile, die aus der Anpflanzung dieser Holzarten für die königlichen Staaten entstehen."

922B. *Review:* Voyages de M. le Marquis de Chastellux dans l'Amerique septentrionale dans les années 1780, 81, et 82. t. I. 390 Seiten, t. II. 362 S. gr. Octav, mit einigen Karten und Aussichten, Paris 1786. (Göttingische Anzeigen von gelehrten Sachen. Göttingen [1787]. 12°. Jahr 1787, p. 1985-1989, **DF.*)

"...Tagebuch eines franz. Offiziers und MitgL der Ac. Franç., der in jenen Jahren den Amerik. Krieg mitgemacht hat und hier seine Abenteuer erzählt."

922C. *Review:* Der Wilde in Frankreich! Ein Schauspiel in vier Aufzügen, von Joh. Fried. Wieting, Schauspieler in Laibach. Laibach: Bey Eger, 1786. 7½ Bogen. 8°. (Allgemeine deutsche Bibliothek. Berlin, 1787. 8°. Bd. 77, p. 113-114, *NAA.*)

"Ziemlich langweiliges Schauspiel nach der Oper Huron, worzu die Musik von Gretry, und das Sujet aus Voltairens Ingenu genommen ist."

1788

923. BEITRAG zu der im 99ten u. f. St. befindlichen Abhandlung: über den Negernhandel. (Hannoverisches Magazin...von Jahre 1788. Hannover, 1789. 4°. Jahrg. 26, col. 1657-1664.)
Title page dated 1789; contents, 1788. * DF
*See* no. 929.

924. BETRACHTUNGEN über die Begriffe der verschiedenen Völker von Ehre, und Schande. (Göttingisches historisches Magazin. Hannover, 1788. 12°. Bd. 3, p. 429-456.) BAA (Neues)
Signed: M (i.e., Christoph Meiners, 1747-1810).
Periodical subsequently called *Neues göttingisches historisches Magazin,* under which it is shelved.

925. BETRACHTUNGEN und Nachrichten über die merkwürdige schlechte Beschaffenheit der Nahrungs-Mittel in America. (Göttingisches historisches Magazin. Hannover, 1788. 12°. Bd. 2, p. 376-380.) BAA (Neues)
Review: *Göttingische Anzeigen von gelehrten Sachen,* Jahr 1788, p. 122, * *DF.*
Periodical subsequently called *Neues göttingisches historisches Magazin,* under which it is shelved.

926. BOUTERWEK, FRIEDRICH. Morgenlied eines Negersklaven aus seinem Kerker. (Musen Almanach. A. MDCCLXXXVIII. Göttingen: Bey Joh. Christ. Dietrich, 1788. 32°. p. 124-127.) NFA
" 'Zur Arbeit', schallt das Donnerwort.
Wir fahren auf; man fährt uns fort
In reiche Zuckerfelder.
Die Frucht, die unser Schweiss gewinnt,
Ist unser nicht — Ha! seelger sind
Die Thiere jener Wälder."

927. CRAMER, PIETER. Herrn Peter Cramers... Sammlung und Beschreibung ausländischer Schmetterlinge aus den drey Welttheilen Asia, Afrika und Amerika, ausgefertiget, herausgegeben und verlegt von Johann Michael Seligmanns sel. Erben... Papillons exotiques des trois parties du monde... à Nuremberg: Chez les héritiers de J. M. Seligmann [1788?]. xlviii, 48 p., 24 col'd plates. 4°. †* KF 1788
Sabin 17383.
A translation of the first three parts only of Cramer's work; no more published.
Title page in German and French; text in German and French, in parallel columns.
Plates engraved by A. F. Happe, and colored by hand.
*See* Heinsius, v. 2, col. 269.

928. EINIGE Betrachtungen über die Schönheit der menschlichen Bildung und über den Hang aller hässlichen Völker, sich noch mehr zu verhässlichen. (Göttingisches historisches Magazin. Hannover, 1788. 12°. Bd. 2, p. 270-292.) BAA (Neues)
Signed: M (i.e., Christoph Meiners, 1747-1810).
Periodical subsequently called *Neues göttingisches historisches Magazin,* under which it is shelved.

929. EINIGE den Negerhandel betreffende Nachrichten und Schilderungen. (Hannoverisches Magazin...vom Jahre 1788. Hannover, 1789. 4°. Jahrg. 26, col. 1569-1604.) *DF
From *Journal de Paris.*
Translated by G. F. Palm of Hannover.
Title page dated 1789; contents, 1788.
*See* no. 923.

930. EINIGE Nachrichten über ehelose Völker. (Göttingisches historisches Magazin. Hannover, 1788. 12°. Bd. 2, p. 385-393.) BAA (Neues)
Signed: M (i.e., Christoph Meiners, 1747-1810).
Periodical subsequently called *Neues göttingisches historisches Magazin,* under which it is shelved.

931. GESCHICHTE der Gesetze des Wohlstandes unter rohen, und halbcultivirten Völkern. (Göttingisches historisches Magazin. Hannover, 1788. 12°. Bd. 3, p. 219-276.) BAA (Neues)
Signed: M (i.e., Christoph Meiners, 1747-1810).
Periodical subsequently called *Neues göttingisches historisches Magazin,* under which it is shelved.

**1788, continued**

932. GESCHICHTE der hieroglyphischen Schrift. (Gôttingisches historisches Magazin. Hannover, 1788. 12°. Bd. 3, p. 456-485.)
BAA (Neues)
Signed: M (i.e., Christoph Meiners, 1747-1810).
Periodical subsequently called *Neues gôttingisches historisches Magazin*, under which it is shelved.

933. ISERT, PAUL ERDMANN. Paul Erdmann Isert's... Reise nach Guinea und den Caribäischen Inseln in Columbien, in Briefen an seine Freunde beschrieben. Kopenhagen: Gedrukt bey J. F. Morthorst, 1788. 8 p.l., 376, lxx p., 5 l., folding frontis. 8°. *KF 1788
Sabin 35243.
"Anhang von meteorologischen Betrachtungen," lxx p. at the end.
Illustrations by Friedrich, sc. Hafniae.
Reviews: *Allgemeine Literatur-Zeitung*, Jahr 1788, Bd. 3, col. 97-104, *NAA*; *Göttingische Anzeigen von gelehrten Sachen*, Jahr 1789, p. 265-269; Jahr 1790, p. 2016, *DF*.

934. KURZE Geschichte der allegorischen Gottheiten. (Gôttingisches historisches Magazin. Hannover, 1788. 12°. Bd. 3, p. 356-379.)
BAA (Neues)
Signed: M (i.e., Christoph Meiners, 1747-1810).
Periodical subsequently called *Neues gôttingisches historisches Magazin*, under which it is shelved.

935. KURZE Geschichte der Meynungen roher Vôlker über die Natur der menschlichen Seelen. (Gôttingisches historisches Magazin. Hannover, 1788. 12°. Bd. 2, p. 742-759.)
BAA (Neues)
Signed: M (i.e., Christoph Meiners, 1747-1810).
Periodical subsequently called *Neues gôttingisches historisches Magazin*, under which it is shelved.

936. KURZE Geschichte der Meynungen roher Vôlker von den Thieren. (Gôttingisches historisches Magazin. Hannover, 1788. 12°. Bd. 3, p. 1-10.)
BAA (Neues)
Signed: M (i.e., Christoph Meiners, 1747-1810).
Periodical subsequently called *Neues gôttingisches historisches Magazin*, under which it is shelved.

936A. LICHTENBERG, GEORG CHRISTOPH. Wundercuren der geweihten Ärzte bei einigen amerikanischen Völkern. [1788.] (In his: Vermischte Schriften. Neue Original-Ausgabe. Goettingen: Dieterich, 1844-67. 12°. Theil 6, p. 416-417.)
NFG
First printed in *Goettingischer Taschenkalender, 1788*, p. 174-177. Not in the Library. Contains a quotation from Jacob Baegert's *Nachrichten von...Californien* (see no. 467). Another quotation from the same work appears in his *Aphorismen. Nach den Handschriften herausgegeben von Albert Leitzmann. Viertes Heft: 1789-1793*, Berlin, 1908, p. 28 (Deutsche Litteraturdenkmale des 18. und 19. Jahrhunderts, No. 140), *NFF*.
References to Franklin, p. 45, 71, 77, 91, 141, 189, 218; to Boston, p. 204; to the geography of North America, p. 117; to a Canadian Indian, p. 29.
In a letter dated Göttingen, den 8. April 1782, Lichtenberg praises "die edle Einfalt der Franklinschen-Theorie." See his *Vermischte Schriften*, Goettingen, 1844-67, v. 8, p. 143, *NFG*.
For G. C. Lichtenberg's attitude towards the American Revolution, see H. S. King, "Echoes of the American Revolution in German literature," in University of California, *Publications in modern philology*, Berkeley, 1929, v. 14, p. 51-54, *STG*. Lichtenberg remarks that "Franklin hat neuerlich nichts physisches geschrieben. Seine 13 rädrige politische Maschine hat ihn wohl die einrädrige elektrische aus dem Sinn gebracht."
See also no. 521A.

937. RÜCKFALL der Deutschen in NordAmerika in die Barbarei. (In: A. L. Schlôzer. Stats-Anzeigen. Gôttingen, 1788. 12°. Bd. 12, p. 480-493.)
BAC
This is the *Anrede an die Deutschen...von den Trustias der besagten Hohen Schule in Philadelphia*. A. L. Schloezer substituted the derogatory title for the original one. See no. 940.

938. SCHOEPF, JOHANN DAVID. Reise durch einige der mittlern und südlichen vereinigten nordamerikanischen Staaten nach Ost-Florida und den Bahama-Inseln unternommen in den Jahren 1783 und 1784 von Johann David Schoepf ... Erster [-Zweyter] Theil. Mit einem Landchärtchen. Erlangen: Bey Johann Jacob Palm, 1788. 2 v. folding map. 8°. *KF 1788
Sabin 77757.
Early issue, on thick paper, with many typographical errors and marginal corrections.
"The first noteworthy German book of travels in America in the eighteenth century. Schoepf as a military surgeon accompanied the Ansbach mercenaries. His work, although written from the standpoint of a scientist is entertaining reading. The author discourses on the climate, mode of living, and sanitary conditions, on public instruction and scientific studies, on natural resources and commerce, and notes the traces left by the war." — *P. C. Weber, America in imaginative German literature*, New York, 1926, *NFCX*.
See also A. J. Morrison, "Doctor Johann David Schoepf," in *German American annals*, Philadelphia, 1910, new series, v. 8, p. 255-264, *NFCA*. A translation into English by A. J. Morrison was issued in Philadelphia, in 1911, entitled *Travels in the Confederation 1783-1784, IID*.
Reviews: *Allgemeine Literatur-Zeitung*, Jahr 1789, Bd. 1, col. 433-438, 441-444, *NAA*; *Allgemeine deutsche Bibliothek*, Bd. 89, p. 535, *NAA*; *Magazin für Botanik*, [Jahr 1790,] Stück 7, p. 157-168, *QEA*; *Göttingische Anzeigen von gelehrten Sachen*, Jahr 1789, p. 1201-1206, *DF*; *Nürnberger gelehrten Anzeigen*, Jahr 1789, p. 689 (not in the Library).
See no. 939, 1099.

939. —— —— Erlangen: Bey Johann Jacob Palm, 1788. 2 v. folding map. 8°. *KF 1788
Sabin 77757.
Corrected issue, on thinner paper, with the typographical errors of the earlier issue corrected in the type.
See no. 938, 1099.

939A. SCHUBART, CHRISTIAN FRIEDRICH DANIEL. Franklin's Grabschrift. 1788. (Reprinted in: J. T. Hatfield and E. Hochbaum, The Influence of the American Revolution upon German literature. New York, London, Berlin [1900?]. p. 19-20.) NFC p.v.4

"Columbia trauert um ihn,
Europa klagt um ihn,
Der kühne Franke hüllt sich in Flor;
Doch Franklins Seele flog empor
Ins Urlicht, Geister drangen
In Schaaren herbei,
Willkommten ihn und sangen:
Wen Gott frei macht,
Ist ewig frei."

The first appearance was in *Deutsche Chronik*, 1790, Stück 52, p. 104.

*1788, continued*

940. SCHULWESEN [der Deutschen] in Pensylvanien. (In: A. L. Schlözer. Stats-Anzeigen. Göttingen, 1788. 12°. Bd. 12, p. 471-480.) BAC
Subtitle: Freiheits Brief der deutschen Hohen Schule (College) in der Stadt Lancaster in dem Staat Pensylvanien, nebst einer Anrede an die Deutschen dieses Stats, von den Trustles der besagten Hohen Schule.
"Hier ist von einer Hohen-Schule die Rede, wo die Leute lesen und schreiben lernen sollen! Von der inneren und äussern Einrichtung derselben, findet sich in diesem Acten Stücke erbärmlich wenig: aber destomer lernt man daraus die gräuliche Barbarei kennen, in die Deutschen in Amerika bereits wieder versunken sind..." — *Schlözer.*

941. SOULÈS, FRANÇOIS. Vollständige Geschichte der Revolution in Nord-Amerika. Aus dem Französischen des Franz Soules, von Karl Hammerdörfer, Prof. in Jena... Zürich: Bey Orell, Gessner, Füsslj und Comp., 1788. 2 v. 1 folding map. 8°. *KF 1788
Sabin 87292.
The original was published in 1787 in Paris.
Reviews:
*Allgemeine Literatur-Zeitung*, Jahr 1789, Bd. 3, col. 865, Jahr 1792, Bd. 1, col. 563-565, *NAA; Gotha gelehrte Zeitung*, Jahr 1788, Bd. 2, p. 538; Jahr 1789, Bd. 1, p. 690 (not in the Library); *Oberdeutsche allgemeine Literatur-Zeitung*, Jahr 1788, Bd. 2, p. 1348; Bd. 4, p. 3162-3165 (not in the Library).

942. [TOPOGRAPHISCH-METEOROLOGISCHE Beschreibung von Cambridge in Amerika.] (Magazin für das Neueste aus der Physik und Naturgeschichte. Gotha, 1788. 12°. Bd. 5, Stück 4, p. 128-129.) 3-OA
Paragraphs are without title.

943. UEBER das Essen des Schweine-Fleisches. (Göttingisches historisches Magazin. Hannover, 1788. 12°. Bd. 3, p. 315-318.) BAA (Neues)
Signed: M (i.e., Christoph Meiners, 1747-1810).
Periodical subsequently called *Neues göttingisches historisches Magazin*, under which it is shelved.

944. UEBER das Essen von stinkenden Fischen, und von gesalzenem Fleische, besonders im heissen Erd-Gürtel, und dann über den Abscheu vieler Völker gegen das Salz. (Göttingisches historisches Magazin. Hannover, 1788. 12°. Bd. 2, p. 57-65.) BAA (Neues)
Signed: M (i.e., Christoph Meiners, 1747-1810).
Periodical subsequently called *Neues göttingisches historisches Magazin*, under which it is shelved.

945. UEBER das Fressen von frischem und rohem Fleisch. (Göttingisches historisches Magazin. Hannover, 1788. 12°. Bd. 3, p. 423-428.) BAA (Neues)
Signed: M (i.e., Christoph Meiners, 1747-1810).
Periodical subsequently called *Neues göttingisches historisches Magazin*, under which it is shelved.

946. UEBER den Hang mancher Völker zum Selbst-Morde. (Göttingisches historisches Magazin. Hannover, 1788. 12°. Bd. 2, p. 104-109.) BAA (Neues)
Signed: M (i.e., Christoph Meiners, 1747-1810).
Periodical subsequently called *Neues göttingisches historisches Magazin*, under which it is shelved.

947. UEBER den Stand der Natur. (Göttingisches historisches Magazin. Hannover, 1788. 12°. Bd. 2, p. 697-714.) BAA (Neues)
Signed: M (i.e., Christoph Meiners, 1747-1810).
Describes the aborigines of California.
Periodical subsequently called *Neues göttingisches historisches Magazin*, under which it is shelved.

948. UEBER die Bevölkerung von America. (Göttingisches historisches Magazin. Hannover, 1788. 12°. Bd. 3, p. 193-218.) BAA (Neues)
Signed: M (i.e., Christoph Meiners, 1747-1810).
Periodical subsequently called *Neues göttingisches historisches Magazin*, under which it is shelved.

949. UEBER die Braut-Preise unter verschiedenen Völkern, nebst einigen Betrachtungen über Probe-Nächte und Probe-Jahre. (Göttingisches historisches Magazin. Hannover, 1788. 12°. Bd. 3, p. 486-515.) BAA (Neues)
Signed: M (i.e., Christoph Meiners, 1747-1810).
Periodical subsequently called *Neues göttingisches historisches Magazin*, under which it is shelved.

950. UEBER die Gesetze der Ess-Lust, oder des Appetits verschiedener Völker, besonders über die Gefrässigkeit der Mongolischen Nationen. (Göttingisches historisches Magazin. Hannover, 1788. 12°. Bd. 3, p. 577-590.) BAA (Neues)
Signed: M (i.e., Christoph Meiners, 1747-1810).
Periodical subsequently called *Neues göttingisches historisches Magazin*, under which it is shelved.

951. UEBER die Rechtmässigkeit des Neger-Handels. (Göttingisches historisches Magazin. Hannover, 1788. 12°. Bd. 2, p. 398-416.) BAA (Neues)
Signed: M (i.e., Christoph Meiners, 1747-1810).
Periodical subsequently called *Neues göttingisches historisches Magazin*, under which it is shelved.

952. UEBER die Strafen des Ehebruchs unter verschiedenen Völkern. (Göttingisches historisches Magazin. Hannover, 1788. 12°. Bd. 2, p. 682-697.) BAA (Neues)
Signed: M (i.e., Christoph Meiners, 1747-1810).
Periodical subsequently called *Neues göttingisches historisches Magazin*, under which it is shelved.

953. UEBER die sympathetische Reizbarkeit, und einige daraus zu erklärende Erscheinungen in den schwächern Völkern. (Göttingisches historisches Magazin. Hannover, 1788. 12°. Bd. 2, p. 40-56.) BAA (Neues)
Signed: M (i.e., Christoph Meiners, 1747-1810).
Periodical subsequently called *Neues göttingisches historisches Magazin*, under which it is shelved.

954. UEBER die Ursachen der Viel-Weiberey. (Göttingisches historisches Magazin. Hannover, 1788. 12°. Bd. 2, p. 417-432.) BAA (Neues)
Signed: M (i.e., Christoph Meiners, 1747-1810).
Periodical subsequently called *Neues göttingisches historisches Magazin*, under which it is shelved.

955. UEBER die Verschmitztheit verschiedener Völker. (Göttingisches historisches Magazin. Hannover, 1788. 12°. Bd. 3, p. 138-159.) BAA (Neues)
Signed: M (i.e., Christoph Meiners, 1747-1810).
Periodical subsequently called *Neues göttingisches historisches Magazin*, under which it is shelved.

1788, continued

956. Von den Mährischen Brüdern in NordCarolina. (Auswahl kleiner Reisebeschreibungen und anderer statistischen und geographischen Nachrichten. Leipzig, 1788. 12°. Theil 8, p. 1059–1062.) KBC
Taken from J. F. D. Smyth's *Tour in the United States of America*, London, 1784, v. 1, p. 213.

957. Von den Meynungen roher Völker über die Entstehung der Menschen. (Göttingisches historisches Magazin. Hannover, 1788. 12°. Bd. 2, p. 293–304.) BAA (Neues)
Signed: M (i.e., Christoph Meiners, 1747–1810).
Periodical subsequently called *Neues göttingisches historisches Magazin*, under which it is shelved.

958. Von einigen Völkern, die Schläge für Merkmaale der Liebe und Freundschafft halten. (Göttingisches historisches Magazin. Hannover, 1788. 12°. Bd. 2, p. 381–383.) BAA (Neues)
Periodical subsequently called *Neues göttingisches historisches Magazin*, under which it is shelved.

959. Von und aus NordAmerika. I. Volks Menge von New York, 30 Dec. 1786. II. Ausfur Handel von Charleston in SüdCarolina, 1786. (In: A. L. Schlözer. Stats-Anzeigen. Göttingen, 1788. 12°. Bd. 12, p. 317–319.) BAC

959A. *Review:* Abbildungen zum Kabinet der vorzüglichsten in- und ausländischen Holzarten, nebst deren Beschreibung von Johann Bartholomäus Bellermann. Erfurt: Auf Kosten des Verfassers, 1788. f°. Nebst 6 Stücken buchförmig geschnitterner Hölzer von Rhus typhina... Juniperus bermudiana. (Allgemeine LiteraturZeitung. Jena, 1788. 8°. Jahr 1788, Bd. 1, col. 475–476, *NAA*.)
Juniperus bermudiana and other American trees.

959B. *Notice:* [Akademie der Wissenschaften und schönen Künste, Richmond, Va.] (Allgemeine Literatur-Zeitung. Jena, 1788. 4°. Jahr 1788, Bd. 3, col. 803, *NAA*.)
This notice is one of several, under the title, "Literarische Nachrichten. Part I. Oeffentliche Anstalten."
"Der Ritter Quesnay, ein Enkel des berühmten Oekonomisten, hat in Virginien, zu Richmond, der Hauptstadt dieses Staates, eine Akademie der Wissenschaften und schönen Künste zu stiften angefangen... Den 24. Junius 1786 ist der Grundstein dazu gelegt worden. Hr. Quesnay ist nun in Paris, und sucht Unterstützung zur ferneren Ausführung seines Plans. Er hat daher eine Schrift *Mémoire et prospectus concernant l'académie des sciences et des beaux arts des Etats-unis de l'Amérique*, dachau drucken lassen, worinn er eine Subscription eröffnet."

959C. *Review:* Allgemeines Archiv für die Länder, Völker und Staatenkunde, deren Litteratur und Hülfsmittel aufs Jahr 1786. herausgegeben von Fr. Gottl. Canzler. Ersten Bandes erstes Stück. Göttingen: Bey Dietrich, 1787. 12 Bogen. 8°. (Allgemeine deutsche Bibliothek. Berlin, 1788. 12°. Bd. 80, p. 516–518, *NAA*.)

959D. *Review:* Amerika, ein geographisch historisches Lesebuch, zum Nutzen der Jugend und ihrer Erzieher von K. Hammerdörfer und C. T. Kosche. Fünfter Band, als eine Fortsetzung von Europa. Nord-Amerika, Erste Abtheilung, 778 S. und 14 S. Vorrede. Südamerika, Zweyte Abtheilung. 694 S. 8°. (Allgemeine LiteraturZeitung. Jena, 1788. 4°. Jahr 1788, Bd. 3, col. 497–500, *NAA*.)
See no. 1057.

959E. *Review:* Antiquedad de la Jubas. Extracto de un Discurso del R. P. M. F. Martin Sarmiento. Madrid, 1788. 32 S. 8°. (Allgemeine Literatur-Zeitung. Jena, 1789. 4°. Jahr 1789, Bd. 2, col. 647–648, *NAA*.)
Opposes the opinion that syphilis was brought to Europe from America. "P. Martyr [i.e., Pietro Martire d'Anghiera] der doch Secretair des Rath von Indien war, sagt kein Wort, dass die Krankheit aus Amerika käme. In keiner Nachricht von Columbus Entdeckungen steht etwas davon... Das zweyte Zeugniss nimmt der Verfasser aus einem französischen Parlaments-Edicte, welches sagt, dass die grosse Verole 1494 in Frankreich gebersscht habe, also zu einer Zeit, da noch kein Franzose mit Columbus Matrosen Gemeinschaft gehabt haben konnte..."

959F. *Review:* Beyträge zur Geschichte des Amerikanischen Krieges aus Originalbriefen und Schriften der damaligen Zeit. Erster Theil. Philadelphia u. Leipzig, 1788. 352 p. 8°. (Allgemeine Literatur-Zeitung. Jena, 1788. 4°. Jahr 1788, Bd. 3, col. 33–34, *NAA*.)
"Bereits 1782 hat der Hr. Prof. Zinner in Kaschau diese Beyträge unter dem Titel: Merkwürdige Briefe und Schriften der berühmtesten Generale in America nebst derselben beygefügten Lebensbeschreibungen zuerst herausgegeben. Sie scheinen aber so wenig bekannt geworden zu seyn, dass... die Verlegerin Kletts Wittwe in Augsburg den Entschluss gefasst, selbige unter einem angemessenen Titel dem Publikum noch einmal anzubieten."

959G. *Review:* Capitain Cooks dritte und letzte Reise, oder Geschichte einer Entdeckungsreise nach dem stillen Ocean... unternommen und unter der Anführung der Capitaine Cook, Clarke und Gore... [n. p.,] 1787. 133, 320 S. 8°. (Allgemeine deutsche Bibliothek. Berlin, 1788. 8°. Bd. 84, p. 174–176, *NAA*.)

959H. *Review:* Christ. Lud. Reinhold... Kurze Geschichte der Schiffahrt, den [*sic!*] Reisen um die Welt, und den [*sic!*] vornehmsten Länderentdeckungen im Süden und Norden. Ein Beytrag zur Geographie. Münster und Osnabrück: Perrenon, 1787. 127 S. 8°. (Allgemeine Literatur-Zeitung. Jena, 1788. 4°. Jahr 1788, Bd. 2, col. 158, *NAA*.)
Of special interest: "Von Entdeckung der neuen Welt."

960. *Review:* Christ. Lud. Reinhold,... mathematisch-politischer Catechismus der Geographie ...Mit Kupf. und einer neuen Weltkarte. Münster und Osnabrück: Bey Perrenon, 1787. 384 p. 8°. (Allgemeine Literatur-Zeitung. Jena, 1788. 4°. Jahr 1788, Bd. 2, col. 292–294, *NAA*.)
Strange geography of America.

960A. *Review:* Christian Ludolph Reinhold... Mathematisch-politisch- und physischer Catechismus der Geographie für Lehrer und ihre Jünger. Nebst einem Anhang von der Geschichte der Schifffahrt, den Reisen um die Welt und den vornehmsten Länderentdeckungen. Münster und Osnabrück: Bey Perrenon, 1787. 24 Bogen. 8°. (Allgemeine deutsche Bibliothek. Berlin, 1788. 12°. Bd. 80, p. 194–198, *NAA*.)
"Die Amerikanischen Besitzungen des Königs in Spanien werden folgendergestalt angegeben. Amerika, 2. in Nordamerika, 3. in Südamerika, 4. in Westindien und 5. caraibische Inseln... Zu Amerika rechnet er Louisiana, Florida und Neumexico, zu Nordamerika Californien und Altmexico." — *p. 196.*

*1788, continued*

960B. *Notice:* Deutsche hohe Schule in Lancaster, P. A. (Allgemeine Literatur-Zeitung. Jena, 1788. 4°. Jahr 1788, Bd. 1, col. 143, *NAA*.)
This title among others under the heading, "Literarische Nachrichten."
It deals with the foundation of a Deutsche hohe Schule in Lancaster, Pa., by Ernst Mühlenberg. The new school received 10,000 acres as a present. The staff consisted of Mühlenberg as the principal, Pastor Hendel as the vice president, Pastor Melzheimer as professor of German, Latin and Greek, Mr. Reichenbach as professor of mathematics and English, and Mr. Hutchins as a teacher of English.
A prayerbook, issued by the Protestant clergymen and published by Leibert and Billmeyer is announced.

960C. *Review:* Diccionario geográfico-historico de las Indias occidentales ó America. Escrito par el Coronel D. Ant. de Alcedo... v. I, 1787. 292 p. v. II, 1788, 344 p. 4°. (Allgemeine Literatur-Zeitung. Jena, 1788. 4°. Jahr 1788, Bd. 4, col. 497-500, *NAA*.)
The author states "was ihm die rüstigen deutschen Geographen wohl nicht zugeben werden, dass die vollständige Beschreibung von America nicht eines Mannes Werk sey..."

961. *Review:* England. Auszug aus einem Briefe an den Herausgeber der Bibliothek. London, d. 26. Nov. 1787. (Neue Bibliothek der schönen Wissenschaften und der freyen Künste. Leipzig, 1788. 12°. Bd. 35, p. 313-326, *NAA*.)
Contains criticisms on "Tarletons Werk über die letzten amerikanischen Feldzüge, 1787, und Andrews Geschichte des amerikanischen Krieges in vier Bänden. 1785," i.e., Sir Banastre Tarleton, *A History of the Campaigns of 1780 and 1781 in the southern provinces of North America*, London, 1787, † * *KF*, and John Andrews, *The History of the war with America, France, Spain and Holland, commencing in 1775 and ending in 1783*, London, 1786, * *KF*.

961A. *Review:* Essai sur l'Administration des Colonies Françaises et particulièrement d'une partie de celles de Saint-Domingue. Avec deux Cartes et deux Tableaux Géographiques et Politiques. Antonina und Paris: Moutory, 1788. 112 p. 8°. (Allgemeine Literatur-Zeitung. Jena, 1788. 4°. Jahr 1788, Bd. 4, col. 695-696, *NAA*.)
"Aller dieser Ursachen wegen ist für die Menschheit in Ost- und Westindien nicht eher etwas zu erwarten, als bis sich alle dortigen Colonien von ihrem Mutterlande losgerissen haben; da sie dann nach und nach die europäischen Kenntnisse zu ihrer Vervollkommnung nutzen werden."

961B. *Review:* Friedrich Ludwig Walthers natürliche und wissenschaftliche Erdkunde. Hof, 1786. 19 Bogen. 8°. (Allgemeine deutsche Bibliothek. Berlin, 1788. 12°. Bd. 82, p. 197-200, *NAA*.)
Contains a "Menschen- und Völkerkunde."

962. *Review:* Geschichte der Seereisen und Entdeckungen, welche auf Befehl Sr. Grosbrittanischen Majestät George des Dritten unternommen sind. Aus den Tagebüchern der Schiffsbefehlshaber und den Handschriften der Gelehrten Sr. J. Bank, Dr. Solander, Dr. J. R. Forster, Dr. G. Forster und Hn. Anderson... herausgegeben. Bd. VI. Aus dem Englischen übersetzt von Hn. Georg Forster. Berlin: Bey Haude u. Spener, 1787. 564 S. ohne 14 Bogen Einl. u. Beylagen. 4°. (Allgemeine Literatur-Zeitung. Jena, 1788. 4°. Jahr 1788, Bd. 1, col. 129-136, *NAA*.)
Note also Banks, *Neueste Reise-Beschreibungen und Entdeckungen des fünften Welttheils, welche sowohl in Gesellschaft der Herren Banks und Solander, als nachher unternommen worden*, Nürnberg, 1786. Sabin 3203. Not in the Library.

963. *Review:* Lehrbücher für die Jugend in Nordcarolina. Zweyte Lieferung; Biblisches Handbuch für selbstprüfende Leser, nebst einem Anhang vom Bibellesen mit Auswahl. Leipzig: Bey Crusius, 1788. 8°. (Göttingische Anzeigen von gelehrten Sachen. Göttingen [1788]. 12°. Jahr 1788, p. 834, * *DF*.)

963A. *Review:* The Life of capitain James Cook by And. Kippis. 2 v. Basel: Thurneysen [n. d.]. (Allgemeine Literatur-Zeitung. Jena, 1788. 4°. Jahr 1788, Bd. 4, col. 527-528, *NAA*.)

963B. *Review:* A List of the Society instituted in 1781 for the purpose of effecting the abolition of the Slave trade. London, 1788. 5¼ Bogen. 8°. (Allgemeine Literatur-Zeitung. Jena, 1789. 4°. Jahr 1789, Bd. 2, col. 433-434, *NAA*.)
"Die Bemühungen der Quäker in Nordamerika, die Einfuhr der Negersklaven zu verbieten, noch mehr aber Hn. Ramsays 1783 gedruckte *Essays on the treatment and conversion of African slaves in British sugar colonies*... haben endlich einen grossen Theil des brittischen Publicums auf das Schicksal der Neger aufmerksam gemacht."

964. *Review:* Medical Commentaries for the year 1785. Collected and published by A. Duncan. v. 10. London, 1786. 496 p. 8°. (Göttingische Anzeigen von gelehrten Sachen. Göttingen [1788]. 12°. Jahr 1788, p. 930-934, * *DF*.)
The Commentaries contain J. Adair's essay on drugs in the West Indies and I. Cochrane's account of a young negro, "der sich aus Missmuth den Unterleib aufschnitt."

965. *Review:* Memoirs of the American Academy of Arts and Sciences to the End of the Year 1785. v. 1. Boston, 1785. 568 p. 6 plates. 8°. (Göttingische Anzeigen von gelehrten Sachen. Göttingen [1788]. 12°. Jahr 1788, p. 825-834, * *DF*.)
"Die amerikanische Akademie hat der Göttingischen Societät der Wissenschaften mit diesem Bande ein angenehmes Geschenk gemacht..."
"Im Eingange: Bildung, Gesetze der Akademie und Verzeichniss der Mitglieder, die europäischen in einer eignen Abtheilung..." Articles on astronomy, mathematics, and medicine by most of the leading American scientists of the day.

965A. *Review:* Neue Quartalschrift zum Unterricht und zur Unterhaltung, aus den besten und neuesten Reisebeschreibungen gezogen. 1stes Stück. Berlin: Bei Wever, 1787. 11 Bogen. 8°. (Allgemeine deutsche Bibliothek. Berlin, 1788. 12°. Bd. 82, p. 196-197, *NAA*.)
Contains "Beytrag zur Geschichte der Russischen Entdeckungsreisen zwischen Asia und Amerika."

965B. *Review:* Neueste Erdbeschreibung aller vier Theile der Welt und der wenig bekannten Länder, nebst einer mathematischen Beschreibung der Erdkugel. Vorzüglich zum Unterricht der Jugend... von H. A. Kunstmann. Berlin: Hesse, 1786. 18 Bogen. 8°. (Allgemeine deutsche Bibliothek. Berlin, 1788. 8°. Bd. 78, p. 197-198, *NAA*.)

*1788, continued*

966. *Review:* Notes on the State of Virginia; written by Thomas Jefferson. London: Bey Stockdale, 1787. 382 p. 8°. (Allgemeine Literatur-Zeitung. Jena, 1788. 4°. Jahr 1788, Bd. 2, col. 33-37, *NAA.*)
A German translation of this work appeared in Leipzig, in 1789.

966A. *Review:* Nouvelle Géographie à l'usage des instituts et des gouvernantes francoises renfermant les productions, les usages, les costumes de chaque pays et tous les changements arrivés sur le Globe jusqu'en 1785 par Mad. Renelle. Berlin: Decker, 1786. tom I. 8°. (Allgemeine Literatur-Zeitung. Jena, 1788. 4°. Jahr 1788, Bd. 2, col. 201-203, *NAA.*)

967. *Review:* Nützliche Anweisung, von dem Landtoback verschiedene gute Sorten Rauch- und Schnupftoback zu fabriciren; nebst einem Anhang, virginische und ungarische Blätter wohl zu zubereiten... Berlin, 1787. 12 p.l., 29 p. 8°. (Allgemeine Literatur-Zeitung. Jena, 1788. 4°. Jahr 1788, Bd. 2, col. 294, *NAA.*)
See no. 785.

968. *Review:* Observations on some parts of Natural History: to which is prefixed an account of several remarkable vestiges of an ancient date, which have been discovered in different Parts of North America. Part I. By Benjamin Smille [*sic!*] Barton... London: auf Kosten des Verf. und in Commission b. Dilly, n.d. 76 p. 8°. (Allgemeine Literatur-Zeitung. Jena, 1788. 4°. Jahr 1788, Bd. 3, col. 879-880, *NAA.*)
The Library's copy of this work by Benjamin Smith Barton is in * KF.

969. *Review:* A Poem on the Bill lately passed for regulating the Slave Trade. By Helen Maria Williams. London: Cadell, 1788. 4°. (Neue Bibliothek der schönen Wissenschaften und der freyen Künste. Leipzig, 1789. 12°. Bd. 39, p. 302, *NAA.*)

970. *Review:* Political Sketches, inscribed to his Exc. John Adams, Ministre plenipotentiary from the united States to the Court of Great-Britain by a Citizen of the United States. London: bey Dilly, 1787. 104 S. 8°. (Allgemeine Literatur-Zeitung. Jena, 1788. 4°. Jahr 1788, Bd. 3, col. 161-164, *NAA.*)
The Library's copy of this work by William V. Murray is in * KF.
This work is a reply to Abbé Mably's *Remarks concerning the government and laws of the United States*, to Raynal and to several other French and English writers who had disseminated false opinions on the thirteen United States.
"Aber in Amerika entstand die Freyheit nicht durch plötzlichen Widerstand gegen Ausschweifungen eines Tyrannen, sondern sie erwuchs langsam aus Grundsätzen"...

971. *Review:* Recherches historiques et politiques sur les états unis de l'amérique septentrionale. Paris: Bey Froulé, 1788. 4 v. 8°.

(Allgemeine Literatur-Zeitung. Jena, 1788. 4°. Jahr 1788, Bd. 4, col. 9-16, *NAA.*)
The Library's copies of this work by Filippo Mazzei are in * KF.
The author was assisted by M. J. A. N. C. Condorcet.
See also Philip Mazzei, *Virginia's agent in Europe; the story of his mission...edited by Howard R. Marraro*, New York: The New York Public Library, 1935, * RB-IGA.

972. *Review:* Recherches historiques et politiques sur les états unis de l'Amérique septentrionale par un citoyen de Virginie. Paris: Froullé, 1788. 4 v. (Göttingische Anzeigen von gelehrten Sachen. Göttingen [1788]. 12°. Jahr 1788, p. 1124-1126, * *DF.*)
See note on preceding entry.

972A. *Review:* Die Reisenden für Länder- und Völkerkunde. Zweyter Band. Nürnberg: Felsecker, 1788. 370 S. ohne Vorrede. 8°. (Allgemeine Literatur-Zeitung. Jena, 1789. 4°. Jahr 1789, Bd. 1, col. 649-650, *NAA.*)
"Die Auszüge aus fremden Reisebeschreibungen, z. B. Poivre, Bartels, Schöpf; wozu diese? — Wer sollte nicht besser thun, diese Reisebeschreibungen selbst zu lesen?"

973. *Review:* Sendschreiben des F. C. de la Roche Callichon...an Hn. Verfasser des politischen Journals, betreffend die Wiederfindung des alten Grönlands, und der unzertrennlich damit verknüpften sogenannten Nordwestlichen Durchfahrt. Kopenhagen: gedruckt auf Kosten des Vf. bey Holm, 1787. 102 Seiten. 8°. (Allgemeine Literatur-Zeitung. Jena, 1788. 4°. Jahr 1788, Bd. 4, col. 615-616, *NAA.*)
The author was a Dutch Landrath. On his instigation, Egede and Rothe were sent to the eastern coast of Greenland in 1786. In this work, he states that ancient Greenland must have been a different island.

973A. *Review:* Statistisch-historisch-geographisches Handbuch zur Grundlegung der Kenntnis der Staaten und Länder und ihrer Geschichte, verfasset von Ant. Albr. Watermeyer. Hamburg: Bey Hofmann [n. d.]. 12 Bogen. 8°. (Allgemeine deutsche Bibliothek. Berlin, 1788. 8°. Bd. 79, p. 202-203, *NAA.*)

973B. *Review:* Taschenatlas, oder geographisches statistisches Handbuch von allen vier Welttheilen, zum lehrreichen Unterricht der Jugend. Nebst 42 Landkarten. Berlin: Bey Wever, 1788. 267 S. 8°. (Allgemeine Literatur-Zeitung. Jena, 1789. 4°. Jahr 1789, Bd. 1, col. 44-46, *NAA.*)
"In Nordamerica fehlt auch manches, z. B. Shelburn in Neuschottland, in und um welcher Stadt 30,000 Einwohner sind."

974. *Review:* Thoughts upon the African Slave trade by John Newton. London: Buckland, 1788. 41 p. 8°. (Allgemeine Literatur-Zeitung. Jena, 1788. 4°. Jahr 1788, Bd. 4, col. 631-632, *NAA.*)
The Library's copies of this essay are in * *KF* and *SEK p.v.2.*

*1788, continued*

975. *Review:* Transactions of the american philosophical Society, held at Philadelphia, for promoting useful Knowledge. Philadelphia: Bey Aitken; auch zu London: Bey Dilly, 1786. Bd. 2, 397 S. 4°. (Magazin für das Neueste aus der Physik und Naturgeschichte. Gotha, 1788. 12°. Bd. 5, p. 158–178, *3–OA*.)

The review contains notes on the history of the Society and criticism on the following articles in the *Transactions:* The White Mountains in New Hampshire, by Belknap; The development of silk worms, by Morgan; A worm living in the retina of a horse, by Hopkinson; A snake [*sic!*] as a parasite in the eye of another horse, by Morgan; Description of an electric eel, the migration of herrings, by Gilpin; Magnetism, by Rittenhouse; The limestone cave at Swatara River, by Miller; Analysis of the water of the springs in Botetourt County, by Madison; Optical illusion, by Rittenhouse; A description of a rock and cascade in Pennsylvania, by Hutchins; An optical instrument, by Rittenhouse; A hygrometer, by Franklin; A theory on a thunderstorm, by Oliver; Oceanic theories, by Oliver and Perkins; and a number of meteorological treatises.
The Library's set of the *Transactions* is in * *EA.* '
See no. 1026.

976. *Review:* Ueber das Rauchen der Kamine u. der Schornsteine in einem Schreiben des Hrn. Dr. Benjamin Franklin an den Hrn. Dr. Ingenhouss, übersetzt und mit Anmerkungen versehen von P. H. C. B[rodhagen]. Hamburg: Bey Bohn, 1788. 116 p. 1 plate. 8°. (Göttingische Anzeigen von gelehrten Sachen. Göttingen [1788]. 12°. Jahr 1788, p. 901–902, **DF*.)

"Hr. Br[odhagen] hat Rustons Schreiben an Fr[anklin] und allerley andere Erfahrungen in den angehängten Anmerkungen beygebracht, auch Bücher genannt, welche diesen Gegenstand betreffen."
Note also *Beschreibung der neuerfundenen pensylvanischen Kamine oder Oefen. 1794. Aus dem Englischen und Holländischen übersetzt,* Gotha, 1794. Sabin 59913. Not in the Library.

977. *Review:* Ueber die auf Jamaika wachsenden, in der Arzneykunst gebräuchlichen Pflanzen, von William Wright. Aus dem Englischen. (Magazin für Botanik. Zürich, 1788– 1790. 12°. Stück 4, p. 111–155; Stück 7, p. 19– 41, *QEA.*)

977A. *Review:* Uebersicht der politischen Lage und des Handelszustandes von St. Domingo, aus dem französischen des Abts Raynal mit Anmerkungen. Leipzig: Haug, 1788. 376 p. 8°. (Allgemeine Literatur-Zeitung. Jena, 1788. 4°. Jahr 1788, Bd. 4, col. 702–704, *NAA.*)

977B. *Notice:* Vermischte Nachrichten. Neuyork, d. 31. Merz, 1788. (Allgemeine Literatur-Zeitung. Jena, 1788. 4°. Jahr 1788, Bd. 4, col. 384, *NAA.*)

This title among others under heading, "Literarische Nachrichten."
"Der ehemalige Buchhändler Magister Reich ist gar nach Amerika gekommen. Er wollte die vor einigen Jahren hereingesandten Bücher gern für Makulatur verkaufen; aber niemand bot ihm etwas.— Nun haben wir auch wieder neue Universitäten, si Diis placet, erhalten; Maryland hat zwey Collegia, wovon ein an einem Ende des Staates, das andere am andern steht, durch ein Landgesetz für die Universität von Maryland erklärt. Neujork hat eine Anzahl Herren, darunter der Gouverneur, General von Steuben, und andere sich befinden, durch ein Gesetz zur Universität vom Staate Neujork erklärt. Sie haben weder Professores noch Studenten, sondern sollen die oberste Aufsicht über alle Schulanstalten im ganzen Staate haben, dabey aber das Recht geniessen, alle akademische Grade zu ertheilen, und Universität heissen. Unter den Procuratoren des Collegii der Stadt Neu York ist unter andern auch der Juden Rabbi, ein Quäkerprediger und ein Bierbrauer."

978. *Review:* The Vision of Columbus: a Poem in nine Books by Joel Barlow, Esq. London: Dilly, 1787. 12°. (Neue Bibliothek der schönen Wissenschaften und der freyen Künste. Leipzig, 1788–1791. 12°. Bd. 36, p. 163; Bd. 42, p. 147–148, *NAA.*)
The Library's copies of this volume are in * *KL.*

979. *Review:* Wilhelm Chamberlain practische Abhandlung von den Kräften des Sbitzolobium oder der Kuhkrätze, ingleichen der Kohlpalmenrinde wider die Würmer. Altenburg: In der Richterischen Buchhandlung. 1786. 84 p. 8°. (Magazin für die Botanik. Zürich, 1788. 12°. [Jahr] 1788, Stück 3, p. 69–70, *QEA.*)

This is a translation of his *On the efficacy of Cowhage in diseases occasioned by worms; to which is added observations on other anthelminitics of the West-Indies,* London, 1785; see "Surgeon General's catalogue," series 1, v. 2, p. 830, for full title and description.

980. *Review:* The Wrongs of Africa. A Poēm. Part I. London: Faulder, 1787. 33 S. 4°. (Allgemeine Literatur-Zeitung. Jena, 1788. 4°. Jahr 1788, Bd. 2, col. 397–398, *NAA.*)
Refers to slave trade.

### 1789

981. ANEKDOTE. (Hannoverisches Magazin... vom Jahre 1789. Hannover, 1790. 4°. Jahrg. 27, col. 319–320.) *DF
A slave-trader repents.
Title page dated 1790; contents, 1789.

982. ANEKDOTE. (Hannoverisches Magazin... vom Jahre 1789. Hannover, 1790. 4°. Jahrg. 27, col. 351–352.) *DF
A slave, given freedom by his master, works for the latter's widow without remuneration.
Title page dated 1790; contents, 1789.

983. ANMERKUNGEN über den Beitrag...dieses Magazins den Negerhandel betreffend. (Hannoverisches Magazin...vom Jahre 1789. Hannover, 1790. 4°. Jahrg. 27, col. 513–528.) * DF
Signed: E. E. Noltemeyer.
"Der... Herr Verfasser ist zweimal in Westindien gewesen... Seit einigen Jahren ist er angesessener Bürger in der Stadt Münder."
Title page dated 1790; contents, 1789.
See no. 929.

984. BALTIMORE in Nord Amerika, 11 Novbr. 1789. (In: A. L. Schlözer. Stats-Anzeigen. Göttingen, 1789. 12°. Bd. 13, p. 527–528.) BAC
Argument against Schoepf's letters.
See no. 812.

985. BEMERKUNGEN über die Wirkungen des Klima, und zwar zuerst des kalten Klima auf die Gesundheit der Menschen. (Göttingisches historisches Magazin. Hannover, 1789. 12°. Bd. 4, p. 1–45.) BAA (Neues)
Signed: M (i.e. Christoph Meiners, 1747–1810).
Periodical subsequently called *Neues göttingisches historisches Magazin,* under which it is shelved.

## 1789, continued

**986.** [CAUSLAND, R.] R. Causland über einige Besonderheiten in der Natur und den Sitten der nordamerikanischen Indianer. (Magazin für die Naturgeschichte des Menschen. Zittau und Leipzig, 1789. 12°. Bd. 2, Stück 2, p. 42–54.) QOA
Discusses the problem of why the Indians have no beards, and describes some Indian customs.

**987.** COOK, JAMES. Des Capitain Jacob Cook dritte Entdeckungs-Reise in die Südsee und nach dem Nordpol. Auf Befehl Sr. Grosbrittann. Majest. George des Dritten unternommen und in den Schiffen Resolution und Discovery während der Jahre 1776 bis 1780 ausgeführt. Aus den Tagebüchern der Schiffsbefehlshaber Herren Cook, Clerke, Gore und King, imgleichen des Schiffswundarztes Herrn Anderson vollständig beschrieben. Aus dem Englischen übersetzt... von Herrn Georg Forster... Berlin: Bey Haude und Spener, 1789. 4 v. table. 8°. *KF 1789

—— Fünf und vierzig Kupfer und Charten zur deutschen Quart-Ausgabe von Cooks dritter Entdeckungsreise... Berlin: Bey Haude und Spener, 1789. 2 p.l., maps, plates, port. 4°.
*KF 1789
Plates engraved by J. F. Bolt, G. W. Hullmann, J. C. G. Fritzsch, F. S. Ringck, I. Nussbiegel and others after J. Webber.

**988.** GRÜNDLICHE Nachrichten von dem Zustande der Negersklaven in den holländischen Kolonien in Amerika. (Hannoverisches Magazin...vom Jahre 1789. Hannover, 1790. 4°, Jahrg. 27, col. 545–560.) *DF
Signed: E. C. Noltemeyer.
Title page dated 1790; contents, 1789.

**989.** KEATE, GEORGE. Nachrichten von den Pelew-Inseln in der Westgegend des stillen Oceans. Aus den Tagebüchern und mündlichen Nachrichten des Capitains Heinrich Wilson ...zusammengetragen von Herrn Georg Keate ...und aus dem Englischen übersetzt von D. Georg Forster... Mit einer Karte und Kupfern... Hamburg: Bei Benjamin Gottlob Hoffmann, 1789. 6 p.l., xii–lviii, 494 p., 1 folding map, 2 plates (1 folding), 3 ports. (incl. frontis.) 8°. (Neuere Geschichte der See- und Land-Reisen. Bd. 1.) *KF 1789 (Neuere)
The original was published in London in 1788 under the title: An account of the Pelew Islands, †*KF.
Review: Göttingische Anzeigen von gelehrten Sachen, Jahr 1794, p. 388–389, *DF.

**990.** KENNEDY, ILDEPHONS. Anmerkungen über die Witterung, besonders der Jahre 1783, 84, 85 und 86. (Bayerische Akademie der Wissenschaften. Neue philosophische Abhandlungen. München, 1789. 4°. Bd. 5, p. 399–457.) *EE
Compares the weather in America with that of the other hemisphere.

**991.** KOSCHE, CHRISTIAN TRAUGOTT. Karakter, Sitten und Religion aller bekannten Völker unsers Erdbodens; ein Handbuch für die Jugend und ihre Erzieher angefangen von C. T. Kosche A.M. und fortgesetzt von F. G. Leonhardi...
Leipzig: Bey Johann Friedrich Junius, 1789–1791. 4 v. 8°. *KF 1789
Bd. 1 has title vignette, engr.
Bd. 2–4 continued by F. G. Leonhardi.
Bd. 1. Die Amerikaner.
Reviews: Allgemeine deutsche Bibliothek, Bd. 99, p. 212–213, NAA; Allgemeine Literatur-Zeitung, Jahr 1788, Bd. 3, col. 497–500, NAA; Göttingische Anzeigen von gelehrten Sachen, Jahr 1790, p. 1365, *DF.

**992.** KOTZEBUE, AUGUST VON. Die Jndianer in England. Lustspiel in drey Aufzügen. Zum ersten Mahle aufgeführt auf dem Liebhaber-Theater zu Reval im Februar 1789. (In his: Theater von August v. Kotzebue. Wien: Jn Commission bey Anton Doll, 1810–19. 16°. Bd. 2, p. 3–112.) NGC
"Das Stück spielt xwar in einer englischen Seestadt... Gurli, die junge Indianerin, wird von dem Sohn des 'ehemals reichen Kaufmannes' Sir John Smith, dem Schiffskapitän Robert, geheiratet." — Constantin Breffka, Amerika in der deutschen Literatur, Coeln, 1917, p. 8, NFF p.v.43.

**993.** KURZE Geschichte des gemässigten Klima. (Göttingisches historisches Magazin. Hannover, 1789. 12°. Bd. 5, p. 703–742.) BAA (Neues)
See "Von dem gemässigten Erd-Gürtel in America," p. 735–742.
Signed: M (i.e., Christoph Meiners, 1747–1810).
Periodical subsequently called Neues göttingisches historisches Magazin, under which it is shelved.

**994.** LOSKIEL, GEORG HEINRICH. Geschichte der Mission der evangelischen Brüder unter den Indianern in Nordamerika durch Georg Heinrich Loskiel. Barby: Zu finden in den Brüdergemeinen, und in Leipzig in Commission bey Paul Gotthelf Kummer, 1789. 8 p.l., 783(1) p. 8°. *KF 1789
Sabin 42109.
First issue with six lines of Errata.
Printed by Lorenz Friedrich Speltenberg.
"Die Materialien zu dieser Beschreibung habe ich theils dem würdigen Bischof August Gottlieb Spangenberg, welcher selbst viele Jahre in Nordamerika, auch im Indianerlande gewesen, theils, und zwar die allermehrsten, dem Missionario David Zeisberger zu danken, welcher nun über 40 Jahre ununterbrochen bey der Mission gedient hat... Der Werth dieser Nachrichten besteht also vornehmlich in ihrer Zuverlässigkeit." — Vorbericht.
Excerpts from this work appear in Magazin für das Neueste aus der Physik und Naturgeschichte, Bd. 6, Stück 2, p. 164–177, *OA.
An English translation by C. I. La Trobe, published in London, in 1794, is in HBC.
See also: J. J. Heim, David Zeisberger, der Apostel der Indianer in Nord-Amerika, wie er unter denselben 60 Jahre lebte und wirkte und starb. Neue und vermehrte Ausgabe, Basel, [pref. 1853], *C p.v.2589; The diary of David Zeisberger...translated from the original German manuscript and edited by Eugene F. Bliss, Cincinnati, 1885 (Historical and Philosophical Society of Ohio, Publications, new series, v. 2–3, IAA) extends from 1781 to 1798. E. A. De Schweinitz, The life and times of David Zeisberger, the western pioneer and apostle of the Indians, Philadelphia, 1870, HBM (Zeisberger). Note also The history of the Moravian Mission among the Indians in North-America [founded on a work by G. H. Loskiel], London, 1740. British Museum catalogue: America, North. Not in the Library.

**995.** —— —— Second issue. *KF 1789
With full page of Errata.

**996.** NACHRICHT über Frasers nordamerikanisches Gras. (Hannoverisches Magazin...vom Jahre 1789. Hannover, 1790. 4°. Jahrg. 27, col. 1357–1360.) *DF
Title page dated 1790; contents, 1789.
See nos. 1090, 1164A.

*1789, continued*

997. NACHRICHT von der ausserordentlichen Fähigkeit eines Negersklaven in Maryland, alles gleich im Kopfe auszurechnen. (Hannoverisches Magazin...vom Jahre 1789. Hannover, 1790. 4°. Jahrg. 27, col. 381-384.) * DF
From the *British mercury*, January, 1789, p. 14. "Mitgetheilt vom Dr. Rush zu Philadelphia..."
Edited by Georg Friedrich Wehrs of Hannover.
Title page dated 1790; contents, 1789.

998. NACHRICHT von einigen Naturmerkwürdigkeiten in Virginien. (Magazin für das Neueste aus der Physik und Naturgeschichte. Gotha, 1789. 8°. Bd. 6, Stück 3, p. 115-125.)
3-OA
Taken from Professor Sprengel's *Beyträgen zur Völker- und Länderkunde*, Theil 8 und 9.
Contents: 1. Der Wasserfall oder der sogenannte Falling Spring in Augusta. 2. Die Maddisens Höhle. 3. Die stürmische Höhle (Blowing Cave). 4. Die natürliche Brücke (Rockbridge). 5. Der Schwefelbrunnen am grossen Kanhaway. 6. Eine sonderbare Naturerscheinung, welche vermuthlich aus einer jählingen Entbindung des Wärmestoffs erklärt werden muss. 7. Eine andere eben so merkwürdige Naturerscheinung... Strahlenbrechung (Looming).

999. [EINE NEUE Art Schildkröte (serrated) aus den Flüssen von Newyork... Ein neuer grauer Frosch aus Carolina... Eine neue geringelte Eidexe...] (Magazin für das Neueste aus der Physik und Naturgeschichte. Gotha, 1789. 12°. Bd. 6, Stück 1, p. 176-179.) 3-OA
Successive paragraph headings used as title.

1000. OTAHEITI. (Der Teutsche Merkur. Weimar, 1789. 12°. Jahr 1789, Vierteljahr 2, p. 275-277.)     * DF (Neue)
Signed: von K.
Poem on the island of Haiti.
Periodical subsequently called *Der Neue teutsche Merkur*, under which it is shelved.

1001. PARIS. Die menschenfreundliche Gesellschaft, welche Abschaffung des Sklavenhandels zur Absicht hat... (Göttingische Anzeigen von gelehrten Sachen. Göttingen [1789]. 12°. Jahr 1789, p. 431-432.)     * DF
Report on "La Société des amis des noirs."

1002. STÖVER, DIETRICH JOHANN HEINRICH. Historisch-statistische Beyträge zur nähern Kenntniss der Staaten und der neuern Weltbegebenheiten. Herausgegeben von Dietrich Heinrich Stöver, Doctor der Philosophie. Hamburg: Bey Benjamin Gottlob Hoffmann, 1789. 8 p.l., 406 p. 12°.     * KF 1789
Neueste Bevölkerungsliste und Häuserzahl der Städte des Nordamericanischen Freystaats, p. 178-179.
Friedens- und Handelstractat zwischen den vereinigten Staaten von Nordamerica und dem Kayser von Marocco, p. 181-185.
Biographische Nachrichten von dem Americanischen General Green, ehemaligen Commandeur en Chef in den beyden Carolinas, p. 248-256.

1003. UEBER den amerikanischen Leinsaamen. (Hannoverisches Magazin...vom Jahre 1789. Hannover, 1790. 4°. Jahrg. 27, col. 255-256.)
* DF
Signed and dated: J. G. Niemann, Gerichtsdirektor, Otterndorf, im Februar 1789.
Title page dated 1790; contents, 1789.
Concerns flax-seed imported from Philadelphia, Pa.
"Jm Betracht der Kultur schreibt mir mein Correspondent, dass man in Amerika den Saamen ungefehr in der Mitte des Aprils in leichtes wohlgedüngtes Land säet, den Flachs vom Unkraut rein hält, und ihn nicht früher her aufziebet, bis er völlig reif und ganz gelb ist."

1004. UEBER den Genuss und die Wirkungen von animalischen und vegetabilischen Speisen. (Göttingisches historisches Magazin. Hannover, 1789. 12°. Bd. 4, p. 355-370.) BAA (Neues)
Signed: M (i.e., Christoph Meiners, 1747-1810).
Periodical subsequently called *Neues göttingisches historisches Magazin*, under which it is shelved.

1005. UEBER die Ausstattungen und Mitgiften unter verschiedenen Völkern. (Göttingisches historisches Magazin. Hannover, 1789. 12°. Bd. 4, p. 46-56.)     BAA (Neues)
Signed: M (i.e., Christoph Meiners, 1747-1810).
Periodical subsequently called *Neues göttingisches historisches Magazin*, under which it is shelved.

1006. UEBER die Entstehung des Eigenthums. (Göttingisches historisches Magazin. Hannover, 1789. 12°. Bd. 5, p. 461-474.) BAA (Neues)
Signed: M (i.e., Christoph Meiners, 1747-1810).
Periodical subsequently called *Neues göttingisches historisches Magazin*, under which it is shelved.

1007. UEBER die Sinnlichkeit, und deren verschiedene Stuffen und Zweige. (Göttingisches historisches Magazin. Hannover, 1789. 12°. Bd. 4, p. 586-606.)     BAA (Neues)
Signed: M (i.e., Christoph Meiners, 1747-1810).
Periodical subsequently called *Neues göttingisches historisches Magazin*, under which it is shelved.

1008. UEBER die Verunstaltungen des Mundes in der Absicht ihn zu verschönern. (Göttingisches historisches Magazin. Hannover, 1789. 12°. Bd. 4, p. 371-376.) BAA (Neues)
Signed: M (i.e., Christoph Meiners, 1747-1810).
Periodical subsequently called *Neues göttingisches historisches Magazin*, under which it is shelved.

1009. VELTHUSEN, JOHANN CASPAR. Nordcarolina. (Hannoverisches Magazin...vom Jahre 1789. Hannover, 1790. 4°. Jahrg. 27, col. 1529-1532.)     * DF
Dated: Rostock, Aug. 10th, 1789.

1009A. *Review*: Abhandlungen über die venerische Krankheit, von Christoph Girtanner. II. und III. Bd. Göttingen: Dietrich, 1789. 933 S. 8°. (Allgemeine Literatur-Zeitung. Jena, 1789. 4°. Jahr 1789, Bd. 4, col. 25-32, *NAA*.)
Where did syphilis originate?

1010. *Review*: Account of the Slavetrade on the Coast of Africa; by Falconbridge, late Surgeon in the Slavetrade. The second Edition. London: B. Philips, 1789. 72 Seiten. 8°. (Allgemeine Literatur-Zeitung. Jena, 1789. 4°. Jahr 1789, Bd. 2, col. 434-437, *NAA*.)
The Library does not have the second edition of Alexander Falconbridge's essay; the first edition, also published in 1788, is in * KF.

1011. *Review*: Arbustum americanum: The American Grove, or a [*sic!*] alphabetical Catalogue of Forest-Trees and Shrubs, natives of the american States. London, 1788. 8°. (Allgemeine Literatur-Zeitung. Jena, 1789. 4°. Jahr 1789, Intelligenzblatt, col. 454, *NAA*.)
The Library has only the Philadelphia, 1785, edition of this *Arbustum americanum*, by Humphry Marshall; class mark, * KD.

*1789, continued*

1012. *Review:* Auszug der Geschichte der aussereuropäischen Welttheile seit den Zeiten Mahomeds und der Entdeckung von Amerika von Ge. Aug. von Breitenbauch. Leipzig: Bey Breitkopf, 1789. 8°. (Göttingische Anzeigen von gelehrten Sachen. Göttingen [1789]. 12°. Jahr 1789, p. 1295–1296, * *DF.*)
See no. 1213.
Note also his *Vorstellung der vornehmsten Völkerschaften der Welt, nach ihrer Abstammung, Ausbreitung und Sprache,* Leipzig, 1786; "a portion is devoted to the aborigines of America." — *Sabin 7708.* Also, his *Religionszustand der verschiedenen Länder der Welt in den ältern und neuern Zeiten,* Leipzig, 1787; Sabin 7707. Neither is in the Library.

1013. *Review:* Beschreibung der wildwachsenden Bäume und Staudengewächse in den vereinigten Staaten von Nordamerika, von Humphry Marschal [*sic!*] Aus dem Englischen, mit Anmerkungen und Zusätzen durch Christian Friedrich Hoffmann. Leipzig, 1788. (Allgemeine Literatur-Zeitung. Jena, 1789. 4°. Jahr 1789, Bd. 4, col. 392, *NAA.*)
*See* note of no. 1011.
"Die reiche Anpflanzung fremder Holzarten, welche der Hr. von Veltheim in Destedt vor Braunschweig seit mehrern Jahren angelegt hat, benutzte der Uebersetzer, um viele Beschreibungen selbst nachzusehen..."

1014. *Review:* Beyträge zur Völker- und Länderkunde, herausgegeben von M. C. Sprengel, Eilfter Theil. Leipzig: Bey Weygand, 1789. 292 S. (Allgemeine Literatur-Zeitung. Jena, 1789. 4°. Jahr 1789, Bd. 4, col. 245, *NAA.*)
In this volume is *Geschichte der seit 1785 von den Engländern meist des Pelzhandels wegen unternommenen Schiffahrten nach der nordwestlichen Küste von Nord-Amerika.*

1015. *Review:* Bibliotheca Americana, or a Chronological Catalogue of the most curious and Interesting Books, Pamphlets, State Papers upon the Subjects of North and South america. 1789. 262 S. 4°. (Allgemeine Literatur-Zeitung. Jena, 1789. 4°. Jahr 1789, Intelligenzblatt, col. 1101; Bd. 4, col. 435–440, *NAA.*)
The Library's copies of this work, ascribed to and catalogued under L. T. Rede, are in * *KF.*

1015A. *Review:* A brief Account of Antigua, together with the Customs and manners of its Inhabitants as well white as black...by John Luffmann. London: B. Cadell, 1789. 180 p. (Allgemeine Literatur-Zeitung. Jena, 1789. 4°. Jahr 1789, Bd. 4, col. 257–262, *NAA.*)
"Da wir von den amerikanischen Zuckerinseln seit Oldendorps Beschreibungen der dänischen Inseln St. Croix etc. nur Fragmente über einige andere, oder den Zustand der dortigen Neger, und nichts vollständiges oder zusammenhängendes über alle Eigenthümlichkeiten dieser Gegenden erhalten haben, so hätte des Vf. Beschreibung der Insel Antigua, welche er zwey Jahre lang bewohnte, wohl reichhaltiger ausfallen können."
A German translation by J. H. Wiedemann appeared as Bd. 15 of the *Bibliothek der neuesten Reisebeschreibungen,* Nürnberg, 1790.

1016. *Review:* Briefe eines amerikanischen Landmanns an den Ritter W. S. in den Jahren 1770–1781, aus dem Französischen übersetzt von Joh. Aug. Ephr. Goetze. Bd. 1. Leipzig: B. Crusius, 1788. 10 Bogen. 8°. (Allgemeine Literatur-Zeitung. Jena, 1789. 4°. Jahr 1789, Bd. 3, col. 565–567, *NAA.*)
*See* no. 1100.

1016A. *Review:* D. Ph. G. Henslers... Geschichte der Lustseuche, die zu Ende des fünfzehnten Jahrhunderts in Europa ausbrach. Zweyten Bandes zweytes Stück. Hamburg, 1789. 92 und 15 S. 8°. (Allgemeine Literatur-Zeitung. Jena, 1789. 4°. Jahr 1789, Bd. 4, col. 25–32, *NAA.*)
Did syphilis originate in America?

1016B. *Review:* De Morbo venereo Analecta quaedam ex M. S. S. Musei Britannici Londinensis Auct. Just. Arnemann, M.D. Göttingen, 1789. 4°. (Allgemeine Literatur-Zeitung. Jena, 1790. 4°. Jahr 1790, Bd. 1, col. 383–384, *NAA.*)
Did syphilis originate in the West Indies?

1017. *Review:* Essay on the Impolicy of the American Slavetrade. The second Edition. By Th. Clarkson. London: Bey Philipps, 1788. 138 p. 8°. (Allgemeine Literatur-Zeitung. Jena, 1789. 4°. Jahr 1789, Bd. 2, col. 445–448, *NAA.*)
The Library's copies of this English work are in * *KF.*

1018. *Review:* Essay on the Slavery and Commerce of the human species particularly the African, the Second Edition, revised and considerably enlarged. London: B. Phillips, 1788. 167 p. 8°. (Allgemeine Literatur-Zeitung. Jena, 1789. 4°. Jahr 1789, Bd. 2, col. 441–445, *NAA.*)
The Library's copies of this English work are in * *KF.*

1018A. *Review:* Geographisches Handbuch in Hinsicht auf Industrie und Handlung, von Paul Joh. Bruns... Neue vermehrte rechtmässige Auflage... Nürnberg: Weigel und Schneider, 1789. 195 S. und 5 S. Verbesserungen und Zusätze. 8°. (Allgemeine Literatur-Zeitung. Jena, 1790. 4°. Jahr 1790, Bd. 1, col. 15–16, *NAA.*)
"Fabriken sind in diesem Staate [America] noch in ihrer Kindheit und werden es auch nach aller Wahrscheinlichkeit (des einträglichen Ackerbaues und hohen Zinsfusses wegen) noch lange bleiben."

1018B. *Review:* Geographisches Handbuch in Hinsicht auf Industrie und Handlung, von Paul Jakob Bruns. Leipzig: Bey Crusius, 1788. 19 Bogen. 8°. (Allgemeine deutsche Bibliothek. Berlin, 1789. 12°. Bd. 90, p. 497–498, *NAA.*)
"Das ist wieder eines von den Lehrbüchern, die eine Gesellschaft Helmstädtischer Gelehrten zum Gebrauche der Schulen in Nordcarolina herauszugeben angefangen hat." The reviewer states that essential matters are missing. "Z, E. fehlt, dass Neu-Jersey auch reichhaltige Kupferertze enthalte; dass der Ort Princetown eine Universität nach Englischer Art, und Lancaster in Pensylvanien seit 1787 eine deutsche hohe Schule hat, dass Nordcarolina starken Schweinshandel nach Virginien treibt, dass Providence auch Ananas und Mahagonyholz liefern..."

1018C. *Review:* Geographisches Kartenspiel für Kinder. Grottkau: Im Verlag und zum Besten der evangelischen Buchanstalt, 1788. (Allgemeine deutsche Bibliothek. Berlin, 1789. 12°. Bd. 89, p. 184–185, *NAA.*)
Geographical games for children.

*1789, continued*

1019. *Review:* Historisch-geographische Monatsschrift, hrsg. v. J. E. Fabri und K. Hammerdörfer. 1788. 12 Stück. 8°. (Allgemeine Literatur-Zeitung. Jena, 1789. 4°. Jahr 1789, Bd. 3, col. 412–416, *NAA.*)
Contains "Beyträge zur Erdbeschreibung und Statistik des nordamerikanischen Freystaats." (Aus amerikanischen Zeitungsblättern.) This periodical, not in the Library, is abundant in articles relating to America, some titles being: Grundgesetze der philadelphischen Gesellschaft zur Verringerung des Elends in den öffentlichen Gefängnissen. Ueber die Finanzen der verschiedenen nordamerikanischen Staaten. Auszug einer ausführlichen Handschrift eines Schlesiers v. J. 1785, die Mohawks, Philadelphia und Baltimore betreffend. Von dem neuen Etablissement der vereinigten nordamerikanischen Staaten am nordwestlichen Ufer des Ohio. Berechnung des Flächeninhalts der Vereinigten Staaten. Friedenstractat des Staats von Georgien und der Creek Indianer. Auszug aus J. Newtons Schrift über den Sklavenhandel. Schreiben aus Virginien in Amerika im Jahre 1788.
The Library does not have J. E. Fabri, *Handbuch der neuesten Geographie. Erste [-Zweyte] Abtheilung,* Halle, 1784–85. Kayser, v. 2, p. 185B.
Note also several articles on America in *Geographisches Magazin [ed. J. E. E. Fabri],* Bd. 1–4, Dessau und Leipzig, 1783–84, and *Neues Geographisches Magazin,* Bd. 1–4, Halle, 1785–89. Not in the Library. Of special interest: J. F. Mallet du Pan, "Ueber einen Zweifel, ob Columbus der erste Entdecker Amerikas war," Bd. 4, Stück 1.

1020. *Review:* L'influence de la decouverte de l'Amerique sur le bonheur du genre humain, par Mr. l'abbé Genty... Paris: B. Nyon d. ält. und Sohn, 1788. 352 p. 8°. (Allgemeine Literatur-Zeitung. Jena, 1789. 4°. Jahr 1789, Bd. 3, col. 358, *NAA.*)
The Library's copies of this English work are in * *KF.*
"Zuerst wird untersucht, ob Amerika's Entdeckung seinen alten Bewohnern nützlich war? welches... verneint wird. Dann wird gefragt: war Amerika's Entdeckung seinen neuen Bewohnern vortheilhaft? Auch dies wird verneint... Auch die letzte Frage: hat Amerika's Entdeckung Europa Vortheil gebracht? wird verneint."

1020A. *Review:* Joh. Christ. Gatterers kurzer Begriff der Geographie in 2 Bänden, Göttingen: Bey Dieterich, 1789. 8°. (Göttingische Anzeigen von gelehrten Sachen. Göttingen [1789]. 12°. Jahr 1789, p. 1761–1767, * *DF.*)
Of special interest: "Eintheilung der Amerikaner in Hauptnationen nach Verschiedenheit der Hauptsprachen (18 Classen)," p. 690–706. "Die nordamerikanischen Länder der Eingeborenen... Der zur Zeit bekanntsten Länder sind 7: Schipiwäer-, Mohaker-, Nadowessier-oder Siuer-, Weissindier-, Missurier-, Illinäer- und Scherokierland," p. 761–782.

1021. *Review:* Lettera allo stampatore Sigr. Pietro Allegrini a nome del'autore del' elogio premiato d'Amerigo Vespucci. Florenz, 1789. 8°. (Allgemeine Literatur-Zeitung. Jena, 1789. 4°. Jahr 1789, Intelligenzblatt, col. 551, *NAA.*)
In this letter, Stanislao Canovai complains of the "unfair" reception of his work on Vespucci; see no. 1058.

1022. *Review:* A List of the Society instituted in 1781 for the purpose of effecting the abolition of the Slave trade. London, 1788. 5¼ Bogen. 8°. (Allgemeine Literatur-Zeitung. Jena, 1789. 4°. Jahr 1789, Bd. 2, col. 433–434, *NAA.*)
Concerns a British society, founded in 1787, for abolishing slave trade, which cooperated with the French "La Société des amis des noirs." See no. 1001. Of special interest: "Wer etwas über den Sklavenhandel an die Gesellschaft gelangen lassen will, kann es ihren Chairman..., Herrn Granville Sharp in the old Jewry einsenden." Among the members of the British society were Lafayette, Brissot de Warville, and Clavière.

1022A. *Review:* Des Pater Labats Reisen nach Westindien, oder den im Amerikanischen Meere liegenden Inseln, nach der neuesten Pariser Ausgabe übersetzt, auch mit nöthigen Anmerkungen und einem vollständigen Register über alle sieben Bände, von Ge. Fried. Casim. Schad. Siebenter und letzter Band. Nürnberg: Auf Kosten der Raspischen Buchhandlung, 1788. 12 Bogen. 8°. (Allgemeine deutsche Bibliothek. Berlin, 1789. 8°. Bd. 89, p. 185–189, *NAA.*)

1023. *Review:* Philosophical Transactions... v. 78 for 1788 Part 1. London, 1788. 218 p. 2 plates. 4°. (Göttingische Anzeigen von gelehrten Sachen. Göttingen [1789]. 12°. Jahr 1789, p. 1617–1621, * *DF.*)
John Hunter's "Some observations on the heat of lands and springs in the Island of Jamaica..." p. 53–65, is noticed; the *Transactions* are in * *EC.*
*See* no. 1042.

1023A. *Review:* Publicistische Uebersicht aller Regierungsarten sämmtlicher Staaten und Völkerschaften auf der Welt, von J. T. Plant. Berlin: Bey Vieweg dem Aeltern, 1788. 5 Bogen. f°. (Allgemeine deutsche Bibliothek. Berlin, 1789. 12°. Bd. 89, p. 217–220, *NAA.*)

1024. *Review:* Reisen durch einige französische, englische, holländische, spanische Besitzungen in der neuen Welt... Leipzig: In der Weygandschen Buchhandlung, 1789. 230 p. 8°. (Allgemeine Literatur-Zeitung. Jena, 1789. 4°. Jahr 1789, Bd. 3, col. 293–295, *NAA.*)
Sabin 6898.
For an abridged translation of the French, see nos. 1030, 1031.
*See also* no. 1112.

1024A. *Review:* Remarks on the Travels of the Marquis of Chatellux, in North-Amerika. London: Wilkie [n. d.]. 80 p. 8°. (Allgemeine Literatur-Zeitung. Jena, 1789. 4°. Jahr 1789, Bd. 1, col. 63–64, *NAA.*)
"Die Reisen des M. von Chatellux...sind ins Englische übersetzt worden, von einem Anhänger der Nordamerikanischen Partey. Gegen das Werk und gegen die Anmerkungen des Uebersetzers, ist gegenwärtige Schrift gerichtet. Sie ist mit gewaltiger Heftigkeit geschrieben. Franklin, Washington und die andern amerikanischen Krieger und Staatsmänner, sind in des Vf. Augen elende Menschen; alle englischen Generals aber Helden und die edelsten Menschen..."

1024B. *Review:* Die Tabaksmanufactur, oder die vollständige Oekonomie des Tabakbaues nach allen seinen Zweigen, von J. S. Halle, Prof. des K. P. C. d. C. in B. 110 p. (Allgemeine Literatur-Zeitung. Jena, 1789. 4°. Jahr 1789, Bd. 1, col. 355–356, *NAA.*)
Contains "Die Tabakspflanzungen in verschiedenen Ländern, wo besonders das in Holland, Frankreich und Amerika gewöhnliche Verfahren beschrieben ist."

*1789, continued*

1025. *Review:* Therese Westen, die Geschichte unglücklich grossmüthiger Treue. Berlin und Leipzig: In der Lindauerschen Buchhandlung, 1786. 156 S. (Allgemeine deutsche Bibliothek. Berlin, 1789. 12°. Bd. 86, p. 126-129, *NAA.*)
One of the characters of this novel goes to America "aus Hoffnungslosigkeit."

1026. *Review:* Transactions of the american philosophical Society, held at Philadelphia for promoting useful knowledge. Vol. II. Philadelphia: B. Aitken, 1786. 394 p. 4°. (Allgemeine Literatur-Zeitung. Jena, 1789. 4°. Jahr 1789, Bd. 4, col. 169-179, *NAA.*)
For details see no. 975.
The Library's set of the *Transactions* is in * *EA*.

1027. *Review:* Travels through the interior parts of America, in a series of letters, by an Officer. London, 1789. 2 v. plates. 8°. (Göttingische Anzeigen von gelehrten Sachen. Göttingen [1789]. 12°. Jahr 1789, p. 1967-1968, **DF*.)
Sabin 1366.
The author of the "Travels" is Thomas Anburey; copies are in * *KF* and *IID*.
See nos. 1115, 1120.

1028. *Review:* A treatise on tropical diseases and on the climate of the West-Indies, by Benjamin Moseley, M.D. London: B. Cadell, 1787. 544 p. 8°. (Allgemeine Literatur-Zeitung. Jena, 1789. 4°. Jahr 1789, Bd. 3, col. 465-469, *NAA.*)
See no. 1029.

1029. *Review:* A treatise on tropical Diseases and on the Climate of the Westindies. By B. Moseley... London, 1788. 544 p. 8°. (Göttingische Anzeigen von gelehrten Sachen. Göttingen [1789]. 12°. Jahr 1789, p. 649-655, **DF*.)
See no. 1028.

1029A. *Review:* Ueber Lebensart, Sitten, Gebräuche und natürliche Beschaffenheit verschiedener Völker und Länder. Ein Lesebuch für Freunde der Erd- und Völkerkunde mit vielen Bemerkungen aus der Naturgeschichte, herausgegeben von Joh. Aug. Donndorf. Erfurt: Keyser, 1789. 676 S. 8°. (Allgemeine Literatur-Zeitung. Jena, 1789. 4°. Jahr 1789, Bd. 4, col. 510-511, *NAA.*)
Of special interest: no. 5. Von den Philippinischen Inseln.

1029B. *Review:* Ursprung und Alter der Lustseuche und ihre Einführung und Verbreitung auf den Inseln der Südsee, nebst einer kurzen Uebersicht der ältesten und neuesten Heilarten dieser Krankheit, von Wilh. Turnbull. Zittau und Leipzig, 1789. 110 S. 8°. (Allgemeine Literatur-Zeitung. Jena, 1789. 4°. Jahr 1789, Bd. 4, col. 22-24, *NAA.*)
Does syphilis come from Hispaniola?

1030. *Review:* Voyages interessans dans différentes Colonies Françoises, Espagnoles, Angloises etc; contenant des Observations importantes relatives à ces contrées, et un Mémoire sur les Maladies les plus communes à Saint-Dominique, leur remèdes, et le moyen de s'en préserver moralement et phisiquement... par M. N. London u. Paris: B. Jean-Francois Bastien, 1788. 2 Th. 507 S. 8°. (Allgemeine Literatur-Zeitung. Jena, 1789. 4°. Jahr 1789, Bd. 3, col. 169-172, *NAA.*)
Sabin (6897) gives Bourgeois as the name of the author. See also *Monthly review*, 1789, v. 80.
See no. 1031.

1031. *Review:* Voyages intéressans dans différentes Colonies Françoises, Espagnoles, Angloises etc. London, 1788. 514 p. 8°. (Göttingische Anzeigen von gelehrten Sachen. Göttingen [1789]. 12°. Jahr 1789, p. 587-591, **DF*.)
See no. 1030.

1031A. *Review:* Wilh. Thomas Raynals philosophische und politische Geschichte der Besitzungen und Handlung der Europäer in beyden Jndien. Nach der neuesten Ausgabe übersetzt und mit Anmerkungen versehen. Kempten: Im Verlag der typographischen Gesellschaft. Erster [-Zweiter] Band, 1783-1784. 8°. (Allgemeine deutsche Bibliothek. Berlin, 1785. 12°. Bd. 85, p. 508-531; Bd. 86, p. 197-227, 471-489, *NAA.*)
Signed: P.

**1790**

1032. BALTIMORE in NAmerika, 30. Aug. 1789. (In: A. L. Schlözer. Stats-Anzeigen. Göttingen, 1790. 8°. Bd. 15, p. 183-186.) BAC
An account concerning the "Tunkers," a religious sect.

1033. BENIOWSKY, MORIZ AUGUST, GRAF VON. Des Grafen Moritz August v. Beniowski Reisen durch Sibirien und Kamtschatka über Japan und China nach Europa. Nebst einem Auszuge seiner übrigen Lebensgeschichte... Mit Anmerkungen von Johann Reinhold Forster. Berlin: Voss, 1790. xxi, 447 p. plates. 8°. (Magazin von merkwürdigen neuen Reisebeschreibungen ... Bd. 3.) KBC
Review: *Allgemeine Literatur-Zeitung*, Jahr 1793, Bd. 2, col. 692-693, *NAA*, where two other German editions are mentioned.
There is a translation by Christoph Meiners mentioned in his *Grundriss der Geschichte der Menschheit*, p. 317; see also no. 1077.

1034. BERICHT von Spanischen Expeditionen zur See und zu Land nach dem nördlichen [Theil von] Californien... in den Jahren 1768, 1769, 1770. [Mit einer Karte von Californien.] (In: P. S. Bruns and E. A. W. Zimmermann, editors. Repositorium für die neueste Geographie, Statistik und Geschichte. Tübingen, 1792. 8°. Bd. 1, p. 1-32.) KBD
Excerpt from Miguel Costanso's *An historical journal of the expeditions by sea and land to the north of California; in 1768, 1769, and 1770...*, London, 1790, † *IXG*.
This German translation was made by Paul Jacob Bruns, 1743-1814.

1035. BRIEF vom Doctor Benjamin Franklin an Herrn Dubourg, den französischen Uebersetzer seiner Werke. (Hannoverisches Magazin... vom Jahr 1790. Hannover, 1791. 4°. Jahrg. 28, col. 1517-1520.) **DF*
Franklin treats the topic, "Death and Revival." Edited by Georg Friedrich Wehrs (1750-1818) in Hannover.
Title page dated 1791; contents, 1790.

*1790, continued*

1036. BURGSDORF, FRIEDRICH AUGUST LUDWIG VON. Abhandlung über die Vortheile vom ungesäumten, ausgedehnten Anbau einiger in den Königl. Preussischen Staaten noch ungewöhnlichen Holzarten. Vor der Königl. Akademie der Wissenschaften zu Berlin gelesen den 14. Januar 1790. von F. A. L. von Burgsdorf. (Forst-Archiv. Ulm, 1790. 8°. Bd. 8, p. 265–293.) VQN

Refers to several species of North American trees.

1037. CAVENDISH. Nachricht von den Versuchen, die Herr John M'Nab zu Albany-Fort über das Gefrieren der Salpeter- und Vitriolsäure angestellt hat. (Journal der Physik. Halle, 1790. 8°. Bd. 1, p. 113–114.) PAA

1038. DOCTOR Franklin. (Hannoverisches Magazin vom... Jahre 1790. Hannover, 1791. 4°. Jahrg. 28, col. 1035–1040.) *DF

About Franklin's last days; by his doctor.
Annotated by Georg Friedrich Wehrs, 1750–1818, of Hannover.
See J. G. Rosengarten, "Franklin in Germany," in *Lippincott's monthly magazine*, Philadelphia, Pa., 1903, v. 71, p. 128–134. *DA.

1039. EGEDE, POUL HANSEN. Nachrichten von Grönland. Aus einem Tagebuche, geführt von 1721 bis 1788 vom Bischof Paul Egede. Aus dem Dänischen. Mit Kupfern. Kopenhagen: Bey Christian Gottlob Proft, 1790. xii p., 1 l., 16–333(1) p., 1 l. frontis. (port.), 1 folding map, 2 folding plates. 8°. *KF 1790

Sabin 22040.
Front. engraved by Clemens after Juel (1787).
"Ich bedarf vielleicht einiger Entschuldigung vor dem Leser, dass das Tagebuch, welches vor 60 Jahren geführet worden, jetzt erst ans Licht komt." (Egede, An den Leser.)
Reviews: *Allgemeine deutsche Bibliothek*, Bd. 104, p. 527, *NAA; Allgemeine Literatur-Zeitung*, Jahr 1790, Bd. 2, col. 406, *NAA; Göttingische Anzeigen von gelehrten Sachen*, Jahr 1790, Bd. 3, p. 1625–1629, *DF; Oberdeutsche allgemeine Literatur-Zeitung*, Jahr 1790, Bd. 2, p. 406 (not in N. Y. P. L.).

1039A. GLEIM, JOHANN WILHELM LUDWIG. Der Amerikaner an den Europäer. 1790. (Americana Germanica. Philadelphia, 1899–1900. 4°. v. 3, p. 382–383.) NFCA (German)

Contains the following warning from America to France to remain moderate:

"Auf Deine Weisheit trotze nicht;
Thu' lieber was du kannst, das, was du bist, zu bleiben!
Ein guter Genius trieb liebend dich zum Licht;
Aus Licht in Finsterniss kann Dich ein böser treiben."

The poem is incorporated in an essay by J. T. Hatfield and E. Hochbaum, "The influence of the American Revolution upon German literature."
Periodical subsequently called *German American annals*, under which it is shelved.
Direct reference to America in Gleim's letter to Herder, dated Sept., 1795. See *Von und an Herder*, Leipzig, 1861, v. 1, p. 194.
See also references to America in two letters addressed to Gleim, dated July 19 and December 9, 1781, by Johannes von Müller, in Körte, *Briefe deutscher Gelehrten*, Zürich, 1806, v. 2, p. 236, NGR; see H. S. King, in University of California, *Publications in modern philology*, Berkeley, 1929, v. 14, p. 161–173, STG.

1040. HISTORISCHE Bemerkungen über die so genannten Wilden, oder über Jäger- und Fischer-Völker. (Göttingisches historisches Magazin. Hannover, 1790. 12°. Bd. 6, p. 273–311.) BAA (Neues)

Signed: M (i.e., Christoph Meiners, 1747–1810).
Periodical subsequently called *Neues göttingisches historisches Magazin*, under which it is shelved.

1041. HISTORISCHE Nachrichten über die wahre Beschaffenheit des Sclaven-Handels, und der Knechtschaft der Neger in West-Indien. (Göttingisches historisches Magazin. Hannover, 1790. 12°. Bd. 6, p. 645–679.) BAA (Neues)

Signed: M (i.e., Christoph Meiners, 1747–1810).
Periodical subsequently called *Neues göttingisches historisches Magazin*, under which it is shelved.

1042. HUNTER, JOHN. Einige Beobachtungen über die Wärme der Brunnen in Jamaica und über die Temperatur der Erde unter ihrer Oberfläche. (Journal der Physik. Halle, 1790. 8°. Bd. 1, p. 111–112.) PAA

Also published in *Magazin für das Neueste aus der Physik und Naturgeschichte*, Bd. 6, Stück 3, 3–OA. *See* no. 1023.

1043. KLOPSTOCK, FRIEDRICH GOTTLIEB. Sie, und nicht Wir. An La Rochefoucauld. 1790. (In his: Werke. Leipzig: Bey Georg Joachim Göschen, 1798–1813. 8°. Bd. 2, p. 141–143.)

"An Amerika's Strömen NFW
Flamt schon eigenes Licht, leuchtet den Völkern umher.
Hier auch winkte mir Trost, er war: In Amerika leuchten
Deutsche zugleich umher! Aber er tröstet nicht."

1043A. MEUSEL, JOHANN GEORG. Litteratur der Statistik. Ausgearbeitet von Johann Georg Meusel. Leipzig: Bey Caspar Fritsch, 1790. 590 p. 8°. *GB

"Sollte diese Bemühung einigen Beyfall erlangen; so würde ich eine neue auf die Litteratur der von mir hier übergangenen grössern und kleinen teutschen Staaten verwenden, vielleicht auch die Litteratur der Statistik von... der nordamerikanischen Republik u.s.w. hinzuthun." — *Vorerinnerungen*. This first volume deals with Europe exclusively; the continuation, published as erster und zweiter Nachtrag in 1793, 1797 respectively (see Kayser, v. 4, p. 95B) is not in the Library.

1044. NORDCAROLINISCHE Kirchennachrichten, herausgegeben von Johann Caspar Velthusen ... Erstes Heft. Leipzig, 1790. (Reprinted in: Der Deutsche Pionier. Cincinnati, O. [1881–82.] 8°. Jahrg. 13, p. 311–317, 352–359.) IEK

Contains: 1. Bericht des Herrn Professor Velthusen über das Wirken der Helmstädtischen Gesellschaft. 2. Brief des Pastors Adolph Nüssmann aus Mecklenburg County, Nord Carolina (dated: Buffalo Creek, 1783, d. 12. November). 3. Auszug aus einem Briefe des Herrn Pastors Christian August Gottlob Storch (dated: May 28th, 1789). 4. Brief von Pastor Friedrich Roschen an Herrn Pastor Johann David Nicolai, Dompredigern in Bremen (dated: Nordcarolina, Rowan County, an der Abbotscreek vom 29sten April – 21sten Junius 1789).
Reviews: *Göttingische Anzeigen von gelehrten Sachen*, Jahr 1793, p. 776, *DF; Allgemeine Literatur-Zeitung*, Jahr 1792, Bd. 1, col. 625–626, NAA.
See no. 1203.

## 1790, continued

1045. POLITISCH philosophische Gespräche. (Der Teutsche Merkur. Weimar, 1790. 16°. Jahr 1790, Vierteljahr 1, p. 297–307; Vierteljahr 3, p. 306–319, 329–340.) *DF (Neue)
Signed: v. K.
How did the large woods of America influence the life of the aborigines?
Periodical subsequently called *Der Neue teutsche Merkur*, under which it is shelved.
See nos. 479, 497, 523, 546, 712.

1046. RAFF, GEORG CHRISTIAN. M. Georg Christians [sic!] Raff's...Geographie für Kinder zum Gebrauch auf Schulen. Nach des Verfassers Tode durchgesehen, verbessert und herausgegeben von Christian Carl Andre... Göttingen: Johann Christian Dietrich, 1790–92. 2 v. in 1. 18 cm. KAM
America, v. 2, p. 183–352.
Review: *Allgemeine Literatur Zeitung*, Jahr 1785, Bd. 1, col. 251, *NAA*.

1046A. STOLBERG, FRIEDRICH LEOPOLD. An Karl Freiherrn von Hompesch. 1790. (Reprinted in: Deutsche National-Litteratur...herausgegeben von Joseph Kürschner. Berlin und Stuttgart, [n. d.] 12°. Bd. 50, Abteilung 2, p. 165–168.) NFF
This volume has individual title: Der Göttinger Dichterbund. Dritter Teil. Friedrich Leopold Graf zu Stolberg. Matthias Claudius.
"Aber sie donnerte nun;
Die sieben Hügel erbebten!
Kühner, als Franklin,
Leitete Luther aus ihr
Zückenden Blitz,
Und labenden Tau!" — p. 166.
Poem first published in the *Hamburger Musen Almanach 1792*, p. 47.

1047. THAYER, JOHN. Nachricht von der Bekehrung des Herrn Johann Thayer, vormaligen protestantischen Wortdieners zu Boston in Nordamerika, der sich zur katholischen Religion in Rom bekehret hat, den 25 May 1783. Von ihm selbst geschrieben. Nebst einem Schreiben an seinen Bruder... Aus dem Französischen. Ofen: Gedruckt bey Katharina Landerin, Wittwe, 1790. 95 p. 8°. *KF 1790

1048. UEBER die Natur der Afrikanischen Neger, und die davon abhangende Befreyung, oder Einschränkung der Schwarzen. (Göttingisches historisches Magazin. Hannover, 1790. 12°. Bd. 6, p. 385–456.) BAA (Neues)
Signed: M (i.e., Christoph Meiners, 1747–1810).
Periodical subsequently called *Neues göttingisches historisches Magazin*, under which it is shelved.

1049. UEBER die Natur der Americaner. (Göttingisches historisches Magazin. Hannover, 1790. 12°. Bd. 7, p. 102–156.) BAA (Neues)
Signed: M (i.e., Christoph Meiners, 1747–1810).
See no. 1053, 1105 (note).
Periodical subsequently called *Neues göttingisches historisches Magazin*, under which it is shelved.

1050. VESPUCCI, AMERIGO. Amerigo Vespuzzi vier Seereisen, von ihm selbst beschrieben. Aus dem Lateinischen übersetzt von Valentin Heinrich Schmidt, Prorector der cölnischen Schule. Berlin, 1790. 1 p.l., 55 p., 1 l. 8°. *KF 1790
From the account of Vespucci's voyages in Grynaeus's *Novus orbis regionum ac insularum veteribus incognitarum*, Basil, 1555, *Reserve (Novus)*.
See no. 57.

1051. VON den Varietäten und Abarten der Neger. (Göttingisches historisches Magazin. Hannover, 1790. 12°. Bd. 6, p. 625–645.)
BAA (Neues)
Signed: M (i.e., Christoph Meiners, 1747–1810).
Periodical subsequently called *Neues göttingisches historisches Magazin*, under which it is shelved.

1052. VON und aus Nord Amerika. (In: A. L. Schlözer. Stats-Anzeigen. Göttingen, 1790. 8°. Bd. 15, p. 483–494, 510.) BAC
From different newspapers.
Contents (from Inhalt, p. 509–510): Titel des Präsid. Washington. Einfur in Newyork. Schulden Stand der Vereinten Staten. Wie das Verbot der Gen. Ass., keine Schauspiele zu spielen, eludiert wird. Kirchenlisten von Salem, New-London, Philadelphia etc. Verhältnis der 13 Ver. Staten unter sich, in Ansehung der Grösse ihrer Contributionen. Kentucky, der 14te Stat, wiewol unter einem andern Namen. Abenteurlicher State of Franklin. Post-Cours und Entfernung der Stationen in den Ver. Staten.

1053. ZWEYTE Abhandlung über die Natur der Americaner, besonders über ihre Gemüthsart. (Göttingisches historisches Magazin. Hannover, 1790. 12°. Bd. 7, p. 209–230.) BAA (Neues)
Note the "Anhang," p. 307–310.
Signed: M (i.e., Christoph Meiners, 1747–1810).
See no. 1049.
Periodical subsequently called *Neues göttingisches historisches Magazin*, under which it is shelved.

1053A. *Review*: Aktenmässige Geschichte der berühmten Salzburgischen Emigration. Aus dem lateinischen Manuskript...übersetzt und mit einem Vorbericht begleitet von Fr. Xav. Huber... Salzburg: Meyer, 1790. 288 S. 8°. (Allgemeine Literatur-Zeitung. Jena, 1790. 4°. Jahr 1790, Bd. 1, col. 481–485, *NAA*.)
"Die Schrift ist übrigens in zwey Bücher vertheilt, wovon das erste die Begebenheiten vor dem Emigrations-Edict auf 123 S., das andere die Folgen desselben (S. 124–141) erzählt."

1054. *Review*: Alex. Falconbridges u. Thomas Clarksons Bemerkungen über die gegenwärtige Beschaffenheit des Sclavenhandels, und dessen Nachtheile für England. Aus dem Englischen herausgegeben und mit Anmerkungen begleitet von M. Chr. Sprengel... Leipzig: Weygand [1789]. 246 S. 8°. (Allgemeine deutsche Bibliothek. Berlin, 1790. 12°. Bd. 94, col. 231–232, *NAA*.)
See no. 1147.

1055. *Review*: L'America divisa nelle sue principali parti. Siena: B. Pazzini Carli, 1788. (Allgemeine Literatur-Zeitung. Jena, 1790. 4°. Jahr 1790, Bd. 2, col. 725, *NAA*.)

1056. *Review*: Americologia, ossia osservazioni storiche e Fisiologiche sopra gli Americani con un breve Ragguaglio delle ultime scoperte fatte da i Russi nel Mar Pacifico, compendie di curiose notizie interessante e scientifiche dato in luce da Ant. Fonticello dedicato alla Società Patria. Mantua: Scionico, 1790. 123 p. 8°. (Allgemeine Literatur-Zeitung. Jena, 1790. 4°. Jahr 1790, Intelligenzblatt, col. 723–724, *NAA*.)
"Das Leben von Columbus und Vespuccius geht voran."

*1790, continued*

**1057.** *Review:* Amerika, ein geographisch historisches Lesebuch zum Nutzen der Jugend und ihrer Erzieher...von K. Hammerdörfer und C. T. Kosche. Leipzig: Weidmann, 1788. (Allgemeine deutsche Bibliothek. Berlin, 1790. 12°. Bd. 93, col. 200–202, *NAA.*)
See *Allgemeine Literatur-Zeitung*, Jahr 1788, Bd. 3, col. 497, *NAA; Allgemeine deutsche Bibliothek*, Bd. 93, p. 200, * *DF; Göttingische Anzeigen von gelehrten Sachen*, Jahr 1788, p. 1008, * *DF.*
See also Sabin 30080.

**1057A.** *Review:* Annalen der brittischen Geschichte des Jahrs 1788. Als eine Fortsetzung des Werks England und Jtalien, von J. W. von Archenholz... Erster Band. Mit dem Bildniss des Staatsm. Pitt. Braunschweig: Auf Kosten des Verf. und in Comm. bey Hofmann in Hamburg, 1789. 498 p. 8°. (Allgemeine deutsche Bibliothek. Berlin, 1790. 12°. Bd. 1, p. 61–69, *NAA.*)
"Der erste Abschnitt liefert eine kurze Uebersicht des Zustandes von Grossbrittanien am Ende des J. 1787. Der Verf. findet ihn glücklich, hoffnungsvoll, und allen Anschein, dass dieser mächtige Staat sein vormalig grosses, durch den amerikanischen Krieg aber sehr geschwächtes Ansehn wieder erhalten werde... Der zweyte Abschnitt enthält die Geschichte des brittischen Staates... Dritter Abschnitt. Geschichte der brittischen Regierung... Der Handel der Amerikaner wird begünstigt, ohnerachtet der fortdauernden Erbitterung derselben gegen die Engländer... Der vierte, fünfte und sechste Abschnitt enthält die Geschichte der Nation, und handelt von den Colonien... Der Verlust der amerikanischen Provinzen war für die Engländer gleichsam die Losung, ihre Jndustrie zu vermehren... Der Erfolg der Expedition nach der Nordwestküste von Amerika war nicht so gar glänzend... Achter Abschnitt. Geschichte der Litteratur. Von Hrn. G. R. Forster... Mit der Sprache selbst sind zwar seit Addison und Steele keine wesentlichen Veränderungen vorgegangen, desto mehr aber ist sie durch verschiedene Vorfälle, z. B. durch die [*sic!*] Fehde der Colonien mit dem Mutterland, das Verkehr mit fremden Hülfsvölkern, die Bekanntschaft mit neuen Gegenständen aus entfernten Welttheilen u. dergl. bereichert worden."

**1057B.** *Review:* Annalen der geographischen und statistischen Wissenschaften, herausgegeben von A. W. Zimmermann, Herzogl. Braunschweigischem Hofrath, Prof. der Mathematik und Naturlehre. 1. Jahrgang. Braunschweig 1790. 1. Stück. Beym Herausgeber und in Commission in der Crusiussischen Buchhandlung in Leipzig. 100 Octavseiten. (Göttingische Anzeigen von gelehrten Sachen. Göttingen [1790]. 12°. Jahr 1790, p. 545–548, * *DF.*)
Aufsatz xi: Portlock and Dixon voyages round the world. Nachrichten aus Briefen von neuen Charten und Tanderen Unternehmungen.

**1057C.** *Review:* Authentic copy of Lieut. Mears Memorial respecting the capture of the Vessels in Nootka-Sound. London: B. Debrett, 1790. 65 p. 8°. (Allgemeine Literatur-Zeitung. Jena, 1790. 4°. Jahr 1790, Bd. 4, col. 546–549, *NAA.*)

**1057D.** *Review:* An authentic Statement of all the Facts relative to Nootka Sound, its discovery, history, settlement and trade. London: B. Debrett, 1790. 26 p. 8°. (Allgemeine Literatur-Zeitung. Jena, 1790. 4°. Jahr 1794, Bd. 4, col. 546–549, *NAA.*)
The reviewer calls himself Argonaut.

**1057E.** *Review:* Beyträge zur Geschichte des Amerikanischen Krieges, aus Originalbriefen und Schriften der damaligen Zeiten. Nebst Skizzen aus dem Leben der berühmtesten Generale und Glieder des Congresses. Erster Theil. 1775 bis 1780. Philadelphia und Leipzig, 1788. 352 S. 8°. (Allgemeine deutsche Bibliothek. Berlin, 1790. 8°. Bd. 97, p. 499–500, *NAA.*)
"Dass der Verfasser dieser Schrift [i.e., Johann Zinner; see no. 727], wie er in dem Vorbericht der ersten genannten Auflage sagt, in Paris die Ehre genossen, mit dem Hn. D. Fränklin genauer bekannt zu seyn, und von ihm und durch seinen gütigen Vorschub vieles zusammen zu bringen, das andern unbekannt ist, kann wohl seyn."
The author speaks also of a possible medical use of Franklin's accordion.

**1057F.** *Review:* Der Capitaine Portlocks und Dixons Reisen um die Welt, besonders nach der nordwestlichen Küste von Amerika, aus dem Englischen übersetzt und erläutert von J. R. Forster. Berlin: Bey Voss und Sohn, 1790. 314 S. 4°. (Allgemeine Literatur-Zeitung. Jena, 1790. 4°. Jahr 1790, Bd. 4, col. 217–224, *NAA.*)
See nos. 1060C, 1060D, 1071, 1072, 1073, 1105G.

**1058.** *Review:* Elogio d'Amerigo Vespucci by P. Stanislaus Canovai. Dissertazione giustificativa di questo celebre navigatore. Florence, 1786. 80 p. 4°. (Göttingische Anzeigen von gelehrten Sachen. Göttingen [1790]. 12°. Jahr 1790, p. 515–518, * *DF.*)
"...von der Akademie zu Cortona gekrönt... Die Preissfrage hatte der Graf von Durfort, Französischer Gesandter am Toskanischen Hofe, aufgegeben..."
See bibliographical notes on the Library's catalogue cards; first published in 1788. Copies are in * *KF.*
See also no. 1021.

**1058A.** *Review:* Geographisches Handbuch in Hinsicht auf Industrie und Handlung, von Paul Joh. [*sic!*] Bruns... Nürnberg: Bey Chr. Weigel und A. S. Schneider, 1789. 20 Bogen. 8°. (Allgemeine deutsche Bibliothek. Berlin, 1790. 12°. Bd. 96, col. 490–491, *NAA.*)
Second edition.
"Der erheblichste Zusatz ist eine Nachricht von der neuen britischen Colonie in Jacksonsbay."

**1059.** *Review:* Geographisches Handbuch in Hinsicht auf Industrie und Handlung, von Paul Joh. Bruns, Prof. und Bibliothekar zu Helmstadt... Nürnberg: B. Weigel und Schneider, 1789. 195, 5 p. Verbesserungen und Zusätze. 8°. (Allgemeine Literatur-Zeitung. Jena, 1790. 4°. Jahr 1790, Bd. 1, col. 16, *NAA.*)
The book contains: "Von der Industrie und dem Handel des Nordamerikanischen Freystaats..."
"Zu Charlestown ist eine Gesellschaft errichtet, welche Sklaven aus Afrika importiert..."
"Unter den Schulbüchern, welche von einigen Professoren in Helmstädt für die deutsche Jugend in Nordcarolina geschrieben werden, um von dem daraus zu erlösenden Gewinn nicht nur eine Sammlung von Büchern als Geschenk dahin zu schicken, sondern auch die Ueberfahrt für 2 bis 3 evangelische Prediger zu bezahlen, ist das hier angezeigte so beschaffen, dass man ihm einen guten Absatz in Deutschland versprechen kann... Da der Nordamerikanische Freystaat der Standpunct ist, von dem aus der Verfasser ausgeht, so ist dieser Welttheil zuerst und verhältnissmässig am vollständigsten beschrieben... Bey Neuschottland ist schon der neue Anbau der Loyalisten bey und um Shelburn beschrieben."

## GERMAN WORKS RELATING TO AMERICA 127

*1790, continued*

1060. *Review:* The History of America by Wm. Robertson. Basel: Turneisen & Le Grand. 3 v. (Göttingische Anzeigen von gelehrten Sachen. Göttingen [1790]. 12°. Jahr 1790, p. 1072, \* *DF.*)

The Library's copy of this 1790 edition is in \* *KF*.

"Die Verbesserungen und Beantwortungen des Don Clavigero von 1788 sind beygebracht."

1060A. *Review:* Joh. Christoph Gatterers kurzer Begriff der Geographie. Erster Band, der von der Erde, ihren Bewohnern und Europa handelt. Zweyter Band, welcher Asien, Afriken, Ameriken und Australien enthält. Göttingen: Dietrich, 1789. lxxx, 902 S. 8°. (Allgemeine Literatur-Zeitung. Jena, 1790. 4°. Jahr 1790, Bd. 1, col. 14–15, *NAA.*)

"In Nordamerika vermissen wir ungern das neue Gouvernement Neu-Braunschweig mit der Stadt Shelburne, welche vor einigen Jahren an 3000 Häuser zählte."

1060B. *Review:* Johann Christoph Gatterers kurzer Begriff der Geographie. Erster Band, welcher von der Erde und ihren Bewohnern überhaupt, und von Europa insonderheit handelt. Göttingen: Dieterich, 1789. 8°. 381 S. Zweyter Band, welcher Asien, Afriken, Ameriken und Australien enthält. 1789. 608 S. (Allgemeine deutsche Bibliothek. Berlin, 1790. 8°. Bd. 92, p. 492–497, *NAA.*)

"Wäre es [i.e., America] eher als die übrigen Welttheile bewohnt und cultiviert worden, so wäre allem Anschein nach Gold und Silber, dessen es so viel hat, nicht zum Massstabe des Werths der Dinge gewählt worden."

1060C. *Review:* Der Kapitaine Portlock's und Dixon's Reise um die Welt, besonders nach der nordwestlichen Küste von Amerika... Aus dem Englischen übersetzt und... erläutert von J. R. Forster. Berlin: Bey Voss und Sohn, 1790. 314 S. 4°. (Allgemeine deutsche Bibliothek. Berlin, 1790. 12°. Bd. 93, p. 191–192, *NAA.*)

See nos. 1057F, 1060C, 1071, 1072, 1073, 1105G.

1060D. *Review:* Der Kapitains Portlock und Dixon Reise um die Welt in den Schiffen König Georg und Königin Charlotte. Von einem Officier am Bord der letzteren. Berlin: Bey Voss und Sohn, 1789. 159 S. 8°. (Allgemeine Literatur-Zeitung. Jena, 1790. 4°. Jahr 1790, Bd. 4, col. 217–224, *NAA.*)

"Die ganze Reise beider Schiffe... ging von London durch das atlantische Meer am Cap Horn in die Südsee nach den Sandwichinseln... und von hier nach der nordwestlichen Küste von Amerika zwischen den neuern russischen Niederlassungen und Californien."

See nos. 1057A, 1060B, 1071, 1072, 1073, 1105A.

1061. *Review:* Läkaren och Naturforskaren. Veckoskrift för Läkare och Naturforskare. v. 9. Stockholm, 1788. (Göttingische Anzeigen von gelehrten Sachen. Göttingen [1790]. 12°. Jahr 1790, p. 2066–2070, \* *DF.*)

The magazine reviewed contains an article by "Mr. Swartz" on "Zubereitung des Ricinusöls in Westindien." An essay by Olof Swarts on the hot springs in Jamaica, was translated by Kästner.

1061A. *Review:* Landwirtschaftliches Magazin. Herausgegeben von S. G. F. Mund. Erstes Quartalstück. Leipzig: Crusius, 1788. 11 Bogen. 8°. (Allgemeine Literatur-Zeitung. Jena, 1788. 4°. Jahr 1788, Bd. 4, col. 649–652, *NAA.*)

No. 12. Amerikanischer Lein aus Virginien, dessen Anbau empfohlen wird. Der Saame ist zu haben bey Jordan in Peine, im Hochstift Hildesheim, der Himte zu 4 Thaler.

1061B. *Review:* Lehrbücher für die Jugend in Nordcarolina, entworfen von einer Gesellschaft Helmstädtischer Professoren. Dritte Lieferung: Religionsgeschichte und geographisches Handbuch... Leipzig: Crusius, 1788. 8°. (Allgemeine Literatur-Zeitung. Jena, 1790. Bd. 2, col. 64, *NAA.*)

"Das geographische Handbuch hat den Herrn Prof. Bruns [i.e., Paul Jacob Bruns] zum Verfasser und führt auch den Titel *Geographisches Handbuch in Hinsicht auf Industrie und Handlung* [see no. 1059]. Es ist, wie in der Vorrede gesagt wird, zunächst für angehende Kaufleute in Nordcarolina bestimmt. Daher wird mit der Beschreibung von Amerika der Anfang gemacht; und dann folgen die Länder Europens, so wie sie mit dem Amerikanischen Freystaate am wenigsten in Verbindung stehen..."

1061C. *Review:* M. Georg Christian Raffs... Geographie für Kinder zum Gebrauch auf Schulen... durchgesehen, verbessert und herausgegeben von Christian Carl Andre... Göttingen: Dieterich, 1790. 8°. (Allgemeine deutsche Bibliothek. Berlin, 1790. 8°. Bd. 95, p. 253–259, *NAA.*)

1061D. *Review:* M. Georg Christian Raffs... Geographie für Kinder. Zweyter Theil. Von Asien, Africa und America, nebst einem Anhange von Südindien und den übrigen wenig bekannten Ländern. Nach dessen Tode ausgearbeitet von Georg August Grohmann. Leipzig: Dykische Buchhandlung, 1790. 15 Bogen. 8°. (Allgemeine deutsche Bibliothek. Berlin, 1790. 12°. Bd. 97, p. 541–547, *NAA.*)

Note also *Kurze Geographie von Asia, Afrika und Amerika und dem Südlande. Versuch einer Fortsetzung von Raffs Geographie für Kinder,* Nürnberg, 1790.

1061E. *Review:* Marano und Quira, oder: die Kette des Schicksals, eine amerikanische Geschichte. Leipzig und Wien: Kleinmayer, 1790. 127 S. 8°. (Allgemeine Literatur-Zeitung. Jena, 1791. 4°. Jahr 1791, Bd. 3, col. 416, *NAA.*)

Fiction.

1061F. *Review:* Materia medica americana potissimum regni vegetabilis. Von Johann David Schoepf. Erlangen: Bey Palm, 1787. 170 p. 8°. (Göttingische Anzeigen von gelehrten Sachen. Göttingen [1790]. 12°. Jahr 1790, p. 776, \* *DF.*)

Schoepf's *Materia Medica* is in the Library (\* *KF*); it is not given a main entry here, because it is in Latin.

*See* no. 910.

*1790, continued*

1062. *Review:* Mémoire en faveur des gens de couleur ou sang mêlés de St. Domingue, et des autres isles françoises de l'Amérique addressée à l'assemblée nationale; par M. Grégoire ...député de Lorraine. Paris: B. Belin. (Allgemeine Literatur-Zeitung. Jena, 1790. 12°. Jahr 1790, Intelligenzblatt, col. 657–658, *NAA.*)
The Library's copies of this *Mémoire* by Henri Grégoire are in *DFD p.v.128* and in the Schomburg Collection *(F-917.29-G).*

1063. *Review:* Memoirs and travels of Mauritius Augustus Count de Benyowski...written by himself translated from the Original Manuscript. London: B. Robinson. T. I, 422 S. T. II, 399 S. 4°. (Allgemeine Literatur-Zeitung. Jena, 1790. 12°. Jahr 1790, Bd. 3, col. 379–384, 395–397, *NAA.*)
The Library has a copy of this work by M. A. Beniowsky in † *DBK.*
See no. 1064.

1064. *Review:* Memoirs and Travels of Mauritius Augustus Count de Benyowsky, written by himself. Translated from the original Manuscript. London, 1790. 2 v. 4°. (Göttingische Anzeigen von gelehrten Sachen. Göttingen [1790]. 12°. Jahr 1790, p. 1129–1136, 1153–1167, * *DF.*)
See preceding note.

1065. *Review:* Le Morelack ou Essay sur les moyens d'abolir la traité et l'esclavage des Negres. London u. Paris: B. Prault, 1790. 288 p. 8°. (Allgemeine Literatur-Zeitung. Jena, 1790. 12°. Jahr 1790, Bd. 4, col. 529, *NAA.*)
See no. 1066.

1066. *Review:* Le More-lack, ou Essays sur les moyens les plus doux et les plus équitables d'abolir le traité et l'esclavage des Negres d'Afrique, en conservant aux Colonies tous les avantages d'une population agricole. London, 1789. 288 p. 8°. (Göttingische Anzeigen von gelehrten Sachen. Göttingen [1790]. 12°. Jahr 1790, p. 362, * *DF.*)
"Um dem Ganzen mehr Energie zu geben, führt er [i.e. der Verfasser, "ein junger Officier"] einen Amerikanischen Neger (More-lack) redend ein..."
See no. 1065.

1067. *Review:* Observations on the Project for Abolishing the Slave-Trade, and on the Reasonableness of attempting some Practical Mode of Relieving the Negroes. London: B. Debrett. 8°. (Allgemeine Literatur-Zeitung. Jena, 1790. 12°. Jahr 1790, Intelligenzblatt, col. 1236, *NAA.*)

1068. *Review:* Philosophical Transactions of the royal Society of London. 1789. Vol. LXXIX, Part I, p. 65–70. (Journal der Physik. Halle, 1790. 8°. Bd. 2, p. 81–88, *PAA.*)
"Nachricht von einer bituminösen Ebene oder See auf der Insel Trinidad von Herrn Alexander Andersen."
The Library's file of the *Philosophical Transactions* is in * *EC.*

1068A. *Review:* The spanish Pretensions fairly discussed by A. Dalrymple. London: B. Elmsly. [n. d.] 19 p. 8°. (Allgemeine Literatur-Zeitung. Jena, 1790. 4°. Jahr 1790, Bd. 4, col. 546–549, *NAA.*)
Deals with the quarrel between Great Britain and Spain concerning the Northwest Coast of America.

1069. *Review:* The Slave Trade Indispensable; an answer to the Speech of William Wilberforce, Esqu. on the 13th of May 1789. By a West-India Merchant. 8°. (Allgemeine Literatur-Zeitung. Jena, 1790. 12°. Jahr 1790, Intelligenzblatt, col. 1236, *NAA.*)

1070. *Review:* Strictures on the Slave Trade, and their Manner of Treatment in the West-India Islands: in a Letter to the Right-Hon. Will. Pitt. By a Gentleman. London: B. Richardson. 8°. (Allgemeine Literatur-Zeitung. Jena, 1790. 12°. Jahr 1790, Intelligenzblatt, col. 1236, *NAA.*)

1070A. *Review:* Taschenatlas, oder geographisch-statistisches Handbuch von allen vier Weltheilen. Zum lehrreichen Unterricht der Jugend. Berlin: Bey Wever, 1788. 267 S. 8°. (Allgemeine deutsche Bibliothek. Berlin, 1790. 12°. Bd. 93, p. 198–199, *NAA.*)

1070B. *Review:* Übersicht der vornehmsten Regierungen der Welt, eine weitere Ausführung der 1788 herausgekommenen Vorstellung der vornehmsten regierenden Stämme der Welt. Leipzig [Böhme], 1789. 2½ Bd. 8°. (Allgemeine Literatur-Zeitung. Jena, 1790. 4°. Jahr 1790, Bd. 1, col. 679–680, *NAA.*)
The author is von Breitenbauch.
Note also *Bemerkungen über die zu Leipzig herausgekommene Vorstellung der vornehmsten Völkerschaften der Welt; eine Beylage zu dieser Schrift,* Leipzig, 1789; see *Allgemeine Literatur-Zeitung,* Jena, 1790, Jahr 1790, Bd. 1, col. 680, *NAA;* also *Geographische statistische Beyträge zur Kenntniss der auswärtigen Europäischen Besitzungen in Asia, Afrika und Amerika, zum Gebrauch auf Schulen,* Duisburg, 1790.

1071. *Review:* Voyage round the World but more particularly to the North West Coast of America. By Captain Nathan Portlock. With twenty Copperplates. London: B. Stockdale, 1789. 384 p. 4°. (Allgemeine Literatur-Zeitung. Jena, 1790. 12°. Jahr 1790, Bd. 4, col. 217–224, *NAA.*)
See note on Library's catalogue cards, under William Bereford, editor; the Library's copies are in * *KF.*

1072. *Review:* Voyage round the World but more particularly to the Northwest Coast of America performed in 1785–1788 by Captain G. Dixon. London: B. Goulding, 1789. 360 p. 4 plates. 4°. (Allgemeine Literatur-Zeitung. Jena, 1790. 12°. Jahr 1790, Bd. 4, col. 217–224, *NAA.*)
See note of no. 1071.

1073. *Review:* Voyage round the World in the years 1785–1788 performed by Capt. Portlock and Dixon. London: B. Randel, 1789. 151 p. 8°. (Allgemeine Literatur-Zeitung. Jena, 1790. 12°. Jahr 1790, Bd. 4, col. 217–224, *NAA.*)
See note of no. 1071.

# GERMAN WORKS RELATING TO AMERICA

## 1791

1074. DER AMERIKANISCHE Wilde und sein Hund. (Neues hannöverisches Magazin...vom Jahre 1791. Hannover, 1792. 4°. Jahrg. 1, col. 309–320.)          *DF
From *Lettres d'un cultivateur americain.*
Title page dated 1792; contents, 1791.

1075. AMERIKANISCHE Zeitungen. (Neues hannöverisches Magazin vom... Jahre 1791. Hannover, 1792. 4°. Jahrg. 1, col. 671–672.) *DF
Signed: W.
Title page dated 1792; contents, 1791.

1076. AUS einem NAmerikanischen Zeitungs-Blatt. (In: A. L. Schlözer. Stats-Anzeigen. Göttingen, 1791. 8°. Bd. 16, p. 128.)   BAC
"Kirchenliste von Philadelphia von 1786–1789."

1077. BENIOWSKY, MORIZ AUGUST, GRAF VON. Des Grafen Moritz August von Benjowsky Begebenheiten und Reisen, von ihm selbst beschrieben. Aus dem Englischen übersetzt von C. D. Ebeling...und Dr. J. P. Ebeling... Mit des erstern Anmerkungen und Zusätzen wie auch einem Auszuge aus Hippolitus Stefanows russisch geschriebenem Tagebuch über seine Reise von Kamtschatka nach Makao... Hamburg: Bei Benjamin Gottlob Hoffmann, 1791. 2 v. frontis. (port.), 1 folding map, 1 plate. 8°. (Neuere Geschichte der See- und Land-Reisen. Bd. 3–4.)      *KF 1789 (Neuere)
Beniowsky's portrait unsigned.
Review: *Göttingische Anzeigen von gelehrten Sachen,* Jahr 1794, p. 389, * DF.
*See* no. 1033.

1078. BERICHTE über den Genesee-Distrikt in dem Staate von Neu-York der vereinigten Staaten von Nord-Amerika nach der im Jahre 1791 Englischen [sic!] herausgegebenen Ausgabe übersetzt. n. p.: Gedruckt im December 1791. 32 p. 18½ cm.      *KF 1791
Photostat reproduction of the original in the Harvard University Library.
"Steht in Zusammenhang mit den Bemühungen von William Berczy, Bevollmächtigtem der Genessee Association, Siedler für das Genessee-Gebiet in New York zu werben."
See Meynen, no. 263.

1079. CAMPE, JOACHIM HEINRICH. Die Entdeckung von Amerika, Ein angenehmes und nützliches Lesebuch für Kinder und junge Leute, von Joachim Heinrich Campe. Zur allgemeinen Schulencyclopädie gehörig. Mit Titelkupfer und Karten. Braunschweig: In der Schulbuchhandlung, 1791. 3 v. fronts., maps. 3. ed., rev. 17 cm. (8°.)     *KF 1791
Sabin 10293.
Illustrations unsigned.
*Contents:* Teil 1. Kolumbus. Teil 2. Kortes. Teil 3. Pizarro.
An English translation of v. 1, by Elizabeth Helme, was published at Dublin in 1800, * KF.
For an American edition with the imprint Boston: Munroe and Francis; New York: Charles S. Francis, [n.d.], see F. H. Wilkens, in *German American annals,* Philadelphia, 1899, old series, v. 3, p. 199, *NFCA,* and Sabin 10284.
See also nos. 762, 850, 1304, 1309.

1080. DEUTSCHE Emigranten nach NAmerica. (In: A. L. Schlözer. Stats-Anzeigen. Göttingen, 1791. 8°. Bd. 16, p. 114–119.)   BAC
Contracts of poor emigrants with the ship owners.
Dated: Baltimore, March 8th, 1791.

1081. DEVALVATION des NAmerikanischen Papir Geldes [in den J. 1777–1781, wo zuletzt 100 Papir Thlr. nur 1⅓ ware Thlr. galten]. (In: A. L. Schlözer. Stats-Anzeigen. Göttingen, 1791. 4°. Bd. 15, p. 287–288.)   BAC
Title completed from Inhalt, p. 507.

1082. EXPORTEN der sämtlichen Vereinten NAmerikanischen Staaten. (In: A. L. Schlözer. Stats-Anzeigen. Göttingen, 1791. 8°. Bd. 16, p. 382–383.)   BAC
From *Maryland journal,* March 8th, 1791, no. 1330.

1083. FORSTER, GEORG, COMPILER. Geschichte der Reisen, die seit Cook an der Nordwest- und Nordost-Küste von Amerika und in dem nördlichsten Amerika selbst von Meares, Dixon, Portlock, Coxe, Long u. a. m. unternommen worden sind. Mit vielen Karten und Kupfern. Aus dem Englischen, mit Zuziehung aller anderweitigen Hülfsquellen, ausgearbeitet von Georg Forster... Berlin: In der Vossischen Buchhandlung, 1791. 3 v. 2 charts, 4 folding maps, 22 plates (part folding), 3 ports. 4°.
Sabin 16274, 25126.      *KF 1791
Illustrations by B. Glasbach, C. C. Glassbach, J. F. Bolt, S. Ringk, Krüger, etc.
Reviews: *Allgemeine Literatur-Zeitung,* Jahr 1793, Bd. 3, col. 153–159, *NAA; Allgemeine deutsche Bibliothek,* Bd. 116, p. 551–568, *NAA; Neue Leipziger gelehrte Zeitung,* Jahr 1792, Bd. 1, p. 143–144 (not in N. Y. P. L.); *Erfurter gelehrte Anzeigen,* Jahr 1791, p. 391–392 (not in N. Y. P. L.); *Annalen der Geographie und Statistik,* Jahr 1791, Bd. 1, p. 94–95; Bd. 4, p. 386–387 (not in N. Y. P. L.).

1084. HÄNDEL zwischen den NAmerikanischen Staten, und ihren benachbarten Wilden. (In: A. L. Schlözer. Stats-Anzeigen. Göttingen, 1791. 8°. Bd. 16, p. 373–379.)   BAC
From *Dunlop's advertiser,* no. 3829.

1085. [HEGNER, JOHANN KONRAD.] Fortsetzung von David Cranzens Brüder-Historie. Barby: Zu finden in den Brüdergemeinen, 1791 [–1816]. 4 parts in 3 v. 8°.      *KF 1791
Sabin 17412.
Part 3, printed at Barby in 1804, wanting.
*See* nos. 412, 460.

1086. JUSTIZ in Spanien gegen Christoph Colons Nachkommen. (Göttingisches historisches Magazin. Hannover, 1791. 12°. Bd. 8, p. 208.)      BAA (Neues)
Periodical subsequently called *Neues göttingisches historisches Magazin,* under which it is shelved.

1087. KURZE Geschichte und Beschreibung der Insel St. Domingo. (Neues hannöverisches Magazin...vom Jahre 1791. Hannover, 1792. 4°. Jahrg. 1, col. 1633–1664.) *DF
Signed: W.
The main source is G. T. F. Raynal's *Essai sur l'administration de St. Dominique,* 1785, * KF.
Title page dated 1792; contents, 1791.

*1791, continued*

1088. LONG, JOHN, INDIAN TRADER. J. Long's westindischen Dollmetschers und Kaufmanns See- und Land-Reisen, enthaltend: eine Beschreibung der Sitten und Gewohnheiten der Nordamerikanischen Wilden; der Englischen Forts oder Schanzen längs dem St. Lorenz-Flusse, dem See Ontario u.s.w.; ferner ein umständliches Wörterbuch der Chippewäischen und anderer Nordamerikanischen Sprachen. Aus dem Englischen. Herausgegeben und mit einer kurzen Einleitung über Kanada und einer erbesserten Karte versehen von E. A. W. Zimmermann, Hofrath und Professor in Braunschweig. Hamburg: Bei Benjamin Gottlob Hoffmann, 1791. xxiv, 334 p., 1 l., 1 folding map. 8°. *KF 1791

Sabin 41881.
The original was published in London in 1791.
Reviews: *Göttingische Anzeigen von gelehrten Sachen*, Jahr 1794, p. 388–389, * DF; *Allgemeine Literatur-Zeitung*, Jahr 1793, Bd. 1, col. 823–824, NAA; *Leipziger gelehrte Zeitung*, Jahr 1791, Bd. 2, p. 516–518 (not in N. Y. P. L.); *Tübinger gelehrte Anzeigen*, Jahr 1792, Bd. 1, p. 64 (not in N. Y. P. L.); *Oberdeutsche allgemeine Literatur-Zeitung*, Jahr 1792, Bd. 2, p. 241–246 (not in N. Y. P. L.).
For German reviews of the English edition, see no. 1119.

1089. —— J. Long's westindischen Dollmetschers und Kaufmanns... Reisen, enthaltend: eine Beschreibung der Sitten und Gewohnheiten der Nordamerikanischen Wilden; der Englischen Forts oder Schanzen längs dem St. Lorenzflusse, dem See Ontario u. s. w.; ferner ein umständliches Wörterbuch der Chippewäischen und anderer Nordamerikanischen Sprachen. Aus dem Englischen. Herausgegeben und mit einer kurzen Einleitung über Kanada und einer verbesserten Karte versehen von E. A. W. Zimmermann,... Hamburg: bei Benjamin Gottlob Hoffmann, 1791. 2 p.l., iv–xxiv, 334 p., 1 l., 1 folding map. 8°. (Neuere Geschichte der See- und Land-Reisen. Bd. 5.)

Sabin 41881. * KF 1789 (Neuere)
See preceding entry for notes.

1090. [NACHRICHT über Frasers nordamerikanisches Gras.] (Neues hannoverisches Magazin... vom Jahre 1791. Hannover, 1792. 4°. Bd. 1, col. 925–928.) *DF

Title from "Rubriken."
Title page dated 1792; contents, 1791.
See nos. 996, 1098.

1091. NOCH etwas von dem Westmeer. (Der Neue teutsche Merkur. Weimar, 1791. 12°. Jahr 1791, Vierteljahr 4, p. 189.) *DF

Ein Auszug aus der "Geschichte der Reisen, die seit Cook an der Nordwest- und Westostküste von Amerika und in dem nördl. Amerika selbst von Meares, Dixon, Portlock, Coxe, Long u. a. unternommen worden sind."
See no. 1095.

1092. PREISE auf Indische Hirn-Häute ausgesetzt. (In: A. L. Schlözer. Stats-Anzeigen. Göttingen, 1791. 8°. Bd. 16, p. 378.) BAC

"We, the subscribers, encouraged by a large subscription, do promise to pay one hundred Dollars for every hostile Indian's scalp with both ears to it taken between this date and the 15th day of June next, by any inhabitant of Alleghany county..."
Taken from the *Maryland gazette*, June 10th, 1791, no. 697.

1093. REUSS, JEREMIAS DAVID. Das Gelehrte England oder Lexikon Der jeztlebenden Schriftsteller in Grosbritannien, Irland und Nord-Amerika nebst einem Verzeichnis ihrer Schriften vom Jahr 1770 bis 1790. Von Jeremias David Reuss... Berlin und Stettin: Bey Friedr. Nicolai, 1791. 2 v. in 1. 21 cm. (8°.) * KF 1791

Main title and text in English; this is an added title page.
A supplement, 1790–1803, issued at Göttingen in 1804, is also in * KF 1791.

1094. SELL, JOHANN JACOB. Versuch einer Geschichte des Negersclavenhandels... Halle: Bei Johann Jacob Gebauer, 1791. 5 p.l., 246 p., 1 l. 8°. *KF 1791

Sabin 79021.
Bibliography, p. 226–244.
Contents of interest: Abschnitt 7: Behandlung der Negersclaven auf der Fahrt nach America. Abschnitt 8: Art des Verkaufs der Sclaven in America und ihr Preiss daselbst. Abschnitt 10: Behandlung der Sclaven in America. Abschnitt 11: Benutzung der Neger in America. Abschnitt 12: Ungefähre Uebersicht der Anzahl der Neger in America.
See Friedrich Kapp, *Geschichte der Sklaverei in den Vereinigten Staaten von Amerika*, New York [1860], SEKK.
Review: *Allgemeine Literatur-Zeitung*, Jahr 1791, Bd. 4, col. 321–324, NAA.

1095. UEBER das wiedergefundene Westmeer. (Der Neue teutsche Merkur. Weimar, 1791. 12°. Jahr 1791, Vierteljahr 2, p. 29–52.) *DF

Signed: V.
See no. 1091.

1096. UEBER die Ausartung der Europäer in fremden Erdtheilen. (Göttingisches historisches Magazin. Hannover, 1791. 12°. Bd. 8, p. 209–268.) BAA (Neues)

Signed: M (i.e., Christoph Meiners, 1747–1810).
Periodical subsequently called *Neues göttingisches historisches Magazin*, under which it is shelved.

1097. VERMISCHTE Anzeigen und Briefe. (In: A. L. Schlözer. Stats-Anzeigen. Göttingen, 1791. 8°. Bd. 16, p. 125–128.) BAC

No. II. Baltimore, 8. März 1791.
Corrects *Stats-Anzeigen*, Bd. 6, p. 131–132.
Baron von Steuben's pension consists of "2500 harten spanischen Thalern."
See no. 774.

1098. [WEHRS, GEORG FRIEDRICH. Nachricht über Frasers nordamerikanisches Gras.] (Neues hannöverisches Magazin... vom Jahre 1791. Hannover, 1792. 4°. Jahrg. 1, col. 925–928.) *DF

Entry from "Rubriken."
Title page dated 1792; contents, 1791.
See nos. 996, 1090.

1098A. *Review:* Actes passés à un Congrès des Etats-Unis de l'Amérique commencé et tenu dans la ville de New-York le mercredi quatre Mars de l'année 1789 et la treizième de l'indépendance des Etats-Unis, traduits par Mr. Hubert... Paris: Hôtel de Thon, 1790. 275 S. 8°. (Allgemeine Literatur-Zeitung. Jena, 1791. Bd. 1, col. 620–621, NAA.)

"An der Spitze steht die neue Constitution... Unter den Acten der ersten Sitzung sind einige, wodurch die Einrichtung der Administration und executiven Gewalt des neuen grossen Staates reguliert wird, und einige andere, die das Verhältnis der einzelnen Colonien und ihr Finanzsystem betreffen."

# GERMAN WORKS RELATING TO AMERICA

*1791, continued*

1098B. *Review:* Annalen der brittischen Geschichte des Jahrs 1789. Als eine Fortsetzung des Werks, England und Italien, von J. W. v. Archenholz u.s.w. Zweyter Band. Mit dem Bildniss des Grosskanzlers Lord Thulow. 348 p. Dritter Band. Mit dem Bildniss des Lord Camden, 384 p. Hamburg: Auf Kosten des Verfassers und in Commission bey Hoffmann, 1790. 8°. (Allgemeine deutsche Bibliothek. Berlin, 1791. 12°. Bd. 103, p. 183–190, *NAA.*)
The reviewer quotes the following from v. 2, p. 137 and considers the judgment untrue and unfair: "Die nach unvernünftiger Freyheit ringenden Amerikaner glaubten diese gegen ihre vormaligen Reichthümer vertauscht zu haben; allein sie fanden sich nicht freyer als ehedem, und ihre eingebildete Glückseligkeit war einem Traum ähnlich gewesen. Anarchie, verletzte Nationalehre u. s. w."

1099. *Review:* Beschreibung einiger nordamerikan. Fossilien von A. G. Schütz. Leipzig, 1791. 16 p. 8°. (Göttingische Anzeigen von gelehrten Sachen. Göttingen [1791]. 4°. Jahr 1791, p. 1872, \**DF.*)
Supplements Schoepf's account; *see* nos. 938, 939.

1099A. *Review:* Beytrag zur deutschen holzgerechten Forstwissenschaft, die Anpflanzung nordamerikanischer Holzarten, mit Anwendung auf deutsche Forste betreffend von F. A. J. von Wangenheim. Göttingen: Bey Dieterich, 1787. 124 S. f°. (Allgemeine deutsche Bibliothek. Berlin [1791]. 12°. Anhang zu Bd. 53/86, p. 634–642, *NAA.*)
"Dieses Werk ist eine Erweiterung des kleinen rühmlich bekannten Traktats, welchen der Verf. 1781 von den nordamerikanischen Holz- und Buscharten herausgegeben hat. — In der ersten [Abtheilung] beschreibt er diejenigen Holzarten, welche in Nordamerika vom 39sten bis 45sten Grad der Breite wachsen, und welche vorzüglich in Forsten, und von Privatpersonen in unserm Klima angebauet zu werden verdienen. Jm zweiten Abschnitt beschreibt er die Holzarten, welche unter eben diesem Grade der Breite in Nordamerika wachsen, von denen es zweifelhaft ist, ob sie zur Aufnahme in unsern Forsten...dienen können."

1100. *Review:* Briefe eines Amerikanischen Landmanns an den Ritter W. S. in den Jahren 1779 bis 1781. Aus dem Engl. ins Franz. von xxx und jetzt aus dem Franz. übersetzt, und mit einigen Anmerkungen begleitet von Joh. August Ephraim Götze. Leipzig: Bey Crusius, 1788. 8°. 1. Bd., 512 S. 2. Bd., 512 S. (Allgemeine deutsche Bibliothek. Berlin, 1791. 12°. Bd. 100, p. 181–184, *NAA.*)

1101. *Review:* The capacity of negroes for religious and moral improvement considered... By Richard Nisbet... London: Philips, 1789. 207 p. 8°. (Allgemeine Literatur-Zeitung. Jena, 1791. 4°. Jahr 1791, Bd. 4, col. 381–384, *NAA.*)
The Library has a copy of this English work in the Schomburg Collection *(326.9-N).*
*See* no. 1016.

1101A. *Review:* Christian Ludolph Reinhold ...Geschichte der Schiffahrt, den (der) Reisen um die Welt, und den (der) vornehmsten Länderentdeckungen in Süden und Norden. Münster und Osnabrück: Bey Perremon, 1787. 8 Bogen. 8°. (Allgemeine deutsche Bibliothek. Berlin [1791]. 12°. Anhang zu Bd. 53/86, p. 1037–1039, *NAA.*)

1101B. *Review:* D[octor] Benjamin Franklin's erweitertes Lehrgebäude der natürlichen Elektricität. Für jedermann fasslich und deutlich dargestellt durch D.E.G. Wien: Bey Rehms, 1790. 6½ Bogen. 8°. (Allgemeine deutsche Bibliothek. Berlin, 1791. 12°. Bd. 105, p. 155–156, *NAA.*)

1102. *Review:* Edw. Umfreville über den gegenwärtigen Zustand der Hudsonbay, aus dem Engl. von E. A. W. Zimmermann. Helmstädt: B. Fleckeisen. 146 p. 8°. (Allgemeine Literatur-Zeitung. Jena, 1791. 4°. Jahr 1791, Bd. 4, col. 294–295, *NAA.*)
Sabin 97703.

1103. *Review:* An Elegy, occasioned by the Rejection of M. Wilberforce's Motion for the abolition of Slave Trade. 1791. 4°. (Neue Bibliothek der schönen Wissenschaften und der freyen Künste. Leipzig, 1791. 12°. Bd. 44, p. 302–303, *NAA.*)

1104. *Review:* Eloge civique de Benjamin Franklin, prononcé le 21 Juil. 1790 dans la Rotonde au nom de la Commune de Paris, par Mr. l'Abbé Fauchet... Paris, 1790. (Neue Bibliothek der schönen Wissenschaften und der freyen Künste. Leipzig, 1791. 12°. Bd. 42, p. 308, *NAA.*)
The Library's copy of this work is in \* *KF.*

1105. *Review:* Friedr. Christian Franz's... Lehrbuch der Länder- und Völkerkunde. Zweeter Theil. Asien, Africa, Amerika, und die neuentdeckten Länder nebst einem Register über beede Theile. Stuttgard: B. Erhard u. Löfland, 1790. 326 p. ohne Register u. Vorrede. 8°. (Allgemeine Literatur-Zeitung. Jena, 1791. 12°. Jahr 1791, Bd. 2, col. 36–38, *NAA.*)
Note also F. C. Franz, *Ueber die Kultur der Amerikaner*, Stuttgart, 1788. Kayser, v. 2, p. 254A. Not in the Library.

1105A. *Review:* Geschichte von Mexico aus spanischen und mexikanischen Geschichtsschreibern, Handschriften und Gemälden der Indianer zusammengetragen, und durch Charten und Kupferstiche erläutert, nebst einigen kritischen Abhandlungen über die Beschaffenheit des Landes, der Thiere und Einwohner von Mexiko. Aus dem Italienischen des Abts D. Franz Xaver Clavigero durch den Ritter Carl Cullen ins Englische, und aus diesem ins Deutsche übersetzt. Leipzig: Im Schwickertschen Verlage, 1789. 1. Alph. 18 Bogen. 8°. (Allgemeine deutsche Bibliothek. Berlin, 1791. 8°. Bd. 102, p. 187–188, *NAA.*)
"...liefert weit mehrere und bessere Materialien zur Kenntnis der Alterthümer, als zur natürlichen Geschichte von Mexico."
See also no. 1148A.

1105B. *Review:* Geschichte der Ynkas, Könige von Peru... Aus den Nachrichten des Ynka Garcillaso de la Vega, verfasset von G. G. Böttger. Erster Theil. Nordhausen: Bey Gerst, 1787. 336 S. Zweyter Theil, ebenda, 1788. 400 S. und Vorrede. (Allgemeine deutsche Bibliothek. Berlin [1791]. 12°. Anhang zu Bd. 53/86, p. 984–986, *NAA.*)

*1791, continued*

1105C. *Review:* Handbuch für Liebhaber englischer Pflanzungen, und Gärtner, oder Anleitung zur Kenntnis aller ausländischer und einheimischer Bäume und Sträucher, deren Cultur bey uns möglich und nützlich ist, nach den neuesten Nachrichten entworfen. Leipzig: Bey Sommer, 1790. 8°. (Allgemeine deutsche Bibliothek. Berlin, 1791. 8°. Bd. 102, p. 460-461, *NAA.*)

"Man kann daraus die verschiedenen Gattungen und Spielarten der mehrsten, vornemlich Nordamerikanischen Holzarten kennen lernen."

1105D. *Review:* Hn. Johann Friedrich Ludwigs neueste Nachrichten von Surinam; als Handbuch für Reisende und Beytrag zur Länderkunde herausgegeben und erläutert von M[agister] Philipp Friedrich Binder... Jena: In der akademischen Buchhandlung, 1790. 260 S. 8°. (Allgemeine Literatur-Zeitung. Jena, 1791. 4°. Jahr 1791, Bd. 2, col. 38-40, *NAA.*)

1105E. *Review:* The History of America, by William Robertson... 3 v. Leipzig: Bei Schwickert, 1786. 8°. (Allgemeine deutsche Bibliothek. Berlin [1791]. 12°. Anhang zu Bd. 53/86, p. 1033-1037, *NAA.*)

1105F. *Review:* Jenne's Reisen von St. Petersburg bis Malta, und von der Donau bis in den Quadalquivir, durch einen Theil von Asien, und einige Städte von Amerika. Drey Theile. Erfurt und Leipzig, 1790. 8°. (Allgemeine deutsche Bibliothek. Berlin, 1791, 8°. Bd. 102, p. 218-226, *NAA.*)

The reviewer does not indicate which American cities are mentioned.

1105G. *Review:* Der Kapitains Portlock's und Dixon's Reise um die Welt in den Jahren 1785 bis 1788 in den Schiffen König Georg und Königin Charlotte... Aus dem Englischen. Berlin: Bey Christian Friedrich Voss und Sohn, 1789. 159 S. 8°. (Allgemeine deutsche Bibliothek. Berlin, 1791. 12°. Bd. 102, p. 518-519, *NAA.*)

See nos. 1057F, 1060C, 1060D, 1071, 1072, 1073.

1106. *Review:* Manners and Customs in the West India Islands, etc. by J. B. Moreton. London: Richardson, 1790. (Göttingische Anzeigen von gelehrten Sachen. Göttingen [1791]. 12°. Jahr 1791, p. 634-636, * *DF.*)

The author of the treatise is a Negro driver on a plantation in the West Indies.

See *Monthly review*, v. 4, p. 337, * *DA.*

Sabin (50621) mentions a German edition: Schilderung des häuslichen Lebens der Sitten und Gebräuche der Einwohner auf der Insel Jamaika. Aus dem Englischen. Prag: Johann Herrl, 1793. 126 p. 12°.

1107. *Review:* Medical Papers, communicated to the Massachusetts medical Society. No. i. Boston in Nordamerika: B. Thomas u. Andrews, 1790. 128 p. 8°. (Allgemeine Literatur-Zeitung. Jena, 1791. 4°. Jahr 1791, Bd. 4, col. 163-165, *NAA.*)

1108. *Review:* Memoirs of the literary and philosophical Society of Manchester. Vol. III. Warrington: B. Eyres; und London: B. C. Cadell, 1790. 648 p., 5 plates. 8°. (Allgemeine Literatur-Zeitung. Jena, 1791. 4°. Jahr 1791, Bd. 2, col. 588-592, *NAA.*)

No. 9: Ueber den Fortgang der Bevölkerung, des Ackerbaues, der Sitten und der Regierungsform in Pensylvania von Dr. Benjamin Rush.

The Library's file of the *Memoirs* is in * *EC.*

1109. *Review:* Nekrolog auf das Jahr 1790, enthaltend Nachrichten von dem Leben merkwürdiger, in diesem Jahre gestorbener Personen, gesammelt von Friedrich Schlichtegroll. Gotha: Perthes, 1791. 2 v. (Göttingische Anzeigen von gelehrten Sachen. Göttingen [1791]. 12°. Jahr 1791, p. 1954-1958, * *DF.*)

v. 1 contains an obituary on Benjamin Franklin. "Franklin; bey aller Unvollständigkeit der Nachrichten wird man das Leben nicht ohne Gefühl lesen."

1109A. *Review:* Neues geographisches Zeitungslexicon, oder kurzgefasste Beschreibung der Länder, Städte, Oerter, Meere, Flüsse und Berge in allen vier Theilen der Welt... Augsburg: Bei Matthäus Riegers sel. Söhnen, 1790. 944 S. 8°. (Allgemeine deutsche Bibliothek. Berlin, 1791. 8°. Bd. 104, p. 270, *NAA.*)

1110. *Review:* Nouveau Voyage dans les etats unis de l'Amerique septentrionale, fait en 1788 par J. P. Brissot. Paris: Buisson, 1791. 3 v. (Allgemeine Literatur-Zeitung. Jena, 1791. 12°. Jahr 1791, Bd. 4, col. 531-536, *NAA.*)

Sabin 8035.

The Library's copy of this work is in * *KF.*

1111. *Review:* The present State of Hudsonbay and its Furtrade with hints for its improvement, by Edward Umfreville. London: B. Stalker, 1791. 230 p. 8°. (Allgemeine Literatur-Zeitung. Jena, 1791. 12°. Jahr 1791, Bd. 1, col. 393-397, *NAA.*)

The Library's copy of this English work is in * *KF.*

Sabin lists an English edition of 1790.

For a German translation, see no. 1102.

1112. *Review:* Reisen durch einige französische, englische, holländische, spanische Besitzungen in der neuen Welt... Leipzig: In der Weygandschen Buchhandlung, 1789. 230 p. 8°. (Allgemeine deutsche Bibliothek. Berlin, 1791. 12°. Bd. 102, p. 206-207, *NAA.*)

*See* no. 1024.

1113. *Review:* A short journey in the West Indies, in which are interspersed curious anecdotes and characters. London: B. Murray, 1790. 2 v. 8°. (Allgemeine Literatur-Zeitung. Jena, 1791. 4°. Jahr 1791, Bd. 4, col. 332, *NAA.*)

1114. *Review:* Slave trade and African hospitality, nach G. Moreland von J. R. Smith. (Neue Bibliothek der schönen Wissenschaften und der freyen Künste. Leipzig, 1791. 12°. Bd. 44, p. 156, *NAA.*)

"Blätter in schwarzer Kunst, 20½ Zoll hoch, 27½ Zoll breit."

# GERMAN WORKS RELATING TO AMERICA 133

*1791, continued*

1115. *Review:* Travels through the interior parts of America in a Series of letters by an Officer. London: B. Lane, 1789. 2 v. 8°. (Allgemeine Literatur-Zeitung. Jena, 1791. 4°. Jahr 1791, Bd. 1, col. 397-400, *NAA.*)
The Library's copies of this edition of Thomas Anburey's work are in * KF.
For a German translation, see no. 1120; *see also* 1027.

1115A. *Review:* Ueber Lebensart, Sitten und natürliche Beschaffenheit verschiedener Völker und Länder: ein Lesebuch für Freunde der Erd- und Völkerkunde, herausgegeben von Johann August Donndorff. Erfurt: Bey Keyser, 1789. 626 S. (Allgemeine deutsche Bibliothek. Berlin, 1791. 8°. Bd. 100, p. 507-508, *NAA.*)
Chap. 5. Von den philippinischen oder manilischen Jnseln.

1116. *Review:* Die Verheerung Westindiens. Beschrieben vom Bischof Bartholomäus de la Casas. Aus dem Span. übersetzt von D. W. Andreä. Berlin: Himburg, 1790. 198 S. in 8°. (Allgemeine deutsche Bibliothek. Berlin, 1791. 12°. Bd. 105, p. 173-175, *NAA.*)
See no. 1156.

1116A. *Review:* Vorstellung der vornehmsten Völkerschaften der Welt nach ihrer Abstammung, Ausbreitung und Sprachen, entworfen von Georg August v. Breitenbauch... Leipzig: Im chursächsischen Jntelligenz Comtoir und bey Lange, 1786. 98 S. 8°. (Allgemeine deutsche Bibliothek. Berlin [1791]. 12°. Anhang zu Bd. 53/86, p. 940-947, *NAA.*)
"IV. Nordamerika: 1. Eskimos, 2. Scusen Sioux in Kanada. 3. Algonkinen. 4. Huronen. 5. Natches. 6. Cherokisen. 7. Apalachen. 8. Mexicaner. 9. Kalifornier." — p. 946.

1117. *Review:* Voyage made in the year 1788 and 1789 from Canton to the North West Coast of America by John Meares. London: Walther, 1790. 382 p. 4°. (Allgemeine Literatur-Zeitung. Jena, 1791. 4°. Jahr 1791, Bd. 2, col. 345-351, *NAA.*)
The Library's copies of this English work are in †* KF.
See also no. 1118.

1118. *Review:* Voyage, made in the Years 1788 and 1789 from China to the Northwest coast of America etc. By John Meares. London: Bey Walter, 1790. xcv, 375, 112 p. plates, maps. 4°. (Göttingische Anzeigen von gelehrten Sachen. Göttingen [1791]. 12°. Jahr 1791, p. 369-380, * *DF.*)
See also no. 1117.

1119. *Review:* Voyages and travels of an Indian Interpreter and trader, describing the Manners and Customs of the North American Indians, by J. Long. London: B. Robson u. Debrett, 1791. 295 p. 4°. (Allgemeine Literatur-Zeitung. Jena, 1791. 4°. Jahr 1791, Bd. 2, col. 225-229, *NAA.*)
The Library's copies of this English work by John Long are in * KF.
For German translations, see nos. 1088, 1089.

1119A. *Review:* Wilhelm Thomas Raynals philosophische und politische Geschichte der Besitzungen und Handlung der Europäer in beyden Jndien. Siebenter Band. Nach der neuesten Ausgabe übersetzt und mit Anmerkungen versehen. Kempten: Im Verlage der typographischen Gesellschaft, 1786. 480 S. 8°. (Allgemeine deutsche Bibliothek. Berlin, 1791. 12°. Anhang zu Bd. 53/86, p. 2205-2220, *NAA.*)

*1792*

1120. ANBUREY, THOMAS. Anburey's Reisen im inneren Amerika. Aus dem Englischen übersetzt von Georg Forster. Berlin: Voss, 1792. 372 p., 1 folding pl. 8°. (Magazin von merkwürdigen neuen Reisebeschreibungen... Bd. 6.)
Sabin 1370. KBC
Translation of his *Travels through the interior parts of America*... London, 1789, * *KF.*
"Thomas Anburey, lieutenant in the army of General Burgoyne, was able to make quite keen observations of America, its forests, roads, qualities and habits of its people. The personal incidents of the writer's travels on foot for more than 1000 miles from Montreal to Virginia, make it a fascinating book." — *Thelma Evans, European impressions of America.* Madison, Wis., 1930, † *I.*
Reviews: *Allgemeine Literatur-Zeitung*, Jahr 1792, Bd. 1, col. 23, *NAA*; *Neue Allgemeine deutsche Bibliothek*, Bd. 1, p. 180-188, 445-461; Bd. 15, p. 244, *NAA*; *Göttingische Anzeigen von gelehrten Sachen*, Jahr 1792, p. 643, * *DF*; *Erlangische gelehrte Anzeigen*, Jahr 1794, p. 316-319 (not in N. Y. P. L.); *Gothaische gelehrte Zeitungen*, Jahr 1792, Bd. 2, p. 818 (not in N. Y. P. L.); *Neue Leipziger gelehrte Zeitung*, Jahr 1791, Bd. 2, p. 809-812; Jahr 1792, Bd. 1, p. 140-143 (not in N. Y. P. L.).

1121. BERICHT von dem was sich am Bord des Amerikanischen Schiffes Elenora, Capt. Metcalfe, während seines Aufenthalts auf den Sandwich-Inseln zugetragen hat. (In: P. J. Bruns and E. A. W. Zimmermann, editors. Repositorium für die neueste Geographie, Statistik und Geschichte. Tübingen, 1792. 8°. Bd. 2, p. 358-365.) KBD
Taken from *Gentleman's magazine*, April, 1792.
"Der Einsender... will aus dem Inhalte beweisen, wie sehr die Amerikanische Menschlichkeit der Brittischen nachstehe." — *E. A. W. Zimmermann's note.*

1122. BERICHT von Spanischen Expeditionen zur See und zu Land nach dem nördlichen Theil [von] Californien... [Mit einer Karte von Californien.] (In: P. J. Bruns and E. A. W. Zimmermann, editors. Repositorium für die neueste Geographie, Statistik und Geschichte. Tübingen, 1792. 8°. Bd. 1, p. 1-32.) KBD
Title variations taken from Inhalt.
Excerpt from Miguel Costanso's *An historical journal of the expeditions by sea and land to the North of California... from a Spanish Ms*... London, 1792, † *IXG.*
The German translation is by Paul Jakob Bruns, 1743-1814.

1123. BOUTERWEK, FRIEDRICH. Der Genius von Otaheiti. (Musen Almanach. Göttingen: Bey J. C. Dietrich [1792]. 32°. p. 40-48.) NFA

*1792, continued*

1124. BRISSOT DE WARVILLE, JACQUES PIERRE. Neue Reise durch die vereinigten Staaten von Nordamerika in dem Jahre 1788. [Berlin: Voss, 1792. 292 p. 8°.] (Magazin von merkwürdigen neuen Reisebeschreibungen... Bd. 7, Theil 1.) Translated by J. R. Forster. KBC
The translation is shortened. Two other translations, namely that by Theophil Friedrich Ehrmann (1762-1811), issued at Dürkheim a. d. H. in 1792, and that by A. Cph. Kayser and J. J. M. Valett, the three volumes of which were published in Bayreuth, 1792-1796, are criticized in the introduction.
See nos. 1110, 1362; also Sabin 8033.

1125. BRUNS, P[AUL] J[AKOB], AND E. A. W. ZIMMERMANN, EDITORS. Repositorium für die neueste Geographie, Statistik und Geschichte ... Erster [-Dritter] Band. Tübingen, 1792-93. 3 v. 8°. KBD
This work contains several articles on North America, which are listed in this compilation.
See nos. 1121, 1122, 1136, 1138, 1144, 1153, 1159, 1184.
Review: *Göttingische Anzeigen von gelehrten Sachen*, Jahr 1793, p. 1620-1623, * DF.

1126. EINIGE neuere Nachrichten von den Pelew- oder Palaos-Inseln. (Neues hannöverisches Magazin...vom Jahre 1792. Hannover, 1793. 4°. Jahrg. 2, col. 113-126.) *DF
"...aus den neuesten Nachrichten des Kapitän MacCluer's von diesem Volk..."
Title page dated 1793; contents, 1792.

1127. FRANKLIN, BENJAMIN. Benjamin Franklin's Jugendjahre, von ihm selbst für seinen Sohn beschrieben, und übersetzt von Gottfried August Bürger. Berlin: Bey Heinrich August Rottmann, 1792. 214 p. 18 cm. *KF 1792
Franklin's autobiography to the year 1731.
For G. A. Bürger's attitude toward America, see J. A. Walz in *Modern language notes*, Baltimore, 1901, v. 16, *RAA*.
Review: *Göttingische Anzeigen von gelehrten Sachen*, Jahr 1792, p. 2003-2004, * DF.

1128. —— Einige für Seereisende nützliche Bemerkungen des Dr. Benjamin Franklin. (Neues hannöverisches Magazin vom... Jahre 1792. Hannover, 1793. 4°. Jahrg. 2, col. 81-94, 97-102.) *DF
A posthumous publication.
Title page dated 1793; contents, 1792.

1129. —— Etwas über den neuesten Zustand der sechzehn vereinigten Staaten von Nordamerika, nach den officiellen Berichten des Generalcongresses von 1791. Nebst Nachrichten über den Geneseedistrikt im Staate von Neu-York und dem darin befindlichen Zucker-Ahornbaum. (Neues hannöverisches Magazin ...vom Jahre 1792. Hannover, 1793. 4°. Jahrg. 2, col. 481-494.) *DF
Signed Fr. [i.e. Benjamin Franklin].
Franklin had died in 1790.
Title page dated 1793; contents, 1792.

1130. GENAUE Nachricht von dem jetzigen Geld Wesen in dem Vereinten Nord Amerika... (In: A. L. Schlözer. Stats-Anzeigen. Göttingen, 1792. 8°. Bd. 17, p. 260-264.) BAC
"Ausgezogen aus 1. *Elliott's Maryland and Virginia Almanac 1791*. 48 S. 2. *The Pennsylvania, Delaware, Maryland and Virginia Almanack 1791*. 48 S."
The survey was made by Dorothea Schlözer [i.e., Dorothea, Freiin von Rodde], daughter of the editor, A. L. Schlözer. See "Zeitgenossen," Bd. 4, Abth. 3, in A. L. and Leopold von Schlözer, *Dorothea von Schlözer, ein deutsches Frauenleben um die Jahrhundertwende, 1770-1825. Mit zwölf Abbildungen*, Gottingen [cop. 1937], *AN* (Rodde).
See also "An Account of Miss D. Schlozer [sic!] a celebrated learned lady...," in *Columbian magazine or Monthly miscellany*, Philadelphia, 1790, v. 4, and "An account of Miss Schlozer," in *Massachusetts magazine or Monthly museum*, Boston, 1791, v. 3, p. 223-234.

1130A. GOETHE, JOHANN WOLFGANG VON. Der Gross-Cophta. Ein Lustspiel in fünf Aufzügen von Goethe. Berlin: Bey Joh. Fr. Unger, 1792. (Reprinted in his: Werke. Herausgegeben im Auftrage der Grossherzogin Sophie von Sachsen. Weimar: Hermann Böhlau, 1887-1919. 8°. Bd. 17, p. 117-250.) NFGK
Act ii, Scene 5. "Ein Freund, der gegenwärtig in Amerika lebt, kam unversehens in grosse Gefahr..."
See Walter Wadepuhl, in *Deutsch-amerikanische historische Gesellschaft von Illinois. Jahrbuch*, Chicago, 1922-23, v. 22-23, p. 77-108, *IEK*.

1131. HERDER, JOHANN GOTTFRIED VON. Franklin's Fragen. Eine Vorlesung. 1792. (Reprinted in his: Sämmtliche Werke. Herausgegeben von Bernhard Suphan. Berlin: Weidmannsche Buchhandlung, 1877-1913. 8°. Bd. 18, p. 503-508.) NFG
See M. B. D. Learned's "Herder and America," in *German-American annals*, new series v. 2, p. 531-570, *NFCA*.
As to a number of Herder's works that appeared in English translation in American magazines of those days, see the "List of translations of German prose," and "List of articles on the German countries," in E. Z. Davis, *Translations of German poetry in American magazines, 1741-1810*, Philadelphia, 1905. (Americana Germanica. Monographs. new series, v. 1, p. 191-214, *NFK*.)
See also D. Jacoby in *Archiv für Litteraturgeschichte*, Leipzig, 1885, v. 18, p. 273-277, *NAA*.

1132. —— Zerstreute Blätter von J. G. Herder. 4. Sammlung. Gotha: Bey Carl Wilhelm Ettinger, 1792. (Reprinted in his: Sämmtliche Werke. Herausgegeben von Bernhard Suphan. Berlin: Weidmannsche Buchhandlung, 1877-1913. 8°. Bd. 16, p. 107-127.) NFG
In part entitled "Gedanken einiger Bramanen," a translation of verses on the prospect of planting arts and learning in America by Dr. Berkeley, bishop of Cloyne (1725) is found. The last stanza in Herder's version reads:

O Muse, nimmst du Westwärts Deinen Flug?
Dort zu beginnen unsern fünften Act:
(Denn vier sind schon vorüber), dass das Werk
Der Zeiten ende mit dem schönsten Schluss?
— *p. 127.*

*See note of preceding entry.*

1133. DIE HEUSCHRECKEN-VERWÜSTUNG Joel II. (Allgemeine Bibliothek der biblischen Literatur. Leipzig, 1792. 12°. Bd. 4, p. 30-79.) *YIA
p. 65 contains references to the customs on the Pelew Islands, taken from George Keate's *Nachrichten von dem Pelew-Inseln...aus dem Englischen übersetzt von D. Georg Forster...* Hamburg, 1789 (* KF 1789 Neuere); *see* no. 989.

# GERMAN WORKS RELATING TO AMERICA

*1792, continued*

**1133A.** HIPPEL, THEODOR GOTTLIEB VON. Ueber die bürgerliche Verbesserung der Weiber. 1792. (Reprinted in his: Sämmtliche Werke. Berlin: G. Reiner, 1828. 12°. v. 6.) NFG
"Eine Schrift kann nie ein mächtiges um sich greifendes Feuer anzünden; und wenn man behauptet: Rousseau, Voltaire und Montesquieu hätten die Französische Revolution zu Stande gebracht, so vergisst man Nordamerica: und es gehört zu den Zeichen dieser Zeit, wenn man mit Büchern bekannter als mit Menschen ist, um zu regieren." — *p. 257.*
"Franklin, ein Mann, desgleichen weder das Griechische noch das Römische Althertum aufzuweisen hat, sagte: 'Gäbe es einen Gottesläugner, er würde sich beim Anblick von Philadelphia, einer so wohleingerichteten Stadt, bekehren'; und die Erde, diese grosse Stadt Philadelphia, sollte so viel nicht über den Gottesläugner vermögen?" — *p. 155.*
See H. S. King, University of California, *Publications in modern philology*, Berkeley, 1929, v. 14, p. 89, STG.

**1134.** DER HÜGEL von Vernon, in Virginien, Wohnsitz des Generals Washington. (Minerva. Hamburg, 1792. 16°. [Jahr] 1792, Bd. 4, No. 18, p. 85–87.) BAA

**1135.** INDIANISCHE Beredsamkeit. (Minerva. Hamburg, 1792. [Jahr] 1792, Bd. 4, No. 18, p. 8–15.) BAA
Signed: P—r.

**1136.** JAMAICA. (In: P. J. Bruns and E. A. W. Zimmermann, editors. Repositorium für die neueste Geographie, Statistik und Geschichte. Tübingen, 1792. 8°. Bd. 2, p. 365–366.) KBD
Excerpt from *Transactions* of the Society Instituted at London for the Encouragement of Arts, Manufactures, and Commerce, v. IX.

**1137.** MITTEL, dessen sich die englischen Bierbrauer bedienen, zu verhindern, dass nach Ost- und Westindien zu verfahrendes Bier nicht sauer werde. (Neues hannöverisches Magazin ... vom Jahre 1792. Hannover, 1793. 4°. Jahrg. 2, col. 1119–1120.) *DF
Title page dated 1793; contents, 1792.

**1138.** REISE in die nördlichen Gegenden zwischen Asien und Amerika. (In: P. J. Bruns and E. A. W. Zimmermann, editors. Repositorium für die neueste Geographie, Statistik und Geschichte. Tübingen, 1792. 8°. Bd. 2, p. 387–388.) KBD
"S. Journal des Savans Juillet 1792."
The author is "Monsieur de la Lande."

**1139.** SCHOEPF, JOHANN DAVID. D. Johann David Schöpfs... Naturgeschichte der Schildkröten mit Abbildungen erläutert... Erlangen: Bey Johann Jacob Palm, 1792. 6 p.l., 160 p., 31 col'd plates. f°. †QLV
American turtles.

**1139A.** SPRENGEL, MATTHIAS CHRISTIAN. Auswahl der besten ausländischen geographischen und statistischen Nachrichten zur Aufklärung der Völker- und Länderkunde... Siebenter Band. Halle: In der Reugerschen Buchhandlung, 1797. 10 x 18cm. *KF 1797
Sabin 31207.
*Contents:* 1. Reisejournal des Herrn Johann Heckewälders, von der Brüdergemeine von Bethlehem in Pensilvanien, nach dem Posten St. Vincent am Wabashfluss, im nordwestlichen Gebiet der vereinigten Staaten von Nordamerika, p. 1–94. 11. Samuel Hearnes Tagebuch seiner Reise von Fort Prinz Wallis in der Hudsonbay nach dem nördlichen Weltmeer, p. 95–325.
Heckewelder "ward en 1792 vom Congress ausersehen, den General Putnam bis zum Wabashfluss zu begleiten, um hier mit mehreren wilden Stämmen Frieden zu schliessen... Seine Nachrichten verbreiten sich zugleich ueber die Sitten und Denkungsart der Wilden, die Lebensart der dort zerstreut wohnenden Europäer, die Unsicherheit, in der sie wegen der feindlichen Einfälle leben, und wie wenig sich die neuen Kolonisten dieser Wüsten, im Denken und Handeln von den ursprünglichen Einwohnern unterscheiden... Die zweyte Reise gieng durch die nördlichen Wüsteneyen der neuen Welt, die bisher kein Europäer betreten hat, und die wegen des dabey unausbleiblichen Elends schwerlich jemand nach Herrn Hearne untersuchen wird." — *Vorrede.*
An English translation of J. Heckewelder's report is in *HBC p.v.123.*
See also P. C. Weber, *America in imaginative German literature*, New York, 1926, p. 25, *NFCX.*
See also nos. 1344, 1371.

**1140.** —— Geschichte der wichtigsten geographischen Entdeckungen bis zur Ankunft der Portugiesen in Japan 1542 von Matthias Christian Sprengel, Professor der Geschichte in Halle... Zweite vermehrte Auflage. Halle: Bei Hemmerde und Schwetschke, 1792. 4 p.l., 420 p., 18 l. 8°. *KF 1792
Sabin 89759.
Contains some account of the discovery of America.
Augmented re-issue of: Grundriss einer Geschichte der wichtigsten geographischen Entdeckungen. Halle: Hemmerde & Schwetschke, 1783. 106 p, 8°.
Note also his *Ueber J. [sic!] Ribero's älteste Weltcharte*, Weimar, 1795, Sabin 89762. Not in the Library.

**1141.** UEBER den Haar- und Bartwuchs der hässlichen und dunkelfarbigen Völker. (Neues göttingisches historisches Magazin. Hannover, 1792. 12°. Bd. 1, p. 484–508.) BAA
Signed: M (i.e., Christoph Meiners, 1747–1810).
Note also *Geschichte des männlichen Barts... Nach dem Französischen frey bearbeitet...1797.* (British Museum catalogue: Geschichte). This is a German version of A. Fangé, *Mémoires pour servir à l'histoire de la barbe de l'homme.* Not in the Library.

**1142.** UEBER die Farben und Schattierungen verschiedener Völker. (Neues göttingisches historisches Magazin. Hannover, 1792. 12°. Bd. 1, p. 611–672.) BAA
Signed: M (i.e., Christoph Meiners, 1747–1810).

**1143.** UEBER die Verschiedenheit der cörperlichen Grösse verschiedener Völker. (Neues göttingisches historisches Magazin. Hannover, 1792. 12°. Bd. 1, p. 697–726.) BAA
Signed: M (i.e., Christoph Meiners, 1747–1810).

**1144.** UNIVERSITÄTEN in dem Nord-Amerikanischen Freistaate. (In: P. J. Bruns and E. A. W. Zimmermann, editors. Repositorium für die neueste Geographie, Statistik und Geschichte. Tübingen, 1792. 8°. Bd. 1, p. 443–448.) KBD
Taken from Jedidiah Morse's *The American geography.* Elizabeth-town, 1789.

*1792, continued*

1145. VOLKS Menge von Pennsylvania. (In: A. L. Schlözer. Stats-Anzeigen. Göttingen, 1792. 8°. Bd. 17, p. 232.) BAC
From Dunlap's *American daily advertiser*, Sept. 2nd, 1791.
Note also *Deutsches Magazin* [ed. *Chr. U. D. v. Eggers*]. Hamburg, 1791-1800. Not in the Library. It contains Chr. U. D. v. Eggers, "Summarische Volksliste der vereinigten Staaten von Nordamerika vom Jahr 1790," Jahrg. 1792, p. 582; "Verschiedenheit der Volksklassen in den europäischen Kolonien in Amerika," Jahrg. 1794, p. 279-281; "Fernere Nachricht von der Bevölkerung der vereinigten Freystaaten von Nordamerika," Jahrg. 1794, p. 351-353.

1146. *Review:* An Address to every Briton on the Slave Trade; being an effectual Plan to abolish this Disgrace to our Country. 1791. 19 p. 4°. (Neue Bibliothek der schönen Wissenschaften und der freyen Künste. Leipzig, 1792. 12°. Bd. 46, p. 316, *NAA.*)

1147. *Review:* Alex. Falconbridges and Thom. Clarksons Bemerkungen über die gegenwärtige Beschaffenheit des Sclavenhandels und dessen politischen Nachtheile für England, aus dem Englischen herausgegeben und mit Anmerkungen begleitet von M. C. Sprengel. Leipzig: B. Weygand, 1790. 8°. (Allgemeine Literatur-Zeitung. Jena, 1792. 4°. Jahr 1792, Bd. 1, col. 574-576, *NAA.*)
See no. 1054.

1147A. *Review:* Allgemeine Weltgeschichte von den ältesten bis auf die neuesten Zeiten. Ein Lesebuch, auch für Nichtgelehrte von Karl Hammerdörfer, Professor zu Jena. Vierter und letzter Band, die Geschichte bis zum Jahre 1783. enthaltend. Halle: In der Buchhandlung des Waisenhauses, 1791. 776 p. 8°. (Allgemeine deutsche Bibliothek. Berlin, 1792. 12°. Bd. 109, p. 197-198, *NAA.*)
"Dieser Band fängt von der Entdeckung Amerikas an und schliesst mit dem Jahre 1783, theils weil die Entstehung und Anerkennung des Nordamerikanischen Freystaats eine neue Periode zu bezeichnen scheint, theils..."

1147B. *Review:* Beyträge zur Geschichte der Erfindungen von Joh. Beckmann... Leipzig: Bey Kummer, 1790. Dritten Bandes zweytes Stück. p. 155-308. (Allgemeine deutsche Bibliothek. Berlin, 1792. 12°. Bd. 109, p. 291-292, *NAA.*)
v, Jndianische Hühner. "... Sie stammen aus Amerika her." The Library has only the first two volumes of this work.
J. Beckmann was the editor of *Beyträge zur Oekonomie, Technologie, Polisey- und Cameralwissenschaften.* v. 1-12. Göttingen, 1779-1791. Not in the Library. The periodical contains a number of articles relating to America.

1147C. *Review:* A Descriptive account of the Island of Jamaica, by William Beckford, Esq. 1. Bd. 404 S. 2. Bd. 405 S. 8°. London, 1791. (Göttingische Anzeige von gelehrten Sachen. Göttingen [1792]. 12°. Jahr 1792, p. 169-176, * *DF.*)
"Beschreibungen des Verfassers, der viele Jahre Pflanzer in Jamaica war, beschäftigen sich nicht nur mit der Natur, den Naturscenen in den Westindischen Inseln, sondern auch mit den Vergnügungen an den Arbeiten der Einwohner und Sklaven."

1148. *Review:* Epistle to William Wilberforce, Esq. on the rejection of the bill for abolishing the Slave Trade. By Anna Letitia Barbauld. 14 p. 4°. London: Johnson, 1791. (Neue Bibliothek der schönen Wissenschaften und der freyen Künste. Leipzig, 1792. 12°. Bd. 46, p. 315-316, *NAA.*)
The Library's copy of this English work is in *Reserve.*

1148A. *Review:* Geschichte von Mexico... Aus dem Italienischen des Abts D. Franz Xaver Clavigero durch den Ritter Carl Cullen ins Englische, und aus diesem ins Deutsche übersetzt. Zweyter und letzter Theil. Leipzig: Bei Schwickert, 1790. (Allgemeine deutsche Bibliothek. Berlin, 1792. 8°. Bd. 106, p. 488-489, *NAA.*)
"...beschäftigt sich insbesondere mit Berichtigung und Widerlegung der Nachrichten und Behauptungen anderer, neuerer Schriftsteller, Pauw, Buffon und Robertson..."
See also 1105A.

1149. *Review:* Karakteristisches Verzeichniss der vorzüglichsten, in Deutschland anzubauenden, einheimischen und nordamerikanischen wildwachsenden Holzarten, für Oekonomen, Forstbediente und Gärtner, bearbeitet von George August Scheppach. Dresden, 1791. 192 Seiten und 1 Tabelle. 8°. (Allgemeine deutsche Bibliothek. Kiel, 1792. 12°. Bd. 111, p. 488, *NAA.*)

1149A. *Review:* M[agister] J. E. Fabri's, Professor zu Jena, Elementar geographie. 3ter und 4ter Band, nebst Vorrede und Register über alle 4 Bände. Halle: Gebauer [n.d.]. (Allgemeine Literatur-Zeitung. Jena, 1792. 4°. Jahr 1792, Bd. 1, col. 300-302, *NAA.*)

1150. *Review:* Nouveau Voyage dans les Etats Unis de l'Amérique septentrionale, fait en 1788, par J. P. Brissot (Warville)... Paris: Bey Buisson, 1791. 3 v. 8°. (Göttingische Anzeigen von gelehrten Sachen. Göttingen [1792]. 12°. Jahr 1792, p. 25-37, 105-120, 129-135, 142-144, * *DF.*)
The Library's copies of this French edition are in * *KF.*

1151. *Review:* Reflexions on the Tomb of Columbus by a Lady. London: Kearsly, 1791. 26 p. 4°. (Neue Bibliothek der schönen Wissenschaften und der freyen Künste. Leipzig, 1792. 12°. Bd. 45, p. 287-288, *NAA.*)

1152. *Review:* S. Holingwirth's Abhandlung von den Sitten der Regierungsart und dem Geiste der Völker in Africa nebst Anmerkungen über die Abschaffung des Sclavenhandels in den brittischen Westindien. Halle: Gebauer, 1789. 8°. (Allgemeine Literatur-Zeitung. Jena, 1792. 4°. Jahr 1792, Bd. 1, col. 574-576, *NAA.*)

*1792, continued*

1153. Review: Sklavenhandel. (In: P. J. Bruns and E. A. W. Zimmermann, editors. Repositorium für die neueste Geographie, Statistik und Geschichte. Tübingen, 1792-93. 8°. Bd. 2, p. 352-358; Bd. 3, p. 63-118, *KBD*.)
Review by P. J. B. (i. e. Paul Jakob Bruns, 1743–1814), of Thomas Clarkson's *Letters on the slave-trade*, London, 1791, an excerpt of which was also printed in this magazine in 1793; *see* no. 1184.

1154. Review: Ueber nordamerikanische Bäume und Sträucher als Gegenstände der deutschen Forstwirthschaft und der schönen Gartenkunst. Von Friedrich Casimir Medicus ... Mannheim, 1792. 7 Bogen. 8°. (Forst-Archiv. Ulm, 1792. 8°. Bd. 13, p. 253–256, *VQN*.)
Sabin 47331.
"In dem gebürgigten Theil von Teutschland verdienen unsere Forstbäume vor den nordamerikanischen den Vorzug... [Es] wird gezeigt, dass die nordamerikanischen Bäume und Sträucher eigentlich nur Gegenstände der schönen Gartenkunst sind..."

1155. Review: Verfassung der vornehmsten europäischen und der vereinigten americanischen Staaten von Hrn. de la Croix mit Berichtigungen des Uebersetzers. Leipzig, 1792. 2 v. 8°. (Göttingische Anzeigen von gelehrten Sachen. Göttingen, 1792. 12°. Jahr 1792, p. 1111–1112, *DF*.)

1156. Review: Die Verheerung Westindiens; beschrieben von Bischof Bartholomäus de la Casas. Aus dem Spanischen übersetzt von D. W. Andreä. Berlin: Himburg, 1790. 198 p. 8°. (Allgemeine Literatur-Zeitung. Jena, 1792. 4°. Jahr 1792, Bd. 1, col. 38, *NAA*.)
See Sabin 11282, in which several more German versions are mentioned.
See no. 1116.

1793

1157. ANREDE der drey Stammhäupter der Seneka's an den Präsidenten des Nordamericanischen Congresses. Philadelphia. Mon. Dec. 1790. [Antwort des Präsidenten der vereinigten Staaten, 29. Dec. 1790. Antwort der Stammhäupter der Senekas, nebst der Replik des Congress-präsidenten. Philadelphia 19. Jan. 1791. Abschiedsrede der Stammhäupter der Senekas.] (Neues göttingisches historisches Magazin. Hannover, 1793. 8°. Bd. 2, p. 734–757.) BAA
Title extended from Verzeichnis.

1158. ARCHENHOLZ, JOHANN WILHELM VON. La Fayette. (Minerva. Hamburg, 1793. 12°. Bd. 5, p. 185–211; Bd. 6, p. 272–277.) BAA

1159. AUSZUG aus Tench Coxe['s] Abhandlung über den jetzigen Handelszustand der vereinigten Staaten von Nordamerika. (In: P. J. Bruns and E. A. W. Zimmermann, editors. Repositorium für die neueste Geographie, Statistik und Geschichte. Tübingen, 1793. 8°. Bd. 3, p. 233–286.) KBD
Excerpts from Tench Coxe's pampblet, *A brief examination on Lord Sheffield's observations on the commerce of the United States*, Philadelphia, 1791. Lord Sheffield's book had appeared in London in 1783.
"Herr Tench Coxe, Beysitzer der Schatzkammer der vereinigten Staaten, fand sich gerade in der gehörigen Lage, durch Kenntniss seines Landes und durch die vor ihm liegenden Zollhaus-, Populations- und Waarenlisten einen solchen Gegner [i.e. Lord Sheffield], wo nicht ganz zu bekämpfen, doch sehr zu schwächen." See the Introduction, by E. A. W. Zimmermann. *See* nos. 809, 1159.

1160. BARTRAM, WILLIAM. William Bartram's Reisen durch Nord- und Süd-Karolina, Georgien, Ost- und West-Florida... Aus dem Englischen. Mit...Anmerkungen von E. A. W. Zimmermann... [Berlin: Voss, 1793.] 494 p. plates (part folding). 8°. (Magazin von merkwürdigen neuen Reisebeschreibungen... Bd. 10, Theil 1.) KBC
Sabin 3872.
Excerpts from Bartram's *Travels through North and South Carolina, Georgia, East and West Florida...*, Philadelphia, 1791, * *KD*.

1161. BÖTTIGER, KARL AUGUST. Washington, Neu-Rom in Amerika. (Der Neue teutsche Merkur. Weimar, 1793. 12°. Jahr 1793, Bd. 3, p. 217–231.) *DF

1162. [DIPPOLD, GOTTFRIED EHREGOTT.] Paul Hennig. Eine wahre Geschichte. Nebst einer merkantilischen Beschreibung von Holland und Surinam. Gräz: Bey Caspar Zaunrieth, Buchhåndler, 1793. 5 p.l., 179 p. 8°. *KF 1793
Preface signed: D. Gottfried Ehregott Dippoldt.
According to the preface, Paul Hennig is the fictitious name of a real person who wrote these letters, but it is more probable that the letters were the work of Dippold himself.

1163. EBELING, CHRISTOPH DANIEL. Christoph Daniel Ebelings, Professors der Geschichte und griechischen Sprache am Hamburgischen Gymnasium, Erdbeschreibung und Geschichte von Amerika. Die Vereinten Staaten von Nordamerika... Hamburg: Bei Carl Ernst Bohn, 1793–1816. 7 v. in 8. 3 folding tables. 8°.
Sabin 21748. *KF 1793
A continuation of Büsching's *Geography*. For bibliographic details of this and another, incomplete, variant, copy; see the Library's catalogue cards.
Bd. I. Einleitung von Neu-England überhaupt; New-Hampshire, Massachusetts, Maine. Bd. II. Rhode-Island, Connecticut, Vermont, New-York. Bd. III. New York, New-Jersey. Bd. IV and VI. Pennsylvania. Bd. v. Delaware, Maryland. Bd. VII. Virginia. "Quellen" and a list of "Landkarten" precede the account of each state.
For decades, this work was the richest source of information on America; see *Allgemeine Literatur-Zeitung*, Jahr 1817, July 31, Appendix, * *DF*.
As to the author, see C. I. Landis, "Charles [*sic!*] Daniel Ebeling," in Pennsylvania German Society, *Proceedings and addresses*, Lancaster, 1929, v. 36, p. 13–27, *IEK*, and W. C. Lane, "Glimpses of European conditions from the Ebeling letters, 1795–1817," in Massachusetts Historical Society, *Proceedings*, Boston, 1926, v. 59, p. 324–376, *IAA*. Of special interest is C. D. Ebeling, *Verzeichnis der von ihm hinterlassenen Büchersammlung*, Hamburg, 1819, * *GO*.
Reviews:
Bd. I–II: *Allgemeine Literatur-Zeitung*, Jahr 1796, Bd. 3, col. 441–449, *NAA*; *Allgemeine geographische Ephemeriden*, Jahr 1800, Bd. 1, p. 136–144, *KAA*; *Göttingische Anzeigen von gelehrten Sachen*, Jahr 1794, p. 1–5; Jahr 1795, p. 1297, * *DF*; *Allgemeines europäisches Journal*, Brünn, Bd. 9, p. 51, * *DF*.
Bd. III. *Allgemeine Literatur-Zeitung*, Jahr 1797, Ergänzungsblätter, col. 33–40, *NAA*; *Neue allgemeine*

### 1793, *continued*

**1163.** EBELING, CHRISTOPH DANIEL, *continued*
*deutsche Bibliothek*, Bd. 30, p. 453–457, *NAA; Allgemeine geographische Ephemeriden*, Jahr 1800, Bd. 1, p. 136–144, *KAA; Greifswalder kritische Nachrichten*, Jahr 1796, p. 247 (not in N. Y. P. L.).
Bd. IV. *Allgemeine Literatur-Zeitung*, Jahr 1797, Ergänzungsblätter, p. 33–40, *NAA; Neue allgemeine deutsche Bibliothek*, Bd. 52, p. 446–452, *NAA; Allgemeine geographische Ephemeriden*, Jahr 1800, Bd. 1, p. 136–144, *KAA*.
Bd. V. *Allgemeine Literatur-Zeitung*, Jahr 1800, Bd. 2, col. 513–518, *NAA; Neue allgemeine deutsche Bibliothek*, Bd. 69, p. 397–403, *NAA; Allgemeine geographische Ephemeriden*, Jahr 1800, Bd. 1, p. 136–144, *KAA*.

**1164.** FISCHEREIEN in NAmerika. (In: A. L. Schlözer. Stats-Anzeigen. Göttingen, 1793. 8°. Bd. 18, p. 416–417.) BAC
Taken from the *American museum*, Philadelphia, August, 1791, Appendix II, p. 9 et seq.

**1164A.** FORSTER, GEORG. Erinnerungen aus dem Jahre 1790 in historischen Gemälden und Bildnissen von D. Chodowiecki, D. Berger, Cl. Kohl, G. F. Bolt und J. S. Ringk. Berlin, 1793. (In his: Sämmtliche Schriften. Leipzig: F. A. Brockhaus, 1843. 12°. v. 6, p. 160–248.) NFG
Of special interest: Cap. 4 entitled "Der Philosoph von Ferney segnet den jungen Gross-Sohn Franklin's," p. 170–172. "Der Stifter des nordamerikanischen Freistaats, der Erfinder des Blitzableiters, der Wohltäter seines Vaterlandes, der Freund und Bruder des Wilden und des Weisen, der humanste Mensch und der glücklichste von allen, die im achtzehnten Jahrhundert zur Mitarbeitern am grossen Vollendungswerke menschlicher Glückseligkeit auserkoren waren, hiess Benjamin Franklin!" See also the illustration of Benjamin Franklin and its description in which Wieland's verses on Franklin are inserted on p. 204–208. Furthermore William Pitt's image and its description, p. 246–248.
Note G. Forster's "Geschichte der englischen Literatur der Jahre 1788–1791," especially his criticism on David Ramsay's *Geschichte der Amerikanischen Revolution* (see no. 1231) and his statement, "Zu einer Zeit, wo man anfing der unzähligen Schriften über die amerikanische Revolution überdrüssig zu werden ..." —v. 6, *p. 75*. Fraser's *Agrostis Cornucopiae* (see no. 996) is discussed, p. 103; Cook's last voyage, p. 107 (see no. 853); Jedidiah Morse's *Geography*, p. 109; Thomas Paine, p. 129; Edmund Burke, p. 131; Wm. Pitt, p. 137; slave-trade, p. 140.
See also H. S. King, in *University of California, Publications in modern philology*, Berkeley, 1929, v. 14, p. 54–56, STG.
See also no. 853A.

**1165.** FORTGESETZTE Betrachtungen über den Sklavenhandel, und die Freylassung der Neger. (Neues göttingisches historisches Magazin. Hannover, 1793. 12°. Bd. 2, p. 1–58, 147–153.) BAA
Signed: M (i.e., Christoph Meiners, 1746–1810).
Note also an article on slave trade in *Deutsches Magazin* [ed. Chr. U. D. v. Eggers], Hamburg, 1791, Bd. 1, p. 580–613. Not in the Library.

**1166.** FRAGMENT eines Briefes aus Neu-York am 20sten July 1792. (Minerva. Hamburg, 1793. 12°. Bd. 6, p. 360–366.) BAA
Signed: ᵡᵡᵣ.
Relates to the Indians.

**1167.** FRAGMENT eines Briefes aus New York an Mr. Pelletier, Kaufmann in London. (Minerva. Hamburg, 1793. 12°. Bd. 8, p. 170–179.)
Dated: New York vom 7ten July 1793. BAA
Pertains to revolts at St. Domingo.

**1168.** FRANKLIN, BENJAMIN. Bemerkungen über die Wilden in Nordamerika. (Neues hannöverisches Magazin...vom Jahr 1793. Hannover, 1794. 4°. Jahrg. 3, col. 169–186.) *DF
Taken from *New London magazine*, April, 1792, p. 164–168.
The translator and annotator is J. F. B. Laur of Goettingen.

**1169.** HERDER, JOHANN GOTTFRIED VON. Briefe zu Beförderung der Humanität. Herausgegeben von J. G. Herder. Erste [-Zweyte] Sammlung. Riga: Bei Johann Friedrich Hartknoch, 1793. (Reprinted in his: Sämmtliche Werke. Herausgegeben von Bernhard Suphan. Berlin: Weidmannsche Buchhandlung, 1877–1913. Bd. 17, p. 5–71, 73–132.) NFG
"Glücklich, wer auf sein Leben zurücksehen kann wie Franklin, dessen Bestrebungen das Glück so herrlich gekrönt hat. Nicht der Erfinder der Theorie elektrischer Materie und der Harmonika ist mein Held, — der zu allem Nützlichen aufgelegte, und auf die bequemste Weise werkthätige Geist, er, der Menschheit Lehrer, einer grossen Menschengesellschaft Ordner sey unser Vorbild."—*p. 9.*
Ueber Benj. Franklins Lebensbeschreibung von ihm selbst, p. 7–10. Franklins Fragen zu Errichtung einer Gesellschaft der Humanität mit Anwendungen, p. 10–16. Klopstocks Ode über den Nordamerikanischen Seekrieg, p. 93–95.
See no. 1372.

**1169A.** HIPPEL, THEODOR GOTTLIEB VON. Kreuz- und Querzüge des Ritters A bis Z. Von dem Verfasser der Lebensläufe. Berlin, 1793–1794. 2 v. 8°. (Reprinted in his: Sämmtliche Werke. Berlin: Reimer, 1828–39. 12°. v. 8.) NFG
"Wen würdest du in Nordamerika aufsuchen? Franklin und Washington? Und wenn der Letztere, so wie der Erstere, nicht mehr im Lande der Lebendigen ist, wirst du nicht nach ihren Kindern fragen? werden dich nicht schon die Namen Washington und Franklin interessiren?"—*p. 331.*
See H. S. King, in *University of California, Publications in modern philology*, Berkeley, 1929, v. 14, p. 89, STG.

**1170.** IMLAY, GILBERT. G. Imlay's...Nachrichten von dem westlichen Lande der Nordamerikanischen Freistaaten, von dem Klima, den Naturprodukten, der Volksmenge, den Sitten und Gebräuchen desselben, nebst einer Angabe der Indianischen Völkerstämme, die an den Gränzen wohnen, und einer Schilderung von den Gesetzen und der Regierung des Staates Kentucky. In Briefen an einen Freund in England. Aus dem Englischen übersetzt...von E. A. W. Zimmermann. [Berlin: Voss, 1793.] 168 p. 8°. (Magazin von merkwürdigen neuen Reisebeschreibungen... Bd. 9, Theil 2.) KBC
Sabin 34359.
Translation of Imlay's *A topographical description of the western territory of North America*..., London: J. Debrett, 1792, * KF.
Reviews: *Allgemeine Literatur-Zeitung*, Jahr 1794, Bd. 4, col. 625–626, *NAA; Göttingische Anzeigen von gelehrten Sachen*, Jahr 1793, Bd. 2, p. 777–780, * DF; *Berliner Monatsschrift*, Bd. 21, p. 398–416 (not in N. Y. P. L.).

**1171.** JEFFERSON, THOMAS. Etat der Bevölkerung der vereinigten Staaten von Nordamerika, nach einer unter öffentlichen Autorität angestellten Zählung. 1790. (Neues göttingisches historisches Magazin. Hannover, 1793. 8°. Bd. 2, p. 758–768.) BAA
Dated: Philadelphia Oct. 20th, 1791.

## GERMAN WORKS RELATING TO AMERICA 139

*1793, continued*

1172. MARMONTEL, JEAN FRANÇOIS. Vertheidigung der Akademie zur Aufrechthaltung der Reinigkeit der französischen Sprache. (Neue Bibliothek der schönen Wissenschaften und der freyen Künste. Leipzig, 1793. 12°. Bd. 51, p. 3–25.) NAA
Suggests a contest to write an eulogy on Benjamin Franklin.

1173. MARSILLAC, JEAN. Leben Wilhelm Penns des Stifters von Pensylvanien aus dem Französischen des Herrn D. Marsillac von Friedrich. Strassburg: Bei Friedrich Spach, 1793. 1 p.l., x, 324 p. 8°. *KF 1793
Sabin 44821.
See Joseph Smith's *A descriptive catalogue of Friends' books*, v. 2, p. 148, * KAB.
The French original, *La vie de Guillaume Penn...*, Paris, 1792, 2 v., is in * KF 1792.
Introduction signed: Friedrich, Strassburg im August 1792.
Karl Julius Friedrich is the translator.

1174. MEINERS, CHRISTOPH. Grundriss der Geschichte der Menschheit. 2. Ausgabe. Lemgo: Meyersche Buchhandlung, 1793. 384 p., 2 l. 16°. BA
"Verzeichniss der vornehmsten Schriften, die in diesem Grundrisse angeführet werden," p. 311–384.

1174A. MICHAELIS, JOHANN DAVID. Lebensbeschreibung, von ihm selbst abgefasst; mit Anmerkungen von Hassencamp... Rinteln: In der Expedition der Theologischen Annalen, 1793. 1 p.l., xxxv(i), 314 p. frontis. (port.) 8°. AN
Im Sommer 1766 bekam ich Gelegenheit zu zwei wichtigen Bekanntschaften. Pringle und Franklin kamen nach Göttingen... *p. 102.* Mit Franklin habe ich einmahl bey Tische eine merkwürdige Unterredung gehabt. Als er bey mir speiste, redeten wir viel von America, den Wilden, dem schnellen Aufblühen der englischen Colonien, ihrer Volksmenge, deren Verdoppelung in 25 Jahren u.s.f., und ich sagte: dass, als ich 1741 in London den Zustand dieser Colonien aus englischen Büchern und Nachrichten genauer kaffte kennen lernen, wäre ich auf den Gedanken gekommen..., sie würden einmahl von England abfallen; man habe mich zwar ausgelacht, ich dächte aber demohngeachtet noch so. Er antwortete mir mit seinem ernsthaften, viel sagenden und klugen Gesichte: darin irrete ich mich, die Americaner hätten eine sehr grosse Liebe zum Mutterlande. Ich sagte: das glaubte ich; allein das allmächtige Interesse würde bald stark wirken, jene Liebe überwiegen, oder gar auslöschen. Er konnte nicht leugnen, dass diess wohl möglich wäre, allein der Abfall sey dennoch unmöglich; denn alles, was die Americaner Wichtiges hätten, Boston, New-york, Philadelphia, läge den englischen Flotten ausgesetzt... — *p. 110–111.*
See also Hassencamp's remarks on Franklin in note on p. 102.

1175. MICHEL WINGLER auf den amerikanischen Inseln. (Neue Bibliothek der schönen Wissenschaften und der freyen Künste. Leipzig, 1793. 12°. Bd. 49, p. 357.) NAA
From the original, *Theatern och Asedderne.*

1176. NACHRICHT an das nach Amerika correspondirende hiesige und auswärtige Publicum. (Allgemeine Literatur-Zeitung. Jena, 1793. 4°. Jahr 1793, Intelligenzblatt, col. 759–760.) NAA
Concerns transatlantic facilities for mail.

1177. NEUE Constitution der Oneida, einer bis zum J. 1788 wilden Nation in NAmerika. (In: A. L. Schlözer. Stats-Anzeigen. Göttingen, 1793. 8°. Bd. 18, p. 115–124.) BAC

1178. DER NEUERE Brutus. Eine Americanische Anecdote. (Minerva. Hamburg, 1793. 12°. Bd. 7, p. 375–376.) BAA
Signed: v. A. [J. W. v. Archenholz.]

1179. [NOUGARET, PIERRE JEAN BAPTISTE.] Honorine Clarins. Eine Geschichte aus dem Amerikanischen Unabhängigkeitskriege... Regensburg: In der Montag- und Weissischen Buchhandlung, 1793. 2 v. in 1. fronts. 8°. *KL
The French original was first published in 1788. The illustration is signed: Ofterloh, sc.

1180. OFICIELLE Nachrichten aus dem Kriegsdepartement der Nordamericanischen Union, betreffend die Feindseligkeiten zwischen den vereinigten Staaten und einigen wilden Stämmen nordwestlich dem Ohioflusse. (Neues göttingisches historisches Magazin. Hannover, 1793. 8°. Bd. 2, p. 708–715.) BAA
"Der Aufsatz ist vom Secretair des Kriegsdepartements H. Knox. 26. Jan. 1792. unterzeichnet... Das Unionsgouvernement liess...zur Belehrung des Publicums diese Nachricht bekannt machen, um zu zeigen, dass man diesen Krieg durchaus habe anfangen müssen."

1181. SCHREIBEN des französischen National-Convents an den Congress der Amerikanischen Freystaaten. (Minerva. Hamburg, 1793. 16°. Bd. 5, p. 123–127.) BAA
Signed: P.
"Der Verfasser dieses Schreibens (address of sympathy) war Guadet. Er hatte dazu den Auftrag vom National-Convent erhalten, der es auch, nachdem am 22sten December 1792 die öffentliche Vorlesung geschehen war, genehmigte, und die Absendung decretirte."

1181A. SHELEKHOV, GRIGORIE IVANOVICH. Grigori Schelechof russischen Kaufmanns Erste und zweyte Reise von Ochotsk in Sibirien durch den östlichen Ocean nach den Küsten von Amerika in den Jahren 1783 bis 1789... Aus dem Russischen übersetzt von J. Z. Logan. St. Petersburg: Bey J. Z. Logan, 1793. 84 p. 8°. *KF
The Library has another German translation by Johann Heinrich Busse (1763–1835) originally published in *Journal von Russland*, St. Petersburg, 1794, IXP. An English translation, London, 1795, is also in *JKP*.
See Avrahm Yarmolinsky, *Shelekhov's voyage to Alaska; a bibliographical note*, New York, 1932, HND (N. Y. P. L.) p.v.15.
Review: *Göttingische Anzeigen von gelehrten Sachen*, Jahr 1794, p. 968, * DF.

1181B. SPRENGEL, MATTHIAS CHRISTIAN, AND G. FORSTER, EDITORS. Neue Beiträge zur Völker- und Länderkunde. Herausgegeben von M. C. Sprengel und G. Forster. Bd. 13. Leipzig: P. G. Kummer, 1793. 1 v. 17½cm. KBC
Of special interest: III. Beschreibung von Neuyork oder Neuniederland und den dortigen Wilden Mohawks oder Maquaas aufgesetzt von Meklenburg. 1644. Taken from v. 1 of Ebenezer Hazard's *Historical collections consisting of state papers, and other authentic documents*, Philadelphia, 1792–94, †* KD.
See no. 1348.

*1793, continued*

1182. STELLER, GEORG WILHELM. G. W. Steller's...Reise von Kamtschatka nach Amerika mit dem Commandeur-Capitän Bering. Ein Pendant zu dessen Beschreibung von Kamtschatka. St. Petersburg: Bey Johann Zacharias Logan, 1793. 2 p.l., 133 p. 8°.  * KF 1793
Reviews: *Der Neue teutsche Merkur*, Jahr 1794, Bd. 3, p. 254, * *DF*; *Göttingische Anzeigen von historischen Sachen*, Jahr 1794, p. 1281–1284; Jahr 1795, p. 645–648. * *DF*.

1183. TAXE europäischer Menschen in NAmerika. (In: A. L. Schlözer. Stats-Anzeigen. Göttingen, 1793. 8°. Bd. 18, p. 416.)  BAC
Signed: C. C. F. Hüpeden.
Concerns difference in price paid to captains for immigrants of different nationalities who could not pay the fare.

1184. UEBER den Sclavenhandel und die Verfassung der Eingebohrnen in der Nähe von den Forts St. Louis and Goree in Afrika. (In: P. J. Bruns and E. A. W. Zimmermann, editors. Repositorium für die neueste Geographie, Statistik und Geschichte. Tübingen, 1793. 8°. Bd. 3, p. 63–118.)  KBD
This is a remodelled translation of Thomas Clarkson's *Letters on the slave-trade*..., London, 1791.
Letter-form is omitted.
The introduction is by Paul Jakob Bruns, professor and librarian in Helmstädt (1743–1814).

1185. UEBER die Aussicht eines Krieges zwischen Frankreich und England. (Minerva. Hamburg, 1793. 12°. Bd. 6, No. 4, p. 52–80.)
Signed: ·r.  BAA
"Eine Rede von Kersaint, gehalten im französischen National-Convent am 1sten Januar 1793." This speech calls for a war with England and alludes to its consequences for America; see p. 68, 74.

1186. UEBER die körperliche Stärke verschiedener Völker. (Neues göttingisches historisches Magazin. Hannover, 1793. 8°. Bd. 2, p. 585–616.)  BAA
Signed: M (i.e., Christoph Meiners, 1747–1810).

1187. UEBER die gymnastischen, und kriegerischen Uebungen verschiedener Völker. (Neues göttingisches historisches Magazin. Hannover, 1793. 8°. Bd. 2, p. 471–523.)  BAA
Signed: M (i.e., Christoph Meiners, 1747–1810).

1188. UEBER die Hagerkeit und Fettheit der verschiedenen Völker der Erde. (Neues göttingisches historisches Magazin. Hannover, 1793. 8°. Bd. 2, p. 154–162.)  BAA
Signed: M (i.e., Christoph Meiners, 1747–1810).

1189. ZUR neuesten Statistick der Americanischen Freystaaten. (Minerva. Hamburg, 1793. 12°. Bd. 6, p. 536–542.)  BAA

1190. *Review*: Bemerkungen über die Krankheiten der Truppen in Jamaica,...durch J. Hunter. Aus dem Englischen übersetzt. Leipzig: Bey Weidmann, 1792. 247 S. 8°. (Neue allgemeine deutsche Bibliothek. Kiel, 1793. 8°. Bd. 3, p. 573–574, *NAA*.)

1191. *Review*: A brief Examination of Lord Sheffield's Observations on the Commerce of the united States. Philadelphia: Carey, 1791. 127 p. 8°. (Göttingische Anzeigen von gelehrten Sachen. Göttingen [1793]. 12°. Jahr 1793, p. 337–340, *NAA*.)
The Library's copy of this English work by Tench Coxe is in * *KD*.
See no. 809, 1159.

1192. *Review*: Columbus or a world discovered. An historical play by Thomas Morton...as it is performed at the Theatre Royal, Covent Garden. London: Miller, 1792. 66 p. 8°. (Neue Bibliothek der schönen Wissenschaften und der freyen Künste. Leipzig, 1793. 12°. Bd. 51, p. 184–186, *NAA*.)
The Library's copies of this English play are in * *KL* and *NCO p.v.68*.

1193. *Review*: The Conspiracy of Kings; a Poem, addressed to the Inhabitants of Europe, from another Quarter of the world. By Joel Barlow...1792. 20 p. 4°. (Neue Bibliothek der schönen Wissenschaften und der freyen Künste. Leipzig, 1793. 12°. Bd. 50, p. 173, *NAA*.)
The Library's copies of this English work are in * *KL*.

1194. *Review*: Debates on the Convention of the State of Pensilvania [*sic!*] on the Constitution proposed for the Government of the united States by T. Lloyd. Philadelphia: James, 1788. 2 v. 8°. (Göttingische Anzeigen von gelehrten Sachen. Göttingen [1793]. 12°. Jahr 1793, p. 782–783, * *DF*.)
Some of the Library's copies of the "Debates," catalogued under Pennsylvania Constitutional Convention, are in * *KD*.
According to the review, the same work was published by Debrett, of London, in 1792 under the title, *Commentaries on the Constitution of the United States of America... By J. Wilson and Thomas M'Kean* (* *KF*); for further historical notes on this work, see the Library's catalogue cards.

1195. *Review*: An enquiry how far the punishment of death is necessary in Pennsylvania with notes and illustrations by William Bradford...to which is added an account of the gaol and penitentiary house of Philadelphia, and of the interior management thereof, by Caleb Lownes. Philadelphia: Bey Dobson, 1793. 108 p. 8°. (Göttingische Anzeigen von gelehrten Sachen. Göttingen [1793]. 12°. Jahr 1793, p. 1771–1774, * *DF*.)
The Library's copy of this English work is catalogued under William Bradford, * *KD 1793*.

1196. *Review*: Fragments of a Poem, intended to have been written in consequence of reading Major Majoribank's Slavery. By the Rev. E. Holder of Bristol. 1792. 20 p. 4°. (Neue Bibliothek der schönen Wissenschaften und der freyen Künste. Leipzig, 1793. 12°. Bd. 50, p. 188–189, *NAA*.)

*1793, continued*

1197. *Review:* Historical Collections consisting of State Papers and other authentic Documents intended as materials for an history of the united States of America, by Ebenezer Hazard. v. 1. Philadelphia: Dobson, 1792. 639 p. 4°. (Göttingische Anzeigen von gelehrten Sachen. Göttingen [1793]. 12°. Jahr 1793, p. 1675-1677, * *DF.*)
"...wir wünschen eine baldige Fortsetzung des Werks, und dass der Verf. bey der Geschichte der Ausbreitung der Deutschen in Pensilvanien und übrigen, [sic!] den Pastorius und andere deutsche Nachrichten benutzen möge."
Hazard's work appeared in 2 volumes, 1792-94, †° *KD*; for review of v. 2, see no. 1291.

1198. *Review:* History civil and commercial of the British Colonies in the West Indies, by Bryan Edwards. London: Stockdale, 1793. 2 v. 4°. (Göttingische Anzeigen von gelehrten Sachen. Göttingen [1793]. 12°. Jahr 1793, p. 1746-1755, * *DF.*)
The Library's copy of this English work is in * *KF.*

1199. *Review:* Indianerne i Engelland. Et Lystspiel i tre Akter af A. v. Kotzebue. Oversatred. Sönnichsen, 1793. 152 p. 8°. (Neue Bibliothek der schönen Wissenschaften und freyen Künste. Leipzig, 1793. 12°. Bd. 51, p. 288-292, *NAA.*)

1200. *Review:* Eine kurze Reise in Westindien, mit verschiedenen Anekdoten und Charakterschilderungen. Aus dem Englischen. Mannheim: Bey Schwan und Götz, 1792. 9½ Bogen. 8°. (Neue allgemeine deutsche Bibliothek. Kiel, 1793. 8°. Bd. 4, p. 342-344, *NAA.*)
For the German original, see no. 992.

1201. *Review:* Letters from America, Historical and descriptive comprising occurences from 1769 to 1777 by Will. Eddis. London: b. Dilly, 1792. 455 S. 8°. (Allgemeine Literatur-Zeitung. Jena, 1793. 4°. Jahr 1793, Bd. 3, col. 159-160, *NAA.*)

1202. *Review:* Neue Quartalschrift aus den neuesten und besten Reisebeschreibungen gezogen. Berlin: B. Wever, 1786, 1787, 1788, 1789, 1790, 1791, 1792. (Allgemeine Literatur-Zeitung. Jena, 1793. 4°. Jahr 1793, Bd. 2, col. 691-692, *NAA.*)
This issue contains excerpts from Coxe, Carli, Carver, Schoepf, Ulloa and others.

1203. *Review:* Nordcarolinische Kirchennachrichten, herausgegeben von Johann Caspar Velthusen... Zweytes und letztes Heft. Stade, 1793. (Göttingische Anzeigen von gelehrten Sachen. Göttingen [1793]. 12°. Jahr 1793, p. 776, * *DF.*)
"Die Einnahme von der kleinen Schrift soll unter seine [Velthusens] drey ärmsten Landschulmeister vertheilt werden."
See no. 1044.

1204. *Review:* Philosophical transactions of the Royal Society of London for the year 1792. P. II. London, 1792. 4°. (Journal der Physik. Leipzig, 1793. 8°. Bd. 7, p. 375-396, *PAA.*)
"Nachricht von den merkwürdigen Wirkungen eines Schiffbruchs auf die Mannschaft des Schiffes; nebst Versuchen und Beobachtungen über den Einfluss des Eintauchens in süsses und salziges, kaltes und warmes Wasser auf die Kräfte des lebenden Körpers, von Herrn D. James Currie," p. 199.
Physical hardships of the crew of a wrecked American ship.
The Library's file of the "Philosophical transactions" is in * *EC.*

1205. *Review:* Political Essays on the nature and Operations of Money, Public Finances and other objects, by Pelatiah Webster. Philadelphia: Bey Cruikshank, 1791. 404 p. 8°. (Göttingische Anzeigen von gelehrten Sachen. Göttingen [1793]. 12°. Jahr 1793, p. 780-782, * *DF.*)
The Library's copies of this English work are in * *KD* and *TIE.*

1206. *Review:* The secret history of the armed neutrality together with memoirs, official letters and state papers, illustrative of that celebrated confederacy: never before published. Written originally in French by a German Nobleman. Translated by Axxxxx Hxxxx. London: J. Johnson and R. Folder, 1792. 260 p. 8°. (Göttingische Anzeigen von gelehrten Sachen. Göttingen [1793]. 12°. Jahr 1793, p. 929-933, * *DF.*)
"(Die Schrift) rühre ursprünglich von einem deutschen Adlichen her, der eine grosse Rolle auf der politischen Schaubühne gespielt, jetzt aber sich zurückgezogen habe; der selbst Zeuge von den Thatsachen gewesen..."
It is also stated that the French manuscript was donated to the Schotten-Bibliothek, in Regensburg, and is just being printed in Germany.

1207. *Review:* Statistische Beschreibung der Besitzungen der Holländer in America. Erster Theil vom Prof. Lueder. Braunschweig: In der Schulbuchhandlung, 1792. 230 p. 8°. (Allgemeine Literatur-Zeitung. Jena, 1793. 4°. Jahr 1793, Bd. 2, col. 218-220, *NAA.*)

1207A. *Review:* Grigori Schelechof's erste und zweyte Reise von Ochotsk durch den östlichen Ocean nach den Küsten von America in den J. 1783-1789... Aus dem Russischen übersetzt von T. Z. Logan. St. Petersburg, 1793. 84 p. (Göttingische Anzeigen von gelehrten Sachen. Göttingen [1794]. 12°. Jahr 1794, p. 968, * *DF.*)

1208. *Review:* Thomas Försters Erzählungen von seinen Reisen in. allen vier Welttheilen. Eine lehrreiche und unterhaltende Monatsschrift... Bd. III Westindien. n. p., 1792. 280 p. 8°. (Allgemeine Literatur-Zeitung. Jena, 1793. 4°. Jahr 1793, Bd. 4, col. 227, *NAA.*)

1209. *Review:* Topographical Description of the Western Territory of North America, by G. Imlay. London: Debrett, 1792. 247 p. 8°. (Göttingische Anzeigen von gelehrten Sachen. Göttingen [1793]. 12°. Jahr 1793, p. 777-780, * *DF.*)
Sabin 34354.
The Library's copies of this English work are in * *KF* and *IID.*
For a German translation, see no. 1170; also no. 1258.

1210. *Review:* Transactions of the Royal Society of Edinburgh v. II. (Journal der Physik. Leipzig, 1793. 8°. Bd. 7, p. 281; *PAA.*)
"Versuche über die ausdehnende Kraft des gefrierenden Wassers, angestellt vom Artilleriemajor Edward Williams, zu Quebek in Canada in den Jahren 1784 und 1785," p. 23-29.
The Library's file of the "Transactions" are in * *EC.*

*1793, continued*

1211. *Review:* Travels through North and South Carolina, Georgia, East and West Florida...by Will. Bartram. Philadelphia: James and Johnson, 1791. 522 p. 8°. (Göttingische Anzeigen von gelehrten Sachen. Göttingen [1793]. 12°. Jahr 1793, p. 422-424, * *DF.*)

1212. *Review:* Ueber den Nordamerikan. Krieg und dessen Folgen für England u. Frankreich von M. C. Sprengel. Leipzig: Weigand, 1781. 126 S. 8°. (Göttingische Anzeigen von gelehrten Sachen. Göttingen [1793]. 12°. Jahr 1793, p. 1251-1254, * *DF.*)
"*Der Schmutztitel: Etwas über die Kosten des jetzigen Nordamerikanischen Krieges und die Vermehrung der englischen und französischen Nationalschulden, bezeichnet den Inhalt dieser Schrift genauer...*"

1213. *Review:* Versuch einer Erdbeschreibung der sechs Welttheile nach den Stämmen ihrer Regenten und Bewohner von Breitenbauch. Leipzig: Bey Richter, 1793. 8°. (Göttingische Anzeigen von gelehrten Sachen. Göttingen [1793]. 12°. Jahr 1793, p. 2039, * *DF.*)

1794

1214. AMERICANISCHE Staatspapiere. (Minerva. Hamburg, 1794. 12°. Jahr 1794, Bd. 2, p. 37-84.) BAA
Jefferson's letter to Mr. Morris, ambassador to Paris.

1215. AMERICANISCHE Staatsschriften... Schreiben des Bürgers Genet, bevollmächtigten Ministers der französischen Republik bey den Vereinigten Staaten von Nordamerica, an den Staatssecretär, Herrn Jefferson. (Minerva. Hamburg, 1794. 12°. Jahr 1794, Bd. 2, p. 466-486.) BAA
Dated: New York am 18ten September 1793, im 2ten Jahr der Einen und untheilbaren französischen Republick.

1216. EIN AMERICANISCHER Staatsbürger an die Staatsbürger in Europa. (Minerva. Hamburg, 1794. 12°. Jahr 1794, Bd. 1, p. 453-464.) BAA
Dated: Philadelphia, den 28sten December 1793, im 18ten Jahre der Unabhängigkeit.

1217. AMERIKANISCHE Handels-Tabelle vom 1. Oktober 92 bis 30. Sept. 1793. (Minerva. Hamburg, 1794. 12°. Jahr 1794, Bd. 3 [i.e., Bd. 4,] p. 555-556.) BAA
"Diese Tabelle (pertaining to American exports) wurde im Juny des jetzt laufenden Jahres (1794) dem Congress vorgelegt."
Bd. 4, Oct.-Dec., incorrectly called Bd. 3.

1218. AUSZUG aus dem officiellen Rapport des Nordamericanischen General-Postmeisters, auf Verlangen des Staats-Secretairs bey dem Nordamericanischen Finanz-Departement erstattet. (Neues göttingisches historisches Magazin. Hannover, 1794. 8°. Bd. 3, p. 464-474.) BAA
Dated: Neuyork, 20. Januar 1790.
Taken from *History of the proceedings and debates of the first house of representatives of the United States of America. Taken in shorthand by Th. Lloyd*, Vol. III, p. 157, et seq.
"Der Rapport bezieht sich hauptsächlich darauf, ob und wie die Post-Revenüen erhöht werden könnten, zugleich aber lernt man manches daraus, wie die dortigen Briefpost-Einrichtungen im Ganzen beschaffen sind."

1219. DIE BILDSÄULE der Freyheit. Eine neue italienische Anecdote. (Minerva. Hamburg,
1794. 12°. Jahr 1794, Bd. 3 [i.e., Bd. 4,] p. 553-555.) BAA
Concerning a plan to erect a monument in praise of American freedom.
Bd. 4, Oct.-Dec., incorrectly called Bd. 3.

1220. ETAT der Erfordernisse für das Jahr 1792 zur Unterhaltung des Generalgouvernements des vereinigten Nordamerica, vom Secretair der Schatzkammer dem Hause der Repräsentanten vorgelegt. (Neues göttingisches historisches Magazin. Hannover, 1794. 8°. Bd. 3, p. 187-189.) BAA

1221. FRANKLIN, BENJAMIN. Benjamin Franklins kleine Schriften meist in der Manier des Zuschauers, nebst seinem Leben. Aus dem Englischen von G. Schatz... Weimar: Im Verlage des Industrie-Comptoirs, 1794. 2 v. 2 ports. (fronts.) 8°. * KF 1794
Sabin 25520.
See P. L. Ford, *Franklin bibliography*, p. 444, * *KAK (Franklin).*
Frontispiece portraits of Franklin by Conrad Westermayer: v. 1, "the fur cap portrait" after Cochin; v. 2, medallion portrait.
*Contents:* Erster Theil. Bj. Franklins Leben, von ihm selbst beschrieben...fortgesetzt vom Dr. Stüber.—Zweyter Theil. Kleine Schriften. I. Ueber frühe Ehen. II. Ueber den Tod seines Bruders, des Mr. John Franklin, III. An den verstorbenen Doctor Mather in Boston. IV. Die Pfeife. Eine wahre Geschichte. v. Bittschrift an diejenigen, die die Oberaufsicht über die Erziehung haben. VI. Der schöne und der hässliche Fuss. VII. Unterhaltung einer Gesellschaft von Tagthierchen, nebst dem Selbstgespräch eines ältern. VIII. Moralen aus dem Schachspiel. IX. Die Kunst, sich angenehme Träume zu verschaffen. X. Guther Rat an einen jungen Handwerker. XI. Nöthige Winke für diejenigen, die gern reich werden möchten. XII. Ein Mittel, aller Welt Beutel zu füllen. XIII. Ein ökonomisches Projekt. XIV. Eine Parabel wider den Verfolgungsgeist. XV. Ein Apolog. XVI. Grabschrift eines Eichhörnchens, das ein Hund getötet hatte. XVII. Der alte, arme Richard, oder Mittel reich zu werden. XVIII. Ueber die Kunst zu schwimmen. XIX. Eine neue Art zu baden. XX. Bemerkung über die allgemein herrschende Lehre von Leben und Tod. XXI. Regeln für die Vorsicht für diejenigen, die im Begriff sind, eine Seereise anzutreten. XXII. Ueber Luxus, Müssiggang und Kunstfleiss. XXIII. Ueber den Sklavenhandel. XXIV. Bemerkungen über den Krieg. XXV. Etwas Spekulatives. XXVI. Sätze zur Prüfung. XXVII. Ueber die Vorkehrungen, die man in China gegen die Hungersnoth trifft. XXVIII. Ueber den Zwist zwischen England und Amerika. XXIX. Ueber peinliche Gesetze und Seekaperey. XXX. Nachricht von den höchsten Gesetzhof in Pennsylvanien. XXXI. Bemerkungen über die Vermehrung der Menschen, Kolonisten usw. XXXII. Ueber den Getreidepreis und die Unterstützung der Armen. XXXIII. Ueber den Schleichhandel und seine Nebenzweige. XXXIV. Bemerkungen über die Nordamerikanischen Wilden. XXXV. Vergleichung des Betragens der alten Juden und der Antifederalisten in den vereinigten Staaten von Amerika. XXXVI. Ueber den innern Zustand von Amerika. XXXVII. Plan einer englischen Schule. XXXVIII. Rede beim Schluss der allgemeinen Staatenversammlung. XXXIX. Unterricht für diejenigen, die nach Amerika auszuwandern gedenken. XL. An Lord Howe. XLI. Gesetze für einen in Philadelphia errichteten Club. XLII. Nach eine Parabel. XLIII. Ueber Musik. XLIV. Ueber eine Ballade. XLV. Der Triumph der Künste. XLVI. Papier. XLVII. Bruchstücke. 1. Ueber den Matrosenpressen. 2. Ueber der Verfolgungsgeist; Vergleichung des Zustandes der Duldung in Alt- und Neuengland. 4. Ueber den Anbau und die Beförderung des Wohlstandes entfernter Länder. 5. Politische Rhapsodien. 6. Zerstreute Ideen über Krieg und Frieden; Abtretung von Ländern; Aussichten auf die künftige Blüte von England und Amerika über Englands Betragen im Kriege mit seinen Kolonien usw.
See the bibliography in B. M. Victory, *Benjamin Franklin and Germany*, Philadelphia, 1915 (Americana Germanica, no. 21), *AN (Franklin).*

*1794, continued*

1222. [GLAUBER, CHRISTIAN GOTTLIEB]. Peter Hasenclever. Landeshut in Schlesien, 1794.] 272 p. 8°. (Reprinted in: Peter Hasenclever. Peter Hasenclever aus Remscheid-Ehringhausen, ein deutscher Kaufmann des 18. Jahrhunderts. Seine Biographie, Briefe und Denkschriften...herausgegeben von Professor Dr. Adolf Hasenclever... Gotha: Perthes, 1922. viii, 252 p. 21½ cm.) AN (Hasenclever)
Only 300 copies of the first edition were printed and presented to friends of the family. It contains a great number of original letters sent from North America and others written in Germany concerning North America.
See also Adolf Hasenclever, "Peter Hasenclever aus Remscheid-Ehringhausen, ein deutscher Kaufmann im 18. Jahrhundert, 1716–1793," in Deutsch-amerikanische historische Gesellschaft von Illinois, *Jahrbuch*, Chicago, 1920/21, v. 20/21, p. 314–337, IEK.

1223. HAMILTON, ALEXANDER. Alex. Hamilton officieller Rapport, dem Hause der Repräsentanten erstattet, in Sachen die neue Accise betreffend. (Neues gőttingisches historisches Magazin. Hannover, 1794. 8°. Bd. 3, p. 171–186.) BBA
Refers to liquor tax.

1224. —— Alex. Hamiltons, Secret. der Schatzkammer der Nordamericanischen Union, officieller Rapport, die Beförderung der Manufacturen betreffend. (Neues gőttingisches historisches Magazin. Hannover, 1794. 8°. Bd. 3, p. 57–110, 193–213.) BBA

1225. KLOPSTOCK, FRIEDRICH GOTTLIEB. Die Denkzeiten. 1795. (Reprinted in his: Werke. Leipzig: Bei Georg Joachim Göschen, 1798–1817. 8°. Bd. 2, p. 176–180.) NFW
Appeared originally in *Hamburg. Neue Zeitung*, Hamburg, 1794, Stück 41.
Verse 9 expresses admiration for Washington.
In the same year appeared "Letter from Mr. Klopstock to the National Convention of France," in *New York magazine or Literary repository*, New York, 1794, v. 5, p. 325.

1226. EINE KURZE Schilderung roher und uncultivirter Sprachen. (Neues gőttingisches historisches Magazin. Hannover, 1794. 8°. Bd. 3, p. 416–443.) BBA
Signed: M (i.e., Christoph Meiners, 1747–1810).

1227. NACHRICHT von der neuesten Reise nach den Pelew-Inseln. (Minerva. Hamburg, 1794. 12°. Jahr 1794, Bd. 1, p. 277–283.) BAA
*See also* no. 1126.

1228. PAINE, THOMAS. Gesunder Menschenverstand. An die Einwohner von America gerichtet... Von Thomas Paine. Aus dem Englischen übersetzt. Kopenhagen: Bey C. G. Proft, Sohn und Comp., 1794. 1 p.l., 140 p. 8°.
\* KF 1794
*Contents*: 1. Vom Ursprunge und der Absicht der Regierung überhaupt, nebst kurzen Anmerkungen über die englische Verfassung. 2. Ueber Monarchie und erbliche Thronfolge. 3. Gedanken über den gegenwärtigen Zustand der Americanischen Angelegenheiten. 4. Ueber das gegenwärtige Vermögen Americas, mit einigen vermischten Anmerkungen.

The introduction is dated: Philadelphia, den 14ten Februar 1776.
The original edition was published at Philadelphia in 1776.
Review: *Allgemeine Literatur-Zeitung*, Jahr 1794, Bd. 4, p. 25–29, NAA.

1229. —— Sammlung verschiedener Schriften über Politik und Gesetzgebung von Thomas Paine, Sekretair der auswärtigen Angelegenheiten bey dem Kongress während des amerikanischen Krieges und Mitglied des Nationalkonvent in Paris 1792. Aus dem Englischen übersetzt. Kopenhagen: Bey C. G. Proft, Sohn und Comp., 1794. 3 p.l., 188 p. 8°. \* KF 1794
*Contents*: 1. Sendschreiben an den Abt Raynal. 2. Sendschreiben an den Grafen von Shelburne. 3. Betrachtungen über den Frieden. 4. Schreiben an die Verfasser des Republikaners. 5. ...Ob die republikanische Staatsverfassung den Vorzug vor der monarchischen habe. 6. Schreiben an den Herrn Dundas.

1230. PFLANZSCHULE zu New-York und Charlestown. (Neues Magazin für die Botanik. Zürich, 1794. 8°. Bd. 1, p. 333.) QEA
"Die Reichthümer des Nationalgartens zu Paris werden durch zwey in Nordamerica, die eine zu New York, die andre zu Charlestown, errichtete Pflanzschulen, von denen Hr. André Michaux der Vorsteher ist, einen grossen Zuwachs erhalten."

1231. RAMSAY, DAVID. Geschichte der amerikanischen Revolution aus den Acten des Congresses der vereinigten Staaten von Dr. David Ramsay, vormaligem Mitgliede des Congresses. Aus dem Englischen... Berlin: In den Vossischen Buchhandlung, 1794–1795. 4 v. in 2. 8°.
Sabin 67688. \* KF 1794
v. IV has added title page: Die Staatsverfassung der Vereinigten Staaten von Nordamerika und historische Beiträge und Belege zu der Geschichte ihrer Revolution. Von G. K. F. Seidel... Berlin, 1795.
"Die Konstitutionen der einzelnen Nordamerikanischen Staaten," v. 4, p. 65–232.
"Konstitutions-Akte der Unions-Regierung der Vereinigten Staaten von Nordamerika," v. 4, p. 233–258.
"Akten und Belege zu der Geschichte der Nordamerikanischen Revolution aus Ramsay's Geschichte der Revolution in Süd-Carolina," v. 4, p. 259–374.
"Des Vizepräsidenten Adams Bemerkungen über die Quellen der Geschichte der amerikanischen Revolution. Mit literarischen Anmerkungen," v. 4, p. 375–396.
"Seidel gives very valuable information about the characteristic features of the United States' government and about the new spirit of liberty that permeates American political social institutions. He discusses the political system of the Union, principles of American government and the character of its population. The second part contains the constitutions of the States, the third the Constitution of the Union." — P. C. Weber, *America in imaginative German literature*, 1926, NFCX.
See also G. C. Hamberger's *Das gelehrte Teutschland*, v. 7, p. 438–439, AGK.
Reviews: *Neue allgemeine deutsche Bibliothek*, Bd. 12, p. 236–241, NAA; *Neue Leipziger gelehrte Zeitung*, Jahr 1796, p. 540 (not in N. Y. P. L.); *Oberdeutsche allgemeine Literatur Zeitung*, Jahr 1796, p. 329–330 (not in N. Y. P. L.); *Nürnberger gelehrte Zeitung*, Jahr 1796, p. 401–405 (not in N. Y. P. L.); *Staats- und juristische Literatur*, Jahr 1794, Bd. 1, p. 44–56 (not in N. Y. P. L.).

1232. REINER Ertrag dessen, was für Einfuhrung von Waaren und Producten in das vereinigte Nordamerica vom 1. Oct. 1789. bis zum 30. Sept. 1790. eingegangen. (Neues gőttingisches historisches Magazin. Hannover, 1794. 8°. Bd. 3, p. 190.) BAA

*1794, continued*

1233. RISLER, JEREMIAS. Leben August Gottlieb Spangenbergs, Bischofs der evangelischen Brüderkirche, beschrieben von Jeremias Risler. Barby: Zu finden in den Brüdergemeinen; und in Leipzig in Commission bey Paul Gotthelf Kummer, 1794. 10 p.l., 516 p., 1 l., frontis. (port.) 8°. *KF 1794
Frontispiece is portrait of Spangenberg, engraved by J. G. Schmidt at Dresden, 1794, after Ant. Graff.
Note "Lebenslauf unseres seligen Bruders August Gottlieb Spangenbergs genannt Joseph, von ihm selbst aufgesetzt," in *Deutsche Literatur. Reihe* [25]. *Deutsche Selbstzeugnisse*, Leipzig, 1933, Bd. 7, p. 52-67.
See also W. M. Beauchamp, *Moravian journals relating to central New York, 1745-1766. Arranged and edited by Rev. Wm. M. Beauchamp...for the Onondaga Historical Association*, 1916, Syracuse, N. Y., [1916], which contains Bishop A. G. Spangenberg's "Journal of a journey to Onondaga in 1745:" A. L. Fries, *Some Moravian heroes*, Bethlehem, Pa., 1936, *ZAE p.v.699*; and A. G. Spangenberg, *An account of the manner in which the Protestant Church of Unitas Fratrum, or United Brethren, preach the gospel, and carry on their missions among the heathen. Translated from the German*, London, 1788, *°KF 1788*, a translation of A. G. Spangenberg, *Von der Arbeit der evangelischen Brüder unter den Heiden*, Barby. 1782. Kayser. v. 5, p. 281A. Not in the Library.

1234. [ROHR, HEINRICH JULIUS LUDWIG VON.] La Fayette als Staatsmann als Krieger und als Mensch. Nach dem Französischen. Mit einer Vorrede von Johann Reinhold Forster, Doktor und Professor auf der Kön. Pr. Friedr. Universität zu Halle. Nebst La Fayette's Bildnisse. Magdeburg: bei Johann Adam Creutz, 1794. 11 p.l., 4-291 p. frontis. (port.) 8°. *KF 1794
Frontispiece: La Fayette Maréchal der französischen Nationalarmée. 1792: by J. C. G. Fritzsch: Hamburg, 1794.
Based upon L. P. Bérenger's *Mémoires historiques et pièces authentiques sur M. de La Fayette*... Paris: Le Tellier, an 11.

1235. UEBER die Nachricht von der Bekehrung des Apostels Paulus zum Christenthum. (Allgemeine Bibliothek der biblischen Literatur. Leipzig, 1794. 12°. Bd. 6, p. 1-22.) *YIA
An account of a Negro in New York who becomes blind by lightning and gets his sight back by another flash, p. 14-15.
Taken from *Richter's chirurgische Bibliothek*, Bd. 4, p. 732.

1236. UEBER die Ursachen der gegenwärtigen Krisis in Europa. (Allgemeines europäisches Journal... Brünn, 1794. 8°. Bd. 2, Stück 2, p. 313-325.) *DF
Important references to America.
"Europa muss...eine allgemeine Vereinigung des Kredits seiner Finanzen, so wie seiner Waffen zu Stande bringen... Man braucht nur die Rede, welche General Washington am 3. Dezember vorigen Jahres im Kongress hielt, zu lesen, um einzusehen, dass Amerika selbst bereit ist, auf diesen Grundsätzen mitzuwirken, um den öffentlichen Kredit zu erhalten..."

1237. UNGEFÄHRE Anzahl der Zeitungen im vereinigten Nordamerica. (Neues gelehrtes historisches Magazin. Hannover, 1794. 8°. Bd. 3, p. 191-192.) BBA
"s. Massach. Magaz. 1790. M. Jun. p. 379."

1238. Voss, JOHANN HEINRICH. Aufmunterung, 1794. (Reprinted in his: Sämmtliche poetische Werke... Neue Ausgabe. Leipzig: Verlag von Immanuel Müller, 1850. 8°. Bd. 4, p. 304-305.)
NFW
"Voss compares the destructive radicalism of the French with the saner conservatism of the American revolution.

Lasst den armen Nachbar schaffen
Was er will und kann!
Lasst ihm Bürger sein den Pfaffen
Und den Edelmann!
Heiliger Gesetze Bürger
Sind ja nicht nothwendig Würger!
Was die Vorwelt sah,
Sieht Amerika!"

See J. T. Hatfield and E. Hochbaum, *The influence of the American Revolution upon German literature*, New York [1900?], p. 45, *NFC p.v.4*.

1238A. —— Chorgesang beim Rheinwein. 1794. (Reprinted in: Americana Germanica. Philadelphia, 1899-1900. 4°. v. 3, p. 338-385.)
NFCA (German)
This periodical subsequently called *German American annals*, under which it is shelved.
J. H. Voss addresses some old wine in a bottle he has just opened:
"Man wird mit jedem Tag nicht schlechter,
Das weisst du ja!
Viel Gutes findest du, und neues!
Zum Beispiel nennen wir ein freies
Amerika!"

1238B. WEST, HANS. Beyträge zur Beschreibung von St. Croix. Nebst einer kurzen Uebersicht benachbarten Inseln, St. Thomas, St. Jean, Tortola, Spanishtown und Krabbeneyland, von Hans West... Aus dem Dänischen, mit Verbesserungen und Vermehrungen des Verfassers. Kopenhagen: Bey C. G. Proft, 1794. 2 p.l., 274 p. 20cm. *KF 1794

1239. *Review*: American Biography. v. 1 by Jeremy Belknap... Published according to an act of Congress. Boston: Isaiah Thomas and Ebenezer T. Andrews, 1794. 416 p. 8°. (Göttingische Anzeigen von gelehrten Sachen. Göttingen [1794]. 12°. Jahr 1794, p. 1617-1621, *DF*.)
The Library's copies of this work are in *AGZ* and *KD*.

1240. *Review*: Auswahl der besten ausländischen und statistischen Nachrichten zur Aufklärung der Völker-und Länderkunde. Von M. C. Sprengel. I. u. II. Band. Halle: in d. Renger Buchhandlung, 1794. (Allgemeine Literatur-Zeitung. Jena, 1794. 4°. Jahr 1794, Bd. 4, col. 603-607, *NAA*.)
Bd. 1 contains: Bryan Edwards Beschreibung der britischen Colonien in Westindien.

1241. *Review*: Beschreibung der wildwachsenden Bäume und Staudengewächse in den vereinigten Staaten von Nordamerika, von Humphry Marschal [sic!]... (Allgemeine deutsche Bibliothek. Kiel, 1794. 8°. Bd. 117, p. 146, *NAA*.)
*See* nos. 1011, 1013, 1248, 1263.

GERMAN WORKS RELATING TO AMERICA 145

*1794, continued*

1242. *Review:* Constitutions des principaux Etats de l'Europe et les Etats Unis de l'Amerique par M. de la Croix... 2. Thl. 8°. (Allgemeine Literatur-Zeitung. Jena, 1794. 4°. Jahr 1794, Bd. 1, col. 545-552, *NAA.*)
The Library's copy of this French work by J. V. Delacroix, published in 6 volumes at Paris, 1791-1801, is in * KF.
For a review and notes on the English translation, see no. 1256.
*See also* no. 1264.

1242A. *Notice:* Ehrenbezeugungen. (Allgemeine Literatur-Zeitung. Jena, 1794. 4°. Intelligenz Blatt, p. 1116, *NAA.*)
"Die deutsche Gesellschaft zu New York in America hat den Hn. Leg. R. Bertuch in Weimar unterm 25. Jan. 1794 zu ihrem Mitgliede aufgenommen."
See also no. 1301B.

1243. *Review:* An Enquiry into the Truth of the Tradition concerning the discovery of America by Prince Madog about the Year 1170. By John Williams. London: Brown, 1791. 82 p. 8°. (Allgemeine Literatur-Zeitung. Jena, 1794. 4°. Jahr 1794, Bd. 1, col. 7-8, *NAA.*)
The Library's copy of this English work is in * KF.

1244-45. *Review:* Historia del nuevo Mundo, escribiatia D. Juan Bautista Muñoz. T. 1. Madrid: b. der Witwe Ibarra, 1793. 364 S. 4°. (Allgemeine Literatur-Zeitung. Jena, 1794. 4°. Jahr 1794, Bd. 4, col. 369-374, *NAA.*)
The Library has copies of the "Historia" in * KF, vol. 1, only, was published, continuation being prohibited by the Spanish government. However, the Library has a transcript of the manuscript of vol. 2 in the Rich Collection (Manuscript Room).
*See* no. 1275.

1246. *Review:* The History of the Origin, Progress and Termination of the American War. By C. Stedman... London: On the expense of the author, 1794. 2 v. plates. (Göttingische Anzeigen von gelehrten Sachen. Göttingen [1794]. 12°. Jahr 1794, p. 1768, *DF.*)
The Library's copies of this English work by Charles Stedman are in *IG*, * *KF*, etc.
The German translation then being published by the Vossische Buchhandlung in Berlin is mentioned in the review; *see* no. 1281.

1247. *Review:* The history of the Origin, Progress, and Termination of the American War by C. Stedman. London: B. Murray, Debrett u. a., 1794. v. I, 399 p., v. II, 449 p. 4°. (Allgemeine Literatur-Zeitung. Jena, 1794. 4°. Jahr 1794, Bd. 4, col. 617-622, *NAA.*)
See note in preceding entry (no. 1246).

1248. *Review:* Humphry Morschal Beschreibung der wildwachsenden Bäume und Staudengewächse in den vereinigten Staaten von Nordamerika. Aus dem Engl... durch Christian Friedrich Hofmann. Leipzig: Bey Crusius, 1788. 8°. (Allgemeine deutsche Bibliothek. Kiel, 1794. 8°. Bd. 117, p. 146, *NAA.*)
*See also* nos. 1011, 1013, 1241, 1263.

1249. *Review:* Journal d'histoire naturelle, ed. by Lamark [*sic!*], Bruguière, Olivier, Havy et Pelletier. Part 5-20. Paris, 1792-1793.
(Göttingische Anzeigen von gelehrten Sachen. Göttingen [1794]. 12°. Jahr 1794, p. 508-519, *DF.*)
"Hr. Bosc giebt eine Beschreibung und Zeichnung vom carolinischen Eichhorn...," *p. 515*.
. J. G. Bruguière was the principal editor of the 3-volume "Histoire naturelle des vers," Paris, 1792-1832, pubished as v. [120-122] of the *Encyclopédie méthodique*, * *AP (Encyclopédie)*.

1250. *Review:* Karl le Beau's Begebenheiten und merkwürdige Reise zu den Nordamerikanischen Wilden. Mit einer genauen Beschreibung von Kanada und den alten Gebräuchen, Sitten und der Lebensart der Kanadier. In zwey Theilen. Leipzig: In der Weygandschen Buchhandlung, 1794. 1 Alphabet. 4 Bogen. 8°. (Neue allgemeine deutsche Bibliothek. Kiel, 1794. 8°. Bd. 11, p. 453-454, *NAA.*)
See no. 340.

1251. *Review:* Eine kurze Nachricht von dem bösartigen Fieber, welches kürzlich in Philadelphia grassirt...von Mathew Carey. Nach der vierten verbesserten Auflage aus dem Englischen übersetzt von Carl Erdmann. Lancaster, 1794. 176 p. 8°. (Göttingische Anzeigen von gelehrten Sachen. Göttingen [1794]. 12°. Jahr 1794, p. 1776, * *DF.*)
*See also* no. 1257.

1252. *Review:* Luigi Castiglionis...Reise durch die vereinigten Staaten von Nordamerika in den Jahren 1785. 1786 u. 1787. Nebst Bemerkungen über die nützlichen Gewächse dieses Landes. Aus d. Ital. von Magnus Peterson. I. Theil. Memmingen: B. Seyler, 1793. 495 S. 8°. (Allgemeine Literatur-Zeitung. Jena, 1794. 4°. Jahr 1794, Bd. 2, col. 388-390, *NAA.*)
Sabin 11414.

1253. *Review:* La Médecine éclairée par les sciences physiques ou journal des decouvertes, relatives aux differentes parties de l'art de guerir, ed. by Fourcroy. v. 2, VII-XII, v. 3, v. 4. Paris: Buisson, 1791-1792. (Göttingische Anzeigen von gelehrten Sachen. Göttingen [1794]. 12°. Jahr 1794, p. 257-271, * *DF.*)
"Hr. Marsillac (spricbt) von einem Kampfer, der seit einigen Jahren auf den Westindischen Inseln aus mehrern Lorbeerarten durch Sublimation gewonnen wird und dem japanischen ganz gleich kommt," *p. 261*.

1254. *Review:* Der Naturforscher. Stck. 27. Halle, 1793. 176 p., 6 pl. (Göttingische Anzeigen von gelehrten Sachen. Göttingen [1794]. 12°. Jahr 1794, p. 558-560, * *DF.*)
"Prof. Losche hat ein amerikanisches schwarzgestreiftes Erdeichhorn zergliedert, und stellt uns die dabey angestellte Wahrnehmungen in sorgfältiger Beschreibung und getreuen Abbildungen dar."

1255. *Review:* Nicol. Joseph Iacquin, selectarum stirpium americanarum historia... Manhemii: In bibliopolio novo academico, 1788. 8°. (Allgemeine deutsche Bibliothek. Kiel, 1794. 8°. Bd. 117, p. 144-145, *NAA.*)
The Library has earlier editions of Jacquin's "Selectarum," in †* *KF 1763* and †††* *KF 1780*, respectively, but not this 1788 edition.
For two German editions, see nos. 819, 1275.

*1794, continued*

1256. *Review:* A review of the Constitutions of the principal states of Europe and of the united States of America...by M. de la Croix. 2 volumes. London: B. Robinson, 1792. 8°. (Allgemeine Literatur-Zeitung. Jena, 1794. 4°. Jahr 1794, Bd. 1, col. 545-552, *NAA.*)
The Library's copies of the first two volumes of Delacroix's work are in *SEC* and * *KF*. For a review and notes on the original French edition, see no. 1242.

1257. *Review:* A short account of the malignant Fever lately prevalent in Philadelphia... By Mathew Carey. Third edition improved. Philadelphia, 1793. 112 p. 8°. (Göttingische Anzeigen von gelehrten Sachen. Göttingen [1794]. 12°. Jahr 1794, p. 1356-1359, **DF*.)
The Library's various issues of this edition of Carey's work are in * *KD*. For a review and notes on the German translation, see no. 1251.

1258. *Review:* A topographical description of the Western Territory of Northamerica, to which are added the discovery, settlement and present state of Kentucky. By George Imlay. 2nd edition. London: Debrett, 1793. 433 p. 8°. (Allgemeine Literatur-Zeitung. Jena, 1794. 4°. Jahr 1794, Bd. 4, col. 625-626, *NAA.*)
Sabin 34355.
The Library's copy of this English work are in * *KF 1195*.
*See also* no. 1170.

1259. *Review:* Transactions of the American Physicians of Philadelphia. v. I. Part I. Philapromoting useful knowledge. v. III. Philadelphia, 1793. 368 p. 4°. (Göttingische Anzeigen von gelehrten Sachen. Göttingen [1794]. Jahr 1794, p. 1705-1717, **DF*.)
The Library's file of the "Transactions" is in * *EA*.
*Contents:* Introduction. Dr. Nicolaus Collin, Was für Untersuchungen in der Naturkunde den vereinigten Staaten in Nordamerica am nützlichsten seyn würden; 1789 vorgelesen. — I. Benjamin Franklin, Muthmassungen über die Bildung der Erde u.d.g. in einem Briefe an den Abbé Soulavie, Passey 1782. II. Benjamin Franklin, Theorie von Licht und Hitze, 1788. III. Benjamin Franklin, Nachricht, wie Chinesen grosse Blätter Papier machen, 1788. IV. Benjamin Franklin, Fragen und Muthmassungen, Magnetismus und die Theorie der Erde betreffend. v. Patterson, Ueber eine sonderbare, zuerst von Franklin beobachtete und noch nicht zulänglich erklärte Erscheinung. VI. Robert McCauselin, Ueber ein erdiges Wesen... Spray of the Falls. VII. William Barton, Ueber die wahrscheinliche Dauer des menschlichen Lebens. VIII. Andrew Ellicot, Looming. IX. Thomas Jefferson, Sugar Maple-tree. x. Jonathan Williams, Vom Gebrauche des Thermometers, Bänke, Untiefen u.d.g. zu entdecken. XI. Benjamin Smith Barton, Von den wirksamsten Mitteln, den tödlichen Folgen des Bisses der Klapperschlange, Crotalus Horridus, zuvorzukommen. XII. S. Williams, Beobachtungen der Abweichung der Magnetnadel 1785, auf der Universität zu Cambridge. XIII. Andrew Ellicot. Genaue Bestimmung der Rectascension... XIV. David Rittenhouse and John Jones, Von Häusern in Philadelphia, wo es den 7. Jun. 1789 eingeschlagen hat. — [Several numbers omitted in review.] — XVII. R. Patterson, Neue Bezeichnung für Musik. Mit Buchstaben statt der Noten...die Amerikanischen Buchdrucker sind mit den Typen zum Notendrucke noch nicht versehen. xviii. W. Warring, Ueber die Theorie der Wassermühlen. XIX. David Rittenhouse, Beobachtungen von Finsternissen 1789, 1791 und Mercurs in der Sonne 1789. xx. David Rittenhouse, Summen von Potenzen der Sinusse. xxi. Harry Muhlenberg, Index Florae Lancastriensis. xxii. William Waring, Berechnung von Dr. Barker's Muehle. xxiii. Jonathan Williams, Thermometrisches Tagebuch ...auf einer Reise nach Oporto und zurueck. xxiv. De Beauvois, Bemerkungen über die cryptogamischen Pflanzen. xxv. Jonathan Heart, Ueber alte Werke der Eingeborenen der westlichen Länder. xxvi. James Greenway, Beschreibung der Cassia Chamaecrista. xxviii. anonym., Von einem Hügel an den Grenzen von Nordcarolina, der sonst ein Vulkan gewesen sein soll. xxix. James Greenway, Von einer giftigen Pflanze, die wild im südlichen Theile von Virginien wächst. xxx. Francis Hopkinson, Beschreibung einer Maschine, den Weg eines Schiffes zu messen. xxxi. Benjamin Smith Barton, Ob die wahre Honigbiene in America einheimisch sey? xxxii. David Rittenhouse, Ein Komet im Cepheus. xxxiii. William Thornton, Cadmus, oder über die Elemente der geschriebenen Sprache... Nebst einem Versuche über die Art, Taubstumme reden zu lehren. xxxiv. William Waring, Bemerkungen über die Theorie des Wassermühlen. (cont'd.) xxxv. Robert Patterson, Verbesserung der metallenen Blitzableiter. xxxvi. Ebenezer Robinson, Schädliche unterirdische Dämpfe zu zerstreuen. xxxvii. Jesse Higgins, Stehendes Wasser in ebenen Boden wegzuschaffen. xxxviii. Matthew Wilson, Beobachtungen bei dem strengen Winter 1779, 1780. xxxix. John Cooke, Eine Mittel allgemeines Maass und Gewicht zu erhalten. xl. Francis Hopkinson, Vorrichtung, vermittelst einer Art von Spiralfeder zu erhalten, dass die Masten eines Schiffes dem Winde ein wenig nachgeben können. xli. Benjamin Smith Barton, Botanische Beschreibung von Linné's Podophyllum Diphyllum. xlii. Le Roy, Ueber den Bau der Hospitäler.

1260. *Review:* Transactions of the College of Physicians of Philadelphia. v. I. Part I. Philadelphia: Dobson, 1793. 254 p. 8°. (Göttingische Anzeigen von gelehrten Sachen. Göttingen [1794]. Jahr 1794, p. 1746-1755, **DF*.)
"Mit Vergnügen hat Rec. die wichtigen Fortschritte bemerkt, welche die practische Arzneywissenschaft in Nordamerika seit einigen Jahren gemacht hat..."
The Library's file of the "Transactions" is in *WAA*.
Medical topics treated by Moses Bartram, George Bensell, Joseph Capelle, William Clarkson, William Currie, Thomas Dolbeare, Benjamin Duffield, Jacob Hall, John Jones, Michael Leib, Benjamin Rush, Benjamin Say, Isaac Senter, Thomas Stockett, Benjamin Tallmann, John Willday.
"Nun erscheint der erste Theil der Verhandlungen dieses Collegiums, dessen Inhalt beweiset, dass jene Amerikanische Societät mit den berühmtesten medicinischen Gesellschaften in Europa wetteifert. Von einer so wichtigen Schrift, die wohl nur in den Händen weniger Leser sich befinden dürfte, wird eine etwas ausführliche Anzeige für Europäische Aerzte interessant sein." For a German translation of the *Transactions* see no. 1295.

1261. *Review:* Transactions of the Society instituted for the encouragement of arts. v. VIII, IX, X. London, 1790-1792. (Göttingische Anzeigen von gelehrten Sachen. Göttingen [1794]. 12°. Jahr 1794, p. 916-919, **DF*.)
Several references to America. "Das in Menge aus Jamaika verschriebene Casher-Gummi wird doch das Senegalsche nicht ganz verdrängen können..." "Der Vorschlag, den Kaffee aus Westindien künftig in seinen Hülsen kommen zu lassen."
Publications of this organization which eventually became the Royal Society of Arts, London, are in *VA*.

1262. *Review:* A treatise on the fevers of Jamaica with some observations on the intermitting fever of America...by Robert Jackson. London: B. Murray, 1791. 424 S. Text und 115 S. Noten. (Allgemeine Literatur-Zeitung. Jena, 1794. 4°. Jahr 1794. Bd. 2, col. 785-791, *NAA.*)
The Library has only the Philadelphia, 1795, edition of this English work.
See nos. 1352, 1402.

*1794, continued*

1263. *Review:* Ueber nordamerikanische Bäume und Sträucher... Mannheim, 1792. 7 Bogen. 8°. (Neue allgemeine deutsche Bibliothek. Kiel, 1794. 8°. Bd. 10, p. 92, *NAA.*)
See also nos. 1154, 1354.

1264. *Review:* Verfassung der vornehmsten Europäischen und der vereinigten Amerikanischen Staaten dargestellt von Herrn de la Croix ... Aus d. Franz. mit Berichtigungen des Uebersetzers. Leipzig: In der Weidmann. Buchh. I. Bd. 1792, 442 S. II. Bd. 1792, 523 S. III. Bd. 1793, 354 S. 8°. (Allgemeine Literatur-Zeitung. Jena, 1794. 4°. Jahr 1794, Bd. 1, col. 545–552, *NAA.*)
See also nos. 1242, 1256.

1265. *Review:* A view of the diseases of the Army in Great Britain, America, the West-Indies... By Thomas Dickson Reid. London: J. Johnson, 1793. 396 p. 8°. (Göttingische Anzeigen von gelehrten Sachen. Göttingen [1794]. 12°. Jahr 1794, p. 1956-1959, * *DF.*)
"Das Ganze zerfällt in zwey Theile. Der erste giebt Nachrichten von den Krankheiten der Englischen Truppen während des letzten Amerikanischen Kriegs; mit einem genauen Tagebuche vom Februar 1776 bis zum December 1787... Im zweyten ist die Rede von den Krankheiten, welchen ein Theil der Englischen Truppen in Westindien und auf der Fahrt dahin ausgesetzt war..."

1266. *Review:* Die wesentlichen Kennzeichen der deutschen und nordamerikanischen Holzarten und Forstkräuter, zum Gebrauch der Oekonomen und Förster von Hrn. von Moser. Leipzig, 1794. 158 Seiten und 3 Kupfertafeln. 8°. (Neue allgemeine deutsche Bibliothek. Kiel, 1794. 8°. Bd. 13, p. 458, *NAA.*)
The book is most probably by Wilhelm Gottfried von Moser, 1729–1793.

1266A. *Review:* Die Wilden. Singspiel in drey Akten; nach dem Französischen von D. Schmieder. Frankfurt: Bey Pech, 1791. 96 S. 8°. (Allgemeine deutsche Bibliothek. Kiel, 1794. 12°. v. 116, p. 102–103, *NAA.*)
Music by d'Alayrac. First performance in the Mainzer Nationaltheater.
The hero expresses his desire to return home in the following lines:
"Ach! kaum kann ich es nun erwarten,
Ins Vaterland zurückzugehen,
Mich da zu pflegen und zu warten,
Früh schlafen gehn, und spät aufstehn..."
For details, see G. Desczyk, in *Deutsch-amerikanische historische Gesellschaft von Illinois, Jahrbuch, 1924–25, IEK.*

1795

1267. AMERIKANISCHES Magazin oder authentische Beiträge zur Erdbeschreibung, Staatskunde und Geschichte von Amerika, besonders aber der vereinten Staaten. Herausgegeben von Professor Hegewisch in Kiel und Professor Ebeling in Hamburg. Band I. Hamburg: Bey Carl Ernst Bohn, 1795-1797. 4 parts in 2 v. 8°. *KF 1795
Sabin 1287.

Intended as a running supplement to Ebeling's *Erdbeschreibung und Geschichte von Amerika*. No more published.
"In this magazine a wealth of information was gathered from the most trustworthy sources, such as official American documents and biographies, published in the United States. Beside news items from across the sea, we find in the first issue a comparative survey of the constitution of the various States of the Union, an economic report concerning the whole country, given by the Federal commissioner of public revenues, an official list of exports from the States, a description of a tour on foot through New Jersey made by Dr. F. H. Antenrieth in 1795, and a list of publications, such as books, charts, engravings, etc., referring to America. The second issue (1795) contains information about immigration and settlements in Pennsylvania, financial reports, and a catalogue of all newspapers and magazines printed in the United States up to 1789. The following issues (1796, 1797) contain stories of the Revolutionary War, especially about Baron von Steuben, essays on American poetry and reviews of letters written by German-Americans." —
P. C. Weber, *America in imaginative German literature*, 1926, *NFCX.*
Reviews:
Erstes Stück: *Allgemeine Literatur-Zeitung*, Jahr 1796, Bd. 1, col. 141–144, *NAA; Neue allgemeine deutsche Bibliothek*, Bd. 25, p. 119–122, *NAA; Erfurter gelehrte Zeitung*, Jahr 1793, p. 281–282 (not in N. Y. P. L.); *Allgemeine geographische Ephemeriden*, Jahr 1800, Bd. 5, p. 144–146, *KAA.*
Zweites Stück: *Erfurter gelehrte Zeitung*, Jahr 1798, p. 281–287 (not in N. Y. P. L.); *Allgemeine Literatur-Zeitung*, Jahr 1798, Bd. 2, Ergänzungsblätter, col. 446–448, *NAA; Neue allgemeine deutsche Bibliothek*, Bd. 31, p. 261–264, *NAA.*
Review of the last two parts: *Allgemeine geographische Ephemeriden*, Bd. 5, p. 144–146, *KAA.*

1268. ATWOOD, THOMAS. Thomas Atwood's Geschichte der Insel Dominica. Aus dem Englischen übersetzt und mit Anmerkungen begleitet von Georg Friedrich Benecke... Göttingen: Bey Johann Christian Dieterich, 1795. 276 p. 18½ cm. (8°.) *KF 1795
Sabin 2345.
The English original was published in London in 1791. The "Vorrede des Uebersetzers" is dated: Göttingen, den 30. Nov. 1794 and signed: G. F. Benecke.
Review: *Göttingische Anzeigen von gelehrten Sachen*, Jahr 1795, p. 72, * *DF.*

1269. BIOGRAPHIEN für die Jugend. Bd. I. Tübingen: In der I. G. Cottaischen Buchhandlung, 1795. 1 v. 8°. *KF 1795
Sabin 25540.
This follows Franklin's account of his life, re-written in the third person.
Issued in two volumes.
Bd. I: B. Franklin, D. B. Franklins Leben.

1270. GENTZ, FRIEDRICH VON. Ueber den Einfluss der Entdeckung von Amerika auf den Wohlstand und die Kultur des menschlichen Geschlechts. (In his: Ausgewählte Schriften. Herausgegeben von Dr. Wilderich Weick. Stuttgart & Leipzig: Druck und Verlag von L. F. Rieger & Comp., 1836-38. 8°. Bd. 5, p. 173–216.) NFG
Appeared originally in *Neue deutsche Monatsschrift*, Berlin, August, 1795, from which it is reprinted.
Another important publication on America by the same author is "Der Ursprung und die Grundsätze der amerikanischen Revolution, verglichen mit dem Ursprung und den Grundsätzen der französischen," published in his *Historisches Journal*, Berlin, 1800, v. 2. Not in the Library. An English translation "The Principles of the American and French Revolutions compared. Translated from the German of Gentz," appeared in *Portfolio*, Philadelphia, 1801, v. 1, p. 193.

*1795, continued*

1271. GOETHE, JOHANN WOLFGANG. Wilhelm Meisters Lehrjahre. Ein Roman. Herausgegeben von Goethe... Berlin: Bey Johann Friedrich Unger, 1795–1796. 4 v. 8°. (Reprinted in his: Werke. Herausgegeben im Auftrage der Grossherzogin Sophie von Sachsen. Weimar: H. Böhlaus Nachfolger, 1887–1919. 8°. Bd. 21–23.) NFGK
See Viertes Buch, sechzehntes Kapitel; Siebentes Buch, drittes Capitel ("hier oder nirgends ist Amerika!"); Siebentes Buch, sechstes Capitel; Achtes Buch, viertes Capitel; Achtes Buch, siebentes Capitel.
See Walter Wadepuhl, "Goethe and America," in Deutsch-amerikanische historische Gesellschaft von Illinois, *Jahrbuch*, Chicago, 1922–23, p. 77–108, *IEK*.

1272. [JACQUIN, NIKOLAUS JOSEPH, FREIHERR VON.] Auswahl schöner und seltener Gewächse als eine Fortsetzung der Amerikanischen Gewächse... Nürnberg: Im Verlag der Raspeschen Handlung, 1795–1796. 5 v. in 3. col'd frontis. (v. 3), 250 col'd plates. 8°. *KF 1795
Sabin 2440.
Edited by Johann Zorn.
Continuation of Jacquin's *Dreyhundert auserlesene amerikanische Gewächse nach Linneischer Ordnung*. Reviews: Erstes Hundert: *Neue allgemeine deutsche Bibliothek*, Bd. 46, p. 342, *NAA*; *Allgemeine Literatur-Zeitung*, Jahr 1795, Bd. 1, col. 128, *NAA*; *Erlanger gelehrte Zeitung*, Jahr 1795, p. 702 (not in N. Y. P. L.). Zweites Hundert: *Allgemeine Literatur-Zeitung*, Jahr 1797, Bd. 3, col. 353–354, *NAA*; *Neue allgemeine deutsche Bibliothek*, Bd. 46, p. 342, *NAA*. Drittes Hundert: *Allgemeine Literatur-Zeitung*, Jahr 1798, Bd. 2, col. 216, *NAA*.

1273. JÄHRLICHER Gewinn, welchen Europa von seinen eignen und den Bergwerken seiner Kolonien an Gold und Silber zieht. (Allgemeines europäisches Journal. Brünn, 1795. 8°. [Jahr] 1795, Bd. 4, p. 23.) *DF
Note also "Kann ein Staat zu viel Geld haben?" by F. J. Bertuch in *Journal des Luxus und der Moden*, Weimar und Gotha, 1795, p. 222. Not in the Library.

1273A. KANT, IMMANUEL. Zum ewigen Frieden. Ein philosophischer Entwurf. 1795. (In his: Sämmtliche Werke. In chronologischer Reihenfolge herausgegeben von G. Hartenstein. Leipzig: Leopold Voss, 1868. 12°. Bd. 6, p. 409.) YBS
"Auch die Verdingung der Truppen eines Staats an einen andern, gegen einen nicht gemeinschaftlichen Feind, ist dahin zu zählen; denn die Unterthanen werden dabei als nach Belieben zu handhabende Sachen gebraucht und verbraucht." Abschnitt 1, §2. See P. C. Weber, *America in imaginative German literature*, New York, 1926, *NFCX*.

1274. LEBENSGESCHICHTE des Benjamin Franklin. (Allgemeines europäisches Journal. Brünn, 1795. 8°. [Jahr] 1795, Bd. 8, p. 86–102; Bd. 9, p. 135–145.) *DF

1275. MUÑOZ, JUAN BAUTISTA. Don Juan Baptista Muñoz Geschichte der Neuen Welt, aus dem Spanischen übersetzt, und mit erläuternden Anmerkungen herausgegeben von M. C. Sprengel... Weimar: Im Verlage des Industrie-Comptoirs, 1795. xvi p., 2 l., 6–493 p., frontis. (port.), maps. 21 cm. (8°.) *KF 1795
Sabin 51344; Medina 5581.
Reviews: *Allgemeine Literatur-Zeitung*, Jahr 1795, Bd. 4, col. 203–205, *NAA*; *Neue allgemeine deutsche*

*Bibliothek*, Jahr 1797, Anhang zu Bd. 1–28, Abth. 2, p. 331–333, *NAA*.

1276. NEUE amerikanische Briefe. (Allgemeines europäisches Journal... Brünn, 1795–96. 8°. [Jahr] 1795, Bd. 9, p. 49–69; Bd. 12, p. 39–46; [Jahr] 1796, Bd. 2, p. 57–67.) *DF
The letters of the first group are dated: Concord in New-Hampshire, August, 1793, and Philadelphia, May 9th, 1794. Taken from the *Deutsche Monatsschrift*. The letter of the second group is dated: Philadelphia, July 13th, 1794, and deals with the town of Philadelphia. Taken from *Deutsche Monatsschrift*. The third group deals with speculation in real estate in America, McKenzie's travels, and miscellaneous matters. One letter is dated: Albany, July 8th, 1794.

1277. POLITISCHE Grabschrift. Aus der americanischen Zeitung the Columbian Centinel. (Minerva. Hamburg, 1795. 12°. Jahr 1795, Bd. 3, p. 164–165.) BAA

1278. RICHTER, JEAN PAUL FRIEDRICH. Hesperus oder 45 Hundsposttage. Eine Lebensbeschreibung. Berlin, 1795. 4 v. 8°. (Reprinted in his: Jean Paul's sämmtliche Werke. Berlin: Bei G. Reimer, 1840–1842. 16°. v. 5–8.) NFG
See 24. Hundsposttag (v. 6, p. 184–235): "Der Nordamerikaner und der alte Deutsche gleichen sich stärker, als Deutsche einander aus benachbarten Jahrhunderten."
See an article, "J. P. F. Richter," in *New England quarterly magazine*, Boston, 1802, no. 2, p. 57.

1279. SCHREIBEN aus Nordamerika. (Allgemeines europäisches Journal. Brünn, 1795. 8°. [Jahr] 1795, Bd. 8, p. 51–58; Bd. 12, p. 46–50.) *DF
The first two letters are dated: Niagarafluss, den 22. April 1794, bezw. den 25. April 1794. About the Niagara Falls. The third is dated: Philadelphia, den 26. Febr. 1795. General American life, especially in Philadelphia. Taken from *Genius der Zeit; ein Journal*. This periodical, published at Altona, 1794–1800 (Bd. 1–21), contains articles relating to America: "Journal eines Reisenden in Nordamerika," Jahr 1795, and "Ueber die Gastfreundschaft der Amerikaner," by Talleyrand Périgord, Jahr 1797. Not in the Library.

1280. SCHREIBEN des Herrn von la Fayette an den Herrn von la Rochefoucault. (Minerva. Hamburg, 1795. 8°. Jahr 1795, Bd. 3, p. 277–288.) BAA
Dated: Nivelles den 25sten August 1792.

1281. STEDMAN, CHARLES. Carl Stedman's Geschichte des Ursprungs, des Fortgangs und der Beendigung des Americanischen Kriegs. Aus dem Englischen übersetzt und mit Anmerkungen begleitet von Julius August Remer Professor in Helmstedt... Berlin: In der Vossischen Buchhandlung, 1795. 2 v. folding plans. 8°. *KF 1795
The English original was published in London in 1794. See Sir Henry Clinton's *Observations on Mr. Stedman's History*, *KF 1794*; see also no. 1246.
Note J. G. Stedman, ...*Nachrichten von Surinam und von seiner Expedition gegen die rebellischen Neger in dieser Kolonie in den Jahren 1772 bis 1777. Ein Auszug aus dem englischen Original*, Hamburg, 1797 (Neuere Geschichte der See- und Land-Reisen, Bd. 8, *KF*). First edition, London, 1796. Sabin 91080. For another edition (Halle, 1772–77), see Sabin 91079. Not in the Library.
Reviews: Bd. 1: *Allgemeine Literatur-Zeitung*, Jahr 1795, Bd. 1, col. 91–92, *NAA*; *Neue allgemeine deutsche Bibliothek*, Jahr 1797, Anhang zu Bd. 1–28, p. 384–397, *NAA*; *Neue Leipziger gelehrte Zeitung*, Jahr 1795, Bd. 4, p. 795–796 (not in N. Y. P. L.), Bd.

## GERMAN WORKS RELATING TO AMERICA 149

*1795, continued*

II: *Neue allgemeine deutsche Bibliothek*, Jahr 1797, Anhang zu Bd. 1–28, p. 384–397, *NAA; Neue Leipziger gelehrte Zeitung*, Jahr 1796, Bd. 3, p. 539–540 (not in N. Y. P. L.); *Der Neue teutsche Merkur*, Jahr 1798, Vierteljahr 1, p. 236, \* *DF; Allgemeine Literatur-Zeitung*, Jahr 1799, Bd. 1, col. 808, *NAA; Gothaische gelehrte Zeitung*, Jahr 1797, Bd. 2, p. 804–805 (not in N. Y. P. L.); *Tübinger gelehrte Zeitung*, Jahr 1797, p. 585 (not in N. Y. P. L.).

1282. TIECK, JOHANN LUDWIG. Geschichte des Herrn William Lovell. Berlin und Leipzig: Bey Carl August Nicolai, 1795–1796. 3 v. 8°. (Reprinted in his: Schriften. Berlin: Bei G. Reimer, 1828–29. 8°. Bd. 6–7.) NFG
The novel ends with the following words spoken by Karl Wilmont: "Adieu — Ich fahre von hier nach Amerika. Der Krieg lockt mich dahin; es wird in der Englischen Armee wohl eine Stelle für einen Lebenssatten übrig sein, der sich dann wenigstens noch einbilden kann, zum Besten seines Vaterlandes zu sterben..."

1283. UIBER den Staat von Neuyork in den vereinigten Staaten von Nordamerika. (Allgemeines europäisches Journal. Brünn, 1795. 8°. [Jahr] 1795, Bd. 1, p. 62–83.) \*DF
Relates especially to the Genesee district.

1284. VERSCHIEDENE Arten der Indianer ihre Zeuge zu malen. (Allgemeines europäisches Journal. Brünn, 1795. 8°. [Jahr] 1795, Bd. 11, p. 86–88.) \*DF
Taken from the *Journal für Fabrik und Handlung.*

1284A. VOSS, JOHANN HEINRICH. Luise, ein ländliches Gedicht in drei Jdyllen. Koenigsberg: Bei Friedrich Nicolovius, 1795. (Reprinted in: Deutsche National Litteratur... herausgegeben von Joseph Kürschner. Berlin und Stuttgart [n. d.]. 12°. Bd. 49, p. 1–68.) NFK
This volume has individual title: Göttinger Dichterbund. Erster Teil. Johann Heinrich Voss.

"Liesest du erst ein wenig im Bett?
ein Kapitel der Bibel
Dort auf der kleinen Riole zur Seite
dir; oder ein Leibbuch
Jener Zeit, da noch Menschen wie Washington lebten und Franklin... — *Zweite Idylle, lines 67–69.*

Glüht mir das Antlitz
Nicht, als hätt' ich im Eifer gepredigt,
oder mit Walter
Über Europa geschwatzt und Amerika,
jenes im Dunkel
Dies im tagenden Lichte der Menschlichkeit..."
— *lines 84–87.*

Both the quotations are missing in "Des Bräutigams Besuch. An F. H. Jacobi," under which title the Zweite Idylle was printed first in *Musenalmanach für 1783. Herausgegeben von Voss und Goeking* [sic!], Hamburg [1783], p. 1–21, *NFA*.
See H. S. King, "Echoes of the American Revolution in German literature," in University of California, *Publications in modern philology*, Berkeley, 1929, v. 14, p. 38–40, *STG*.

1285. WINTERBOTHAM, WILLIAM. Amerika. Heftweise. (Allgemeines europäisches Journal. Brünn, 1795. 8°. [Jahr] 1795, Bd. 9, p. 51.) \*DF
Translation (first Heft, only) of Winterbotham's *An historical... view of the American United States*, London, 1795, \* *KF*.

1286. ZIMMERMANN, EBERHARD AUGUST WILHELM VON. Frankreich und die Freistaaten von Nordamerika. Verglichen in Hinsicht ihrer Länder, ihrer Natur-Produkte, ihrer Bewohner und der Bildung ihrer Staaten. Von E. A. W. Zimmermann, Hofrath und Professor in Braunschweig. Berlin: In der Vossischen Buchhandlung, 1795–1800. 2 v. frontis. 8°. \* KF 1795
Bd. I has also engraved title page which reads: Frankreich und die Freistaaten von Nordamerika. Vergleichung beider Länder... Berlin: In der Vossischen Buchhandlung, 1795.
Bd. II has an additional title page which reads: Allgemeine Uebersicht Frankreichs von Franz I. bis auf Ludwig XVI. und der Freistaaten von Nord-Amerika von ihrem Entstehen bis auf die heutigen Zeiten... nebst einer Gegeneinanderstellung ihrer Revolutionen von Eberh. Aug. Wilh. von Zimmermann. Braunschweig: Gedruckt und verlegt bei Carl Reichard, 1800.
Frontis. engraved by D. Berger.
Reviews: *Neue allgemeine deutsche Bibliothek*, Bd. 27, p. 428–433, *NAA; Erlanger gelehrte Zeitung*, Jahr 1797, p. 29–32 (not in N. Y. P. L.); *Nürnberger gelehrte Zeitung*, Jahr 1796, p. 652–656 (not in N. Y. P. L.); *Tübinger gelehrte Zeitung*, Jahr 1796, p. 591 (not in N. Y. P. L.); *Neueste kritische Nachrichten*, Jahr 1796, p. 25–28 (not in N. Y. P. L.).
For a German review of the French edition, see no. 1431.
"E. A. W. von Zimmermann, court-councillor in the duchy of Brunswick, a scientist and geographer. Later he was professor at the Collegium Carolinum in Brunswick. The author was well informed about the United States through his activity as an editor of a number of important books of travel and through his frequent correspondence with friends in Boston and New York. The background of his work is the revolution in France and America. The author compares these countries with regard to the nature of their soil, their physical products, their population, their form of government, and discusses the radical differences in the character of the countries and their inhabitants, and the consequent divergent course which the revolution took in each." — *P. C. Weber, America in imaginative German literature*, New York, 1926, *NFCX*. See also Otto Vossler, "Die Amerikanischen Revolutionsideale in ihrem Verhältnis to den europäischen," in *Historische Zeitschrift*, München und Berlin, 1929, Beiheft 17, *BAA*.
Note also the periodical *Annalen der Geographie und Statistik* [ed. *E. A. W. Zimmermann*], Bd. 1–3, Braunschweig und Leipzig, 1790–1792. Not in the Library. Of special interest, "Kurze Beschreibung der 4 Comitate Harkemann, Otsego, Tioga und Ontario in Nord Amerika, des künftigen 16ten Staats," Jahr 1791, Bd. 4, p. 485–492.

1287. *Review:* American edition of the Encyclopaedia. n. p. n. d. 4°. (Göttingische Anzeigen von gelehrten Sachen. Göttingen [1795]. 12°. Jahr 1795, p. 1275–1277, \* *DF*.)
"Mit diesem Schmutztitel haben wir bereits eilf Quartbände erhalten... ohne Haupttitel, ohne Vorrede, ohne Anzeige des Druckorts und Jahrs, ohne irgend eine Angabe des Plans oder der Absicht des Verfassers. Es ist aber offenbar darauf angelegt, alle menschlichen Kenntnisse in einem Wörterbuch zu vereinigen..."

1288. *Review:* The American Kalendar, or United States Register for the year 1795. London: B. Debrett. 192 Seiten. 8°. (Allgemeine Literatur-Zeitung. Jena, 1795. 4°. Jahr 1795, Bd. 3, col. 308–309, *NAA*.)
The Library has a copy of this work in *Reserve.*

1289. *Review:* American universal Geography or a View of the present State of all the Empires, Kingdoms and Republics of the known World, by Jedidiah Morse. Boston: J. Thomas & Ebenezer Andrewes, 1793. 2 v. 8°. (Göttingische Anzeigen von gelehrten Sachen. Göttingen [1795]. 12°. Jahr 1795, p. 1785–1792, \* *DF*.)
Thorough review of the second edition of Morse's work, since the first edition had not been reviewed. The Library's copy of this American work is in \* *KD*.

1795, *continued*

1290. *Review:* An Essay on Colonisazion...by C. B. Wadstrom. In two parts... London: B. Vf., gedr. b. Darton u. Harvey, 1794. 4°. (Allgemeine Literatur-Zeitung. Jena, 1795. 4°. Jahr 1795, Bd. 3, col. 305–308, *NAA.*)
References to the American Indians.
The Library has copies of this English work in *Reserve* and in the Schomburg Collection, *325-W.*

1291. *Review:* Historical Collections consisting of State Papers and other authentic Documents intended as Materials for an History of the United States of America, by Ebenezer Hazard. v. 2. Philadelphia: Dobson, 1794. 654 p. 4°. (Göttingische Anzeigen von gelehrten Sachen. Göttingen [1795]. 12°. Jahr 1795, p. 604–606, * *DF.*)
The Library's copy of this 2-volume work, 1792–94, is in † * *KD.*

1292. *Review:* Eine kurze Nachricht von dem bösartigen Fieber, welches kürzlich in Philadelphia grassiret... Von Mathew Carey. Nach der vierten verbesserten Auflage aus dem Englischen übersezt, von Carl Erdmann Lancaster: Bailey, 1794, 176 S. 8°. (Journal der Erfindungen, Theorien und Widersprüche in der Natur- und Arzneiwissenschaft. Gotha, 1795. 12°. Bd. 3, Intelligenzblatt No. v, p. 5–6, *WAA.*)

1293. *Review:* Letters on Emigration. By a Gentleman lately returned from America. London: Printed for Kearsly, 1794. (Allgemeines europäisches Journal. Brünn, 1795. 8°. [Jahr] 1795, Bd. 9, p. 50, * *DF.*)
The Library's copy of the "Letters," by Hodgkinson, is in *Reserve.*

1294. *Review:* Luigi Castiglioni's...Reise durch die vereinigten Staaten von Nordamerika in den Jahren 1785, 1786 und 1787... Aus dem Italienischen von Magnus Petersen. Erster Theil. Mit Kupfern. Memmingen: Bey Seyler, 1793. 495 S. 8°. (Neue allgemeine deutsche Bibliothek. Kiel, 1795. 8°. Bd. 15, p. 244–249, *NAA.*)

1295. *Review:* Medicinische Verhandlungen des Kollegiums der Aerzte zu Philadelphia. Ersten Bandes erster Theil. Aus dem Englischen übersetzt von Christian Friedrich Michaelis. 1795. xxviii und 132 S. 8°. (Journal der Erfindungen, Theorien und Widersprüche in der Natur- und Arzneiwissenschaft. Gotha, 1795. 12°. Bd. 3, Intelligenzblatt No. vi, p. 30, *WAA.*)

1296. *Review:* Memoirs of the American Academy of Arts and Sciences. v. ii. part i. Boston: 1793. 200 p. 4°. (Göttingische Anzeigen von gelehrten Sachen. Göttingen [1795]. 12°. Jahr 1795, p. 1265–1274, * *DF.*)
The Library's file of the *Memoirs* is in * *EA.*
*Contents:* John Lowell, Lobschrift auf James Bowdoin. 1. Theil: Mathematik und Astronomie. 1. James Winthrop, Geometrische Methoden, mittlere Proportionallinien zwischen gegebenen äussern zu finden. 2. James Winthrop, Einen Winkel geometrisch in drey Theile zu theilen. 3. William Croswell, Aus zwey Seiten eines Kugeldreyecks mit dem eingeschlossenen Winkel die dritte Seite zu finden. 4. Samuel Webber, Beobachtung der ringförmigen Sonnenfinsternis den 3. April 1791. Joseph Willard, Beobachtung des Durchganges Merkurs durch die Sonne am 5. Nov. 1789. ii. Theil: Naturkunde. 1. Samuel Tenney, Ueber die prismatischen Farben. 2. Samuel Tenney, Nachricht von einer Anzahl Gesundwasser bey Saratoga in New-york. 3. Samuel Hale, Muthmassungen, warum Nordwestwinde im Winter in Neuengland kälter und häufiger sind. 4. Samuel Hitchcock, Scheintote Froesche. 5. Edward Augustus Holyoke, Von dem Ueberschusse der Hitze und Kälte der Amerikanischen Atmosphäre über die Europäische. 6. Asa Packard, Vom Aufenthalte der Schwalben im Winter. 7. [omitted in review.] 8. Severyn J. Bruyn [Tote Schwalben in einem Baum gefunden]. 9. A. Crocker, Praktischer Versuch, Apfelbäume zu ziehen und Apfelwein zu machen. 10. anonymous, Witterungsbeobachtungen zu Montreal in Canada. 11. General Samuel Parson, Entdeckungen in dem westlichen Lande. 12. James Winthrop, Barometrische Bemerkungen auf einer Reise zum See Champlain. 13. Edward Wigglesworth, Lebenswahrscheinlichkeit in den Staaten Massachusets und Neu-Hampshire. 14. Caleb Gannet, Merkwürdiges Nordlicht den 27. März 1781. 15. William Heath, Dunkelheit in Canada im October 1785. 16. Hugh Maxwell, Ueber Bäume als Leiter des Blitzes. 17. John Vinall, [Negative Electricität als Mittel gegen Brandschäden.] 18. James Warren, Beweis von der Wirkung des Lichts auf das Wachsthum der Pflanzen. 19. Samuel West, Von einem Hügel, Gay Head. 20. William Baylies, Beschreibung von Gay Head. 21. Winthrop Sargent, Verzeichniss von Wald- und andern Bäumen, nordwestlich vom Strome Ohio. 22. Robert Annan, Nachricht von dem Knochengerüste eines grossen Thiers. 23. Timothy Edwards, Beschreibung eines Horns oder Knochens, den man neuerdings in...einem abendlichen Aste des Susquehanna...gefunden hat. 24. Aaron Dexter, Beobachtungen über die Manufactur der Pottasche. 25. M. Feron, Zweyter Versuch über die Wasser bey Boston. 26. Noah Webster, Ueber die Theorie der Vegetation. iii. Theil: Arzneykunde. 1. Edward Augustus Holyoke, Nachricht von einer ungewöhnlichen Luftgeschwulst. 2. Aaron Dexter. Nachricht von einem Kinnbackenzwang.

1297. *Review:* The natural and civil History of Vermont. By Samuel Williams. Walpole in Newhampshire: Isaiah Thomas and David Carlisle, 1794. (Göttingische Anzeigen von gelehrten Sachen. Göttingen [1795]. 12°. Jahr 1795, p. 1337–1342, * *DF.*)
The Library has various copies of this American work in *IQE.*

1298–99. *Review:* Reliquiae Houstonianae seu Plantarum in America meridionali a Guilielmo Houston collectarum Icones, manu propria aere incisae. Norimbergae: Ex offic. Raspeana, 1794. 24 Seiten in 8°. 26 Tafeln. (Neue allgemeine deutsche Bibliothek. Kiel, 1795. 8°. Bd. 19, p. 249, *NAA.*)
The Library does not have this 1794 edition, which the *Catalogue général* of the Bibliothèque nationale calls the first German edition; it does, however, have the first edition, London, 1781, * *KF 1781.*
See note on no. 1400.

1300. *Review:* A short Account of the malignant fever lately prevalent in Philadelphia... by Mathew Carey. Philadelphia: B. Vf., 1793. Third edition. 112 S. ohne die Sterbelisten. 8°. (Allgemeine Literatur-Zeitung. Jena, 1795. 4°. Jahr 1795, Bd. 4, col. 409–412, *NAA.*)
The Library has various issues of this third edition in * *KD.*

1301. *Review:* Statistisch historisches Archiv. Hrsg. v. E. A. W. Zimmermann. Erster Band. Leipzig: In der Schäferschen Buchh., 1795. 163 S. (Allgemeine Literatur-Zeitung. Jena, 1795. 4°. Jahr 1795, Bd. 3, col. 453–454, *NAA.*)
*Contains:* No. 6. Kurze Geschichte und Generalregeln des in Nordamerika, England, Holland und Russland bestehenden Jerusalemsordens. No. 7. Authentische Nachricht von der Schadloshaltung der Lojalisten in Nordamerika durch die grossbritanische Regierung.

# GERMAN WORKS RELATING TO AMERICA 151

*1795, continued*

1301A. *Review:* Verkauf von Ländereien in Amerika. Hamburg, 1793 (mit einem Kårtchen). (Allgemeines europäisches Journal. Brünn, 1795. 12°. [Jahr] 1795, Bd. 9, p. 52, \*DF.)
"Nur an die Theilnehmer einer Länderkaufsgesellschaft vertheilt, die in Bremen und Hamburg oktroyiert wurde, um 99 992 Acres Neu Territory in Virginien zu kaufen."

1301B. *Notice:* Vermischte Nachrichten. (Allgemeine Literatur-Zeitung. Jena, 1795. 4°. Intelligenz Blatt, p. 1188, *NAA.*)
"Die deutsche Gesellschaft in New York, deren in no. 139 des Intel. Bl. S. 1116 gedacht wird [see no. 1243A] ist 1787 daselbst von den angesehensten deutschen Kaufleuten und Landbesitzern errichtet und hat die menschenfreundliche Absicht, den fremden Ankömmlingen in Amerika durch Rath und That beyzustehen, und überhaupt die Nordamerikanischen Deutschen mit dem Mutterlande und unter sich selbst in freundschaftliche, zu wechselseitiger Unterstützung abzweckende Verhältnisse zu setzen."
The statutes of the Deutsche Gesellschaft are in \* *KD (Grundregeln).*

1302. *Review:* Vermischte Sammlungen aus der Naturkunde zur Erklärung der H. Schrift. Fünftes Heft, von Samuel Oedmann... Rostock und Leipzig, 1793. xxviii und 140 S. Sechstes Heft, ebendas., 1795. 180 S. in 8°. (Allgemeine Bibliothek der biblischen Literatur. Leipzig, 1795. 8°. Bd. 7, p. 652–693, \* *YIA.*)
On p. 659, mute dogs which are supposed to live in America are referred to.

1303. *Review:* View of the United States of America in a Series of papers written in various times between the Years 1787 and 1794. By Tench Coxe... Philadelphia: Bey Wilhelm Hall, 1794. 513 p. 8°. (Göttingische Anzeigen von gelehrten Sachen. Göttingen [1795]. 12°. Jahr 1795, p. 1739–1742, \* *DF.*)
The Library has various copies of this American work in \* *KD.*

## 1796

1304. ALLGEMEINES Historien-Buch von den Merkwürdigsten Entdeckungen fremder ehedem ganz unbekannter Länder und Inseln; Nebst Beschreibung ihrer Einwohner, derselben Sitten und Gebräuche, Religions-Meynungen, Regierungsformen, Natur- und Kunsterzeugnisse, Thiere, Pflanzen und anderer Seltenheiten. Ein angenehmes und lehrreiches Lesebuch für alle Stände; Zur Beförderung der Menschenkenntniss, Menschengeschichte, Erdbeschreibung und Naturgeschichte. Wien: Zu finden beym Buchdrucker Chr. Gottlob Tåubel, 1796. 2 parts in 1 v. 616 p. 8°.  \* KF 1796
*Contents:* Bd. 1, 1 [Campe, J. H.] Die Entdeckung der neuen Welt. Bd. 1, 2 [Campe, J. H.] Fortsetzung der Entdeckung der neuen Welt. Entdeckung und Eroberung des Königreichs Mexiko in Amerika.
See nos. 762, 850, 1079.
Was also published under the title *Geschichte der Entdekkung von Amerika. Ein durchaus verständliches Lesebuch für Jedermann, mit einem historischen Kupferstich,* Halle, 1795, Sabin 27210. Not in the Library. The Library, however, has German editions of 1830, 1868, 1882, and translations into English (1800), French (1783, 1836), Dutch (1838), Spanish (1845).
A continuation of J. H. Campe's *Die Entdeckung von Amerika* was published as *Vierter Theil mit einem Kupfer und einer Karte,* Prag, 1815. See T. C. Enslin, *Bibliotheca paedagogica,* Berlin, 1824, p. 15, *SSB.*
Note also his *Robinson's Reise um die Welt: Amerika,* Nürnberg, 1816, Sabin 10308. Not in the Library.
J. H. Campe also enhanced the interest of German youth in America by his edition of Marie Sophie von La Roche's *Erscheinungen am See Oneida,* Leipzig, 1797–1798. It is "rédigé pour l'instruction et l'amusement de la jeunesse." The Library has the French version with the imprint, Paris: J. E. G. Dufour, 1803, in \* *KF,* but not the German original.

1305. AUSZUG aus einem Briefe des Herrn Pastors Storch in Nordcarolina, datirt Salisbury vom 20ten Jan. bis zum 25ten Febr. 1796. (Neues Hannöverisches Magazin... vom Jahre 1796. Hannover, 1797. 4°. Jahrg. 6, col. 1185–1192.)  \* DF
"Auch diese authentische Beschreibung bestätigt die im 47ten St. [see no. 1325] aus einer amerikanischen Zeitung mitgetheilten Warnungen vor dem berufiosen Auswandern nach Nordamerika, in täuschender Erwartung eines grössern Glücks mit minderer Anstrengung als im Vaterlande; — und lehrt zugleich, dass leider die Grundsätze, welche jetzt Europa zerrütten, auch bis zu jenem entlegenen Erdwinkel hinzudringen anfangen."
Deals with Pastor Nüssmann's death, a new church building, a new university, the Library Society, a Latin school in Salem, discovery of an old wall under the earth, influence of reading of Thomas Paine's book, and botanical matters (sensitive briars).
"Mitgetheilt vom Generalsuperintendenten Velthusen in Stade" (i.e. Johann Caspar Velthusen, 1740–1814).
Title page dated 1797; contents, 1796.

1306. BARTL, FRANZ KONRAD. Nachricht von der Harmonika, nebst einer Kupfertafel. (Allgemeines europäisches Journal. Brünn, 1796. 8°. [Jahr] 1796, Bd. 11, p. 155–164.)  \* DF
Taken from Bartl's book of the same title, published at Olmütz in 1796. See *Deutscher Gesamtkatalog,* v. 12, p. 179. Kayser, in his *Allgemeines Bücher-Lexikon,* Theil 1, p. 154, gives place of publication as Prague.
Bd. 11, November, of *Allgemeines europäisches Journal,* incorrectly called Bd. 12.

1307. BLUMENBACH, JOHANN FRIEDRICH. Abbildungen naturhistorischer Gegenstände. Heft 1. Göttingen: Bey H. Dieterich, 1796. 17 l., 20 plates. illus. 8°.  QGF
Bound with the ensuing 9 Hefte and issued in book form in 1810.
The second chapter, entitled "Tayadaneega," and the representation of this leader of the Mohawks (frequently called Joseph Brant), are intended to define Blumenbach's notion of an American race. He deals with the same subject more substantially in *Beyträge zur Naturgeschichte,* Göttingen, 1806–11, QOD.
See also his *Über die natürliche Verschiedenheit im Menschengeschlechte,* Leipzig, 1798, p. 2–10, 217. British Museum catalogue. Not in the Library.

1308. BÜLOW, DIETRICH VON. Briefe eines Deutschen in America. (Minerva. Hamburg, 1796-97. 12°. Jahr 1796, Bd. 2, p. 73–103, 486–517; Bd. 4, p. 385–424; Jahr 1797, Bd. 1, p. 105–113.)  BAA

1309. CAMPE, JOACHIM HEINRICH. Fortsetzung der Campischen Reisebeschreibungen für die Jugend... Reise des Grafen von Benjowsky aus dem Englischen von neuem frei übersetzt und abgekürzt... Theil 1–2. Reutlingen: Gedrukt bey Johannes Grözinger, 1796. 2 v. in 1. 8°.  \* KF 1796
*Contents:* Theil 1–2: Beniowsky, M. A. von. Reise des Grafen von Benjowsky.
*See* nos. 1033, 1077.

*1796, continued*

1310. FORSTER, GEORG. Nathaniel Portlocks und Georg Mortimers Reisen an die Nordwestküste von Amerika; nebst den Reisen eines Amerikanischen Dolmetschers und Pelzhändlers, welche eine Beschreibung der Sitten und Gebräuche der Nordamerikanischen Wilden enthalten, herausgegeben von John Long. Aus dem Englischen übersetzt...von Georg Forster ... Berlin: In der Vossischen Buchhandlung, 1796. viii, 74, 384 p., 1 l., 1 map, 6 plates. 4°.
Sabin 64394. \*KF 1796
*Contents:* 1. Des Schiffskapitains N. Portlocks Reise an die Nordwestküste von Amerika und um die Welt. 2. Des Lieutenents G. Mortimer Bemerkungen auf seiner Reise, in der Brigantine Merkur, unter Anführung des Herrn J. H. Cox. 3. Reisen eines amerikanischen Dolmetschers und Pelzhändlers, welche eine Beschreibung der Sitten und Gebräuche der nordamerikanischen Eingebornen, und einige Nachricht von den Posten am St. Lorenz-Flusse, dem See Ontario u. s. w. enthalten. Herausgegeben von J. Long.
*See also* nos. 1083, 1088, 1089.

1311. [IMPRIMEUR ou la fête de Franklin.] (Neue Bibliothek der schönen Wissenschaften und der freyen Künste. Leipzig, 1796. 8°. Bd. 57, p. 238.) NAA
Account of a celebration at Paris in honor of Benjamin Franklin.

1312. JOURNAL eines Reisenden in Nordamerika. (Allgemeines europäisches Journal. Brünn, 1796. 8°. [Jahr] 1796, Bd. 1, p. 39-54.) \*DF
Itinerary from Baltimore to Virginia (Dec. 1st, 1794) and back by way of Philadelphia.

1313. KOTZEBUE, AUGUST VON. Die Negersclaven. Ein historisch-dramatisches Gemählde in drey Aufzügen. 1796. (In his: Theater... Wien: Jn Commission bey Anton Doll, 1810-19. 16°. Bd. 6, p. 153-239.) NGC
"Die Scene ist auf der Jnsel Jamaica." — "Der Dichter hat bloss eingekleidet, aber nicht erfunden. Raynal's Histoire philosophique, Selle's Geschichte des Negerhandels, Sprengel vom Negerhandel. Jaert's Reise nach Guinea, der famöse Code noir, und einige in periodischen Schriften zerstreute Aufsätze haben ihm den Stoff geliefert." — *Vorbericht.*
"1791 hatte dann Kotzebue in dem Schauspiel Die Sonnenjungfrau den Weg betreten, ausschliesslich ineramerikanische Zustände der Urzeit dramatisch zu gestalten... Er hat dann etliche Jahre später zur Sonnenjungfrau noch eine Fortsetzung geliefert (1795): *Die Spanier in Peru oder Rollas Tod* und damit einen Gegenstand aufgegriffen, der etliche Male in der deutschen Literatur dramatisiert worden ist." — *Gerhard Descsyk, in Deutsch-amerikanische historische Gesellschaft von Illinois, Jahrbuch,* Chicago, 1924-25, IEK.

1314. MARINE Grossbritanniens und deren Vertheilung, zur Epoche des 1. Januar 1796. (Allgemeines europäisches Journal. Brünn, 1796. 8°. [Jahr] 1796, Bd. 3, p. 71.) \*DF

1315. MOSER, HEINRICH CHRISTOPH. Versuch einer Geschichte der deutschen Forstwirthschaft. Von den ältesten bis auf die neuesten Zeiten. (Forst-Archiv. Ulm, 1796. 8°. Bd. 16, p. 179-244.) VQN
Refers to American trees imported into and planted in Germany. The author who was a "Forstlehrer zu Bayreuth" should not be confused with Wilhelm Gottfried von Moser, 1729-1793, editor of the *Forst Archiv sur Erweiterung der Forst- und Jagdwissenschaft.*
See T. C. F. Enslin in *Bibliothek der Forst- und Jagd-Wissenschaft,* Leipzig, 1843, p. 56, VQP.
*See also* no. 1266.

1316. NACHRICHT von dem Gehalte und Preise derer in London zu habenden Kasten, worinnen Sämereyen von nordamerikanischen Bäumen befindlich sind. (Neues Forst-Archiv. Ulm, 1796. 8°. Bd. 1, p. 47.) VQN (Forst)

1317. NEUE Entdeckungsreise. (Minerva. Hamburg, 1796. 12°. Jahr 1796, p. 125-130.) BAA
Signed: v. A. [Archenholz.] Pertains to Spillard's travels.
Spillard "wollte America eben so practisch kennen lernen, als die andern drey Weltheile, und schiffte sich daher im Jahre 1790 zu Gibraltar nach Boston ein. Jn diesen sechs Jahren bereisete er alle vereinigte Staaten in Nord-America, nahm hernach seinen Weg über Ost-Florida, und über den Fluss St. Mary, durch die Wildnisse, wo alle Stämmer der Creek-Nation...ihren Wohnsitz haben..."
There is a full-page article about "Mr. Spillard, the celebrated pedestrian traveller, so frequently mentioned in the European and American publications" in the *Gentlemen's magazine,* January, 1796.

1318. PROCLAMATION der Commissarien der französischen Republik in St. Domingo. (Minerva. Hamburg, 1796. 12°. Jahr 1796, p. 324-337.) BAA

1319. ROTERMUND, HEINRICH WILHELM. Beitrag zur Geschichte des Tabackrauchens. (Neues Hannöverisches Magazin...vom Jahre 1796. Hannover, 1797. 4°. Jahrg. 6, col. 1601-1607.) \*DF
Treats the first import of tobacco into Europe and several orders of German governments to forbid smoking.
Title page dated 1797; contents, 1796.

1320. RUSH, BENJAMIN. Beschreibung des gelben Fiebers, welches im Jahre 1793 in Philadelphia herrschte, von Benjamin Rush, Professor der Arzneikunde auf der Universität von Pensylvanien. Aus dem englischen übersezt und mit einigen Zusätzen begleitet von P. Fr. Hopfengärtner, herzogl. Würtemberg. Hofmedicus und Stadtphysicus in Stuttgard und J. F. H. Autenrieth, herzogl. Würtemberg. Hofmedicus in Stuttgard. Tübingen: in der J. G. Cottaischen Buchhandlung, 1796. xlviii, 472 p. incl. folding tables. 8°. \*KF 1796
Sabin 74209.
Bemerkungen über die wahrscheinlichen Ursachen der verschiedenen Formen des gelben Fiebers von Dr. Autenrieth, p. 439.
Review: *Allgemeine Literatur-Zeitung,* Jahr 1796, Bd. 4, col. 313-314, NAA.

1321. SCHILLER, JOHANN FRIEDRICH. Columbus. (Musenalmanach für das Jahr 1796. Herausgegeben von Schiller. Neustrelitz: Bei dem Hofbuchhändler Michaelis [1796]. 32°. p. 179. NFGV

"Steure, muthiger Segler! Es mag der Witz
    dich verhöhnen
Und der Schiffer am Steu'r senken die
    lässige Hand.
Jmmer nach West! Dort muss die Küste
    sich zeigen,
Liegt sie doch deutlich und liegt schim-
    mernd vor deinem Verstand.
Traue dem leitenden Gott und folge dem
    schweigenden Weltmeer!
Wär sie noch nicht, sie stiegt jetzt aus den
    Fluten empor.
Mit dem Genius steht die Natur in ewigem
    Bunde;
Was der eine verspricht, leistet die
    andre gewiss."

# GERMAN WORKS RELATING TO AMERICA 153

*1796, continued*

In Schiller's *Werke*, Leipzig und Wien, 1865, Bd. 1, p. 110, Anmerkung, p. 328-329, *NFCY*, a passage from "Briefe des Julius an Raphael" is cited: "Auf die Unfehlbarkeit seines Kalküls geht der Weltentdecker Kolumbus die bedenkliche Wette mit einem unbefahrenen Meere ein, die fehlende zweite Hälfte zu der bekannten Hemisphäre, die grosse Insel Atlantis zu suchen. Er fand sie, diese Insel seines Papiers, und seine Rechnung war richtig."

1322. SCHREIBEN an Herrn xxx. Was ist ein Philosoph? (Neue Bibliothek der schönen Wissenschaften und der freyen Künste. Leipzig, 1796. 8°. Bd. 57, p. 70-100.) NAA
Slave trade to America is discussed.

1323. SCHREIBEN des jungen la Fayette aus Philadelphia an seinen Vater in Olmütz. (Minerva. Hamburg, 1796. 12°. Jahr 1796, Bd. 2, p. 251-257.) BAA
Dated: Philadelphia, den 3. Febr. 1796. Signed: George la Fayette.
Lafayette's son expresses his grief at the imprisonment of his father.

1324. TIMAEUS, JOHANN JACOB KARL. Nordamerikanischer Staats-Kalender, oder statistisches Hand- und Adressbuch der Vereinigten Staaten von Nordamerika. Von J. J. C. Timaeus, Hofmeister und öffentlichem Lehrer an der Ritterakademie in Lüneburg. Hamburg: In der amerikanischen Postexpedition bei Ulrich Hencke; und in Leipzig in Commission bei A. L. Reinicke, 1796. xxxviii, 544 [i.e. 540] p. tables. 8°. * KF 1796
A statistical handbook of the United States, being an altered and enlarged edition of "The United States register for the year 1795" (see note in no. 1288).
Bibliography, p. xii-xiv.
Reviews: *Allgemeine Literatur-Zeitung*, Jahr 1796, Bd. 3, col. 153-156, *NAA*; *Gothaische gelehrte Zeitung*, Jahr 1796, Bd. 2, p. 486-487 (not in N. Y. P. L.); *Göttingische Anzeigen von gelehrten Sachen*, Jahr 1796, Bd. 2, p. 1043-1044, * *DF*; *Oberdeutsche allgemeine Literatur Zeitung*, Jahr 1796, Bd. 2, p. 153-155 (not in N. Y. P. L.); *Erlanger gelehrte Zeitung*, Jahr 1797, p. 7-8 (not in N. Y. P. L.); *Gothaische gelehrte Zeitung*, Jahr 1796, Bd. 2, p. 486-487 (not in N. Y. P. L.).

1325. UEBER das Auswandern nach Nordamerika und den Ankauf dortiger Ländereien. (Neues Hannöverisches Magazin...vom Jahre 1796. Hannover, 1797. 4°. Jahrg. 6, col. 737-751.) *DF
Signed: A. zu Hzb.
Title page dated 1797; contents, 1796.

1326. UIBER den Ahornzucker und seine Kultur in Deutschland. (Allgemeines europäisches Journal. Brünn, 1796. 8°. [Jahr] 1796, Bd. 8, p. 58-75.) *DF

1327. UIBER den Zucker, den man in den vereinigten Staaten von Nordamerika aus der daselbst im Uiberfluss vorhandenen Ahornbaumart verfertigt. (Allgemeines europäisches Journal. Brünn, 1796. 8°. [Jahr] 1796, Bd. 6, p. 67-70.) *DF

1328. WASHINGTON, GEORGE. George Washington's beständigen Präsidenten und Protektors, officielle und eigenhändige Briefe und Berichte, welche er während des ganzen Krieges zwischen den Amerikanischen Freystaaten und England als Generalissimus an den Congress geschrieben,
nebst andern, welche er von diesem und andern Hauptpersonen erhalten hat. Aus dem Englischen, als die wichtigste und documentierte Geschichte dieses merkwürdigen Krieges. Leipzig: In der Weygandschen Buchhandlung, 1796 [-97]. 2 v. 8°. * KGW 1796
Sabin 101708.
v. 1, only, in N. Y. P. L.
Original: Official letters to the Honourable American Congress... London, 1795, * *KGW 1795*.
Reviews: *Neue allgemeine deutsche Bibliothek*, Bd. 29, p. 391-392, *NAA*; *Allgemeine Literatur-Zeitung*, Jahr 1796, Intelligenzblatt, col. 939, *NAA*.
The letters are the fundamental source for the accusations of Frh. von Bülow; see no. 1363 and especially the note on no. 1409.

1329. WASHINGTON. (Minerva. Hamburg, 1796. 12°. Jahr 1796, Bd. 1, p. 393-411.) BAA
"Der Verfasser ist der jetzt aus Amerika zurückkommene Graf v. Burkhausen [i.e., Graf Conrad Johann August von Burghaus, who died in 1804]." — *Introduction by the editor, J. W. Archenholz.*
"Er ging im Jahre 1794, nachdem er seinen Geburts-Vorrechten entsagt hatte, nach Philadelphia, um als Wallfahrer nach jener mehr oder weniger eingebildeten Freyheits-Region, sondern um allda sein Leben zu beschliessen. Die Ursachen seiner Sinnesänderung sind sehr belehrend, und liegen grösstentheils in dem jetzigen sittlichen, durchaus verkannten Zustande von America..."
Another article on Washington — not in the Library — had been published in *Journal von und für Deutschland* [ed. Bisbra], Ellrich, 1784, Stück 1, p. 19, taken from a letter of John Bell of Maryland to a friend in England. See H. S. King in *University of California, Publications in modern philology*, Berkeley, 1929, v. 14, p. 137-144, *STG*.

1330. WASHINGTON'S Adresse an das Volk der Vereinigten Staaten in America. (Minerva. Hamburg, 1796. 12°. Jahr 1796, Bd. 4, p. 489-525.) BAA
Dated: Vereinigte Staaten, den 17ten September 1796.
Note also *Politische Annalen* [ed. C. Girtanner], Berlin, 1793-1794, Bd. 1-8. Not in the Library. Bd. 6, p. 486-488, contains "Schreiben des General Washington;" Bd. 7, p. 67-70, "Beschlüsse des Ausschusses der Bürgerschaft der Stadt Newyork."

1331. *Review:* An account of the bilious remitting yellow fever, as it appeared in the city of Philadelphia in the year 1793. By Benjamin Rush... Philadelphia: Dobson, [1794]. 8°. (*Allgemeine Literatur-Zeitung*, Jena, 1796. 4°. Jahr 1796, Bd. 1, col. 209-214, *NAA*.)
The Library's copy of this English work is in * *KD*.

1332. *Review:* An account of the Sugar-Maple-Tree of the united states and of the methode [*sic!*] of obtaining Sugar from it...by Benjamin Rush. Philadelphia, 1792. 1 Bogen. 8°. (Neues Forst-Archiv. Ulm, 1796. 8°. Bd. 2, p. 35, *VQN Forst*.)
The Library does not have this letter by Thomas Jefferson in separate form. It does, however, have the *Transactions* of the American Philosophical Society, v. 3, p. 64-81, * *EA*, from which it was extracted; *see* Sabin 74201.
For a German translation, see no. 1381.

1333. *Review:* American State Papers being a Collection of original and authentic Documents, relative to the war between the united States and Great-Brittain [*sic!*]. 2 v. n. p., 1795. (Göttingische Anzeigen von gelehrten Sachen. Göttingen [1796]. 12°. Jahr 1796, p. 443-446, * *DF*.)
The Library's copies of this set — catalogued under George Washington — are in * *KGW 1796*.
For the German translation and notes, see no. 1328.

*1796, continued*

1334. *Review:* Arbustum americanum: The American Grove, or a [*sic!*] alphabetical Catalogue of Forest-Trees and Shrubs, natives of the american States. London, 1788. 8°. (Neues Forst-Archiv. Ulm, 1796. 8°. Bd. 1, p. 153, *VQN Forst.*)
*See* no. 1015.

1335. *Review:* Beschreibung der wildwachsenden Bäume und Staudengewächse in den Vereinigten Staaten von Nordamerika, von Humphry Marschal... (Neues Forst-Archiv. Ulm, 1796. 8°. Bd. 1, p. 153, *VQN Forst.*)
"...eine recht gute Übersetzung, in welcher die beschriebenen Gewächse nach dem Alphabete der lateinischen Geschlechts-Namen des Linnéschen Systems geordnet sind."
*See* nos. 1011, 1013, 1241, 1248, 1263, 1354.

1336. *Review:* Beyträge zum Archiv der medicinischen Polizey und der Volksarzneykunde, hrsg. v. J. C. F. Scherf. 6ter Band. Leipzig: Bey Weigand. 1. Sammlung 1795. 142 S.–2. Sammlung 1796. 182 S. (Allgemeine Literatur-Zeitung. Jena, 1796. 4°. Jahr 1796, Bd. 4, col. 377–380, *NAA.*)
The second Sammlung contains: Medicinal-taxe in Charlestown in Nordamerika, übers. v. Dr. Hunnold in Cassel.
"Während sich Reichthum dort [i.e., in Charleston, S. C.] überall verbreite, könne man, wenigstens in Charlestown, nicht zwey Aerzte nennen, welche sich durch ihre Praxis unabhängig gemacht haben... Die Arzneyen werden nicht nach ihren verschiednen Ingredienzen und Bereitungsarten, sondern nach ihrer Wirkung oder Form bezahlt... Ein Krankenbesuch wird mit 5 Schilling bezahlt; des Nachts zur Schlafenszeit aber, je nachdem das Wetter oder andere Umstände ihn erschweren, mit 1–2 Pfund Sterling. Zahnausziehen und Aderlassen kostet einem Sklaven weniger als einem Weissen... Armen wird alles umsonst geleistet."

1337. *Review:* Beyträge zur Geographie, Geschichte und Staatenkunde, herausg. v. J. E. Fabri u. s. f. Nürnberg: Bei Schneider u. Weigel, 1795. Viertes Stück 1795; Fünftes Stück 1796. 8°. (Allgemeine Literatur-Zeitung. Jena, 1796. 4°. Jahr 1796, Bd. 2, col. 548–550, *NAA.*)
Stück 5: Handel der Vereinigten Staaten von Nordamerika vom J. 1790 und 1793.

1338. *Review:* Faunae Insectorum Americes Borealis Prodromus, auctore G. W. F. Panzero... Norimbergae, 1794. 4°. (Neue allgemeine deutsche Bibliothek. Kiel, 1796. 8°. Bd. 23, p. 504, *NAA.*)

1339. *Review:* A geographical and historical Account of Bulam, by Andrew Johannsen. London, 1794. 43 p. 8°. (Allgemeine Literatur-Zeitung. Jena, 1796. 4°. Jahr 1796, Bd. 1, col. 66, *NAA.*)
The book contains excerpts from *View on the United States of America*, by Tench Coxe.
"Den Beschluss des Bandes macht eine Nachricht von der neuen Stadt Washington, und Morse's Aufsatz über die vornehmsten Religionspartheien in den amerikanischen Freystaaten..."
*See* no. 1404.

1340. *Review:* Geschichte und Beschreibung von Westindien. Ein Lesebuch zum Nutzen und Vergnügen für den Bürger und Landmann. Weissenfels: Bey Friedrich Severin, 1792. 12. Bd. 8°. (Neue allgemeine deutsche Bibliothek. Kiel, 1796. 8°. Bd. 22, p. 227, *NAA.*)
Also published under the title: Thomas Försters Erzählungen von seinen Reisen in allen Welttheilen. Bd. 6.

1341. *Review:* Graf Meaupois und seine Freunde. Eine französische Geschichte aus den Zeiten der Revolution. Zweyter und letzter Theil. Leipzig: Bey Voss und Compagnie, 1795. 277 S. 8°. (Neue allgemeine deutsche Bibliothek. Kiel, 1796. 8°. Bd. 25, p. 270–271, *NAA.*)
"Am Ende geht, was von der Gesellschaft sich retten konnte, über Hamburg nach Nordamerika."

1342. *Review:* The History of the District of Maine by James Sullivan. Boston: Andrews, 1795. 421 p. 8°. (Göttingische Anzeigen von gelehrten Sachen. Göttingen [1796]. 12°. Jahr 1796, p. 884–886, * *DF.*)
The Library's copies of this American work are in * KD.

1343. *Review:* J. J. C. Bode's literarisches Leben. Nebst dessen Bildniss von Lips. Berlin: Bey Lagarde, 1796. 8°. 144 S. (Neue Bibliothek der schönen Wissenschaften und der freyen Künste. Leipzig, 1796. 8°. Bd. 58, p. 93–102, *NAA.*)
Bode's "Westindier" mentioned on page 99.

1344. *Review:* A Journey from Prince of Wales's fort in Hudsonsbay to the Northern Ocean undertaken in the Years 1769, 1770, 1771 und 1772 by Samuel Hearne. London: B. Strahan u. Cadell, 1795. 458 p. 4°. (Allgemeine Literatur-Zeitung. Jena, 1796. 4°. Jahr 1796, Bd. 3, col. 601–606, *NAA.*)
The Library's copies of this English work are in † * *KF* and † *HBO.*

1345. *Review:* Karakteristisches Verzeichniss der vorzüglichsten, in Deutschland anzubauenden, einheimischen und nordamerikanischen wildwachsenden Holzarten, für Oekonomen, Forstbediente und Gärtner, bearbeitet von George August Scheppach. Dresden, 1791. 8°. 192 Seiten und 1 Tabelle. (Neues Forst-Archiv. Ulm, 1796. 8°. Bd. 1, p. 134, *VQN Forst.*)
See T. C. F. Enslin in *Bibliothek der Forst- und Jagd-Wissenschaft*, Leipzig, 1843, p. 56, *VQP.*

1346. *Review:* Eine kurze Reise in Westindien, mit verschiedenen Anekdoten und Charakterschilderungen. Aus dem Englischen. Manheim: B. Schwan u. Götz, 1796. 152 S. 8°. (Allgemeine Literatur-Zeitung. Jena, 1796. 4°. Jahr 1796, Bd. 2, col. 150–152, *NAA.*)

1347. *Review:* A memoir concerning the fascinating faculty, which has been ascribed to the rattlesnake and other american serpents, by Benj. Smith Barton. Philadelphia, 1796. 70 p. 8°. (Göttingische Anzeigen von gelehrten Sachen. Göttingen [1796]. 12°. Jahr 1796, p. 1959–1960, * *DF.*)
Appeared originally in the *Transactions* of the American Philosophical Society, v. 4, p. 74–113, * *EA*; the Library does not have a copy of this privately distributed issue (see Sabin 3816).

## GERMAN WORKS RELATING TO AMERICA  155

1796, continued

1348. *Review:* Neue Beyträge zur Völker- und Länderkunde herausg. von M. C. Sprengel und G. Forster. Leipzig: Kummer, 1793. Eilfter Theil 286 S. Zwölfter Theil 295 S. Dreyzehnter Theil 298 S. (Allgemeine Literatur-Zeitung. Jena, 1796. 4°. Jahr 1796, Bd. 2, col. 257–261, *NAA.*)
Theil 12, No. 11: "Bruchstücke zur Staatskunde des amerikanischen Freystaats im Auszuge aus dem Columbian Magazin und der Prüfung eines Ungenannten 1791 in Philadelphia über Lord Sheffields Darstellung des nordamerik. Handels."
See no. 1181B.

1349. *Review:* Nordamerikanische schwarze Wallnuss (Iuglans nigra L.). Joach. Frider. Plappart Dissertatio de Iuglande nigra. Viennae, 1777. 8°. mit Kupfern. (Neues Forst-Archiv. Ulm, 1795. 8°. Bd. 2, p. 32, *VQN Forst.*)

1350. *Review:* Official Letters to the Honourable American Congress, written during the War between the United Colonies and Great Britain by G. Washington. London: Cadell, 1795. 2 v. 8°. (Allgemeine Literatur-Zeitung. Jena, 1796. 4°. Jahr 1796, Intelligenzblatt, col. 939, *NAA.*)
See entries and notes of nos. 1328 and 1333.

1351. *Review:* Salomon Gessner von Johann Jacob Holtinger. Zürich: Bey Gessner, 1796. 270 S. 8°. (Neue Bibliothek der schönen Wissenschaften und der freyen Künste. Leipzig, 1796. 8°. Bd. 58, p. 325–345, *NAA.*)
Gessner's continuation of Bodmer's Inkel und Yariko is discussed on p. 332.

1351A. *Review:* Systematisches Verzeichniss derjenigen ausländischen, grösstentheils nordamerikanischen Bäume und Gesträuche, welche in dem amerikanischen Garten auf dem hochfürstlichen Gute Hohenheim befindlich sind, und daselbst im freyen Grund den Winter ausdauren [*sic!*]... Stuttgart, 1780. 16°. (Neues Forst-Archiv. Ulm, 1796. 8°. Bd. 1, p. 54, *VQN* [*Forst*].)
Hohenheim is located in the Duchy of Württemberg.

1352. *Review:* Ueber die Fieber in Jamaica. Aus dem Englischen übersezt, mit Anmerkungen und Zusätzen von Kurt Sprengel. 1796. 262 S. 8°. (Journal der Erfindungen, Theorien und Widersprüche in der Natur- und Arzneiwissenschaft. Gotha, 1796. 12°. Bd. 4, Intelligenzblatt XII, p. 40–41, *WAA.*)
The author's name is Robert Jackson.
See nos. 1262, 1402.

1353. *Review:* Ueber die Humanität. Von Ferdinand Delbrück: Magdeburg, 1795, 134 S. kl. 8°. (Neue Bibliothek der schönen Wissenschaften und freyen Künste. Leipzig, 1796. 8°. Bd. 58, p. 318–324, *NAA.*)
Franklin's society at Philadelphia is discussed on p. 321.

1354. *Review:* Ueber nordamerikanische Bäume und Sträucher... Mannheim, 1792. 7

Bogen. 8°. (Neues Forst-Archiv. Ulm, 1796. 8°. Bd. 1, p. 136, *VQN Forst.*)
"Diese...Abhandlung befindet sich auch im liten Bande der staatswirtschaftlichen Vorlesung der churpfälz. physikalisch-ökonomischen Gesellschaft zu Heidelberg."
See nos. 1154, 1263.

1355. *Review:* Ueber die Verläumdung der Wissenschaften. Eine poetische Epistel an Herrn Professor Garve von J. C. F. Manso, Leipzig: Dyck, 1796. 4°. (Neue Bibliothek der schönen Wissenschaften und der freyen Künste. Leipzig, 1796. 8°. Bd. 57, p. 302–343, *NAA.*)
Discusses the American revolution on p. 325.

1356. *Review:* Die wesentlichen Kennzeichen der deutschen und nordamerikanischen Holzarten und Forstkräuter, zum Gebrauch der Oekonomen und Förster von Hrn. von Moser. Leipzig: 1794. 158 Seiten und 3 Kupfertafeln. 8°. Zweyte verbesserte Auflage. Leipzig, 1795. 8° mit illuminirten Kupfern. (Neues Forst-Archiv. Ulm, 1796. 8°. Bd. 1, p. 34, *VQN Forst.*)
See also no. 1266.

### 1797

1357. Aus dem Tagebuche eines Reisenden, gleich nach Beendigung des Amerikanischen Krieges. (Allgemeines europäisches Journal. Brünn, 1797. 8°. [Jahr] 1797, Bd. 4, p. 102–119.) *DF
Shows the danger of travel on American roads.

1358. Auszüge aus Briefen. (Der Neue teutsche Merkur. Weimar, 1797. 12°. Jahr 1797, Bd. 2, p. 168–172.) *DF
The first letter concerning literature and entertainment in Philadelphia is dated: January 26th, 1797 and signed: S... It commences, "Die Menschen hier zu Lande haben etwas solideres zu thun, als Bücher zu schreiben und zu lesen."

1359–60. Auszug eines Briefes aus Philadelphia vom 11ten August 1794. (Neues Hannöverisches Magazin...vom Jahre 1797. Hannover, 1798. 4°. Jahrg. 7, col. 797–800.) *DF
Translated from the Swedish by Johann Georg Ludolph Blumhof of Göttingen, 1774–1825.
Accounts of Connecticut, Massachusetts, and New Hampshire.
Title page dated 1798; contents, 1797.

1361. Ein Besuch beym Präsidenten Washington. (Der Neue teutsche Merkur. Weimar, 1797. 12°. Jahr 1797, Bd. 2, p. 5–11.) *DF
Taken from Henry Wansey's *An excursion to the United States of North America in the summer of 1794.*
Translated from the English manuscript by Joh. Christ. H. Hüttner, 1766–1847.
See also no. 1387.

1362. Brissot de Warville, Jacques Pierre. ...Neue Reise in die vereinten Staaten von Nordamerika, gemacht im Jahr 1788 von dem französischen Bürger J. P. Brissot (de Warville) Theil 1–2. [Reutlingen: J. Grözinger,] 1797. 2 v. in 1. 12°.    *KF 1797
At head of title: Fortsetzung der Campischen Reisebeschreibungen für die Jugend. Theil 3–4.

*1797, continued*

**1362. BRISSOT DE WARVILLE, J. P.**, *continued*
Published originally under the title: Nouveau voyage dans les États-Unis... Paris, 1791, * KF.
The third volume is not included in this translation. The first German translation appeared in 1792; see no. 1124.
There are two other German translations extant: one by Alb. Cp. Kayser, Bayreuth: Zeitungsdr. Theil 1 and 2, 1792; Theil 3, 1793 (reviews in *Allgemeine Literatur-Zeitung*, Jahr 1793, Bd. 2, col. 693–694, *NAA*; *Neue allgemeine deutsche Bibliothek*, Bd. 9, p. 165–168, *NAA*). Another translation (Sabin 8038) by K. Jul. Friedrich, "mit der kurzen Lebensgeschichte des Verf. und mit einigen Zusätzen und Erläuterungen vermehrt von Thph. F. Ehrmann," appeared in Dürkheim: Bey Pfähler, 1792 (reviews in *Allgemeine Literatur-Zeitung*, Jahr 1793, Bd. 2, p. 693–694, *NAA*; *Neue allgemeine deutsche Bibliothek*, Bd. 9, p. 168–172, *NAA*; *Gothaische gelehrte Zeitungen*, Jahr 1792, Bd. 1, p. 86–93 (not in N. Y. P. L.); *Tübinger gelehrte Anzeigen*, Jahr 1793, p. 300 (not in N. Y. P. L.).
For the translation by J. R. Forster, Berlin, 1792, see no. 1124 (Sabin 8033), and for *Neue unveränderte Auflage*, Hof: G. A. Grau, 1796, see Sabin 8032.

**1363. BÜLOW, DIETRICH, FREIHERR VON.** Der Freistaat von Nordamerika in seinem neuesten Zustand, von D. von Bülow. Berlin: Bei Johann Friedrich Unger, 1797. 2 v. 8°. *KF 1797
Sabin 9149.
For a summary of the work, see P. C. Weber's *America in German imaginative literature*, 1926, p. 28–30: "From him [i.e. Bülow] and his work a powerful and persistent current, hostile to America, was set in motion, in public opinion as well as in imaginative literature;" see also note on no. 1387.
Reviews: See Ebeling's thorough criticism, first printed in *Beyträge von gelehrten Sachen, welche mit der Hamburgischen neuen Zeitung ausgegeben worden*, 1797, Stück 3 zu No. 112 (July 12th), and reprinted in *Amerikanisches Magazin*, Hamburg, Jahr 1797, Bd. 1, p. 172–184, *Reserve*; see also Archenholz in *Beyträge von gelehrten Sachen*... Jahr 1797, Febr. 1st.
Other reviews appear in: *Der Neue teutsche Merkur*, Jahr 1798, Bd. 1, p. 236–237, * *DF*; *Neue allgemeine deutsche Bibliothek*, Bd. 33, p. 487–501; Bd. 40, p. 422–429, *NAA*; *Göttingische Anzeigen von gelehrten Sachen*, Jahr 1797, Bd. 3, p. 1955–1960, * *DF*; *Oberdeutsche allgemeine Literatur Zeitung*, Jahr 1800, Bd. 2, p. 353–358 (not in N. Y. P. L.); *Nürnbergische gelehrte Zeitung*, Jahr 1797, p. 401–407 (not in N. Y. P. L.).
Note also *Der Freistaat von Nord-America; or The Free-State of North America*, described by D. von Bülow, noticed in *Philadelphia magazine and review*, Philadelphia, 1799, p. 224; and *Interesting travels in North America*. Translated from the German of Bulow, Philadelphia, 1801, in v. 2, p. 337.

**1364.** —— Noch ein paar Worte über America. (Minerva. Hamburg, 1797. 12°. Jahr 1797, Bd. 4, p. 540–551.) BAA
Dated: Hamburg den 1sten December 1797.

**1365. EINEM, JOHANN KONRAD VON.** Auf Franklin. Nach dem Französischen des du Bourg. (Musen Almanach, 1797. Göttingen: Bei J. C. Dieterich [1797]. 32°. p. 62.) NFA
"Dem Himmel raubt' er seine Blitze;
Er ist's, durch den die Kunst'in wilden Ländern blühn;
Ihn stellt Amerika an seiner Weisen Spitze:
Gezählet hätt' Athen zu seinen Göttern ihn."

**1366. FRANKLIN, BENJAMIN.** Erhöhung des Arbeitslohns in Europa; eine Folge des Wohlstandes von America. Ein aufgefundenes Manuscript Franklins. (Minerva. Hamburg, 1797. 12°. Jahr 1797, Bd. 1, p. 533–553.) BAA
A translation of Franklin's essay published in the *Journal d'oeconomie publique, de morale et de politique*, March, 1797.

**1367. FROHBERGER, CHRISTIAN GOTTLIEB.** Briefe über Herrnhut und die evangelische Brüdergemeine; nebst einem Anhange. Von Christian Gottlieb Frohberger... Budissin: Gedruckt bey G. G. Monse [1797]. 430, 136 p. 12°. ZXHC
"Brüdergemeinen in den vereinigten Staaten von Nordamerika," Anhang, Abschnitt 1, p. 32–39.
Also published with the imprint Bauzen: Schöps, 1797. See T. C. F. Enslin in *Bibliotheca theologica*, Stuttgart, 1833, p. 89, ZE.
Review: *Allgemeine Literatur-Zeitung*, Jahr 1798, Bd. 1, col. 145–148, *NAA*.

**1368. GESCHICHTE** des See Krieges in den Jahren 1796 und 1797. (Europäische Annalen. Tübingen, 1797. 8°. Jahrg. 1797, Bd. 3, p. 295–352.) BTA
A chapter on "West Indien," p. 316–323.

**1369. GROS BRITANNIEN.** (Europäische Annalen. Tübingen, 1797. 8°. Jahrg. 1797, Bd. 2, p. 247–312.) BTA
References to the West Indies.

**1370. GROS BRITANNIENS** Finanz Wesen vor und seit dem jezigen Kriege. (Europäische Annalen. Tübingen, 1797. 8°. Jahrg. 1797, Bd. 2, p. 109–142.) BTA
Debts incurred during the American revolutionary war, p. 121.

**1371. HEARNE, SAMUEL.** Reise von dem Prinz von Wallis-Fort an der Hudsons-Bay bis zu dem Eismeere in den Jahren 1769–1772. Aus dem Englischen übersetzt. Mit Anmerkungen von Johann Reinhold Forster... Berlin: Voss, 1797. 284 p., 1 folding plate. 8°. (Magazin von merkwürdigen neuen Reisebeschreibungen... Bd. 14.) KBC
Abridged translation of Hearne's *A Journey from Prince of Wales's Fort in Hudson's Bay, to the northern Ocean*... London, 1795, † *KF*.
Another translation, by Christian Matthias Sprengel (1746–1803), which is part of "Auswahl der besten ausländischen, geographischen und statistischen Nachrichten, zur Aufklärung der Völker- und Länderkunde," is listed under no. 1139A.
Reviews: *Der Neue teutsche Merkur*, Jahr 1798, Bd. 1, p. 236, * *DF*; *Allgemeine Literatur-Zeitung*, Jahr 1798, Bd. 4, col. 445–446; Jahr 1799, Bd. 3, col. 817–824, *NAA*; *Neue allgemeine deutsche Bibliothek*, Bd. 42, p. 469–478, *NAA*; *Oberdeutsche allgemeine Literatur Zeitung*, Jahr 1799, Bd. 2, p. 708–716; Jahr 1800, Bd. 1, p. 625–629 (not in N. Y. P. L.); *Nürnberger gelehrte Zeitung*, Jahr 1797, p. 793–799 (not in N. Y. P. L.); *Tübinger gelehrte Anzeigen*, Jahr 1798, p. 476–478 (not in N. Y. P. L.).

**1372. HERDER, JOHANN GOTTFRIED VON.** Briefe zu Beförderung der Humanität. Herausgegeben von J. G. Herder. Neunte[-Zehnte] Sammlung. Riga: Bei Johann Friedrich Hartknoch, 1797. (Reprinted in his: Sämmtliche Werke. Herausgegeben von Bernhard Suphan. Berlin: Weidmannsche Buchhandlung, 1877–1913. 8°. Bd. 18, p. 141–302.) NFG
Herder's aversion to sending German auxiliaries to America, p. 211. "Neger-Idyllen," p. 224–234. Many other allusions to the American aborigines, p. 223. Among the Neger-Idyllen, "Der Geburtstag" is of special importance. Walter Miflin, who acts as liberator of slaves, is an historical personality, the son of a governor of Pennsylvania. Fifteen years after Herder (1812), Kotzebue made him the hero of his drama, *Die Quaker*; see *German-American annals*, v. 6, p. 541, *NFA*. With regard to the "Neger-Idyllen," see also P. A. Shelley's "Crèvecœur's contribution to Herder's Neger-Idyllen," in the *Journal of English and Germanic philology*, v. 37, p. 48–69, *RKA*.
Herder's "Der deutsche Nationalruhm," originally intended for the *Humanitätsbriefe*, but doubtless withheld from publication for political reasons did not

*1797, continued*

appear before 1810. See his *Sämmtliche Werke*, ed. Suphan, v. 18, p. 208–211, *NFG*.

Und doch sind sie [the Germans] in ihrer
Herren Dienst
So hündisch treu! Sie lassen willig sich
Zum Mississippi und Ohio-Strom
Nach Candia und nach dem Mohrenfeld
Verkaufen. Stirbt der Sklave, streicht der
Herr
Den Sold Indess: und seine Witwe darbt.
Die Waisen ziehn den Pflug und hungern.
Doch
Das schadet nichts; der Herr braucht einen
Schatz.

See no. 1169.

1373. DES HERRN Saint-Jean de Creve-Coeur Abhandlung von der Kultur und der Benutzung des unächten Acazienbaums in den vereinigten Staaten von Nordamerika, welche in der öffentlichen Sitzung der königlichen Ackerbaugesellschaft zu Paris den 30ten März vorgelesen worden. (Neues Hannöverisches Magazin... vom Jahre 1797. Hannover, 1798. 4°. Jahrg. 7, col. 273–296.) *DF
Translated by Johann Georg Ludolph Blumhof of Göttingen, 1774–1825, from the *Mémoires de la Société royale d'agriculture de Paris*, 1786, trimestre d'hyver, p. 122 et seq.
Title page dated 1798; contents, 1797.

1374. LENZ, JAKOB MICHAEL REINHOLD. Der Waldbruder, ein Pendant zu Werthers Leiden von dem verstorbenen Dichter Lenz. (Reprinted in his: Gesammelte Schriften. Herausgegeben von Franz Blei. München und Leipzig: Georg Müller, 1909–13. 8°. Bd. 5, p. 107–146.) NFG
Appeared originally in: *Schillers Horen*, 1797, Bd. 10, Theil 4, p. 85–102; Bd. 11, Theil 5, p. 2–30.
"Eben erhalte ich einen wunderbaren Brief von einem Obristen in hessischen Diensten, der...mir eine Stelle als Adjutant bei ihm anträgt, wenn ich ihn nach Amerika begleiten will...dieser Sprung aus dem Schulmeisterleben auf die erste Staffel der Leiter der Ehre und des Glücks, ist Himmelsleiter, auf der ich alle meine Wünsche zu ersteigen hoffe..." — *p. 127*.
Cf. p. 128, 130, 137–138.
"Sie wollen das Schicksal des armen Herz wissen und was ihn zu einem so schleunigen und seltsamen Entschluss als der ist, nach Amerika zu gehen, hat bewegen können. Lieber Pfarrer, um das zu beantworten, muss ich...eine ziemlich weitläuftige Erzählung anfangen." — *p. 132*.

1375. LITERARISCHE Durchflüge. (Der Neue teutsche Merkur. Weimar, 1797. 12°. Jahr 1797, Bd. 1, p. 293–300.) *DF
References to Benjamin Franklin, p. 294–295.

1376. [MOREAU DE SAINT-MÉRY, MÉDÉRIC LOUIS ÉLIE.] Die nach englischen Grundsätzen verbesserte Pferdezucht in Amerika zur Nachahmung anderer Länder. Nebst einer Nachricht von den Sächsischen Stuttereien. Ein Lehrbuch für Pferdeliebhaber und Oekonomen. Leipzig: In Commission der Müllerschen Buchhandlung, 1797. xiv p., 1 l., 63 p. 17½cm. (8°.) *KF 1797
See Evans 29108.
"Vorrede des Verfassers" dated: Philadelphia, den 8. October 1795.
The French original appeared in Philadelphia, in 1795; in the same year the work was issued in an English translation.
See J. G. Rosengarten, *Moreau de Saint Méry and his French friends in the American Philosophical Society*, Philadelphia, 1911, *AN p.v.*116, no. 6.
See also no. 1437.
Review: *Allgemeine Literatur-Zeitung*, Jahr 1798, Bd. 1, col. 759–760, *NAA*.

1377. NEUESTE Geschichte des innern Frankreichs. (Europäische Annalen. Tübingen, 1797. 8°. Jahrg. 1797, Bd. 4, p. 22–74.) BTA
Relation between France and North America, p. 62.

1378. NOCH ein kleiner Beitrag zur Geschichte des Tabackrauchens. (Neues Hannöverisches Magazin...vom Jahre 1797. Hannover, 1798. 4°. Jahrg. 7, col. 669–673.) *DF
Deals with Professor Tapp's Latin oration, given as early as 1653, in which he tries to prove the detriment of smoking tobacco and laments the general indulgence in the custom.
Signed: v. R.
Title page dated 1798; contents, 1797.

1379. PRÜFUNG der Vortheile, welche die deutsche Forstwirthschaft durch den Anbau nordamerikanischer Holzarten zu erwarten hat. (Neues Hannöverisches Magazin...vom Jahre 1797. Hannover, 1798. 4°. Jahrg. 7, col. 129–154.) *DF
Signed: J. v. U—r.
Title page dated 1798; contents, 1797.

1380. ROYER, BARBAULT. Ueber den neuesten Zustand von St. Domingo. (Minerva. Hamburg, 1797. 12°. Jahr 1797, Bd. 1, p. 403–408.) BAA
Dated: Geschrieben im Januar 1797.
Barbault Royer was secretary to a French commission sent to Santo Domingo.

1381. RUSH, BENJAMIN. Nachricht von dem Zucker-Ahorn in den Nordamerikanischen Freystaaten, und von der Art und Weise, Zucker aus demselben zu erhalten... In einem Briefe an Thomas Jefferson...von Benjamin Rush... Philadelphia, 1792. (Neues Forst-Archiv. Ulm, 1797. 8°. Bd. 3, p. 49–88.) VQN (Forst)
"Anmerkungen des Herausgebers," p. 73–88.
"Dieser Aufsatz ist eine Uebersetzung der im 11ten Bande des Neuen Forstarchivs S. 35, § 30 angezeigten englischen Schrift."
See note of no. 1332.

1382. SCHICKSALE eines muhamedanischen Imam aus der Gegend des Gambra Flusses, und seine Gefangenschaft in Amerika und England. (Allgemeines europäisches Journal. Brünn, 1797. 8°. Jahr 1797, Bd. 10, p. 67–77.) *DF
Experiences of an Arabian Imâm, by the name of Job, in several states of America, as Maryland, Delaware, etc., and in England during the thirties of the eighteenth century. The report is based on Thomas Bluett's *Memoirs of the Life of Job, the Son of Solomon, the high Priest of Boonda in Africa*, London, 1734; a German translation appeared in 1747 as the third volume of *Allgemeine Historie der Reisen zu Wasser und zu Lande*, Buch VI, Cap. VII, *KBC*.

1383. TAFEL, zur Uibersicht des auswärtigen Handels der fränkischen Republik im Jahre 1796. (Europäische Annalen. Tübingen, 1797. 8°. Jahrg. 1797, Bd. 2, p. 91–95.) BTA
Imports of France from the United States, p. 93.

1384. UEBER die vermeinten alten Festungswerke in Nord-Amerika. (Der Neue teutsche Merkur. Weimar, 1797. 12°. Jahr 1797, Bd. 2, p. 50–58.) *DF
With a bibliography of books on whether there were "ancient works of art" in North America.
Signed: v. K.

*1797, continued*

1385. UIBER Belgien, besonders in Rücksicht auf den Handel... (Europäische Annalen. Tübingen, 1797. 8°. Jahrg. 1797, Bd. 2, p. 3-14.)
References to America, p. 10 and 11. BTA

1386. UIBER den Ursprung und die wahre Beschaffenheit der neuesten Weiterungen zwischen den Frei Staaten Frankreich und Nord Amerika. (Europäische Annalen. Tübingen, 1797. 8°. Jahrg. 1797, Bd. 4, p. 203-212.) BTA

1387. WANSEY, HENRY. Heinrich Wansey's Tagebuch einer Reise durch die vereinigten Staaten von Nord-Amerika, im Sommer des Jahres 1794. Aus dem Englischen. Mit Anmerkungen des Uebersetzers, und einer Vorrede über Auswanderung und Länderkauf in Nord-Amerika von C. A. Böttiger. Berlin: Voss, 1797. 220 p. 8°. (Magazin von merkwürdigen neuen Reisebeschreibungen... Bd. 14, Theil 2.) KBC
There is an "Anhang," entitled: Regeln für die Deutsche Gesellschaft in dem Staate von Neu York, Germantown 1787.
The introduction, dated Weimar, June the 15th, 1797, is of great value, as it contains a criticism of Bülow's work (*see* no. 1363) and a bibliography of literature on emigration. The book itself is a translation of Wansey's *The journal of an excursion to the United States of America, in the summer of 1794* ... Salisbury, 1797, * KF 1796.
This slightly abridged translation is by Johann Christ. Hüttner of London (1766-1847).
Reviews: *Allgemeine Literatur-Zeitung*, Jahr 1798, Bd. 4, col. 445-446; Jahr 1799, Bd. 3, col. 817-824, *NAA; Neue allgemeine deutsche Bibliothek*, Bd. 42, p. 469-478, *NAA; Oberdeutsche allgemeine Literatur-Zeitung*, Jahr 1799, Bd. 2, p. 708-716; Jahr 1800, Bd. 1, p. 625-629 (not in N. Y. P. L.); *Nürnberger gelehrte Zeitung*, Jahr 1797, p. 793-799 (not in N. Y. P. L.); *Tübinger gelehrte Anzeigen*, Jahr 1798, p. 476-478 (not in N. Y. P. L.).

1388. WICHTIGE Belehrung über Nordamerika überhaupt und über Pensilvanien insbesondere von L. J. Jardine, Doktor der Arzneiwissenschaft, in einem Schreiben an seinen Freund in England, aus dem Englischen übersetzt vom Prof. Leonhardi. (Allgemeines europäisches Journal. Brünn, 1797. 8°. Jahr 1797, Bd. 6, p. 27-35.) *DF
Dated: Burlington, Dec. 16th, 1794.
The announced continuation did not appear.

1389. *Review:* An Account of the Campaign in the West Indies 1794 — with the reduction of Martinique... by Caspar [*sic!*] Willyams. London: Nicol, 1797. 230 p. 4°. (Allgemeine Literatur-Zeitung. Jena, 1797. 4°. Jahr 1797, Intelligenzblatt, col. 1372-1373, *NAA.*)
The Library's copy of this work by Cooper Williams is in † *KF*.

1390. *Review:* The American Remembrancer, or an Impartial Collection of Essays, Resolves, Speeches, etc. relative to the Treaty with Great-brittain. Philadelphia: M. Carey, 1795. 3 v. 8°. (Göttingische Anzeigen von gelehrten Sachen. Göttingen [1797]. 12°. Jahr 1797, p. 1825-1829, *DF.*)
The Library's copies of this American collection are in *ICM (Great Britain)* and * *KD.*

1391. *Review:* Annalen der Arzneymittellehre. Herausgegeben von D. Joh. Jakob Römer. Ersten Bandes zweytes Stück. Leipzig: B. Schäfer, 1796. 207 Seiten. 8°. (Allgemeine Literatur-Zeitung. Jena, 1797. 4°. Jahr 1797, Bd. 2, col. 583, *NAA.*)
No. 9: "Von den beyden amerikanischen Gewächsen, der Agave americana und Begonia balmisiana als specifischen Mitteln gegen die Lustseuche."

1391A. *Notice:* Bálmis, Franz Xaver. Über die Amerikanischen Pflanzen... als zwey neuentdeckte specifische Mittel gegen die Lustseuche, Scropheln und andere dahin sich beziehende Krankheiten; aus dem Spanischen ins Italienische, aus diesem ins Deutsche übersetzt, nebst Anmerkungen von... Prof. Friedr. Ludw. Kreissig. Leipzig: Baumgärtner, 1797. 8° mit 2 Kupfern in folio. (Europäische Annalen. Tübingen, 1797. 8°. Jahrg. 1797, Bd. 3, Advertisement at end, *BTA.*)
Sabin 2982.
The established form of this author's name is Francisco Xavier de Bálmis. The Library has the original edition, *Demonstracion de los eficaces nuevamente descubiertas...*, 1794, * *KP.*

1392. *Review:* A concise and impartial History of the American Revolution. By John Lendrum. Boston, 1795. 2 v. 8°. (Göttingische Anzeigen von gelehrten Sachen. Göttingen [1797]. 12°. Jahr 1797, p. 1862-1863, * *DF.*)
The Library's copy of this English work is in * *KD.*

1393. *Review:* Geschichte des Revolutionskrieges in Sanct Domingo, von Bryan Edward. Aus dem Englischen. Theil 1... Leipzig: In der Dyckischen Buchhandlung, 1798. 220 p. 8°. (Göttingische Anzeigen von gelehrten Sachen. Göttingen [1797]. 12°. Jahr 1797, p. 2000, * *DF.*)
Sabin 21898.
An essay on Europe's interest in the welfare of the American colonies is added.

1394. *Review:* History of the Insurrection in the four western Counties of Philadelphia. in the Year 1794, by Will. Findley. Philadelphia, 1796. 328 p. 8°. (Göttingische Anzeigen von gelehrten Sachen. Göttingen [1797]. 12°. Jahr 1797, p. 1533-1536, * *DF.*)
The Library's copies of this English work are in *ISC* and * *KD.*

1395. *Review:* An historical Survey of the French Colony of the Island of St. Domingo comprehending a short Account of its political State, Productions and Export... By Bryan Edwards. London: Stockdale, 1797. 247 p. 4°. (Allgemeine Literatur-Zeitung. Jena, 1797. 4°. Jahr 1797, Intelligenzblatt, col. 1371-1372, *NAA.*)
Sabin 21894.
The Library's copy of this English work is in * *KF.*

1396. *Review:* An inaugural botanico-Medical Dissertation on the Phytolacca decandra of Linneus. By Benj. Schultz of Pensylvania. Philadelphia: Th. Dobson, 1795. 55 p., plate (in folio). 8°. (Göttingische Anzeigen von gelehrten Sachen. Göttingen [1797]. 12°. Jahr 1797, p. 1456, * *DF.*)
"Um der Seltenheit willen gedenken wir dieser Gelegenheitsschrift; auch als Beytrag zur Mat. med. americana. Der Verf. klagt über Mangel an Untersuchungen einheimischer Mittel in der neuen Welt, wie wir in der alten gegen die Einführung neuer Arzneymittel."

# GERMAN WORKS RELATING TO AMERICA

*1797, continued*

1396A. *Review*: A Message of the President of the united States to Congress relative to France and Great-Britain with the Papers therein referred to. Philadelphia, 1795. 291 p. 8°. (Gôttingische Anzeigen von gelehrten Sachen. Gôttingen [1797]. 12°. Jahr 1797, p. 1417–1421, *DF.)
The Library's copies of this compilation, catalogued under United States. — Department of State, are in * KD 1795.

1397. *Review*: A Narrative of the successful manner of cultivating the Clove tree, in the Island of Dominica, one of the windward Charibbee Islands. By W. Urb. Bruée... London, 1797. 31 p. 8°. (Gôttingische Anzeigen von gelehrten Sachen. Gôttingen [1797]. 12°. Jahr 1797, p. 1454–1456, *DF.)
Die "für die Statistik wichtige Schrift verdient um so mehr eine baldige Anzeige in unsern Blättern, da sie nicht in den Buchhandel kommt, sondern auf Veranstaltung des königl. geb. Conseil bloss für die Pflanzer im Britt. Westindien...gedruckt worden."
This work is not listed in the British Museum *Catalogue* under this author.

1398. *Review*: The proceedings of the Governor and Assembly of Jamaica in regard to the Maroon Negroes: published by order of the Assembly... London: Printed for J. Stockdale, 1796. lxxxix, 109 p. 8°. (Gôttingische Anzeigen von gelehrten Sachen. Gôttingen [1797]. 12°. Jahr 1797, p. 457–464, *DF.)
The Library's copy of these *Proceedings* is in * KF.

1399. *Review*: Quashy or the Coal-Black Maid. A Tale. By Captain Thomas Morris. 1796. 8°. 26 S. (Neue Bibliothek der schönen Wissenschaften und der freyen Künste. Leipzig, 1797. 8°. Bd. 60, p. 134–135, *NAA.*)
The Library's copy of this poem is in * KL.

1400. *Review*: Reliquiae houstounianae seu plantarum in america meridionali, a Guilielmo Houstoun. Nürnberg: Raspe, 1794. 42 S. 8°. (Allgemeine Literatur-Zeitung. Jena, 1797. 4°. Jahr 1797, Bd. 1, col. 188–189, *NAA.*)
The Library has the London, 1781, edition of this work (* KF), but not the later German edition.

1401. *Review*: Réponse aux principales questions qui peuvent être faites sur les états unis de l'Amerique, par un Citoyen des états unis. Lausanne: B. Vincent u. Laquiers, 1795. T. I, 311 S. ausser 82 S. Einleitung. T. II, 468 S. 8°. (Allgemeine Literatur-Zeitung. Jena, 1797. 4°. Jahr 1797, Bd. 3, col. 193–196, *NAA.*)
The Library's copy of this French work by J. E. Bonnet is in *IID*.

1402. *Review*: Robert Jackson über die Fieber in Jamaica. Aus dem Englischen übersetzt mit Anmerkungen und Zusätzen von Kurt Sprengel. Leipzig: b. Schäfer, 1796. 262 S. 8°. (Allgemeine Literatur-Zeitung. Jena, 1797. 4°. Jahr 1797, Bd. 4, col. 633–636, *NAA.*)
See nos. 1262, 1352.

1403. *Notice*: Some Information respecting America, collected by Thomas Cooper. London, 1795. 240 p. 8°. (Allgemeine Literatur-Zeitung. Jena, 1797. 4°. Jahr 1797, Bd. 3, col. 196–200, *NAA.*)
The *Allgemeines europäisches Journal*, Jahr 1797, Bd. 6, p. 28 (*BAA*), announces a German translation of the above for New Year, 1798.
The Library's copy of this English work is in *IID*. *Contents:* Letters from America to a friend in England. [Tables of American currency; prices duties, etc.]; Constitution of the United States. Extract from a work not yet published...entitled A view of the United States of America, by Tench Coxe. — Information to those who would remove to America, written some time since by Benjamin Franklin.

1404. *Review*: View of the united States of America in a Series of Papers written at various times between 1787 and 1794, by Tench Coxe. London, 1795. 512 p. 8°. (Allgemeine Literatur-Zeitung. Jena, 1797. 4°. Jahr 1797, Bd. 3, col. 196–200, *NAA.*)
The Library's copies of this English work are in * KF.
See also no. 1339.

## 1798

1405. ACTENSTÜCKE zur Geschichte der Unterhandlungen der amerikanischen Minister in Paris, mit der französischen Regierung im Jahr 1797. (Minerva. Hamburg, 1798. 12°. Jahr 1798, Bd. 2, p. 393–466; Bd. 3, p. 67–137, 234–302, 448–494.) BAA

1406. AMERIKANISCHE Staats-Papiere, den neulichen Aufenthalt und die Unterhandlungen der drei ausserordentlichen Abgesandten der vereinigten Frei Staaten in Paris betreffend. (Europäische Annalen. Tübingen, 1798. 8°. Jahrg. 1798, Bd. 2, p. 97–140.) BTA

1407. BÜLOW, DIETRICH, FREIHERR VON. Fragmente eines Briefes aus Lancaster in Pensylvanien, vom 16ten May 1798. (Minerva. Hamburg, 1798. 12°. Jahr 1798, Bd. 3, p. 166–177.) BAA

1408. —— Ueber die politische Lage von America. (Minerva. Hamburg, 1798. 12°. Jahr 1798, Bd. 3, p. 536–550.) BAA
A postscriptum by J. W. Archenholz is added. It contains his opinion on D. von Bülow's book (see no. 1363) and evaluates criticisms on it.

1409. —— Ueber Washingtons Briefe und N. Amerika. (Der Neue teutsche Merkur. Weimar, 1798. 12°. Jahr 1798, Bd. 2, p. 128–136.) *DF
Dated: Hamburg, Febr. 14th, 1798.
"The essay not only deals with the title subject, but is a self-defence of the author's work on America [see no. 1363]. Ebeling had charged Bülow with ignorance of the history and laws of the U. S. A., and had criticized him for having based his presentation of America more on personal experience and observation and for having made use of letters of Washington evidently fictitious [*see* no. 1328]. Bülow answers that the shadows in his picture of America were by no means dark enough, that, e.g. the climate in this country was much more unhealthy than he had indicated in his work." — *P. C. Weber, America in imaginative German literature, 1926, NFCX.*
Bülow continued his attacks against the United States in his essay "Despotismus in dem Freistaat Nordamerikas," which was published in Karl Ludwig von Woltmann's *Geschichte und Politik, eine Zeitschrift*, Berlin, 1800, p. 181 (not in the Library). In the same periodical, p. 112, another article derogatory to the leading statesmen of America, will be

*1798, continued*

**1409.** Bülow, Dietrich, Freiherr von, *cont'd*
found, viz., "Bemerkungen über die berühmtesten Männer des Freistaats Nordamerika." The author is a Mr. Kierrulf who resided in America for five years (1793–1798). He writes: "Kinder der Freiheit hoffte ich zu finden, aber betrogen sah ich mich bald in meiner frohen Erwartung. Habsucht, Selbstliebe und Unwissenheit waren die Pflanzen, die in diesem Boden der Freiheit üppig gewuchert hatten." See Hildegard Meyer, "Nord Amerika im Urteil des deutschen Schrifttums bis zur Mitte des 19. Jahrhunderts... Mit einer Bibliographie," in *Uebersee-Geschichte*, Hamburg, 1929, Bd. 3, *BAA*.

**1410.** Constitution der Batavischen Republik. (Europäische Annalen. Tübingen, 1798. 8°. Jahrg. 1798, Bd. 3, p. 285–344.) BTA
Many references to America.

**1411.** Die Constitutionen der neuesten Frei Staaten, in Vergleichung unter sich und mit der fränkischen. (Europäische Annalen. Tübingen, 1798. 8°. Jahrg. 1798, Bd. 3, p. 185–220.) BTA

**1412.** Cultur der Chemie. Die chemische Societät in Philadelphia... (Allgemeines Journal der Chemie. Leipzig, 1798. 4°. Bd. 1, p. 569.)
3-PKA

**1413.** Engel, Johann Jacob. Fürstenspiegel. Berlin: Mylius, 1798. 8°. (Reprinted in his: Schriften. Berlin: In der Myliusschen Buchhandlung, 1801–1806. 8°. Bd. 3.) NFG
In "Culturgrad," p. 154–165, the question of sending German auxiliaries to America is discussed.
"Princess Kunigunde watches from her window the sad parting of the soldiers bartered away by her father. She is moved to tears. At her next geography lesson she reproaches her teacher for giving her wrong information. He had taught her, she claims, that human beings were sold in Africa only, but now she knows that in Germany, too, human beings were sold for money. She cannot see the difference between the soldier traffic of her father and the slave trade carried on "von den afrikanischen Hungerleidern von Prinzen, die um eines geringen nichtswürdigen Gewinst willen das Blut ihrer Untertanen an ein fremdes Volk nach einem fremden Weltteil hin verkaufen."
*cf.* J. A. Walz in *Modern language notes*, Baltimore, 1901, v. 16, p. 349, *RAA*.

**1414.** Euphrasén, Bengt Anders. Herrn Bengt And. Euphraséns Reise nach der schwedisch-westindischen Jnsel St. Barthelemi, und den Jnseln St. Eustache und St. Christoph... Aus dem Schwedischen von Joh. Georg Lud. Blumhof... Göttingen: Bey Johann Christian Dieterich, 1798. vi, 308 p., 10 l. plates. 16°.
Sabin 23107. HRR 1798
See Amandus Johnson, *The Swedes in America, 1638–1900*, Philadelphia, 1914, *IEP*.

**1415.** Ferrer, Joseph Joachim von. Geographische Ortsbestimmungen. (Allgemeine geographische Ephemeriden. Weimar, 1798. 8°. Bd. 2, p. 393–400.) KAA
Ortsbestimmungen von New York, New Haven, &c.: Meerestiefen auf den Küsten des nördlichen Amerika, p. 395. Meerestiefen an der Küste von Nordamerika, p. 400.

**1416.** Das Gelbe Fieber. (Allgemeines Journal der Chemie. Leipzig, 1798. 4°. Bd. 1, p. 567.)
3-PKA
Discusses whether yellow fever does not originate in deteriorating remainders in storage houses.

**1417.** Gros Britannien. (Europäische Annalen. Tübingen, 1798. 8°. Jahrg. 1798, Bd. 1, p. 38–116.) BTA
References to America, p. 39.

**1418.** Gros Britannien und Frankreich in Bezug auf Nordamerika. (Europäische Annalen. Tübingen, 1798. 8°. Jahrg. 1798, Bd. 2, p. 140–153.) BTA

**1419.** Klinger, Friedrich Maximilian von. Geschichte eines Teutschen der neuesten Zeit. Leipzig: Bei Johann Friedrich Hartknoch, 1798. 568 p. 8°. (Reprinted in his: Werke. Leipzig: Verlag von Gerhard Fleischer, 1832. 8°. Bd. 8.)
NFG
Hadem, the broadminded, big hearted tutor of a young nobleman, is removed from his position on a trumped-up charge. He enlists as chaplain of a German regiment about to sail for America. Ernst, his pupil, who dearly loved Hadem, goes to Paris to complete his education. "Franklin war um diese Zeit in Paris. Ernst hatte das Glück, diesem seltenen Manne zu gefallen und von ihm geachtet zu werden. Als sich dieser nun zu seiner Abreise fertig machte, bat ihn Ernst um die Bestellung eines Briefes an Hadem, von dem er den edlen Greis so oft unterhalten hatte. Franklin versprach ihm, wenn Hadem in dem ungeheuren Bezirke von Amerika lebte, so sollte er diesen Brief gewiss bekommen..." Later Ernst receives a note from Franklin with a letter from Hadem enclosed: "er habe den jungen deutschen Mann auch in Amerika nicht vergessen, seinen Auftrag erfüllt und sende ihm hiermit einen Beweis davon." — *J. A. Walz in Modern language notes, Baltimore, 1901, v. 16, p. 173–174, RAA.*
"Abscheu vor dem Soldatenhandel deutscher Fürsten und dem Elend der gesellschaftlichen und familiären Verhältnisse in Europa bewegt...den Feldprediger Hadem nach seiner Heimkunft aus dem amerikanischen Kriege zusammen mit seinem Zögling Ernst v. Falkenberg, dem die Fäulnis des europäischen Wesens fast das Herz zerfressen hat, dem Vaterlande zum zweitenmale und für immer den Rücken zu kehren." — *G. Descryk, in Deutsch-amerikanische historische Gesellschaft von Illinois. Jahrbuch. 1924–1925, p. 45, IEK.*

**1420.** Klopstock, Friedrich Gottlieb. Zwey Nordamerikaner. 1795. (In his: Werke. Leipzig: Bei Georg Joachim Göschen, 1798–1817. 8°. Bd. 2, p. 223–224.) NFW
"Wer an dem Frühlingsmorgen der neugeborenen Freyheit
Meine Freuden empfand,
Der allein und kein anderer fühlt den innigen Schmerz auch,
Welcher jetzo die Seele mir trübt."
"Two Americans deplore the bloodthirsty nature of the French revolution, being introduced as citizens of a republic where liberty did not become wantonness." — *J. T. Hatfield and E. Hochbaum, The influence of the American Revolution upon German literature, New York, [1900?], p. 45, NFC p.v.4.*

**1421–22.** Kotzebue, August von. Die Verwandtschaften. Ein Lustspiel in fünf Aufzügen. Erschien 1798. (In his: Theater. Wien: Jn Commission bey Anton Doll, 1810–19. 16°. Bd. 9, p. 105–186.) NGC
"Halbe Amerikaner sind auch die Kaufleute, die wie (Louis Sebastien] Merciers *L'habitant de Guadeloupe* [for an English translation see *NCO p.v.74*] von den reichen Inseln mit gefüllter Börse heimkehren, deren Jnhalt sie zunächst verheimlichen und dann zur Belohnung der Tugend und Bestrafung des Lasters verwenden. Georg von Reinbeck versucht als erster diesen Stoff für die deutsche Bühne zu gewinnen (1796 *Der Virginier*) [not in the Library] nach ihm Kotzebue (1798 *Die Verwandtschaften*)." — *Gerhard Descryk in Deutsch-amerikanische historische Gesellschaft von Illinois, Jahrbuch, Chicago, 1924–25, IEK.*

*1798, continued*

1423. MARSH, HERBERT. Wer ist Fox, der Staatsmann? (Der Neue teutsche Merkur. Weimar, 1798. 12°. Jahr 1798, Bd. 2, p. 271-285.)
\* DF
The letter, arguing against Archenholz, is dated: Leipzig, May 22, 1798; Archenholz had attacked Marsh in the April issue of his *Minerva*, Jahr 1798, p. 188. Discusses, with reference to G. R. Harper's *Observations on the dispute between the United States and France*, Philadelphia and Dublin, 1798 (*KF 1798*) and writings, by John Erskine (see *KF*), the war between the United States and France, 1798-1800, and how far Charles Fox was instrumental. Herbert Marsh, B.D., was Fellow of St. John's College, Cambridge, translated and edited one of J. D. Michaelis's theological works into English. See notice in *American monthly review*, Philadelphia, 1795, v. 3, p. 304.

1424. PATJE, CHRISTIAN LUDWIG ALBRECHT. Ueber die Entbehrung ausländischer Bedürfnisse. (Neues Hannöverisches Magazin...vom Jahre 1798. Hannover, 1799. 4°. Jahrg. 8, col. 1591-1604.)
\* DF
Title page dated 1799; contents, 1798.
Concerns imports from America.

1425. SCHILLER, JOHANN FRIEDRICH. Nadowessiers Totenlied. (Reprinted in his: Sämmtliche Werke. Stuttgart: Cotta, 1860. 16°. Bd. 1, p. 207-209.)
NFGV
Appeared originally in *Musen Almanach für das Jahr 1798*, Tübingen 1798, p. 237.
As to Goethe's, Schiller's, and Herder's opinion on the poem, see *Der Briefwechsel zwischen Schiller und Goethe, hrsg. von H. G. Graef und Albert Leitzmann*, Leipzig, 1912, Theil 1, p. 354, 357, 358, 360, 361, 365.
See also *Der Teutsche Merkur*, Weimar, 1780, Jahr 1780, Bd. 3, p. 77, \* DF.
The source for the poem is Jonathan Carver's *Reisen*. See no. 642.
In Theil 2, p. 26-30 of the *Briefwechsel* Goethe describes, in his letter to Schiller of Jan. 26, 1798, a poem by Erasmus Darwin, entitled, "The Botanic Garden, London, 1791." He mentions "Doktor Franklin's Erfindung, dem Gewitter seine Blitze zu nehmen," the "Freiheit Amerikas, Irlands, Frankreichs" and the "Zerstörung von Mexico." — *p. 28.*

1426. SCHREIBEN des Herrn Hofrath Blumenbach an den Herausgeber über die Lage von Schekomeko in Nordamerika. (Allgemeine geographische Ephemeriden. Weimar, 1798. 8°. Bd. 1, p. 353-354.)
KAA
Schekomeko is located on the Hudson, "eine kleine Tagesreise von Rheinbeck, nicht weit von Livingstone."
The article states that this Indian name of a place near Rhinebeck on the Hudson River is on no map of that period; even people who were near it, did not know the name. There had been a house of missionaries there. Cranz, Spangenberg, and Loskiel mention it. But at the time the article was written, both the Indians and the missionaries had abandoned the place.
See Friedrich Kapp, *Die Deutschen im Staate New York während des achtzehnten Jahrhunderts*, Leipzig, 1884 (Geschichtsblätter, Bilder und Mittheilungen aus dem Leben der Deutschen in Amerika. Bd. 1, *IEK*). See especially Zehntes Kapitel: Die Herrnhuter in Schekomeko, p. 200-220.

1427. TRIESNECKER, FRANZ VON [DE PAULA]. Zweyter Nachtrag zu den geographischen Längen Bestimmungen aus beobachteten Sonnen-Finsternissen und Stern-Bedeckungen. (Allgemeine geographische Ephemeriden. Weimar, 1798. 8°. Bd. 1, p. 532-541.)
KAA
Relating to the longitude of Cambridge, Mass. (Sonnenfinsternis d. 3. April 1791). See also *Allgemeine geographische Ephemeriden*, Bd. 3, p. 161, *KAA*.

1428. UEBER den Anbau des Zuckerahorns, zu Beantwortung der Frage: ob er in Deutschland möglich sey, oder ob man mit der Anpflanzung Versuche gemacht habe, und welches der Erfolg gewesen sey? (Neues Forst-Archiv. Ulm, 1798. 8°. Bd. 4, p. 230-233.)
VQN (Forst)
Signed: St...l in Z.
Excerpt from *Reichsanzeiger*, August, 1796, p. 5519-5521.
Note also *Goldgrube Deutschlands, oder durch welche inländische Erzeugnisse kann der fremde Kaffee, Thee und Zucker möglichst ersetzt werden? Und was ist insbesondere von der Zuckerbereitung aus Runkelrüben und Ahornbäumen zu erwarten?* Berlin, 1799; F. W. Kühne, *Ueber den Zuckerahornbaum, und die leichte Methode, wie man Zucker aus seinem Safte verfertigt, und von den grossen Vortheilen, welche die Anpflanzung dieses Baumes darbietet*, Altenburg, 1801; Graf von C. F. Sponeck, *Ueber den Anbau und die forstliche Behandlung des wein- und spitzblättrigen Ahorns, mit Rücksicht auf Zuckerbenutzung*, Mannheim, 1811; Theodor von Walberg, *Ueber der Cultur und Benutzung des in- und ausländischen Ahornbaums, zur Gewinnung des Saftes zum Rohzucker in den österreichischen Staaten*, Wien, 1810; F. Wehrs, *Der Ahornzucker*, Hannover, 1814 (reprinted from his *Neue ökonomisch-technologische Entdeckungen*, Hannover, 1812). None of these titles is in the Library.

1429. WAS ist Volkssouveränität? (Der Neue teutsche Merkur. Weimar, 1798. 12°. Jahr 1798, Bd. 2, p. 232-242.)
\* DF
References to North America.

1430. *Review:* The case of the manufacturers of soap and candles, in the city of New York, stated and examined. Published by the Association of Tallow Chandlers and soap Makers. New York, 1797. 61 S. 8°. (Allgemeines Journal der Chemie. Leipzig, 1798. 4°. Bd. 1, p. 325-326, *3-PKA.*)
The Library catalogues this pamphlet under the author's name, S. L. Mitchill, \* *KD 1797*.

1431. *Review:* Essay de Comparaison entre la France et les Etats-Unis de l'Amerique septentrionale par Mr. E. A. W. de Zimmermann... Traduit de l'Allemand...par l'Auteur meme. v. 1. n. p.: Bey Heinicke und Hinrichs, 1797. 494 p. 8°. (Göttingische Anzeigen von gelehrten Sachen. Göttingen, 1798. 12°. Jahr 1798, p. 127-128. \* *DF.*)
The Library's copy of the French edition of Zimmermann's work is in \* *KF*. For the German translation of the work itself, see no. 1286.

1432. *Review:* Howards praktisches System auf die Gefängnisse in Philadelphia angewandt, zum Besten der Menschheit und als Beyspiel für andere Staaten. Aus dem Englischen übersetzt. Leipzig: Bei Hilscher, 1797. 132 p. 8°. (Allgemeine Literatur-Zeitung. Jena, 1798. 4°. Jahr 1798, Bd. 4, col. 796-799, *NAA.*)
A thorough review of "Howard" appeared as late as 1801 in *Neue allgemeine deutsche Bibliothek*, Jahr 1801, Bd. 61, p. 255-260, *NAA*.
See no. 1470.

1433. *Review:* An inaugural dissertation on the operation of pestiential fluids within the large testines, termed by Nosologists Dysentery. Submitted to the public examination, by W. Bay. New York: Swords, 1797. 109 S. in 8°. (Allgemeines Journal der Chemie. Leipzig, 1798. 4°. Bd. 1, p. 325, *3-PKA.*)
"Eine Fortsetzung der Saltonstall'schen Abhandlung [i.e., Winthrop Saltonstall's *An inaugural dissertation on the chemical and medical history of septon...*, New York, 1796]. Am Ende befinden sich auch Briefe von Mitchill über einen ähnlichen Gegenstand."

*1798, continued*

**1434.** *Review:* The Massachuset [*sic!*] Magazine. Boston: J. Adams and E. T. Andrews, 1789–1796. 8 v. (Göttingische Anzeigen von gelehrten Sachen. Göttingen [1798]. 12°. Jahr 1798, p. 525–527, \**DF.*)
The Library's file of the *Massachusetts magazine* is in \* *KSD*, Isaiah Thomas and Ebenezer T. Andrews were the original publishers.

**1435.** *Review:* Memoirs of the Medical Society of London. v. IV. London: C. Dilly, 1795. 447 p., 5 pl. 8°. (Göttingische Anzeigen von gelehrten Sachen. Göttingen [1798]. 12°. Jahr 1798, p. 585–595, \* *DF.*)
Articles by Js. Senter of Philadelphia, Dr. Hubbard of New Haven, Connecticut, and Dr. J. Warren of Boston, are treated.

**1436.** *Review:* Précis sur l'établissement des Colonies de Sierra Léona et Bonlama à la côte occidentale de l'Afrique. Par C. B. Wadström. Paris, 1798. (Allgemeine geographische Ephemeriden. Weimar, 1798. 8°. Bd. 1, p. 653–662, *KAA.*)
Relates to American slavery.
The Library's copy of this French work is in *Reserve.*

**1437.** *Review:* A topographical and political description of the Spanish part of Saint-Domingo ... by M. L. E. Moreau de St. Mery. Translated by W. Corbett. Philadelphia, 1796. 2 v. (Allgemeine geographische Ephemeriden. Weimar, 1798. 8°. Bd. 1, p. 570–575, *KAA.*)
The Library's copies of this work by M. L. E. Moreau de Saint-Méry, are in the Schomburg Collection, *971.294-M.*
See no. 1376.

**1438.** *Review:* A Treatise on the Yellow Fever as it appeared in the Island of Dominica in the Years 1793–1796...and some other West India Diseases, also the chemical Analysis and medical Properties of the hot Mineral Waters in the same Islands. By James Clarke... London, 1797. 168 p. 8°. (Göttingische Anzeigen von gelehrten Sachen. Göttingen [1798]. 12°. Jahr 1798, p. 777–781, \* *DF.*)

**1439.** *Review:* Voyage de La Pérouse autour du Monde... Par Milet-Mureau. A Paris, 1798. Theil 1–4. (Allgemeine geographische Ephemeriden. Weimar, 1798. 8°. Bd. 2, p. 35–50, *KAA.*)
Accounts of California.
The Library's copies of this French work, catalogued under J. F. de G. / comte de Lapérouse, are in \* *KF.*
*See also* no. 1450.

**1440.** *Review:* A Voyage of discovery to the North Pacific Ocean and round the World... under the command of Captain George Vancouver. (Allgemeine geographische Ephemeriden. Weimar, 1798. 8°. Bd. 2, p. 330–349, *KAA.*)
Relating to the Northwest Coast of North America.
The Library's copies of this English work are in \* *KF.*
For a German translation, *see* no. 1456; *also* no. 1471.

*1799*

**1441.** AUSZUG aus einem Briefe über das Neu-Jerseyer Kupferbergwerk das zehen Englische Meilen von New-York liegt. (Gesellschaft Naturforschender Freunde zu Berlin. Neue Schriften. Berlin, 1799. 8°. Bd. 2, p. 361.)
Dated: Oct. 25th, 1795. 3–\* *EE*
"Mitgetheilt von dem Herrn Bergrath Becher zu Dillenburg."

**1442.** BUACHE, PHILIPPE. Ueber die Entdeckungen, welche im Grossen Ocean oder Süd-Meere zu machen sind. (Allgemeine geographische Ephemeriden. Weimar, 1799. 8°. Bd. 3, p. 329–347.) *KAA*
Relates to the northwestern coast of America.

**1443.** BÜLOW, CARL VON. Berichtigung. (Minerva. Hamburg, 1799. 12°. Jahr 1799, Bd. 3, p. 190–192.) *BAA*
Pertains to Dietrich von Bülow's letter; see *Minerva,* Jahr 1798, Bd. 3, p. 166–177 (no. 1407).

**1444.** DONNANT, DENIS-FRANÇOIS. Azakia, eine Canadische Geschichte. (Minerva. Hamburg, 1799. 12°. Jahr 1799, Bd. 3, p. 170–184.) *BAA*
*See* no. 778.

**1445.** ETWAS über westindischen und deutschen Kaffee. (Neues Hannöverisches Magazin... vom Jahre 1799. Hannover, 1800. 4°. Jahrg. 9, col. 1289–1292.) \* *DF*
Recommends innocuous German coffee instead of West Indian coffee, which is considered detrimental to health.
Signed: Dr. Roebler, Rudolstadt.
Title page dated 1800; contents, 1799.

**1446.** GELBES Fieber; und chemische Charakteristik des männlichen und weiblichen Geschlechts. (Allgemeines Journal der Chemie. Leipzig, 1799. 4°. Bd. 3, p. 124–125.) 3–PKA
An essay in *Allgemeines Journal der Chemie,* Bd. 1, p. 567, is continued in a humorous vein; *see* no. 1416.

**1447.** JANISCH, DANIEL. Das achtzehnte Jahrhundert; eine Satyre. (Deutsche Literaturdenkmale des 18. und 19. Jahrhunderts. Berlin, 1901. 12°. No. 91–104 [Neue Folge No. 41–54], p. 473–508.) NFF (Deutsche)
No. 91–104 have separate title: Die Deutschen Säcularidichtungen an der Wende des 18. und 19. Jahrhunderts. Herausgegeben von August Sauer.
Janisch's satire originally appeared in *Diogenes-Laterne,* Leipzig, 1799, p. 1–110.
"Den sich mit eigener Hand Europa's Genius selbst schuf,
glücklicher Phocion deines Amerika, einziger Weiser,
Franklin! Heil! du erfandest, ein in besserer Salmoneus,
Gegenmittel der grauszerstörenden Rache des Himmels,
und bedecktest die Hütten der armen Menschen weit mehr als
ehernen Schilden, mit Blitzableitern gegen den Donner.
O dass dein genialischer Geist ein Mittel ersonnen,
auch die moralischen Ungewitter der Rauh- und der Habsucht
und der unseligen Zwiste der Völker, wie der Parteyen,
und des allvergiftenden Luxus verderbliche Folgen abzuleiten! du hättest den selbstgeschaffenen Freystaat
unerschütterlich dann gegründet, *der jetzo schon anfault.*" — *p. 505–506.*

*1799, continued*

1448. JANISCH, DANIEL. Wünsche an das neunzehnte Jahrhundert: eine satyrisch-sentimentalische Apostrophe. (Deutsche Litteraturdenkmale des 18. und 19. Jahrhunderts. Berlin, 1901. 12°. No. 91-104 [Neue Folge No. 41-54], p. 509-530.) NFF (Deutsche)
No. 91-104 have separate title: Die Deutschen Säculardichtungen an der Wende des 18. und 19. Jahrhunderts. Herausgegeben von August Sauer.
Janisch's satire originally appeared in *Diogenes-Laterne,* Leipzig, 1799, p. 111-172.

"Und du, o schmählich-unterjochte einst,
nun freygestrittene Columbia!
dass du die edlen Washington's nicht kränkest!
dass Franklin's Name dir stets theuer sey,
und theuer seiner Sprüche goldne Wahrheit!
Nie locke dich Brittanien ins Joch
zurück. Doch zoll' auch keinen Dollar nur
an deine Räuber-Schwester, Gallien.
Traun! Wahre der erstrebten Freyheit, wahre.
Wenn dann die Tugend tief gewurzelt ist:
dann ruf' die Musen und die Charitinnen
in deine Comtoire! dann veredele
die stärkste Freybeit durch die schönen Künste!
Der Irokese, der Hurone komm'!
und sonn' und wärme sich an deinem Licht,
des bessern Menschen-Lebens sich mitfreuend." — *p. 529.*

In the same collection two poems (nos. 17, 18 respectively) by Johann Jsaak Freiherr von Gerning (1767-1837), relating to Washington and Franklin, are noteworthy. They were, however, not published before 1801, 1802 respectively.

1449. [KOEHLER, ANDREAS RUDOLF.] Beschreibung des Hallischen Waisenhauses und der übrigen damit verbundenen Frankischen Stiftungen nebst der Geschichte ihres ersten Jahrhunderts... Halle: Im Verlage der Waisenhaus Buchhandlung, 1799. xvi, 214 p., 2 l. map. illus. 8°. SHS (Hallisches)
Refers to American congregations on p. vi and vii.

1450. LAPÉROUSE, JEAN FRANÇOIS DE GALAUP, COMTE DE. La Perouse'ns Entdeckungsreise in den Jahren 1785, 1786, 1787 und 1788 herausgegeben von M. C.-A. Milet-Mureau. Aus dem Französischen übersetzt und mit Anmerkungen begleitet von J. R. Forster und C. L. Sprengel. Berlin: Voss, 1799-1800. 2 v. plates (part folding). 8°. (Magazin von merkwürdigen neuen Reisebeschreibungen... Bd. 16, 17.) KBC
As to the bibliography of this work see the Société de géographie, *Bulletin,* Paris, 1888, série 7, tome 9, p. 325-351; this translation is listed under no. 85.
See also no. 1439.

1451. LA ROCHEFOUCAULD LIANCOURT, FRANÇOIS ALEXANDRE FRÉDÉRIC, DUC DE. De la Rochefoucauld Liancourt Reisen in den Jahren 1795, 1796 und 1797 durch alle an der See belegenen Staaten der Nordamerikanischen Republik; imgleichen durch Ober-Canada und das Land der Irokesen. Nebst zuverlässigen Nachrichten vom Unter-Canada. Aus der französischen Handschrift übersetzt... Hamburg: Bei Benjamin Gottlob Hoffmann, 1799. 3 v. 8°. (Neuere Geschichte der See- und Land-Reisen. Bd. 9-11.) *KF 1789 Neuere
Sabin 39058.
La Rochefoucauld's "Voyage" was originally published at Paris in 1799. *KF.
Reviews: *Allgemeine Literatur-Zeitung,* Jahr 1800, Bd. 4, col. 17-23, 25-32, *NAA; Neue allgemeine deutsche Bibliothek,* Bd. 49, p. 163-169, *NAA;*

*Gothaische gelehrte Zeitungen,* Jahr 1798, Bd. 2, p. 931-935; Jahr 1799, Bd. 1, p. 195-199 (not in N. Y. P. L.); *Der Neue teuttsche Merkur,* Jahr 1799, Bd. 1, p. 279-280, *DF; Erlangische gelehrte Zeitung,* Jahr 1799, Bd. 1, p. 95-96 (not in N. Y. P. L.).
See no. 1507.

1452. MERKWÜRDIGER Scheintod. (Athenaeum. Berlin, 1799. 8°. Bd. 2, p. 336.) *DF
This humorous little note about the *Berlinische Monatsschrift* shows how the Romantic Movement criticised Benjamin Franklin.

1453. NEW-BARBADOES-NECK in der Provinz New-Jersey in Nord America. (Gesellschaft naturforschender Freunde zu Berlin. Neue Schriften. Berlin, 1799. 8°. Bd. 2, p. 357-360.)
Dated: March 29th, 1795. 3-*EE
"Mitgetheilt von dem Herrn Bergrath Becher zu Dillenburg."

1454. TAURINIUS, ZACHARIAS. Beschreibung einiger See- und Landreisen nach Asien, Afrika und Amerika...von einem gebohrnen Aegyptier Zacharias Taurinius. Mit einer Vorrede von Johann Jacob Ebert, Professor in Wittenberg. Leipzig: Bey Friedrich Gotthold Jacobäer, 1799-1800. 2 v. 20½ cm. BKD
A fictitious voyage, written in collaboration with a certain "Magister Judge," who also assisted the author in compiling two other fictitious voyages published under titles: 1. See- und Landreise nach Ostindien und Aegypten (etc.) in den Jahren 1795-1799. Von Joseph Schrödter. Leipzig: Wolf und Compagnie, 1800; 2. Christian Friedrich Damberger Landreise in das Innere von Afrika (etc.). In den Jahren 1781 bis 1797. Zwey Theile... Leipzig: Martini, 1801.
Review: *Neue allgemeine deutsche Bibliothek,* Bd. 58, p. 442-459, *NAA,* in which the similarity between Taurinius's and the fictitious voyages of de la Porte is observed, and Professor Ebert is challenged to prove that the voyage was actually made.

1455. UEBER die Art und Weise, beim Mahlen das feinste und schönste Mehl zu erhalten, nach dem Verfahren der geschicktesten Müller in Amerika. (Neues Hannöverisches Magazin... vom Jahre 1799. Hannover, 1800. 4°. Jahrg. 9, col. 1517-1532, 1565-1604.) *DF
"Zur Beherzigung für die Müller und gesammte Publikum in Deutschland aus dem Englischen übersetzt von J. H. M. Poppe."
Translation of the fourth part of Oliver Evans's *The young mill-wright and miller's guide,* Philadelphia, 1795.
Title page dated 1800; contents, 1799.
Evidence of continued German interest in American flour mills are the following works: *Beiträge zur Kenntniss des amerikanischen Mühlenwesens und der Mehlfabrikation,* Berlin, 1832, and atlas (Sabin 4383); J. C. Leuchs, *Beschreibung und Abbildung der verbesserten amerikanischen Malmühlen. Nebst Angabe der Erfindungen im Mühlenbau seit den letzten 30 Jahren,* Nürnberg, 1828; *Ueber die Einrichtung der amerikanischen Mühlen und die Verfahrungsart bei der Mehlbereitung in denselben,* München, 1837. These are not in the Library.

1456. VANCOUVER, GEORGE. George Vancouvers Reisen nach dem nördlichen Theile der Südsee während der Jahre 1790 bis 1795. Aus dem Englischen übersetzt und mit Anmerkungen begleitet von Joh. Friedrich Wilh. Herbst. Berlin: Voss, 1799. 2 v. 8°. (Magazin von merkwürdigen neuen Reisebeschreibungen... Bd. 18, 19.) KBC
Translation of Vancouver's *A voyage of discovery to the north Pacific Ocean and round the world...* London, 1798, † *KF 1798.
For a German review of this original English edition, see no. 1440.

*1799, continued*

1457. VOM Herrn G. N. Lutgens zu Lutgenhude, Luzern-County, Wilkesbarre in Pensilvanien an den Herrn Oberforstmeister v. Burgsdorf. (Gesellschaft naturforschender Freunde zu Berlin. Neue Schriften. Berlin, 1799. 8°. Bd. 2, p. 362–369.)   3–* EE
Dated: June 17th, 1798.
A settler tells about trees and plants.
Sabin (42741) lists his *Etwas über den gegenwärtigen Zustand der Auswanderungen und Ansiedlungen im Staate von Pennsylvanien*, Hamburg, 1796. Not in the Library. See also Kayser, v. 1, p. 613B.

1458. ZIMMERMANN, [EBERHARD AUGUST WILHELM VON.] Bruchstück aus "Frankreich und die Freistaaten von Nordamerika, verglichen in Hinsicht ihrer Länder, Bewohner etc." (Der Neue teutsche Merkur. Weimar, 1799. 12°. Jahr 1799, Bd. 2, p. 39–48.)   * DF
*See* no. 1286. This excerpt does not deal with America.

1459. *Review:* Albert der Selbstmörder. Gotha: Bey Eltinger, 1798. 226 S. 8°. (Neue allgemeine deutsche Bibliothek. Berlin, 1799. 8°. Bd. 24, p. 58–59, *NAA.*)
Signed: Zb.
The main character of this novel instead of committing suicide, as the title makes believe, goes to America where George Washington embraces him as a sign of welcome.

1460. *Review:* Beiträge zur Philosophie und Geschichte der Religion und Sittenlehre überhaupt, und der verschiedenen Glaubensarten und Kirchen insbesondere. Herausgegeben von C. F. Stäudlin. Fünfter Band. Lübeck: Bey J. F. Bohn, 1799. 407 p. 8°. (Göttingische Anzeigen von gelehrten Sachen. Göttingen [1799]. 12°. Jahr 1799, p. 916–918, * DF.)
The Beiträge contain: Nachrichten zur Religionsgeschichte aus de la Rochefoucauld Liancourt Reisen durch die an der See gelegenen Staaten der Nordamericanischen Republik, imgleichen durch Ober-Canada und das Land der Irokesen.
*See* no. 1451.

1461. *Review:* Benjamin Smith Bartons... Abhandlung über die vermeinte Zauberkraft der Klapperschlange und anderer amerikanischer Schlangen. (Neue allgemeine deutsche Bibliothek. Kiel, 1799. 8°. Bd. 46, p. 144–149, *NAA.*)
*See* no. 1462 and note on no. 1347.

1462. *Review:* Benjamin Smith Barton's... Abhandlungen über die vermeynte Zauberkraft der Klapperschlange und anderer amerikanischen Schlangen... Aus dem Englischen übersetzt, mit einer Einleitung und erläuternden Anmerkungen versehen von E. A. W. Zimmermann... Leipzig: Reinicke und Hinrichs, 1798. xxiv, 102 p. 8°. (Allgemeine Literatur-Zeitung. Jena, 1799. 4°. Jahr 1799, Bd. 1, col. 512, *NAA.*)
*See* no. 1461.
"A translation also appeared in *Amerikanisches Magazin*, Hamburg, 1797 [see no. 1267], v. 1, p. 1–13."
— Sabin 3818.

1463. *Review:* An excursion to the united States of North America, in the Summer 1794 by Henry Wansey. 2nd ed. with additions. Salisbury: Easton, 1798. 270 S. (Allgemeine Literatur-Zeitung. Jena, 1799. 4°. Jahr 1799, Bd. 3, col. 9–10, *NAA.*)
The Library's copies of this English work are in IID and * KF.
*See also* no. 1387.

1464. *Review:* An inaugural dissertation, shewing on what manner pestilential vapours acquire their acid quality... Submitted to the public examination of the faculty of physic under the authority of the trustees of Columbia College, in the state of New York. W. Sam. Johnson, LLD President, For the degree of D. of Physic on the 2. day of May 1798. By Adolph C. Lent. Citizen of the state of New York. Printed by Swords, 1798. 54 S. 8°. (Allgemeines Journal der Chemie. Leipzig, 1799. 4°. Bd. 2, p. 330, *3-PKA.*)

1465. *Review:* Lametherie's Journal de physique, de chémie et d'histoire naturelle. v. 3. Paris: bey Cuchet, 1799. 480 p. 4°. (Göttingische Anzeigen von gelehrten Sachen. Göttingen [1799]. 12°. Jahr 1799, p. 1262–1266, * DF.)
The journal contains an essay by Proust on "ein sehr gemischtes Silbererz aus America."
This is the periodical founded by François Rozier. It is catalogued under *Journal de physique*... 3–OA.

1466. *Review:* The natural History of the rarer lepidopterous Insects of Georgia: including their systematic characters, the particulars of their several metamorphoses, and the plants on which they feed. Collected from the observations of Mr. John Abbot, many years resident in that country, by Jam. Edw. Smith... London, 1797. 2 v. 104 col'd plates. 4°. (Göttingische Anzeigen von gelehrten Sachen. Göttingen [1799]. 12°. Jahr 1799, p. 277–280, * DF.)
"Die Beeren von Prinos verticillatus sollen im Ohio-Kriege den Englischen Soldaten gute Dienste gegen den Durchfall gethan haben."
Sabin (25) gives the publication dates as 1796–98.

1467. *Review:* Neues bergmännisches Journal. Bd. 1. Stck. 1, 2, 3, 4. Freyberg, 1795-1797. (Göttingische Anzeigen von gelehrten Sachen. Göttingen [1799]. 12°. Jahr 1799, p. 347–350, * DF.)
Stück 1 contains "Hrn. Walther's Nachrichten von dem Bergbau und Gebürgen in den vereinigten Staaten von Nordamerica; eigentlich ein Auszug aus Hrn. Jefferson's Aufsätzen, welche 1788 zu Philadelphia herausgekommen sind."
*See* no. 1468.

1468. *Review:* Neues bergmännisches Journal, herausgegeben von Köhler und Hoffmann. Erster Band. Freyberg: b. Cratz, 1795. 576 p. 4°. (Allgemeine Literatur-Zeitung. Jena, 1799. 4°. Jahr 1799, Bd. 1, col. 717–720, *NAA.*)
*See* no. 1467.

1469. *Review:* Travels through the States of Northamerica and the Province of Upper and Lower Canada during the Years 1795–1797, by Isaac Weld. London: B. Stockdale, 1799. 464 p. 4°. mit 16 Karten. (Allgemeine Literatur-Zeitung. Jena, 1799. 4°. Jahr 1799, Bd. 4, col. 305–311, *NAA.*)
The Library's copies of this English work are in * KF.
For the German translation, *see* nos. 1489, 1490.

*1799, continued*

1470. *Review:* Versuch über Strafen, in vorzüglicher Hinsicht auf Todes- und Gefängnissstrafen. Nebst einer aus dem Englischen angehängten Nachricht über die Strafgesetze und Gefängnisse Pensylvaniens. Von Justus Gruner. Göttingen: Bey Rosenbusch, 1799. 179 p. 8°. (Göttingische Anzeigen von gelehrten Sachen. Göttingen [1799]. 12°. Jahr 1799, p. 1408, *DF.*)

"Die angehängte Nachricht ist eine Übersetzung von Caleb Lowne's *Darstellung der Veränderung und des gegenwärtigen Zustandes der Strafgesetze in Pensylvanien.* Wenn diese Gesetze so ausgeführt werden, wie sie abgefasst sind, so ist für die Erreichung des edelsten Nebenzweckes menschlicher Strafen, d. i. für die Besserung der Verbrecher selbst, an keinem Orte in der Welt so gut gesorgt, wie in Philadelphia."

There is another review in *Neue allgemeine deutsche Bibliothek,* Bd. 61, p. 260–261, *NAA.*

As to German interest in American penitentiaries, note F. Cuningham, *Notizen über die Gefängnisse in der Schweiz...Dann als Nachtrag: die Beschreibung der verbesserten Gefängnisse von... Philadelphia, Bury, Ilchester und Millbank... Aus dem Französischen übersetzt,* Luzern, 1821; G. de Beaumont und A. de Tocqueville, *Amerika's Besserungs-System und dessen Anwendung auf Europa. Mit einem Anhang über Straf-Ansiedlungen, und 22 Beilagen. Aus dem Französischen, nebst Erweiterungen und Zusätzen von N. H. Julius. Mit 4 Kupfertafeln,* Berlin, 1833; N. H. Julius, *Die amerikanischen Besserungs-Systeme,* Leipzig, 1837; Eduard Ducpetiaux, *Das Besserungs-System, oder der gegenwärtige Zustand des Gefängnisswesens in den vereinigten Staaten... Nach dem Französischen frei bearbeitet...herausgeg. von Conrad Samhaber,* Frankfurt a. M., 1839. None of these titles is in the Library.

See no. 1432.

1471. *Review:* A Voyage of Discovery to the North Pacific Ocean and round the World... under the Command of Capt. George Vancouver. London: B. Robinson u. Edward. Vol. I, 432 p.; Vol. II, 504 p. Vol. III, 515 p.; mit Kupfern... 4°. (Allgemeine Literatur-Zeitung. Jena, 1799. 4°. Jahr 1799, Bd. 1, col. 185–192, 193–200, *NAA.*)

The Library's copies of this English work are in * KF 1798.

See nos. 1440, 1456.

**1800**

1472. ANFRAGE. (Neues Hannöverisches Magazin...vom Jahre 1800. Hannover, 1801. 4°. Jahrg. 10, col. 1661–1664.)   * DF

Also "Einiges zur Beantwortung der Anfrage im 91sten Stück," col. 1827–1834.

Concerning spruce-beer.

Title page dated 1801; contents, 1800.

1472A. BAGGENSEN, JENS. Der Tag der Freiheit oder der jüngste Tag. Nach Gott weiss wie vielen Jahrhunderten zu singen. (Musenalmanach für 1800. Von Johann Heinrich Voss. Neustrelitz: Beym Hofbuchhändler Ferdinand Albans [1800]. 32°. p. 219–222.)   NFA

"Es huldigt dir, o Tag, Tyrannenwürger!
 Westinders Morgenroth;
 Und deiner Fahne schwört
 Europa's Bürger
 Laut: Freiheit oder Tod!"

1473. BEITRÄGE zur Geschichte der teutschen Sitte für fremde Staaten zu streiten. (Europäische Annalen. Tübingen, 1800. 8°. Jahrg. 1800, Bd. 3, p. 231–248.)   BTA

German mercenaries fighting in America, p. 245–248.

1474. BEYTRAG zur Geschichte der Nordamerikanischen Länder-Entdecker. (Monatliche Correspondenz zur Beförderung der Erd- und Himmelskunde. Gotha, 1800. 8°. Bd. 1, p. 348–354.)   3–OMA

In fine: Obige Auszüge sind meinen Beobachtungen gemäss Josiah Roberts. Auch den meinigen Bernard Magee. Boston, den 6. Nov. 1795.

Taken from *Collections of the Massachusetts Historical Society,* 1795, v. 4.

1475. BRIEFE über Nordamerika, aus dem handschriftlichen Tagebuche eines Reisenden. (Der Neue teutsche Merkur vom Jahre 1800. Weimar, 1800. 12°. Jahr 1800, Bd. 1, p. 18–32, 205–213.)
* DF

Erster Brief, "Im Octobr. 1798: Ueber die auswandernden Teutschen." Zweiter Brief, "M. Nov. 1799: Schicksale eines teutschen Zimmermanns in Filadelfia."

Both letters tend to warn emigrants.

Signed: G.

1476. CHARADEN und Rätsel No. 10. (Almanach und Taschenbuch zum geselligen Vergnügen. Herausgegeben von W. G. Becker. Leipzig: Bei Roch und Weigel, 1800. 24°. p. 393.)

Solution: Achordion.   NFA (Taschenbuch)

1477. CHARADEN und Rätsel No. 11. (Almanach und Taschenbuch zum geselligen Vergnügen. Herausgegeben von W. G. Becker. Leipzig: Bei Roch und Weigel, 1800. 24°. p. 393.)

Signed: B.   NFA (Taschenbuch)

"Pulver und Dampf hast du in Europa vermehret, du wilder Amerikaner, und ach! mehr noch des Widerspruchs Wuth. Widerspruch schufst du an Thoren der Stadt, in Magen und Nase, Widerspruch jüngst in Berlin, ach! zwischen Vater und Sohn."

Solution: Tobacco.

1478. EBELING, CHRISTOPH DANIEL. Ebelings America Band I. Zweyte Auflage. (Allgemeine geographische Ephemeriden. Weimar, 1800. 8°. Bd. 6, p. 282–284.)   KAA

"Selbstanzeige;" originally published in *Hamburger Neue Zeitung.*

See no. 1163.

1479. ———. Ueber Portugiesische und Amerikanische Landkarten und eine neue Berechnungs-Methode des Flächen-Inhalts der Länder. (Monatliche Correspondenz zur Beförderung der Erd- und Himmels-Kunde. Gotha, 1800. 8°. Bd. 1, p. 158.)   3–OMA

Dated: Hamburg, Dec. 20th, 1799.

"v. Z." [i.e. Franz Xaver von Zach, 1754–1832] in a note to the above, mentions a letter sent by Professor Samuel Webber from Cambridge, Mass.

The latter and Mr. Patterson, secretary of the Academy in Philadelphia, consider the progress of science in America very slow.

1480. EINIGE Nachrichten über die neue Colonie des Capitäns Williamson, am See Ontario in Nordamerica. Aus London mitgetheilt. (Allgemeine geographische Ephemeriden. Weimar, 1800. 8°. Bd. 5, p. 113–122.)   KAA

Review: *Allgemeine Literatur-Zeitung,* Jahr 1802, Intelligenzblatt, col. 1476, *NAA.*

*1800, continued*

1481. KURZE topographische Beschreibung der Provinz Ober-Canada. Mit einer Charte. (Allgemeine geographische Ephemeriden. Weimar, 1800. 8°. Bd. 6, p. 289-317.) KAA

From D. W. Smyth, *A short topographical description of His Majesty's Province of Upper-Canada in North America...*, London, 1799, * KF.

1482. MÜHLENBERG, HEINRICH ERNST MELCHIOR. Kurze Bemerkungen über die in der Gegend von Lancaster in Nordamerika wachsenden Arten der Gattungen Iuglans, Fraxinus und Quercus... Mit Anmerkungen vom Herrn Professor C. L. Willdenow. (Gesellschaft naturforschender Freunde zu Berlin. Neue Schriften. Berlin, 1800. 8°. Bd. 3, p. 387-402.) 3-* EE

The Library catalogues this author's work under Henry Melchior Muhlenberg.

1483. MÜNCHHAUSEN, KARL LUDWIG AUGUST HEINO, FREIHERR VON. Werbungslied der[!] jungen nordamerikanischen Wilden bei dem Vater der Braut. Nach dem Huronischen. (Musenalmanach für 1800. Von Johann Heinrich Voss. Neustrelitz: Beym Hofbuchhändler Ferdinand Albans [1800]. 32°. p. 131-132.) NFA

"Der Verfasser sammelte dieses Lied mit mehreren auf seinem Feldzuge in Amerika. Er versichert, den vollen Sinn, und fast auch das Silbenmass, wiedergegeben."

Münchhausen was forced to join the auxiliary army and met there another German poet, Johann Gottfried Seume (1763-1810). See Albert von Pfister, *The voyage of the first Hessian army from Portsmouth to New York, 1776,* New York, 1915, *IG,* containing abstracts from Seume's diaries. Seume's famous poem "Der Wilde" (in his *Sämmtliche Werke,* Leipzig, 1839, Bd. 7, p. 72-75, *NFG*) did not appear before 1801. A book entitled *Rückerinnerungen von Seume und Münchhausen,* Frankfurt am Mayn, 1797 (second edition, 1823) is not in the Library. The mutual experiences during the expedition to America was described in an article by J. G. Seume, in *Neue Litteratur- und Völkerkunde,* 1789, v. 2, p. 361-381, and later in his "Mein Leben," (*Prosaische und poetische Werke,* Berlin [n. d.], Erster Teil, *NFG*). Seume's two poems "Abschiedsschreiben an Münchhausen" and "Erinnerung. An Münchhausen" deal with remembrances of the American war. The following characteristic lines are quoted from the "Abschiedsschreiben":

"Erinn're dich, wie Arm in Arm wir gingen,
Und an dem Blick der Abendsonne hingen,
Die bei Neufundland niedersank,
Und wie wir hoch auf Adlerbergen sassen,
Und in der Dämmlung Klopstocks Hermann lasen,
Auf einer grauen Felsenbank. (p. 20.)

Between 1783 and 1810, Seume thought it more to his credit to try to forget and make others forget that he voluntarily entered the Hessian service; he pretended that he had been forced to it, as a palliation for serving with the Yankees, and boasted of his desertion, as if that, too, were to his credit. See J. G. Rosengarten, *A defence of the Hessians,* Philadelphia, 1899, p. 27, *IG p.v.8.*

See also Julius Goebel, *Amerika in der deutschen Dichtung,* n. p., 1894, p. 108-111, *NFI p.v.I.*

1484. REISE von Hamburg nach Philadelphia. Hannover: Ritschersche Buchhandlung, 1800. 208 p. 16°. * KF 1800

The anonymous author, a young merchant, starts his voyage from Hamburg in 1796. He visits Baltimore, Annapolis, Boston, New York, Charleston and the West Indies (Porto Rico, Domingo, etc.). He also visits Ex-President Washington. There are accounts of the election campaign of President Adams, the trade in the different places, the yellow fever, disappointment of immigrants, etc. The *Neue allgemeine deutsche Bibliothek* calls the author "einen etwas excentrischen Panegyricus auf Amerika."

Reviews: *Allgemeine Literatur-Zeitung,* Jahr 1801, Bd. 4, col. 118-119, *NAA; Neue allgemeine deutsche Bibliothek,* Bd. 64, col. 451-454, *NAA; Göttingische Anzeigen von gelehrten Sachen,* Jahr 1800, Bd. 3, p. 1694-1696, * DF.

1484A. RIEDESEL, FRIEDERIKE CHARLOTTE LUISE (VON MASSOW), FREIFRAU VON. Auszüge aus den Briefen und Papieren des Generals Freyherrn von Riedesel und Seiner Generalin, gebornen von Massow. Ihre beyderseitige Reise nach America und ihren dortigen Aufenthalt betreffend. Zusammengetragen und geordnet von ihrem Schwiegersohne Heinrich dem XLIV. Grafen Reuss. [Berlin:] Gedruckt als Manuscript für die Familie [1800]. 1 p.l., 386 p. 19 cm.
Sabin 71299. * KF 1800

For later editions see the Library's catalogue.

There are several translations of these letters in the Library: 1827; * KF 1827 and *IGE;* 1867 *IGE* and *IAG.*

See also John Burgoyne, "Letters to Gen. Riedesel, 1776-1777, on military matters, the greater part during the Saratoga campaign," in French, 27 items, mostly A. L. S., unbound: Bancroft Mss. One of these letters is a copy, and two are written in English. Five of them are printed (in German) in Max von Eelking, *Leben und Wirken des herzoglich braunschweigischen General Lieutenents Friedrich Adolph Riedesel,* Leipzig, 1856, p. 256-264, and *NA.* Von Loos, "Letters to Gen. Riedesel, 1781-1783, on military affairs in Canada and on personal matters," in German, 45 A.L.S., unbound: Bancroft mss. There is also one in the Myers Collection, "British and Hessian Officers." Twenty-three of these letters are printed in Eelking's *Riedesel,* Leipzig, 1856, p. 266-284.

See also Friedrich Kapp, "Die Deutschen in der Amerikanischen Revolution," an appendix to J. F. Schroeder, *Washington und die Helden der Revolution,* New York, 1857, † *AN (Washington),* and Georges Monarque, *Un général allemand au Canada. Le baron Friedrich Adolphus von Riedesel,* Montréal, 1927, *IAG p.v.370.*

1485. —— Die Berufs-Reise nach America. Briefe der Generalin von Riedesel auf dieser Reise und während ihres sechsjährigen Aufenthalts in America zur Zeit des dortigen Krieges in den Jahren 1776 bis 1783 nach Deutschland geschrieben. Berlin: Bei Haude und Spener, 1800. x, 352 p. 16°. * KF 1800
Sabin 71300.

Includes letters from General Riedesel to his wife and an abstract of his account of Burgoyne's invasion.

See the chapter entitled, "Baroness Riedesel suffers at Saratoga" (Book III, 12), in Mark Van Doren, *An autobiography of America,* New York, 1929, *AGZ.*

Title page engraved, with a vignette taken from Weld's *Travels,* representing Cape Diamond on the St. Lawrence.

Reviews: *Allgemeine Literatur-Zeitung,* Jahr 1802, Bd. 3, col. 575-576, *NAA; Neue allgemeine deutsche Bibliothek,* Bd. 61, p. 403-407, *NAA; Göttingische Anzeigen von gelehrten Sachen,* Jahr 1800, Bd. 3, p. 1649-1651, * DF; Oberdeutsche allgemeine Literatur-Zeitung,* Jahr 1801, Bd. 1, p. 513-520 (not in N. Y. P. L.); *Leipziger Jahrbuch der neuesten Literatur,* Bd. 4, p. 281-283 (not in N. Y. P. L.); *Nürnbergische gelehrte Zeitung,* Jahr 1801, p. 569-574 (not in N. Y. P. L.); *Tübinger gelehrte Anzeigen,* Jahr 1801, p. 57-59 (not in N. Y. P. L.).

*1800, continued*

1486. TRIESNECKER, FRANZ VON (DE PAULA). Geographische Ortsbestimmungen und vermischte astronomische Bemerkungen. (Monatliche Correspondenz zur Beförderung der Erd- und Himmels-Kunde. Gotha, 1800. 8°. Bd. 1, p. 596–605; Bd. 2, p. 474–491.) 3–OMA
Dated: Wien, den 29. Febr., 22. März und 29. April 1800.
Several references to America, especially in Bd. 1, p. 604.
A continuation of no. 1427.

1487. UIBER den Zustand Frankreichs zu Ende des Jahres 8. (Europäische Annalen. Tübingen, 1800. 8°. Jahrg. 1800, Bd. 4, p. 99–310.) BTA
Translation of A. M. B. de L., comte Hauterive's *De l'état de la France, à la fin de l'an VIII,* Paris, 1800, *DFT*.
References to America, p. 180–181.

1487A. Voss, JOHANN HEINRICH. Die Kartoffelernte. (Musenalmanach für 1800. Von Johann Heinrich Voss. Neustrelitz: Beym Hofbuchhändler Ferdinand Albans [1800]. 32°. p. 51–53.) NFA
"Nein, ein Mann ward ausgesandt,
Der die neue Welt erfand!
Reiche nennens Land des Goldes;
Doch der Arme nennts sein holdes
Nährendes Kartoffelland!"

1488. WASHINGTON. (Minerva. Hamburg, 1800. 12°. Jahr 1800, Bd. 1, p. 528–544.) BAA
Excerpts from Fontane's obituary, read in the Rotonde à Paris; with a postscriptum by J. W. v. Archenholz.
Archenholz discusses two more obituaries on Washington, one by Friedrich von Gentz, published in his *Historisches Journal*, and another by an anonymous author in K. L. v. Woltmann's *Zeitschrift für Geschichte und Politik*. Neither journal is in the Library.

1489. WELD, ISAAC. Isaac Weld's des Jüngern Reisen durch die Staaten von Nordamerika und die Provinzen Ober- und Nieder-Canada, während den Jahren 1795, 1796 und 1797. Aus dem Englischen übersetzt. Mit Kupfern. Berlin: Voss, 1800. 536 p. 8°. (Magazin von merkwürdigen neuen Reisebeschreibungen... Bd. 20.) KBC
For another translation, see the following entry, no. 1490.
The Library's copies of the original, *Travels through the states of North America*... London, 1799, are in IID, * KF, etc.
See also no. 1469, 1490, 1506.

1490. —— Reise durch die nordamerikanischen Freistaaten und durch Ober- und Unter-Canada in den Jahren 1795, 1796 und 1797 von Isaac Weld, aus dem Englischen frei übersetzt. Mit sechs Kupfern. Berlin: Bei Haude und Spener, 1800. iv p., 2 l., 410 p., 5 plates, 1 plan. 8°.
* KF 1800
"Da von Welds Reisen drei verschiedene deutsche Uebersetzungen erschienen sind; so ist es um so nöthiger, dass jeder Unternehmer von der seinigen Rechenschaft ablege. Diejenige, welche wir dem Publikum hier liefern, enthält auf 410 gedruckten Octav-Seiten alles, was die englische Urschrift auf 462 Quartseiten von grösserem Druck liefert." Nachschrift der Verleger, signed and dated: Haude und Spener. Berlin den 5 Junius, 1800.
The third German translation, not in the Library, was published in Berlin: b. Oehmigke d. j., 1800. Bd. I, 395 p. 8°.

Plan of the "Grundriss der Unions-Stadt Washington" and the plates, unsigned, are reduced in size from the originals.
Reviews: *Allgemeine Literatur-Zeitung,* Jahr 1799, Bd. 4, col. 305–311; Jahr 1801, Bd. 1, col. 677–678, *NAA; Göttingische Anzeigen von gelehrten Sachen,* Jahr 1800, Bd. 1, p. 217–228, 257–265; Bd. 3, p. 1912, * *DF; Allgemeine geographische Ephemeriden,* Bd. 4, p. 6–19, *KAA; Oberdeutsche allgemeine Literatur-Zeitung,* Jahr 1801, Bd. 1, p. 49–72 (not in N. Y. P. L.); *Erlangische gelehrte Zeitung,* Jahr 1800, Bd. 1, p. 493–494 (not in N. Y. P. L.).
See no. 1489.

1491. *Review:* American Gazetteer... by Jedidiah Morse. 2nd edition. London: Dilly, 1798. 8°. (Allgemeine Literatur-Zeitung. Jena, 1800. 4°. Jahr 1800, Intelligenzblatt, col. 1117, *NAA*.)
The Library's copies of this English work are in * *KF.*

1492. *Review:* Annals of Medicine for the Year 1796 exhibiting a concise View of the latest and most important Discoveries in Medicine and medical Philosophy, by Andrew Duncan sen. and Andrew Duncan jun. v. 1–2. Edinburgh, 1796–1797. 469 p. 8°. (Göttingische Anzeigen von gelehrten Sachen. Göttingen [1800]. 12°. Jahr 1800, p. 1034–1040, 1073–1078, * *DF*.)
The *Annals* contain several articles dealing with medical cases in America, especially in the West Indies.

1493. *Review:* Bildliche Abbildung aller bekannten Völker nach ihren Kleidertrachten, Sitten, Gewohnheiten, und mit Beschreibung aus den besten englischen, französischen und italienischen Werken bearbeitet von M. Friedrich Gottlob Leonhardi... Heft 1 [–4]. Leipzig: Bey Baumgärtner, 1798[–99]. (Neue allgemeine deutsche Bibliothek. Kiel, 1800. 8°. Bd. 54, p. 428–430, *NAA*.)

1494. *Review:* The Caffee [*sic!*] Planter of St. Domingo, with an Appendix, containing a View of the Constitution, Government, Laws and State of the Colony previous to the year 1789. to which are added some hints on the present state of the Island under the british Government by P. J. Laborie. London: Cadell, 1798. 8°. (Allgemeine Literatur-Zeitung. Jena, 1800. 4°. Jahr 1800, Intelligenzblatt, col. 1116–1117, *NAA*.)
The Library's copy of Laborie's *The Coffee planter of Saint Domingo* is in * *KF.*

1495–96. *Review:* A descriptive Sketch of the present State of Vermont, one of the united States of America by J. A. Graham... London: Foy [*sic!*] 1792 [*sic!*]. 186 p. 8°. (Allgemeine Literatur-Zeitung. Jena, 1800. 4°. Jahr 1800, Intelligenzblatt, col. 1117, *NAA*.)
Imprint should read: London: Fry, 1797.
The Library's copies are in *IQE* and * *KF.*

1497. *Review:* Emigration to America, candidly considered; in a series of Letters from a Gentleman resident there to his friend in England. London: Rickman, 1798. 62 p. 8°. (Allgemeine Literatur-Zeitung. Jena, 1800. 4°. Jahr 1800, Intelligenzblatt, col. 1117, *NAA*.)
The Library's copy of this English work by T. C. Rickman is in * *KF.*

*1800, continued*

1498. *Review:* Essays literary, moral and philosophical. By Benjamin Rush... Philadelphia, 1798. 378 p. 8°. (Göttingische Anzeigen von gelehrten Sachen. Göttingen [1800]. 12°. Jahr 1800, p. 1076–1078, * *DF.*)

The Library's copy of this English work is in *NBQ.*
"...zu wünschen wäre, dass einmal ein Mann ohne Vorurtheil, aber von practischer Einsicht, einen Entwurf von der ganzen Bildung eines Volks...machen wollte, wenn darin alle alte Literatur und aller gelehrter Sprachunterricht abgeschafft, dagegen die ganze Erziehung bloss auf unmittelbar nützliche Kenntnisse gerichtet sein müsste. Dass eine solche Volksbildung sich denken lässt, hat keinen Zweifel." Beside pedagogical topics the work treats questions of law (public punishment), government (creation of a Peace Office, supplementing the War Office), immigration (advice for immigrants), Germans in Pennsylvania, Indians, effect of tobacco on health, maple sugar and several personalities known for longevity, such as Ed. Drinker, Anne Woody, Quaker Benjamin Lee and Anthony Benezet. Finally, literary works are added.

1499. *Review:* An experimental dissertation on the Rhus venix . By Thom. Horsfield. Philadelphia, 1798. 80 p. (Allgemeines Journal der Chemie. Leipzig, 1800. 4°. Bd. 4, p. 405, *3-PKA.*)

1500. *Review:* Joh. Johnson, An experimental inquiry into the properties of carbonic acid gas or fixed air. — Benjamin de Witt, An explanation of the Effects of Oxygene or the base of vital air on the human body. Philadelphia, 1797. (Allgemeines Journal der Chemie. Leipzig, 1800. 4°. Bd. 4, p. 513, *3-PKA.*)

1501. *Review:* Journals of Congress. Philadelphia: Follwell, 1800. 3 v. 8°. (Göttingische Anzeigen von gelehrten Sachen. Göttingen, 1800. 12°. Jahr 1800, p. 2037–2040, * *DF.*)

The Library's copy of the *Journals* is in *Reserve.*

1502. *Review:* Eine kurze Geschichte, die Natur und Heilart des gelben Americanischen Fiebers betr., von Constanz Didier, aus Brabant. Manuscript. (Göttingische Anzeigen von gelehrten Sachen. Göttingen [1800]. 12°. Jahr 1800, p. 993–996, * *DF.*)

The essay won the prize of the Königliche Stiftung, Göttingen.
According to Kayser, v. 2, p. 44, the work was published under the title, *Commentat. med. de febre flava Americana,* Göttingen, 1800.

1503. *Review:* The natural and political History of the State of Vermont etc. by Ira Allen ... London: West, 1798. 300 p. 8°. (Allgemeine Literatur-Zeitung. Jena, 1800. 4°. Jahr 1800, Intelligenzblatt, col. 1117, *NAA.*)

The Library's copy of this English work is in * *KF.*

1504. *Review:* A sketch of the revolutions in chemistry. By T. Smith. Philadelphia, 1798. 40 S. 8°. (Allgemeines Journal der Chemie. Leipzig, 1800. 4°. Bd. 4, p. 405, *3-PKA.*)

The Library's copy of this English work by Thomas P. Smith is in * *KD.*

1505. *Review:* Sketches of the History of America, by J. T. Callender. Philadelphia: Snowdon & Mac Corkle, 1798. 263 p. 8°. (Göttingische Anzeigen von gelehrten Sachen. Göttingen [1800]. 12°. Jahr 1800, p. 651–653, * *DF.*)

The Library's copy of this American work is in * *KD.*

1506. *Review:* Travels through North America and the Provinces of Upper and Lower Canada during the Year 1795–1797 by J. Weld junior. London: Stockdale, 1798. 464 p. 4°. (Allgemeine Literatur-Zeitung. Jena, 1800. 4°. Jahr 1800, Intelligenzblatt, col. 1117, *NAA.*)

*See* nos. 1469, 1489, 1490.

1506A. *Notice:* Vermischte Nachrichten. New York, den 30. März 1800. (Allgemeine Literatur-Zeitung. Jena, 1800. 4°. Intelligenzblatt, p. 675, *NAA.*)

"Unter den vielen bisher gedruckten Lobreden, Predigten und Freymaurerreden auf Washington zeichnet sich die vom Gouverneur Morris durch Beredtsamkeit, die vom Südcarolinischen Senator Dr. Ramsay durch historische Schilderung seiner Verdienste aus. Der Geograph Dr. Jed[idiah] Morse arbeitet an einer umständlichen Lebensbeschreibung desselben. Washington selbst hat keine hinterlassen, sondern nur ein Tagebuch... Auf den Vorschlag des Kriegs-Secretairs soll eine Kriegsschule errichtet werden, die aus einer Fundamental-, einer Infanterie- und Cavallerie-, und einer Marineschule bestehen, und ausser Zeichenmeistern, Bereitern u. dgl. 20 Professoren, nämlich 6 für die Mathematik, 4 für Geographie und Naturkunde, 2 für Chemie und Mineralogie, und 8 für Kriegs- und Schiffsbaukunst haben wird.
Den Preis für die beste Abhandlung Ueber das gelbe Fieber hat Dr. Brown in Boston erhalten.
Die deutschen Theaterstücke werden jetzt in Nordamerika eben so beliebt als in England. Man druckt das German Theatre nach, und nebenbey erscheint zugleich eine Uebersetzung der Kotzebueschen Stücke, die hier und in andern Städten mit vielem Beyfall gegeben werden."

1507. *Review:* Voyage dans les États-Unis d'Amerique, fait en 1795, 1796 et 1797, par La Rochefoucauld-Liancourt. L'an VII. Paris. 8 v. maps. 8°. (Göttingische Anzeigen von gelehrten Sachen. Göttingen [1800]. 12°. Jahr 1800, p. 617–628, * *DF.*)

The Library's copy of this French work is in * *KF 1799.*

*See* no. 1451.

1508. *Review:* Die wilde Europäerinn, oder Geschichte der Frau von Walwille von A. C. x x x, einem alten Seeofficier. Aus dem Französischen. Meissen: bey Erbstein, 1799. 18 Bogen. 8°. (Neue allgemeine deutsche Bibliothek. Kiel, 1800. 8°. Bd. 52, p. 327–329, *NAA.*)

Sabin 101130.
Signed: Bg.
"The probably fictitious story of the captivity and marriage of an English woman among the Iroquois, from about 1755 to 1759, her escape, later experiences among the Indians, and marriage to a certain 'Walville'. Told after the death of the latter for the information of officers from a ship who encountered her while she was living near St. John, Newfoundland, in 1778. After the introduction the story is told in the first person." — *Sabin.* For a later edition, see Sabin 101129.

Among the totally forgotten novels of those days dealing with American matters is also *Walter oder kurze Geschichte eines nordamerikanischen Pflanzers,* Schleswig, 1797, mentioned in Kayser, *Vollständiges Bücher Lexicon,* 1836, "Index Locupletissimus Librorum," p. 148A. The author is unknown.

# SUPPLEMENTARY LIST

NOTE: The preceding list of numbered entries includes German books before 1800, articles in German periodicals to 1800, and books reviewed in German journals to 1800, in The New York Public Library. The following is an alphabetical list of German titles relating to America, gleaned from various sources — principally Sabin and Kayser — not in the Library. It is included to make the record of German literature relating to America before 1800 as complete as possible. The statement that they are not in the Library is the compiler's responsibility; no search has been made by a member of the staff.

The form of entry in the source has been retained for ease in identification. The shortest possible title is given (generally, a fuller title appears in the source), and the list is not represented in the Index.

DIE ABENTHEUERINNEN im Lande der Esquimaux... Leipzig, 1793. *Sabin 22845.*

ALDENBURGK. West-Indianische Reisze und Beschreibung... Coburgk, 1627. *Sabin 710.*

ALLERLEY für Deutschlands Jünglinge in allen Ständen. Stendal, 1783. *Kayser, v. 1, p. 45A.*

ALLERNEUSTER Kriegsstaat oder gründliche Nachrichten von den heutigen Kriegsbegebenheiten. Leipzig, 1731, &c. *Sabin 911.*

ALLGEMEINE Geschichte der Handlung und Schiffahrt, der Manufacturen und Künste, des Finanz und Cameralwesens... Bresslau, 1751–1754. *British Museum catalogue. (Geschichte.)*

AMERIKANISCHE Anekdoten aus den neuesten Zeiten... Leipzig, 1789. *Sabin 1285a.*

DIE ANKUNFT der Deutschen aus Amerika... Hof, 1784. *Sabin 42725.*

ANSON. Des Herrn Admiral, Lord Ansons Reise um die Welt... Leipzig und Göttingen, 1749. *Sabin 1640.*

ANTERSEN, JOHANN PETER VON. Fataler Schiffs-Capitain... Erfurt, 1742. *Sabin 1669.*

ARCHONTOLOGIA Cosmica, das ist Beschreibung ... Frankfurt am Mayn, 1695. *Sabin 1917.*

ARNOULD, AMBROISE MARIE. Frankreichs Handlungs-Bilanz und auswärtige Handlungsbeziehungen... Lübeck, 1792. *Sabin 2091.*

—— System der Seehandlung und Politik Europa's während... Erfurt, 1798. *Sabin 2090.*

AUGSPURGER, JOHANN PAUL. Kurtze und wahrhaffte Beschreibung der See Reisen von Amsterdam in Holland nacher Brasilien in America und Angola in Africa... Schleusingen, 1644. *Sabin 2379.*

AUSERLESENE Aufsätze zur geographischen, statistischen, politischen und sittlichen Völkerkunde... Berlin, 1789-1790.

AUSWAHL der besten ausländischen geographischen und statistischen Nachrichten zur Aufklärung der Völker- und Länderkunde. Halle, 1794–1800. *British Museum catalogue. (Collection.)*

BACKHAUS, JOHANN GOTTLIEB. Neue...Abhandlung vom Tabacksbau, worin die einzige ... Darmstadt, 1799. *Sabin 2620.*

BANKS, JOSEPH. Neueste Reisebeschreibungen und Entdeckungen des fünften Weltheils... Nürnberg, 1786. *Sabin 3203.*

BARBA. Berg-Büchlein von den Metallen und Mineral... Hamburg, 1676. *Sabin 3255b.*

—— Docimasia, oder Probier- und Schmelzkunst... Wien, 1775. *Sabin 3255c.*

BARTON, ROBERT. Der Englische Held und Ritter Franciscus Drake in einer Beschreibung von dessen Leben, Thaten und See Reisen... Leipzig [1690]. *Sabin 9501.*

BAWIER, FRANZ URBAN. Fr. Urban Bavier's, des See-Capitäns, merckwürdige Reisen und Begebenheiten... Franckfurt und Linz, 1752; Nürnberg, 1752. *Sabin 4001.*

BEATTY, CHARLES. Tagebuch einer Zween Reise ... Frankfurt und Leipzig, 1771. *Sabin 4150.*

BECHER, JOHANN JOACHIM. Politische [sic!] Discvrs... Frankfurt, 1668. *Sabin 4221.*

BECKFORD, WILLIAM. Mahlerische Beschreibung der Insel Jamaica... Berlin, 1790. *Sabin 4250.*

BEHRENS, KARL FRIEDRICH. Reise nach den unbekannten Sud-Landern und rund um die Welt ... Hamburg, 1735. *Sabin 4377.*

BERTIUS, PETRUS. Beschreibung der gantzen Welt abgebildet... Amsterdam [1605?]. *Sabin 5012.*

BESCHREIBUNG der dreizehn unabhängigen Nordamerikanischen Staaten... Köln, 1783. *Sabin 5041.*

BESCHREIBUNG der neuerfundenen pensylvanischen Kamine oder Oefen... Gotha, 1794. *Sabin 59913.*

BESCHREIBUNG der Spanischen Macht in America... Sorau, 1763–71. *British Museum catalogue. (America, Spanish Power in...)*

BISSET, ROBERT. Edmund Burkes Leben in hist.-litt.-polit. Hinsicht... Gera, 1799. *Sabin 5649.*

BLOME, RICHARD. Englisch America. Leipzig, 1697. *Sabin 5971.*

[BOLLAN.] Die Wichtigkeit und Vortheil des Kap-Breton... Leipzig, 1747. *Sabin 6217.*

BOSSU, N. Neue Reisen nach West-Indien... Frankfurt, Leipzig, und Helmstädt, 1771–74. *Sabin 6468.*

—— Helmstädt, 1776. *Sabin 6469.*

BOUGAINVILLE, LOUIS DE. Reise um die Welt... Leipzig, 1772; Zweite Auflage. Leipzig, 1783. *Sabin 6871.*

BRUCE, PETER HENRY. Nachrichten von seinen Reisen in Deutschland, Russland, der Tartarei, Westindien etc... Leipzig, 1784. *Sabin 8727.*

[ 169 ]

BULLEN, CHRISTIAN. Christians Bullen eines seefahrenden journal... Bremen, 1668. *Sabin 9124.*

CAMPBELL, JOHN. Leben und Thaten der Admirale und anderer berühmten Britanischen See-Leute... Göttingen, 1755. *Sabin 10238.*

CARLI, D. Der nach Venedig überbrachte Mohr... Augspurg, 1693. *Sabin 10910.*

CELLARIUS, F. Geographischer Unterricht über den Welttheil von Europa... Eichstädt, 1787. *Sabin 11656.*

[CHETWOOD, W. R.] Reisen und Begebenheiten... Leipzig, 1793. *Sabin 12557.*

CHRONICON, das ist Beschreibung der Occidentalischen und Indianischen Ländern... Wittenberg, 1606. *Sabin 12959.*

COOK, JAMES. Entdeckungsreise nach der Südsee 1776-1780... Berlin, 1781. *Sabin 16267.*

—— Nachricht von den neuesten Entdeckungen der Engländer in der Süd-See... Berlin, 1772. *Sabin 16234.*

COXE, TENCH. Die neueren Entdeckungen der Russen zwischen Asien und America... Frankfurt und Leipzig, 1783. *Sabin 17311.*

CURIEUSE Anmerckungen über den Staat von Frankreich... [Leipzig,] 1720. *Sabin 39308.*

CURIOSE Beschreibung der auserlesensten Merckwürdigkeiten... Augsburg, 1784. *Sabin 17986.*

DALRYMPLE, ALEXANDER, Historische Sammlung der Reisen... Hamburg, 1786. *Sabin 18339.*

DAMPIER, WILLIAM. Dampiers Reise um die Welt... Celle, 1783. *Sabin 18390.*

—— Neue Reise um die Welt... Leipzig, 1702. *Sabin 18389.*

DE l'Amérique et des Americains. Berlin, 1774. *Kayser, v. 1, p. 52A.*

DELAPORTE, M. Reisen eines Franzosen... Leipzig, 1774. *Sabin 19361.*

DE L'ISLE, J. N. Erklärung der Charte von den Neuen Entdeckungen... Berlin, 1753. *Sabin 41417.*

—— Schreiben eines Russischen Officiers... Berlin [175-?].

DES WESTINDIANISCHEN Kleinen Albertus... Frankfurt und Leipzig, 1757. *Library of Congress card.*

DIRRHAIMER, ULRICH. Kirchen-Geschichte... Wien, 1725. *Sabin 20224.*

DIXON, GEORGE. Reisen nach der nordwestlichen Küste von Amerika... Nürnberg, 1795. *Sabin 20367.*

DUCHÉ, JACOB. Briefe, welche Beobachtungen über verschiedene Gegenstände der Literatur, Religion und Moral enthalten... Leipzig, 1778. *Sabin 21049.*

EHRMANN, THEOPHIL FRIEDRICH. Geschichte der merkwürdigsten Reisen... Frankfurt, 1791. *Sabin 22074.*

EIGENTLICHE Beschreibung des Lands Guiana... Bärn, 1677. *Sabin 22078.*

EIGENTLICHER...Bericht...derjenigen Uneinigkeiten, so in America... *British Museum catalogue. (America.)*

ELLIS, WILLIAM. Zuverlässige Nachricht von der dritten und letzten Reise des Kap. Cook und Clerke... Frankfurt und Leipzig, 1783. *Sabin 22334.*

ENDHOVEN, JAN VAN. Denkwürdige und ausführliche Erzehlung Der glucklichen und Siegreichen See Reise... [n. p. 1665.] *Sabin 22558.*

ENGEL, S[AMUEL]. Anmerkungen über den Theil von Cap. Cooks Reise-relation... n. p., 1780. *Sabin 22567.*

EXTRACT vnd Augsszug. Der Grossen vñ wunderbarlichen Schifffarth, Buelij Cataloni, eines Abbten, dess heyligen Orden A. Benedicti... Lintz, 1624. *Sabin 23512.*

FABRI, J. E., Abriss der natürl. Erdkunde. Nürnberg, 1800. *See T. C. F. Enslin, Bibliotheca Paedagogica, Berlin, 1824, p. 28, SSB.*

FRAGMENT sur les colonies en général... Basel, 1778. *Kayser, v. 2, p. 245.*

FRANKLIN, BENJAMIN. Freier Wille, ein Werk für denkende Menschen... Leipzig, 1787. *Kayser, v. 2, p. 252B.*

FRITSCH, J. G. Disput. histo. georgr., in qua quaeritur... Hof, 1796. *See T. C. F. Enslin, Biblioteca historico-geographica, Berlin, 1825, p. 103B.*

GALLOWAY, J. Briefe über den in Amerika... Hamburg, 1780. *See T. C. F. Enslin, Biblioteca historico-geographica, Berlin, 1825, p. 108B.*

GEGENWAERTIGER Zustand derer Finantzen von Franckreich... Leipzig, 1720. *Sabin 26837.*

GESCHICHTE, neuere, von Amerika... Berlin, 1778. *Kayser, v. 2, p. 355A.*

GESCHICHTE, neueste, d. Welt... Augsburg, 1775-77. *Kayser, v. 2, p. 368A.*

GESCHICHTE u. Handlung d. engl. Colonien im nördl. Amerika. Frankf. a. M., 1758. *Kayser, v. 2, p. 359B.*

GESCHICHTE der neuesten Weltbegebenheiten im Grossen... Leipzig, 1778-90. *Kayser, v. 2, p. 368A.*

GESCHICHTE und polit. Verfassung d. vereinigten Staaten von Nordamerika... Leipzig, 1788. *Kayser, v. 2, p. 363A.*

GESCHICHTE der Schiffbrüche... Berlin, 1791-94. *Kayser, v. 2, p. 365B.*

GESCHICHTE der Staatsveränderungen in Amerika... Leipzig, 1782. *Kayser, v. 4, p. 440B.*

DIE GLAUBWUERDIGKEIT von Maldonados nordwestlicher Schiffahrt... Gotha, 1712. *Sabin 38375.*

GREGORIUS, S. G. Die curieuse Geographia... Frankfurt, 1715. *Sabin 28738.*

GROSS-BRITTANISCHES America nach seiner Erfindung, Bevölckerung und allerneuestem Zustand... Hamburg, 1710. *Sabin 57158.*

GRÜNDLICHER Bericht von Beschaffenheit... Frankfurt, 1669. *Sabin 29011.*

# GERMAN WORKS RELATING TO AMERICA 171

HAPPEL, EBERHARD WERNER. E. G. Happelii grösseste Denkwürdigkeiten der Welt... Hamburg, 1683–1708. *Sabin 30277.*

HAWKESWORTH, JOHN. Ausführlich und glaubwürdige Geschichte der neuesten Reisen um die Welt... Berlin, 1775. *Sabin 30943.*

—— Geschichte der See-Reisen und Entdeckungen im Süd-Meer... Berlin, 1774. *Sabin 30942.*

HAZART, C. Kirchen-Geschichte, das ist... Wienn in Oesterreich, 1678–1701. *Sabin 31114.*

HENDY, [JAMES], AND [JOHN] ROLLO. Ueber die Drüsenkrankheit in Barbados oder über Wilhelm Hillary's Elephantiasis. Frankfurt, 1788. *Sabin 31336.*

HERRLIBERGER, DAVID. Heilige Ceremonien, Gottes- und Götzen-Dienste aller Völcker der Welt. Zürich, 1748. *Sabin 31581.*

HISTORISCH-GEOGRAPHISCHE Beschreibung von America für Jünglinge. Nürnberg, 1784. *Sabin 32102.*

HISTORISCHER Bericht von den sämmtlichen durch die Engländer geschehenen Reisen um die Welt... Leipzig, 1775–80. *Sabin 32107.*

JEVER, J. Verzeichniss Allerhand Pietistischer Intriguen und Unordnungen... 1731. *Sabin 36097.*

KENT, JOHN. See-u. Handlungs-Geschichte von England... Leipzig, 1777. *Kayser, v. 3, p. 328A.*

[KOLB, JOHANN ERNST.] Erzählungen von... Negersklaven. Bern, 1789. *Sabin 38226.*

KOLUMBUS, nach der Wahrheit geschildert. (Archiv für den Menschen und Bürger in allen Verhältnissen. Leipzig, 1781. Bd. 3.)

KÜHN, J. M. Merkwürdige Lebens- und Reisebeschreibung... Gotha, 1741. *Sabin 38339.*

KURZE Beschreibung des Generaldistrikts in Nordamerika. Bremen, 1792. *Sabin 38359.*

KURZE Nachricht von dem mittägigen Carolina... Leipzig, 1734. *Sabin 87855.*

KURZGEFASSTE historisch-geographische Nachrichten von den Englischen Kolonien in Nord Amerika... Hamburg, 1778. *Sabin 38364.*

LEBEN und Thaten George Washingtons... Hamburg, 1783. *Kayser, v. 3, p. 498A.*

LEBEN des Waltumseglers und Entdeckers James Cook... Frankfurt und Leipzig, 1781. *Sabin 16265.*

LEBENSBESCHREIBUNG von Gualtero Bodano, Prediger in Amsterdam... Creveld, 1738. *Sabin 39587.*

LEUBELFING, J. VON. Ein schön lustig Reissbuch vorniemals in Truck kommen... Ulm, 1612. *Sabin 40727.*

LOBSPRUCH. Ueber die Herrliche Victori... 1629. *Sabin 41714.*

LUDOLFF, H. Allgemeine Schaubühne der Welt... Frankfurt a. M., 1701–31. *Sabin 42659.*

LÜDER, A. F. Statistische Beschreibung der Besitzungen der Holländer in Amerika. Braunschweig, 1792. *Sabin 42640.*

LUFFMAN, [JOHN]. Kurze Beschreibung der Insel Antigua... Leipzig, 1790. *Sabin 42666.*

LUTYENS, GOTTHILF NICHOLAS. Etwas über den gegenwärtigen Zustand der Auswanderungen und Ansiedlungen im Staate von Pennsylvanien. Hamburg, 1796. *Sabin 42741.*

[MAJOR, J. D.] Vorstellung etlicher Kunst- und Naturalien-kammern in America und Asia... Kiel [1674]. *Sabin 44067.*

MENOLOGIUM Societatum Jesu... München, 1669. *Sabin 47866, 24811.*

MEYEN, JOHANN JACOB. Franklin der Philosoph und Staatsmann... Alt-Stettin, 1787. *Sabin 48668.*

[MICHEL, FRANZ LUDWIG.] Kurzer Bericht über die Amerikanische Reiss... (Neues Berner Taschenbuch auf das Jahr 1898. Bern, 1897. p. 59–144.) *Meynen 631.*

MILBILLER, JOSEPH. Allgemeine Geschichte der berühmtesten Königreiche und Freistaaten in und ausserhalb Europas... Leipzig, 1796.

MILIUS, A. Merckwürdiger Discurss von dem Ursprung der Thier, und Auszzug der Völcker... Saltzburg, 1670. *Sabin 48983.*

MURSINNA, F. S. Geschichte der Entdeckung von Amerika. Halle, 1795. (Vaterländische Geschichte. Theil 7.) See *T. C. F. Enslin, Biblioteca historico-geographica, Berlin, 1825, p. 236B.*

NACHRICHTEN und Erinnerungen an verschiedene deutsche Völker... n. p., 1778. *Sabin 51693.*

NEUE Nachricht alter und neuer Merkwürdigkeiten... Zürich, 1734. *Sabin 10974.*

NEUE Nachrichten von dene neuentdeckten Insuln in der See zwischen Asien und Amerika... Hamburg und Leipzig, 1766. *Sabin 78015.*

NEUE Sammlung der merkwürdigen Reisegeschichten... Frankfurt, 1748–80. *Sabin 52370.*

NEUESTE Staatsbegebenheiten mit historischen und politischen Anmerkungen... Frankfurt, 1775–81.

NEUESTER Zustand der Engländischen Schiffarth... n. p., 1731. *Sabin 52383.*

NIGRINUS or SCHWARTZ, FRANZ. Schauplatz der gantzen Welt... Aysch, 1679. *Sabin 55306.*

DER NUNMEHRO in der Neuen Welt vergnügt... Bern, 1711. *Sabin 10975.*

OCHS, JOHANN RUDOLFF. Amerikanischer Wegweiser oder Kurtze und eigentliche Beschreibung der Engelischen Proviντzen in Nord America... Bern, 1579. *Sabin 56647.*

OLDMIXON, JOHN. Das Gross-Brittanische Scepter in der Neuen Welt... Hamburg, 1715. *Sabin 57159.*

ORVILLE, ANDRÉ GUILLAUME C. D'. Geschichte der verschiedenen Völker... Hof, 1773–77. *Sabin 57731.*

PAGÈS, PIERRE MARIE FRANÇOIS. Herrn De Pagès Reisen um die Welt... Frankfurt und Leipzig, 1786. *Sabin 58169.*

PENNANT, THOMAS. Thiergeschichte der Nördlichen Polarländer... Leipzig, 1787. *Sabin 59760.*

PETERS, BERNHARD MICHAEL. Eine besonders merkwürdige Reise von Amsterdam nach Surinam... Bremen, 1788-90. *Sabin 61187.*

PFENNIG, JOHANN CHRISTOPH. Anleitung zur ...Kenntniss d. neuesten Erdbeschreibung. Berlin, 1770. *Kayser, v. 4, p. 334A.*

PIEROTS, ROBERT. Americanische Freybeuter oder Leben Robert Pierots... Copenhagen, 1772. *Sabin 62752.*

PLANT, JOHANN TRAUGOTT. Handbuch d. vollständ. Erdbeschreibung u. Gesch. des 5n Welttheils od. Polynesiens... Gera, 1793-99. *Kayser, v. 4, p. 356A.*

PLEISSNER. Der Amerikaner. Lustspiel in einem Aufzuge... Frankfurt und Leipzig, 1783. *Sabin 63415.*

PORTLOCK, NATHANIEL. Der Kapitaine Portlock und Dixon's Reise... Berlin, 1789. *Sabin 64393, 20367.*

—— —— Berlin, 1790. *Sabin 64392.*

PRENTIES, S. W. Seereise eines jungen Officiers ... Strassburg, 1786. *Sabin 65080.*

PRICE, RICHARD. Anmerkungen über die Natur der bürgerlichen Freyheit... Braunschweig, 1777. *Sabin 65454.*

PRIESTLEY, JOSEPH. Briefe, welche kürzlich von Personen in Paris an Doctor Priestley in America geschrieben... [London,] 1798. *Sabin 65501.*

RAYNAL, [GUILLAUME THOMAS FRANÇOIS]. Die politische Lage und der Handel von St. Domingo. Leipzig, 1788. *Sabin 68096.*

REICHARD, [H. A. O.]. Ueber den gesetzlichen Zustand der Negersklaven in Westindien... Leipzig, 1779. *Sabin 68977.*

REICHART, JOHANN PETER. Johann Peter Reicharts ,.. Zwanzigjährige Wanderschafft und Reisen in West und Ost Indien... Onolzbach, 1755. *Sabin 68981.*

REISE nach allen 4 Welttheilen, od. Geschichte d. vornehmsten Völker. v. Europa, Asien, Afrika u. Amerika... Leipzig, 1798. *Kayser, v. 4, p. 479B.*

REISE nach der Jnsel Malta in d. J. 1776... Hamburg, 1783. *Kayser, v. 4, p. 477B.*

REISE, e. kurze, nach Westindien... Mannheim, 1792. *Kayser, v. 4, p. 479B.*

REISE in das Südmeer, ein Beitrag zu Ansons Reisen... Nürnberg, 1772. *Sabin 69135.*

REISENDEN, die, f. Länder- und Völkerkunde... Nürnberg, 1788. *Kayser, v. 4, p. 480B.*

ROSS, ALEXANDER. Der gantzen Welt Religionen oder Beschreibung aller Gottes- und Götzendienste... Amsterdam, 1667. *Sabin 73322.*

—— Der Wunderwürdige Juden- und Heiden-Tempel... Nürnberg, 1701. *Sabin 73323.*

RUYTER. Relation von der Reise des Herrn Admiral-Leutnant Reiters. n. p., 1665. *Sabin 74513.*

SAMMLUNG der besten und neuesten Reisebeschreibungen... Berlin, 1763-1802. *Sabin 75902; Kayser, v. 5, p. 33.*

SAURIUS, ABRAHAM. Abrahami Saurii Stätte-Buch... Frankfurt am Main, 1653. *Sabin 77201.*

SCHAU-BÜHNE der Welt, Oder Beschreibung der Welt-Geschichte... Franckfurt a. M., 1699. *Sabin 77517.*

SCHAUPLATZ der Welt... Stuttgard, 1765. *Sabin 77522.*

SCHULZ, FRIEDRICH. Aufsätze zur Kunde ungebildeter Völker... Weimar, 1789. *Sabin 78011.*

SCHWARZ, J. L. Beschreibung der Reisen um die Welt und Entdeckungen im Südmeers... Hamburg, 1775. *Sabin 78097.*

SEELIG, JOHANN GOTTFRIED. Copia eines Sendschreibens aus der neuen Welt... n. p., 1695. *Meynen 227.*

SEMLER, J. S. Allgemeine Geschichte der Ost- und Westindischen Handlungsgesellschaften in Europa... Halle, 1764. *Sabin 79072.*

SEWEL, WILLIAM. Die Geschichte von dem Ursprung, Zunehmen und Fortgang des Christlichen Volcks... [Jena,] 1742. *Sabin 79616.*

SEYFRIED, JOHANN HEINRICH. Poliologia, Das ist Beschreibung aller berühmten Städte in der gantzen Welt... Sutzbach, 1683. *Sabin 79635, 79636.*

STAAT Von America. [Halle, 1717?] *Sabin 90016.*

STAIR, NIL. Des weitberühmten Seeländers... Frankfurt u. Leipzig, 1778. *Sabin 90103.*

TOBLER, JOHANN. Beschreibung von Süd-Carolina. (In: Alter und verbesserter Schreib-Calender, auf das...Christ-Jahr mdccliv mit einer merkwürdigen Beschreibung von Süd-Carolina versehen. St. Gallen, 1754, p. 32-42.) *Meynen 257.*

UCHTERITZ, HEINRICH VON. Kurtze Reise Beschreibung Hr. Heinrich von Uchteritz... Schlesswig bey Johann Holwein, 1666. *Sabin 97662.*

UHLAND, LUDWIG JOSEPH. Rede vom Ursprung der Bevölkerung in Amerika. Tübingen, 1767. *Sabin 97676.*

VALENTINI, MICHAEL BERNHARD. Museum Museorum... Frankfurt am Mäyn, 1704 [-14]; Zweyte Edition. Franckfurt am Mäyn, 1714. *Sabin 98357.*

VERSUCH einer systemat. Erdbeschreibung der entfernten Welttheile, Afrika, Amerika u. Südindien. Frankfurt und Nürnberg, 1791-99. *See T. C. F. Enslin, Biblioteca historico-geographica, Berlin, 1825, p. 325B.*

VERTHEIDIGUNG der französischen Regierung gegen gewisse Beschuldigungen in den Berichten der amerikanischen Gesandten... Hamburg, 1798. *Sabin 99303.*

VON den Hessen in Amerika, ihrem Fürsten und den Schreyern... 1782. *Sabin 31617.*

WARHAFFTIGE Contrafey einer wilden Frawen ... Nüremberg [1566]. *Sabin 101422.*

WEBER, LUDWIG. Der hinckende Bott von Carolina... Zürich, 1735. *Meynen 195.*

# INDEX

(Authors, Anonymous Titles of Books,[1] and Subjects)

Numbers refer to entries

## A

A., v. *See* Archenholz.
Abbildung Nordamericanischer Länder, 364.
Abbot, John, 1750–1840, contributor. *See* Smith, Sir J. E., The natural history of the rarer lepidopterous insects of Georgia.
Abbots Creek, N. C.: German (Evangelical Lutheran) settlement, 1044, 1203.
Abelin, Johann Philipp, d. 1643: *note of authorship*, 175, 177.
Abhandlung über die Kolonien überhaupt, und die amerikanischen besonders (*review*), 653.
Abhandlungen zur Naturgeschichte, Physik und Oekonomie (*review*), 625A.
Abnaki Indians. *See* Indians.
Aborigines. *See* Indians.
Abrégé de la révolution de l'Amérique angloise. *See* Du Buisson, P. U.
Académie des sciences et beaux arts des États-Unis de l'Amérique. *See* Akademie der Wissenschaften und schönen Künste.
Académie des sciences, belles-lettres et arts de Lyon, 700.
Academy and Learned Society Publications Cited:
American, 474, 492, 821, 965, 975, 1026, 1296, 1474.
foreign, 261, 354, 366, 377, 697, 700, 843, 844, 856, 875, 919, 965, 990, 1023, 1044, 1056, 1058, 1068, 1108, 1210, 1261, 1435, 1453, 1457, 1482, 1502.
*See also* the names of individual academies and societies.
Acadia, 271.
*See also* Nova Scotia.
Accademia etrusca, Cortona, Italy, 1058.
Accordion, 419, 428, 1306, 1476.
Account of the European settlements in America. *See* Burke, Edmund.
An Account of the present state of Nova-Scotia (*review*), 907.
Accounts, Early. *See* Early Accounts of the New World.
Achenwall, Gottfried, 1719–1772:
Anmerkungen. *See his* Entwurf einer politischen Betrachtung.
Einige Anmerkungen über Nordamerika, 427.
Entwurf einer politischen Betrachtung, 333.
Acosta, José de, ca. 1539–1600:
America, 124.
Geographische vnd historische Beschreibung, 102.
*See also* Francisci, Guineischer und Americanischer Blumen-Pusch.
Actes passés à un Congrès des Etats-Unis de l'Amérique (*review*), 1098A.
Adair, James, 1735–1775:
Geschichte der Amerikanischen Indianer, 699.
History of the American Indians. *See* Etwas von den Nordamerikanischen Indianern, 699.
Adair, James Makittrick, 1728–1802: Ueber die Vorbereitung und Lebensordnung. *See* Duncan, Medical commentaries.
Adams, John, 1735–1826, contributor. *See* Ramsay, Geschichte; Untersuchung der Frage, 724.
*election*, 1484.
*See also* Murray, W. V., Political sketches.
Adams, Samuel, 1722–1803: Eine Rede die auf dem Staatshause zu Philadelphia (*review*), 671.

An Address to every Briton on the slave trade (*review*), 1146.
Adelung, Johann Christoph, 1734–1806:
Geschichte der Schiffahrten, 435.
Versuch einer Neuen Geschichte, 441.
Adelung, Johann Christoph, 1734–1806, translator. *See* Venegas, Natürliche und bürgerliche Geschichte von Californien.
Adultery: Indian penalties, 952.
Das Aelteste deutsch-amerikanische Kirchenbuch, 234A.
Agave americana, 1391, 1391A.
Agricultural Schools, 1230.
Agriculture:
American farmers, 1016, 1100.
German American farmers, 487, 647, 1457.
Haiti, 859, 1393, 1395.
Pennsylvania, 225, 226, 229, 230, 231.
United States, 768, 854, 917.
*See also* Country Life; also various products, as Flax; Flour; Tobacco; also various activities, as Horse Breeding.
Akademie der Wissenschaften und schönen Künste, Richmond, Va., 959B.
"Akensas." *See* Indians.
Alaska: description and travel, 1450.
Albert der Selbstmörder (*review*), 1459.
Albertinus, Aegidius, 1560–1620, translator. *See* Botero, Allgemeine Historische Weltbeschreibung.
Alcedo, Antonio de, 1735–1812: Diccionario geográfico-historico (*review*), 960C.
Alexander, William, d. 1783: Geschichte des weiblichen Geschlechts. *See* Von der Art, 759.
Algemeine Geschichte der Länder und Völker von America. *See* Schröter, J. F.
Algonquian Indians. *See* American Languages.
"Alkermes" (confection), 429, 443.
Allen, Ira, 1751–1814: The natural and political history of... Vermont (*review*), 1503.
Allerhand...Brief. *See* Jesuits.
Allerneuste Beschreibung. *See* Lawson, John.
Allgemeine Amerikanische Kriegsgeschichte. *See* Huske, John.
Allgemeine Historie. *See* Prévost d'Exiles, Erste Reisen.
*See also* Charlevoix, Allgemeine Geschichte und Beschreibung; Charlevoix, Fortsetzung der Reisen; Charlevoix, Reisen und Niederlassungen in dem nordlichen America.
Allgemeine Sammlung von Reisebeschreibungen. *See* Prévost d'Exiles, Erste Reisen.
*See also* Charlevoix, Allgemeine Geschichte und Beschreibung; Charlevoix, Fortsetzung der Reisen; Charlevoix, Reisen und Niederlassungen in dem nordlichen America.
Allgemeines Historien-Buch, 1304.
Almanach americain (*reviews*), 761, 829A, 908.
Aloes, 271.
Alphabet. *See* Picture Writing.
Alte und Neue Schwarm-Geister-Bruth, und Quäcker-Greuel, 227.
Amat. *See* Haiti.
America, Discovery of, 87, 94, 106, 144, 202, 214, 235, 341, 353, 385, 386, 393, 536, 667, 700, 762, 822, 1012, 1020, 1079, 1140, 1243, 1245, 1270, 1275, 1304, 1474.
L'America divisa nelle sue principali parti (*review*), 1055.

---

[1] Anonymous titles of periodical articles listed under subject, only; supplementary list not included.

America in Drama, 437, 439, 475, 476, 514, 517, 520, 533, 571, 716, 797, 818, 849, 992, 1175, 1192, 1313, 1351, 1421.
America in Fiction, 265, 336, 425, 432, 529, 678, 681, 820, 1074, 1179, 1271, 1278, 1282, 1399, 1419, 1444, 1447, 1454, 1459, 1508.
America in Poetry, 2, 3, 4, 5, 77A, 96, 174, 442, 478, 482, 485, 487, 496, 499, 500, 500A, 508, 517A, 519, 528, 541, 547, 549, 551, 556A, 558, 586, 611, 616, 635, 645A, 645C, 652, 674, 705, 717, 744, 745, 749, 775, 792, 798, 805, 851, 861, 879, 926, 978, 969, 980, 1043, 1103, 1123, 1132, 1225, 1238, 1321, 1365, 1420, 1425, 1447, 1448, 1476, 1477, 1483.
America, oder wie mans zu Teutsch nennet Die Neuwe Welt. *See* Acosta, J. de.
American Academy of Arts and Sciences: Memoirs:
 v. 1 (*review*), 965.
 v. 2 (*review*), 1296.
American Colonies. *See* Colonies in America.
American edition of the Encyclopaedia (*review*), 1287.
American history, 60, 65, 204, 205, 234, 341, 554, 566, 1012, 1244/45, 1275.
The American Kalendar, or United States register for the year 1795 (*review*), 1288.
American Languages (Indian), 188, 435, 1226.
 aboriginal specimens, 327.
 Algonquian, 236, 241, 1088, 1089, 1119, 1310.
 Canada, 213, 214.
 Chippewa, 1088, 1089, 1119, 1310.
 Eskimo, 320, 324.
 Florida, 213, 214.
 Lord's Prayer, 327.
 Nipissing, Ont., Can., 241, 1088, 1089, 1119, 1310.
 Pokonchi, 221.
 Virginia, 213, 214.
 *See also* Picture Writing.
American Literature, 1093, 1358.
 *See also* Literature.
American Philosophical Society, Philadelphia, Pa.: Transactions:
 v. 1 (*reviews*), 474, 492.
 v. 2 (*reviews*), 922, 975, 1026.
 v. 3 (*reviews*), 1259.
 *See also* Auszug der Artikeln, 377; Auszug aus den Philosophisch. Transactions, 376A; Delbrück, Ueber die Humanität; Nachricht, 856; Neue Mitglieder, 821; Philadelphia, 348.
An American remembrancer (*review*), 1390.
American Revolution, 516A, 518, 523, 531, 543, 546, 561, 565, 594, 627, 654, 663, 682, 695, 701, 712, 737, 832, 834, 860, 941, 961, 971, 972, 1231, 1246, 1247, 1281, 1286, 1357, 1370, 1392, 1431, 1458, 1484A.
 anecdotes, 488, 503, 750, 752, 776.
 beginnings, 497, 534, 543, 628, 663.
 bibliography, 505.
 biography and rosters, 612, 672, 727, 908, 959E, 1057E, 1267, 1485.
 American naval officers, 823, 824.
 British officers, 494, 550, 672, 787.
 British participation, 494, 550, 649, 672, 739, 751, 758, 889, 1212.
 campaigns. *See* military operations.
 commerce, 703, 704, 789.
 *See also* Commerce with and relating to America.
 contemporary accounts, 505A, 505B, 541A, 585, 606, 630, 657, 662, 701, 759F, 1057E, 1267.
 contemporary opinions, 479, 484, 485, 504, 512, 524, 539, 543, 561, 609, 660, 663, 671, 714, 720, 744, 775, 788, 798, 834, 896, 1221.
 drama, 533, 571, 892.
 European participation, 710.
 fiction, 820, 1179, 1282.
 finance (including national debt), 659, 1205.
 French participation, 708, 739, 766, 767, 783, 1212, 1448.

American Revolution, *continued*
 German mercenaries. *See* German Mercenaries.
 hospitals, 550, 919.
 letters, 516, 522, 553, 564, 572, 582, 585, 589, 590, 602, 606, 614, 618, 620, 621, 622, 623, 631, 639, 641, 643, 657, 673, 683, 703, 704, 727, 730, 760, 845, 1484A, 1485.
 Loyalists, 1301.
 map, 513.
 medical and sanitary affairs, 597.
 military operations, 1775–1778, 695.
 Boston, Mass., 582, 602.
 Canada, 585, 606, 618, 622.
 Forts Mercer and Mifflin, 583.
 Jamaica, W. I., 621.
 New England, 618.
 New York, 505B, 553, 582, 643, 683.
 Newburgh, 760.
 Philadelphia, Pa., 582, 614, 657.
 Saratoga, N. Y., 623.
 Staten Island, N. Y., 516.
 Vermont, 582.
 Yorktown, Va., 708.
 naval operations, 789, 845, 876.
 Negroes, 489.
 Netherlands' participation, 613, 724, 889.
 officers. *See* Officers, Military and Naval.
 pensions, 1097.
 personal narratives, 727, 876.
 *See also* letters.
 poetry, 484, 485, 496, 528, 611, 616, 652, 674, 675, 676, 717, 744, 745, 775, 798, 820, 879, 1043, 1355, 1448.
 portraits, 691, 838.
 predictions. *See* contemporary opinion.
 prisoners, British and Hessian, Staunton, Va., 620.
 reconciliation. *See* contemporary opinion.
 results, 739, 766, 767.
 *See also* United States: history.
 songs. *See* poetry.
 sources, 789, 1333, 1350.
 treaties, preliminary, 515, 753.
 *See also* Paris, Treaty of, 1783; Versailles, Treaty of.
 *See also* Declaration of Independence.
The American traveller. *See* Cluny, Alexander.
Der Americaner (*review*), 864A.
Gli Americani (*review*), 437.
Der Americanische Robinson, 265.
Americanische Urquelle, 382.
Amerikanische Bibliothek. *See* Ebeling, C. D., editor.
Amerikanisches Archiv. *See* Remer, J. A., editor.
Amerikanisches Magazin. *See* Hegewisch, D. H., and C. D. Ebeling, editors.
Amtsdiarium vom Januar 1759. *See* Boltzius, J. M.
Analecta historico-litterario-curiosa, 259.
Anatomy: squirrel, 1254, 1296.
Anburey, Thomas:
 Reisen im inneren Amerika, 1120.
 Travels through the interior parts of America (*review*), 1027, 1115.
The Ancient right of the English nation. *See* Bollan, William.
Anderson, Alexander, d. 1811:
 Nachricht von einer bituminösen Ebene. *See* Royal Society of London, Philosophical transactions, v. 79.
 *See also* Cook, Dritte Entdeckungs-Reise; Geschichte der Seereisen und Entdeckungen.
Anderson, James. Beschreibung des Berges Morne-Garou auf der Jnsel St. Vincent, und des Feuerberges auf seinem Gipfel. Jn einem Briefe von Hrn. James Anderson, 843A.
Anderson, Johann, 1674–1743: Nachrichten von Island, Grönland, 320, 324.
Andre, Christian Karl, 1763–1831, editor. *See* Raff, Geographie.

# GERMAN WORKS RELATING TO AMERICA — INDEX 175

Andreae, Dietrich Wilhelm, d. 1813, translator. See Casas, Die Verheerung Westindiens.
Andrews, John, 1736–1809: History of the war in America. See England.
Anecdotes, 488, 503, 750, 752, 776, 786, 826, 916, 981, 982, 1074, 1113, 1178, 1200, 1219, 1346.
Anghiera, Pietro Martire d', 1455–1526:
 'Ander Theil, Der Newen Welt, 82.
 See also Angliara, Die schiffung; Cortés, Von dem Newen Hispanien.
 biography, 82, 536.
Angliara, Juan de: Die schiffung mitt dem Lanndt der Gulden Insel gefundē, 44.
Animals:
 diseases. See Veterinary Medicine.
 Mexico, 852.
 North America, 411.
 St. Bartholomew (island), 1414.
 See also Zoology; also individual animals, as Squirrels.
Animals, Prehistoric: Hudson River, 1296.
Ankündigung einiger Schriften, 844.
Anmerkungen zu den Briefen des Hrn. Benjamin Franklins von der Elektricität. See Wilcke, J. C.
Anmerkungen über die vornehmsten Acten des dreyzehnten Parlements von Grossbritannien. See Remer, J. A.
Annalen der Arzneymittellehre. See Römer, J. J., editor.
Annan, Robert, contributor. See American Academy of Arts and Sciences, Memoirs, v. 2.
Annapolis, Md.: description and travel, 1484.
Annapolis Royal, Nova Scotia: British garrison, 550.
Anthropology: Indians, 1056, 1141, 1142, 1143, 1186, 1187, 1188.
Antill, Edward, contributor. See American Philosophical Society, Transactions, v. 1.
Antilles:
 climate, 868.
 commerce with France, 397.
 description and travel, 188, 397.
 health, 868.
 history, 397, 685.
 natural history, 188.
 Negroes, 868.
 See also various islands of the Antilles.
Antilles, Lesser:
 British possession, 398, 399, 400, 405, 407.
 See also various islands of the Lesser Antilles.
Anwanden, Christoff Ludwig Dietherr von. See Dietherr von Anwanden, C. L.
Apollonius, Levinus, fl. 1565–1583: Dritte Theil der Newen Welt, 83A.
Apple Cider, 965, 1296.
Appleton, Nathaniel, 1693–1784: Predigt. See Urlsperger, Der Ausführlichen Nachrichten.
Arabian Slave, 1382.
Archaeology:
 America, 968, 1305.
 bibliography, 1384.
 Peru, 830, 831.
 Susquehanna valley, 1296.
Archenholz, Johann Wilhelm von, 1743–1812:
 Annalen der brittischen Geschichte (review), 1057A.
 Anzeiger des Teutschen Merkur, 878A.
 La Fayette, 1158.
 Neue Entdeckungsreise, 1317.
 Der neuere Brutus, 1178.
 See also Bülow, Fragmente; Bülow, Der Freistaat; Bülow, Ueber die politische Lage von America; Der Hügel von Vernon; Indianische Beredsamkeit; Marsh, Wer ist Fox?; Washington.
Arctic Regions, 202, 412, 538, 1039:
 America, 468.
 climate, 985.
 discovery, 568.

Arctic Regions, continued
 exploration, 312, 320, 324, 328, 332, 552, 569, 570, 575, 807, 813, 1033, 1077, 1083, 1091, 1095, 1138, 1182, 1310, 1344, 1371.
 zoology, 320, 321, 324.
Arctic zoology (review), 908A.
Army, 761.
American colonial, 612, 672, 908, 1180.
British in America, 182, 183, 379, 494, 550, 562, 597, 644, 672, 683, 787, 862, 1265.
 See also German Mercenaries.
French in America, 708.
 See also United States: army.
Arnemann, Justus A., 1763–1786. De Morbo venereo (review), 1016B.
Arnold, Christoph, 1627–1685, translator. See Rogerius, Offne Thür.
Arthus, Gotthard, 1570–1630? translator. See Bry, Additamentvm; Bry, Appendix; Bry, Neundter vnd Letzter Theil Americæ; Bry, Neundter Theil Americæ; Hudson, Zwölffte Schiffahrt.
Artus. See Arthus.
Association of Tallow Chandlers and Soap Manufacturers. See Mitchill, S. L.
Astronomy, 474, 492, 965, 1296.
 See also Latitude and Longitude.
Atlantis, 830, 831, 867, 867A.
Atlas Minor. See Mercator, Gerardus.
Atwood, Thomas, d. 1793: Geschichte der Insel Dominica, 1268.
d'Auberteuil. See Hilliard d'Auberteuil.
Augusta, Ga.: hot springs, 998.
Ausführliche Beschreibung. See La Peyrère.
Ausführliche Historie Derer Emigranten, 275.
Ausführliche Historie und Geographische Beschreibung Des...Landes Louisiana, 251.
 Dritte Auflage, 252.
Ausführlicher Bericht wie es mit der Silber Flotta hergangen, 157.
Ein Auszug ettlicher sendbrieff...von wegen einer newgefundenen Inseln, 45.
Auszug eines Schreibens aus Amerika. See Heeringen, von.
Autenrieth, Johann Heinrich Ferdinand von, 1772–1835, contributor. See Hegewisch, D. H., and C. D. Ebeling, editors, Amerikanisches Magazin.
Autenrieth, Johann Heinrich Ferdinand von, 1772–1835, translator. See Rush, Beschreibung.
An authentic statement of all the facts relative to Nootka Sound (review), 1057D.
Authors, American: biography, 1093.
 See also American literature.
Auxiliaries. See German Mercenaries.
Avis aux Hessois et autres peuples de l'Allemagne. See Mirabeau, H. G. R., comte de.

# B

B., J. N. C. See Buchenröder, J. N. C.
B., P., z. S. & E. See Ein Kleiner Versuch.
Babo, Franz Joseph Marius, 1756–1822: Das Winterquartier in Amerika, 571.
Bach. See Back.
Back, Jacob Conrad, fl. 1755–61, engraver. See Huske, Allgemeine Amerikanische Kriegsgeschichte.
Baegert, Jacob, 1717–1772: Nachrichten von der Amerikanischen Halbinsel Californien, 467, 477.
Baggesen, Jens, 1764–1826: Der Tag der Freiheit, 1472A.
Bahama Islands, 875.
 climate, 938, 939.
 description and travel, 938, 939.
Bálmis, Franz Xavier de: Uber die amerikanischen Pflanzen (notice), 1391A.
Baltimore, Md.: description, 1312, 1484.
Bandini, Angelo Maria, 1726–1803: Americus Vespucci, 325.

Banks, Sir Joseph, bart., 1743-1820, contributor. See Geschichte der Seereisen und Entdeckungen.
Banks and Banking:
United States, 722, 814, 858.
See also Credit, International; Money and Coinage.
Barbados:
description and travel, 197.
trade, 234.
Barbauld, Anna Letitia Aikin, 1743-1825: Epistle to William Wilberforce (review), 1148.
Barbault-Royer, P. F.: Ueber den neuesten Zustand von St. Domingo, 1380.
Barbeau-Dubourg, Jacques, 1709-1779, translator. See Einem, Auf Franklin; Franklin, Brief vom Doctor Benjamin Franklin; Franklin, Sämmtliche Werke.
Bard, Samuel, contributor. See American Philosophical Society, Transactions, v. 1.
Bardeleben, Heinrich von, d. 1835: Tagebuch, 505B.
Barendsz. See Barents.
Barents, Willem, d. 1597: voyages, 107.
Barlow, Joel, 1754-1812:
The Conspiracy of kings (review), 1193.
The Vision of Columbus (review), 978.
Barrington, Daines, 1727-1800, contributor. See Engel, Geographische und Kritische Nachrichten.
Barron, William, d. 1803:
Geschichte der Kolonisirung der freyen Staaten des Alterthums (reviews), 664, 665.
History of the colonization of the free states of antiquity (review), 631, 665.
Bartl, Franz Konrad, d. 1813: Nachricht von der Harmonika, 1306.
Barton, Benjamin Smith, 1766-1815:
Abhandlung über die vermeinte Zauberkraft der Klapperschlange (review), 1461.
Abhandlungen über die vermeynte Zauberkraft der Klapperschlange (review), 1462.
A Memoir concerning...the rattlesnake (review), 1347.
See also American Philosophical Society, Transactions, v. 1, part 1; v. 3.
Bartram, Isaac, contributor. See American Philosophical Society, Transactions, v. 1.
Bartram, John, contributor. See Iwan Al...z, 715.
Bartram, Moses, contributor. See American Philosophical Society, Transactions, v. 1; College of Physicians of Philadelphia, Medicinische Verhandlungen, Bd. 1.
Bartram, William, 1739-1823:
Reisen, 1160.
Travels (review), 1211.
Basin, Jean, 16th century, translator. See Vespucci, Diss büchlin saget wie.
Batiscamp, Quebec, Canada, 585, 606.
Bauhin, Kaspar, 1560-1624, contributor. See Theodorus, Neuw vollkommentlich Kreuterbuch.
Baumann, Ludwig Adolph, 1734-1802: Abriss der Staatsverfassung...in Amerika, 669.
Baumgarten, Siegmund Jakob, 1706-1757, contributor. See Schröter, Algemeine Geschichte.
Bay, William, 1773-1865: An inaugural dissertation on...dysentery (review), 1433.
Bayerische Akademie der Wissenschaften, 990.
Baylies, William, 1743-1826, contributor. See American Academy of Arts and Sciences, Memoirs, v. 2.
Beaver, Quebec[?], Canada, 861.
Becher, Johann Philipp, 1752-1831:
Auszug aus einem Briefe, 1441.
New-Barbadoes-Neck, 1453.
Beckford, William, d. 1799: A descriptive account of the Island of Jamaica (review), 1147C.
Beckmann, Johann, 1739-1811: Beyträge zur Geschichte der Erfindungen (review), 1147B.
Beer, Ferdinand Wilhelm, translator. See Prévost d'Exiles, Erste Reisen.

Beer, Johann Christoph, 1638?-1712, supposed translator. See Duval, Geographiae; Montanus, Die unbekante Neue Welt.
Beer:
English, 1137.
spruce, 384, 402, 1472.
West Indies, 1137.
Bees in the West Indies, 625A.
Begebenheit eines jungen Englischen Officiers, 418.
Begebenheiten eines americanischen Passagiers. See Des Zu Wasser und Lande.
Begonia, 1391, 1391A.
Behaim, Martin, 1459?-1506: discoveries, 1, 94, 274A, 382, 385, 393, 580, 1019.
Der Bekannte Wasserfall zu Niagara (review), 490.
Belcher, Jonathan, 1681-1757: Extract. See Urlsperger, Der Ausführlichen Nachrichten.
Belgium: commerce and communication with the United States, 1385.
Belknap, Jeremy, 1744-1798:
American biography (review), 1239.
The History of New-Hampshire (review), 872A.
See also Die Art der Indianer, 846.
See also American Philosophical Society, Transactions, v. 2.
Bellegarde, Jean Baptiste Morvan de, 1648-1734: Allgemeine historische Einleitung, 235.
Bellermann, Johann Bartholomäus: Abbildungen zum Kabinet der vorzüglichsten in- und ausländischen Holzarten (review), 959A.
Benecke, Georg Friedrich, 1762-1844, translator. See Atwood, Geschichte der Insel Dominica.
Benezet, Anthony, 1714-1784: biography, 1498.
Beniowsky, Moriz August, Graf von, 1741-1786:
Begebenheiten (review), 1077.
Memoirs and travels (reviews), 1063, 1064.
Reisen, 1033.
See also Campe, J. H., Fortsetzung der Campischen Reisebeschreibungen für die Jugend.
Bensell, George, contributor. See College of Physicians, Philadelphia, Medicinische Verhandlungen, Bd. 1; College of Physicians of Philadelphia, Transactions, v. 1.
Benzoni, Girolamo, b. 1519:
Erste Theil Der Newenn Weldt, 82A, 83.
Der Newenn Welt, 79.
Novae Novi Orbis Historiae, 89.
See also Bry, Das vierdte Buch; Bry, Americae, Pars Quarta; Bry, Americæ Das Fünffte Buch; Bry, Das sechste Theil; Doppelmayr, Historische Nachricht, 274A (note).
Berckenmeyer, Paul Ludolph, 1667-1732: Fortsetzung des Curieusen Antiqvarii, 239.
Berczy, William, contributor. See Berichte über den Genesee-Distrikt.
Beresford, William, fl. 1788, editor. See Portlock and Dixon, Voyage.
Bérenger, Laurent Pierre, 1749-1822: Mémoires historiques. See Rohr, La Fayette.
Berger, Daniel, 1744-1824, engraver. See Zimmermann, Frankreich und die Freistaaten von Nordamerika.
Berger, Friedrich Ludwig von, 1701-1735, contributor. See Gründliche Erweisung.
Bericht für diejenigen, welche nach Nord-Amerika sich begeben...wollen (review), 865.
Bericht von dem was sich am Bord des Amerikanischen Schiffes Elenora...zugetragen hat, 1121.
Bericht eines englischen Amerikaners von Philadelphia (review), 657.
Bericht von Spanischen Expeditionen, 1122.
Berichte über den Genesee-Distrikt, 1078.
Bering, Vitus, 1680-1741: explorations, 1182.
Berkeley, George, 1685-1753, bishop of Cloyne: Gedanken einiger Bramanen. See Herder, Zerstreute Blätter.
Berkeley, Sir William, 1606-1677: biography, 193.
Berkly. See Berkeley.

# GERMAN WORKS RELATING TO AMERICA — INDEX 177

Bermuda Islands, 158, 160, 161.
British garrison, 550.
whaling, 625A.
Bertin, Dr. *See* Des Moyens de conserver la santé des Blancs et des Nègres... aux Antilles.
Bertius, Petrus, 1565–1629: Geographischer eyn oder zusammengezogener Fabeln fünff vnterschiedliche Bücher, 125B.
Bertram, John. *See* Bartram, John.
Beschreibung Der in America neu-erfundenen Provinz Pensylvanien. *See* Penn, William.
Beschreibung der Europäischen Kolonien in Amerika (*reviews*), 626, 658.
Beschreibung des Hallischen Waisenhauses. *See* Koehler, A. R.
Beschreibung Der schiffart. *See* Settle, Dionyse.
Besonderes Gespräche In dem Reich der Lebendigen, 276.
Bethabara, N. C., 344.
Bethlehem, Pa., 344.
Moravian Brethren, 461.
Betrachtungen über den gegenwärtigen Zustand der französischen Colonie. *See* Hilliard d'Auberteuil.
Betuleius, Xystus. *See* Birck, Sixt.
Beverages. *See* various beverages, as Beer, Coffee, etc.
Ein Bewert Recept, 50.
Beyträge zur Geschichte des Amerikanischen Krieges (*reviews*), 959F, 1057E.
Beyträge zur Sittenlehre, Oekonomie, Arzneywissenschaft, Naturlehre und Geschichte (*review*), 466.
Beyträge zur Völker- und Länderkunde (*reviews*), 866, 1014.
Bible: Old Testament: Psalms: German, 483.
Biblical Literature: Lutheran catechisms and Biblical reader, 844.
Bibliographies:
America, 349, 642, 802, 825, 1015, 1093.
American Revolution, 505.
archaeology: America, 1384.
geography: America, 349.
immigration, 1387.
Indians, 1174.
science: American works, 349.
slavery, 1094.
Steuben, 829.
Biblioteca Americana. *See* Rede, L. T.
Biddle, Owen, contributor. *See* American Philosophical Society, Transactions, v. 1.
Bierling, Fr. Immanuel, translator. *See* Prévost d'Exiles, Erste Reisen.
Bigges, Walter, d. 1586: Relation, 88.
Biography:
American, 204, 205, 1093, 1239, 1267.
naval, 204, 205.
writers, American, 1093.
*See also* Diaries; Letters; Portraits; *also* various classes, as Officers, Military and Naval; *also* individual names, as Columbus; Franklin.
Biology. *See* Mortality; Natural History; Physiology; Zoology.
Birck, Sixt, 1500–1554, translator. *See* Cortés, Von dem Newen Hispanien.
Blackford, Dominique de, contributor. *See* Vom Deutschen-Handel.
Blindness Caused by Lightning, 1235.
Bluett, Thomas: Some memoirs. *See* Schicksale eines muhamedanischen Imam, 1382.
Blumenbach, Johann Friedrich, 1752–1840:
Abbildungen naturhistorischer Gegenstände, 1307.
Schreiben...über die Lage von Schekomeko, 1426.
Blumhof, Johann Georg Ludolph, 1774–1825, translator. *See* Auszug eines Briefes, 1350; Crèvecœur, Abhandlung; Euphrasén, Reise.
Bock, Friedrich Samuel, 1716–1786: Kurz gefasste Missions Geschicht, 316.
Bock, J. Ch., contributor. *See* Antwort auf die... gethane Anfrage "Ueber den Canadischen Zuckerbaum," 637.

Bockenhoffer, Johann Joachim, contributor. *See* Richshoffer, Brassilianisch- und West Indianische Reisse Beschreibung.
Bode, Johann Joachim Christoph, 1730–1793:
Literarisches Leben (*review*), 1343.
Der Westindier. *See his* Literarisches Leben (*review*).
biography, 1343.
Bode, Johann Joachim Christoph, 1730–1793, translator. *See* Cumberland, Der West-Indianer.
Bodmer, Johann Jacob, 1689–1783: Inkel und Yariko. *See* Holtinger, Salomon Gessner.
Boehme, Anton Wilhelm, 1673–1722: Das verlangte ...Canaan, 240.
Böttger. *See* Boetticher.
Boetticher, Gottfried Conrad, 1704?–1783, translator. *See* Garcilaso de la Vega, Ferdinand von Soto; Garcilaso de la Vega, Geschichte der Ynkas.
Böttiger, Karl August, 1760–1835: Washington, 1161.
Böttiger, Karl August, 1760–1835, editor. *See* Wansey, Tagebuch.
Boie, Heinrich Christian, 1744–1806: Amerika, 775.
Bollan, William, d. 1776:
The Ancient right of the English nation (*review*), 416.
Coloniae Anglicae illustratae (*review*), 417.
Bolt, Johann Friedrich, 1769–1836, engraver. *See* Cook, Dritte Entdeckungs-Reise; Forster, Geschichte.
Boltzius, Johann Martin, 1703–1765:
Amtsdiarium. *See* Urlsperger, Americanisches Ackerwerk Gottes.
Beschreibung des...Dankfestes. *See* Urlsperger, Der Ausführlichen Nachrichten.
Briefe. *See* Urlsperger, Der Ausführlichen Nachrichten.
Nebendiarium. *See* Urlsperger, Der Ausführlichen Nachrichten.
Reise-Diarium. *See* Urlsperger, Der Ausführlichen Nachrichten.
Tageregister [1747–1751]. *See* Urlsperger, Der Ausführlichen Nachrichten.
Tageregister vom Jahre 1751. *See* Urlsperger, Americanisches Ackerwerk Gottes.
Tageregister vom Jahre 1752. *See* Urlsperger, Americanisches Ackerwerk Gottes.
Tageregister vom Jahre 1753. *See* Urlsperger, Americanisches Ackerwerk Gottes.
Zuverlässige Antwort. *See* Urlsperger, Der Ausführlichen Nachrichten.
Zweyte Probe einiger...Anmerkungen. *See* Urlsperger, Der Ausführlichen Nachrichten.
Boltzius, Johann Martin, 1703–1765, and I. C. Gronau:
Auszüge einiger Schreiben. *See* Urlsperger, Der Ausführlichen Nachrichten.
Einige Briefe. *See* Urlsperger, Der Ausführlichen Nachrichten.
Einige merckwürdige hieher gehörige Briefe. *See* Urlsperger, Der Ausführlichen Nachrichten.
Nachricht vom Einfall der Spanier. *See* Urlsperger, Der Ausführlichen Nachrichten.
Reise-Diarium. *See* Urlsperger, Der Ausführlichen Nachrichten.
Tage-register [1734–1743]. *See* Urlsperger, Der Ausführlichen Nachrichten.
Boltzius, Johann Martin, 1703–1765, and others: Briefe und Extracte. *See* Urlsperger, Americanisches Ackerwerk Gottes.
Bond, Thomas:
Défense de l'inoculation (*review*), 831A.
*See also* American Philosophical Society, Transactions, v. 1.
Bonnet, J. Esprit: Réponse aux principales questions ...sur les États Unis (*review*), 1401.
Bonneville, C. de. *See* Pazzi de Bonneville, Zacharie de.
Book of Common Prayer, 855.
Boone, Daniel, 1734–1820: biography, 815, 871, 872.
Bordeaux, France: commerce with Maryland, 748.

Born, Ignatz, Edler von, 1742-1791: Physikalische Arbeiten (*review*), 875.
Borowski, Georg Heinrich: Ueber die Anpflanzung ausländischer Holzarten zum Nutzen der Forsten (*review*), 922A.
Borrhaus, Martin, 1499-1564: Elementale Cosmographicum. *See* Doppelmayr, Historische Nachricht.
Bos, Lambert van den, 1610-1698: Leben und Tapffere Thaten, 204.
Leben und Thaten, 205.
Bosc, Louis Augustin Guillaume, 1759-1828, contributor. *See* Bruguière and others, Journal.
Bossart, Johann Jakob, editor. *See* Oldendorp, Geschichte der Mission.
Boston, Mass., 525, 582, 602, 1107.
American revolution, 582, 602.
Catholic church, 1047.
description and travel, 513, 1484.
Evangelical Lutheran Church, 1047.
German mercenaries, 602.
map, 513.
Botany, 135, 187, 189, 354, 819, 1255, 1259, 1396, 1466, 1482, 1499.
America, 688, 819, 886, 909, 1304, 1400.
Leeward Islands, 1414.
Mexico, 1299.
North America, 411, 470, 1299.
Pennsylvania, 715, 1259, 1457.
United States, 738, 1090, 1098, 1230, 1252, 1272, 1294, 1298/99.
West Indies, 625A.
*See also* Herbs; Trees and Shrubs; *also* various plants, as Agave americana; Begonia; etc.
Botany, Economic, 187, 271, 414, 415, 421, 429, 430, 443, 459, 1003, 1305, 1397.
Botany, Medical, 977, 979, 1391, 1391A, 1396.
*See also* Herbs, Medicinal; Plants, Poisonous.
Botero, Giovanni, 1540-1617: Allgemeine Historische Weltbeschreibung, 125.
Bourgeois, Nicholas Louis, 1710-1776: Voyages intéressans (*review*), 1030.
Bourignon, Xaverius von, contributor. *See* Philorthodoxo, Ungeheuchelte Theologische Unterredung.
"Bourlardiere, Herr de la:" *biography*, 253.
Bouterwek, Friedrich, 1766-1828:
Der Genius von Otaheiti, 1123.
Morgenlied, 926.
Bowdoin, James, 1727-1790, contributor. *See* American Academy of Arts and Sciences, Memoirs, v. 1.
*biography*, 1296.
Bradford, William, 1755-1795:
An Enquiry how far the punishment of death is necessary (*review*), 1195.
*See also* Gruner, Versuch über Strafen.
Bradley, John, contributor. *See* American Philosophical Society, Transactions, v. 1.
Brahl, Johann, b. 1754, translator. *See* Mirabeau, Des Grafen von Mirabeau Sammlung.
Brandywine Creek, Pennsylvania, 688, 909.
Brant, Captain Joseph. *See* Thayadanega.
Brant, Sebastian, 1457-1521: Das Narrenschiff, 2, 3, 4, 5.
Braun, Nicolaus, d. 1639, contributor. *See* Theodorus, Neuw vollkommentlich Kreuterbuch.
Brawer. *See* Brouwer.
Brazil, 34, 35, 36, 37, 38, 39, 40, 41, 55, 86, 158, 180, 184, 187, 196.
aboriginal religion, 793.
early accounts, 69, 70, 71/72, 92, 93, 144.
Indians, 793.
poetry, 746, 747.
Breitenbauch, Georg August von, 1731-1817:
Auszug der Geschichte der aussereuropäischen Welttheile (*review*), 1012.
Versuch einer Erdbeschreibung (*review*), 1213.
Vorstellung der vornehmsten Völkerschaften der Welt, 1116A.

Bretzner, Christian Friedrich, 1748-1807: Das Räuschgen, 849.
Briars, Sensitive, 1305.
Bridges, Natural, 998.
Briefe eines amerikanischen Landmanns (*reviews*), 1016, 1100.
Briefe und Extracte derselben, von denen Herren Predigern in Ebenezer. *See* Boltzius, J. M.
Briefe über gegenwärtigen Zustand von England (*review*), 659.
Briefe, den gegenwärtigen Zustand von Nordamerika betreffend. *See* Sprengel, Christian.
Briefe vom J. 1757, 539.
Briefe über die jetzige Uneinigkeit zwischen den Amerikanischen Colonien und dem Englischen Parlament (*review*), 590.
Briefe über die jezige Uneinigkeit zwischen den amerikanischen Kolonien und dem englischen Parlament (*review*), 660.
Brissot de Warville, Jacques Pierre, 1754-1793:
De La France et des Etats unis (*review*), 867B.
Neue Reise, 1124, 1362.
Nouveau voyage (*review*), 1110, 1150.
*See also* Society instituted in 1781...
British Colonies in America, 182, 183, 219, 233, 238, 242, 245, 247, 257, 273, 301, 330, 351, 352, 362, 363, 364, 367, 373, 379, 381, 382, 417, 423, 429, 481, 494, 497, 502, 507, 513, 515, 521, 523, 526, 535, 554, 566, 567, 577, 578, 591, 592, 609, 653, 661, 662, 664, 665, 757, 780, 1024, 1030, 1031, 1112, 1198.
agricultural products, 534, 663.
British quarrel, 505.
commerce, 534, 770.
culture, 446.
ministers to America, 721.
statistics, 565, 595.
taxation, 472.
British West Indies. *See* West Indies.
Brodhagen, Peter Heinrich Christian, 1753-1805, translator. *See* Franklin, Ueber das Rauchen der Kamine.
"Brookland, bei Neu York," 641.
Brouwer, Hendrik, 1580-1643: *voyages*, 175, 176.
Brown, Roberto, pseud. *See* Crouch, Nathaniel.
Bruchstück aus "Frankreich und die Freistaaten von Nordamerika." *See* Zimmermann, E. A. W.
Bruée, W. Urb: A narrative of the successful manner of cultivating the clove tree (*review*), 1397.
Brühl, Johann Benjamin, 1691-1763, engraver. *See* Die Krafft und Wahrheit.
Bruguière, Jean Guillaume, 1750-1799, and others:
Journal d'histoire naturelle (*review*), 1249.
Bruns, Paul Jakob, 1743-1814:
Geographisches Handbuch (*reviews*), 1018A, 1018B, 1058A, 1059.
*See also* Bericht von Spanischen Expeditionen; Bericht von dem was sich am Bord des Amerikanischen Schiffes Elenora...zugetragen hat; Clarkson, Ueber den Sclavenhandel; Coxe, Auszug aus Tench Coxe's Abhandlungen; Jamaica; Reise in den nördlichen Gegenden zwischen Asien und Amerika; Sklavenhandel; Universitäten.
Bruns, Paul Johann [i.e., Paul Jakob], 1743-1814, and E. A. W. Zimmermann, editors: Repositorium, 1125.
Brunswick. — Army: Returns of the Brunswick troops in British pay. *See* Great Britain. — Treaties, Die drey vollständigen Subsidien-Tractaten.
Brunswick Papers: Letters and documents relating to the service of the Brunswick troops in America, 1776-1777. *See* Great Britain. — Treaties, Die drey vollständigen Subsidien-Tractaten.
Bruyn, Severyn J., contributor. *See* American Academy of Arts and Sciences, Memoirs, v. 2.

# GERMAN WORKS RELATING TO AMERICA — INDEX 179

Bry, Theodor de, 1561-1623, editor:
Achter Theil Americæ, 154.
Additamentvm; Das ist, Zuthuung zweyer fürnemer Reysen oder Schiffarten Herrn Francisci Draken, 111.
Additamentvm, Oder Anhang dess neundten Theils Americæ, 117.
America, Das ist, Erfindung, 138.
Americæ Achter Theil, 108.
Americæ Das Fünffte Buch, 95, 131.
Americae, Pars Quarta, 132.
Der ander Theil, der Newlich erfundenen Landschafft Americæ, 91, 120.
Appendix Dess eilfften Theils Americæ, 150.
Dreyzehnder Theil Americae, 158.
Dritte Buch Americæ, 92, 93.
Historische Beschreibung, Der wunderbarlichen Reise, 146.
Neundter vnd Letzter Theil [Americæ], 114, 164, 165.
Das VII. Theil America, 98, 139.
Das sechste Theil der neuwen Welt, 97.
Das sechte Theil Americæ, 147.
Das vierdte Buch Von der neuwen Welt, 94.
Vierzehender Theil Americanischer Historien, 162.
Warhafftige Abconterfaytung der Wilden in America. *See his* Der ander Theil.
Wunderbarliche, doch Warhafftige Erklärung, Von der Gelegenheit vnd Sitten der Wilden in Virginia, 90, 112, 149.
Zehender Teil Americæ, 143.
Zwölffter Theil der Newen Welt, 152.
*See also* Casas, Umbständige warhafftige Beschreibung; Gottfried, Newe Welt; Hudson, Zwölffte Schiffahrt.
Buchenröder, Johann Nicolaus Carl: Grundriss von Nordamerika (*review*), 629.
Buchenröder, Johann Nicolaus Carl, supposed author: Das Nord-Amerika, 554.
Buckwheat, Siberian, 414.
Büdingische Sammlung, 313A.
Bülow, Carl von, 1776-1841: Berichtigung, 1443.
Bülow, Dietrich, Freiherr von, 1757-1807:
Briefe, 1308.
Fragmente eines Briefes, 1407.
Der Freistaat von Nordamerika, 1363.
Noch ein paar Worte über America, 1364.
Ueber die politische Lage von America, 1408.
Ueber Washingtons Briefe, 1409.
*See also* Wansey, Tagebuch; Washington, Beständigen.
Buerger, Gottfried August, 1747-1794, translator. *See* Franklin, Jugendjahre.
Büsch, Johann Georg, 1728-1800: Allgemeine Anmerkungen über den Zustand, 448.
Büsching, Anton Friedrich, 1724-1793. *See* Ebeling, Erdbeschreibung und Geschichte von Amerika.
Burghaus, Conrad Johann August, Graf von, d. 1804: Washington, 1329.
Burgoyne, John, 1722-1792:
*biography*, 623.
*campaign*, 1485.
*See also* Remer, Amerikanisches Archiv.
Burgsdorf, Friedrich August Ludwig von, 1747-1802: Abhandlung über die Vortheile vom ungesäumten ...Anbau einiger...Holzarten, 1036.
Ueber die in den Waldungen der Kurmark-Brandenburg befindlichen...Holzarten, 886.
Versuch einer vollständigen Geschichte vorzüglicher Holzarten in systematischen Abhandlungen (*review*), 911B.
*See also* Vom Herrn G. N. Lutgens an den Herrn... v. Burgsdorf, 1457.
Burke, Edmund, 1729-1797:
Account of the European settlements in America (*review*), 372.
Edmund Burkes Jahrbücher (*review*), 591, 592, 661.
*See also* Remer, Amerikanisches Archiv.

Burkhausen. *See* Burghaus.
Burnaby, Andrew, 1734?-1812: Reisen durch die Mittlern Kolonien der Engländer in Nord-Amerika, 507.
Burton, Robert, pseud. *See* Crouch, Nathaniel.
Butel-Dumont, Georges Marie, 1725-1788: Der Engländischen Pflanzstädte in Nord-America, 351.
Butterflies: America, 927.
Byrne, Wilhelm, 1743-1805, engraver. *See* Der bekannte Wasserfall zu Niagara.

## C

Cabot, Sebastian, ca. 1474-1557: *voyages*, 204, 205, 502, 535.
Calancha, Antonio de la, 1548-1654, contributor. *See* Francisco, Guineischer und Americanischer Blumen-Pusch.
Calendars, 463.
California, 477, 1034.
description and travel, 1439, 1450.
discovery, 467, 1122.
exploration, 1122.
government, 1122.
history, 445, 454.
Indians, 467, 947.
natural history, 445, 454.
California, Lower. *See* Lower California.
Callender, James Thomas, 1758-1803: Sketches of the history of America (*review*), 1505.
Callichon, Friedrich Christian de la Roche, 1726-1789: Sendschreiben (*review*), 973.
Calueto, Urbanus. *See* Chauveton, Urbain.
Cambridge, Mass., 618, 623, 965, 1427, 1479.
climate, 942.
German mercenaries, 623.
topography, 942.
Camerarius, Rudolf Jacob, 1665-1721: Von dem Gebrauch der Beere des Americanischen...Nachtschattens, 429.
Campaigns, Military. *See* various wars, as American Revolution; French and Indian War; etc.
Campe, Joachim Heinrich, 1746-1818:
Die Entdeckung der neuen Welt. *See* Allgemeines Historien-Buch.
Die Entdekkung von Amerika (*review*), 762, 1304.
Fortsetzung der Campischen Reisebeschreibungen, 1309.
Geographisches Kartenspiel (*review*), 872B.
Sammlung, 850.
*See also* Brissot de Warville, Neue Reise.
Camphor: West Indies, 1253.
Canada, 213, 214, 236, 241, 320, 324, 332, 416, 606, 618, 770.
American Revolution, 585, 606, 618, 622, 751, 788.
British aspects, 242, 243, 423, 751.
British garrison, 550.
colonies, 213, 214, 236, 241, 723, 907, 1444, 1480.
description and travel, 213, 214, 222, 224, 236, 241, 328, 334, 340, 347, 351, 355, 357, 363, 364, 367, 378, 490, 513, 545, 554, 781, 1088, 1089, 1119, 1250, 1276, 1285, 1310, 1344, 1371, 1451, 1469, 1489, 1490, 1506, 1507.
fiction, 778, 1444.
foreign relations: Great Britain, 1487.
French and Indian War, 371, 380, 381, 382, 395, 423.
geography, 213, 357, 423, 629, 781.
German mercenaries, 585, 618, 622.
history, 236, 241, 352, 357, 367, 378, 562, 723.
Indians, 213, 214, 236, 238, 241, 271, 334, 340, 371, 1250, 1276, 1344, 1371.
Jesuit missions, 271.
natural history, 347, 1344, 1371.

Canada, *continued*
    pictorial works, 313, 214, 417.
    song, 861.
    topography. *See* Topography.
    *See also* various provinces, regions, etc.; *also* French and Indian War.
Canada, Upper:
    description and travel, 1481.
    Indians, 1460.
Canal: Delaware river and Chesapeake bay, 474, 492.
Candisch, Thomas. *See* Cavendish, Thomas.
Cannibals, Indian-American, 73, 74.
Canovai, Stanislao, 1740-1811:
    Elogio d'Amerigo Vespucci (*review*), 1058.
    Lettera (*review*), 1021.
Canzler, Friedrich Gottlieb, 1764-1811: Allgemeines Archiv (*reviews*), 907A, 959C.
Cape Breton, 416.
    French and Indian War, 381.
Capell, Rudolf, 1635-1684: Vorstellungen des Norden, 195A.
Capelle, Joseph, contributor. *See* College of Physicians of Philadelphia, Transactions, v. 1.
Captives of Indians. *See* Indian Captivities.
Carey, Mathew, 1760-1839:
    Eine kurze Nachricht (*reviews*), 1251, 1292.
    A Short account (*reviews*), 1237, 1300.
    *See also* An American remembrancer.
Carli, Carlo, conte. *See* Carli, Giovanni Rinaldo, conte.
Carli, Giovanni Rinaldo, conte, 1720-1795:
    Briefe über Amerika (*reviews*), 830, 831, 867, 867A.
    *See* Neue Quartalschrift aus den neuesten und besten Reisebeschreibungen gezogen.
Carolina, 244, 331, 488A, 880.
    description, 267, 351, 693.
    discovery, 193.
    geography, 693.
    German settlements, 240, 305, 306, 307, 308, 318, 337, 339, 487, 777, 903, 937, 1044, 1203, 1305.
    history, 247, 693.
    Indians, 699.
    Moravian Brethren, 344.
    Palatines, 240.
    slaves, 305; 306.
    *See also* North Carolina; South Carolina.
Carter, Landon, contributor. *See* American Philosophical Society, Transactions, v. 1.
Cartier, Jacques, 1491-1557: *voyages*, 144.
Carver, Jonathan, 1732?-1790:
    Johann Carvers Reisen, 642.
    *See also* Campe, Sammlung; Neue Quartalschrift aus den neuesten und besten Reisebeschreibungen gezogen; Schiller, Nadowessiers Totenlied.
    *biography*, 640.
Casas, Bartolomé de las, 1474-1566, Bishop of Chiapa:
    Newe Welt, 99, 109.
    Umbständige warhafftige Beschreibung, 185.
    Die Verheerung Westindiens (*review*), 1116, 1156.
    Warhafftiger vnd gründlicher Bericht, 133.
Castellux. *See* Chastellux.
Castiglioni, Luigi, conte, 1757-1832: Reise durch die vereinigten Staaten (*reviews*), 1252, 1294.
Castleton, Vt.: American Revolution, 582.
Castor Oil: manufacture: West Indies, 1061.
Catholic Church. *See* Roman Catholic Church.
Cattle, 713.
Causland, R.: R. Causland über einige Besonderheiten, 986.
Cavendish: Nachricht von den Versuchen...über das Gefrieren der Salpeter- und Vitriolsäure, 1037.
Cavendish, Thomas, 1555?-1592: *voyages*, 108, 111, 121, 145, 154, 155, 204, 205.
Caves: Virginia, 998.
Caxa, Quiritius: Noch ein anderer Sendbrieff. *See* Cysat, Warbafftiger Bericht.
Cellarius, Martinus. *See* Borrhaus, Martin.
Celler, Johann Peter. *See* Moralischer Artikel.

Census. *See* as sub-head under Colonies in America; United States; *also* various states.
Central America:
    description and travel, 221.
    Indians. *See* Indians.
    natural history, 189.
Cérisier, Antoine Marie, d. 1828, translator. *See* Barron, History.
Chalmers, George, 1742-1825: Schätzung der verhältnismässigen Stärke von Grossbritannien (*review*), 921E.
Chamberlain, William: Practische Abhandlung (*review*), 979.
Champlain, Lake, 1296.
    topography of district, 606.
Charaden und Rätsel:
    No. 10, 1476.
    No. 11, 1477.
Charakter, Zustand und Anzahl der Indianer, 887.
Charaktere, oder unpartheyische Musterung (*review*), 628.
Charleston, S. C., 305, 306, 318, 688, 752, 959, 1484.
    shipping, 358.
    slave trade, 358, 1059.
Charlevoix, Pierre François Xavier de, 1682-1761:
    Allgemeine Geschichte und Beschreibung, 355.
    Fortsetzung der Reisen, 378.
    Histoire et description generale de la Nouvelle France. *See* Schröter, Algemeine Geschichte.
Charlevoix, Pierre François Xavier de, 1682-1761, and others: Reisen und Niederlassungen in dem nordlichen America, 367/68.
Chastellux, François Jean, marquis de, 1734-1788:
    Reise (*review*), 870.
    Voyage (*reviews*), 840, 840A.
    Voyages (*review*), 922B.
    *See also* Literatur und Völkerkunde.
Chatham, William Pitt, 1st earl of. *See* Pitt, William, first earl of Chatham.
Chauveton, Urbain, 16th century, translator. *See* Benzoni, Novae Novi Orbis Historiae.
Chemical Society in Philadelphia, 1412, 1504.
Chemistry, 1037, 1412, 1438, 1464, 1499, 1500, 1504.
Children's Books. *See* Juvenile Literature.
Chimneys, 922, 976, 1088.
Chippewa Indians. *See* Indians; *also* American Languages.
Chittenden, Lucius Eugene, 1824-1900, translator. *See* Crespel, Merkwürdige Reisen.
Chodowiecki, Daniel, 1726-1801, illustrator. *See* Sprengel, Allgemeines historisches Taschenbuch.
Christian IV, 1577-1648, king of Denmark: *voyage*, 202.
Christianity, 1460.
    *See also* Church in America; Religion.
Chronica. *See* Egenolf, Christian.
Chronologen. *See* Wekhrlin, 625.
Church in America:
    American colonies, 87, 761.
    New England, 855.
    North Carolina, 908, 1044, 1203.
    United States, 1460.
    Virginia, 249, 843.
    *See also* Catholic Church; Dunkers; Evangelical Lutheran Church; Freethinkers; Jesuits; Jews; Mennonites; Missons; Moravian Brethren; Protestant Episcopal Church; Reformed Church; Schwenckfeldians; Society of Friends.
Church Records: New London, Conn.; Philadelphia, Pa.; Salem, Mass., 1052.
Churches: United States, 1339.
Cieza de León, Pedro de, 1518-1560, contributor. *See* Francisci, Guineischer und Americanischer Blumen-Pusch.
Cincinnati, Order of: Statutes, 784.
    *comment on*, 896.
Cities, American, 1415.
Cladera, Cristóbal, 1760-1816: Investigationes bistoricas. *See* Doppelmayr, Historische Nachricht.

Claesz, Johan, contributor. *See* Exquemelin, Die Americanische See-Räuber.
Clarke, James: A treatise on the yellow fever (*review*), 1438.
Clarkson, Thomas, 1760–1846:
Essay on the impolicy of the American slave trade (*review*), 1017.
Letters on the slave trade. *See* Sklavenhandel (*review*).
Ueber den Sclavenhandel, 1184.
Clarkson, William. *See* College of Physicians of Philadelphia, Medicinische Verhandlungen, Bd. 1; College of Physicians of Philadelphia, Transactions, v. 1.
Claudius, Matthias, 1740–1815:
Asmus omnia sua Secum portans, 482.
Erdäpfellied, 743A.
Urians Reise um die Welt, 851.
Clavière, Étienne, 1735–1793, contributor. *See* Society instituted in 1781.
Clavigero. *See* Clavijero.
Clavijero, Francisco Javier, 1731–1787:
Abhandlung, 852.
Geschichte von Mexico (*reviews*), 1105A, 1148A.
Clemens, Gottfried, 1706–1776, editor. *See* Des Ordinarii Fratrum.
Clemens, Johann Friedrich, 1749–1831, engraver. *See* Egede, Nachrichten.
Clerke, Charles, 1741–1779, contributor. *See* Anführung des Capitains Cook, Clerke [etc.]; Cook, Dritte Entdeckungs-Reise; Cook, Voyage; Geschichte der Seereisen und Entdeckungen.
Climate, 990, 1170.
America, 922, 993.
Antilles, 868.
Arctic regions, 985.
Bahama Islands, 938, 939.
Cambridge, Mass., 942.
Louisiana, 1030.
Montreal, Can., 1296.
Santo Domingo, 1030, 1031.
United States, 768, 795, 938, 939.
West Indies, 1028, 1029.
*See also* Meteorological Observations.
Clinton, Sir Henry, 1738?–1795:
Observations on Mr. Stedman's History. *See* Stedman, Charles, Geschichte des Ursprungs.
*See also* Geisler, A. F., Geschichte und Zustand der Königl. Grosbrittannischen Kriegsmacht.
Clove Tree: Dominica, 1397.
Clubs: Pennsylvania laws, 1221.
Clüver, Philipp, 1580–1622, contributor. *See* Welper, Compendium.
Cluny, Alexander:
The American traveller (*review*), 446.
Le Voyageur americain (*review*), 770.
Cochin, Charles Nicolas, 1715–1790, engraver. *See* Franklin, Kleine Schriften.
Cochrane, I., contributor. *See* American Academy of Arts and Sciences, Memoirs, v. 1.
Cod Fisheries: Newfoundland, 332, 638, 801.
Coffee, 493, 521, 544, 1445.
Martinique, 422.
Santo Domingo, 1494.
West Indies, 1261.
Coinage. *See* Money and Coinage.
Collection des portraits des hommes (*review*), 691.
College of Physicians of Philadelphia:
Medicinische Verhandlungen, Bd. 1 (*review*), 1295.
Transactions, v. 1 (*review*), 1260.
Colleges and Universities:
Lancaster, Pa., 940, 960B.
New York, N. Y., 1464.
Salem, N. C., 1305.
United States, 1144.
*See also* Schools; Schoolbooks.
Collin, Nicolaus, contributor. *See* American Philosophical Society, Transactions, v. 3.

Collyer, Joseph, d. 1776, joint author. *See* Fenning, Daniel, and others.
Colman, Benjamin, 1673–1747: Schreiben. *See* Urlsperger, Der Ausführlichen Nachrichten.
Colon. *See* Columbus.
Coloniæ Anglicæ illustratæ. *See* Bollan, William.
Colonies in America, 337, 339, 632, 633, 639, 658, 663, 664, 723, 1096, 1124.
British. *See* British Colonies in America.
British West Indies, 1198.
Canada, 213, 214, 236, 241, 723.
census, 948.
*See also* United States: census.
church history. *See* Church in America.
Compagnie d'Occident, 251, 252, 253, 254.
Connecticut, 733.
Danish. *See* Danish Colonies in America.
Delaware, 562.
Dutch. *See* Dutch Colonies in America.
finance, public, 356.
*See also* Finance, Public.
Florida, 342.
French. *See* French colonies in America.
geography. *See* Geography.
Georgia, 301, 305, 306, 307, 308, 318, 350, 494.
government, 669.
*See also* United States: government.
Indians, 1290.
Jews, 756.
Louisiana, 252.
Massachusetts, 1480.
Mississippi Valley, 260, 472.
Moravian Brethren, 365, 891.
New York, 370.
Newfoundland, 435, 453.
North America, 187, 189, 190, 629, 866.
Ontario Lake, region, 1480.
Pennsylvania, 225, 226, 230, 231, 1388.
Portuguese. *See* Portuguese Colonies in America.
St. Bartholomew, 884.
slaves, 690, 735, 1014.
social life and customs, 1096.
Spanish. *See* Spanish Colonies in America.
Swedish. *See* Swedish Colonies in America.
Venezuela, 68.
Virginia, 839.
Welsh. *See* Welsh Colonies in America.
West Indian companies. *See* West-Indische Compagnie (generic term): colonization.
*See also* Provinces.
Columbia University, New York, N. Y., 1464.
Columbus, Christopher:
Eyn schön hübsch lesen von etlichen insalen, 6.
Der Deutsche Kolumbus-Brief, 7.
*See also* Schreiben des Christoph Columbus, 822.
biography, 31, 32, 48, 49, 89, 94, 104, 106, 175, 176, 204, 205, 385, 386, 393, 519, 548, 563, 576, 667, 674, 675, 676, 836, 1056, 1079, 1086, 1151.
discovery of America, 6, 7, 31, 32, 48, 87, 94, 104, 144, 204, 205, 385, 386, 393, 519, 536, 548, 576, 667, 674, 675, 676, 732, 762, 822, 836, 978, 1079, 1086, 1129, 1170, 1299.
drama, 1192.
poetry, 674, 675, 676, 978, 1321.
Comet, 1259.
Commerce:
America, 57, 534, 663, 770, 788, 1176, 1273, 1366.
America: Europe, 448, 481, 609, 632, 633.
America: France, 251, 252, 253, 254, 255, 256, 260, 1383.
America: Germany, 448, 511, 521, 646, 686, 1003, 1315, 1316, 1424, 1487A.
America: Great Britain, 446, 521, 609, 646, 780, 799, 800, 809, 817, 900, 1137.
America: Spain, 157, 191, 273, 399, 400.
America: Sweden, 651.
American Revolution, 703, 704, 789.
Antilles: France, 397.

Commerce, *continued*
British colonies, 446, 448, 511, 534, 609, 663, 770, 780, 789, 799, 1198.
Cuba, 398, 400.
Jamaica, W. I., 1136.
Jamaica, W. I.: Great Britain, 817.
Louisiana, 251, 252, 253, 646.
Maryland: Bordeaux, France, 748.
New York, 959, 1052.
North America: Sweden, 581.
Nova Scotia, 863, 907.
Pennsylvania, 211, 231.
Santo Domingo, 859, 1395.
South Carolina, 959.
statistics, 511, 799, 800, 1217, 1324.
United States, 707, 780, 809, 858, 938, 939, 1002, 1058A, 1059, 1082, 1159, 1191, 1217, 1224, 1228, 1232, 1276, 1324, 1337, 1348, 1403.
Belgium, 1385.
France, 893.
Germany, 886, 1003.
Great Britain, 809, 900.
Morocco, 1002.
Portugal, 893.
West Indies, 167, 168, 181, 191, 250, 255, 256, 310, 400, 481, 609, 632, 633, 780, 893, 1137, 1198.
France, 827.
Netherlands, 173.
*See also* Communication; Free Ports; Shipping; Trade; Transportation; also various articles of commerce, as tobacco.
Commercial Treaties. *See* Trade Treaties.
Communication:
America: Spain, 157.
United States, 1224, 1228, 1232, 1324.
United States: Belgium, 1385.
*See also* Postal Service; Shipping; Transportation.
Compagnie d'Occident, 250, 260.
colonization, 251, 252, 253, 254.
Company of Mississippi, 253.
Compass, 548, 1259.
A Compendious extract... *See* Zinzendorf, Sieben letzte Reden.
A Concise account of voyages for the discovery of a north-west passage *(review)*, 731.
Condorcet, Marie Jean Antoine Nicolas de Caritat de, marquis, 1743–1794, contributor. *See* Mazzei, Recherches historiques.
Connecticut:
census, 584.
description and travel, 729, 1163, 1478.
geography, 729.
history, 733, 1359, 1360.
Constitutions, State, United States, 694, 806, 823, 824, 854, 877, 1098A, 1155, 1194, 1242, 1256, 1264, 1267, 1411.
*See also* United States: Constitution.
The Constitutions of the several independent states of America. *See* Jackson, William, bp. of Oxford.
The Contest in America. *See* Mitchell, John.
Cook, James, 1728–1779:
Captain Cooks dritte und letzte Reise *(review)*, 887A, 959G.
Des Capitain Jacob Cook dritte Entdeckungs-Reise, 987.
Neueste Reisebeschreibungen, 853.
Voyage to the Pacific Ocean *(reviews)*, 841, 841A.
*See also* Anführung des Capitains Cook, Clerke [etc.]; Auszug aus Cooks Reise; Auszug aus lezter Reise; Campe, Sammlung; Forster, Geschichte der Reisen; Forster, Reise; Geschichte und Entdeckungen; Noch etwas von dem Westmeer; Ueber das Wiedergefundene Westmeer; Zimmermann, Heinrich Zimmermanns...Reise um die Welt.
Cooke, John, contributor. *See* American Philosophical Society, Transactions, v. 3.

Coombe, Thomas, contributor. *See* American Philosophical Society, Transactions, v. 1.
Cooper, Thomas, 1759–1840: Some information respecting America *(review)*, 1403.
Copey etlicher brieff, 59.
Copia Desjenigen Brieffes, 277/278.
Copia der newen zeytung, 36, 37, 38, 39, 40.
*See also* New Zeutung.
Copper Mines and Mining:
America, 356.
New Jersey, 1441, 1453.
Corbett, W., translator. *See* Moreau de St. Méry, A topographical and political description of...Saint-Domingo.
Córdoba, Francisco Hernandez, fl. 1517: *explorations*, 45.
Cortés, Hernando, 1485–1547:
Briefe, 604, 605.
Translation, 46.
Von dem Newen Hispanien, 67.
*See also* Ein Auszug ettlicher sendbrieff; Campe, Die Entdeckung von Amerika; Francisci, Guineischer und Americanischer Blumen-Pusch; Kurzgefasste Geschichte; Meer oder Seehanen Buch; Zur "Neuen Zeitung."
biography, 424, 447.
Cosmographia: das ist. *See* Neue Zeyttung, 78.
Costanso, Miguel: *expedition*, 1122.
Costume. *See* Dress; *see also* Pictorial Works.
Courts: Pennsylvania Supreme Court, 1221.
Courtship:
Indians, 759.
*See also* Marriage.
Coxe, J. H. [?], *explorations*, 1083, 1091, 1095, 1202.
Coxe, Tench, 1755–1824:
Auszug aus Tench Coxe's Abhandlung, 1159.
A Brief examination *(review)*, 1191.
View of the United States of America *(review)*, 1303.
*See also* Johannsén, A geographical and historical account of Bulam.
*See also* Sprengel, M. C., and J. R. Forster, editors, Neue Beyträge.
Cramer, Pieter, d. 1780: Sammlung und Beschreibung ausländischer Schmetterlinge, 927.
Cranz, David, 1723–1777:
Alte und Neue Brüder-Historie, 460.
Historie von Grönland, 412, 449.
*See also* Hegner, Fortsetzung.
Credit, International, 1236.
Crespel, Louis, b. 1700: Des Ehrwürdigen Pater Emanuel Crespels merkwürdige Reisen, 334.
Crèvecœur, Michel Guillaume St. Jean de, 1735–1813: Abhandlung von der Kultur...des Acazienbaums, 1373.
Letters from an American farmer. *See* Etwas von den Schlangen in Nordamerika; Iwan Al...z.
*See also his* Sittliche Schilderungen von Amerika.
Lettres. *See* Literatur und Völkerkunde.
Lettres d'un cultivateur américain *(reviews)*, 837, 915.
Sittliche Schilderungen von Amerika, 782.
*See also* Der amerikanische Wilde und sein Hund; Briefe eines amerikanischen Landmanns; Filson, Historie; Herder, Briefe.
Crime and Punishment. *See* Penitentiaries; Punishment, Capital.
Crocker, A., contributor. *See* American Academy of Arts and Sciences, Memoirs, v. 2.
Croix, de la. *See* Delacroix.
Crome, August Friedrich Wilhelm, 1753–1833: Ueber die Grösse, Volksmenge, Klima und Fruchtbarkeit des nordamerikanischen Freistaats *(review)*, 768.
Croswell, William, contributor. *See* American Academy of Arts and Sciences, Memoirs, v. 2.
Crouch, Nathaniel, 1632?–1725: Der Englische Held und Ritter Franciscus Dracke, 268.

# GERMAN WORKS RELATING TO AMERICA — INDEX 183

Cuba, 221, 398, 400, 621.
  commerce, 398, 400.
  description, 398, 400.
  history, 162.
Culture in America, 413.
Cumberland, Richard, 1732-1811: Der Westindier (reviews), 475, 476.
Currie, James, 1756-1805, contributor. *See* Royal Society of London, Philosophical transactions, 1792, part 2.
Currie, William, contributor. *See* College of Physicians of Philadelphia, Medicinische Verhandlungen, Bd. 1; College of Physicians of Philadelphia, Transactions, v. 1.
Customs. *See* social life and customs, as sub-head under various countries, races, etc.
Customs [tariff]. *See* Tariff.
Cysat, Renwart, 1545-1614: Warhafftiger Bericht, 86.

## D

Dahlmann, Sven: Beschreibung der...Insel St. Barthelemy, 884.
Dalibard, Thomas François, 1703-1779, contributor. *See* Auszug aus dem Philosophisch. Transactions, 376A.
Dalrymple, Alexander, 1737-1808: The Spanish pretensions fairly discussed (*review*), 1068A.
Dances:
  Haitian aborigines, 816.
  Indian, 816.
Danish Colonies in America, 545.
Danish Expedition of 1606 to Greenland, 202.
Dapper, Olfert, 1636-1689: Dappervs Exoticvs Cvriosvs, 248.
Dapper, Olfert, 1636-1689, translator. *See* Montanus, Die unbekante Neue Welt.
Das über die Glückliche Ankunfft etlicher hundert Saltzburger Emigranten Sich Höchsterfreute Meissen. *See* Novellarius, pseud.
Davis. *See* Davys.
Davys, John, 1550?-1605: explorations, 204, 205.
Deaf and Dumb: language, 1259.
Deane, Silas, 1737-1789:
  Betrachtungen über den künftigen Handel, 703.
  Schreiben, 703A, 703B.
  Ein vertrauter Brief, 704.
  *biography*, 703, 704.
  *portrait*, 838.
Death. *See* Mortality; Suicide.
De Bry. *See* Bry.
Declaration of Independence, 694, 714, 806.
  *See also* American Revolution, etc.
Deerfield, Mass., 305, 306, 318.
Delacroix, Jacques Vincent, 1743-1832:
  Constitutions des principaux États (*review*), 1242.
  A Review of the constitutions of the principal states of Europe (*review*), 1256.
  Verfassung der vornehmsten europäischen und der vereinigten americanischen Staaten (*reviews*), 1155, 1246.
Delaware:
  colony, 562.
  description and travel, 1163, 1478.
  finance, public, 1130.
Delaware river: American Revolution, 583.
Delbrück, Johann Friedrich Ferdinand, 1772-1848: Ueber die Humanität (*review*), 1353.
Democracy, 720.
De Normandie. *See* Normandie.
Des Moyens de conserver la santé des Blancs et des Nègres...aux Antilles (*review*), 868.
Des Ordinarii Fratrum. *See* Zinzendorf, N. L., Graf von.
De Soto. *See* Soto.
Des Zu Wasser und Lande, 336.

Deshayes, Gérard Paul, joint author. *See* Bruguière and others, Journal.
Deutsche Gesellschaft in dem Staate von Neu York:
  By-laws. *See* Wansey, Tagebuch.
Deutsche hohe Schule in Lancaster P. A. (*notice*), 960B.
De Witt, Benjamin, 1774-1819, contributor. *See* Johnson, John, An experimental inquiry.
Dexter, Aaron, contributor. *See* American Academy of Arts and Sciences, Memoirs, v. 2.
Diaries [known authors]: Anderson, 962, 987; Clarke, 962, 987; Cook, 575, 962, 987; Doehla, 541A; Egede, 1039; Gore, 962, 987; King, 962, 987; Naas, 300; Stefanov, 1077; Urlsperger, 350; Weiser, 319; Wilson, 989.
Diarrhoea, 1466.
Dickinson, John, 1732-1808: *portrait*, 838.
Didier, Constanz: Ein kurze Geschichte, die Natur... des gelben Fiebers betr. (*review*), 1502.
Diet:
  Indians, 943, 944, 945, 1004.
  Negroes, 881.
Diether, Andreas, 16th century, translator. *See* Cortés, Von dem Newen Hispanien.
Diether von Anwanden, Christoff Ludwig, 1619-1687, editor. *See* Hammersam, West-Jndianische Reissbeschreibung.
Dieze, Johann Andreas, translator. *See* Ulloa, Physikalische und historische Nachrichten.
Dippold, Gottfried Ehregott, 1751-1804: Paul Hennig, 1162.
Discoverers, 869, 1474.
  *See also* various discoverers, as Columbus.
Discovery [also listed under names of individual discoverers and places], 2, 3, 4, 5, 6, 7, 8, 9, 10, 11, 12, 13, 14, 15, 16, 17, 18, 19, 20, 21, 22, 23, 24, 24A, 25, 26, 27, 28, 29, 30, 31, 32, 33, 34, 36, 37, 38, 39, 40, 41, 44, 45, 46, 48, 49, 51, 52, 53, 57, 59, 66, 68, 77A, 90, 91, 92, 93, 95, 97, 98, 101, 108, 111, 112, 114, 117, 120, 131, 132, 138, 139, 143, 146, 147, 149, 150, 152, 154, 158, 162, 1473.
  history, 836.
  imaginative, 2, 3, 4, 5.
  *See also* Discoverers; Voyages and Travels; also various countries and regions, subhead, discovery.
Dise figur anzaigt vns das volck (Woodcut of South American Indians), 19, 20.
Diseases in America, 1265.
  army, 597, 919, 1190, 1265.
  cattle, 713, 965.
  *See also* Veterinary Medicine.
  Jamaica, W. I., 1190.
  Negro slaves, 1336.
  tropical, 1028, 1029.
  West Indies, 596, 598, 979, 1028, 1029, 1265.
  *See also* various diseases, as Yellow Fever; *also* Drugs; Medicine.
Diss büchlin saget wie. *See* Vespucci, 33, 34.
Dixon, George, d. 1800?, joint author. *See* Portlock, Nathaniel, and G. Dixon.
  *See also* Forster, George, compiler, Geschichte der Reisen; Noch etwas von dem Westmeer, 1091; Ueber das wiedergefundene Westmeer, 1095; Voyage round the world (*review*), 1072.
Dobereiner, Philipp, translator. *See* Jesuits, Sendtschreyben vnd warhaffte zeytungen.
D[octor] Benjamin Franklin's erweitertes Lehrgebäude der natürlichen Elektricität (*review*), 1101B.
Doctor Franklin, 1038.
Doehla, Johann Konrad [or Conrad], 1750-1820: Tagebuch, 541A.
Doernberg, Karl Ludwig von, Freiherr. Journal d'un voyage en Amérique, 605A.
Dogs, 394, 1074, 1302.
Dohm, Christian Wilhelm von, 1751-1820:
  Briefe nordamerikanischen Inhalts, 542.
  Einige der neuesten politischen Gerüchte, 543.

Dohm, Christian Wilhelm von, *continued*
  Etwas Apologetisches wegen der englisch-amerikanischen Handlung, 509.
  Die fünfte Lieferung der Materialien für die Statistik (*review*), 834.
  Geschichte des fünften Welttheils im Kleinen, 510.
  Nordamerikanische Handlung, 511.
  Ueber die Kaffeegesetzgebung, 544.
  *See also* Raynal, Geschichte.
Dohm, Christian Wilhelm von, 1751-1820, compiler. *See* Die fünfte Lieferung, 834.
Dolbeare, Thomas, contributor. *See* College of Physicians of Philadelphia, Medicinische Verhandlungen, Bd. 1; College of Physicians of Philadelphia, Transactions, v. 1.
Dominica:
  clove tree, 1397.
  history, 1268.
Donnant, Denis François: Azakia, 1444.
Donndorf, Johann August; 1754-1777: Ueber Lebensart, Sitten, Gebräuche und natürliche Beschaffenheit verschiedener Völker und Länder, 1029A, 1115A.
Donop, Carl Emil Curt von: Letters. 1776-1777, 511A.
Doppelmayr, Johann Gabriel, 1671-1750: Historische Nachricht, 274A.
Dowry. *See* Marriage: dowry.
Drake, Sir Francis, 1540?-1596: *explorations*, 88, 106, 108, 111, 121, 145, 154, 155, 204, 205, 268.
Drama relating to —:
  America, 1192.
  American revolution, 533, 571, 892.
  Columbus, 1192.
  German mercenaries, 797.
  immigrants, 520, 818.
  slavery, 1313.
Dramas [authors and anonymous titles]: Anekdote, 503; Babo, 571; Barlow, 1193; Bode, 1343; Bretzner, 849; Cumberland, 475, 476; Gli Americani, 437; Goethe, 514, 892; Heinrich, 172; Holtinger, 1351; Iffland, 818; Inkle und Yariko, 439; Klinger, 517, 716; Kotzebue, 992, 1199, 1313, 1421, 1422; Lenz, 520; Michel Wingler, 1175; Morton, 1192; Schiller, 797; Wagner, 533.
Drayton, William Henry, 1742-1799: *portrait*, 838.
Dress, Indian, 1493.
Dresser, Matthaeus, 1536-1607: Historien vnd Bericht Von dem Newlicher Zeit erfundenen Königreich China, 100, 103.
Die Drey vollständigen Subsidien-Tractaten. *See* Great Britain. — Treaties.
Dreyhundert auserlesene amerikanische Gewächse. *See* Jacquin, N. J.
Drugs [also under specific names], 42, 43, 50, 51, 62, 187, 426, 458, 910, 918, 1061, 1253, 1391, 1466.
Jamaica, 977.
prices, 1336.
West Indies, 964.
*See also* Botany, Medical.
Drury, Dru, 1725-1803: Abbildungen und Beschreibungen exotischer Insekten (*review*), 832.
Dryander, Johann, 1500-1550, contributor. *See* Staden, Warhafftige Historia.
Dubourg. *See* Barbeu-Dubourg.
Du Buisson, Paul Ulric, 1746-1794:
  Abrégé de la révolution de l'Amérique angloise (*review*), 654.
  Vorstellung der Staatsveränderung in Nordamerika, 783.
Dumplers. *See* Dunkers.
Duncan, Andrew, 1744-1828, editor: Medical commentaries (*reviews*), 873, 964.
Dunkers, 916, 1032.
Dunlap, John, 1747-1812, editor: American daily advertiser. *See* Volks Menge von Pennsylvania, 1145.
Dunmore, John Murray, earl, 1732-1809, 796.
Durfort, Giovanni Luigi, conte: *prise*, 1021, 1058.
Du Roi, the elder: Journal, 511B.

Du Roi, Johann Philipp, 1741-1785: Die Harbkesche wilde Baumzucht (*review*), 480A.
Du Roy, editor. *See* Vertrauliche Briefe aus Kanada.
Du Simitière, Pierre Eugène, 1736-1784, artist. *See* Collection des portraits; Sammlung von Bildnissen.
Dutch Colonies in America, 182, 183, 204, 205, 233, 247, 1024, 1207.
slaves, 988.
Duval, Pierre, 1618-1683: Geographiæ universalis, 200.
Dyes and Dyeing: Night-shade, 429, 443.
Dysentery, 1433.

# E

E., A., compiler. *See* Lied eines Negersklaven in Amerika, 792.
Early Accounts of the New World, 31, 32, 36, 37, 38, 39, 40, 41, 45, 46, 49, 51, 53, 57, 59, 67, 68, 69, 70, 71/72, 73, 74, 75, 88, 89, 92, 93, 95, 96, 97, 98, 101, 102, 105, 106, 107, 108, 122, 126, 127, 128, 139, 144, 184, 218, 262; *see also* as subhead of various countries and states.
Earth: Indian myths, 894.
Ebeling, Christoph Daniel, 1741-1817:
  Ebelings America Bd. 1, 1478.
  Erdbeschreibung und Geschichte von Amerika, 1163.
  Ueber Portugiesische und Amerikanische Landkarten, 1479.
  *See also* Bülow, Der Freistaat von Nordamerika; Bülow, Ueber Washingtons Briefe; Burnaby, Reisen; Carver, Reisen; Fragen.
Ebeling, Christoph Daniel, 1741-1817, editor: Amerikanische Bibliothek (*review*), 587.
Amerikanisches Magazin. *See* Hegewisch, D. H., and C. D. Ebeling, editors.
Ebeling, Christoph Daniel, 1741-1817, translator. *See* Beniowsky, Begebenheiten und Reisen.
Ebeling, J. P. *See* Ebeling, Johann Dietrich Philipp Christian.
Ebeling, Johann Dietrich Philipp Christian, 1753-1795, translator. *See* Beniowsky, Begebenheiten und Reisen; Rush, Untersuchung.
Eben, Johann Michael, 1716-1761, engraver. *See* Huske, Allgemeine Amerikanische Kriegsgeschichte.
Ebenezer, Ga.:
  Evangelical Lutheran Church, 350.
  German settlement, 275, 276, 277, 278, 279, 280, 281, 282, 283, 284, 285, 286, 287, 288, 289, 291, 292, 293, 294, 295, 296, 297, 298, 299, 301, 303, 308, 322, 326, 668, 1449.
  immigration, 305, 306, 307, 318.
Ebenezer Creek, Ga. *See* Ebenezer, Ga.
Ebert, Johann Jacob, 1737-1805, supposed author. *See* Taurinius, Beschreibung einiger See- und Landreisen.
Eclipses, 1259.
Economic History: United States, 1401, 1403, 1404.
Economics. *See* various phases of economics, as Commerce, Money, etc.
Eddis, William, b. 1745: Letters from America (*review*), 1201.
Education, Religious:
  Lutheran catechism and biblical reader, 844, 914, 963.
  Protestant instruction in Pennsylvania, 361.
Education in America, 413, 938, 939, 1221.
  German schools in Pennsylvania, 940.
  Philadelphia, Pa., 532.
  Salem, N. C., 1305.
  school books, 914, 963.
  *See also* Colleges and Universities; Scholarship.
Edwards, Bryan, 1743-1800:
  Beschreibung der britischen Colonien in Westindien. *See* Sprengel, Auswahl der besten ausländischen und statistischen Nachrichten.
  Geschichte des Revolutionskrieges in Sanct Domingo (*review*), 1393.

# GERMAN WORKS RELATING TO AMERICA — INDEX 185

Edwards, Bryan, *continued*
An Historical survey (*review*), 1395.
History civil and commercial of the British colonies (*review*), 1198.
Edwards, Timothy, contributor. *See* American Academy of Arts and Sciences, Memoirs, v. 2.
Eel, Electric, 574, 975.
Egede, Hans Poulsen, 1689–1758: Ausführliche und wahrhafte Nachricht, 312.
*See also* Andersen, Nachrichten; Bock, Kurz gefasste Missions Geschicht.
Egede, Poul Hansen, 1708–1789: Nachrichten von Grönland, 1039.
Egenolf, Christian, d. 1565: Chronica, 60.
Ehrmann, Theophil Friedrich, 1762–1811, translator. *See* Brissot de Warville, Neue Reise.
Einem, Johann Konrad von, d. 1799: Auf Franklin, 1365.
Einige Anmerkungen über Nordamerika. *See* Achenwall, Gottfried.
Einige Nachricht von der Evangelischen Kirchenverfassung in Nordcarolina (*review*), 911.
Einige den Negerhandel betreffende Nachrichten, 929.
Eintraechtige Freunde in Wien, 875.
Electricity, 366, 369, 452, 839, 965.
An Elegy, occasioned by the rejection of M. Wilberforce's motion for the abolition of slave trade (*review*), 1103.
Ellicott, Andrew, 1754–1820, contributor. *See* American Philosophical Society, Transactions, v. 3.
Ellis, Henry, 1721–1806: Reise nach Hudsons Meerbusen, 328.
Ellis, John, 1710?–1776, contributor. *See* American Philosophical Society, Transactions, v. 1.
Ellis, John, 1710?–1776, joint author. *See* Lettsom, J. C., and J. Ellis, Geschichte des Thees und Koffees.
Elogj storici di Christoforo Colombo e di Andrea d'Oria (*review*), 732.
Elucidarius. *See* Lucidarius.
Emigration and Immigration, 192, 207, 240, 865, 1221, 1293, 1387, 1497, 1498.
America, 319, 1325, 1419.
bibliography, 1387.
British, 271, 365.
drama, 520, 818.
Dutch, 772.
Ebenezer, Ga., 305, 306, 307, 318.
fares, 1183.
fiction, 681, 1341.
Genesee region, New York, 1078.
Georgia, 322.
German, 337, 338, 339, 529, 754, 754A, 777, 861A, 1080, 1305, 1325.
Massachusetts, 313.
Moravian Brethren, 365.
North America, 866.
Palatine Germans, 240, 249, 257, 271.
Pennsylvania, 531, 1267, 1388.
Philadelphia, Pa., 1475.
Protestants, 313.
Salzburgers. *See* Salzburgers.
song, 916A.
United States, 865, 1497.
Endner, Gustav Georg, 1754–1824, illustrator. *See* Fenning, Neue Erdbeschreibung.
Engel, Johann Jacob, 1741–1802: Fürstenspiegel, 1413.
Engel, Samuel, 1702–1784: Geographische und Kritische Nachrichten, 468.
Engel, Samuel, 1702–1784, editor. *See* Mulgrave, Reise.
Engelbrecht, Johann Andreas, 1733–1803, translator. *See* Hilliard d'Auberteuil, Betrachtungen.
Engelschall, Joseph Friedrich, 1739–1797: Malchens Loblied auf den Zucker, 705.
Der Engländischen Pflanzstädte in Nord-America Geschichte. *See* Butel-Dumont, G. M.
England. *See* Great Britain.
England (*review*), 961.

Der Englische Held und Ritter Franciscus Dracke. *See* Crouch, Nathaniel.
English Colonies. *See* Colonies: British.
Ens, Gaspar, b. ca. 1570: West- vnnd Ost Jndischer Lustgart, 144.
Entertainment: United States, 1358.
Entick, John, 1703(?)–1773: The present state of the British Empire. *See* Dohm, Nordamerikanische Handlung.
Ephemeriden der Menschheit (*review*), 593.
Erdman, Carl, translator. *See* Carey, Ein Kurze Nachricht.
Eremita, Jacobus. *See* L'Hermite, Jacques.
Erläuterung für Herrn Caspar Schwenckfeld, 461.
Erskine, John, 1721(?)–1803, contributor. *See* Marsh, Wer ist Fox?
Erst theil dieses Weltbuchs. *See* Franck, Sebastian.
Eskimos, 202, 312, 1039.
languages, 320, 324.
missions, 312, 320, 324, 1116A.
L'Espion américain en Europe (*review*), 432.
L'Espion Turc. *See* L'Espion américain en Europe.
Essai sur l'Administration des Colonies Françaises (*review*), 961A.
Essay on the slavery and commerce of the human species (*review*), 1018.
Ethnography. *See* various races.
Ethnology, 991.
Etliche zu dieser Zeit nicht unnütze Fragen über einige Schrifft-Stellen. *See* Büdingische Sammlung.
Etrennes aux des oeuvrés; ou, Letre d'un Quaker (*reviews*), 433, 434.
Euphraséń, Bengt Anders: Reise nach der schwedischwest-indischen Jnsel St. Barthelemi, 1414.
Europe:
American revolution, 710.
commerce with America, 632, 633.
foreign relations of various countries, 599.
Evangelical Lutheran Church, 258.
Abbots Creek, N. C., 1044, 1203.
Boston, Mass., 1044, 1047.
catechism and Biblical reader, 864, 914, 963.
Ebenezer, Ga., 350.
Massachusetts, 313, 317.
Mecklenburg County, N. C., 1044, 1203.
New York, 903.
North Carolina, 844, 864, 914, 963, 1009, 1044, 1305.
constitution, 864, 911.
Pennsylvania, 361, 506, 897.
Philadelphia, Pa.: church records, 1076.
United States, 903.
Virginia, 249.
*See also* Education, Religious; Pietists; Salzburgers.
Evans, Oliver, 1755–1819: The young mill-wright and miller's guide. *See* Ueber die Art and Weise.
Ewald, Schack Hermann, 1745–1824, translator. *See* Adair, Geschichte der Amerikanischen Indianer.
Ewing, John, contributor. *See* American Philosophical Society, Transactions, v. 1.
Exploration. *See* as sub-head under various countries, regions, etc.
Explorers of America, 204.
individual explorers: Behaim, 385, 580; Bering, 1182; Cabot, 204, 205, 502; Cavendish, 108, 111, 145, 155, 204, 205; Clerke, 121, 145; Columbus. *See* Columbus; Cook, 538, 689, 728, 813, 841, 850, 853, 987, 1038, 1091; Cordova, 45; Cortés, 45, 46, 67, 424, 447, 579, 604, 605, 680, 1079; Coxe, 1083, 1091; Davis, 204, 205; Dixon, 1072, 1073, 1083, 1091; Drake, 88, 108, 121, 145, 155, 204, 205, 368; Frobisher, 80, 202, 204, 205; Gore, 728, 841, 987; Grenville, 90, 122; Grijalva, 45; Lapérouse, 1439, 1450; La Salle, 218; Madog, 1243; Magalhaes, 121, 145, 155; Meares, 1083, 1091, 1117, 1118; Mortimer, 1310; Noort, 121, 145, 155, 204, 205; Pizarro, 58, 680, 1079; Portlock, 1073, 1083, 1091, 1310; Pretty, 108, 111; Ruyter, 204,

Explorers of America, *continued*
205; Schmidt, 98, 111, 139; Schouten, 146; Soto, 342, 869; Spielbergen, 150; Vancouver, 1440, 1456; Vespucci, 10, 11, 12, 13, 14, 15, 16, 17, 18, 19, 20, 21, 22, 23, 24, 25, 26, 27, 28, 29, 30, 31, 32, 33, 34, 99, 143, 204, 205, 262, 325, 386, 393, 536, 1021, 1050, 1058.

Exports and Imports of America [entries also under commodities]:
Germany, 448, 686, 688, 909, 1003, 1036, 1149, 1316, 1345, 1424, 1487A.
Great Britain, 521, 780, 1137.
New York, 1052.
Santo Domingo, 1395.
South Carolina, 959.
Sweden, 651.
United States, 686, 707, 1082, 1217, 1424.
West Indies, 780, 1137.
*See also* Commerce.

Exquemelin, Alexandre Olivier: Die Americanische See-Räuber, 201.

## F

Fabri, Johann Ernst, 1755–1825: Elementar geographie (*review*), 1149A.
Fabri, Johann Ernst, 1755–1825, editor: Beyträge zur Geographie, Geschichte, und Staatenkunde (*review*), 1337.
Fabri, Johann Ernst, 1755–1825, and K. Hammerdörfer, editors: Historisch-geographische Monatsschrift (*review*), 1019.
Fairy Tales, 425.
Falckner, Daniel, 1666–ca. 1741: Curieuse Nachricht, 229.
Falconbridge, Alexander, d. 1792: Account of the slave trade on the coast of Africa (*review*), 1010.
*explorations*, 1054, 1147.
Farms and Farming. *See* Agriculture.
Fauchet, Claude, 1744–1793: Eloge civique de Benjamin Franklin (*review*), 1104.
Fauquier, Francis, 1704?–1768, contributor. *See* Burnaby, Reisen.
Faust, Bernhard Christoph, 1755–1842, contributor. *See* Scherf, Beyträge.
Faustin, oder das philosophische Jahrhundert (*review*), 806A.
Federmann, Nicolaus, d. 1555: Indianische Historia, 68.
Feldzug der vereinigten Franzosen und Nordamerikaner in Virginien, 708.
Fenning, Daniel, d. 1767: Neue Erdbeschreibung, 545.
Fenning, Daniel, and others: A new system of geography. *See his* Neue Erdbeschreibung von ganz Amerika.
Fenwick, George, 1603–1656/7: *biography*, 733.
Feron, M., contributor. *See* American Academy of Arts and Sciences, Memoirs, v. 1, v. 2.
Ferrer, Joseph Joachim von: Geographische Ortsbestimmungen, 1415.
Fevers:
Jamaica, W. I., 1261, 1352, 1402.
*See also* Yellow Fever.
Feyerabend, Sigmund, 1528–1590:
Cosmographia, 77.
General Chronica, 81.
Fiction [author and anonymous titles]: Albert der Selbstmörder, 1459; Der Amerikanische Robinson, 265; Der Amerikanische Wilde und sein Hund, 1074; Azakia, 778; Des Zu Wasser und Lande, 336; Dippold, 1162; Donnant, 1444; L'Espion américain en Europe, 432; Goethe, 1271; Graf Meaupois, 1341; Janisch, 1447; Jung-Stilling, 678; Die Junge Amerikanerin, 425; Klinger, 1419; Lenz, 1374; Merck, 681; Moritz, 820; Morris,

Fiction, *continued*
1399; Nougaret, 1179; Richter, 1278; Sprickmann, 529; Taurinius, 1454; Therese Westen, 1025; Tieck, 1282; Die wilde Europäerinn, 1508.
*See also* Anecdotes; Fairy Tales.

Fiction relating to ——:
America, 1459.
American revolution, 820, 1179, 1282.
Canada, 778, 1444.
German mercenaries, 1374, 1419.
immigrants, 681, 1341.
Iroquois Nation, 1508.
Miemacs (Indians), 1508.
Washington, 1459.

Files [tools], 474, 492.
Filson, John, 1747?–1788: Histoire de Kentucke (*reviews*), 871, 872.

Finance:
American colonies, 356.
American revolution, 659.
British possessions, 702, 1370.
Delaware, 1130.
Dutch possessions, 718.
French possessions, 718, 722.
Pennsylvania, 1130.
Spanish possessions, 718.
states (individual), 718.
United States, 718, 814, 1052, 1130, 1205, 1220, 1223, 1228, 1267.
public debts, 1019, 1052.
*See also* Banks and Banking; Credit, International; Money and Coinage; Taxation.

Findley, William, 1751–1821: History of the insurrection in the four western counties of Pennsylvania (*review*), 1394.
Fireplaces. *See* Chimneys.
Fischart, Johann, ca. 1550–1590?: Das Glückhafft Schiff, 77A.
Fischer, Johann Gottlob: Reise-Beschreibung Der Saltzburg-Dürnberger Emigranten, 303.
Fish and Fishing, 898, 975.
fishing rights, 416.
Indian diet, 943, 944, 945.
North America, 1164.
United States, 854, 917.
Whales, 804.
*See also* Cod Fisheries.
Flax Culture, 414.
Flaxseed. *See* Linseed.
Floods: Virginia, 469.
Florida, 83, 89, 91, 120, 615, 621.
British garrisons, 550.
British possession, 398, 399, 400, 405, 407, 757.
colonies, 342.
conquest, 342, 869.
description and travel, 213, 214, 407.
discovery, 869.
geography, 213.
history, 342.
Indians, 213, 214, 699.
pictorial works, 213, 214.
Florida, East: description and travel, 1160, 1211, 1317.
Florida, West: description and travel, 1160, 1211.
Flour, 187.
grinding, 1019.
Fm. *See* Krausneck, J. C.
Förster, Thomas, editor: Erzählungen (*review*), 1208; *see also* Geschichte und Beschreibungen von Westindien.
Fogs: Kensington, Conn., 376.
Fontana, Felice, 1730–1805:
Traité sur le vénin de la vipere (*review*), 738.
*See also* Royal Society of London, Philosophical transactions, v. 70.
Fontane, Louis Jean Pierre, marquis de, contributor. *See* Washington, 1488.
Fonticelli, Antonio: Americologia (*review*), 1056.

Food [also indexed under specific foods], 187, 259, 384, 402, 422, 436, 521, 544, 636, 637, 686, 705, 817, 902, 925, 1137, 1261, 1326, 1327, 1332, 1381, 1445, 1472, 1494.
See also Diet.
Forberger, Georg, 16th century, translator. See Giovio, Warhafftige Beschreibunge aller Chronickwirdiger Historien.
Foreign Relations. See as sub-head under various countries.
Forestry [also entered under various smaller subjects], 187, 346, 470, 607, 636, 637, 686, 688, 886, 909, 1011, 1013, 1036, 1045, 1149, 1154, 1230, 1241, 1248, 1255, 1263, 1266, 1315, 1316, 1326, 1327, 1345, 1356, 1373, 1379, 1381, 1457, 1482.
See also Trees and Shrubs.
Forster, Georg, 1754–1794:
Erinnerungen aus dem Jahre 1790, 1164A.
Nathaniel Portlocks and Georg Mortimers Reisen, 1310.
Noch etwas über die Menschenrassen, 853A.
Reise, 575.
Forster, Georg, 1754–1794, compiler: Geschichte der Reisen, 1083.
Forster, Georg, 1754–1794, translator. See Anburey, Reisen *(review)*; Cook, Dritte Entdeckungs-Reise; Geschichte der Seereisen und Entdeckungen; Keate, Nachrichten.
Forster, Johann Reinhold, 1729–1798:
Anführung des Capitains Cook, Clerke, Gore und King *(review)*, 728.
Flora Americae Septentrionalis *(review)*, 470.
Geschichte der Entdeckungen und Schiffahrten im Norden *(review)*, 807.
See also Beniowsky, Reisen; Forster, Georg, Reise; Geschichte der Seereisen und Entdeckungen; Rohr, La Fayette.
Forster, Johann Reinhold, 1729–1798, translator. See Hearne, Reise; Lapérouse, Entdeckungsreise; Portlock, N., and G. Dixon, Der Kapitains Portlock's und Dixon's Reise.
Forster, Johann Reinhold, 1729–1798, and M. C. Sprengel, editors:
Beyträge zur Länder- und Völkerkunde *(review)*, 729.
See also Sprengel, M. C., and J. R. Forster, editors, Neue Beyträge.
Forts and Fortifications:
American prehistoric, 1384.
Mercer and Mifflin, 583.
St. Lawrence river, 1088, 1089, 1119, 1310.
See also Garrisons.
Fortsetzung des Curieusen Antiqvarii. See Berckenmeyer, P. L.
Fortsetzung von David Cranzens Brüder-Historie. See Hegner, J. K.
Fortsetzung der Reisen. See Charlevoix, P. F. X. de.
Fossils. See Paleontology.
Fourcroy, Antoine François, comte de, 1755–1809: La médecine éclairée *(review)*, 1253.
Fox, Charles James, 1749–1807: *biography*, 1423.
Fracanzano da Montalboddo, compiler: Newe vnbekanthe landte, 31, 32.
France. — Convention Nationale, 1792–1795: Schreiben des französischen National-Convents an den Congress der Amerikanischen Freystaaten, 1181.
France, 250, 676, 1286, 1431.
American Revolution, 708, 739, 767, 783, 1212, 1448.
colonies. See French Colonies in America.
commerce with America, 251, 252, 253, 254, 255, 256, 1338.
West Indies, 255, 827.
foreign relations, 718, 1286, 1423.
shipping, 748.
See also French and Indian War.

Francisci, Erasmus, 1627–1694:
Guineischer und Americanischer Blumen-Pusch, 189.
New-polirter Geschicht- Kunst- und Sitten-Spiegel ausländischer Völcker, 190.
Ost- und West-Jndischer, 187.
See also Bos, Leben und Tapffere Thaten; Kimayer, Neu-Eröffnetes Raritäten-Cabinet.
Franck, Sebastian, 1499–1542:
Ander theil dieses Weltbuchs, 73.
Erst theil dieses Weltbuchs, 74.
Westbůch, 36, 63.
Francke, August Hermann, 1663–1727, contributor. See Falckner, Curieuse Nachricht.
Franckenstein, Jacob August, 1689–1733: Unmassgebliche Gedancken, 303A.
Francus, Jacobus, pseud. See Memmius, Conrad.
Der Fränkische Robinson. See Der Americanische Robinson.
Franklin, Benjamin, 1706–1790:
Anecdoten, 786.
Bemerkungen, 1168.
Brief vom Doctor Benjamin Franklin, 1035.
Briefe von der Elektricität, 369.
Ein Brif die Rechtschreibung betreffend, 709.
Einige für Seereisende nützliche Bemerkungen, 1128.
Erhöhung des Arbeitslohns in Europa, 1366.
Etwas über den neuesten Zustand, 1129.
The Internal state of America. See Bericht für Diejenigen.
Jugendjahre, 1127.
Kleine Schriften, 1221.
Sämmtliche Werke, 645.
A Triumph of the arts, 442.
Ueber das Interesse und die Politik der vereinigten amerikanischen Staaten. See Literatur und Völkerkunde.
Ueber das Rauchen der Kamine *(review)*, 976.
Verfassung und das Interesse von Nordamerika, 854.
See also Achenwall, Einige Anmerkungen; American Philosophical Society, Transactions, v. 2, v. 3; Auszug aus den Philosophisch. Transactions, 376A; Bericht für diejenigen, welche nach Nord-Amerika sich begeben... wollen; Cooper, Some information; Literatur und Völkerkunde.
*biography*, 366, 369, 419, 423, 427, 428, 442, 452, 645, 650, 704, 709, 786, 854, 865, 917, 976, 1038, 1052, 1104, 1109, 1127, 1128, 1129, 1131, 1168, 1169, 1172, 1221, 1269, 1274, 1311, 1365, 1366, 1375, 1448, 1452.
*poetry*, 1046A, 1365, 1447, 1448.
Franklin, Benjamin, 1706–1790, and Richard Jackson: The interest of Great Britain consider'd *(review)*, 423.
Franz, Friedrich Christian, 1766–1847: Lehrbuch der Länder- und Völkerkunde *(review)*, 1105.
Fraser, John, 1750–1811. See Nachricht über Frasers nordamerikanisches Gras, 996.
See also Wehrs, Nachricht.
Frederick II, the Great, king of Prussia, 1712–1786: Mémoires, 511C.
Free Ports:
French West Indies, 827.
St. Mauritius, 893, 896.
Freedom, Religious. See Church History.
Freethinkers, 227.
Freezing Point:
acids, 1037.
water, 1210.
French Colonies in America, 223, 250, 251, 252, 256, 260, 355, 363, 364, 367, 373, 378, 380, 381, 382, 395, 406, 545, 708, 890, 1024, 1030, 1031, 1377, 1386.
French and Indian War, 1755–1763, 352, 362, 364, 373, 379, 382, 397, 399, 407, 427.
Canada, 371, 380, 382, 395, 423.
Cape Breton, 381.
treaty, Mobile, Ala., 405.
See also Paris, Treaty of, 1783.

French West Indies. *See* West Indies, French.
Fresenius, Johann Philip, 1705-1761: Bewährte Nachrichten von Herrnhutischen Sachen, 321.
Die Freundliche Bewillkommung der Saltzburgischen Emigranten in Leipzig, 279.
Fricius, Valentinus: Indianischer Religionstandt, 87.
Friedrich, Karl Julius, b. 1756, translator. *See* Brissot de Warville, Neue Reise; Marsillac, Leben Wilhelm Penns.
Friends, Society of. *See* Society of Friends.
Friendship: Indian practices, 958.
Fries, Lorenz, d. 1532:
  Ynderweisung vnd vaslegunge Der Cartha Marina, 53.
  Yslegung der Mercarthen, 51, 52.
Fritz, Johann Friedrich, contributor. *See* Schultze, Orientalisch- und occidentalischer Sprachmeister.
Fritzsch, J. C. G., engraver. *See* Cook, Dritte Entdeckungs-Reise.
Fritzsch, Johann Christian, 1720-1802, illustrator. *See* Rohr, La Fayette.
Frobisher, Sir Martin, 1535?-1594: *explorations*, 80, 202, 204, 205.
Frogs, 743, 828, 1296.
Frohberger, Christian Gottlieb, d. 1827: Briefe, 1367.
Fruits. *See* various fruits, as Apples.
A Full and impartial account of the Company of Mississippi. *See* Historische und Geographische Beschreibung des an dem grossen Flusse Mississipi.
Funck, David, editor: Der in Europa und America verehrliche Thron und Kron Gross-Britanniens, 219.
Fur Trade, 1014, 1088, 1089, 1310, 1371.
Furlij, Benjamin. *See* Furly, Benjamin.
Furly, Benjamin, 1636-1714, contributor. *See* Penn, Beschreibung Der... Provinz Pensylvanien.

## G

G., D. E. *See* D[octor] Benjamin Franklin's erweitertes Lehrgebäude der natürlichen Elektricität.
Gage, Thomas, d. 1656: Neue merckwürdige Reise-Beschreibung, 221.
Galloway, Joseph, 1731-1803: Briefe an einen vornehmen Herrn und Pair von Grossbritannien (*review*), 730.
Gannet, Caleb, contributor. *See* American Academy of Arts and Sciences, Memoirs, v. 2.
Der Gantzen Welt abcontrafetung, 104.
Garcilaso de la Vega, El Inca, 1540-1616:
  Ferdinand von Soto (*reviews*), 869, 921C.
  Geschichte der Eroberung von Florida, 342.
  Geschichte der Ynkas (*review*), 1105B.
Gardens and Gardening, 408A.
Garrisons, British, 550.
Garve, Christian, 1742-1798. *See* Manso, Ueber die Verläumdung der Wissenschaften.
Gates, Horatio, 1728/29-1806: *portrait*, 838.
Gatterer, Johann Christoph, 1727-1799: Johann Christoph Gatterers kurzer Begriff der Geographie (*reviews*), 1020A, 1060A, 1060B.
Gedanken über den Aufstand der englischen Colonien, 512.
Geiger, Wolfgang Jacob, compiler. *See* Theatri Europæi Zehender Theile.
Geisler, Adam Friedrich, b. 1757: Geschichte und Zustand der Königl. Grosbrittannischen Kriegsmacht, 787.
Genaue Nachricht von dem jetzigen Geld Wesen, 1130.
General history of Connecticut. *See* Peters, S. A.
General Washington, 677.
Generale Nederlandsche Geoctroyeerde West-Indische Compagnie. *See* West-Indische Compagnie.
Genesee Region, New York, 1129, 1283.
  immigration, 1078.

Genest. *See* Genet.
Genet, Edmond Charles, 1763-1834: Americanische Staatsschriften, 1215.
Genty, Louis, 1743-1817, abbé: L'Influence de la decouverte de l'Amérique (*review*), 1020.
Gentz, Friedrich von, 1764-1832: Ueber den Einfluss der Entdeckung von Amerika, 1270.
Geodetic Survey: North American coast, 1415.
Geographical Position. *See* Latitude and Longitude.
Geographie zum Gebrauch der Schulen in den evangelischen Brüdergemeinen (*review*), 869A.
Geographische Belustigungen, 513.
Geographische vnd historische Beschreibung. *See* Acosta, José de.
Geographische Tabellen für die Jugend zur Vorbereitung und Wiederholung (*review*), 834A.
Geographisches Kartenspiel für Kinder (*review*), 1018C.
Geography, 31, 32, 35, 51, 52, 53, 56, 63, 64, 65, 73, 74, 75, 77, 81, 96, 101, 104, 110, 113, 115, 116, 122, 125, 126, 127, 128, 129, 166, 169, 171, 200, 213, 228, 239, 248, 264, 311, 341, 626, 835, 852, 869D, 872C, 873C, 913A, 1046, 1057, 1213, 1267, 1289, 1414, 1427, 1486, 1491.
  America, 60, 77, 102, 110, 114, 117, 124, 125, 134, 138, 144, 146, 147, 163, 164, 165, 175, 176, 187, 194, 195, 200, 228, 235, 239, 248, 264, 311, 341, 410, 451, 545, 554, 761, 960, 1055, 1105, 1140, 1163, 1258, 1478.
  bibliography, 349, 802, 825.
  European settlements, 372.
  Northeastern, 684.
  American cities, 1415.
  American colonies, 594, 626, 653, 658, 662.
  British colonies, 363, 364, 507, 545, 566, 567.
  Canada, 213, 629, 690, 696, 781.
  Connecticut, 729.
  Florida, 213.
  French colonies, 363, 364, 545.
  Haiti, 859, 883.
  Kentucky, 1170, 1209, 1252, 1258.
  Louisiana, 251, 252, 253, 254, 357.
  Mexico, 852.
  Mississippi valley, 473.
  North America, 261, 629.
  St. Bartholomew, W. I., 884.
  United States, 768, 795, 1019, 1286, 1303, 1404, 1431, 1486.
  Vermont, 1297, 1495/96, 1503.
  Virginia, 213.
  West Indies, 1200, 1340, 1346, 1491.
  *See also* description and travel (as subhead); Discovery.
Geology, 696, 908.
  America, 761.
  Haiti, 859.
  New Jersey, 1441.
  Northeastern America, 684.
  Trinidad, 1068.
  United States, 899, 1467, 1468.
Georgia, 1160, 1466.
  colonization, 301, 350, 693.
  description and travel, 351, 1211.
  geography, 693.
  Germans in. *See* Germans in America.
  history, 305, 306, 307, 308, 318, 350, 693.
  immigration, 322.
  Indians, 699.
  slaves, 305, 306.
  *See also* Salzburgers.
German Baptist Brethren. *See* Dunkers.
German Belles-Lettres relating to America. *See* Anecdotes; Drama; Fiction; Poetry; Satire; Songs and Hymns.
German Commerce with America, 448, 511, 521, 646, 686, 688, 886, 909, 1003, 1036, 1149, 1315, 1316, 1345, 1424, 1487A.

# GERMAN WORKS RELATING TO AMERICA — INDEX 189

German Mercenaries, 508, 515, 516, 539, 540, 572, 573, 575A, 583, 586, 616, 644, 645A, 674, 688, 709, 734, 742A, 774, 829, 938, 939, 1097, 1372, 1374, 1413, 1473, 1483, 1484A, 1485.
Boston, Mass., 602.
British budget, 644.
"Brookland, bei Neu York," 641.
Cambridge, Mass., 623.
Canada, 585, 618, 622.
drama, 797.
fiction, 1419, 1374.
Long Island, N. Y., 537, 624.
losses, 779.
New England, 618.
New York, 683.
officers, 787.
Pensacola, Fla., 615.
Philadelphia, Pa., 614.
poems and songs, 500, 508, 519, 541, 547, 549, 551, 586, 635, 672, 749.
Staunton, Va., 620.
treaty, 515.
West Indies, 621.
German Settlements. See Germans in America; also various settlements and religious sects.
Germanna, Va., 258.
Germans in America, 249, 258, 319, 487, 810, 937, 1026, 1267.
agriculture, 487, 647.
Carolina, 240, 305, 306, 307, 308, 318, 337, 339, 487, 777, 903, 937, 1044, 1203, 1305.
Ebenezer Creek, Ga. See Ebenezer Creek, Ga.
education and schools, 940.
Georgia, 275, 276, 277/78, 279, 280, 281, 282, 283, 284, 285, 286, 287, 288, 289, 291, 292, 293, 294, 295, 296, 297, 298, 299, 301, 303, 305, 306, 307, 308, 318, 322, 326, 350, 668, 1449.
immigration, 337, 338, 339, 529, 754, 754A, 1080, 1305, 1325.
Jamaica, W. I., 464.
New York, 1387.
Palatines. See Palatine Germans.
Pennsylvania, 209, 210, 225, 226, 229, 230, 231, 240, 300, 309, 315, 359, 388, 461, 463, 506, 531, 532, 572, 614, 812, 897, 940, 1475, 1498.
Pietists. See Pietists.
religious life, 903.
See also various denominations and sects.
rural life, 647.
Salzburgers. See Salzburgers in America.
schools. See education and schools.
Schwenckfeldians. See Schwenckfeldians.
Virginia, 258.
See also German Mercenaries.
Germantown, Pa., 300.
Pietists, 258, 313.
See also Pietists.
Germany. — Statutes: Auswanderungen aus Deutschland, 777.
Gesammlete Nachrichten von den Englischen Kolonien in Nordamerika (review), 662.
Geschichte und Beschreibung von Westindien (review), 1340.
Geschichte der Englischen Colonien in Nord America (reviews), 502, 535.
Geschichte und Handlung der französischen Pflanzstädte in Nordamerika, 357.
Geschichte der Kolonisirung der freyen Staaten des Alterthums. See Barron, William.
Geschichte der Kriege in und ausser Europa. See Korn, C. H.
Geschichte der neuesten Weltbegebenheiten im Grossen (reviews), 733A, 834B, 869C.
Geschichte der Seereisen und Entdeckungen (reviews), 911C, 962.
Geschichte der Weltbegebenheiten im Grossen (review), 834C.

Gesellschaft Helmstaedtischer Professoren, 844, 1044.
Gesellschaft naturforschender Freunde, Berlin, 1457, 1482.
Gessner, Salomon, 1730-1788: biography, 1351.
Ghethel, Henning, of Lübeck, translator. See Fracanzano da Montalboddo, compiler, Newe vnbekanthe landte.
Gilpin, Thomas, 1728-1778, contributor. See American Philosophical Society, Transactions, v. 2.
Giovio, Paolo, 1483-1552, bishop of Nocera: Warhafftige Beschreibunge aller Chronickwirdiger, Historien, 75.
Girod-Chantrans, Justin, 1750-1841:
Reise eines Schweitzers in verschiedene colonien in America (review), 876.
Voyage d'un Suisse dans différentes colonies d'Amérique:
excerpt: Physikalische Beschaffenheit, 859.
review, 877C.
Girtanner, Christoph, 1760-1800: Abhandlungen über die venerische Krankheit (review), 1009A.
Glasbach, Benjamin, b. 1757, illustrator. See Forster, Georg, compiler, Geschichte der Reisen.
Glassbach, Carl Christian, b. 1751, illustrator. See Forster, Georg, compiler, Geschichte der Reisen.
Glauber, Christian Gottlieb, 1755-1804: Peter Hasenclever, 1222.
Gleditsch, Johann Gottlieb, 1714-1786: Neu vermehrte Erläuterung, 607.
Gleim, Johann Wilhelm Ludwig, 1719-1803: Der Amerikaner an den Europäer, 1039A.
Gloster, Archibald, contributor. See American Philosophical Society, Transactions, v. 1.
Gluttony, Indian, 901, 950.
Goebel, Julius, contributor. See Bardeleben, Tagebuch.
Goeckinck, Leopold Friedrich Günther von, 1748-1828: Kriegeslied eines Provinzialen, 645A.
See also Schreiben eines deutschen Juden, 756.
Goecking, Gerhard Gottlieb Guenther: Vollkommene Emigrations Geschichte. See Huebner, Johann Hübners Kurtze Einleitung.
Goethe, Johann Wolfgang von, 1749-1832:
An Silvie von Ziegesar. See Gregor, Meiner Tochter.
Der Gross-Cophta, 1130A.
Liebes Lied eines Amerikanischen Wilden, 746.
Die Mitschuldigen, 892.
Das Neueste von Plunderweilern, 677A.
Stella, 514.
Todeslied eines Gefangenen, 747.
Wilhelm Meisters Lehrjahre, 1271.
See also Schiller, Nadowessiers Totenlied.
Goettingische Societaet der Wissenschaft, 965.
Die Göttliche Allmacht In der Wunderthätigen Ausbreitung, 280.
Goetze, August Ephraim, 1731-1793, translator. See Briefe eines amerikanischen Landmanns.
Golaw, Salomon von, pseud. See Logau, Friedrich von.
Gold:
American shipments, 333, 1273.
mining, 356.
Gonzaga, Francesco, d. 1620, bishop of Mantua: De origine seraphicae religionis franciscanae. See Fricius, Indianischer Religionstandt.
Gore, John, d. 1790, contributor. See Cook, Entdeckungs-Reise; Geschichte der Seereisen und Entdeckungen.
See also Anführung des Capitains Cook, Clerke [etc.]; Cook, Voyage.
Gottfried, Johann Ludwig, pseud., 17th century:
Historische Chronica, 177, 237.
Newe Welt, 163, 175, 176.
Gottwaldt, Christoph: Physikalisch-anatomische Bemerkungen (review), 762A.
Gourgues, Dominique de, 1530?-1593, contributor. See Bry, Der ander Theyl.
Gout: American remedy, 458.

Government, 666, 921, 1023A, 1228, 1229.
  American states, 770, 795.
  Haiti, 859.
  United States, 720, 854, 970, 971, 972.
  See also various forms of government, as Democracy.
Graf Meaupois und seine Freunde (review), 1341.
Graff, Anton, 1736–1813, artist. See Risler, Leben August Gottlieb Spangenbergs.
Graham, John Andrew, 1764–1841: 'A descriptive sketch of the present state of Vermont (review), 1495/96.
Grass: Agrostis cornucopiae, 187, 996, 1090, 1098.
Great Britain. — Treaties:
  Accords-Puncta, 182, 183.
  Die drey vollständigen Subsidien-Tractaten, 515.
  See also Präliminair-Friedensartikel zwischen Sr. Grossbrittannischen Majestät und den Generalstaaten, 753.
Great Britain [as subject], 711.
  American revolution. See American Revolution.
  army in America, 182, 183, 379, 494, 550, 597, 644, 672, 683, 787, 862, 1265.
  beer, 1137.
  colonial legislation, 599.
  colonies. See British Colonies in America.
  commerce with America, 355, 446, 521, 609, 686, 780, 799, 800, 809, 817, 900, 1137. See also Commerce.
  emigration, 271, 365/66.
  See also Emigration and Immigration.
  foreign relations: Canada, 1487.
    Netherlands, 613, 753, 889.
  Indians visit, 238, 271.
  Jews, 207.
  navy, 597, 725, 758, 787, 1314.
  quarrel with American colonies. See American Revolution.
  resources, 900.
  shipping, 1314.
  statistics, 494, 565, 595.
  trade, 273.
  trade treaty with France and West Indies, 255.
  treaties. See Treaties.
  See also French and Indian War; Navy; United States: foreign relations.
Green, Valentine, 1739–1813, engraver. See General Washington.
Greene, Nathanael, 1742–1786: biography, 1002.
Greenland, 332.
  Danish expedition of 1606, 202.
  description and travel, 202, 312, 320, 324, 1039.
  discovery, 202.
  history, 202, 412, 449, 973.
  missions, 312, 320, 324, 412, 449, 1039.
  Moravian Brethren, 412, 449.
  whaling, 332.
Greenway, James, contributor. See American Philosophical Society, Transactions, v. 3.
Grefve Grasses Sjö-Batailler och Kriegsoperationerne uti Westindien (review), 911D.
Grégoire, Henri, 1750–1831: Mémoire (review), 1062.
Gregor, Christian, 18th century: Meiner Tochter, 462.
Greinuile. See Grenville.
Grenada, West Indies: British possession, 399.
Grenville, Sir Richard, 1541–1591: voyages, 90, 112, 144, 149.
Grijalva, Juan de, d. 1638: explorations, 45.
Gronau, Israel Christian, d. 1745, joint author. See Boltzius, J. M., and I. C. Gronau, Ausxüge einiger Schreiben; Boltzius, J. M., and I. C. Gronau, Einige Briefe; Boltzius, J. M., and I. C. Gronau, Einige Merckwürdige hieher gehörige Briefe; Nachricht; Reise-Diarium; Tage-register.
Gronovius, Johannes Fredericus, 1690–1760, contributor. See Forster, Flora Americae Septentrionalis.
Gründliche Erweisung, 266.
Grundriss von Nordamerika. See Buchenröder, J. N. C.

Gruner, Karl Justus von, d. 1820: Versuch über Strafen (review), 1470.
Grynaeus, Simon, 1493–1541, editor. See Novus Orbis Regionum, Die New welt.
Guadeloupe:
  British capture, 397, 423.
  description and travel, 397.
  geography, 423.
Guadet, Marguerite Élie, 1758–1794. See France. — Convention Nationale, 1792–1795, Schreiben.
Guiana, 110, 115, 116, 122, 126, 127, 128, 129, 158, 180, 189, 493, 1105D.
  colonization, 192.
  description and travel, 933.
  early accounts, 129.
  meteorological observations, 933.
  New Netherlands compared to, 192.
Guiana, Dutch, 1162, 1281.
Gymnastics, Indian, 1187.

# H

H. See Heise, J. C. F.
Haebler, Konrad, 1857–    , contributor. See New zeutung, 41.
Hagen, Caspar: Memoriae philosophorum. See Doppelmayr, Historische Nachricht.
Hagendorp, Gisbert Karl von: Einige Anmerkungen über die Aufbringung, 888.
Hager, Johann Georg, 1709–1777: Geographischer Büchersaal, 410.
Haid, Johann Jacob, 1704–1767, engraver. See Urlsperger, Americanisches Ackerwerk Gottes.
Haiti, 621, 883, 1000, 1123.
  aboriginal dances, 816.
  agriculture, 859, 1393, 1395.
  slaves and slavery, 859.
  See also Santo Domingo.
Hale, Samuel, contributor. See American Academy of Arts and Sciences, Memoirs, v. 2.
Halen, O., translator. See Bry, Der ander Theil.
Hales, Stephen, 1677–1761: Nachricht von dem grossen Vortheile des Ventilators. See Auszug aus den Philosophische Transactions, 366.
Halifax, Nova Scotia: British garrison, 550.
Hall, captain: The history of the civil war in America (review), 695.
Hall, Jacob, contributor. See College of Physicians of Philadelphia, Medicinische Verhandlungen, Bd. 1; College of Physicians of Philadelphia, Transactions, v. 1.
Halle, Johann Samuel, 1727–1810: Die Tabaksmanufactur (review), 1024B.
Hallische Nachrichten. See Kurtze Nachricht.
Hallisches Waisenhaus, 1449.
Halverius, Hieronymus, 16th century, translator. See Giovio, Warhafftige Beschreibunge aller Chronickwirdiger Historien.
Hamilton, Alexander, 1757–1804:
  Officieller Rapport, 1223, 1224.
  See also An American remembrancer.
Hammerdörfer, Karl: Allgemeine Weltgeschichte (review), 1147A.
Hammerdörfer, Karl, joint editor. See Fabri and Hammerdörfer, editors, Historisch-geographische Monatsschrift.
Hammerdörfer, Karl, translator. See Soulès, Vollständige Geschichte.
Hammerdörfer, Karl, and C. T. Kosche: Amerika (reviews), 959D, 1057.
Hamor, Ralph, the younger:
  Dreyzehente Schiffahrt, 140, 141.
  See also Bry, Zehender Teil Americæ.
Hand, Edward, contributor. See Rush, Untersuchung der Arzneykunde.

# GERMAN WORKS RELATING TO AMERICA — INDEX

Handbuch für Liebhaber englischer Pflanzungen (review), 1105C.
Happe, Andreas Friedrich, b. 1733, engraver. See Cramer, Sammlung.
Happel, Eberhard Werner, 1647–1690:
Der Insularische Mandorell. See his Mundus Mirabilis Tripartitus.
Mundus Mirabilis Tripartitus, 213.
Thesaurus Exoticorum, 214.
See also Kimayer, Neu-Eröffnetes Raritäten-Cabinet.
Hariot, Thomas. See Harriot, Thomas.
Harlem, N. Y., 553.
Harper, Robert Goodloe, 1765–1825: Observations on the dispute between the United States and France. See Marsh, Wer ist Fox?
Harriot, Thomas, 1560–1621:
A Briefe and true report. See Dresser, Historien vnd Bericht.
Wunderbarlicher doch Warhafftiger Bericht, 105.
See also Bry, Wunderbarliche.
Hasenclever, Peter, 1716–1793:
Bemerkungen über Amerika. See Das politische Journal.
See also Glauber, Peter Hasenclever.
Hauterive, Alexandre Maurice Blanc de Lanautte, comte d', 1754–1830: De l'état de la France. See Uiber den Zustand Frankreichs, 1487.
Haüy, René Just, 1743–1822, joint author. See Bruguière and others, Journal.
Havana, Cuba, 221.
description and travel, 398, 400.
Negroes, 221.
Haveckens, Iohan. See Hawkins, Sir John.
Havy. See Haüy.
Hawkins, Sir John, 1719–1789: voyages, 108, 154.
Hazard, Ebenezer, 1744–1817: Historical collections (review), 1197.
Health, 985, 1498.
Antilles, 868.
Charleston, S. C., 1336.
Pennsylvania, 922.
Santo Domingo, 1030, 1031.
See also Diseases; Sanitation; etc.
Hearne, Samuel, 1745–1792:
A Journey (review), 1344.
Reise, 1371.
Heart, Jonathan, contributor. See American Philosophical Society, Transactions, v. 3.
Heath, William, 1737–1814, contributor. See American Academy of Arts and Sciences, Memoirs.
Hecking, Gottfried, 1687–1773, contributor. See Ausführliche Historie, 275.
Heer. See Herr.
Heerbrand, Jakob Friedrich, captain, contributor. See Abschrift einer Vollmacht; Formular eines Kontrakts.
Heeringen, von: Auszug eines Schreibens aus Amerika, 516.
Hegard, S. L.: Geographisches Spiel für die Jugend (review), 869B.
Hegewisch, Dietrich Hermann, 1746–1812, and C. D. Ebeling, editors: Americanisches Magazin, 1267.
Hegner, Johann Konrad, b. 1748: Fortsetzung von David Cranzens Brüder-Historie, 1085.
Heiden, Franz Janszoon van der: Erstaunens-würdige Beschreibung. See Crouch, Der Englische Held.
Hein, Pieter Pieterszoon, 1578–1629, contributor. See Bry, Vierzehender Theil Americanischer Historien.
Heinrich, Heinrich, 1614–1682: Ferdinandina, 172.
Heise, Johann Christoph Friedrich, 1718–1804: Von der Nation der Caraïben, 450.
Heister, von: Auszüge aus dem Tagebuche, 516A.
Helme, Elizabeth, translator. See Campe, Die Entdeckung von Amerika.
Helmuth, Justus Henry Christian, 1745–1825, contributor. See Briefe von deutschen Geistlichen in Pensylvanien, 506.

Hemmersam, Michael, 17th century:
West-Indianische Reissbeschreibung, 180.
See also Francisci, Guineischer und Americanischer Blumen-Pusch.
Hemp Culture, 474, 492.
Hennemann, William Johann Konrad, translator. See Fenning, Neue Erdbeschreibung.
Hennepin, Louis, 17th century:
Beschreibung, 218.
Neue Entdeckung, 224.
Neue Reise-Beschreibung, 222.
Hennig, Christian Gottfried, translator. See Carli, Briefe.
Hennings, August Adolf Friedrich, 1746–1826: Sammlung von Staatsschriften, 789.
Henry XLIV, count of Reuss, b. 1753, compiler. See Riedesel, Auszüge aus den Briefen und Papieren; Riedesel, Die Berufs-Reise nach Amerika.
Henry, William, contributor. See American Philosophical Society, Transactions, v. 1.
Hensler, Philipp Gabriel, 1733–1805: Geschichte der Lustseuche (review), 1016A.
Herbs: North America: catalogue, 470.
Herbs, Medicinal, 42, 43, 50, 61, 62.
Jamaica, 977.
See also Botany, Medical; Drugs; also various herbs, as Sbitzolobium.
Herbst, Johann Friedrich Wilhelm, 1743–1807, translator. See Vancouver, Reisen.
Herckemann, Elias, 17th century: voyage, 175, 176.
Herder, Johann Gottfried von, 1744–1803:
Briefe zu Beförderung der Humanität, 1169, 1372.
Dissertation (review), 645B.
Franklin's Fragen, 1131.
Ideen, 790.
Zerstreute Blätter, 1132.
Hermes, Johann Timotheus, 1738–1821: Sophiens Reise von Memel nach Sachsen, 575B.
Hermite. See L'Hermite.
Herr, Michael, 16th century, translator. See Novus Orbis Regionum, Die New welt; Vespucci, Alleräalteste Nachricht.
Herrera y Tordesillas, Antonio de, 1559–1625: Achtzehender Theil der Newen Welt, 153.
Herrera y Tordesillas, Antonio de, 1559–1625, translator. See Bry, Zwölfter Theil.
Herring, 975.
Herrman, Augustine, artist. See Montanus, Die unbekante Neue Welt.
Hessians. See German Mercenaries.
Hewatt, Alexander: Historical account (review), 693.
Heyde, Frantz Janss von der. See Heiden, Franz Janszoon van der.
Higgins, Jesse, contributor. See American Philosophical Society, Transactions, v. 3.
Hilliard d'Auberteuil, Michel René, 1751–1789:
Betrachtungen, 608.
Essais historiques (reviews), 763, 764.
See also Etwas von der Volksmenge, 707; Portrait du Général Washington.
Hinrichs, Johann: Extracts from the letter-book of Captain Johann Heinrichs, 575B.
Hippel, Theodor Gottlieb von, 1741–1796:
Kreuz- und Querzüge des Ritters A bis Z, 1169A.
Ueber die bürgerliche Verbesserung der Weiber, 1133A.
Hispaniola, W. I., 621.
Histoire impartiale des evenements militaires et politiques de la dernière guerre (review), 835A.
Histoire naturelle et politique de la Pensylvanie. See Rousselot de Surgy, P. J.
Histoire philosophique & politique (review), 481.
Historical account of the rise and progress of the colonies of Carolina and Georgia. See Hewatt, Alexander.
An Historical essay on the English constitution. See Ramsay, Allan.

Historisch-geographische Beschreibung der in diesem Krieg, 397.
Historisch- und Geographischer Calender, 261.
Historisch-statistische Notiz. *See* Schirach, G. B.
Historische und Geographische Beschreibung des an dem grossen Flusse Missisipi gelegenen herrlichen Landes Louisiana, 253.
Historische und Geographische Beschreibung von Neu-Schottland, 330.
Historische und geographische Beschreibung der zwölf vereinigten Colonien von Nordamerika (*review*), 594.
Historische Litteratur für das Jahr 1781 (*review*), 694, 734.
Historische und politische Betrachtungen über die Colonien, 609.
Historischer Beweis der in Nordamerika vorgefallenen Staatsveränderung (*review*), 630.
History, 60, 63, 64, 75, 89, 177, 203, 208, 215, 237, 274, 341, 559, 580.
*See also* various countries, states, etc., sub-head, history.
History, Natural. *See* Natural History.
The History of the civil war in America. *See* Hall, captain.
History of the colonization of the free states of antiquity. *See* Barron, William.
History of the origin and progress of the present war (*review*), 395.
Hitchcock, Samuel, contributor. *See* American Academy of Arts and Sciences, Memoirs, v. 2.
Hodgkinson: Letters on emigration (*review*), 1293.
Höen, Moritz Wilhelm, contributor. *See* Boehme, Das verlangte Canaan.
Hoeniger, Nicholaus, 16th century, translator. *See* Apollonius, Dritte Theil; Benzoni, Der Newenn Weldt.
Hoffmann, Carl August Siegfried, editor. *See* Neues Bergmännisches Journal, Bd. 1.
Hoffmann, Christian Friedrich, translator. *See* Marshall, Beschreibung.
Holder, Henry Evans: Fragments of a poem (*review*), 1196.
Holland. *See* Netherlands.
Hollingworth, Henry, contributor. *See* American Philosophical Society, Transactions, v. 1.
Hollingsworth, S.:
  Abhandlung (*review*), 1152.
  An Account of the present state of Nova-Scotia, 907.
Holme, Thomas, 1624–1695, contributor. *See* Penn, Beschreibung.
Holtinger, Johann Jacob, 1750–1819: Salomon Gessner (*review*), 1351.
Holyoke, Edward Augustus, 1728–1829, contributor. *See* American Academy of Arts and Sciences, Memoirs, v. 2.
Holzhalb, Johann Rudolf, b. 1730?, illustrator. *See* Kurze, zuverlässige Nachricht.
Homar. *See* Hamor.
Hondius, Jodocus, 1546–1611, cartographer. *See* Bertius, Petri, Bertii geographischer eyn oder zusammengezogener Fabeln; Raleigh, Die Fünffte Kurtze Wunderbare Beschreibung; Raleigh, Kurtze Wunderbare Beschreibung.
Honorine Clarins. *See* Nougaret, P. J. B.
Hopfengärtner, Philipp Friedrich, d. 1807, translator. *See* Rush, Beschreibung.
Hopkinson, Francis, 1737–1791, contributor. *See* American Philosophical Society, Transactions, v. 2, v. 3.
"Hornhuck," N. Y., 553.
Horses, 975, 1376.
Horsfield, Thomas, 1773–1859: An experimental dissertation (*review*), 1499.
Hospitals:
  American Revolution, 919, 1108.
  construction, 1259.
Houston. *See* Houstoun.

Houstoun, William, 1695?–1733: Reliquiae Houstonianae (*review*), 1299, 1400.
Howard, John, 1726?–1790: Howards praktisches System (*review*), 1432.
Howe, Sir William, 1729–1814: *biography*, 488, 528, 1221.
Hubbard, Thomas, 1776–1838, contributor. *See* Medical Society of London, Memoirs, v. 4.
Huber, Franz Xaver: Aktenmässige Geschichte der berühmten Salzburgischen Emigration (*review*), 1053A.
Hubert, translator. *See* Actes passés à un Congrès des États-Unis de l'Amérique.
Hudson, Henry, d. 1611:
  Zwölffte Schiffahrt, 136, 137, 156.
  *See also* Adelung, Geschichte.
Hudson River: prehistoric animals, 1296.
Hudson's Bay, 328, 1102, 1111, 1344, 1371.
Huebner, Johann, 1668–1731:
  Kurtze Einleitung, 274.
  Neuvermehrtes und verbessertes Reales Staats-Zeitungs- und Conversations-Lexicon, 391.
Hüpeden, C. C. F.: Taxe europäischer Menschen in N Amerika, 1183.
Hüttner, Johann Christian, 1766–1847, translator. *See* Wansey, Ein Besuch beym Präsidenten Washington; Wansey, Tagebuch.
Hullman, G. W., engraver. *See* Cook, Dritte Entdeckungs-Reise.
Hulsius, Levinus, d. 1605, editor:
  Sechste Theil, Kurtze, Warhafftige Relation, 121, 145, 155.
  *See also* Hamor, Dreyzehente Schiffahrt; Hudson, Zwölffte Schiffahrt; Herrera y Tordesillas, Achtzehender Theil; Muencken, Die XVII Schiff-Fahrt; Ortelius, Ausszůg; Raleigh, Die Fünffte Kurtze Wunderbare Beschreibung; Smith, Viertzehende Schiffart; Whitbourne, Zwantzigste Schifffahrt.
Humberger, Johann, translator. *See* Acosta, America; Bry, Neundter Theil Americæ.
Hume, David, 1711–1776: *biography*, 433, 434.
Humor. *See* Wit and Humor.
Hunnius, Christoph Friedrich:
  Das aufgemunterte Crannichfeldt, 299.
  Der gläubige Emigrant, 281.
Hunold, Ph., d. 1808: Medicinal-taxe in Charlestown in Nordamerika. *See* Scherf, Beyträge.
Hunter, John, 1728–1793:
  Bemerkungen über die Krankheiten der Truppen in Jamaica (*review*), 1190.
  Einige Beobachtungen, 1042.
  Ueber die Wärme der Brunnen und Quellen in Jamaika. *See* Royal Society of London, Philosophical transactions, v. 78.
Huntington, Samuel, 1731–1796: *portrait*, 838.
Hurons. *See* Indians.
Huser, Heinrich, 1638–1684, joint author. *See* Zeller and Huser, Jamaica.
Huske, John, 1721?–1773, supposed author: Allgemeine Amerikanische Kriegsgeschichte, 352.
Hutchins, Thomas, 1730–1789, contributor. *See* American Philosophical Society, Transactions, v. 2.
Huttich, Johann, 1480?–1544, compiler. *See* Novus Orbis Regionum.
Hygiene, Public: New York, 1430.
Hygrometer, 975.
Hymns. *See* Poetry and Songs.

# I

Iceland, 332.
  description and travel, 320, 324.
  zoology, 312.
Iffland, August Wilhelm, 1759–1814: Die Jäger, 818.
Illustrations. *See* Pictorial Works.
Imlay, Gilbert, fl. 1755–1796:
  Nachrichten von dem westlichen Lande, 1170.
  Topographical description (*review*), 1209, 1258.

# GERMAN WORKS RELATING TO AMERICA — INDEX 193

Immigration. *See* Emigration and Immigration.
An Impartial and succinct history of the origin and progress of the present war. *See* History of the origin and progress of the present war.
Imports and Exports. *See* Commerce.
Incas. *See* Indians.
Incle and Yarico. *See* Inkle und Yariko.
Indian Captivities, 184, 603.
Indian Languages. *See* American Languages.
Indians, 20, 21, 51, 52, 53, 79, 80, 82, 83, 84, 90, 91, 95, 97, 99, 109, 112, 120, 125, 131, 133, 138, 144, 147, 149, 163, 175, 176, 185, 187, 189, 190, 194, 195, 214, 232, 244, 328, 341, 411, 455, 456, 457, 491, 495, 610, 642, 699, 768, 795, 830, 831, 867, 887, 948, 991, 992, 1040, 1074, 1116A, 1168, 1174, 1199, 1221, 1259, 1290, 1304, 1317, 1425.
Abenakis, 418, 603.
adaptability, 905.
adultery, 952.
Akensas, 735, 857.
Algonquians, 1116A.
*See also* American Languages.
American revolution, 489.
anecdotes, 786, 1074.
anthropology, 1056.
Apalachians, 1116A.
arts, 440, 1284.
beliefs, 957.
bibliography, 1174.
Brazil, 793.
California, 947, 1116A.
Canada, 213, 214, 236, 238, 241, 271, 334, 340, 371, 1116A, 1250.
cannibalism, 73, 74.
Caribbeans, 450, 678, 891.
Carolina, 247, 699.
character, 951, 955, 1049, 1053, 1056.
Cherokees, 1116A.
Chippewa, 1089.
*See also* American Languages.
dress and adornment, 928, 1008, 1493.
eloquence, 498, 1135.
emotions, 951.
Eskimo. *See* American Languages.
ethnography, 455, 456, 457, 491.
fictitious address to Spanish Cortes, 579.
Florida, 213, 699.
food. *See* diet.
forest life, 1045.
friendship, 958.
Georgia, 305, 306, 699.
gluttony, 901, 950.
Guiana, 420.
Haiti, 816.
honor and shame, 924.
Hurons, 556A, 678, 1116A, 1448.
illustrations. *See* pictorial works.
Iroquois. *See* Iroquois Nation.
Kentucky, 815.
languages. *See* American Languages.
Long Island, N. Y., 624.
Lower California, 467, 477.
manners and customs, 392, 435, 440, 557, 885, 916, 986, 1088, 1089, 1119, 1310, 1493.
marriage, 930, 949, 1005.
meat as food, 943, 944, 945.
medicine and medicine men, 420, 527.
Mexico, 47, 67, 467, 477, 493, 1116A.
missions. *See* Missions.
Mississippi, 218, 222, 224, 699.
Mohawks, 1307.
mutilation, voluntary, 885.
myths and legends, 894, 934, 947, 957.
Natchez, 1116A.
nature. *See* character, etc.
New England, 206, 227.
New Mexico, 857.
nobility, 895.

Indians, *continued*
North America, 786, 887, 1221.
North Carolina, 193, 244, 699.
Northeastern America, 684.
Nova Scotia, 330.
Ohio valley, 815, 1180.
Oneidas, 673, 1177.
origin, 560.
Pennsylvania, 211, 225, 226, 230, 231, 673.
Peru, 793.
physical attributes, 1141, 1142, 1143, 1186, 1187, 1188.
pictorial works, 213, 214, 311, 364, 451.
poetry and songs by and about Indians, 485, 519, 556A, 1425, 1448, 1483.
property, 1005.
religion, 87, 181, 316, 793, 849, 934, 935, 1304.
revolt. *See* warfare.
Santo Domingo, 1166.
scalp bounty, 1092.
Senecas, 1157.
Six Nations. *See* Iroquois Nation.
social life and customs, 790, 887.
South America, 579.
South Carolina, 699.
Spanish America, 221.
Stockbridge, Mass., 305, 306, 307, 318.
suicide, 946.
treatment of, 1116, 1156.
Tupi, 69, 71/72.
vices, 1498.
Virginia, 193, 213, 214, 796.
virginity, 904.
warfare and wars, 489, 679, 846, 1084, 1166, 1180.
*See also* French and Indian War.
wealth, 931.
Western United States, 1170, 1209, 1258.
*See also* Micmacs (Indians).
Industries:
British colonies, 534.
United States, 1059, 1224.
taxation of, 1203, 1224.
Ingenhouss. *See* Ingenhousz.
Ingenhousz, Jan, 1730–1799: Vermischte Schriften physisch-medicinischen Innhalts (*review*), 807A.
Inkle und Yariko (*review*), 439.
Insects, 1338, 1466.
illustrations, 832.
*See also* Butterflies; Wasps.
Instruction. *See* Education.
Instruction, Religious. *See* Education, Religious.
Instructions for the treatment of Negroes (*review*), 913.
Inter-state Relations. *See* United States: state relations.
Irenico-Polemographia. *See* Theatrum Europæum.
Iron Manufactures, 1222.
Iroquois Nation, 856, 890, 1448, 1451, 1460, 1461, 1507.
fiction, 1508.
London visit, 246.
picture writing, 932.
songs, 374/375.
Iselin, Isaak, 1728–1782: Geschichte der Menschheit, 610.
Isert, Paul Erdmann, 1757–1789:
Reise, 933.
*See also* Kotzebue, A. von, Die Negersclaven.
Isle Royale, 253.

# J

J. *See* Beschreibung der europäischen Kolonien in Amerika.
J., J., of Chippenham, contributor. *See* Penn, Beschreibung.
Jackson, Richard, d. 1787, joint author. *See* Franklin, Benjamin, and R. Jackson, The interest of Great Britain consider'd.

Jackson, Robert, 1750-1827:
A Treatise on the fevers of Jamaica (*review*), 1262.
Ueber die Fieber in Jamaica (*reviews*), 1352, 1402.
Jackson, William, bishop of Oxford, 1751-1815, compiler. *See* The Constitutions of the several independent states of America.
Jacquin, Nikolaus Joseph, Freiherr von, 1727-1817:
Auswahl schöner und seltener Gewächse, 1272.
Dreyhundert auserlesene amerikanische Gewächse, 819.
Selectarum stirpium americanarum historia (*review*), 1255.
Die Jahr Blum. *See* Quad, Matthias.
Jamaica, W. I.: Proceedings of the Governor and Assembly (*review*), 1398.
Jamaica, W. I. [as subject], 464, 466, 522, 687, 725, 822.
American revolution, 621.
commerce, 817, 1136.
description and travel, 199.
diseases, 1190.
fevers, 1262, 1352, 1402.
German settlement, 464.
hot springs, 1023, 1042.
medicinal herbs, 977.
negroes and slavery, 687, 1106, 1313, 1398.
pepper-tree, 625A.
pictorial works, 600.
social life and customs, 1106.
Jamaica (title), 1136.
Janisch, Daniel, 1762-1847: Das achtzehnte Jahrhundert, 1447, 1448.
Jardine, L. J.: Belehrung über Nordamerika, 1388.
Jay, John, 1745-1829, contributor. *See* An American remembrancer.
*portraits*, 838.
Jean Paul. *See* Richter, Jean Paul.
Jefferson, Thomas, 1743-1826:
Etat der Bevölkerung der vereinigten Staaten von Nordamerika, 1171.
Notes on the state of Virginia (*review*), 966.
*See also* American Philosophical Society, Transactions, v. 3; Americanische Staatspapiere, 1406; Neues bergmännisches Journal, Bd. 1.
Jenne's Reisen von St. Petersburg (*review*), 1105F.
Jenssen, Lorents: Waren Preis, 651.
Jesuit Missionary and Other Activities, 172, 441.
Brazil, 87.
Lower California, 389, 445, 467, 477.
Mexico, 389, 445.
Jesuits:
Allerhand...Brief, 269, 272.
Aus America, 151.
Letters édifiantes. *See their* Allerhand.
Der neüwe Welt-Bott. *See their* Allerhand.
Sendtschreyben vnd warhaffte zeytungen, 76.
Jews:
colonies in America, 756.
England, 207.
North America, 791.
United States, 1221.
Johannsen, Andrew: A geographical and historical account of Balum, 1339.
Johnson, Joseph, 1776-1862: An experimental inquiry into the properties of carbonic acid gas (*review*), 1500.
Johnson, Samuel, 1709-1784: Taxation no tyranny. *See* Remer, Amerikanisches Archiv.
Jollet, Louis, 1645-1700: Beschreibung. *See* Hennepin, Beschreibung.
Jones. Ueber die physischen Merkwürdigkeiten des Sumpfs Diomal Swamp in Nordamerika, 854A.
Jones, John, 1729-1791, contributor. *See* American Philosophical Society, Transactions, v. 1, v. 3; College of Physicians of Philadelphia, Medi*zi*nische Verhandlungen, Bd. 1; College of Physicians of Philadelphia, Transactions, v. 1.

Joseph II, 1741-1790, emperor of Germany. *See* Germany. — Statutes.
Jubilæum Theatri Europæi. *See* Theatrum Europæum.
Juel, Jens, 1745-1802, illustrator. *See* Egede, Nachrichten.
Jung-Stilling, Johann Heinrich, 1740-1817: Die Geschichte Florentins v. Fahlendorn, 678.
Die Junge Amerikanerin. *See* Villeneuve, G. S.
Juvenile Literature, 762, 835, 850, 872C, 913A, 965, 991, 1046, 1057, 1079, 1105, 1269, 1309, 1362.

## K

K., C. C. *See* Begebenheit eines jungen Englischen Officiers.
Kästner, Abraham Gotthelf, 1719-1800, editor. *See* Rohr, Julius Bernhards von Rohr Physikalische Bibliothek.
Kästner, Abraham Gotthelf, 1719-1800, translator. *See* Prévost d'Exiles, Erste Reisen.
Kalm, Pehr, 1716-1779:
Beschreibung, 347.
Resa till Norra Amerika. *See* Rousselot de Surgy, Histoire naturelle.
Kant, Immanuel, 1724-1804: Zum ewigen Frieden, 1273A.
Karsch, C., engraver. *See* Bos, Leben und Thaten.
Karsten, Franz Christian Lorenz, 1751-1829: Europens Handel (*review*), 692.
Kayser, Albrecht Christoph, d. 1811, translator. *See* Brissot de Warville, Neue Reise.
Keate, George, 1729-1797:
Nachrichten von den Pelew-Inseln, 989.
*See also* Die Heuschrecken-Verwüstung Joel II.
Keller, Franciscus, 1700-1762, compiler. *See* Jesuits, Allerband...Brief.
Kempe, John Tabor: Allerhand Briefe und Anzeigen, 774.
Kemys, Lawrence, d. 1618, contributor. *See* Bry, Americæ Achter Theil.
Kennedy, Ildephons: Anmerkungen über die Witterung, 990.
Kensington, Conn.: fogs, 376.
Kentucky:
discovery, 1170, 1209, 1258.
geography, 1170, 1209, 1258.
government, 1170, 1209, 1258.
history, 871, 872, 1052.
Indians, 815.
settlement, 1170, 1209, 1258.
Kersaint, Armand Simon de Coetnempren, comte de, 1742-1793: Ueber die Aussicht eines Krieges zwischen Frankreich und England, 1185.
Keye, Otto: Kurtzer Entwurff von Neu-Niederland, 192.
Kiefhaber, Jean. *See* Kiffhaber, Hans.
Kiffhaber, Hans, 16th century, editor. *See* Federmann, Indianische Historia.
Kimayer, Thomas: Neu-Eröffnetes Raritäten-Cabinet, 232.
King, James, 1750-1784, contributor. *See* Cook, Dritte Entdeckungs-Reise; Forster, Anführung des Capitains Cook, Clerke [etc.]; Geschichte der Seereisen und Entdeckungen.
Kingston, W. I.: shipping, 621.
Kippis, Andrew, 1725-1795: The life of Captain James Cook (*review*), 963A.
Das Kleine Brüder-Gesang-Buch. *See* Moravian Brethren.
Klinger, Friedrich Maximilian von, 1752-1831:
Die Falschen Spieler, 716.
Geschichte eines Teutschen der neuesten Zeit, 1419.
Sturm und Drang, 517.
Klopstock, Friedrich Gottlieb, 1724-1803:
Die Denkzeiten, 1225.
Der jezige Krieg, 717.

Klopstock, Friedrich Gottlieb, *continued*
Sie, und nicht Wir, 1043.
Zwey Nordamerikaner, 1420.
*See also* Herder, Briefe; Stolberg, Mein Vaterland.
Knox, Henry, 1750-1806: Oficielle Nachrichten, 1180.
Koblenz, G. von. Gebeugter Vaterlandsstolz, 517A.
Koch, Johann Gottlieb Franz Friedrich, 1755-180-?:
Versuch eines Kriegs-Rechts der Negern in Afrika, 679.
Kocherthal, Josua von, d. 1719, contributor. *See* Boehme, Das verlangte.
Koehler, agent for emigration, translator. *See* Historische und Geographische Beschreibung von Neu-Schottland.
Köhler, Alexander Wilhelm, d. 1832, editor. *See* Neues bergmännisches Journal, Bd. 1.
Koehler, Andreas Rudolf, d. 1827: Beschreibung, 1449.
Köhler, Johann Tobias, 1720-1768:
Beschreibung der Insel Cuba, 398.
Beschreibung des Landes Florida, 407.
Kurze Beschreibung, 399.
Von dem Handel der Spanier nach Westindien, 400.
Koelling, Johann Friedrich: Die Thränen derer standhafften Bekenner des Evangelischen Glaubens, 282.
Konge Vetenskaps Academiens. *See* Kungliga svenska Vetenskapsakademien, Stockholm.
Korn, Christian Heinrich, 1726-1783: Geschichte der Kriege, 518.
Kosche, Christian Traugott, 1754-1789:
Karakter, Sitten und Religion aller bekannten Völker, 991.
*See also* Hammerdörfer, K., and C. T. Kosche, Amerika.
Kotzebue, August von, 1761-1819:
Indianerne i Engelland *(review)*, 1199.
Die Indianer in England, 992.
Die Negersclaven, 1313.
Die Verwandtschaften, 1421, 1422.
*See also* Herder, Briefe.
Kraemer, Matthias. *See* Kramer, Matthias.
Krafft, John Charles Philip von: Journal, 518A.
Die Krafft und Wahrheit des Göttlichen Wortes, 283.
Kramer, Johann Matthias: Neueste und richtigste Nachricht von der Landschaft Georgia, 322.
Kramer, Matthias, fl. 1672-1727, translator: *See* Bos, Leben und Tapffere Thaten; Bos, Leben und Thaten.
Krauseneck, Johann Christoph, 1738-1799:
Columbus, 519.
Die Werbung für Engeland, 564A.
Kreysig, Friedrich Ludwig, 1770-1839, translator. *See* Bálmis, Uber die amerikanischen Pflanzen.
Kriegslied eines Provinzialen. *See* Goeckinck, L. F. G. von.
Krüger, Andras Ludwig, 1743-ca. 1805, illustrator.
*See* Forster, Geschichte der Reisen.
Küttner, Johann David, 1693-1769: Der Allervortheilhafteste und Seeligste Verlust Derer Nachfolger Jesu, 284.
Kungliga svenska Vetenskapsakademien, Stockholm:
Nya handlingar *(reviews)*, 872D, 913B.
Kunstmann, H. A.: Neueste Erdbeschreibung aller vier Theile der Welt *(reviews)*, 873B, 965B.
Kunze, Johann Christoph, 1744-1807:
Ueber den Religionszustand unter den Deutschen in Nordamerika, 903.
Von der bei den Deutschen in Philadelphia angelegten lateinischen Schule, 532.
*See also* Briefe von deutschen evangelischen Geistlichen in Pensylvanien, 506.
Kurtze Nachricht, 317.
Kurtze Remarqves, 254.
Eine kurze Reise in Westindien *(reviews)*, 1200, 1346.
Kurze topographische Beschreibung der Provinz Ober-Canada, 1481.
Kurze, zuverlässige Nachricht, 365/66.

Kurzgefasste Geschichte des Christoph Columbus *(review)*, 667.
Kurzgefasste Geschichte der drey ersten Entdecker von Amerika. *See* Ring, F. D.
Kurzgefasste Geschichte des Ferdinand Cortez, 680.
Kuttner. *See* Küttner.

## L

L, M. de. *See* Histoire impartiale des evenements militaires et politiques de la dernière guerre.
Labat, Jean Baptiste, 1663-1738: Reisen nach Westindien *(reviews)*, 837C, 874, 921, 921A, 921B, 1022A.
Labor. *See* Wages.
Laborie, Pierre Joseph: The caffee planter *(review)*, 1494.
La Croix, de. *See* Delacroix.
Låkeren och Naturforskaren *(review)*, 1061.
La Fayette, Georges Washington Louis Gilbert de Motier, marquis de, 1779-1849:
Schreiben das jungen la Fayette, 1323.
*biography*, 1234, 1323.
Lafayette, Marie Joseph Paul Roch Yves Gilbert de Motier, marquis de, 1757-1834:
Schreiben, 1280.
*biography*, 1022, 1158, 1234, 1323.
La Fayette als Staatsmann als Krieger und als Mensch. *See* Rohr, J. L. von.
Lafitau, Joseph François, 1681-1746: Mœurs des sauvages amériquains. *See* Schröter, Algemeine Geschichte.
Lafosse, J. F. Avis aux habitans des Colonies *(review)*, 908B.
La Hontan, Louis Armand de Lom d'Arc, baron de, 1681-1746: Des berühmten Herrn Baron De Lahontan Neueste Reisen nach Nord-Indien, 236, 241.
Lamarck, Jean Baptiste Antoine de Monet de, 1744-1829, joint author. *See* Bruguière, J. G., and others, Journal d'histoire naturelle.
Lametherie's journal de physique, v. 3 *(review)*, 1465.
Lancaster, Pennsylvania, 506, 916, 1407, 1484.
college, 940.
German settlement, 940.
Land:
Pennsylvania, 1388.
purchase of, 1387.
United States, 1325.
*See also* Real Estate.
Landessbergk. *See* Landsberg.
Landsberg, Martin, editor. *See* Vespucci, Von den newen Insulen vnd landen.
Lange, Jean Georg, translator. *See* Hennepin, Neue Entdeckung; Hennepin, Neue Reise-Beschreibung.
Languages:
aboriginal, 213.
deaf and dumb, 1259.
Indian. *See* American Languages.
*See also* Phonetics.
Lapérouse, Jean François de Galaup, comte de, 1741-1788:
Entdeckungsreise, 1450.
Voyage *(review)*, 1439.
La Peyrère, Isaac de, 1594-1676: Ausführliche Beschreibung, 202.
La Rochefoucauld Liancourt, François Alexandre Frédéric, duc de, 1747-1827:
Reisen, 1451.
Voyage dans les États-Unis *(review)*, 1507.
*See also* Klopstock, Sie, und nicht Wir; Schreiben des Herrn la Fayette; Stäudlin, Beiträge.
La Salle, Robert Cavelier, sieur de, 1643-1687: *explorations*, 218.
Latitude and Longitude: United States, 1414, 1427, 1486.

Latomus, Sigismund, firm, publishers, Frankfurt am Main: Relationis Historicæ, 203, 208, 215.
Die Laube. *See* Lenz, Henriette von Waldeck.
Laudonnière, René Goulaine de, 16th century, contributor. *See* Bry, Der ander Theyl. *expeditions*, 91.
Laur, J. F. B., translator. *See* Franklin, Bemerkungen.
Laurel: West Indies, 1253.
Laurens, Henry, 1724-1792: *portrait*, 838.
Law, John, 1671-1729: *West Indian Company*, 250, 251, 252, 253, 254, 260.
Law, 970.
  fishery rights, 416.
  military, 679.
  *See also* Courts.
Lawson, John, d. 1712: Allerneuste Beschreibung der Provintz Carolina, 244.
Learned Societies. *See* Academies and Learned Societies.
Le Beau, Claude: Begebenheiten und merkwürdige Reise *(review)*, 1250.
  Neue Reise, 340.
Le Beau, Karl. *See* Le Beau, Claude.
Leben und Tapffere Thaten der aller-berühmtesten See-Helden. *See* Bos, Lambert van den.
Leben und Thaten Der Durchläuchtigsten See-Helden. *See* Bos, Lambert van den.
Lederer, John: The discoveries of John Lederer, 193.
Lee, Benjamin: *biography*, 1498.
Lee, Charles, 1731-1782, contributor. *See* Remer, Amerikanisches Archiv.
Legends. *See* Myths and Legends.
Lehrbücher für die Jugend in Nordcarolina *(reviews)*, 914, 963, 1061B.
Leib, Michael, contributor. *See* College of Physicians of Philadelphia, Medicinische Verhandlungen, Bd. 1; College of Physicians of Philadelphia, Transactions, v. 1.
Leiste, Christian, 1738-1815: Beschreibung, 577, 578.
Lemke, Hermann Heinrich: Briefe und Extracte. *See* Urlsperger, Der Ausführlichen Nachrichten.
Le Moyne de Morgues, Jacques, d. 1588, artist. *See* Bry, Der ander Theyl.
Lendrum, John: A concise and impartial history of the American Revolution *(review)*, 1392.
Lent, Adolph C.: An inaugural dissertation *(review)*, 1464.
Lenz, Jakob Michael Reinhold, 1751-1792: Henriette von Waldeck, 520.
  Der Waldbruder, 1374.
Leonhardi, Friedrich Gottlieb, d. 1814, translator. *See* Jardine, Belehrung über Nordamerika.
Lercher, Laux: Ein neůwe zeitung, 66.
Le Roy, Jacques, b. 1739, engraver. *See* Portrait du Général Washington.
LeRoy, Jean Baptiste, 1724-1800, contributor. *See* American Philosophical Society, Transactions, v. 3.
Lerpinière, Daniel, 1745-1785, engraver. *See* Robertson, Sechs Blätter *(review)*.
Léry, Jean de, 1534-1611: *expedition*, 92.
Lesser, Friedrich Christian, 1692-1754: Umständliche Nachrichten, 285.
Lessing, Gotthold Ephraim, 1729-1781: Ernst und Falk, 645C.
Lessing, Karl Gotthelf, 1740-1812: Die Mätresse, 645D. A Letter from new Iersey *(notice)*, 379B.
Lettera allo stampatore Sigr. Pietro Allegrini. *See* Canovai, Stanislao.
Letters [specified authors, only; anonymous letters are under appropriate subjects]: Bülow, 1308, 1364, 1407; Columbus, 6, 7; Cortés, 46, 604, 605; Crèvecœur, 782; Cysat, 86; Dohm, 542; Galloway, 730; Gregor, 463, Hasenclever, 1222; Isert, 933; Jefferson, 1214; Jesuits, 76, 151, 269, 272; Lafayette, 1323; Latomus, 203, 208, 215; Kay, 59; Kunze, 532; Losberg, 641; Montcalm,

Letters, *continued*
  539; Pastorius, 209, 210; Penn, 211; Pinto, 522; Rochefort, 188; Schiller, 754, 754A; Schlözer, 618; Schöpf, 812; Steuben, 643.
Letters from an American farmer. *See* Crèvecœur, M. G. St. J. de.
Letters on emigration. *See* Hodgkinson.
Letters and essays on several diseases of the West-Indies *(review)*, 596.
Letters from Illinois. *See* L'Espion américain en Europe.
Lettre du Landgrave de Hesse, 550A.
Lettres d'un cultivateur américain. *See* Crèvecœur.
Lettres ilinoises. *See* L'Espion américain en Europe.
Lettsom, John Coakley, 1744-1815, and J. Ellis: Geschichte des Thees und Koffees, 521.
L'Hermite, Jacques, d. 1624: *voyage*, 162.
Liberty, Religious. *See* Religious Freedom.
Library Society, Salisbury, N. C., 1305.
Lichtenberg, Georg Christoph, 1742-1799: Briefe aus England, 521A.
  Wundercuren der geweihten Arzte, 936A.
Liebe, Gottlob August, 1746-1819, engraver. *See* Russell, Geschichte des Ursprunges.
Light, 965.
Lightning: blindness, 1235.
Lightning rod, 452.
Lind, John, 1737-1781: Remarks upon the principal acts of the 13th Parliament *(review)*, 599.
  *See also* Aussöhnungs-Plan, 504.
Lindemann, Johann Gottlieb: Geschichte der Meinungen älterer und neuerer Völker, 793.
Lindenau, Gotzke, d. 1612: *voyage*, 202.
Lingen, von: Contrast alter und neuer Zeit, 793A.
Linschoten, Jan Huygen van, 1563-1611: voyages, 114, 164, 165.
Linseed, 1003.
Lintschoten. *See* Linschoten.
Lips, Johann Heinrich, 1758-1817, etcher. *See* Bode, Literarisches Leben.
Liquor Tax, 1223, 1224.
List, Gottlieb Christian Heinrich, 1752-1821, translator. *See* Fenning, Neue Erdbeschreibung.
Literarische Blätter, Nürnberg. *See* Rauw, Cosmographia.
Literary and Philosophical Society of Manchester: Memoirs, v. 2 *(review)*, 919.
—— v. 3 *(review)*, 1108.
Literatur und Völkerkunde, Vierter Jahrgang: Bd. 7 u. 8 *(review)*, 916.
Bd. 9 *(review)*, 917.
Literature. *See* American Literature; German Literature; *also* various forms of literature, as Drama, Fiction, Poetry, etc.; *also* Juvenile Literature.
Litteratur und Völkerkunde *(review)*, 735.
Liturgy: Reformed Church, 483.
Lizards, 999.
Lloyd, Thomas, 1756-1827, editor. *See* Pennsylvania.
—— Constitutional Convention, Debates *(review)*, 1194.
  *See also* Auszug aus dem officiellen Rapport.
Lobwasser, Ambrosius, 1515-1585, translator. *See* Reformed Church in the United States, Neuvermehrt- und vollständiges Gesang-Buch.
Lochner, Michael Friedrich: Memoria Behaimia. *See* Doppelmayr, Historische Nachricht.
Loew, Conrad, translator. *See* Meer oder Seehanen Buch.
Löwe, Andr. J., b. 1752, contributor. *See* Historische und Geographische Beschreibung.
Logan, Johann Zacharias, translator. *See* Schelekhov, Erste und zweyte reise.
Logau, Friedrich von, 1604-1655: Deutscher Sinn-Getichte Drey Tausend, 174.

Lonck. *See* Loncq.
Loncq, Hendrick Cornelius: *biography*, 162, 196.
London, England: Indian visit, 238, 246.
Long, John, Indian trader:
Westindischen Dollmetschers und Kaufmanns See- und Land-Reisen, 1088, 1089.
Voyages and travels (*review*), 1119.
*See also* Forster, Geschichte der Reisen; Forster, Reisen an die Nordwestküste; Noch etwas von dem Westmeer; Ueber das wiedergefundene Westmeer.
Long Island, N. Y., 516.
description and travel, 537.
German mercenaries, 537, 624.
Indians, 624.
map, 513.
López de Gómara, Francisco, 1510–1560?, contributor. *See* Francisci, Guineischer und Americanischer Blumen-Pusch.
López de Velasco, Juan, 16th century: *manuscript*. *See* Herrera y Tordesillas, Achtzehender Theil der Newen Welt.
The Lord's Prayer in eight American languages, 327.
Lorimer, John, contributor. *See* American Philosophical Society, Transactions, v. 1.
Losberg, von: Auszug eines Schreibens aus Amerika. *See* "Brookland, bei Neu York."
Loschge, Friedrich Heinrich, 1755–1840, contributor. *See* Der Naturforscher.
Loskiel, Georg Heinrich, 1740–1814: Geschichte der Mission der evangelischen Brüder, 994, 995.
Louisburg, Nova Scotia: British garrison, 550.
Louisiana, 218, 357, 406, 473.
bibliography, 253.
colonization, 218, 251, 252, 253, 254.
commerce, 646.
description and travel, 213, 218, 316, 357.
early accounts, 218, 222, 224.
geography, 251, 252, 253, 254, 357.
history, 218, 251, 252, 253, 254, 357.
Indians, 213, 214.
pictorial works, 213, 214.
products, 646.
Love: Indian practices, 958.
Lowell, John, 1743–1802, contributor. *See* American Academy of Arts and Sciences, Memoirs, v. 2.
Lower California:
description and travel, 389, 445, 467, 477.
Indians, 467, 477.
Jesuits, 389, 445, 467, 477.
"Jnsul California," 214.
natural history, 389, 445.
Lownes, Caleb, pseud. *See* Bradford, William.
Loyalists, 1301.
Lucidarius: Von allerhandt geschöpffen Gottes, 64.
Luckenbach, Abraham: *biography*. *See* Urlsperger, Der Ausführlichen-Nachrichten Von der Königlich-Gross-Britannischen Colonie Saltzburgischer Emigranten in America.
Ludwig, Johann Friedrich; Neueste Nachrichten von Surinam (*review*), 1105D.
Lueder, August Ferdinand, 1760–1819: Statistische Beschreibung (*review*), 1207.
Luffman, John: A brief account of Antigua (*review*), 1015A.
Lutgens, Gotthilf Nicholas: *biography*, 1457.
Luther, Martin, 1483–1546: *teachings*, 844.
Lutheran Church, Evangelical. *See* Evangelical Lutheran Church.
Lutz, Johann Friedrich: Unterricht vom Blitz und den Blitz-oder Wetterableitern (*review*), 839.
Luzac, Elie, 1723–1796, translator. *See* Untersuchung der Frage, 724.
Lyson, Edward, contributor. *See* Abhandlungen zur Naturgeschichte, Physik und Oekonomie.

# M

M. *See* Meiners, Christoph.
M., M. D. L. R. C. A. L. T. de. *See* Poncelin de La Roche-Tilhac, J. C.
M., N. *See* Bourgeois, N. L.
Mably, Gabriel Bonnot de, abbé, 1709–1785: Remarks concerning the government and laws of the United States. *See* Murray, Political sketches.
McCauslin, Robert, contributor. *See* American Philosophical Society, Transactions, v. 3.
McCluer, John, d. 1794?: Einige neuere Nachrichten von den Pelew, 1126.
M'Kean, Thomas, 1734–1817, joint author. *See* Wilson, James, 1742–1798, and T. M'Kean, Commentaries.
Mackenzie, Sir Alexander, 1763–1820, contributor. *See* Neue amerikanische Briefe, 1276.
Madison, James, 1749–1812, contributor. *See* American Philosophical Society, Transactions, v. 2.
Madog ab Owain Gwynedd, 1150–1180?: *voyage*, 1243.
Männling, Johann Christoph, 1658–1723, editor. *See* Dapper, Dappervs Exoticvs Cvriosvs.
Märter, Prof.: Nachrichten von den Bahamischen Inseln. *See* Born, Physikalische Arbeiten.
Magalhães, Ferñao de, ca. 1480–1521: *explorations*, 106, 121, 145, 155.
Magallanes: discovery, 87.
Magee, Bernard, contributor. *See* Beyträge zur Geschichte der Nordamerikanischen Länder-Entdecker.
Magellan, Ferdinand. *See* Magalhães, Ferñao de.
Magnetism, 975.
Mail. *See* Postal Service.
Maine:
description and travel, 1163, 1478.
history, 1342.
Malsburg: Vor 100 Jahren, 578A.
Mammals, 634.
Mexico, 625A.
*See also* various mammals.
Manso, Johann Caspar Friedrich, 1760–1826: Ueber die Verläumdung der Wissenschaften (*review*), 1355.
Maple Trees and Maple Sugar, 636, 637, 686, 1129, 1259, 1326, 1327, 1332, 1373, 1381, 1428, 1498.
Maps, 193.
America, 1055, 1479.
American revolution, 513.
Boston, Mass., 513.
Long Island, N. Y., 513.
Marano and Quira (*review*), 1061E.
Marmontel, Jean François, 1723–1799: Vertheidigung der Akademie, 1172.
Marperger, Paul Jakob, 1656–1730, supposed author. *See* Kurtze Remarqves.
Marquette, Jacques, 1637–1675: Beschreibung. *See* Hennepin, Beschreibung.
Marriage:
Indians, 930, 949.
dowry, 1005.
*See also* Polygamy.
Marschal. *See* Marshall.
Marsh, Herbert, 1757–1837: Wer ist Fox, 1423.
Marshall, Humpry, 1722–1801:
Arbustum americanum (*reviews*), 1011, 1334.
Beschreibung der wildwachsenden Bäume und Staudengewächse (*reviews*), 1013, 1241, 1248, 1335, 1354.
Marsillac, Jean:
Leben Wilhelm Penns, 1173.
*See also* Fourcroy, La médecine éclairée.
Martini, Joh. Jacob, contributor. *See* Neu eingerichtete und vermehrte Bilder-Geographie.
Martinique (island), 390.
British capture, 397.
campaign of 1794, 1389.
coffee exports, 422.
description and travel, 397, 403.

Martyr, Peter. See Anghiera, Pietro Martire de.
Maryland, 670, 812, 814, 984, 1032, 1484.
 commerce, 748.
 description and travel, 193, 1163, 1201, 1312, 1478.
 discovery, 193.
 Negroes, 997.
Maskelyne, Nevil, contributor. See American Philosophical Society, Transactions, v. 1.
Mason, James, 1710-1780, artist. See Robertson, Sechs Blätter.
Massachusetts, 305, 306.
 description and travel, 1163, 1478.
 history, 1359/60.
 immigration, 313.
 Indians, 759.
 See also Boston; Cambridge.
Massachusetts Bay Colony. See Massachusetts Colony.
Massachusetts Colony, 313, 759, 1480.
Massachusetts Historical Society, 1474.
Massachusetts magazine (review), 1434.
Massachusetts Medical Society: Medical papers, no. 1 (review), 1107.
Matanzas, Cuba: Spanish Silver Fleet, 162.
Mathematics, 965, 1259, 1296.
Mauss, Isaak, 1748-1833: Auf Amerika. See Auszug aus einem Briefe, 879.
Mauvillon, Jakob, 1743-1794: Sammlung (review), 666.
Mauvillon, Jakob, 1743-1794, translator. See Raynal, Philosophische und politische Geschichte.
Maxwell, Hugh, 1733-1799, contributor. See American Academy of Arts and Sciences, Memoirs, v. 2.
Mazzei, Filippo, 1730-1816: Recherches historiques et politiques (review), 971.
Meares, John, 1756-1809:
 Authentic copy of Lieut. Meares memorial (review), 1057C.
 Voyage made in the year 1788 and 1789 (reviews), 1117, 1118.
 See also Forster, G., Geschichte der Reisen; Noch etwas von dem Westmeer; Ueber das wiedergefundene Westmeer.
Mears. See Meares.
Meat as Food: Indian diet, 943, 944, 945.
Mechel, Christian von, 1737-1818, engraver. See Urlsperger, Americanisches Ackerwerk Gottes.
Mecklenburg County, North Carolina: Evangelical Lutheran Church, 1044, 1203.
Medical Fees, 1336.
Medical Instruments. See various instruments, as Syringe.
Medical Society of London: Memoirs, v. 4 (review), 1435.
Medicine (entries also under specific subjects), 420, 474, 492, 527, 550, 597, 735, 868, 873, 881, 910, 985, 1107, 1204, 1235, 1253, 1260, 1295, 1296, 1336, 1435, 1492.
 See also Diseases; Drugs; Herbs, Medicinal; Hospitals; Veterinary Medicine.
Medicus, Friedrich Casimir, 1736-1809: Ueber nordamerikanischen Bäume und Sträucher (reviews), 1154, 1263, 1354.
Meer oder Seehanen Buch, 106.
Megiser, Hieronymus, ca. 1553-1618: Septentrio Novantiquus, 134.
Meier, Heinrich Ludwig, translator. See Garcilaso de la Vega, Geschichte.
Meiners, Christoph, 1747-1810:
 Bemerkungen über die Wirkungen des Klima, 985.
 Betrachtungen über die Begriffe der verschiedenen Völker von Ehre, 924.
 Betrachtungen über Männer-Wochen, 885.
 Einige Betrachtungen über die Schönheit der menschlichen Bildung, 928.
 Fortgesetzte Betrachtungen über den Sklavenhandel, 1165.
 Geschichte der Gesetze des Wohlstandes unter rohen Völkern, 931.

Meiners, Christoph, continued
 Geschichte der hieroglyphischen Schrift, 932.
 Grundriss der Geschichte der Menschheit, 1174.
 Historische Bemerkungen über die so genannten Wilden, 1040.
 Historische Nachrichten, 1041.
 Kurze Geschichte des Adels, 895.
 Kurze Geschichte der allegorischen Gottheiten, 934.
 Kurze Geschichte des gemässigten Klima, 993.
 Kurze Geschichte der Meynungen roher Völker von der Natur des Himmels, 894.
 Kurze Geschichte der Meynungen roher Völker von den Thieren, 936.
 Eine kurze Schilderung roher und uncultivirter Sprachen, 1226.
 Ueber die Ausstattungen und Mitgiften unter verschiedenen Völkern, 1005.
 Ueber die Begriffe verschiedener Völker von dem Werthe der Jungfrauschafft, 904.
 Ueber die Bevölkerung von America, 948.
 Ueber die Braut-Preise unter verschiedenen Völkern, 949.
 Ueber die cörperliche Stärke verschiedener Völker, 1186.
 Ueber die Entstehung des Eigenthums, 1006.
 Ueber das Essen des Schweine-Fleisches, 943.
 Ueber die Farben und Schattierungen verschiedener Völker, 1142.
 Ueber den Genuss und die Wirkungen von animalischen und vegetabilischen Speisen, 1004.
 Ueber die Gesetze der Ess-Lust, 950.
 Ueber die grosse Verschiedenheit der Biegsamkeit und Unbiegsamkeit, 905.
 Ueber die gymnastischen und kriegerischen Uebungen verschiedener Völker, 887.
 Ueber den Haar- und Bartwuchs der hässlichen und dunkelfarbigen Völker, 1141.
 Ueber die Hagerkeit und Fettheit der verschiedenen Völker der Erde, 1188.
 Ueber den Hang mancher Völker zum Selbst-Morde, 946.
 Ueber den Hang verschiedener Völker zur Völlerey, 901.
 Ueber den Hang vieler Völker zu fetten Speisen, 902.
 Ueber die Natur der Afrikanischen Neger, 1048.
 Ueber die Natur der Americaner, 1049.
 Ueber die Rechtmässigkeit des Neger-Handels, 951.
 Ueber die Sinnlichkeit, 1007.
 Ueber den Stand der Natur, 947.
 Ueber die Strafen des Ehebruchs unter verschiedenen Völkern, 952.
 Ueber die sympathetische Reizbarkeit, 953.
 Ueber die Ursachen der Viel-Weiberey, 954.
 Ueber die Verschiedenheit der cörperlichen Grösse verschiedener Völker, 1143.
 Ueber die Verschmitztheit verschiedener Völker, 955.
 Ueber die Verunstaltungen des Mundes in der Absicht ihn zu verschönern, 1008.
 Von den Meynungen roher Völker über die Entstehung der Menschen, 957.
 Von den Varietäten und Abarten der Neger, 1051.
 Zweyte Abhandlung über die Natur der Americaner, 1053.
 See also Beniowsky, Reisen.
Meissner, August Gottlieb, 1753-1807: Anrede einiger Indianer an den Cortes, 579.
Meister, Albert Ludwig Friedrich, 1724-1788: Nachricht von einem neuen musikalischen Instrumente, 419.
Melsheimer, Frederick Valentine, 1749-1814, supposed author. See Tagebuch der Seereise.
Memmius, Conrad, fl. 1594, contributor. See Latomus, Relationis Historicae.
Memoriale oder Rechtliche Ansuchungs-Schreiben, 286.
Mennonites:
 Netherlands, 794.
 North America, 803.

# GERMAN WORKS RELATING TO AMERICA — INDEX

Mercator, Gerardus, 1512-1594: Atlas Minor, 169, 171.
Mercenaries. *See* German Mercenaries.
Mercer, Fort. *See* Mifflin and Mercer, Forts.
Merchant Marine: Nova Scotia, 863.
Mercier, Louis Sébastian, 1740-1814:
L'Habitant de Guadeloupe. *See* Kotzebue, Die Verwandtschaften.
Merck, Johann Heinrich, 1741-1791: Herr Oheim der Jüngere, 681.
Merian, Matthæus, 1593-1650, editor. *See* Bry, Neundter Theil; Bry, Vierzehender Theil; Gottfried, Historische Chronica; Gottfried, Newe Welt; Irenico-Polemographia...Continuati Septennium; Irenico-Polemographiæ, Continuatio I; Irenico-Polemographiæ, Continuatio II; Theatri Europæi Continuati Dreyzehnder Theil; Theatri Europæi Continuati Zwölffter Theil; Theatri Europæi Sechster Theil; Theatri Europæi Vierdter Theil; Theatri Europæi, Zehender Theil; Theatrum Europæum; Welper, Compendium Geographicum.
Merian, Matthæus, 1593-1650, engraver. *See* Gottfried, Newe Welt; Theatrum Europæum.
Metcalf, Simon, d. 1794: *biography*, 1121.
Meteorological Observations, 474, 492, 975, 985, 993.
Cambridge, Massachusetts, 942, 965.
Guiana, 933.
Haiti, 859.
United States, 795.
(eastern), 998.
Virginia, 507, 998.
West Indies, 187, 933.
*See also* Climate; Electricity; Geography; Lightning; Magnetism; Weather.
Meusel, Johann Georg, 1743-1820: Litteratur der Statistik, 1043A.
Meusel, Johann Georg, 1743-1820, editor. *See* Du Roi, J. P., Die Harbkesche wilde Baumzucht.
Mexico, 48, 49, 172, 187.
aboriginal religion, 793.
animals, 852.
botany, 1298/99.
Catholic church, 54, 55.
conquest, 604, 605, 1304.
description and travel, 214, 221, 852.
discovery, 680.
geography, 852.
government, 494A.
history, 1105A, 1148A.
Indians, 47, 67, 1116A.
Jesuits, 389, 445.
manuals, 625A.
natural history, 389, 445, 852.
pictorial works, 214.
*See also* New Mexico.
Meyer, Martin, 17th century, editor. *See* Irenico-Polemographiæ.
Michaelis, Christian Friedrich, 1754-1814, contributor. *See* College of Physicians of Philadelphia, Medicinische Verhandlungen, Bd. 1.
Michaelis, Johann David, 1717-1791: Lebensbeschreibung, von ihm selbst abgefasst, 1174A.
Michaux, André, 1746-1802: Pflanzschule, 1230.
Micmacs (Indians): fiction, 1508.
Mifflin, Walter: *biography*, 1372.
Mifflin and Mercer, Forts, 583.
Miggrode, Jacques de, translator. *See* Casas, New Welt; Casas, Umbständige warhafftige Beschreibung; Casas, Warhafftiger vnd gründlicher Bericht.
Milet-Mureau, Louis Marie Antoine Deshouff, baron de, 1756-1825, editor. *See* Lapérouse, Entdeckungsreise; Lapérouse, Voyage.
Military Art:
primitive, 679.
*See also* Army; Forts and Fortifications; Navy; etc.
Military Campaigns. *See* various wars, as American Revolution; French and Indian War.

Military Law, 679.
Miller, John Peter, 1709-1796, contributor. *See* American Philosophical Society, Transactions, v. 2.
Mills. *See* Flour (grinding); Water Mills.
Mineralogy: Pennsylvania, 231.
Mines and Mining, 356, 1065, 1273, 1467, 1468.
Mirabeau, Honoré Gabriel Riquetti, comte de, 1749-1791:
Avis aux Hessois et autres peuples d'Allemagne, 551A.
Considérations. *See his* Sammlung.
Sammlung einiger philosophischen und politischen Schriften, 896.
Mirificus, Leonhardus, fictitious character, 336.
Missions:
Brazil, 87.
Caribbean Islands, 555.
Eskimo, 312, 320, 324.
Greenland, 312, 320, 324, 412, 449, 1039.
Indian, 54, 55, 151, 227, 269, 272, 316, 994, 995.
Jesuit, 87, 269, 272, 316.
Mexico, 54, 55.
Moravian Brethren, 412, 449, 994, 995.
Negro, 355, 555.
"Neu-Herrnhut und Lichtenfels," Greenland, 412, 449.
New England, 227.
New York, 994, 995.
Pennsylvania, 994, 995.
Virgin Islands, 555.
West Indies, 76.
Mississippi River, 251, 252, 253, 473.
Mississippi Valley:
colonies, 260, 472.
description and travel, 218, 222, 224, 250, 251, 252, 253, 254.
geography, 472.
history, 1170, 1258, 1290.
Indians, 218, 222, 224, 699.
Mitchell, John, d. 1768:
The Contest in America (*notice*), 379A.
(*review*), 373.
Mitchill, Samuel Latham, 1764-1831: The case of the manufacturers of soap and candles (*review*), 1430.
Mittelberger, Gottlieb:
Reise nach Pennsylvanien, 359.
*See also* Rousselot de Surgy, Histoire naturelle.
Mobile, Ala.:
British garrison, 550.
British possession, 398, 399, 400, 405, 407.
French and Indian War, 405.
Mocquet, Jean, b. 1575: Wunderbare Jedoch Gründlich- und warhaffte Geschichte, 216, 217.
Mohawks. *See* Indians.
Molitor, Nicolaus Carl [or Karl], 1754-1826, editor. *See* Ingenhousz, Vermischte Schriften.
Money and Coinage [also entered under more specific headings], 263, 333, 862, 1081, 1130, 1205.
Money, Paper: United States, 862, 1081.
Montaigne, Michel Eyquem, 1533-1592: Essais. *See* Goethe, Liebes Lied; Goethe, Todeslied.
Montanus, Arnoldus, 1625?-1683: Die unhekante Neue Welt, 194, 195.
Montcalm-Gozon, Louis Joseph de, marquis de Saint-Véran, 1712-1759: *letters*. *See* Briefe von J.
Montreal, Canada:
British garrison, 550.
climate, 1296.
Moore, Sir John, 1718-1779: *naval action*, 152.
Moravian Brethren: Das Kleine Brüder-Gesang-Buch, 408.
Moravian Brethren [as subject], 287, 294, 304, 313A, 315, 388, 460, 461, 462, 480, 486, 555, 640, 1233, 1367.
Bethlehem, Pa., 461.
bibliography, 304.
Carolina, 344.

Moravian Brethren, *continued*
  colonies, 365, 891.
  Greenland, 412, 499.
  history, 1085.
  hymns, 408.
  immigration, 365.
  missions, 412, 449, 994, 995.
  New York, 994, 995.
  North Carolina, 906, 956.
  Pennsylvania, 304, 309, 994, 995.
  Philadelphia, Pa., 323.
  prayer-book, 408.
  Virgin Islands, 555.
Moreau de Saint-Méry, Médéric Louis Élie, 1750–1819.
  Die nach englischen Grundsätzen verbesserte Pferdezucht in Amerika, 1376.
  A Topographical and political description (*review*), 1437.
Morel, John, contributor. *See* American Philosophical Society, Transactions, v. 1.
Le Morelack (*reviews*), 1065, 1066.
Moreland, George, 1763–1804, and J. R. Smith: Slave trade and African hospitality (*review*), 1114.
Moreton, J. B.: Manners and customs in the West India islands (*review*), 1106.
Morgan, John, contributor. *See* American Philosophical Society, Transactions, v. 1, v. 2.
Moritz, Karl Philipp, 1756–1793:
  Anton Reiser, 820.
  *See also* Neue Reisen eines Deutschen.
Morris, Gouverneur, 1752–1816: *portrait*, 838.
Morris, Robert, 1733–1806:
  Authentischer Bericht von den Finanzen der Amerikaner, 718.
  *biography*, 703, 718, 1214.
Morris, Thomas, 1776–1844: Quashy (*review*), 1399.
Morschal. *See* Marshall.
Morse, Jedidiah, 1761–1826:
  American gazetteer (*review*), 1491.
  American geography. *See* Universitäten.
  American universal geography (*review*), 1289.
Mortality: Salem, Mass., 965.
Mortimer, George: *explorations*, 1310.
Morton, Thomas, 1764?–1838: Columbus; or, A world discovered, 1192.
Moseley, Benjamin, 1742–1819: A treatise on tropical diseases (*review*), 1028, 1029.
Moser, Heinrich Christoph: Versuch einer Geschichte der deutschen Forstwirthschaft, 1315.
Moser, Johann Jacob, 1701–1785: Nord-America, 795.
Moser, Wilhelm Gottfried von: Die wesenlichen Kennzeichen der deutschen und nordamerikanischen Holzarten (*reviews*), 1266, 1356.
Moss, 1259.
Mount Vernon, Va., 1134.
Mountains. *See* names of various mountains.
Mud-Island, Fort, Red Bank, N. J. *See* Mifflin and Mercer, Forts.
Mühlenberg, Heinrich Ernst Melchior, 1711–1781: Kurze Bemerkungen, 1482.
Müller, Gerhard Friedrich, 1705–1783: Voyages from Asia to America (*review*), 409.
Müller, Johann Gottfried: Extract. *See* Urlsperger, Der Ausführlichen Nachrichten.
Müller, Johann Gottfried, translator. *See* Prévost d'Exiles, Erste Reisen.
Müller, Johann Ulrich: Neu-ausagefertigter Kleiner Atlas, 228.
Müller, Peter, contributor. *See* American Philosophical Society, Transactions, v. 1.
Münchhausen, Karl Ludwig August Heino, Freiherr von, 1759–1836: Werbungslied der jungen nord-amerikanischen Wilden, 1483.
Muencken, Johann [i.e., Munck, Jens], 1579–1628: Die xxvi. Schiff-Fahrt, 170.
Muenster, Sebastian, 1489–1552: Cosmographia, 65.
Muhlenberg, Harry, contributor. *See* American Philosophical Society, Transactions, v. 3.

Mulgrave, Constantine John Phipps, 2nd baron, 1744–1792: Reise nach dem Nordpol, 552.
Munck, Jens. *See* Muencken, Johann.
Mund, Sebastian Georg Friedrich, editor: Landwirtschaftliches Magazin (*review*), 1061A.
Mundus Mirabilis. *See* Happel, E. W.
Munk, Jens. *See* Muencken, Johannes.
Muñoz, Juan Bautista, 1745–1799:
  Geschichte der Neuen Welt, 1275.
  Historia del nuevo Mundo (*review*), 1245.
Murr, Christoph Gottlieb, 1733–1811:
  Diplomatische Geschichte, 580.
  *See also* Doppelmayr, Historische Nachricht.
Murray, Johan Andreas, 1740–1791?, translator. *See* Kalm, Beschreibung.
Murray, Johan Filip, 1726–1776, translator. *See* Kalm, Beschreibung.
Murray, William Vans, 1762–1803: Political sketches (*review*), 970.
Music:
  German tunes, 483.
  Iroquois songs, 375, 383.
  *See also* Poetry and Songs.
Musical Instruments. *See* Accordion.
Mutilation, Self:
  Indian, 885.
  Negro, 964.
Mylius, Christlob, 1722–1754: Nachrichten, 343.
Myths and Legends, Indian, 894, 934, 947, 957.

N

Naas, Johannes: Reisetagebuch, 300.
Die nach englischen Grundsätzen verbesserte Pferdezucht in Amerika. *See* Moreau de Saint-Méry, M. L. E.
Nach dem jetzigen Staat eingerichtete Bilder-Geographie, 451.
Nachricht von einigen Naturmerkwürdigkeiten in Virginien, 998.
Nachricht über Frasers nordamerikanisches Gras. *See* Wehrs, G. F.
Nachricht von der Provinz Virginien in Nord-America, 469.
Nachrichten von der Amerikanischen Halbinsel Californien. *See* Baegert, Jacob.
Nachrichten zum Nuzen und Vergnügen, 682.
Nachrichten von den vereinigten Deutschen Evangelisch-Lutherischen Gemeinen in Nord-America, 897.
Nack, Johann Bernhard, 1724–179–?, translator. *See* Le Beau, Neue Reise.
Nairne, Edward, 1726–1806, contributor. *See* American Philosophical Society, Transactions, v. 2.
Nantucket, Mass.: description and travel, 782, 837.
Natürliche und bürgerliche Geschichte von Californien. *See* Venegas, Miguel.
Natural History, 735B, 1302.
  America, 451, 684, 743, 1304, 1465.
    bibliography, 349.
  Antilles, 188.
  California, 445, 454.
  Canada, 347.
  Central and South America, 189.
  Lower California, 389, 445.
  Mexico, 389, 445, 852.
  North America, 411, 469, 696, 740.
  Pennsylvania, 231, 438.
  United States, 795.
  Vermont, 1297, 1495/96.
  Virginia, 998.
  West Indies, 187, 188, 874.
  *See also* Biology; Botany; Geology; Mineralogy; Paleontology; Zoology.
Der Naturforscher (periodical):
  1784 (*review*), 808.
  1793 (*review*), 1254.

# GERMAN WORKS RELATING TO AMERICA — INDEX 201

Nautical Instruments, 1259.
Naval Battles:
  American Revolution, 659, 789, 845, 876.
  British, 1796–97, 1370.
Naval Biography, 204, 205, 787, 823, 824.
Navigation, 51, 52, 53.
  American, 534, 663.
Navy:
  American, 758, 789, 823, 824.
  American biography, 204, 205.
  British, 597, 725, 758, 787, 1314.
  French, 708.
  warships, 758.
Nazareth, Pa., 812.
Neander, Joachim, 1650–1680, contributor. *See* Reformed Church in the United States, Neuvermehrt- und vollständiges Gesang-Buch.
Negroes, 1101.
  American Revolution, 489.
  Antilles, 868.
  character, 1048.
  customs and manners, 881.
  diet and food, 735, 881.
  Havana, Cuba, 221.
  importation, 358.
  *See also* Slavery; Slave Trade.
  Jamaica, West Indies, 687, 1398.
  liberation, 1048.
  Maryland, 997.
  medicine, 735, 881.
  missions, 355, 555.
  Nicaragua, 221.
  poetry and songs, 519, 616, 926, 1372, 1399.
  religion, 735, 881.
  revolt of, 489.
  self-mutilation, 964.
  social life and customs, 735.
  treatment of, 913.
  varieties, 1051.
  West Indies, 335, 866, 1041.
Nensinger, Johann Leonhard: Erdbeschreibung für Kinder (*reviews*), 872C, 913A.
Nestler, Carl Gottfried, 1730–1780, illustrator. *See* Franklin, Sämmtliche Werke.
Netherlands, 718, 724.
  American Revolution, 613, 889.
  colonies. *See* Dutch Colonies in America.
  commerce, 173.
  emigration, 772.
  foreign relations: Great Britain, 613, 753, 889.
  United States, 613, 718, 724.
  Mennonites, 794.
  treaties. *See* Treaties.
Neu-aussgefertigter Kleiner Atlas. *See* Müller, J. U.
Neu-eingerichtete und vermehrte Bilder-Geographie, 311, 451.
Neu-Gefundenes Eden von der Landschaft Georgia. *See* Kramer, Neueste und richtigste Nachricht.
Neu-Schottland. *See* Nova Scotia.
Neu-Schwedē (island), 212.
Neu Windsor. *See* New Windsor.
Neue Erdbeschreibung von ganz Amerika. *See* Fenning, Daniel.
Neue Nachrichten von denen neuentdeckten Insuln (*review*), 568.
Neue Nordische Beyträge von Pallas (*reviews*), 735A, 735B.
Neue Nordische Beyträge zur physikalischen und geographischen Erd- und Völkerbeschreibung (*review*), 696.
Neue Quartalschrift aus den neuesten und besten Reisebeschreibungen gezogen (*review*), 1202.
Neue Quartalschrift zum Unterricht und zur Unterhaltung (*review*), 965A.
Neue Reisen eines Deutschen nach und in England im Jahr 1783 (*review*), 919A.

Neuere Beobachtungen über fremde Länder und Sitten (*reviews*), 837A, 873A.
Neues bergmännisches Journal, Bd. 1 (*reviews*), 1467, 1468.
Neues geographisches Zeitungslexicon (*review*), 1109A.
Ein Neues Lied von Amerika, 478.
Neueste Erdkunde, welche Asien, Afrika, Europa, Amerika (*reviews*), 837B, 873C.
Neueste Litteratur der Geschichtkunde, 580A.
Neueste und richtigste Nachricht von der Landschaft Georgia. *See* Kramer, J. M.
Der Neüwe Welt-Bott. *See* Jesuits, Allerhand...Brief.
Neutral Trade, 789.
Neutrality: United States, 789.
New Amsterdam, 182, 183, 192.
  description and travel, 194, 195.
  recapture by Dutch, 204, 205.
  *See also* New York City.
New England:
  American Revolution, 618.
  church, 855.
  description and travel, 142, 143, 158, 159, 160, 161, 197, 351.
  German mercenaries, 618.
  history, 351.
  Indian war of 1675, 206.
  Indians, 227, 684.
  missions, 227.
  Protestant Episcopal Church, 855.
New France. *See* Canada.
New Hampshire, 582.
  description and travel, 1163.
  history, 846, 1359/60.
  White Mountains, 975.
New Jersey:
  church records, 1052.
  description and travel, 1163, 1267, 1478.
  geology, 1441.
  mines and mining, 1441, 1453.
New Mexico, 162, 163, 218, 222, 224.
  Indians, 857.
New Netherlands, 194, 195.
  colonies and colonization, 192, 213, 214, 370.
  Guiana compared with, 192.
  pictorial works, 213, 214.
  *See also* New Amsterdam; New York.
New Orleans: Treaty of Paris, 406.
New Spain: description, 221.
Die New welt. *See* Novus Orbis Regionum.
New Windsor, N. Y., 643.
New World. *See* America.
New York [City and Colony], 683, 718, 725, 999, 1167, 1219, 1230, 1283, 1415, 1464.
  American Revolution, 553, 643, 683.
  city census, 959.
  commerce, 1052.
  description and travel, 404, 490, 1163, 1478, 1484.
  German mercenaries, 583, 641, 683.
  Germans in, 1387.
  history, 370.
  imports. *See* commerce.
  missions, 994, 995.
  Moravian Brethren, 994, 995.
  public hygiene, 1430.
  treaties: Great Britain, 182–183.
  war with Vermont rumored, 774.
  *See also* New Amsterdam and various villages which now compose New York City.
New zeutung, 41.
Newburgh, N. Y.: American Revolution, 760.
Newe vnbekanthe landte. *See* Fracanzano da Montalboddo.
Newe Zeittung auss Venedig, 84, 85.
Newe Zeittung: von dem lande, das die Sponier funden haben ym 1521, 47.
*See also* Zur "Neuen Zeitung."
Newe Zeyttung auss den New erfundnen Jnseln, 78.
Newe Zeytung aus Hispanien und Italien, 58.

Newfoundland, 332.
  British garrison, 550.
  cod fisheries, 332, 638, 801.
  colonization, 453.
  description, 396.
  history, 453.
Newspapers [as subject, only], 66, 78.
  United States, 1075, 1237.
    bibliography, 1267.
Newton, John, 1725-1807: Thoughts upon the African slave trade (*review*), 974.
Niagara Falls, 735:
  American falls, 848.
  Canadian falls, 848.
  description, 490, 1279.
  pictorial works, 490.
Niagara River, 848.
Nicaragua: Negroes, 221.
Nicola, Lewis, contributor. *See* American Philosophical Society, Transactions, v. 1.
Nicolai, Eliud: Newe vnd warhaffte relation, 148.
Nicolas, John, 1756?-1819. *See* An American remembrancer.
Nicolls, Richard, 1624-1672: biography, 182, 183.
Niederelbisches historisch-politisch-literarisches Magazin (*review*), 920.
Niemann, J. G.: Ueber den amerikanischen Leinsaamen, 1003.
Night-shade (botany): dye, 429, 443.
Nipissing, Ontario, Canada: Indians, 1088, 1089.
  *See also* American Languages.
Nisbet, Richard, 1746-1813: The capacity of Negroes (*review*), 1101.
Nitric Acid, freezing of, 1037.
Nobility: Indian conception, 895.
Noch ein kleiner Beitrag zur Geschichte des Tabackrauchens, 1378.
Noltemeyer, E. C., f. 1780:
  Anmerkungen über den Beitrag, 983.
  Gründliche Nachrichten von dem Zustande der Negersklaven, 988.
Noort, Olivier van, 1558?-1627: *voyages and explorations*, 117, 121, 145, 155, 204, 205.
  Das Nord-Amerika Historisch und Geographisch beschrieben, 554.
Normandie, Johann von, contributor. *See* American Philosophical Society, Transactions, v. 1.
North America:
  animals, 411.
  botany. *See* Botany.
  colonization. *See* Colonies in America.
  commerce. *See* Commerce.
  description and travel, 108, 111, 112, 114, 117, 120, 131, 132, 138, 139, 143, 146, 147, 149, 150, 152, 154, 158, 164, 165, 166, 235, 341, 343, 351, 355, 364, 451, 507, 513, 545, 554, 566, 567, 577, 578, 642, 658, 684, 761, 782, 795, 800, 830, 831, 840, 840A, 867, 870, 916, 1024, 1027, 1030, 1031, 1115, 1163, 1201, 1450, 1451, 1475, 1478, 1489, 1490.
  fisheries, 416, 1164.
  geography, 261, 629.
  *See also* Geography.
  immigration. *See* Emigration and Immigration.
  Indians. *See* Indians.
  Jews. *See* Jews.
  Mennonites, 803.
  natural history. *See* Natural History.
  paleontology, 431, 1099.
  pictorial works, 417; *see also* Pictorial works.
  prehistoric remains, 968, 1305.
  statistics. *See* Statistical Information.
  taxation. *See* Taxation.
  transportation. *See* Transportation.
  whaling, 804.
  *See also* Northeast Coast of North America; Northwest Coast of North America; *also* various countries of North America, etc.

North American Colonies. *See* Colonies in America.
North Carolina, 469, 1009.
  church, 908, 1044, 1203.
  description and travel, 193, 244, 344, 1160, 1211, 1233.
  Evangelical Lutheran Church, 844, 864, 911, 914, 963, 1009, 1044, 1305.
  Germans in, 240.
  Indians, 193, 244, 699.
  Moravian Brethren, 906, 956.
  volcanoes, 1259.
  *See also* Carolina.
Northeast Coast of North America, 1083, 1091, 1095, 1310.
Northeast Passage, 107, 118, 119, 130, 178, 435, 468, 807.
  *See also* Northeast Coast of North America.
Northwest Coast of North America, 409, 1014, 1056, 1083, 1091, 1095, 1310.
  discovery, 1071, 1072, 1073, 1440, 1442, 1456, 1471.
  exploration, 1117, 1118.
Northwest Passage, 80, 136, 137, 156, 170, 202, 328, 387, 468, 731, 742, 807, 841, 853, 973, 1371.
  *See also* Northwest Coast of North America.
Nostitz, C. W. G. von, engraver. *See* La Hontan, Des berühmten Herrn Baron De Lahontan Neueste Reisen.
Noticia de la California. *See* Venegas, Miguel.
Nougaret, Pierre Jean Baptiste, 1742-1823: Honorine Clarins, 1179.
Nova Scotia:
  British and French differences, 330.
  British garrison, 550.
  commerce, 863, 907.
  description and travel, 907, 920.
  geography, 330, 907.
  history, 330.
  Indians, 330.
  merchant marine, 863.
  *See also* Acadia.
Novellania, pseud.: Das über die Glückliche Ankunfft etlicher hundert Saltzburger Emigranten Sich Höchsterfreute Meissen, 287.
Novus Orbis Regionum:
  Die New welt, 57.
  *See also* Vespucci, Vier Seereisen; Von Walter Raleigh, 563.
Nüssman, Adolph, 1739-1794:
  Einige Nachricht, 911.
  *See also* Velthusen, Einige Nachricht; Velthusen, Nordcarolinische Kirchennachrichten.
  biography, 1305.
Nützliche Anweisung, von dem Landtoback (*review*), 967.
Numismatics. *See* Money and Coinage.
Nusbiegel, 1713-1776, illustrator. *See* Oldendorp, Geschichte der Mission der evangelischen Brüder.
Nussbiegel, Johann, 1750-ca. 1830, engraver. *See* Cook, Dritte Entdeckungs-Reise.

# O

Observations on the project for abolishing the slave-trade (*review*), 1067.
Oedmann, Samuel: Vermischte Sammlungen (*review*), 1302.
Officers, Military and Naval:
  American, 612, 672, 823, 824.
  British, 672, 787.
Ofterloh, illustrator. *See* Nougaret, Honorine Clarins.
Ohio Valley, 815.
  description and travel, 1170, 1209, 1258.
  Indians, 815, 1180.
Oldendorp, Christian Georg Andreas, 1721-1787: Geschichte der Mission der evangelischen Brueder, 555.

# GERMAN WORKS RELATING TO AMERICA — INDEX 203

Oliver, Andrew, 1731-1799, contributor. *See* American Philosophical Society, Transactions, v. 2.
Olivier, Guillaume Antoine, 1756-1814, editor. *See* Bruguière and others, Journal.
Oneida Indians. *See* Indians.
Ontario, Canada: description and travel, 1481.
Ontario, Lake, 377, 1088, 1089, 1310.
   tides, 377.
Williamson colony, 907, 1444, 1480.
Ophthalmology: horses, 975.
Optics, 975, 998.
Ordoñez de Cevallos, Pedro, b. ca. 1550, contributor. *See* Bry, Zwölffter Theil.
Orientalisch- und occidentalischer Sprachmeister. *See* Schultze, Benjamin.
Ortelius, Abraham, 1527-1598: Ausszūg auss des Abrahami Ortelÿ Theatro, 123.
Orthography. *See* Phonetics.
Osterwald, Friedrich: Historische Erdbeschreibung (*reviews*), 835, 869D.
Otto, Bodo, 1711-1787, contributor. *See* American Philosophical Society, Transactions, v. 1.
Otto, Louis Guillaume, comte de Mosley, 1754: A letter...to Dr. Franklin. *See* Doppelmayr, Historische Nachricht.

## P

P**. *See* Pauw, Cornelius de.
P., Christophorus, translator. *See* Bry, Wunderbarliche...; Dresser, Historien vnd Bericht; Harriot, Wunderbarlicher doch Warhafftiger Bericht.
Pabst, Jobann Georg Friedrich: Die Entdeckungen des fünften Welttheils (*review*), 832A.
Pacific Coast, North. *See* Northwest Coast of North America.
Pacific Ocean, 962, 987.
   discovery, 1056.
   *See also* various discoverers, as Cook.
Packard, Asa, contributor. *See* American Academy of Arts and Sciences, Memoirs, v. 2.
Paine, Thomas, 1737-1809:
   Age of reason. *See* Auszug aus einem Briefe des Herrn Pastors Storch.
   Berichtigung dessen, was der Abbt Raynal. *See* Dohm, Die Fünfte Lieferung.
   Gesunder Menschenverstand, 1228.
   Sammlung verschiedener Schriften, 1229.
   *See also* Raynal, Geschichte.
Palairet, Jean, 1697-1774: A concise description of English and French possessions (*review*), 363.
Palatines in America, 257, 271.
   Carolina, 240.
   immigration, 249.
   Pennsylvania, 240.
Paleontology: North America, 431, 1099.
Palm, Georg Ferdinand, 1760-1798, translator. *See* Einige den Negerhandel.
Panzer, Georg Wolfgang Franz, 1729-1804: Faunae insectorum (*review*), 1338.
Panzer, Georg Wolfgang Franz, 1729-1804, translator. *See* Drury, Abbildungen.
Paper Money. *See* Money, Paper.
Paris, Treaty of 1763, 405, 406, 502, 535.
Paris, Treaty of 1783, 745, 799, 800.
Parraud, J. P., translator. *See* Filson, Histoire de Kentucke.
Parsons, Samuel Holden, 1737-1789, contributor. *See* American Academy of Arts and Sciences, Memoirs, v. 2.
Paschall, Thomas, 1634-1718, contributor. *See* Penn, Beschreibung.
Paskell. *See* Paschall.
Pastorius, Francis Daniel, 1651-1719:
   Beschreibung von Pennsylvanien, 325.
   Copia, 209.

Pastorius, Francis Daniel, *continued*
   Sichere Nachricht auss America, 210.
   Umständige geographische Beschreibung, 226, 230.
   *See also* Falckner, Curieuse Nachricht; Hazard, Historical collections; Thomas, Continuatio.
Pastorius, Melchior Adam, b. 1624, contributor. *See* Pastorius, F. D., Beschreibung; Pastorius, F. D., Umständige geographische Beschreibung.
Patje, Christian Ludwig Albrecht, 1748-1817: Ueber die Entbehrung ausländischer Bedürfnisse, 1424.
Patterson, Robert, 1743-1824, contributor. *See* American Philosophical Society, Transactions, v. 3.
Paul Hennig. Eine wahre Geschichte. *See* Dippold, G. E.
Pausch, Georg: Journal, 521B.
Pauw, Cornelius de, 1739-1799:
   Defense de recherches philosophiques. *See his* Recherches philosophiques.
   Philosophische Untersuchungen über die Amerikaner (*reviews*), 455, 456.
   Recherches philosophiques sur les Americains (*reviews*), 457, 491; *see also* Carli, Briefe.
Pazzi de Bonneville, Zacharie de, b. 1710?, contributor. *See* Recherches philosophiques.
Peace. *See* War and Peace.
Peletier, Bertrand, 1761-1797, joint editor. *See* Bruguière and others, Journal.
Pelew Islands, 1126, 1133, 1227.
   description and travel, 989.
Pendleton, Edmund, 1721-1803: *speech. See* Authentischer Beweis.
Penitentiaries: Philadelphia, Pa., 1195, 1432, 1470.
Penn, William, 1644-1718:
   Beschreibung Der in America, 211.
   Eine Nachricht Wegen der Landschafft, 207.
   *See also* Pastorius, Umständige Geographische Beschreibung.
   biography, 207, 211, 225, 226, 238, 433, 434, 1173.
   poetry, 503A.
Pennsylvania (colony). — Treaties. Minutes of conferences. *See* Weiser, Tagebuch.
Pennsylvania. — Constitutional Convention: Debates on the convention of the State of Pensilvania (*review*), 1194.
Pennsylvania, 506, 920.
   agriculture, 225, 226, 229, 230, 231.
   botany, 715, 1259, 1457.
   census, 1108, 1145, 1171.
   colonies, 207, 209, 210, 225, 226, 230, 231, 1388; *see also* Colonies in America.
   commerce, 211, 231.
   description and travel, 211, 225, 226, 230, 231, 344, 351, 359, 469, 1163, 1312, 1388.
   education, 940.
   Evangelical Lutheran Church, 897.
   finance, public, 1130.
   Friends. *See* Society of Friends.
   German school, 940.
   German settlements, 209, 210, 225, 226, 229, 230, 231, 240, 300, 309, 315, 359, 388, 461, 463, 506, 531, 532, 572, 614, 812, 897, 940, 1358, 1475, 1498.
   health, 922.
   history, 207, 209, 210, 225, 226, 230, 231, 438, 1394.
   immigration, 531, 1267, 1329.
   Indians, 211, 225, 226, 230, 231, 673.
   land, 1325.
   minerals, 231.
   missions, 994, 995.
   Moravian Brethren. *See* Moravian Brethren.
   natural history, 231, 438.
   Palatines, 240.
   Protestants, 361, 531.
   religious instruction, 361.
   slavery, 1372.
   statistics, 1145, 1171.
Pensacola, Fla.:
   British garrison, 550.
   German Mercenaries, 615.

Pensions: American Revolution, 1097.
Pepper tree: Jamaica, W. I., 625A.
Perch, 808.
Perkins, Elisha, 1741–1799, contributor. *See* American Philosophical Society, Transactions, v. 2.
Pernety, Antoine Joseph, 1716–1801:
Dissertation sur l'Amérique. *See* Pauw, Recherches philosophiques.
Examen des Recherches philosophiques. *See* Pauw, Recherches philosophiques.
Peru, 58, 59, 83, 187.
aboriginal religion, 793.
archaeology, 830, 831, 967.
description and travel, 830, 831, 867.
discovery, 680.
Indians, 793.
social life and customs, 232.
Peter Hasenclever. *See* Glauber, C. G.
Peters, Samuel Andrews, 1735–1826: General history of Connecticut (*review*), 733.
Petersen, Magnus, translator. *See* Castiglioni, Reise.
Petrified Objects, Prehistoric, 431.
Peyers, Junker Casper: *voyage*, 197.
Pfeffel, Gottlieb Konrad, 1736–1809:
Lied eines Negersklaven, 616.
Recept wider den Krieg, 556A.
Philadelphia, Pa., 572, 582, 584, 614, 648, 657, 671, 769, 812.
American revolution, 582, 614, 657.
charities, 593.
church records, 1052, 1076.
description and travel, 211, 359, 401, 1276.
Evangelical Lutheran Church, 1076.
Friends, 715, 720.
German mercenaries, 614.
German settlement, 532, 1475, 1498.
immigration, 1475.
Latin school, 532.
Moravian Brethren, 323.
penitentiaries, 1195, 1433, 1470.
Pietists. *See* Pietists.
Protestant Church, 506.
social life and customs, 1279, 1308, 1358.
social work, 593.
*See also* Germantown, Pa.
Philology. *See* Languages.
Philorthodoxo, Christian, pseud.: Ungeheuchelte Theologische Unterredung, 323.
Philosophical transactions. *See* Royal Society of London.
Philosophische und politische Geschichte der Besitzungen und des Handels der Europäer in beyden Indien. *See* Raynal, G. T. F.
Philosophische und politische Geschichte der europäischen Handlung. *See* Raynal, G. T. F.
Philosophische Untersuchungen über die Amerikaner (*reviews*), 455, 456.
Phonetics, 709.
Physicians: Charleston, S. C., 1336.
Physics. *See* various branches of physics.
Physiology, 1204.
Phytolacca Decandra, 1396.
Pickersgill, Richard, supposed author. *See* A Concise account of voyages for the discovery of a north-west passage.
Pictorial Works:
Canada, 213, 214.
Florida, 213, 214.
Indians, 213, 214.
insects, 832.
Jamaica, W. I., 600.
Louisiana, 213, 214.
New Netherlands, 213, 214.
Niagara Falls, 490.
slaves, 1114.
Virginia, 213, 214.
Picture Writing, Indian, 890, 932.

Pietists, 305, 306, 307, 308, 318, 1449.
Germantown, Pa., 313.
Philadelphia, Pa., 314, 315.
Pinckney, Charles, 1758–1824. *See* An American remembrancer.
Pineapple: West Indies, 459.
Pinto, Isaac de, 1715–1787:
Réponse. *See* Anekdote, 503.
Schreiben über die Empörung der Nord-Amerikaner, 522.
*See also* Dohm, Etwas Apologetisches; Politische Weissagungen, 524.
Pirates, 201.
Pithou, Nicolas, 1524–1598, translator. *See* Settle, Beschreibung Der schiffart.
Pitman. *See* Pittman.
Pitt, William, 1st earl of Chatham, 1708–1778:
Strictures on the slave trade (*review*), 1070.
*See also* Litteratur und Völkerkunde.
Pittman, Philip: The present state of European settlements on the Mississippi (*review*), 473.
Piyot, admiral, 725.
Pizarro, Francisco, marqués, 1475?–1541: *explorations*, 58, 97, 102, 680, 762, 1079.
Placentia, Newfoundland: British garrison, 550.
Plant, J. T. Publicistische Uebersicht aller Regierungsarten sämmtlicher Staaten und Völkerschaften auf der Welt (*reviews*), 921D, 1023A.
Plants. *See* Botany.
Plants, Poisonous, 187, 738, 1259, 1499.
*See also* Botany, Medicinal; Herbs, Medicinal.
Plays. *See* Dramas.
A Poetical epistle to His Excellency George Washington. *See* Wharton, C. H.
Poetry and Songs [Authors and Anonymous Titles]:
Abendfantasien, 635; Amerika, 775; Barlow, 978; Berkeley, 1132; Bouterwek, 926, 1123; Brand, 2, 3, 4, 5; Canovai, 1021; Cbaraden und Rätsel, 1476, 1477; Claudius, 482, 743A, 851; Columbus und der Abenwind, 674; La Compagnie de Mississippi, 253; Die Deutsche Hülfstruppen nach Amerika, 508, 541; Einem, 1365; An Elegy, 1103; Engelschall, 705; Fischart, 77A; Franklin, 442; Die Freiheit Amerika's, 744, 798; Gesang, 547; Gespräch derer europäischen Mächte, 745; Goethe, 746, 747; Herder, 1132, 1372; Die Hessen nach Amerika, 549, Holder, 1196; Janisch, 1447, 1448; Klopstock, 717, 1043, 1225, 1420; Koelling, 282; Krauseneck, 519; Kunz und Hinz 1776, 749; Lied einer Amerikanerin, 611; Lied eines Deutschen in Fremden Kriegsdiensten, 551; Lied eines jungen Engländers in Amerika, 496; Lied eines Negersklaven in Amerika, 792; Logau, 174; Manso, 1355; Mauss, 879; Moravian Brethren, 408; Moritz, 820; Morris, 1399; Münchausen, 1483; Ein Neues Lied von Amerika, 478; Otaheiti, 1000; Pfeffel, 556A, 616; Psalm Boek voor die tot, 810A; Quad, 96; Die Quaker, 558; Reformed Church in the United States, 483; Schaitberger, 291; Schiller, 1321, 1425; Schmidt, 861; Schubart, 484, 485, 499, 499A, 528, 851A; Stolberg, 487, 500, 620A, 757A, 1046A; Voss, 1238, 1238A; Wekhrlin, 652; Weppen, 596, 805; Wharton, 670; Williams, 969; The Wrongs of Africa, 980; Zachariae, 424, 447; Zinzendorf, 388.
Poetry and Songs relating to —
America, 744, 745, 798, 1043, 1447, 1448.
American Revolution, 484, 485, 496, 528, 611, 652, 717, 744, 745, 775, 798, 820, 1043, 1355.
Brazil, 746, 747.
Canada, 861.
Columbus, 674, 732, 987, 1321.
Franklin, 1365, 1447, 1448.
German mercenaries, 500, 508, 519, 541, 547, 549, 551, 586, 635, 672, 749.
immigrants, 916A.
Indians, 485, 519, 1448, 1483.
Iroquois, 375.

# GERMAN WORKS RELATING TO AMERICA — INDEX

Poetry and Songs relating to, *continued*
Negroes, 519, 616, 926, 1372, 1399.
slave trade, 969, 980, 1103, 1196.
slavery, 616, 792, 926, 1399.
Society of Friends, 558.
sugar, 705.
Treaty of Paris, 745.
Treaty of Versailles, 805.
Vespucci, 1021, 1085.
Washington, 670, 1225, 1448.
Poison: rattlesnake, 738; *see also* Ticunas.
Poivre, Pierre, 1719–1786: Voyage d'un Philosophe (*review*), 440.
Pokonchi Indians. *See* American Languages.
Poliander, pseud., editor. *See* Analecta historico-litterario-curiosa.
Political sketches. *See* Murray, W. V.
Politics, 1221.
American, 1308. *See also* United States: government and politics.
Santo Domingo (Haiti), 1494.
Das politische Journal (periodical), 1783 (*review*), 810.
Polygamy: Indians, 954.
Poncelin de La Roche-Tilhac, Jean Charles, 1746–1828, editor. *See* Almanach americain.
Poor, Care of: Philadelphia, Pa., 593.
Popp, Stephan: Popp's journal, 556B.
Poppe, Johann Heinrich Moritz von, 1776–1854, translator. *See* Ueber die Art und Weise, 1455.
Poppy Juice, 740.
Population. *See* Census under various places.
Pork: Indian diet, 943, 944, 945.
Portlock, Nathaniel, 1748?–1817:
Der Kapitains [*or* e] Portlock's und Dixon's Reise (*reviews*), 1057F, 1060C, 1060D, 1105G.
Voyage round the world (*reviews*), 1071, 1073.
*See also* Forster, Georg, Geschichte der Reisen; Forster, Georg, Nathaniel Portlocks und Georg Mortimers Reisen; Noch etwas von dem Westmeer, 1091.
Portrait du Général Washington (*review*), 736.
Portraits, American Revolutionary, 691, 838.
*See also* various persons, as Washington, subhead, portraits.
Portugal:
commerce, 893.
foreign relations: United States, 893.
trade treaty with United States, 893.
Portuguese Colonies in America, 545.
Postal Service, 1052, 1176, 1218, 1288, 1324.
Postell, Guillaume, 1510–1581: Cosmographia disciplina. *See* Doppelmayr, Historische Nachricht.
Potatoes, 436, 743A, 1296, 1487A.
Practical remarks on Westindia diseases (*review*), 598.
Prayer-book: Moravian Brethren, 408.
Predigten von einem Bostonschen Geistlichen, 525.
Prehistoric Remains. *See* Archaeology.
Prettie. *See* Pretty.
Pretty, Francis, 1599–1742: *explorations*, 108, 111, 154.
Preussische Akademie der Wissenschaften zu Berlin. *See* Historisch- und Geographischer Calender.
Prévost, Benoit Louis, 1735–1804, engraver. *See* Collection des portraits (*review*).
Prévost d'Exiles, Antoine François, 1697–1763: Erste Reisen, 353.
Prices: United States, 1403.
Prism, 1296.
Prisons. *See* Penitentiaries.
Probst, Peter, 1699–1750, compiler. *See* Jesuits, Allerhand...Brief.
Property: Indian conceptions, 1006.
Protestant Church, 506, 531.
Protestant Episcopal Church:
New England, 855.
*See also* Book of Common Prayer.

Protestants:
immigration, 313.
Pennsylvania schools, 361.
Waldoboro, Me., 313.
*See also* various Protestant denominations.
Proust, Louis Joseph, 1754–1826, contributor. *See* Lametherie's journal de physique.
Providence, R. I.: British garrison, 550.
Provinces in America:
British, 219.
European, 372.
*See also* Colonies in America.
Psalm Boek voor die tot die evangelische Broeer-Kerk (*review*), 810A.
Public Finance. *See* Finance, Public.
Punishment, 1432.
capital: Pennsylvania, 1195, 1470.
officials, 1498.
Purmann, Johann Georg, 1733–1813: Sitten und Meinungen der Wilden in America, 557.
Purry, Jean Pierre, fl. 1718–1731: Memoire presenté à Sa Gr. Mylord Duc de Newcastle. *See* Von Gross-Britannien, 267.
Puzzles (actual), 1476, 1477.

## Q

Quad, Matthias, 1557–1609:
Geographisch Handtbuch, 113.
Die Jahr Blum, 96.
Quakers, 558. *See also* Society of Friends.
Quebec, Canada, 530, 1210.
British garrison, 550.
English attack, 271.
topography, 606.

## R

Raff, Georg Christian, 1748–1788: Geographie für Kinder (*reviews*), 1046, 1061C, 1061D.
Rahn, Johann Rudolff, joint compiler. *See* Simler, J. W., and J. R. Rahn, Vier loblicher Statt Zürich Verbürgerter Reissbeschreibungen.
Raleigh, Sir Walter, 1552–1618:
Die Fünffte Kurtze Wunderbare Beschreibung, 122, 126, 127, 128, 129.
Kurtze Wunderbare Beschreibung, 110, 115, 116.
*See also* Bry, Achter Theil Americæ; Bry, Wunderbarliche; Ens, West- und Ost Jndischer Lustgart; Von Walter Raleigh, 563.
Ramsay, Allan, 1733–1784: An historical essay on the English constitution (*review*), 472.
Ramsay, David, 1749–1815: Geschichte der Amerikanischen Revolution, 1231.
Ramsay, James, 1733–1789: An essay on the treatment and conversion of African slaves in the British sugar colonies (*review*), 833; *see also* Sprengel, Beyträge.
Rapp, Johann Heinrich, contributor. *See* Richshoffer, Brasslianisch-und West Indianischer Reise Beschreibung.
Rarop, Simon Gilde von: *biography*, 182, 183.
Rattlesnakes, 331, 1259, 1347, 1461, 1462.
anatomy, 625A.
poison, 738.
Rauw, Johannes, d. 1600:
Cosmographia, 101.
Weltbeschreibung. *See his* Cosmographia (*note*).
Raynal, Guillaume Thomas François, 1713–1796:
Geschichte der Revolution von Nord-Amerika, 860.
Philosophische und politische Geschichte (*reviews*), 632, 633, 1031A, 1119A.
Révolution de l'Amérique (*review*), 737.
Staatsveränderung von Amerika. *See his* Geschichte der Revolution von Nord-Amerika.

Raynal, Guillaume Thomas François, *continued*
  Uebersicht der politischen Lage und des Handelszustandes von St. Domingo (*review*), 977A.
  *See also* Der Akademie der Wissenschaften, 700; Dohm, Die fünfte Lieferung; Karsten, Europens Handel; Kotzebue, Die Negersclaven; Kurze Geschichte und Beschreibung der Insel St. Domingo, 1087; Paine, Gesunder Menschenverstand; Paine, Sammlung verschiedener Schriften.
  *biography*, 481, 737, 860.
Real Estate:
  speculation, 1276.
  *See also* Land.
Ain Recept von ainem holtz, 42, 43.
Recherches philosophiques sur les Americains (*reviews*), 457, 491.
Den Rechten weg auss zu faren, 8, 9.
Reck, Philipp Georg Friedrich von, 1710–1798:
  Diarium. *See* Urlsperger, Der Ausführlichen Nachrichten.
  Eine...kurtze Nachricht. *See* Urlsperger, Der Ausführlichen Nachrichten.
  Kurz gefasste Nachricht (*review*), 668.
  Reise-Diarium. *See* Urlsperger, Der Ausführlichen Nachrichten.
Rede, Leman Thomas, d. 1810: Bibliotheca Americana (*review*), 1015.
Reed, Joseph, 1741–1785: *portrait*, 838.
Reflexions on the tomb of Columbus (*review*), 1151.
Reformed Church in the United States:
  Neuvermehrt- und vollständiges Gesang-Buch, 483.
  *catechisms*, 483.
  *Pennsylvania*, 483.
Reid, Thomas Dickson: A view of the diseases of the army (*review*), 1265.
Reina, Cassiodoro de, ca. 1520–1594, translator. *See* Bry, Americæ Achter Theil.
Reinbeck, Georg von. Der Virginier. *See* Kotzebue, Die Verwandtschaften.
Reinhold, Christian Lodolf, 1737–1791:
  Kurze Geschichte der Schiffahrt (*reviews*), 959H, 1101A.
  Mathematisch-politischer Catechism der Geographie (*reviews*), 960, 960A.
Reinius, Cassiodorus. *See* Reina, Cassiodoro de.
Reise von Hamburg nach Philadelphia, 1484.
Reise in den nördlichen Gegenden zwischen Asien und Amerika, 1138.
Reise eines Schweitzers in verschiedene Kolonien in America. *See* Girod-Chantrans, Justin.
Reise nach dem stillen Ocean auf Befehl des Königs von Grossbrittanien unternommen (*review*), 876A.
Reisecorrespondenz in, durch und aus allen fünf Theilen der Welt (*review*), 876B.
Reisen durch Amerika (*review*), 810B.
Reisen durch einige französische, englische, holländische, spanische Besitzungen in der Welt (*reviews*), 1024, 1112.
Reisen und Niederlassungen in dem nordlichen America. *See* Charlevoix, P. F. X.
Die Reisenden für Länder- und Völkerkunde (*review*), 972A.
Relation. *See* Bigges, Walter.
Religion, 181, 276, 277/78, 843, 934, 935, 1304.
  Brazilian aborigines, 793.
  Indians, 87, 181, 793, 934, 935, 1304.
  Mexican aborigines, 793.
  Negroes, 735, 881.
  Peruvian aborigines, 793.
  United States, 795.
  *See also* Christianity; Church in America.
Religious Denominations: United States, 1339.
Religious Freedom: Virginia, 843.
Religious Instruction. *See* Education, Religious.
Remarks upon the principal acts of the XIIIth Parliament. *See* Lind, John.
Remarks on the travels of the Marquis de Chatellux, in North-America (*review*), 1024A.

Remer, Julius August, 1738–1803, editor:
  Amerikanisches Archiv (*review*), 588, 655.
  Anmerkungen über die vornehmsten Acten des dreyzehnten Parlements (*review*), 656.
Remer, Julius August, 1738–1803, translator. *See* Stedman, Geschichte des...Amerikanischen Kriegs.
Renelle, Lucie Elizabeth Bouillon, 1745–1823: Nouvelle géographie (*review*), 966A.
Reptiles and Amphibia. *See* Frogs; Lizards; Snakes; Turtles.
Resolute (ship), 575.
Reuss, Jeremias David, 1750–1837: Das Gelehrte England, 1093.
Revolution. *See* American Revolution; Indians: warfare and wars.
Rheumatism: American remedy, 458.
Rhode Island, 573.
  description and travel, 1163.
Ribaut, Jean, ca. 1520–1585, contributor. *See* Bry, Der ander Theyl.
Riccioli, Giovanni Battista, 1598–1671:
  Geographiae. *See* Doppelmayr, Historische Nachricht.
Rice Culture: South Carolina, 817.
Richard, Christian. *See* Richardson, Carsten.
Richardson, Carsten: *explorations*, 202.
Richart-sohn, Karsten or Christian. *See* Richardson, Carsten.
Richmond, Va.: academy established, 959B.
Richshoffer, Ambrosius, b. 1612: Brassilianisch-und West Indianische Reisse Beschreibung, 196.
Richter, Jean Paul Friedrich, 1763–1825: Hesperus, 1278.
Rickman, Thomas Clio, 1761–1834: Emigration to America (*review*), 1497.
Riedesel, Friederike Charlotte Luise (von Massow), Freifrau von, 1746–1808:
  Auszüge aus den Briefen und Papieren, 1484A.
  Die Berufs-Reise nach America, 1485.
Riedesel Friedrich Adolph, Freiherr von, 1738–1800; *biography*, 1484A, 1485.
Ring, Friedrich Dominik, d. 1809: Kurzgefasste Geschichte der drey ersten Entdecker von Amerika (*review*), 836.
Ringk, F. S., engraver. *See* Cook, Dritte Entdeckungs-Reise.
Ringk, Johann Samuel, d. 1814, illustrator. *See* Forster, Georg, Geschichte der Reisen; Forster, Georg, Nathaniel Portlocks und Georg Mortimers Reisen.
Risler, Jeremias, 1720–1811: Leben August Gottlieb Spangenbergs, 1233.
Rittenhouse, David, 1732–1796, contributor. *See* American Philosophical Society, Transactions, v. 1, v. 2.
*See also* College of Physicians of Philadelphia, Medicinische Verhandlungen, Bd. 1.
Rivers. *See* various rivers, as Mississippi River.
Roberts, Josiah, contributor. *See* Beyträge zur Geschichte der Nordamerikanischen Länder-Entdecker, 1474.
Robertson, George, ca. 1742–1788: Sechs Blätter (*review*), 600.
Robertson, William, 1721–1793:
  Geschichte von Amerika, 559.
  The History of America (*reviews*), 912, 1060, 1105E.
  *See also* Kurzgefasste Geschichte der drey ersten Entdecker von Amerika.
Robin, Claude, b. 1750: Voyage dans l'Amérique septentrionale (*review*), 769.
Robinson, Ebenezer, contributor. *See* American Philosophical Society, Transactions, v. 3.
"Robinsonaden," 265.
Rochambeau, Donatien Marie Joseph de Vimeur, vicomte de, d. 1813: *voyage*, 769.
Rochefort, Charles de, b. 1605: Historische Beschreibung Der Antillen Inseln, 188.

# GERMAN WORKS RELATING TO AMERICA — INDEX

Rochefoucauld. *See* La Rochefoucauld.
Roehler: Etwas über westindischen und deutschen Kaffee, 1445.
Römer, Johann Jakob, 1763-1819, editor:
Annalen der Arzneymittellehre (*review*), 1391.
*See also* Bálmis, Uber die Amerikanischen Pflanzen.
Roeslin, Helisaeus, 1544-1616. Mitternächtige Schiffarth, 125A.
Rogerius, Abrabam, d. 1649: Offne Thür zu dem verborgenen Heydenthum, 181.
Rogers, Robert, 1731-1795: Ueber die Sitten und Gebräuche der wilden Völker in Nordamerika. *See* Literatur und Völkerkunde, 1786.
Rohr, Heinrich Julius Ludwig von, d. 1811: La Fayette, 1234.
Rohr, Julius Bernhard von, 1688-1742: Physikalische Bibliothek, 349.
Rolffsen, F., engraver, 325.
Rollenhagen, Gabriel, 1583-1619?: Vier Bücher Wunderbarlicher, 122 (*note*).
Roman Catholic Church:
Boston, Mass., 1047.
history, 87.
Mexico, 54, 55.
*See also* similar subjects, as Jesuits.
Roschen, Friedrich: Brief. *See* Velthusen, editor, Nordcarolinische Kirchennachrichten.
Rosler. *See* Rossler.
Rossler, Wilhelm Ernst Burkhard, translator. *See* Le Beau, Neue Reise.
Rostermund, Heinrich Wilhelm, 1761-1848: Beitrag zur Geschichte des Tabackrauchens, 319.
Rosters, Military. *See* American Revolution: biography and rosters.
Roubaud, Pierre Joseph Antoine, b. 1724, supposed author. Letters. *See* Briefe vom J. 1757.
Rousseau, Jean Jacques, 1712-1778, 433.
Rousselot de Surgy, Jacques Philbert, d. 1737, compiler: Histoire naturelle et politique de la Pensylvanie (*review*), 438 (*note*).
Rowley, William, 1742-1806: Medical advice (*review*), 597.
Royal Society of Arts. *See* Society instituted for the Encouragement of Arts.
Royal Society of Edinburgh: Transactions, v. 2 (*review*), 1210.
Royal Society of London:
Philosophical transactions, v. 70 (*review*), 697.
v. 78 (*review*), 1023.
v. 79 (*review*), 1068, 1204.
*See also* Abhandlungen zur Naturgeschichte, Physik und Oekonomie; Auszug der Artikeln, 376A, 377.
Royer. *See* Barbault-Royer.
Rozier, François, 1734-1793, contributor. *See* Lametherie's journal de physique.
R-r: Aussicht in die Zukunft, 503A.
Ruchamer, Jobst, translator. *See* Fracanzano da Montalboddo, compiler, Newe vnbekanthe landte.
Rural Life: German American, 647, 1457.
Rusch. *See* Rush.
Rush, Benjamin, 1745-1813:
An Account of the bilious remitting yellow fever (*review*), 1331.
An Account of the sugar-maple-tree (*review*), 1332.
Beschreibung des gelben Fiebers, 1320.
Essays (*review*), 1498.
Nachricht von der ausserordentlichen Fähigkeit eines Negersklaven in Maryland, 997.
Nachricht von dem Zucker-Ahorn, 1381.
Untersuchung der Arzneykunde unter den Indiern in Nordamerika, 527.
*See also* American Philosophical Society, Transactions, v. 1; College of Physicians of Philadelphia, Medicinische Verhandlungen, Bd. 1; College of Physicians of Philadelphia, Transactions, v. 1; Literary and Philosophical Society of Manchester, Memoirs, v. 1-2.
Russell, William, 1741-1795:
Geschichte von Amerika. *See his* Geschichte des Ursprunges und des Fortganges.
Geschichte des Ursprunges und des Fortganges, 649.
Ruyter, Michael Adriaanszoon de, 1607-1676: *explorations*, 204, 205.
Ryff, Walther Hermann, 16th century:
New erfundne Heyslame, vnd bewärte artzney, 62.
Wjn wolgegründt nutzlich vnd heylsam handtbüchlin, 61.

## S

S., W. *See* Seton, William.
Die Säugthiere in Abbildungen (*review*), 634.
St. Augustine, Fla.: British garrison, 550.
St. Bartholomew (island):
animals, 1414.
colonization, 884.
description and travel, 884.
geography, 884.
St. Christopher (island), 1414.
St. John, J. Hektor. *See* Crèvecoeur, Michel Guillaume St. Jean de.
St. John's, Newfoundland: British garrison, 550.
St. Lawrence River, 1485.
fortifications, 1088, 1089, 1119, 1310.
St. Lucia: British possession, 399.
St. Mauritius: free port, 893.
St. Vincent: British possession, 399.
Ste. Anne de Beaupré, Quebec, 622.
Salem, Mass.: mortality, 965.
Salem, N. C.: college and Latin school, 1305.
Salisbury, N. C.: German settlement, 1305.
Saltonstall, Winthrop: An inaugural dissertation. *See* Bay, An inaugural dissertation.
Salzburgers in America, 275, 276, 277, 278, 279, 280, 281, 282, 283, 284, 285, 286, 287, 288, 289, 291, 292, 293, 294, 295, 296, 297, 298, 299, 301, 303, 303A, 305, 306, 307, 308, 317, 318, 326, 350, 363, 668, 1053A.
Sammlung von Bildnissen der im amerikanischen Kriege, 838.
San Domingo. *See* Santo Domingo.
San Salvador, 158.
Sanches, Antonio Nunes Ribiero, 1699-1783: Dissertation sur l'origine de la maladie vénerienne (*review*), 345.
Sanchez. *See* Sanches.
Sanfleben, Georg: Extract aus dem... Reise-Diario. *See* Urlsperger, Der Ausführlichen-Nachrichten.
Sanitation:
American Revolution, 597.
West Indies, 873.
*See also* Health; Medicine; etc.
Santo Domingo, 67, 608, 836, 1268, 1397.
climate, 1030, 1031.
coffee, 1494.
commerce, 859, 1393, 1395.
description and travel, 859, 883, 1030, 1031, 1087, 1380, 1393, 1395, 1484.
exports, 1393, 1395.
geography, 859, 883.
geology, 859.
government, 859, 1318, 1437, 1494.
health, 1030, 1031.
history, 1087, 1318, 1494.
meteorological observations, 859, 877C.
poetry, 1000, 1123.
politics, 1494.
revolts, 1166, 1167.
slavery and slave trade, 868, 1062, 1393, 1395.
social life and customs, 1437, 1494.
*See also* Haiti.
Saratoga, N. Y.:
battle of: Burgoyne's defeat, 623.
water analysis, 1296.

Sargent, John. *See* Sergeant, John.
Sargent, Winthrop, 1753–1820, contributor. *See* American Academy of Arts and Sciences, Memoirs, v. 2.
Sarmiento, Martin, 1695–1772: Antiquedad de la Jubas (*review*), 959E.
Sauorgnan. *See* Savorgnano.
Savannah, Ga., 617.
Savorgnano, Pietro, 16th century, translator. *See* Cortés, Von dem Newen Hispanien.
Say, Benjamin, 1755–1813, contributor. *See* College of Physicians of Philadelphia, Medicinische Verhandlungen, Bd. 1; College of Physicians of Philadelphia, Transactions, v. 1.
Sbitzolobium, 979.
Scales, Automatic, 474, 492.
*See also* Weights and Measures.
Scalp Bounties, Indian, 1092.
Schad, Georg Friedrich Casimir, translator. *See* Labat, Jean Baptiste.
Schäffer, Johann Gottlieb, 1720–1795: Der Nutzen und Gebrauch des Tobakrauchclystieres (*review*), 426.
Schagen, Gerrett van, 17th century, cartographer. *See* Montanus, Die unbekante Neue Welt.
Schaitberger, Joseph, 1658–1733: Ich bin ein armer Exultant. *See* Die Treuen.
Schatz, Georg, 1763–1795, translator. *See* Franklin, Kleine Schriften.
Schedel, Hartmann, 1440–1514:
Das Buch der Chroniken, 1.
*See also* Doppelmayr, Historische Nachricht.
Scheibler, Karl Friedrich: Reisen, Entdeckungen u. Unternehmungen (*review*), 765.
Schekomeko, New York, 1426.
Schelechof. *See* Shelekhov.
Schenk, Peter, 1645–1715, engraver. *See* Mocquet, Wunderbare.
Scheppach, Georg August: Karakteristisches Verzeichniss der vorzüglichsten...nordamerikanischen... Holzarten (*reviews*), 1149, 1345.
Scherdiger, Abel, translator. *See* Benzoni, Novae Novi Orbis Historiae.
Scherf, Johann Christian Friedrich, d. 1818: Beyträge zum Archiv der medizinischen Polizey (*review*), 1336.
Schiller, Johann Christoph Friedrich, 1759–1805:
An Henriette von Wolzogen, 754.
An einen Stuttgarter Freund, 754A.
Columbus, 1321.
Kabale und Liebe, ein bürgerliches Trauerspiel, 797.
Nadowessiers Totenlied, 1425.
Der Venuswagen, 683A.
Vermischte Neuigkeiten und Nachrichten zum Nuzen und Vernügen. *See* Nachrichten zum Nuzen und Vernügen.
Schiller, Johann Friedrich, translator. *See* Robertson, Wilhelm Robertson's Geschichte, 559.
Schirach, Gottlob Benedikt, 1743–1804: Historisch statistische Notiz (*reviews*), 565, 595.
Schleder, Johann Georg, fl. 1652–1663, compiler. *See* Irenico-Polemographiæ Continuatio, 186; Theatri Evropæi Sechster vnd letzter Theil, 173.
Schlesische privilegirte Staats-Kriegs- u. Friedens-Zeitungen, 380.
Schlichtegroll, Adolf Heinrich Friedrich von, 1765–1822, compiler. *See* Nekrolog auf das Jahr 1790.
Schlözer, August Ludwig, 1735–1809:
An die Hrn. Herausgeber der Berlinischen Monatschrift, 798.
Vertrauliche Briefe aus Kanada, 618.
Schlözer, Dorothea, 1770–1825, compiler. *See* Genaue Nacbricht.
Schmaus, Leonardus: Lucubrati uncula. *See* Aln Recept von ainem holtz.
Schmidel, Ulrich, 1510?–1579?:
Wahrhaftige Beschreibung. *See* Franck, Erst theil dieses Weltbuchs.
*explorations*, 73, 98, 111, 139, 144.

Schmidt, Clamor Eberhard Karl, 1746–1824: An den Biber, 861.
Schmidt, Johann Gottfried, 1764–1803, engraver. *See* Risler, Leben August Gottlieb Spangenbergs.
Schmidt, Ulrich. *See* Schmidel, Ulrich.
Schmidt, Valentin Heinrich, b. 1756, translator. *See* Vespucci, Amerigo Vespuzzi vier Seereisen.
Schmieder, Heinrich Gottlieb, 1763–1811?: Die Wilden (*review*), 1266A.
Schmohl, Johann Christoph: Ueber Nordamerika und Demokratie, 720.
Schneider, Johann Gottlieb, d. 1822:
Allgemeine Naturgeschichte der Schildkröten, 755.
*See also* Vom Wallfisch.
Schoch, Johann Georg, 17th century, translator. *See* Mocquet, Wunderbare.
Ein Schön hübsch lesen von etlichen insslen. *See* Columbus.
Ein Schöne Newe zeytung, 48.
Ein Schöne Richtige vnd volkomliche Beschreibung dess Göttlichen Geschöpffs. *See* Rauw, Cosmographia.
Schöner, Johann, 1477–1547, contributor. *See* Doppelmayr, Historische Nachricht.
Schoensperger, Johann, 16th century, translator. *See* Vespucci, Von der gefunden Region.
Schöpf, Johann David, 1752–1800:
Beschreibung des Amerikanischen Barschings. *See* Die Naturforscher, 1784.
Beschreibungen einiger Nord-Amerikanischer Fische, 898.
Beyträge zur mineralogischen Kenntniss, 899.
Materia medica americana (*review*), 910, 1061I.
Naturgeschichte, 1139.
Reise durch einige der mittlern und südlichen vereinigten nordamerikanischen Staaten, 938, 939.
Von der Wirkung des Mohnsaftes in der Lustseuche (*review*), 740.
*See also* Aus Nord Amerika, 812; Baltimore in Nord Amerika, 984; Neue Quartalschrift aus den neuesten und besten Reisebeschreibungen Gezogen; Schütz, Beschreibung.
Scholarship in United States, 1409.
*See also* Colleges and Universities.
School Books, 914, 963, 1058A, 1059, 1061B.
Schools, 1305, 1348.
*See also* Colleges and Universities.
Schouten, Willem Corneliszoon, d. 1625: *explorations*, 146.
Schreiben eines deutschen Patrioten, 757.
Schreiben über die Empörung der Nord-Amerikaner. *See* Pinto, Isaac de.
Schreiben an einen guten Freund, 560.
Schreiber, Johann Georg, 1676–1750, engraver. *See* Ausführliche Historie Derer Emigranten.
Schröter, Johann Friedrich, 1710–1788: Allgemeine Geschichte der Länder und Völker von America, 341.
Schubart, Christian Friedrich Daniel, 1739–1791:
Der Britte an Howe nach der Schlacht bey Flatland, 528.
[Excerpts from contributions to the *Deutsche Chronik*,] 484.
Franklin's Grabschrift, 939A.
Die Freiheit, 499.
Freiheitslied eines Kolonisten, 499A.
Ein Gespräch auf dem Schiffe, 798A.
Der kalte Michel, 861A.
Der sterbende Indianer an seinen Sohn, 485.
Schütz, Andreas Gotthelf von, baron, d. 1807: Beschreibung einiger nordamerikan. Fossilien (*review*), 1099.
Schultz, Benjamin: An inaugural botanico-medical dissertation (*review*), 1396.
Schultze, Benjamin, 1689–1760: Orientalisch- und occidentalischer Sprachmeister, 327.
Schulz, Gottfried: Vom Americanischen traubentragenden Nachtschatten, 443.
Schulze, Johann Ludewig, editor. *See* Nachrichten von den vereinigten Deutschen Evangelisch-Lutherischen Gemeinen in Nord-America.

# GERMAN WORKS RELATING TO AMERICA — INDEX

Schurtz, Cornelius Nicholas, fl. 1670?-1689, engraver. *See* Francisci, Neu-polirter Geschicht- Kunst- und Sitten-Spiegel ausländischer Völcker; Francisci, Ost- und West-Jndischer Lust- und Stats-Garden.
Schwabe, Johann Joachim, 1714–1784, translator. *See* Prévost d'Exiles, Erste Reisen.
Schwartz, Olaus [or Olof], 1760–1817: Zubereitung des Ricinusöls in Westindien. *See* Läkaren och Naturforskaren.
Schwenckfeld, Caspar, 1490?–1561: Erläuterung, 461.
Schwenckfeldians, Society of, 329, 461.
Science:
bibliography of American works, 349.
*See also* various scientific subjects.
The Secret history of the armed neutrality together with memoirs...by a German nobleman (*review*), 1206.
Seeds of Plants: American, 1316.
*See also* the names of various plants; also such subjects as Botany; Trees and Shrubs; etc.
Seidel, Günther Karl Friedrich: Die Staatsverfassung der Vereinigten Staaten von Nordamerika. *See* Ramsay, Geschichte der Amerikanischen Revolution.
Sell, Johann Jacob, 1754–1816: Versuch einer Geschichte des Negersclavenhandels, 1094, 1313.
Semitière. *See* Du Simitière.
Ein Sendbrieff. *See* Zumarraga, Juan de.
Senden, Ernst Johann Friedrich Schüler von, 1753–1827: Denkwürdigkeiten, 528A.
Sendtschreyhen vnd warhaffte zeytungen. *See* Jesuits.
Seneca Indians: addresses to Congress, 1157.
Senter, Isaac, 1755–1779, contributor. *See* College of Physicians of Philadelphia, Transactions, v. 1; Medical Society of London, Memoirs, v. 4.
Sergeant, John, 1710–1749: *ordination*, 305, 306, 318.
Sermons: Zinzendorf, 388, 525.
Serpents. *See* Snakes.
Seton, William, 1746–1798. *See* Crèvecœur.
Settle, Dionyse, 16th century: Beschreibung der schiffart des Haubtmans Martini Forbissher, 80.
Die Seufftzende Saltzburger, 288.
Sheffield, John Baker Holroyd, 1st earl of, 1735–1821: Observations on the commerce of the American states (*review*), 809.
*See also* Auszug aus Tench Coxe['s] Abhandlung; Coxe, A brief examination; Sprengel, M. C., and J. R. Forster, editors, Neue Beyträge.
Shelekhov, Gregorii Ivanovich, 1748–1795: Erste und zweyte Reise (*review*), 1181A, 1207A.
Shipping:
America: Britain, 1314.
Barbados, 234.
Charleston, S. C., 358.
France, 748.
Kingston, W. I., 621.
Maryland: Bordeaux, France, 748.
neutrality law, 789.
Virginia, 234.
West Indies: Great Britain, 186, 212, 1314.
*See also* Commerce; Trade.
Ships: ventilators, 376A.
Shipwrecks, 1204.
A Short journey in the West Indies (*review*), 1113.
Shrubs. *See* Trees and Shrubs.
Sickness. *See* Health.
Sierra Leone: slavery, 1436.
Silberflotte. *See* Spanish Silver Fleet.
Silkworms, 474, 492, 975.
Silver:
American exports, 1273.
mining, 333, 356, 1465.
Silver Fleet, Spanish. *See* Spanish Silver Fleet.
Simler, Johann Wilhelm, 1605–1672, and J. R. Rahn, compilers: Vier Loblicher Statt Zürich Verbürgerter Reissbeschreibungen, 197, 199.
Simmendinger, Ulrich, b. 1672: Warhaffte und glaubwürdige Verzeichnüss, 249.

Sitten und Meinungen der Wilden in America. *See* Purmann, J. G.
Sivers, Heinrich, 1626–1691, translator. *See* La Peyrère, Ausführliche Beschreibung.
Six Nations. *See* Iroquois Nation.
A Sketch of the history of Jamaica (*review*), 876C.
Sklavenhandel (*review*), 1153.
Sky: Indian myths, 894.
Slave Trade, 335, 882, 929, 951, 974, 981, 982, 983, 1001, 1010, 1017, 1018, 1022, 1054, 1069, 1114, 1147, 1153, 1184, 1221, 1322.
abolition, 923, 1065, 1066, 1067, 1146, 1148, 1165.
poetry and songs, 969, 980, 1103, 1196.
Santo Domingo, 893, 1062.
slave ships, 366.
West Indies, 1041, 1062, 1070, 1152.
The Slave trade indispensable (*review*), 1069.
Slaves and Slavery, 981, 982, 1018.
abolition, 1048.
American colonies, 690, 1014.
Antigua, 1015A.
Antilles, 868.
bibliography, 1094.
Carolina and Georgia, 305, 306.
diseases, 882, 1336.
drama, 1313.
Dutch colonies, 988.
Haiti, 859.
Jamaica, W. I., 1106, 1313, 1398.
liberation, 1372.
Maryland, 997.
moral improvement, 1101.
origin, 619.
pictorial works, 1114.
poetry and songs, 616, 792, 926, 1313, 1372, 1399.
revolt, 489, 1393, 1395.
Santo Domingo, 859, 1393, 1395.
Sierra Leone, 1436.
treatment of, 913.
West Indies, 555, 833, 866.
*See also* Negroes; Slave Trade.
Sloane, Sir Hans, 1660–1753, contributor. *See* Abhandlungen zur Naturgeschichte, Physik und Oekonomie.
Smallpox: West Indies, 873.
Smille. *See* Smith, Benjamin.
Smith, Benjamin, 1766–1815: Observations on some parts of natural history (*review*), 968.
Smith, Sir James Edward, 1759–1838: The natural history of the rarer lepidopterous insects of Georgia (*review*), 1466.
Smith, John, 1580–1631:
Viertzehende Schiffart, 142, 159.
*See also* Bry, Zehnder Teil Americæ; Scheibler, Reisen, Entdeckungen u. Unternehmungen.
Smith, John Raphael, 1752–1812, joint author. *See* Moreland, G., and J. R. Smith, Slave trade.
Smith, Robert, contributor. *See* American Philosophical Society, Transactions, v. 1.
Smith, Thomas: A sketch of the revolutions in chemistry (*review*), 1504.
Smith, William, 1727–1803, contributor. *See* American Philosophical Society, Transactions, v. 1.
Smith, William, 1728–1793: The history of the province of New-York (*notice*), 370.
Smoking. *See* Tobacco.
Smuggling, 650.
Smyth, David William, 1764–1837: A short topographical description of...Upper-Canada. *See* Kurze topographische Beschreibung.
Smyth, John Ferdinand Dalziel, 1745–1814: Tour of the United States. *See* Charakter und Anzahl der Indianer; Von den Mährischen Brüdern in Nord-Carolina.
Snakes, 706.
*See also* Rattlesnakes.

Social Life and Customs, 782, 810, 837, 915, 938, 939, 1221, 1279.
*See also* as subhead of various countries, races, etc.
Social Work: Philadelphia, Pa., 593.
Società Patria, 1056.
Societät der Wissenschaft, Philadelphia, Pa. *See* American Philosophical Society, Philadelphia, Pa.
Société des amis des noirs, Paris, 1001.
Societies, Learned. *See* Academies and Learned Societies.
Society of the Cincinnati. *See* Cincinnati, Order of.
Society of Friends, 227, 433, 434, 715, 1173, 1372, 1449.
  Pennsylvania, 438.
  Philadelphia, Pa., 715, 920.
  poetry, 503A, 558.
  *See also* Penn, William.
Society Instituted for the Encouragement of Arts: Transactions, v. 8-10 (*review*), 1251.
Society Instituted at London for the Encouragement of Arts, Manufactures, and Commerce, 1136.
Society Instituted in 1781 for the Purpose of Effecting the Abolition of the Slave Trade: List (*review*), 963B, 1022.
Soil: fertility, 768.
Solander, Daniel Charles, 1736-1782, contributor. *See* Geschichte der Seereisen und Entdeckungen.
Soldiers. *See* Army.
Songs. *See* Poetry and Songs.
Sorghum (grass): culture, 415, 421, 430.
Soto, Hernando de, ca. 1500-1542: *explorations*, 342, 869, 921C.
Soulavie, Jean Louis Giraud, 1752-1813, contributor. *See* American Philosophical Society, Transactions, v. 3.
Soulès, François, 1748-1809: Vollständige Geschichte der Revolution in Nord-Amerika, 941.
South America:
  Indians. *See* Indians.
  natural history, 189.
South Carolina:
  British garrison, 550.
  commerce and slave trade, 358.
  description and travel, 244, 1160, 1211.
  exports and imports, 959.
  Germans in, 240.
  history, 1231.
  Indians, 699.
  rice culture, 817.
South River: prehistoric walls, 1305.
Spain:
  colonies. *See* Spanish Colonies in America.
  commerce with America, 157, 191, 255, 273.
  communication with America, 157.
  conquest of Florida, 342, 869, 921C.
  trade, 273, 290, 398, 400.
  treaty with West Indies, 255.
Spangenberg, August Gottlieb, 1704-1792:
  Leben des Herrn Nicolaus Ludwig Grafen und Herrn von Zinzendorf und Pottendorf, 480, 486.
  *See also* Blumenbach, Schreiben; Loskiel, Geschichte der Mission.
  *biography*, 480, 486, 994, 1233.
Spanish America, 221.
  Indians, 221.
  *See also* Central America; South America.
Spanish Colonies in America, 79, 82, 82A, 83, 83A, 84, 85, 87, 89, 98, 99, 109, 133, 147, 148, 162, 185, 201, 223, 271, 398, 545, 822, 1024, 1030, 1031.
  *See also* various Spanish colonies.
Spanish Silver Fleet, 157, 162.
Speelhoven, Martin: Die Glücks- und Unglücksfälle, 444.
Spelling. *See* Orthography.
Spielbergen. *See* Spilberghen.
Spilberghen, Joris van, d. 1620: *explorations*, 148, 150.
Spillard, Mr.: *travels*, 1317.

Spörri, Felix Christian: Americanische Reiss-beschreibung, 197.
Sprengel, Christian Ludolph, editor. *See* Lapérouse, Entdeckungsreise.
Sprengel, Kurt, 1765-1833, editor. *See* Jackson, Ueber die Fieber in Jamaica.
Sprengel, Matthias Christian, 1746-1803:
  Allgemeines historisches Taschenbuch, 799, 800.
  Auswahl der besten ausländischen und statistischen Nachrichten (*review*), 1240.
  Briefe (*reviews*), 564, 589, 627.
  Geschichte der Europäer in Nordamerica, 723.
  Geschichte der Revolution von Nord-America, 823, 824.
  *See also* Neuere Beobachtungen über fremde Länder und Sitten.
  Geschichte der wichtigsten geographischen Entdeckungen, 1140.
  Kurze Schilderung der Grossbrittanischen Colonien (*reviews*), 566, 567.
  Ueber den jetzigen Nordamerikanischen Krieg (*reviews*), 739, 766, 767.
  Ueber den Nordamerikan. Krieg (*review*), 1212.
  Vom Ursprung des Negerhandels, 619.
Sprengel, Matthias Christian, 1746-1803, editor. *See* Alex. Falconbridges u. Thomas Clarksons Bemerkungen; Beyträge zur Völker- und Länderkunde; Muñoz, Geschichte.
  *See also* Forster, J. R., and M. C. Sprengel, editors.
Sprengel, Matthias Christian, 1746-1803, translator. *See* Hearne, Reise.
Sprengel, Matthias Christian, 1746-1803, and J. R. Forster, editors.
  Neue Beyträge zur Völker- und Länderkunde (*reviews*), 1181B, 1348.
  *See also* Forster, J. R., and M. C. Sprengel, editors, Beyträge.
Sprickmann, Anton Matthias: Nachrichten aus Amerika, 529.
Springs. *See* Wells and Springs.
Spruce Beer. *See* Beer: spruce.
Squirrel, 1249, 1254.
  anatomy, 1254.
Staatsgesetze der dreyzehn vereinigten amerikanischen Staaten (*review*), 877.
Staden, Hans, 16th century:
  Warhafftige Historia, 70, 71-72.
  *See also* Bry, Dritte Buch Americæ; Franck, Ander theil dieses Weltbuchs; Roeslin, H., Mitternächtige Schiffarth; Winckelmann, Der Americanischen Neuen Welt Beschreibung.
Staehlin von Storcksburg, Jakob, 1710-1785: Das von den Russen...entdeckte...Nordamerika (*review*), 569.
Stäudlin, Karl Friedrich, 1761-1826: Beiträge zur Philosophie und Geschichte der Religion (*review*), 1460.
Stars: Indian myths, 894.
Staten Island, N. Y.: American Revolution, 516.
Statistical Information [also entered under subject]:
  America, 584.
  Great Britain, 494, 565, 595.
  North America, 799, 800, 1019.
  Pennsylvania, 1145, 1171.
  United States, 707, 726, 768, 834, 847, 1002, 1019, 1082, 1189, 1217, 1288, 1324, 1383.
Statistische Uebersicht der vornehmsten deutschen und sämtlichen europäischen Staaten (*review*), 877A, 877B, 921G.
Statue of Liberty: anecdote, 1219.
Staunton, Virginia: German mercenaries, 620.
Stedman, Charles, 1753-1812:
  Geschichte des...Americanischen Krieges, 1281.
  The History of the origin, progress, and termination of the American war (*review*), 1246, 1247.
Stefanov, Hippolitus, d. 1778, contributor. *See* Beniowsky, Begebenheiten und Reisen.

Steindecker, Johann, 1654–1733, publisher. *See* Latomus, Relationis Historicæ continuatio.
Steinhoewel, Heinrich, 1412–1482?: Chronica. *See* Egenolf, Chronica.
Steller, Georg Wilhelm, 1709–1746: Reise von Kamtschatka nach Amerika, 1182.
Steuben, Friedrich Wilhelm August Heinrich Ferdinand von, 1730–1794:
Copia eines Schreibens, 643.
*bibliography*, 829.
*biography*, 643, 773, 829, 1097, 1267.
*portrait*, 838.
Stilling, Heinrich. *See* Jung-Stilling, J. H.
Stockbridge, Mass.: Indians, 305, 306, 307, 318.
Stockett, Thomas, contributor. *See* College of Physicians of Philadelphia, Medicinische Verhandlungen, Bd. 1; College of Physicians of Philadelphia, Transactions, v. 1.
Stoecklein, Joseph, 1676–1733, compiler. *See* Jesuits, Allerhand... Brief.
Stöver, Dietrich Johann Heinrich, 1767–1822: Historisch-statistische Beyträge, 1002.
Stolberg, Friedrich Leopold, 1750–1819:
An Karl Freiherrn von Hompesch, 1046A.
Lied eines deutschen Soldaten, 500.
Mein Vaterland, 487.
Der Prüfstein, 757A.
Die Zukunft, 620A.
Storch, Carl August Gottlieb, b. 1764:
Auszug aus einem Briefe, 1305.
*See also* Velthusen, Nordcarolinische Kirchennachrichten.
Storch, Christian August Gottlieb. *See* Storch, Carl August Gottlieb.
Stoves. *See* Fireplaces.
Stuck, Gottlieb Heinrich, d. 1787:
Gottlieb Heinrich Stuck's Nachtrag, 825.
Verzeichnis von aeltern und Land- und Reisebeschreibungen, 802.
Stueber, Henry, 1770?–1792, contributor. *See* Franklin, Kleine Schriften.
Stüven, Joannes Fridericus. De vero novi orbis. *See* Doppelmayr, Historische nachricht.
Sturm, Johann Georg, 1742–1793, engraver. *See* Oldendorp, Geschichte der Mission der evangelischen Brüder.
Sturz, Helferich Peter, 1736–1779: Ueber den Vaterlandsstolz, 500A.
Stuss, Johann Heinrich, 1686–1775: Schrifftmässige Anrede, 289.
Stuvenius. *See* Stüven.
Stuyvesant, Peter, 1602–1682: *biography*, 182, 183.
Sugar:
maple, 636, 637, 686, 1326, 1327, 1332, 1381, 1428.
poetry, 705.
West Indies, 259, 780, 1393, 1395.
Suicide: Indians, 946.
Sullivan, James, 1744–1808: The history of the district of Maine *(review)*, 1342.
Surinam. *See* Guiana.
Surveys: United States: states, 847.
Susquehanna River, 462.
Susquehanna valley, archaeology, 1296.
Swatara Creek, Pa., 975.
Sweden: commerce with North America, 581, 651.
Swedish Colonies in America, 884.
Sweet Spring Mountain, Botetourt County, Va., 975.
Syphilis, 42, 43, 50, 61, 62, 345, 1391, 1391A.
remedy, 740.
slaves, 882.
Syringe, 426.
Systematisches Verzeichniss derjenigen ausländischen, grösstentheils nordamerikanischen Bäume *(review)*, 1351A.

## T

"Tabacksklystier", 426.
Tabernæmontanus, called Jacobus Theodorus. *See* Theodorus, Jacobus.
Tableau général du commerce *(reviews)*, 921H, 921I.
Tagebuch der Seereise von Stade nach Quebec in Amerika, 530.
Tageregister vom Jahre 1751 [1752, 1753]. *See* Urlsperger, Americanisches Ackerwerk Gottes.
Talbot, Sir William, translator. *See* Lederer, The discoveries of John Lederer.
Tallmann, Benjamin H., contributor. *See* College of Physicians of Philadelphia, Medicinische Verhandlungen, Bd. 1; College of Physicians of Philadelphia, Transactions, v. 1.
Tappe, Jacob T., 1603–1680: [Latin oration.] *See* Noch ein kleiner Beitrag.
Tariff:
United States, 1223, 1232.
*See also* Smuggling.
Tarleton, Sir Banastre, bart., 1754–1833: A history of the campaigns of 1780 and 1781 *(review)*. *See* England.
Taschenatlas *(reviews)*, 973B, 1070A.
Taube, Friedrich Wilhelm, 1728–1778:
Abschilderung der Englischen Handlung *(review)*. *See his* Geschichte.
Geschichte der Engländischen Handelschaft *(reviews)*, 534, 663.
Taurinius, Zacharias, pseud.: Beschreibung einiger See- und Landreisen nach... Amerika, 1454.
Taxation:
British colonies, 472.
industries, 1224.
liquor, 1223.
North America, 888.
United States industries, 1223.
Taxation no tyranny. *See* Johnson, Samuel.
Tayadaneega. *See* Thayadanega.
Tea, 521:
Carolina, 408A.
Tennessee: history, 1170, 1209, 1258.
Tenney, Samuel, 1748–1816, contributor. *See* American Academy of Arts and Sciences, Memoirs, v. 2.
Tentzel [or Tenzel], Wilhelm Ernst, 1659–1707: Monatliche Unterredungen. *See* Pastorius, Beschreibung von Pennsylvanien.
Terre Neuve [or Terreneuf]. *See* Newfoundland.
Teutelieb, pseud. *See* Schreiben eines deutschen Patrioten.
Thayadanega [Joseph Brant], 1307.
Thayer, John, 1755–1815: Nachricht von der Bekehrung, 1047.
Theatre, 1052.
Theatrum Europæum [variations in title], 167, 168, 173, 179, 186, 191, 198, 206, 212, 220, 223, 234, 255, 271, 290, 310.
Theodorus, Jacobus, ca. 1520–1590: Neuw vollkommentlich Kreuterbuch, 135.
Therese Westen *(reviews)*, 921J, 1025.
Thermometer: nautical use, 1259.
Theüs, Jeremiah, 1720–1774, artist. *See* Urlsperger, Americanisches Ackerwerk Gottes.
Thörigten Abzug einiger Untertanen nach Pensilvaniam betreffend, 236A.
Thomas, Gabriel, 17th century: Continuatio der Beschreibung der Landschafft Pensylvaniæ, 231.
Thornton, William, 1759–1827, contributor. *See* American Philosophical Society, Transactions, v. 3.
Thunderstorms, 965, 975, 1259.
*See also* Meteorological Observations.
Ticunas, 697.
Tides: Lake Ontario, 377.
*See also* Meteorological Observations.
Tieck, Johann Ludwig, 1773–1853: Geschichte des Herrn William Lovell, 1282.

Timaeus, Johann Jacob Karl, d. 1809: Nordamerikanischer Staats-Kalender, 1324.
Tobacco, 826, 1319, 1378, 1477, 1498.
 America, 1016, 1100.
 medicinal aspects, 426.
 Virginia, 785, 799, 800, 967.
Topography:
 Canada, 1481.
 Lake Champlain district, 606.
Toxicodendron, 607.
Toze, Eobald, 1715–1789:
 Beweis, das...Martin Behaim, 385.
 Von den Betrügereyen des Americus Vespucci, 386.
 Der wahre und erste Entdecker, 393.
 *See also* Doppelmayr, Historische Nachricht.
Trade [with or relating to America]:
 Barbados, 234.
 British colonies, 534, 663.
 Cuba: Spain, 398, 400.
 Great Britain: Spain, 273.
 neutral America, 789.
 Portugal, 893.
 Sweden, 651.
 United States, 703.
 West Indies: Spanish, 290, 398, 400.
 *See also* Banks and Banking; Commerce; Communication; Free Ports; Industries.
Trade Treaties:
 Portugal: United States, 893.
 United States: Morocco, 1002.
 West Indies: France and Spain, 255.
Transportation:
 immigrant fares, 1183.
 North America, 1052.
Travel Dangers in United States, 1357.
Travels. *See* Voyages and Travels.
Travels through the interior parts of America. *See* Anburey, Thomas.
Treaties, 182, 183.
 German mercenaries, 515.
 Great Britain: Netherlands, 753.
 Portugal, 893.
  Great Britain, 1390.
 Netherlands, 724.
 *See also* French and Indian War: treaty; Paris, Treaty of; Versailles, Treaty of; *also* Trade Treaties.
Trees and Shrubs, 187, 408A, 1255, 1373, 1482.
 America, 346, 1011, 1013, 1241, 1248, 1266, 1356.
 Canada, 636, 637.
 Charleston, S. C.: nurseries, 1230.
 German importations, 688, 886, 1036, 1149, 1154, 1263, 1315, 1316, 1345, 1354, 1379.
 Lancaster, Pa., 1482.
 Middle West, 1296.
 New Jersey, 909.
 New York state, 909.
 New York nurseries, 1230.
 North America, 909.
  catalogue, 470.
 Ohio river, 1296.
 Pennsylvania, 909.
 Wilkes-Barre, Pa., 1457.
 *See also* various trees and shrubs, as Maple Trees.
Die Treuen Bekenner Christi Das ist gründliche Beschreibung derer Saltzburger, 291.
Tribbeckow, Johannes, 1677–1712, contributor. *See* Boehme, Das verlangte.
Tribecko. *See* Tribbeckow.
Triesnecker, Franz von (de Paula), 1745–1817:
 Geographische Ortsbestimmungen, 1486.
 Zweyter Nachtrag, 1427.
Trinidad:
 geology, 1068.
 lakes, 1068.
The Triumph of the arts. *See* Franklin, Benjamin.
Tröltsch, Karl Friedrich, d. 1807: Der fränkische Robinson. *See* Der Americanische Robinson.

Tropical Diseases, 1028, 1029.
 *See also* Diseases in America.
Trumbull, John, ca. 1756–1843, artist. *See* General Washington; Portrait du Général Washington.
Tucker, Josiah, 1712–1799: *writings*. *See* Remer, Amerikanisches Archiv.
Tübingen. — Universität: Engelisch-theologische Facultæt: Der Theologischen Facultæt, 304.
Tunkers. *See* Dunkers.
Tupi Indians. *See* Indians.
Turgot, Anne Robert Jacques, baron de l'Aulne, 1737–1781: Betrachtungen über den Cincinnatus-orden-Schreiben. *See* Mirabeau, Sammlung.
Turnbull, Wilhelm: Ursprung und Alter der Lustseuche und ihre Einführung und Verbreitung auf den Inseln der Südsee (*review*), 1029B.
Turtles, 755, 999, 1139.

## U

Ueber den Aufstand der englischen Colonien in Amerika (*review*), 601.
Ueber Nordamerika und Demokratie. *See* Schmohl, J. C.
Ueber nordamerikanische Bäume und Sträucher (*reviews*), 1154, 1263, 1354.
Ueber den Vaterlandsstolz. *See* Sturz, H. P.
Übersicht der vornehmsten Regierungen der Welt (*review*), 1070B.
Uffenbach, Peter, 1566?–1635, translator. *See* Mercator, Atlas Minor.
Uhlich, fl. 1719–1740, illustrator. *See* Ausführliche Historie.
Ulloa, Antonio de, 1716–1795:
 Physikalische und historische Nachrichten, 684.
 *See also* Neue Quartalschrift.
Die Um das [*sic!*] Evangelii willen vertriebene Saltzburger, 292.
Die Um des Evangelii Willen verjagte...Saltzburger, 293.
Umfreville, Edward:
 Gegenwärtiger Zustand der Hudsonbay (*review*), 1102.
 The Present state of the Hudson Bay (*review*), 1111.
Umständliche Nachricht...[Salzburger,] 294.
Umständliche Und Wahrhafftige Nachrichten [Salzburger,] 295.
Die Unbekante Neue Welt. *See* Montanus, Arnoldus.
United States. — Congress:
 [Various publications of Congress (*reviews*)], 789, 1098A, 1229, 1231, 1267, 1501.
 *as subject*, 703A, 703B, 756, 799, 1218, 1228, 1229, 1239, 1277, 1328, 1350, 1406, 1501.
 *presidents*, 799, 800.
United States. — Constitution: text and commentary, 806, 823, 824, 854, 877, 917, 1155, 1194, 1218, 1228, 1229, 1242, 1256, 1264, 1267, 1348, 1403, 1411, 1429.
United States. — President:
 Message (*review*), 1396A.
 *as subject*, 1052.
United States [as subject] 594, 1197, 1206, 1286, 1291, 1431, 1485.
 agriculture, 786, 917.
 *See also* Agriculture.
 army, 727, 823, 824, 908.
 *See also* Army.
 banks and banking, 722, 814, 858, 959, 1236.
 biography, 1093, 1239.
 botany, 1252, 1272, 1294, 1298/99.
 *See also* Botany.
 census, 707, 726, 768, 799, 800, 1002, 1189, 1231, 1286, 1431.
 *See also* Colonies in America: census.
 church history, 1460.
 *See also* Church in America.

United States, *continued*
climate, 768, 795, 938, 939.
*See also* Climate; Meteorological Observations.
colleges and universities, 1144.
colonial history, 182, 183, 192, 223, 245, 247, 257, 270, 271, 351, 357, 427, 446, 471, 479, 481, 494, 497, 502, 512, 523, 526, 531, 534, 535, 542, 543, 546, 554, 563, 565, 590, 591, 592, 594, 595, 599, 609, 626, 628, 630, 631, 653, 654, 657, 659, 660, 661, 662, 663, 664, 665, 669, 712, 714, 723, 770.
*See also* Colonies in America.
commerce. *See* Commerce with or relating to America.
communication. *See* Communication.
description and travel, 769, 770, 782, 795, 810, 876, 1110, 1124, 1129, 1150, 1252, 1294, 1303, 1357, 1362, 1363, 1364, 1387, 1388, 1401, 1414, 1451, 1463, 1469, 1475, 1484, 1489, 1490, 1506, 1507.
*See also* North America, *also* various regions, states, etc., sub-head, description and travel.
economic history, 854, 917, 1401, 1403, 1404.
education. *See* Education in America.
entertainment, 1358.
Evangelical Lutheran Church, 903.
*See also* Evangelical Lutheran Church.
finance, public, 718, 814, 1052, 1130, 1205, 1220, 1223, 1228, 1236, 1267.
*See also* Finance, Public.
fisheries, 416, 854, 917.
foreign relations, 1386.
France, 718, 1181, 1286, 1341, 1377, 1401, 1417, 1418.
Great Britain, 594, 595, 609, 613, 618, 656, 659, 702, 711, 721, 767, 900, 970, 1014, 1185, 1240, 1301, 1370, 1390, 1396A, 1417, 1418, 1423.
Netherlands, 613, 718, 724.
Portugal, 893.
geography, 768, 795, 1002, 1189, 1286, 1303, 1431, 1458, 1469, 1486, 1489, 1490, 1606.
*See also* Geography.
geology. *See* Geology.
Germans in. *See* Germans in America.
government and politics, 720, 761, 764, 854, 970, 971, 972, 1197, 1220, 1228, 1229, 1286, 1291, 1308, 1324, 1333, 1348, 1401, 1410, 1414, 1429, 1431, 1458, 1501.
*See also* Colonies in America: government.
history, 559, 698, 771, 806, 811, 842, 878, 912, 1060, 1163, 1185, 1197, 1201, 1206, 1214, 1215, 1291, 1301, 1333, 1403, 1478, 1505.
post-Revolutionary period, 799, 800.
sources, 1405, 1406.
immigration, 865, 1497.
*See also* Emigration and Immigration.
industries, 1058A, 1059, 1224.
Jews. *See* Jews.
land. *See* Land.
meteorological observations. *See* Meteorological Observations.
money. *See* Money and Coinage; Money, Paper.
Moravian Brethren. *See* Moravian Brethren.
natural history. *See* Natural History.
navy. *See* America: navy.
neutrality law, 789.
politics. *See* government and politics.
population. *See* census.
products, 1286, 1431, 1458.
religion, 795, 1339.
*See also* Church in America; *also* various denominations.
silver exports, 1273.
social life and customs, 782, 810, 938, 939, 1279.
state constitutions. *See* Constitutions, State.
state governments, 770, 795, 806.
state relations, 1052.
state surveys, 847.
statistics. *See* Statistical Information.
tariff, 1223, 1232.
taxation. *See* Taxation.

United States, *continued*
trade. *See* Commerce; Trade.
travel dangers, 1357.
*See also* description and travel; *also* North America: description and travel.
treaties, 893.
*See also* Treaties.
*See also* Northeast Coast of North America; Northwest Coast of North America.
United States register. *See* The American Kalendar, or United States register.
*See also* Timaeus, Nordamerikanischer Staats-Kalender.
Universitäten in dem Nord-Amerikanischen Freistaate, 1144.
Universities. *See* Colleges and Universities.
U-r, J. v. *See* Uslar, J. J. von.
Urlsperger, Johann August, 1728–1806, contributor. *See* Urlsperger, Samuel, Americanisches Ackerwerk Gottes.
Urlsperger, Samuel, 1685–1772:
Americanisches Ackerwerk Gottes, 350.
Der Ausführlichen Nachrichten, 305, 306, 318.
Copien von den Vocationen der Herren Prediger. *See his* Der Ausführlichen Nachrichten.
Die den 17. mai 1751. *See his* Der Ausführlichen Nachrichten.
Eine Erinnerung. *See his* Der Ausführlichen Nachrichten.
Eine kurtze Aufmunterung. *See his* Der Ausführlichen Nachrichten.
Die Sammlung, 307.
Eine schriftmässige Ermunterungsrede. *See his* Der Ausführlichen Nachrichten.
Umständliche Nachricht. *See his* Der Ausführlichen Nachrichten.
Umständlicher Vorbericht. *See his* Der Ausführlichen Nachrichten.
Zuverlässiges Sendschreiben, 308.
Uslar, Johann Jacob von: Prüfung der Vortheile, 1379.

V

Vaccination, 873.
Valdés, Diego, fl. 1580: Rhetorica christiana. *See* Fricius, Indianischer Religionstandt.
Vancouver, George, 1758–1798:
Reisen, 1456.
A Voyage of discovery *(reviews)*, 1440, 1471.
Vaughan, Benjamin, 1751–1835, translator. *See* Franklin, Brief vom Doctor Benjamin Franklin; Franklin, Sämmtliche Werke.
Veer, Gerrit de, fl. 1600:
Dritte Theil, 118, 119, 130, 178.
Warhafftige Relation, 107.
*See also* Bry, Neundter vnd Letzter Theil Americæ.
Velasco, Juan Lopez de. *See* Lopez de Velasco, Juan.
Veltheim, Friedrich von, d. 1805. *See* Marshall, Beschreibung.
Velthusen, Johann Caspar, 1740–1814:
Einige Nachricht von...Nordcarolina, 864. *(review)*, 1009.
Nordcarolina, 1009.
Nordcarolinische Kirchennachrichten *(review)*, 1203.
*See also* Ankündigung einiger Schriften; Lehrbücher für die Jugend in Nordcarolina.
Velthusen, Johann Caspar, 1740–1814, editor. *See* Nordcarolinische Kirchennachrichten; Storch, Auszug aus einem Briefe.
Venegas, Miguel, 1680–1764:
Natürliche und bürgerliche Geschichte von Californien, 445.
A Natural and civil history of California *(review)*, 389.
Noticia de la California *(review)*, 454.
Venereal Diseases. *See* Syphilis.

Venezuela, 68.
Verazzano, Giovanni da, 1485-1527: *voyages*, 144.
Verelst, Egidius, 1742-1818, illustrator. *See* Baegert, Nachrichten von der Amerikanischen Halbinsel Californien.
Verhelst. *See* Verelst.
Verkauf von Ländereien in Amerika (*review*), 1301A.
Vermischte Nachrichten (*notices*), 977B, 1301B, 1506A.
Vermont:
description and travel, 1163, 1495, 1496, 1503.
geography, 1297, 1495, 1496, 1503.
history, 1297, 1495, 1496, 1503.
natural history, 1297, 1495, 1496, 1503.
war with New York rumored, 774.
Versailles, Treaty of, 1783: poem, 805.
Versuch einer Beschreibung u. Geschichte der Antillischen Inseln, 685.
Versuch einer Neuen Geschichte des Jesuiter-Ordens. *See* Adelung, J. C.
Vertrauliche Briefe aus Kanada, 622.
Vespucci, Amerigo, 1451-1512:
Allerälteste Nachricht, 262-263.
Amerigo Vespuzzi vier Seereisen, 1050.
Diss büchlin saget wie, 33, 34.
Das sind die new gefundē menschē, 18.
Von der neū gefunden Region, 10, 11, 12, 13, 14, 15, 21, 22, 23, 24.
*See also* Woodcut, 19, 20.
Von den nüwē Insulē vnd lāden, 16, 17, 25, 26, 27, 28, 29, 30.
*See also* Bandini, Americus Vespucci; Bry, Zehnder Teil Americæ.
biography, 836, 1056.
explorations, 31, 32, 99, 104, 144, 204, 205, 325, 385, 386, 393, 536.
poem, 1021, 1058.
portrait, 104.
Veteres Migrate Coloni, 296.
Veterinary Medicine, 979.
*See also* Cattle: diseases; also various animals, subhead, diseases.
Vigera: Diarium. *See* Urlsperger, Der Ausführlichen Nachrichten.
Villeneuve, Gabrielle Suzanne Barbot, dame de, 1695?-1755, supposed author: Die Junge Amerikanerin (*review*), 425.
Villermont, contributor. *See* Abhandlungen zur Naturgeschichte, Physik und Oekonomie.
Vinal, John, contributor. *See* American Academy of Arts and Sciences, Memoirs, v. 2.
Virgin Islands: Moravian Brethren, 555.
Virginia [Old and New], 90, 112, 134, 149, 158, 507, 708, 916, 966.
agriculture, 1061A.
American Revolution, 799, 800.
caves, 998.
church history, 258, 843.
description and travel, 143, 160, 161, 213, 214, 469.
discovery, 100, 103, 105, 193.
early accounts, 100, 103, 105, 134.
Evangelical Lutheran Church, 258.
floods, 469.
geography, 213.
Germans in, 258.
history, 100, 134, 140, 141, 785.
Indians, 193, 213, 214, 796.
*See also* American Languages.
natural history, 998.
pictorial works, 213, 214.
religious freedom, 843.
tobacco, 785, 799, 800, 967.
trade, 234.
Virginity: Indians, 904.
Vischer, Ludwig Friedrich, translator. *See* Bellegarde, Allgemeine historische Einleitung; La Hontan, Des Berühmten ... Reisen nach Nord-Indien; Lawson, Allerneuste Beschreibung der Provintz Carolina.

Vitriolic Acid: freezing of, 1037.
Vivares, Thomas, ca. 1735-ca. 1790, artist. *See* Robertson, Sechs Blätter.
Volcanoes:
North Carolina, 1259.
West River Mountain, 965.
Volcksmann. *See* Volkmann.
Volkmann, Johann Jacob, 1732-1803: Neueste Reisen durch England (*review*), 735C.
Vollständige So Wohl Historisch- als Theologische Nachricht Von der Herrnhuthischen Brüderschafft, 309.
Voltaire, François Marie Arouet de, 1694-1778: biography, 433, 434.
Vom Wallfisch, 804.
Von der bei den Deutschen in Philadelphia angelegten lateinischen Schule, 532.
Von den Mährischen Brüdern in Nord-Carolina, 906, 956.
Von der Nation der Caraiben. *See* Heise, J. C. F.
Von der neū gefunden Region. *See* Vespucci, Amerigo.
Von den newen Jnsulen vnd landen. *See* Vespucci, Amerigo.
Vopelius, Georg Christoph: Das Hochzupreisende Werck, 297.
Voss, Johann Heinrich, 1751-1826:
Aufmunterung, 1238.
Die Kartoffelernte, 1487A.
Luise, 1284A.
Vossius, Martin Friedrich, editor. *See* Vespucci, Allerälteste Nachricht.
*See also* Allererste Nachrichten, 536.
Voyage d'un Suisse dans différentes colonies d'Amérique. *See* Girod-Chantrans, Justin.
Voyages intéressans. *See* Bourgeois, N. L.
Voyages and Travels, 216, 217, 235, 530, 639, 1128.
accounts. *See* Angliara; Bartram; Beniowsky; Bering; Bigges; Bos; Brawer; Brissot de Warville; Carli; Carver; Casas; Clerke; Cook; Coxe; Crouch; Dixon; Drake; Federman; Forster, Georg; Forster, J. R.; Franck; Gage; Gore; Hearne; Hemmersam; Hennepin; Herckemann; Heyde; Hudson; La Hontan; Lapérouse; La Peyrère; Long; Meares; Metcalfe; Mocquet; Mortimer; Munck; Naas; Portlock; Raleigh; Richshoffer; Schoepf; Shelekhov; Smith, John; Speelhoven; Spörri; Ulloa; Veer; Vespucci; Weld; Zeller and Huser.
bibliography, 802, 825.
collections, 82, 82A, 83, 106, 204, 205, 409, 435, 962, 1014, 1083.
history, 807.
Pacific ocean, 841.
*See also* Discovery; *also* various continents, countries, and other geographical divisions, subhead, description and travel.
Voyages and Travels, Fictitious, 1454.
Voyages around the World, 121, 145, 155, 1440, 1471.
Le Voyageur Americain. *See* Cluny, Alexander.
Vries, Simonde, b. 1630, editor. *See* La Peyrère, Ausführliche Beschreibung.

# W

W. *See* Wieland, C. M.
W., J., translator. *See* Penn, Beschreibung, 211.
Wadström, Carl Bernhard, 1746-1799:
An Essay on colonisazion, 1290.
Précis sur l'établissement des colonies de Sierra Léone (*review*), 1436.
Wadsworth, Jeremias, 1743-1804. *See* Deane, Schreiben.
Waerdenburch. *See* Waerdenburgh.
Waerdenburgh, Dirk van: *naval action*, 196.
Wagenseil, Johann Christoph, 1633-1705, contributor. *See* Doppelmayr, Historische Nachricht.
Wages, 1366.

Wagner, Heinrich Leopold, 1747-1779: Die Kindermörderin, 533.
Walbaum, Johann Julius, 1724-1799: Verzeichniss einiger ausländischen Frösche, 828.
Walch, Johann Georg: Erweckungs-Rede, 298.
Waldo, Samuel, 1696-1759: Kurtze Beschreibung derer Landschafft Massachusetts Bay, 313.
Waldoboro, Me.: Protestants, 313.
Walls, Prehistoric, 1305.
Walther, Friedrich Ludwig, 1759-1824: Natürliche und wissenschaftliche Erdkunde (review), 961B.
Von menschenfressenden Völkern und Menschenopfern (reviews), 833A, 833B.
Wangenheim, Friedrich Adam Julius von, 1747-1800: Beschreibung einiger Nordamericanischen Holtz- und Buscharten, 688.
Beytrag zur deutschen holzgerechten Forstwissenschaft, 909.
(review), 1099A.
Wansey, Henry, 1752-1827: Ein Besuch beym Präsidenten Washington, 1361.
An Excursion to the United States (review), 1463.
Tagebuch einer Reise, 1387.
War and Peace, 1498.
See also various wars, as American Revolution.
Warfare, Indian art of, 846.
Warhaffte Nachricht von einer Hochteutschen Evangelischen Colonie zu Germantown, 258.
Warhafftige vnnd liebliche Beschreibung etlicher fürnemmen Jndianischen Landschafften vnd Jnsulen.
See Bry, Das vii. Theil America.
Warhafftiger Bericht. See Cysat, Renwart.
Waring, William, contributor. See American Philosophical Society, Transactions, v. 3.
Warren, James, contributor. See American Academy of Arts and Sciences, Memoirs, v. 2; Medical Society of London, Memoirs.
Warships, 758.
See also Navy.
Washington, George, 1732-1799:
American state papers (review), 1333.
Beständigen Präsidenten und Protektors...Briefe, 1328.
Circularschreiben, 760.
Official letters (review), 1350.
See also Bülow, Ueber Washingtons Briefe; Uiber die Ursachen der gegenwärtigen Krisis in Europa; Washington; Washington's Adresse.
biography, 649, 670, 677, 719, 736, 760, 1052, 1134, 1225, 1328, 1329, 1330, 1361, 1448, 1484, 1484A, 1488.
fiction, 1459.
poetry, 670, 1225, 1448.
portraits, 649, 677, 719, 736, 838.
Washington, D. C., 1161, 1339, 1490.
Wasps, 360.
Wassenaer, Jacob van, jonkheer, 1610-1665: biography, 204, 205.
Water, 1206.
analysis: Saratoga, N. Y., 1296.
freezing, 1210.
See also Wells and Springs.
Water Mills, 1259.
Water Spouts, 975.
Watermeyer, Albrecht Anton: Statistisch-historisch-geographisches Handbuch (reviews), 921F, 973A.
Wealth:
Indians, 931.
See also Money; etc.
Weather, 990.
See also Meteorological Observations.
Webber, J., illustrator. See Cook, Dritte Entdeckungs-Reise.
Weber, Samuel, 1760-1810, contributor. See American Academy of Arts and Sciences, Memoirs, v. 2; Ebeling, Ueber Portugiesische und Amerikanische Landkarten.

Webster, Noah, 1758-1843, contributor. See American Academy of Arts and Sciences, Memoirs, v. 2.
Webster, Pelatiah, 1725-1795: Political essays (review), 1205.
Wedderburn. See Inkle und Yariko.
Wedekind, E. C.: Aufgabe [von einer Krankheit der americanischen Hundel, 394.
Wehrs, Georg Friedrich, 1750?-1818: Nachricht über Frasers nordamerikanisches Gras, 996, 1090, 1098.
Wehrs, Georg Friedrich, 1750?-1818, editor. See Franklin, Brief vom Doctor Benjamin Franklin; Doctor Franklin; Rush, Nachricht.
Weights and Measures, 1259.
See also Scales.
Weiser, Conrad, b. 1696:
Tagebuch, 319.
Weiss: Beantwortung der...Preisfrage über das Anstecken der Viehseuche, 713.
Weissiger, Daniel:
Kurtze Nachricht. See Kurtze Nachricht.
Sammlungen auserlesener Materien. See Bock, Kurz gefasste Missions Geschichte.
Wekhrlin, Wilhelm Ludwig, 1739-1792:
Chronologen, 625.
Über die Insurgenten, 652.
Weld, Isaac, 1774-1856:
Reise durch die nordamerikanischen Freistaaten, 1490.
Reisen durch die Staaten von Nordamerika, 1489.
Travels through the states of North America (reviews), 1469, 1506.
Wells, Richard, contributor. See American Philosophical Society, Transactions, v. 1.
Wells and Springs:
Augusta, Ga., 998.
hot: Jamaica, W. I., 1023, 1042.
Welper, Eberhard, fl. 1630: Compendium Geographicum, 166.
Welsch, Georg Hieronymus, 1624-1677: Von dreyen Amerikanischen Früchten, 354, 1677.
Welsers, of Augsburg, Colonization by, 68.
Der Welt kugel, 35.
Wenzel, G. T., annotator. See Franklin, Sämmtliche Werke.
Wepfer, Johann Jakob, 1620-1695, contributor. See Camerarius, Von dem Gebrauch der Beere des Americanischen...Nachtschattens.
Weppen, Johann August, 1741-1812:
Der Hessische Officier in Amerika. See his Klage einer Hessin.
Klage einer Hessin, 586.
Eine Parabel, 805.
Wernitz, F. H., translator. See Raynal, Geschichte der Revolution von Nord-Amerika.
Wesley, John, 1703-1791, contributor. See Achenwall, Einige Anmerkungen, über Nordamerika; Du Buisson, Vorstellung.
West, Benjamin, contributor. See American Philosophical Society, Transactions, v. 1.
West, Hans, 1758-1811: Beyträge zur Beschreibung von St. Croix, 1238B.
West, Samuel, contributor. See American Academy of Arts and Sciences, Memoirs, v. 2.
West India Company. See West-Indische Compagnie.
West Indies, 67, 111, 152, 158, 180, 269, 271, 272, 450, 466, 555, 780, 893, 1156, 1240, 1393.
administration, 179.
beer, 1137.
bees, 625A.
botany, 625.
British colonies, 1198.
British garrisons, 550.
camphor, 1253.
castor oil manufacture, 1061.
climate, 1028, 1029.
coffee, 1261.
commerce, 167, 168, 173, 191, 310, 481, 780, 827, 1136, 1198.

West Indies, *continued*
  description and travel, 153, 194, 195, 196, 197, 201, 685, 874, 921, 933, 1113, 1200, 1340, 1346, 1494.
  discovery, 353.
  diseases, 596, 598, 873, 979, 1028, 1029, 1265.
  drugs, 964.
  French attack on English colonies, 233.
  geography, 1200, 1340, 1346, 1494.
  German mercenaries, 621.
  government, 494A, 1494.
  history, 188, 206, 220, 471, 685, 1198, 1340, 1368, 1369, 1389, 1393.
  laurel, 1253.
  meteorological observations. *See* Meteorological Observations.
  mission, 555.
  natural history, 187, 188, 874.
  Negroes, 335, 866, 1041.
  *See also* Slave Trade; Slaves and Slavery.
  sanitation, 873.
  slave trade. *See* Slave Trade.
  slavery. *See* Slaves and Slavery.
  smallpox, 873.
  sugar, 259, 780.
  trade, 198, 290, 390, 398, 400.
  *See also* various islands of the West Indies.
West Indies, French: free ports, 827.
West-Indische Compagnie [generic term], 157, 167, 182, 183, 252, 253.
  colonization, 168, 191, 250, 251, 254, 256, 260.
  Danish quarrel, 191.
  *See also* Compagnie d'Occident; Swedish West Indian Company.
West-vnnd Ost Jndischer Lustgart. *See* Ens, Gaspar.
Westermayer, Conrad, 1765–1826, artist. *See* Franklin, Kleine Schriften, 1221.
Western United States: description and travel, 1170, 1209, 1258.
Westfeld, Christian Friedrich Gotthold, 1746–1823: Von dem Coffee, 422.
Whales and Whaling:
  Bermuda Islands, 625A.
  Greenland, 332.
  North America, 804.
Wharton, Charles Henry, 1748–1833: A poetical epistle to His Excellency George Washington (*review*), 670.
Whiskey Insurrection, 1394.
Whitbourne, Sir Richard, fl. 1579–1626: Zwantzigste Schifffahrt, oder Gründliche vnd sattsame Beschreibung dess Newen Engellands, 160, 161.
White, John, fl. 1585–1593, artist. *See* Bry, Wunderbarliche...
White Mountains, N. H., 975.
Widemann, Samuel, b. 1691: Rede bey der Ordinationshandlung. *See* Urlsperger, Americanisches Ackerwerk Gottes.
Wiederholdt, Captain. Tagebuch, 533A.
Wieland, Christoph Martin, 1733–1813:
  Unterredungen zwischen W**, 501.
  *See also* Fortsetzung der Neuesten Politischen Gerüchte, 546; Gespräche über einige neueste Weltbegebenheiten, 712; Politische Nachrichten, 479; Politische Neuigkeiten, 497, 523.
Wieting, Johann Friedrich: Der Wilde in Frankreich! 922C.
Wigglesworth, Edward, 1732–1794, contributor. *See* American Academy of Arts and Sciences, Memoirs, v. 2.
Wilberforce, William, 1759–1833: *motion to abolish slave trade. See* Barbauld, Epistle; An Elegy; The Slave trade indispensable.
Wilcke, Johan Carl, 1732–1796: Anmerkungen zu den Briefe des Hrn. Benjamin Franklins von der Elektricität. *See* Franklin, Brief.
Willard, Joseph, 1738–1804, contributor. *See* American Academy of Arts and Sciences, Memoirs, v. 2.

Willday, John, contributor. *See* College of Physicians of Philadelphia, Medicinische Verhandlungen, Bd. 1; College of Physicians of Philadelphia, Transactions, v. 1.
Willdenow, Carl Ludwig, 1765–1812, editor. *See* Muhlenberg, Kurze Bemerkungen.
Williams, Cooper. *See* Willyams, Cooper.
Williams, Edward:
  Versuche über die ausdehnende Kraft des gefrierenden Wassers. *See* Royal Society of Edinburgh, Transactions, v. 2.
  *biography*, 1210.
Williams, Helen Maria, 1762–1827: A poem on the Bill lately past (*review*), 969.
Williams, John, 1727–1798: An enquiry into the truth of the tradition concerning the discovery of America by Prince Madog (*review*), 1243.
Williams, Jonathan, 1750–1815, contributor. *See* American Philosophical Society, Transactions, v. 3.
Williams, Samuel, 1743–1817:
  The natural and civil history of Vermont (*review*), 1297.
  *See also* American Philosophical Society, Transactions, v. 3.
Williamson, Charles, 1757–1808: *biography*, 1480.
Williamson, Hugh, 1735–1819, contributor. *See* American Philosophical Society, Transactions, v. 1.
Willyams, Cooper, 1762–1816: An account of the campaign in the West Indies (*review*), 1389.
Wilson, Capt. Henry, contributor. *See* Keate, Nachrichten.
Wilson, James, 1742–1798, and T. M'Kean, 1734–1817: Commentaries on the Constitution of the United States of America. *See* Pennsylvania. — Constitutional Convention, Debates.
Wilson, Matthew, 1731–1790, contributor. *See* American Philosophical Society, Transactions, v. 3 (*review*).
Wilson, Richard, 1714–1782, artist. *See* Der Bekannte Wasserfall zu Niagara.
Winckelmann, Johann Just, 1620–1699: Der Americanischen Neuen Welt Beschreibung, 184.
Wind, 975, 1296.
  *See also* Meteorological Observations.
Windmills, Horizontal, 474, 492.
Winghe, Jodocus, 1544–1603, artist. *See* Casas, Umbständige warhafftige Beschreibung.
Winter, Jacob, editor. *See* Vespucci, Van den nygē Jnsulen vnd landen.
Winterbotham, William, 1763–1829: Amerika, 1285.
Das Winterquartier in Amerika. *See* Babo, F. J. M.
Winthrop, James, 1752–1821, contributor. *See* American Academy of Arts and Sciences, Memoirs, v. 1, v. 2.
Wit and Humor. *See* Anecdotes.
With, Johann. *See* White, John.
Woman [also under appropriate subjects], 425, 533, 611, 746, 750, 752, 759, 904, 949, 952, 954, 958, 1005, 1025, 1508.
Woodcut of South American Indians: Dise figur anzaigt vns das volck, 19, 20.
Woog, Moritz Carl Christian, 1684–1760, translator. *See* Prévost d'Exiles, Erste Reisen.
World, New. *See* America.
Wright, Benjamin, engraver. *See* Bertius, Geographischer eyn oder zusammengezogener Fabeln.
Wright, William, 1735–1819: Ueber die auf Jamaika wachsenden...Pflanzen (*review*), 977.
Writers, American, 1093.
The Wrongs of Africa (*review*), 980.
Wynn. *See* Wynne.
Wynne, John Huddleston, 1743–1788: A general history of the British Empire in America (*review*), 471.

# GERMAN WORKS RELATING TO AMERICA — INDEX

## Y

Yaws (disease), 713.
Yellow Fever, 1416, 1446, 1484, 1502.
  Dominican Republic, 1438.
  Philadelphia, Pa., 1251, 1257, 1292, 1300, 1320, 1331.
Yucatan, 45, 46, 49.
  history, 47.

## Z

Zach, Franz Xaver von, 1754–1832, contributor. *See* Ebeling, Ueber Portugiesische und Amerikanische Landkarten.
Zachariae, Friedrich Wilhelm, 1726–1777: Cortes *(reviews)*, 424, 447.
Zedler, Johann Heinrich, 1706–1763: Grosses vollständiges Universal Lexicon, 302.
Zeisberger, David, 1720–1808, contributor. *See* Loskiel, Geschichte der Mission.
Zell, Johann Michael, 1740–1815, illustrator. *See* Purmann, Sitten und Meinungen.
Zeller, Hans Jacob, d. 1692, and Heinrich Huser: Jamaica, 199.
Ziegler, Philip. *See* Zigler, Philip.
Zigler, Philip, compiler. *See* Bry, America, Das ist, Erfindung.
Zimmermann, Eberhard August Wilhelm von, 1743–1815:
  Annalen der geographischen und statistischen Wissenschaften, 1057B.
  Bruchstück aus "Frankreich und die Freistaaten von Nordamerika," 1458.
  Essay de comparaison entre la France et les États-Unis de l'Amérique *(review)*, 1431.
  Frankreich und die Freistaaten von Nordamerika, 1286.
  Statistisch historisches Archiv *(review)*, 1301.
Zimmermann, Eberhard August Wilhelm von, 1743–1815, editor. *See* Bericht von dem...Schiffes Elenora...zugetragen hat; Clarkson, Ueber den Sclavenhandel; Coxe, Auszug aus Tench Coxe's Abhandlung; Long, Westindischen Dollmetschers und Kaufmanns See- und Land-Reisen; Reise in den nördlichen Gegenden zwischen Asien und Amerika;
Zimmermann, Eberhard August Wilhelm von, *continued*
  Sklavenhandel; Universitäten; *see also* Bruns, P. J., and E. A. W. Zimmermann, editors, Repositorium.
Zimmermann, E. A. W., translator. *See* Barton, Abhandlungen; Bartram, Reisen; Imlay, Nachrichten; Umfreville, Uber den gegenwärtigen Zustand der Hudsonbay.
Zimmermann, Heinrich: Heinrich Zimmermanns von Wissloch in der Pfalz, Reise um die Welt mit Capitain Cook, 689.
Zimmermann, Johann Georg: Ueber die Einsamkeit, 805A.
Zimmermann, Peter Carl: Reise nach Ost- und West-Indien, 465.
Zincke, G. H. *See* Leipziger Sammlungen.
Zinner, Johann, editor: Merkwürdige Briefe und Schriften der berühmtesten Generäle Amerika, 727.
Zinzendorf, Nicolaus Ludwig, Graf von, 1700–1760:
  Des Ordinarii Fratrum Öffentliche Reden, 388.
  Sieben Letzte Reden, 314.
  Pennsylvanische Nachrichten, 315.
  *See also* Büdingische Sammlung; Philorthodoxo, Ungeheuchelte Theologische Unterredung; Spangenberg, Leben.
Zollickhoffer, Jacob, clergyman, 258.
Zoology, 189, 574, 975.
  Arctic regions, 320, 324.
  Iceland, 312.
  *See also* Natural History.
Zorgdrager, Cornelius Gijsbertsz, fl. 1700: Beschreibung des Grönländischen Wallfischfangs und Fischerey, 332.
Zorn, Johann, 1739–1799, editor. *See* Jacquin, Auswahl schöner und seltener Gewächse als eine Fortsetzung der Amerikanischen Gewächse: Jacquin, Dreyhundert.
"Zuckerbaum," 636–637.
  *See also* Maple Tree.
Zumarraga, Juan de, 1468–1548, bishop of Mexico: Ein Sendbrieff, 54, 55.
Zur Kunde fremder Völker und Länder *(review)*, 810C.
Zur "Neuen Zeitung," 49. *See also* Newe Zeitung; New Zeutung.
Zusammenkünfte am Atlas zu Kenntniss der Länder, Völker und ihrer Sitten herausgegeben für die Jugend *(review)*, 841B.
Zuverlässiger Briefwechsel *(review)*, 493.

Selective Bibliography

Dippel, Horst. Americana Germanica: 1770-1800: Bibliographie deutscher Amerikaliteratur. (Stuttgart, 1976).

Palmer, Philip M. "German Works on America," in: In Honorem Lawrence Marsden Price: Contributions by His Colleagues and by His Former Students. (Berkeley: University of California Pr., 1952), pp. 271-412.

Pochmann, Henry. Bibliography of German Culture in America to 1940. (Madison: University of Wisconsin Pr., 1953).

Ritter, Alexander. Deutschlands literarisches Amerikabild: Neuere Forschungen zur Amerikarezeption der deutschen Literatur. (Hildesheim: Olms, 1977).

Tolzmann, Don Heinrich. Catalog of the German-Americana Collection, University of Cincinnati. (München: K.G. Saur, 1990).

_____. The First Germans in America, With A Biographical Directory of New York. (Bowie, MD: Heritage Books, Inc., 1992).

_____. German-Americana: A Bibliography. (Metuchen, NJ: Scarecrow Pr., 1975).

_____. Germany and America (1450-1700): Julius Friedrich Sachse's History of the German Role in the Discovery, Exploration, and Settlement of the New World. (Bowie, MD: Heritage Books, Inc., 1991).

_____. In der Neuen Welt: Deutsch-Amerikanische Festschrift zur 500-Jahrfeier der Entdeckung von Amerika. New German-American Studies, Vol. 5. (New York: Peter Lang Pub. Co., 1992).

# Heritage Books by Don Heinrich Tolzmann:

*Amana: William Rufus Perkins' and Barthinius L. Wick's History of the Amana Society, or Community of True Inspiration*

*Americana Germanica: Paul Ben Baginsky's Bibliography of German Works Relating to America, 1493–1800*

*Biography of Baron Von Steuben, the Army of the American Revolution and Its Organizer: Rudolf Cronau's Biography of Baron von Steuben*

*CD: German-American Biographical Index (Midwest Families)*

*CD: Germans, Volume 2*

*CD: The German Colonial Era (four volumes)*

*Cincinnati's German Heritage*

*Covington's German Heritage*

*Custer: Frederick Whittaker's Complete Life of General George A. Custer, Major General of Volunteers, Brevet Major General U.S. Army and Lieutenant-Colonel Seventh U.S. Cavalry*

*Dayton's German Heritage: Karl Karstaedt's Golden Jubilee History of the German Pioneer Society of Dayton, Ohio*

*Early German-American Newspapers: Daniel Miller's History*

*German Achievements in America: Rudolf Cronau's Survey History*

*German Americans in the Revolution*

*German Immigration to America: The First Wave*

*German Pioneer Life and Domestic Customs*

*German Pioneer Lifestyle*

*German Pioneers in Early California: Erwin G. Gudde's History*

*German-American Achievements: 400 Years of Contributions to America*

*German-Americana in Europe: Two Guides to Materials Relating to American History in the German, Austrian, and Swiss Archives*

*German-Americana: A Bibliography*

*Germany and America, 1450–1700*

*Kentucky's German Pioneers: H. A. Rattermann's History*

*Lives and Exploits of the Daring Frank and Jesse James: Thaddeus Thorndike's Graphic and Realistic Description of Their Many Deeds of Unparalleled Daring in the Robbing of Banks and Railroad Trains*

*Louisiana's German Heritage: Louis Voss' Introductory History*

*Maryland's German Heritage: Daniel Wunderlich Nead's History*

*Memories of the Battle of New Ulm: Personal Accounts of the Sioux Uprising. L. A. Fritsche's History of Brown County, Minnesota (1916)*

*Michigan's German Heritage: John Andrew Russell's History of the German Influence in the Making of Michigan*

*Ohio's German Heritage*

*Ohio Valley German Biographical Index*

*Ohio Valley German Biographical Index: A Supplement*

*Outbreak and Massacre by the Dakota Indians in Minnesota in 1862: Marion P. Satterlee's Minute Account of the Outbreak, with Exact Locations, Names of All Victims, Prisoners at Camp Release, Refugees at Fort Ridgely, etc. Complete List of Indians Killed in Battle and Those Hung, and Those Pardoned at Rock Island, Iowa*

*The German-American Soldier in the Wars of the U.S.: J. G. Rosengarten's History*

*The German Element in Virginia: Herrmann Schuricht's History*

*The German Immigrant in America*

*The Pennsylvania Germans: James Owen Knauss, Jr.'s Social History*

*The Pennsylvania Germans: Jesse Leonard Rosenberger's Sketch of Their History and Life*

www.ingramcontent.com/pod-product-compliance
Lightning Source LLC
Chambersburg PA
CBHW062016220426
43662CB00010B/1356